LEON
RUSSELL

OTHER BOOKS BY BILL JANOVITZ

The Rolling Stones' Exile on Main St.
(33⅓ Series)

Rocks Off: 50 Tracks
That Tell the Story of the Rolling Stones

LEON RUSSELL

THE MASTER OF SPACE AND TIME'S JOURNEY THROUGH ROCK & ROLL HISTORY

Bill Janovitz

hachette
BOOKS
New York

Hachette Books
Hachette Book Group
1290 Avenue of the Americas
New York, NY 10104
HachetteBooks.com
Twitter.com/HachetteBooks
Instagram.com/HachetteBooks

First Edition: March 2023

Published by Hachette Books, an imprint of Perseus Books, LLC, a subsidiary of Hachette Book Group, Inc. The Hachette Books name and logo is a trademark of the Hachette Book Group.

The Hachette Speakers Bureau provides a wide range of authors for speaking events.

To find out more, go to www.hachettespeakersbureau.com or call (866) 376-6591.

The publisher is not responsible for websites (or their content) that are not owned by the publisher.

Print book interior design by Jeff Williams.

Library of Congress Control Number: 2022917456

ISBNs: 9780306924774 (hardcover), 9780306923029 (ebook)

Printed in the United States of America

LSC-C

Printing 3, 2023

For Laura, Lucy, and Will, who put up with me while I was working on this book, during which there was no escape; we were all locked down together during the pandemic. Happy hour in my house became known as Leon hour, as after a few sips of a cocktail, I would launch into unsolicited Leon lessons.

This book is also dedicated to the late great Jimmy Karstein.

Contents

Preface

SIR ELTON JOHN INDUCTED HIS most important influence, Leon Russell, into the Rock & Roll Hall of Fame in 2011. "He was my idol," Elton said before bringing Leon up to the podium to give his acceptance speech. The once-lithe super-hippie rock star ambled to the stage with the help of a cane—heavyset, dark sunglasses contrasting with his pale face, all framed by his long snowy white hair and beard, looking even older than his sixty-nine years.

"About a year ago, Elton came and found me in a ditch by the side of the highway of life," Leon said, haltingly, humbly, his voice breaking with emotion. "He took me up the high stages with big audiences and treated me like a king. And the only thing I can say is, 'Bless your heart.' Also, I want to say thank you very much, I appreciate it and, uh, hallelujah."

The induction was a satisfying bookend to Leon Russell's career, but it had been no easy task. It really came down to the intense lobbying efforts of Elton John.

There has been much angst about the Rock & Roll Hall of Fame since its inception. Admission and inclusion in the Hall of Fame are entirely subjective, and the nominating process is mired down in biases and politics. Nevertheless, it has become meaningful to many of the artists inducted and a bone of contention for fans of artists—and some artists themselves—who are excluded.

From the outset, the only criterion was that an artist had to have released a record at least twenty-five years ago. That's it.

"The criteria were deliberately left open," said Jon Landau, Bruce Springsteen's manager and head of the nominating committee. Landau described the factors as "a mix of quality and influence. . . . We have artists with mass appeal, and artists with a very narrow audience." Discussing the J. Geils Band, Landau—who started out as one of *Rolling Stone's* earliest editors—noted, "I'm still trying to get them into the Hall of Fame, unsuccessfully. Peter [Wolf] is my oldest friend. We go back to 1967."

I mean, who do you gotta know around here?

Elton John was among a third wave of slam-dunk Hall of Famers. He was inducted in 1994. Around 2008, he started to plead for Leon's inclusion, which just based on Leon's career from 1959 to 1975 would seem a pretty obvious case. But he kept going.

If it pleases the court: Leon started in 1959 with Jerry Lee Lewis; moved to LA and became the first-call piano player among the A-list of the so-called Wrecking Crew session musicians, backing the Beach Boys and Frank Sinatra and playing on almost all of Phil Spector's hits. He was one of the most critical forces for bringing together one of America's most underappreciated bands, Delaney & Bonnie and Friends—the band that directly changed the career trajectories of George Harrison and Eric Clapton, among others. Leon pulled together Mad Dogs & Englishmen for Joe Cocker; cofounded Shelter Records, a powerhouse independent label that discovered Tom Petty, the Dwight Twilley Band, and Phoebe Snow, signed J. J. Cale, and was crucial in introducing reggae to America; commenced his solo career with an almost flawless run of three solo albums, the first of which featured two Beatles, two Rolling Stones, Clapton, and Steve Winwood; was a top international concert draw during rock's golden era; helped Harrison organize rock music's first major all-star charity concert, also a Grammy-winning album; wrote no fewer than three evergreen standards, including a song that topped all of the major commercial charts; racked up six gold records; crossed over from rock to country before that was a popular career move, scoring a number one on the country chart; presented the funk/R&B Gap Band and renegade progressive bluegrass New Grass Revival; spearheaded innovation in recording, music video, and music gear such as the drum machine; helped launch countless music-biz careers; continued a dedicated career long after the spotlight had moved on; and then roared back in his late sixties with a Grammy-nominated hit collaboration with his most celebrated protégé. There really shouldn't have been much to deliberate.

But he seemingly had vanished from the public eye. What happened? How did this genuine rock star end up in "a ditch by the side of the highway of life"?

Chapter 1

Killer Education

ONE NIGHT IN THE DEAD of winter in Cheyenne, Wyoming, 1960, Russell Bridges stood on the side of the stage watching a riot unfold.

Bridges had just warmed up the crowd of about four hundred with his band, the rest of whom were at that moment blazing onstage with Jerry Lee Lewis now at the piano. The truth is, this crowd had not needed any warming up. Despite the icy conditions outside, these cowboys and cowgirls were primed and pumped to see The Killer, no matter that Lewis was now at the nadir of a career that had taken off like a rocket, only to crash down to earth. Only three years earlier, the news of his marriage—already his third, at the age of twenty-two—to his thirteen-year-old cousin, Myra, daughter of his bandmate and cousin, J. W. Brown, had caused an uproar.

Old Jerry Lee was determined to get back on top, but for now, he would drive his Cadillac to wherever he could collect a few hundred bucks, performing solo or with a local pickup band. Or, as on this cold night in Cheyenne, with whatever musicians he could afford to take along.

Like Russell Bridges, who had been playing the clubs and bars of Tulsa since he was fourteen. Oklahoma was a dry state, with liquor sales prohibited. So, being an "underage" performer at nightclubs was not a pressing issue. In the postwar years, Tulsa was the "Oil Capital of the World," even weathering the Great Depression pretty well (unlike the rest of the Dust Bowl state), with a flourishing Art Deco building boom through the 1930s. Bridges's own Will Rogers High School is a prime example of the architectural style. Although ostensibly "dry," the clubs were filled with beer and illegal hard booze, and young performers had no trouble getting a drink at these gigs.

"I worked a beer joint club from six till eleven and then a private club from midnight to five a.m. I barely had time to sober up for school," Bridges recalled later. "One club I played at quite a lot paid ten dollars a night and all you could drink, and I drank all of it. By the time I finished high school, I was drinking at least a pint of hard liquor a day."

It was at a gig at Tulsa's legendary Cain's Ballroom where Bridges and his band, the Starlighters, had first met and performed with Jerry Lee Lewis. The place had been put on the map by Bob Wills and His Texas Playboys, who broadcast their unique brand of western swing on KVOO from 1934 to 1942.

The Starlighters were a top band in Tulsa, too. "We were mostly an instrumental band," sax player Johnny Williams said. And they would back national acts who came through. "Anybody that would come into town, whether it was Frogman Henry or really anybody, it didn't matter."

Bridges was already commonly regarded as the best pianist in Tulsa, and the first on the scene to mic his instrument and run it through an amplifier. At some of the clubs the Starlighters played, they would be lucky to show up and the piano was playable, never mind in tune. But Bridges could make an old box sound like a Steinway.

As fans, the band was understandably thrilled to back Jerry Lee Lewis for his Cain's Ballroom show. By the time he'd reached Tulsa, Jerry Lee was exasperated, battling the bottle, and at his lowest ebb, having done a stretch of about ten shows with ten different bands. When he heard the Starlighters, his mood swung to exuberance.

Bridges had made sure the band knew all of Jerry Lee's material in the correct keys by showtime. After their first warm-up set, Lewis came up onto the bandstand and, indicating Bridges, declared, "I'm not gonna set down at that piano. He plays a lot better piano than I do!"

The Starlighters had ripped through one song after another that first performance together; when they were done, a sweaty and spent Jerry Lee said, "Well, shit. You guys have got to come on the road with me." Lewis was not sure how, economically, he'd be able to take the band out. The boys would have gone for nothing, and that's not much less than what they ultimately got. Bridges had just completed three days of entrance exams for the University of Tulsa but quickly decided college and ROTC were not as compelling as a chance to hit the road with one of his heroes.

Bridges changed the oil in his '51 Chrysler Imperial limousine, hitched a trailer to it, threw the instruments in, and the Starlighters hit the road. "We didn't know about cases, drove about fifty miles, looked in back—all our instruments were in pieces," he said later.

They toured on and off with Lewis over the last half of 1959 into 1960, going out for runs of twenty to thirty days, sometimes just opening the shows and sometimes backing Lewis, who occasionally had with him the rest of his three-piece combo, J. W. Brown and Russell Smith. "We were on the road with him when he was down and out and married the little cousin, you know," said Williams. "Russell [Bridges], a lot of times, would stay on the bandstand and play. . . . Lewis was not bashful about having him play. They got along good. I'm not sure that Russell didn't give him a pointer or two on the piano!"

But there were times when the young band struggled to get paid by Lewis's booking agent; once, they had to file charges against his manager to get him to pay up. Several times they slept in the car outside a gas station, out of fuel, waiting for it to open so they could get back on the road. These were sobering lessons in the business of music.

Thus, the Starlighters found themselves in Cheyenne that wintry night in early 1960. After the band finished their set, Bridges watched from the side of the stage as The Killer brought the crowd to a boil. Jerry Lee might have fallen from his pinnacle, but he could still whip an audience into a frenzy, glaring at the crowd like a cornered and wounded wild beast, kicking back the bench and playing with his feet.

The atmosphere was combustible. Cheyenne "turned into a complete riot," recalled drummer Chuck Blackwell. "It was unbelievable. People just fighting and crashing and breaking bottles across the bar. It looked like something out of the movies. Then they turned on the band and started throwing things at us." The band kept cooking and Jerry Lee stood on the piano bench singing with a gun in his hand as the melee continued.

"When the fighting started to spill over onto the stage, we thought, 'Oh shit, we're not gonna make it out of here alive,'" Blackwell recalled. "Then all of a sudden [bassist] Lucky Clark recognized a guy he'd been in prison with." Lucky had done time for "some kind of robbery," Williams recalled. "He was a little wild and was apt to jump on to someone." Lucky's jailhouse friend "got us, and our instruments, through that mass riot and out the exit to the parking lot," said Blackwell. But not before Jerry Lee himself escaped. Instructing his band of teenagers to keep vamping, he slipped off the stage with his gun in hand, snuck out the stage entrance, and split in his Caddy, leaving the kids to fend for themselves.

The tour with Lewis gave Bridges a glimpse of what it felt like to be the star of the show. Before they had left Tulsa, the Starlighters sometimes featured guest vocalists like local legends Jumpin' Jack Dunham or Jimmy "Junior" Markham. Sometimes Lucky sang. Fellow Tulsa musicians always discouraged Bridges from singing, telling him his voice was "too nasal." But at a packed Vets Memorial Hall in Kiowa, Kansas, on November 5, 1959, Russell Bridges had changed a few minds, perhaps even his own, about his ability to be a front man.

The showbill portentously announced:

IN PERSON

The Jerry Lee Lewis Show & Dance
Star of Movies, TV, and Records
With Johnny Williams and the HOLLYWOOD STARLIGHTERS
Featuring Russell Bridges

The Killer had begged off this particular show, claiming appendicitis, though the musicians speculated that it was more likely related to rotgut moonshine and amphetamines. Rightfully fearing another riot, the promoter had a local doctor announce the bad news and offered to return patrons' money if they decided to leave. "Well, the crowd did not like that," Blackwell recalled. "So Russell got up and did the whole Jerry Lee show. He just rocked the house, even kicked the piano bench back a couple of times."

In retrospect, that was the night Russell Bridges began transforming into Leon Russell. Nobody asked for their money back.

Chapter 2

Okies

CLAUDE RUSSELL BRIDGES WAS BORN on April 2, 1942, at Southwestern Hospital in Lawton, Oklahoma. But his family—his mother, Hester; father, John; and brother, Jerry—lived in Apache, about twenty miles away. Hester and John had married in 1935.

Apache, in southwestern Oklahoma, was the last town in the territories settled during the land runs that began in 1889, with white settlers arriving chaotically via wagons, often killing each other and Native Americans who legally owned the land. The discovery of oil under the Oklahoma red dirt fueled bamboozling and bloodbaths. The run on Apache occurred on August 6, 1901, and according to the Oklahoma Historical Society, "within hours there were five lumberyards and six saloons."

Apache's population in 1940 was only around 1,100, about a quarter of which was Native American. John Bridges had registered for the draft at age twenty-seven, listing "Farmer's Union Coop" as his occupation. Two years later, John and Hester's second son, Claude, was born. They called him by his middle name, Russell, after one of his mother's brothers, Russell Claude Whaley. (For clarity, we will refer to him henceforth by his stage name, Leon.)

John Bridges's father was Irish with some Cherokee blood. A DNA test on Leon's brother's family indicated that Leon and his brother, Jerry, were one-sixteenth Cherokee, and the balance of their lineage was primarily Irish.

Hester said Leon didn't speak for his first few years, starting later than most kids. Years later, she told Leon's wife, Jan Bridges, that the first thing he said was, "What's the matter, little birdie, you cry?" Jan recalled the conversation with her mother-in-law: "He was watching the birds, and something was going on with the birds. And she [Hester] said she was just shocked because he never spoke."

At around four years old, Leon started to show interest in the family piano. Both of his parents played. "My dad and mom had a duo," Leon told filmmaker Denny Tedesco. "He played the bass on the piano, she played the top end, and so I saw that from an early age. All my aunts, actually I think on both sides of the family, played piano. One, in particular, Aunt Bertha, I stole a lot of stuff from her. She was great." Hester was amazed to hear four-year-old Leon picking out the melody of "Trust and Obey," a hymn he had heard in church. Hester, noting that neither she nor John pushed the piano on either of their sons, said she thought Leon was a prodigy. "He just sat down one day and started playing by ear," Hester said. She drove him to nearby Anadarko, to the best piano teacher in the area, Dora Popejoy. "I don't want many four-year-olds, but I want Leon," Popejoy had said to Leon's mother.

One of Leon's first memories was a scarring and formative one. "I have always experienced severe stage fright, not only on stages, but in crowded rooms, lines for movies, and just about any place there's a lot of people who can be, by any stretch of the imagination, considered an audience," he recalled. "The psychologists call this 'agoraphobia.' . . . I have to give credit for this paralyzing condition to one of my aunts on my father's side. At the age of four, I had discovered my sexual organs, and shortly thereafter, discovered that my female cousin had a completely different set."

At a family gathering in Duncan, just to the east of Lawton, Leon found the opportunity to explore this discovery in greater depth with his cousin in a secluded playhouse. His "rather severe Aries aunt" arrived just as Leon was taking off his cousin's underwear. "She promptly paraded me in front of each individual adult family member and disclosed the nature of my research with scorching charges and descriptions.

"That incident has affected me for my entire life. It has had an immeasurable detrimental effect on my career in show business in that I tend to freeze up around any situation that involves people watching me, even in an audition or interview. I've always harbored the suspicion that my audiences come to watch me deal with my secret phobia onstage."

When Leon was five, the family moved to Maysville for about a year, and he continued lessons with two more teachers. When they settled in

Tulsa, he was around twelve, and Leon started lessons with Margaret Freeze.

Hester observed that he was favoring his left hand, as he would all his life. She had discovered when he was around eighteen months old what Leon would later describe as a birth injury that had damaged his second and third vertebrae, causing a slight paralysis on his right side. "I was born with spastic paralysis," he said, "now called cerebral palsy." He suspected the doctor delivered him with forceps, causing the injury. This paralysis to his right side resulted in "very limited neurological connections. I had to devise ways to play that I could sort of get around that limitation. I kind of play a little bit of a thing with my left hand . . . like Chet Atkins or Merle Travis, just an octave thing. But the way I use it is some sort of bass things on my left hand and more of a rhythmic horn-like parts [on the right]. I am a left-handed piano player for sure."

The condition made him "very aware of the duality involved in our plane of existence here." He later explained, with his hallmark self-deprecation, "My chops have always been sort of weak, because the right side of my body was paralyzed a little bit. I have damaged nerve endings on the right side, so my piano style comes from designing stuff I can play with my right hand."

"I know that sounds like an excuse," he said. "But you play the hand that you got. I know I sound like Mahatma Gandhi. I don't mean to."

Leon had the drive to overcome any limitations, imagining himself strapped to the front of a train that would run straight into the face of a cliff if he made a mistake during practicing. Playing the piano "helped his three fingers on his right hand," Hester said. Fairly early on, he developed the ability to identify the notes as he heard them—a skill that was at least relative pitch, but not perfect pitch. "They had this one tuner who meant to be doing something good," he said. "It was an upright, an old upright piano, so he tuned the piano down one step because he said it would stay in tune better, and I suppose it would stay in tune better except it was one step flat. So my pitch has always been off plus or minus one step for my whole life. Otherwise, I would have had perfect pitch, but you can't have everything, I guess."

He admitted that his unique style "effectively mimicked classical stuff." Leon said he "studied classical music, and thought some of those guys were incredible. I also thought Harpo Marx was pretty great—that comedy versus great harp playing going on." And he was struck early by religious music. He recalled being at his grandmother's house. "She was a very elegant lady, and she was doing her hair in the bathroom," he said. "It came down and hit the floor and went over about six or seven feet, and she wore it in a bun. So while she was messing with her hair, I went into her bedroom, and she had a little phonograph record by her bed, and it had a little record on there called 'Blood on Your Hands.' I said, 'Lord, Grandma's listening to murder songs?' I played that record . . . that was my first knowledge of what the family music background was."

Don Copeland, a classmate, remembered young Leon as bright, quiet, introspective, and well liked. Leon found out that Don sang, and they bonded over music. Don recalled that the Bridges, like most in Maysville, lived in a small house, but he was struck by the presence of a piano on his first visit when he and Leon were both around nine or ten years old. Leon performed Debussy's masterpiece, "Clair de Lune," for his friend. Leon's mother would hear the two boys singing together and showed them how to harmonize.

Leon also played the cornet in the elementary school band, then picked up the alto sax and became good enough to gain membership in the high school marching band when he was nine. The town's music director, Joe Reed, a tremendous influence on Leon, promoted him.

But Leon had a chip on his shoulder, feeling more than challenged by his paralysis, which resulted in a lifelong limp, mistaken by most of his friends as an aftereffect of polio. "I felt like the world cheated me big time," he said. "I took piano lessons for ten years and there's girls taking piano lessons for three years and they were playing at Carnegie Hall. And I was still trying to figure out how to play."

He added: "If I hadn't had the problem, I probably wouldn't have gotten into music at all and would have been an ex-football player today, selling insurance in Des Moines."

Chapter 3

Tulsa Time

AFTER LEON'S SIXTH-GRADE YEAR, IN August 1953, the Russell family relocated to Tulsa, following his father John's career move to the Texas Company, soon to be known as Texaco. But John Bridges had been having an affair, and four years later, when Leon was fifteen, his parents started a divorce that took several years to complete. "It went on, and apparently that house, I think, must have been just a powder keg," said Leon's first child, his daughter Baby Blueagle Bridges-Fox, who goes by Blue. "And, you know, those are pretty formative years. I don't think my grandpa really had much to do with the boys at that time." Hester would remarry in 1963 to Eugene Fulbright. By then, Leon was well established in California.

"I've never had a great deal of family involvement," Leon said. "The deep involvements I've had with people have been through musical relationships rather than blood." We see this in action later in his life when he formed musical "families" in communal situations at his home studio and on the road, with Mad Dogs & Englishmen and his own Shelter People band.

His widow, Jan Bridges, said that Leon always liked going to other people's houses as a kid because his was too quiet. His parents were on the stern side. "When we got together," Jan said, talking about 1979 or so, "first he took me to meet his mom, and then he took me to meet his dad, who had remarried. I only saw his father one more time before he passed, when I had taken our daughter, Sugaree, to meet him. But they weren't close. He really wasn't close to either of his parents."

Leon's brother, Jerry, was seven years older. "They weren't close at all,"

9

Jan said. Later in life, when Leon was successful, "I think [Jerry] really wanted to be a part of Leon's life. But I think it was the same as anybody who might be a fan. But Leon didn't have fond memories of his brother. He really didn't have any love for him because evidently, he did mean things to Leon when Leon was a kid. . . [Jerry] sort of picked on him." Jerry joined the Air Force out of high school and went to work for a prosthetics company in Texas.

In Tulsa, the Bridges settled into a two-bedroom ranch home at 1958 North Marion Avenue, on the city's northeast side, but soon it was Leon and Hester alone there after his father left and Jerry moved on. "The first night we moved to Tulsa, I laid in my lonely bed, and I heard all those sirens going by outside, and it just chilled me to the bone," Leon said. "I thought, 'I'm in the big city!'" And like most rock 'n' rollers, he had lain in bed listening to the radio. Specifically, he recalled R&B disc jockey Frank Berry on KAKC, which later became Tulsa's first full-time rock 'n' roll radio station. "I was probably about twelve or thirteen, and his show was like from midnight till six," he recalled. "He played blues all night. It was an unusual show. Of course, in the South, there were a lot of stations that had that blues format, but it was kind of a bonus in Tulsa."

The music of Tulsa would have a profound impact on the trajectory of Leon Russell's life. The city had been home to Bob Wills and His Texas Playboys, the leader of western swing, since the 1930s. Wills married jazz and blues with country music, adding dashes of the mariachi music that was filtering over the border and polka that was popular with Czech settlers in Texas. He was one of the first country artists to bring a drummer into his band. The resulting music was almost always ebullient, even when the lyric was melancholy.

"Bob Wills was on the radio . . . every day on KVOO," recalled future star J. J. Cale, who was part of Leon's scene of high school musicians. "And you know, I don't think I liked it or disliked it. It was just what you *heard*. The only thing that raised my attention span was when rock 'n' roll started coming in."

Western swing was waning in popularity as rock 'n' roll gained traction. Texas Playboy Leon McAuliffe went on to open his own club, the Cimarron Ballroom, and form his Cimarron Boys. The Cimarron would later play host to rock 'n' roll acts, including Ronnie Hawkins and the Hawks, which included a teenaged Levon Helm.

"Tulsa has always had that energy for me that has come from the ground," said Jim Halsey, who booked McAuliffe, his first promotion, in 1949, on his way to becoming the biggest agent in country music. Halsey started booking Leon Russell in the 1970s. "And a lot of that comes from native people who were here and are still here and the sacred earth we live on. Now, that produces a certain energy." Tulsa sits geographically, psychologically, and spiritually at the crossroads of the South, the West, and the Midwest. Route 66, "America's Highway," ran through it.

When he entered Will Rogers High School, Leon was still intimidated by Tulsa's "big city" aspects. "This was just about the time that *Blackboard Jungle* came out, and I used to slide along the lockers and keep 'em all shined up trying to get out of the way of all those boys with those motorcycles and chains and switchblades. It was really terrifying." His fellow students at Will Rogers High included musician David Gates and singer Anita Bryant, Miss Oklahoma 1958—probably not quite the hoodlums Leon described. Leon and Gates, who was two years older, played together in the Accents, mostly playing high school hops. Gates had formed the Accents with drummer Don Kimmel, bassist Gerald Goodwin, and Leon. Their first publicity photo from 1957 (Leon at fifteen or sixteen) shows them dressed in white tuxes sporting crew cuts, except for Leon, whose proud pompadour soars above his horn-rim-bespectacled smiling face.

Leon played in a few different bands. Some played high school parties and dances, and some played clubs. "I got a little bit of an education playing those joints," said Leon's bandmate Starlighters drummer Chuck Blackwell. "I remember them being packed. People packed into a booth, and the women would be carrying on. Ah, smoke. Fights."

"Even though we were not famous," Johnny Williams, another bandmate in the Starlighters, said, "we were stars of the bars."

Some of these clubs were in or near the Greenwood Avenue district, which historically had been an economic powerhouse in North Tulsa. Once known as Black Wall Street, so named by Booker T. Washington, the area is now remembered for one of the worst race massacres in the country's history. Credible estimates range from fifty to three hundred Black people died in the massacre in 1921.

Despite the massacre and subsequent efforts of white people to forcibly relocate the survivors, many of them remained and rebuilt. By the 1930s, the neighborhood was hopping again. Cain's Ballroom was only a few blocks away from the border of Greenwood and remains today, though the neighborhood has long since been divided by the I-244 expressway. In his country standard "Take Me Back to Tulsa," Wills gives a shout-out to Greenwood: "Would I like to go to Tulsa, boy I sure would / Let me off at Archer and I'll walk down to Greenwood." The Gap Band, whom Leon later signed to his Shelter Records label, named themselves in tribute to their hometown neighborhood, with "Gap" standing for Greenwood, Archer, and Pine Streets.

Growing up, Leon probably knew nothing of the Tulsa Massacre. That appalling chapter in history was erased for decades and not taught in the city's segregated schools. But he was drawn to the Greenwood neighborhood by the music. "There was a club on Greenwood Avenue in Tulsa called the Flamingo," Leon explained. "It was the local version of many Black music halls that proliferated throughout America before all the commotion about civil rights. In those days, the ghetto was invisible and nonexistent to the white power structure. The philosophy was, 'If they stay on their side of town, they can do anything they want,' and that's exactly what 'they' did."

As drummer Jim Karstein, a few years younger than Leon and who later played and recorded, and even lived with him in Los Angeles, recalled, "It was before liquor was illegal, and no closing hours. Places could just go around the clock, especially once you'd go over to the north side."

But once the white musicians stepped out of the clubs after hanging out and jamming with Black musicians, bigotry was never far away. "I didn't understand Southern Bible Belt Protestant racism, in terms of brotherhood, which they preached simultaneously," Leon said in 1970. "That was perhaps the first indication I had that something was amiss." As for his family's reaction at the time, he described them as "the normal, average, Christian Midwestern bag . . . and racism as well." Leon's wife and daughters said his mother, Hester, was racist, as were her two husbands.

At about age sixteen, Leon and his more adventurous buddies stayed out at the Flamingo watching full-blown R&B revues that lasted until dawn. He recalled, "The place was a gold mine of influence for a young musician." He saw shows like the Lloyd Price Show of Stars, with Price's twenty-five-piece band, revues that featured other stars like Ruth Brown, Chuck Berry, and Fats Domino. He was also exposed to some of the titans of R&B at the Big Ten Ballroom, on the north side of the city, including

Bobby "Blue" Bland with Junior Parker, Ray Charles, and Jackie Wilson. In 1971, Leon called Charles "one of the great innovators": "He was so unique in his early days before everybody started being influenced by him, so I always went and saw him as often as I could. I suppose I listened to his early records and Elvis Presley's more than anybody else's."

Elvis broke nationwide in 1956 with "Heartbreak Hotel," his first single for RCA, and played the Tulsa Fairgrounds in April the same year. But a few guys in Tulsa were already hip to Elvis's Sun Records sides before '56. Leon first saw Cale, who lived in the same part of town, on local television playing with the Valentines, led by Bobby Taylor, an Elvis impersonator. "I thought he was quite spectacular," Leon said. He and Cale did not play much together before they both ended up in LA years later.

Elvis, as a white performer translating the blues and merging it with country to form rockabilly while mixing in gospel and Tin Pan Alley–type popular ballads, was a revelation for the young white musicians of Tulsa. But as a pianist, Leon had two foundational pillars: Jerry Lee Lewis and Little Richard. Not very well known was another influence, Esquerita, the stage name of Eskew Reeder, from whom Little Richard took a great deal of his sound and image, including the hair piled high in a pompadour. "He made Little Richard look like a choirboy," Leon recalled. "Esquerita's standard wardrobe consisted of toreador pants that looked as though they were painted on and a see-through blouse covered with sequins, along with high-heeled pumps, jewelry, mascara, and false eyelashes that would make even Tammy Faye Bakker blush. . . . He came up to me one night and said, 'Honey, come up to my room at the Small Hotel, and if I can't make you scream in thirty seconds, I'll give you my TV.'"

Leon's expanding record collection represented his broadening interests. And he had opinions. "Back when I was a kid, I got mad at Nat King Cole because he didn't sound Black enough to me, you know what I mean? But then later on, when I matured and grew up somewhat, I heard the Nat King Cole Trio, which is some of the most astonishing piano playing on the face of the earth, which was piano, drums, and guitar. And you know, same thing with Lou Rawls. I played on a lot of his records. And I don't know, I mean, I was racially prejudiced in sort of a backward way. I didn't much care for Black singers that sang like white people."

Tulsa was a small city, but one with a thriving music scene. Around age fourteen, Leon was also playing with some of the wilder groups at clubs "where people could go and drink twenty-four hours a day," Leon explained. "The police didn't pay any attention, and there weren't any kind of rules. . . . When something like that happens, when people don't get caught up in that political morality, it creates kind of a hotbed of musical experience."

Oklahoma was not a completely dry state. Some nightclubs were allowed to serve beer with 3.2 percent alcohol by volume, but nothing stronger. Enforcement was weak, leaving the doors open for bootleggers and patrons to sneak in their own bottles. Many bootleggers owned some of the nightspots, so the whole scene was sketchy. Gambling and territorial disputes led to shootings—even bombings.

"Another club I played all the time exploded one night, quite unexpectedly and completely," Leon recalled. "One minute it was there, and the next minute it covered about three square blocks. . . . After that initial explosion, there were six bombings and five fires in a ten-week period. Each and every club owner was convinced that his club was destroyed by a neighbor down the street to eliminate competition."

Another explosion took place at the Casa Del in the Glenhaven neighborhood along Route 66. Leon discussed it with a "famous Arkansas rocker" (Levon Helm of The Band) who'd once told him about one night while drumming for Ronnie Hawkins: "Yeah, I worked at that fucking joint," Helm said. "They wouldn't pay me, so I put thirty-five sticks of dynamite in there and blew up their fucking joint." Helm described the same event with similar details in his memoir.

David Gates, who went to Leon's high school, is described by many as the most business-minded and ambitious of the young Tulsa rock 'n' rollers. Gates's music was meticulous and polished. Leon learned a great amount from their collaboration, when they recorded a couple of locally released singles as the Accents, likely the earliest recordings that feature Leon, and they would continue their collaborative efforts in Los Angeles into the mid-1960s. In the meantime, Gates graduated in 1958 and went off to the University of Oklahoma, and Leon met drummer Chuck Blackwell. "One night while I was playing on a flatbed trailer in downtown Tulsa," Blackwell said, "a young guy by the name of Russell Bridges came by and asked me if I'd be interested in joining a small group he was putting together." They referred to this group as the second version of the Accents, which Gates would continue to use for gigs between classes and semesters at college. "We played jazz standards at the Momar Supper Club east of Peoria on 51st Street."

Leon also recalled the Momar, which held jam sessions on the weekends that started about midnight and went well into the following mornings, with many of the jazz-loving musicians who played the earlier country music shows around town letting loose after hours. "Of course, they [the musicians] couldn't get jobs playing jazz. So they played hillbilly music. And so they'd go out to the Momar club and played jazz for eight or ten hours. I learned a lot listening to those guys."

Leon also enlisted Blackwell in the newly formed Starlighters, the band that would go on tour with Jerry Lee Lewis. Lucky Clark was on bass and, though Leon seemed to have forgotten it, Johnny (later known as J. J.) Cale was on guitar. Later, Leo Feathers, a teenage Cherokee rodeo cowboy who happened to be a hotshot guitar picker, replaced Cale. And there was the man later billed on show posters as "Hollywood" Johnny Williams on sax. ("I don't know *where* the 'Hollywood' came from," Williams said with a laugh.)

By the time Leon was in ninth grade, the Starlighters and other combos of the same pool of musicians were playing every night. "We were playing the Birdcage, the Paradise, and we had the Club A-Go-Go, the Fondalite," Johnny Williams said. There was an impressive number of evocative mid-century club names like the Peppermint Lounge, the Continental, the Orbit, the House of Blue Lights, the Morocco, and Club Sahara.

And then there was the Tropicana Club, where one of the most famous photos in Tulsa music history was taken. From left to right: Leo Feathers, jacket and tie, his Cherokee features in profile. On the drums, in shirt and tie, is Blackwell, dirty blond hair swept back. Behind him is Ron Ryles on bass, sitting in that night for Lucky Clark. Johnny Williams stands at the ready, holding his sax, in a dark plaid jacket and tie. And there, on a folding wooden chair—with an upside-down crate as a booster—sits Russell Bridges, soon to be known as Leon Russell, looking kind of like Dave Brubeck: horn-rimmed glasses, French cuffs peeking from his jacket sleeves, hunched over the upright piano opened to the soundboard.

In the photo, Leon appears to be listening intently to the two men who share a single microphone, Jumpin' Jack Dunham and Jimmy "Junior" Markham, two of the early rock 'n' roll singers in Tulsa, who sat in with the Starlighters that night.

Drummer Jim Karstein recalled the first time he met Leon, at Griff's Supper Club, where Leon was playing with the Starlighters. "They were such accomplished musicians. I was just completely flabbergasted. They were playing a few of the hits of the day, but they would also dip into the old standards. They weren't playing what you would call hard rock 'n' roll."

Unless you stuck around until after dinner. "Russell was especially good at playing Erroll Garner–style jazz during dinner," said Blackwell. "But then, after everybody got through eating, he'd break into Jerry Lee Lewis."

Nineteen fifty-nine was the big year for Leon and the Starlighters. Leon graduated high school at seventeen, and that's the summer they played the gig at Cain's, opening for and backing Jerry Lee Lewis.

Hitting the road with Jerry Lee Lewis sure beat going to college for Leon. Leon "had about a 144 IQ," Williams said. "I talked him out of going to college."

But the tour ended abruptly after the Kiowa, Kansas, show, when The Killer really did have appendicitis that required surgery. The two remaining shows of roughly two months of touring were canceled and the Starlighters returned to Tulsa. In an attempt to capitalize on the band's momentum, their manager, Jack Shaw, tried to get the Starlighters traction nationally. A booking agent heard them perform and suggested the band should make a record.

The band booked Gene Sullivan's Hi-Fi Studio in Oklahoma City, where they recorded Leon's "Creepin'," backed with "Hot Licks," penned by Feathers. The bluesy "Creepin'" sounds like a striptease in a haunted house. Leon launches the track with a tongue-in-cheek ersatz classical two-chord intro. The band sounds taken by surprise at the way Leon ends the track. "Hot Licks" sounds like early Duane Eddy.

An even better recording was "All Right" backed with "Swanee River," with Leon tearing it up very much like his mentor Jerry Lee, with a twist of Ray Charles. This was recorded for the WKY label. Leon wrote "All Right," and the act was billed as "Russell Bridges and the Starlighters." It was not released widely until many years later, after Leon was famous, on the Chess label. Leon sounds fully confident taking the vocals for the first time on record. Both tracks display a Jerry Lee Lewis influence, not only on the breathtaking piano work but also in the arrangement, production, and Leon's vocals. "All Right" is a screamer, and Leon wails on the keys while howling like The Killer had on "Great Balls of Fire."

Released in 1959, "Creepin'"/"Hot Licks" charted locally, got a notice in *Billboard* magazine, and resulted in a tour of Oklahoma and Louisiana. But after that, "We had broke up the band because I got married in March of 1960," said Williams.

Chapter 4

Oklahoma's Lonesome Cowboys Are Turned On in Tinseltown

BACK IN TULSA AFTER THE tour with Jerry Lee Lewis, Chuck Blackwell said, "We heard that there were some Tulsa musicians who had gone to California. Leon and I decided to also go out to California to find out what was going on."

As the fifties flipped into the sixties, Hollywood was on the cusp of becoming a hotbed for rock 'n' roll's second wave. Leon went out to Los Angeles in June 1960. A singer and guitarist, Bill Pair, had gone out first, immediately after graduating from Will Rogers High. Jimmy "Junior" Markham, who went to LA in 1961, said there was enough work in night-clubs there and in Orange County to keep any capable musician booked every night of the week. Pair helped fellow migrant musicians get gigs and a place to stay. Musicians went back to Tulsa and spread the word. "Our style went over real good out there," recalled Pair.

"I loaned him forty dollars," Johnny Williams said, "him [Leon] and a guitar player, Lee Weir, to go to California, put them on a bus. He never did pay me back the forty dollars! He owes me a lot of interest." Williams laughed.

"It's amazing that I didn't end up in jail, or dead, or both after I arrived in California for the first time," Leon wrote in a memoir he started (but never completed). "Except for the Jerry Lee Lewis tour, I had never been away from home for any length of time and was completely inexperienced and naïve about the ways of the world." His promised job at the Golden

Arms in Torrance lasted only one night, and he did not find work again for months. He crashed on people's floors, including Bill Pair's.

Leon went out to LA and back three times over eighteen months before staying permanently. Chuck Blackwell and Johnny Williams joined him. They worked as the Starlighters at the Dollhouse in North Hollywood and other area nightclubs their first summer of 1960. Leon was drinking heavily by the time he reached California, up to a pint of whiskey a day. "I don't know how many nights I took him home because he'd be drunk out of his little old mind," Williams said. "He was the nastiest drunk."

With his relocation came his transition into the Leon Russell name. "My ID card that I borrowed to play when I was underage was from a Cajun man, Lionel Debreaux," he said. Debreaux was a friend who would cook for Russell and his friends and help them haul their gear to gigs. When Leon told the story in *The Union*—Cameron Crowe's documentary about making the album of the same name—he pronounced it "Leon-el." "But people called me Russell, cuz my real name is Russell Bridges, and I wanted to make it look like that was part of my name."

Leon would make connections at various after-hours jam sessions on Friday and Saturday nights around LA. Top session guitarist James Burton was the most pivotal. Burton first met Leon in Louisiana, and then again at a club in the San Fernando Valley.

"He was working at Sun Valley Rancho out there in the Valley," Burton said. "I went out one night to sit in, and Leon was playing piano. . . . We got to be the best of friends. . . . I'd go out and set in and play, and I'd drive him back to his apartment over there and in the Valley. . . . He didn't even have a car at that time."

Leon recalled it differently, that they met at jam sessions at the Palomino in North Hollywood, a legendary venue famous for country and western and, later, country rock. Tommy Allsup, another Okie, hooked Leon up with a weekly gig there. Allsup would also soon connect Leon with his earliest studio session work. "That's where I met James," Leon said. "James played for a month or two and then got a job with Bob Luman in Vegas."

Burton knew rockabilly singer Luman from adolescence in Louisiana. Burton was fifteen when he wrote the classic riff to "Suzie Q," a hit for Dale Hawkins. He was sixteen when he accompanied Luman out to

Hollywood to appear in the 1957 movie *Carnival Rock*, directed by the king of low-budget teen films Roger Corman. While in town, they played a show that teen heartthrob Ricky Nelson, star of *The Adventures of Ozzie and Harriet*, attended. Nelson had already had a hit record and hired Burton to stay in Hollywood in Nelson's band. Every week, *Ozzie and Harriet* signed off with Nelson performing a song. His appearances on national television made Burton an early guitar hero for kids across the country, and he would go on to become one of the most legendary sidemen and session players in rock 'n' roll and country music.

Though still a very young man himself, Burton was three years older than Leon when he befriended the young Tulsan. Leon said, "James'd come pick me up the next day and take me down to see Ricky Nelson, take me out to eat, take care of me." Burton got Leon on some of the Nelson sessions.

Leon also credited Burton with teaching him guitar, perhaps indirectly. When he'd first arrived in LA, Leon took up guitar, playing along endlessly to a Freddie King record. The paralysis on his right side meant it took a year to learn how to hold a pick properly. "He watched me a lot," Burton acknowledged. "But he would always ask me, 'How do you do this? How'd you do that?' And I would sit down with him and show him stuff. . . . He just *really* locked into it, man." Leon would sit in with Burton on club dates playing guitar.

The Palomino was fruitful ground for Leon. The house band was made up of guys who gigged at night while working sessions during the day, including Gene Davis (guitar, vocals), Red Rhodes (steel guitar), Delaney Bramlett (bass, vocals), Mel Taylor (drums), and Glen D. Hardin (piano). Bramlett and Hardin would soon be members of the Shindogs, the house band on *Shindig!*, the 1964 show that Leon was part of as well. And Hardin went on to play with the Crickets (years after Buddy Holly's death) and in 1970 joined Burton in Elvis Presley's TCB band.

In these early days in LA, Leon also became close friends with Sonny Curtis of the Crickets, who had collaborated with and played alongside Holly. "There was a kind of a movement from Tulsa out to California and Leon sort of headed that movement," Curtis said. "And we of course— J. I. [Allison] and Glen Hardin, another piano player, and I—lived in California to pursue our record career. And Leon and those guys like J. J. Cale and Jimmy Karstein, and Chuck Blackwell, they all lived around there, so it was kind of inevitable that we ran into each other because we're from roughly the same part of the country, us being from West Texas."

Via the Valley connections, Leon appeared on a local television show during this period. "He was on *Cal's Corral*," said composer/singer-songwriter Randy Newman, who got to know Leon in his early days in LA. "He was on television. *That* was of some significance." Leon played on the show with permutations of the ever-evolving Palomino house bands.

Like most of the Tulsans, Leon was back and forth between LA and Tulsa as the little drips of money came and went, as they chased gigs and popped Benzedrine to keep themselves alert.

Eventually, Leon and Chuck settled in LA together and had steady work in the Downey and Norwalk area. David Gates and Jim Karstein soon followed, having hatched the plan to motor west over the summer of 1961. Karstein recalled, "Gates was really an instigator. Gates was a man with a plan. He knew exactly what he was going to do." After a period when Chuck and Leon rented a room next to a laundromat at a trailer park, the two and Tulsa bassist Carl Radle eventually moved to the downstairs rooms in a house that Gates leased when he'd arrived in Hollywood with his wife and child.

The Tulsa guys were networking at jam sessions. Over the autumn of 1961, Leon and David Gates fell in with a crew of musicians at the Crossbow out in the Valley, including Glen Campbell, Tommy Allsup, and Jim Seals and Dash Crofts, who later became a soft rock duo. During these early days in California, Leon met a guitarist with whom he would collaborate through his peak as a rock star, Don Preston, who sat in for J. J. Cale one night. One of Leon's first (and relatively few) road gigs took him on the road with Paul Revere and the Raiders. In late 1960, the Boise, Idaho, band had recorded an instrumental called "Like, Long Hair," a boogie-woogie sendup of Rachmaninoff's "Prelude in C-sharp minor." By early '61, the record was a Top 40 hit, leading to the Raiders' first appearance on *American Bandstand*. But just as they were getting this early taste of success, their leader Paul Revere Dick was drafted, which took him out of the group for about two years while his partner Mark Lindsay held the band together. On one tour, Lindsay had Leon filling in for Paul Revere.

But they were still relatively inexperienced, and Lindsay was a nervous wreck. He got a big lesson from Leon, whose experience sitting in for Jerry Lee Lewis was still fresh. "I'm dying up there," Lindsay recalled. "At intermission, I said, 'Man, this is a tough crowd.' Leon says, 'Look, when we get back out there, if you get in trouble, just kick it to me. I'll show you.' So I sang a couple of songs, and it was just dead. So I went, 'Okay, Leon.' So he jumps up and shouts, 'Hey! What the fuck's goin' on? Didn't you come here to have a good time?' The audience answers, 'Yeah!' So he goes, 'Yeeoww!' kicks over the stool, throws up the lid to the piano, and goes into 'Great Balls of Fire.' I said, 'I get it.'"

Leon and crew were back in Tulsa for the holidays at the end of 1961. Don Nix and his band the Mar-Keys—the Memphis group that included Donald "Duck" Dunn and Steve Cropper of the classic Stax Records house band Booker T. & the MG's—first met Leon and the Tulsa guys when the Mar-Keys had a weeklong stint at the Fondalite Hotel for New Year's week 1961–1962. Though the Mar-Keys had already enjoyed a hit single, "Last Night," Nix felt a kinship with the Oklahomans, "playing the same music at local clubs and dances in Tulsa, a town not all that different from Memphis." It was the beginning of some meaningful friendships; Nix and Leon would become especially close by the late sixties.

Leon soon returned to LA, and word of his talent got around the studio scene there. He began getting hired for recording sessions. Between gigs, he and Gates were also starting to make inroads recording demos for songwriters, thanks partly to connections like James Burton and session bassist and producer Joe Osborn.

Another key figure from the Palomino was Tommy Allsup, about ten years older than Leon, who had played with Bob Wills and His Texas Playboys. Allsup played guitar on "It's So Easy" for Buddy Holly and was on the tour that ended Holly's life in the plane crash on February 3, 1959. Allsup and Waylon Jennings played in the band, backing Holly and the others, and had gotten bus seats instead of a coveted spot on the plane. Legend has it that Allsup lost a coin toss to Ritchie Valens for the last seat on the plane. Allsup had gone out to LA in 1960 to become an A&R rep for Liberty Records, which had a publishing company called Metric Music. Liberty was founded by violinist Simon "Si" Waronker and became one of the most successful independent record labels of the fifties and sixties.

Leon started doing demos for Metric's songwriters at the company's modest studio in Hollywood, above a Carolina Pines restaurant, a late-night hangout on the corner of Sunset and LaBrea. By 1962–1963, as he worked his way into big-time recording sessions with the group of musicians later nicknamed (by top drummer Hal Blaine) the Wrecking Crew, Leon brought Jim Karstein and other Tulsa buddies into the Metric demo sessions. Karstein explained, "We probably averaged five or six songs a week that he would demo. I would give anything to hear some of those tapes again because Carl [Radle] and I were on bass and drums. Leon a lot of the time on piano, but by the time Leon Russell was in Wrecking Crew, he couldn't always make it, so sometimes it was Gates on piano. If Gates couldn't make it, it was Randy Newman. Glen Campbell or James Burton on guitar, and Jackie DeShannon, who sang a lot of them." Newman recalled, "I was down there and Leon was there. Jimmy Smith, who was P. J. Proby, changed his name and became a star in England. Glen Campbell played on those demos. Fanita [Jones] and those girls [the Blossoms] who became the Crystals, Darlene Love."

Starting out in Chicago, DeShannon had a hit record and was promoting it when she met Eddie Cochran. Cochran was signed to Liberty and gave that label some of its biggest hits. "Jackie's best girlfriend was Sharon Sheeley, who, just as a sidenote, was Eddie Cochran's girlfriend," Karstein said. "In fact, I think she was in the cab when he got killed." Sheeley was a songwriter, penning Ricky Nelson's "Poor Little Fool," the first ever *Billboard* Hot 100 number one song in 1958. She was eighteen at the time, which made her the youngest woman to write a number one hit in America, but it was a long time coming; she had written the song around age fifteen, encouraged by none other than The King. She'd met Elvis Presley as a fan, and he said she should write her own songs.

DeShannon, following Cochran's advice, went to LA and signed with Liberty Records. But they were more interested in her songwriting: Metric Music needed writers to build up their catalog as a prime revenue source. Aside from a memorable tour supporting the Beatles on their first trip through America, DeShannon mostly stayed in LA to churn out songs.

In 1962, Leon, Karstein, Gates, and bassist Carl Radle got a steady gig for about a month as DeShannon's band at Pandora's Box on the Sunset Strip. "Jackie was dating Leon, and Sharon Sheeley was dating Jimmy O'Neill," Karstein explained. "Jimmy O'Neill was the number one disc jockey in LA on the number one station, KRLA. They decided to commandeer Pandora's Box and have a big promo deal. . . . It was a big success. I mean, there were lines down Sunset to get in that place." Around the same time, O'Neill hosted Leon, Radle, and Blackwell on a local television show, *Stepping Out*. The tracks they performed were prerecorded at Liberty's studios. In a couple of years, O'Neill would host *Shindig!*, which would also feature Leon and members of his circle.

Tommy LiPuma, who became a hugely successful record producer—he would work with Leon on his final album *Life Journey* in 2014—recalled being taken to the club on his first night in LA by Liberty Records promo man Bud Dain to see DeShannon. But, LiPuma wrote, "I was immediately taken by the band, especially the acoustic piano player who was razor thin and was wearing a blue seersucker suit with a burgundy tie and a pompadour hairdo, with a very serious expression on his face. It was Leon."

Karstein said that the Pandora's Box run of shows was supposed to be an ongoing showcase for DeShannon. "It was going swimmingly till Jackie remembered that she had set up a surgery to get her nose job and forgot to tell everyone about it." But the show went on. Instead of DeShannon being featured every night, different singers rotated in, including Jan and Dean and Bobby Rydell. This run of shows became *the* place to be in LA and was lousy with movie stars, including Clint Eastwood (who would remain friendly with Leon for decades), Sal Mineo, and Shelley Fabares. On this unnamed house band's nights off, a nascent act called the Beach Boys filled in. In fact, the venue has a place in Beach Boys lore. Brian Wilson said the song "All Summer Long" was inspired by his wife, Marilyn, after he spilled a Coke all over her at Pandora's Box.

Karstein said the Beach Boys performed like such an amateurish garage band that Leon and Carl Radle would snicker to each other while watching them. "I came home for Christmas, '62, and I was listening to the radio, in January or February," Karstein recalled. "One day I call up Leon, I say, 'Hey, Leon! You know that band that used to come in there [Pandora's Box]? What's the deal with those guys? They've had two number one hit records!' He said, 'Yeah, I know. But that piano player's [Brian Wilson] a genius.'"

Leon and Jackie dated for several months after the run of shows, according to Karstein. "Jackie was wonderful, and I was excited with the knowledge that I was going to be working with her," LiPuma said. "But I couldn't get Leon out of my mind. He had a style that even then was very unique and I made it my business to find out his whereabouts."

LiPuma got to know Leon better while the pair hung around the Liberty offices with producer Snuff Garrett, Leon playing piano on most of the song demos. Many of these recordings can be heard on a collection of Sheeley songs released later by RPM Records. Roughly half of them were cowritten by Sheeley and DeShannon. The band on most of the tracks consists of Leon, Gates on bass, Hal Blaine on drums, and Glen Campbell on guitar. And the vocalists include Mac Davis, Herb Alpert, P. J. Proby, Campbell, and Delaney Bramlett. Even Jeff Beck and Jimmy Page show up. LiPuma got to see Leon and these other future stars at work. "When I started to make demos with some of the staff songwriters myself, I hired Leon to help me as I didn't know my ass from the sound console at the time," LiPuma wrote.

Tommy "Snuff" Garrett would become Leon's most valuable connection at Liberty. Starting in Dallas as a DJ, he'd struck up a friendship with Buddy Holly. After Holly died in 1959, Garrett needed a change and looked to get into the record business. Al Bennett, president of Liberty, gave him a job as an A&R rep and producer. Garrett quickly started producing hits. In 1960, "You're Sixteen" and "Dreamin'" for Johnny Burnette and "Devil or Angel" for Bobby Vee, whom he styled after Holly. Garrett and Vee hit again the following year with "Rubber Ball."

In Vee's touring band was a young saxophonist named Bobby Keys, from the Lubbock, Texas, area, who grew up idolizing his neighbor, Holly. Keys hung out in Tulsa between Vee tour dates and became friends with the musicians in Leon's orbit, eventually making his way to LA and a friendship and multiple collaborations with Leon before heading to England to work with George Harrison, John Lennon, and the Rolling Stones.

The first track Snuff Garrett hired Leon to play on was a 1961 demo of "Old Rivers," pitched to Tommy Allsup by friend Cliff Crofford. "I'd sent it to everybody—Johnny Cash, [Tennessee] Ernie Ford—everybody turned the fucking song down," Garrett said. "Finally I cut it myself in kind of a classy way." Actor Walter Brennan did the vocal, a recitation. Allsup had Leon demo it. "That was Leon's piano work," Garrett noted of the final recording. "I fell in love with his playing." It was released in 1962.

As with producers who followed, Garrett could just tell Leon a direction, and he would run with it. They didn't have to give him charts (basic sheet music with arrangements). On "Old Rivers," Leon shows a distinct Floyd Cramer, Nashville influence. Leon, though, was not credited on the track—he was nineteen and still too young to join the American Federation of Musicians (AFM) Union, Local No. 47, which required members to be twenty-one or older. Though Garrett implied Leon is playing piano, Leon had likely formulated the part and demoed it for Gene Garf to execute, per the AFM contract. Or it is possible they just wrote in Garf's name. Union credits were commonly inaccurate, and musicians often swapped credits as favors.

"I had to borrow IDs to get in clubs, borrow union cards and all that stuff," Leon said. "The union was real rough, they called that 'homesteading.' The guy who used to be president was Liberace's bass player. . . . I kind of yelled at him pretty bad and called him a 'Nazi.'"

The demo sessions kept Leon working most days of the week. "We would go in," said Don Randi, "both of us, he and I would do two for twenty-five, or 'twofers,' to help out songwriters." Randi was a fellow pianist who was already working sessions and who would sometimes have Leon sub in for him at live gigs on the Strip. "We would do that in the other studio, like Gold Star [Studio] B. Sometimes on Saturday, we would do—God, I don't know how many writers and songwriters. We'd have to figure out the chord changes, and we were jumping all over it."

Leon had the phony "Lionel Debreaux" ID to gig at nightclubs in the LA area. He soon obtained more convincing identification, with his actual name on it, which he took to the Tulsa local of the AFM on one of his trips back home. That allowed him to join the union via a back door, so when Leon returned to LA, he could receive credit on sessions under his actual name, Russell Bridges. With this, he graduated from the minor to the major league. His talent was too great to keep hacking out demos. By the autumn of 1962, he was working almost every day on AFM-contracted sessions, sometimes two or more a day, a pace that would only grow more intense and that he would maintain for about five years solid.

In addition to playing on others' demos, Randy Newman was himself a young songwriter at Metric. He benefited from having Leon play on demos of his first copyrighted songs. "Leon would play on them, and Gates would arrange them," Newman said. "Sometimes there would be a couple of horns or more. They were kind of elaborate demos." He was impressed by Leon's ability. "I was meek and mild, a kid at the time, and deferred to him on my own songs because he was just great. The octaves he could play was something that was beyond me and still are."

When pianists talk about the ability to play octaves, they mean playing the same notes in two octaves with one hand, and maybe two more with the other, and playing chords or melodic runs in parallel. "And he had a good left hand, as I recall," Newman said. "But it was the *gospel* sort of right hand that I had not heard a great deal of—some. I don't remember the first time I heard Ray Charles; it was '59, I think. But this was seven years from when rock 'n' roll started for white America. I mean, it had *just* started in a lot of ways, but it was all there pretty quick. And his gospel playing was kind of a revelation to me. And octaves are hard. You've got to practice and do a lot of playing to do it, and I don't know how he did it."

In 1998, Leon told *Musician* magazine that the octaves playing was influenced by composer Edvard Grieg. "I worked real hard on certain things because I didn't have other things, and that's one example. I felt that they could work as a melodic tool. I used to practice lines and octaves on both hands," simultaneously as well as alternately. He also explained that he would approach the piano beyond the perspective of a typical pianist. "I tried harmonica-like solos in my right hand on the piano because the harmonica has certain built-in limitations. You really have to have an overview of some kind to make that work because not all the notes are there, so there's just a few acceptable licks you can do. . . . Floyd Cramer was playing pedal steel licks. Blues is different; that's what I was doing."

"You see those hands, which are enormous," said Leon's most famous protégé, Elton John, calling Leon's "the biggest hands I've seen apart from [Bruce] Hornsby and Keith Jarrett. They're the largest fingers I've ever seen. You know he's got a pretty big span. I, of course, have little sausage fingers. I'm happy if I've got an octave."

Randy Newman noted that rock 'n' roll "hit the public like a square white-sounding kind of thing" after the movie *Blackboard Jungle*. Plus, it was turning into big business and Los Angeles was emerging as serious competition to New York City as a powerhouse in music and television, adding to the thriving Hollywood movie industry. And though Liberty/Metric's first hit was Julie London's torch ballad "Cry Me a River," the label had 1958 rock 'n' roll hits with Eddie Cochran's "Summertime Blues" and "C'mon Everybody," making it as good a place as any to be in the early-sixties rock 'n' roll biz.

Musicians were flocking to Hollywood from places like Texas, Oklahoma, Chicago, and New Orleans. Newman, who grew up visiting his mother's hometown of New Orleans, said he wasn't sure how much music he consciously picked up there. "But I love Fats Domino. And I loved the way Leon played. I think the whole world did eventually." Newman said Leon had it all, including the sense of time. "Leon had time like a rock." The famously self-deprecating Newman contrasted himself with Leon in the matter of keeping steady time. When asked if he had played with drummer Jim Gordon during those days, he replied, "Yep. You bet—quite a bit. I've played with him or *against* him. I'm sorry to say it was my time. Ask [Jim] Keltner about it. Every step I've taken, I was pulled and dragged or pushed. I didn't feel confident about playing on my own records until Leon said, 'You know, you should play on your own, you're fine.'"

Also pushing Newman early on was Lenny Waronker, son of Liberty/Metric's owner Simon Waronker. Lenny and Randy had been hanging around music since they were children, first on Twentieth Century–Fox movie sets, where Newman's uncle, Al, was a composer and conductor (he composed the famous Twentieth Century–Fox fanfare) and Si Waronker, an instrumentalist, and then later at Liberty and Metric. "Randy and I met Leon and Dave Gates, I guess, when they just got here," Waronker said. "They were young." They *were* young—Leon was about the same age as both Newman and Waronker—but Leon and Gates seemed much further developed to Newman, who said, "I was still living at home. [Leon] seemed like a grown-up, he and Gates both. . . . They were a different kind of people, it seems, even then. Gates was foursquare, and Leon was on the hip side. . . . Look at the both of them; radically different paths they took."

Lenny Waronker started as a promo man at Liberty but quickly changed into A&R and publishing at Metric. He became a successful producer and eventual head of Warner Bros. Records through the label's prolific growth period of the 1970s and 1980s. "I thought I needed to learn some stuff, so I tried promotion, which was awful," he said. "Then the publishing thing opened up."

A well-regarded songwriter, still obscure as a performer, named Willie Nelson was signed to Liberty Records as a recording artist in 1961. Though Leon and Willie would not meet for another nine or ten years, Leon played piano on Willie's *...And Then I Wrote*, recorded September 11–12, 1961, at Radio Recorders, with Joe Allison producing. Allison had started the record in Nashville the previous month but was unhappy with the results, so he brought the sessions to LA, where Glen Campbell,

Red Callender, Billy Strange, and others contributed. The album includes songs that have become standards, like "Hello Walls," "Funny How Time Slips Away," and "Crazy." Leon shines on "Mr. Record Man," reintroducing the track with that slip-note style that Floyd Cramer pioneered, slipping quickly from a note below the target note in a way that makes the piano approximate the bends of a guitar.

As with many of the sessions he would do over the years, Leon had no idea which artist would be singing over the rhythm tracks he recorded. At Nelson's house in the 1970s, he heard this album and half-jokingly protested that whoever played piano on the record was stealing his riffs—until the two friends figured out it was Leon himself.

One of if not the first session Leon got union credit for was a Snuff Garrett–produced Johnny Burnette recording of "Just Out of Reach," on December 11, 1961, at Liberty's Custom Recorders. Leon provides a relaxed sixteenth-note cadence in the higher register of the loping arrangement. Tommy Allsup and Dick Glasser are the guitarists; the great Earl Palmer is on drums. Palmer had already cemented his legacy with his early work on classics by Little Richard, Fats Domino, and Lloyd Price. His backbeat on Domino's 1949 boogie "The Fat Man" is one of rock 'n' roll's foundational underpinnings.

There are also a couple of well-known jazz players on the Burnette recording. Bassist Red Callender had played with a couple of Leon's influences, Erroll Garner and Nat King Cole. There's also the jazz luminary Barney Kessel—who grew up in Muskogee, Oklahoma—on guitar. Among other highlights, Kessel had played the smooth accompaniment to Julie London's hit "Cry Me a River," a song Leon would later feature in the *Mad Dogs & Englishmen* set with a markedly different arrangement.

Leon was high on the experience of his first "real sessions" with the "main guys" at the studio where he had been working almost every day. "Many nights I had stood outside one studio or another and watched people like Earl Palmer, who would arrive in his new Cadillac," Leon remembered. "Now here I was on the 'inside,' with Earl playing drums and Barney Kessel on guitar."

Leon's session work had just started, but his star rose quickly, and he became one of three or four top LA pianists always in demand. His calendar would have few openings until the 1970s. He was not only technically impressive but also brought an earthy personality to his playing. First-call

Wrecking Crew guitarist Tommy Tedesco recalled an early session with Glen Campbell and Leon Russell. "They brought Leon in and, I'll never forget, Leon panicked and was sitting there, and Glen said, 'Leon, just play that shit you did in Oklahoma. They don't know *nothing* here.' So Leon played Leon Russell, and all of a sudden, they *don't* know nothing, that was his style, that's what they loved, and that's what he did from there on in."

Keith Allison—a young guitarist who migrated out from Texas and later joined Paul Revere & the Raiders—said Leon was hanging out over at producer Gary Paxton's studio in Hollywood around the time Leon took that gig as a substitute Paul Revere. "It was an old Craftsman house that they turned into a studio. There was a bunch of hits coming out of that little funky studio on a side street in Hollywood."

Paxton hired Leon for some sessions. "He was known for hiring the down-and-out and was a big supporter of musicians in general," Leon said. "The first Paxton session I played on was for Bobby 'Boris' Pickett of 'Monster Mash' fame, for the album that followed Pickett's hit single." (Contrary to some reports, Leon is not on the "Monster Mash" single itself.) "Those days came well before [Paxton's] resurgence as a religious re-cording artist, and he was drinking a lot of whiskey then, as well as taking the odd Benzedrine tablet," Leon wrote.

Paxton was the first producer to give David Gates and Leon a shot as recording artists, releasing the Paxton-penned "Sad September" backed with (b/w) "Tryin' to Be Someone" in October 1962, credited to "David and Lee" (Lee being Leon). "They had a house band," Allison said. "It was guys crashing there. You came in with a song, and for a few bucks, [Paxton] would cut there. If it was good enough, he would release it." "Sad September" is a moody number that sounds like a transition from the Everly Brothers' tight-harmony sound into something new. David and Leon's duet is surrounded by reverb-soaked strings, which ebb and flow while Leon teases out piano accents. It is a link to the chamber pop of the mid-1960s: the Walker Brothers, the Left Banke, and the Association, the latter group produced by Paxton.

The B-side "Tryin' to Be Someone" features James Burton pulling twangy licks from his Telecaster, while Gates and Russell sound a little like the Everly Brothers fronting Buck Owens's Buckaroos. The song was written by Gates, and he and Leon formed a music publishing company called Dragonwyck in 1962.

In October, instrumental surf masters the Ventures were in town and recorded *The Ventures Play Telstar and the Lonely Bull*, with Leon playing organ on the soaring Joe Meek–penned earworm "Telstar." His melody jumps out on the recording. Gates played bass on the record, which became the biggest seller for the Ventures, selling over five million copies worldwide.

Leon's work accelerated as 1962 rolled on. He wrote a letter to Jimmy Markham that November 19 on Dragonwyck Music Company letterhead, in part:

> Carl probably told you about our new house. It really is kind of
> a gas but still mainly an experiment and how to live above your
> means.
>
> David and I are in the process of signing a production deal
> with a Walt Disney subsidiary called Colosseum Records. We
> would have a pretty gassey position if we get the percentage we
> are trying for.
>
> I played a gig Saturday night in Pismo Beach with perhaps the
> heaviest group I have ever played with. Glenn [*sic*] Campbell was
> on guitar, Steve Douglas was on saxophone (he is the West Coast
> representative for Leiber and Stoller Productions), David played
> bass and a fellow named Hal Blaine played drums. He works
> with Patty Page and Tammy Sands. It was a pretty wild group.
> All the guys are studio cats and hardly ever take regular gigs, but
> we all decided that it would be fun and Glenn had the gig as the
> "Champs" so we took it and had a ball.

The letter must have been enough of a siren song, for soon, Leon and Markham were renting a one-bedroom house off of La Cienega Boulevard together.

Other notable 1962 sessions included the Everly Brothers' "Little Hollywood Girl" and Jackie DeShannon's "Breakaway." On November 5, Leon recorded "Everybody but Me" with Johnny Rivers, a songwriter who was soon a star in his own right.

Leon and David Gates finished off the year with a session for Liberty's producer, Dick Glasser. They put together an instrumental band of the Tulsa fellows billed as the Fencemen, with Chuck Blackwell, Gates, and

Leon. The first single was a Gates cowrite, "Swingin' Gates," backed with Leon's "Bach n' Roll," which features overdubs of organ trading off with a tack piano (thumbtacks fastened to the hammers in an upright piano for a more percussive sound). Leon played both parts.

The Fencemen was one of dozens of studio-only "bands" made up of session musicians, with Leon, Tommy Tedesco, Billy Strange, and Glen Campbell often contributing. Other records made by different combinations of these musicians included the De-Fenders, the Routers, the Deuce Coups, and other surf/hot rod–inspired releases. There was even a "band" led by drummer Hal Blaine called Hal Blaine & the Young Cougars. Almost every track on the resulting album, *Deuces, "T's," Roadsters & Drums*, opens with the revving of engines and peeling of tires of drag strips. Leon recalled, "It was a lot of fun doing those stupid records."

Chapter 5

The Wall of Sound

AS THE SOUNDS OF PEELING tires and revving engines from drag races fade in your mind, cue in the famous Hal Blaine *boom, boom, boom, BANG! Boom, boom, boom, BANG!* beat that kicks off the Ronettes' 1963 smash "Be My Baby" and settle into that lush Wall of Sound. This is one of the Phil Spector sessions that Leon played on in July 1963.

There's an argument to be made that the most significant American bands were not really bands at all; they were the now-legendary studio session players who formed core groups in Detroit, Muscle Shoals, Memphis, Nashville, New York, Chicago, and Hollywood. Even the Byrds and Beach Boys, two of the most innovative and successful American bands, had the regular session musicians later referred to as the Wrecking Crew play on their biggest records.

Session musicians were technically independent and interchangeable. But the nicknamed house bands—the Funk Brothers at Motown, the Swampers in Muscle Shoals, the Wrecking Crew in Hollywood—did have core members. These A-listers played together with a measurable chemistry. Songwriter Jeff Barry explained that Hal Blaine "was the nucleus of some guys who just all *thought* the same time. I mean, time is more than a metronome."

Leon worked his way into this burgeoning group of elite players-for-hire in Hollywood, variously described as the Regulars, the Clique, the Guys, or early on with Phil Spector, the Wall of Sound. When Blaine published his book *Hal Blaine and the Wrecking Crew* in 1990, they started being referred to as the Wrecking Crew. Though Leon received his official membership in the AFM Local 47 musicians union on July 3,

33

1963, he had already established a reputation. Musicians like Leon were slowly replacing "the Suits," as the younger musicians called them—that buttoned-up bunch who had little patience for rock 'n' roll, for improvisation, and for the looseness that the younger breed displayed. The old group felt the new louche bunch was going to "wreck the business," hence the nickname.

But Dean Torrence explained that a regular group of the people known as the Wrecking Crew started by playing on the records by his duo, Jan and Dean. That duo began in high school by forming doo-wop groups with future actor James Brolin and future Beach Boy Bruce Johnston. "Jan [Berry] kind of handpicked the guys. Originally, we used to use a lot of Black guys that were normally doing jazz records, the Ernie Freeman Band. They were good—really, really good. And then somewhere along the line, we ran into Hal [Blaine] and then, once we ran into Hal, it was all over. We started from scratch and just built people, we handpicked people around Hal or would use—if he had suggestions—if Hal said, 'Well, I've worked with this guy, this guy, and this guy,' we'd say, 'Okay, let's try to form some sort of chemistry,' which we did. Quite honestly, the Wrecking Crew—and this was 1962—I give Jan credit for putting most of the Wrecking Crew together. A lot of those guys had sometimes played with one another. But there wasn't a cohesive unit, and we were the first ones to pick out a core bunch of maybe six guys, seven guys, and those were the only guys we would use until they didn't want to play anymore."

The basic unit grew, fully coalesced, and came to prominence under the irreverent humor and calculated chaos of Spector, a rising Midas in the record biz. "Phil Spector had a comedic style similar to Don Rickles, using it in sessions at the expense of the players," Leon said. No producer had harnessed the full power of this young group of studio musicians like Spector would. It led to more than twenty consecutive hit records. The quietly wry, wildly talented, and increasingly outré-looking Leon quickly found his place with this new crew. "Everybody fell in love with him too, because he was a real character," Lenny Waronker recalled. "Interesting guy; scary in a way. . . . He was very cool and reserved—smart as hell."

Jack Nitzsche took credit for landing Leon on Planet Spector. They'd met via Jackie DeShannon at Pandora's Box. Nitzsche was at the beginning of an illustrious career, contributing to hundreds of records by the likes of the Rolling Stones, Neil Young, the Monkees, Graham Parker, and

Tom Petty. "[Leon] was an innovative piano player," Nitzsche said. "In those days, it was real hard to find rock 'n' roll piano players who didn't play too much."

In 1963, Nitzsche got a deal with Frank Sinatra's Reprise label to record his own LP, *The Lonely Surfer*. The band included Leon, David Gates on bass, Hal Blaine on drums, and Tommy Tedesco and Ray Pohlman on guitars. Influenced by "The Lonely Bull," Herb Alpert's instrumental smash from the year before, it was surf guitar by way of Ennio Morricone, an immense-sounding production, leagues above the disposable fizz that Leon had largely been recording.

"I had heard about Phil for a long time," said Nitzsche in 1988. "I put the band together for the session, a lot of the same guys I had been working with for years. Phil didn't know a lot of these people; he had been in New York in 1960 to 1962. Leon Russell, Harold Battiste, Earl Palmer, Don Randi, Hal Blaine, Glen Campbell: a lot of the players came out of my phone book." Randi also recalled hiring Leon for Spector sessions. "During the Spector sessions, a lot of the time we had two or three piano players going at once," Nitzsche said. "I played piano as well. Phil knew the way he wanted the keyboards played. It wasn't much of a problem who played. Leon was there for the solos and the fancy stuff, rolling pianos. The pianos were interlocking and things would sound cohesive. I knew Leon would emerge as a band leader."

In August 1962, Leon played on his first session for Spector: "Zip-a-Dee-Doo-Dah," from Walt Disney's 1946 film *Song of the South*, remade as a funky dirge. Leon said, "Phil came up to me and made some sort of hand sign, as if he might be warding off a vampire, and said, 'Dumb. Play dumb.'" The song was a top ten hit. "From that time forward, I played on almost every record he made."

The Spector sessions were recorded at Gold Star Studios, a cozy storefront on Santa Monica Boulevard that was once a dentist's office but that soon became the magic room where everyone wanted to record. Leon noted that Gold Star's Studio A was designed to hold "about five musicians, six at the most. Phil managed to get in twenty-five, with almost enough room left over for someone to walk." Spector envisioned pop symphonies and therefore required a rock 'n' roll orchestra. On their breaks, musicians had to tiptoe over cables, duck under microphones, and limbo under boom stands. Because this was before multitracking enabled the

extensive overdubbing that came later in the decade, mammoth productions like Spector's required as many musicians playing together, cheek by
jowl. If anyone made a glaring error, the take would be halted, and they'd
restart the performance. In more traditional recording sessions, classic
singers like Sinatra would appear and sing live, with the expectation that
the master recording would be done in one, maybe two takes, so musicians
had little margin for error. But Spector's tracking sessions could result in
dozens of takes, sometimes over a hundred before the producer was satisfied and the vocalists could be overdubbed. His principal engineer, Larry
Levine, theorized that wearing down the musicians was part of Spector's
MO. As the takes and hours accumulated, instrumentalists would play
less as individuals and more as a team, a system, the Wall.

Spector's controlled-chaos approach extended to sound leakage. Drums
were picked up by piano mics, while guitar and bass amps washed into the
overhead drum mics. All of it was fed into the famous Gold Star echo chamber, two rooms with walls coated in a highly reflective cement-and-plaster
mixture, located behind Studio A. This wondrous chamber was never seen
by anyone aside from the members of the studio crew. "Not even Phil,"
said studio cofounder David Gold. That's how it remained until the final
session at the studio: Maurice Gibb begged Gold to see the chamber. "He
told me that in their early days back in England when he and his brothers
used to listen to Phil's music, they'd lie in bed and wonder what the chambers looked like. So I allowed him to be the first and only other person to
ever see the inside."

Spector also dialed in tape echo (think early Elvis/Sun Studios "slap-
back" effect). The echo and reverb would be mixed with that lush Wall of
Sound. Often, a mix would be bounced down to a track or two to open
up one for overdubs, degrading the tape signal on each generation. The
vocals, particularly the lead, would be up front in the mix, popping from
the speakers, while all else receded to the background, a comfortable fuzzy
bed for tales of teenage lust, love, and heartache.

"The hardest part was convincing people it could be done," Spector
said. "The hardest part in life is people who don't get it. . . . About anything. I would explain what I was doing to people and they just didn't get
it. If I wanted three pianos, I couldn't get three pianos in the studio, so I'd
get three piano players sitting at one piano, fighting to get their hands on
it. Leon Russell, Brian Wilson sometimes."

Playing sessions with Spector and others, Leon became so busy that he faded out of the club gigs at night. "Once he got on that train, it was nonstop," said Karstein. "It was at least six days a week, maybe sometimes seven. . . . He would probably average at least three sessions a day." Studio musicians were accustomed to producers trying to get them to do extra takes and overtime under the table. But Spector paid well and made sure to adhere to union rules. "We were union men, so that later on in our lives, we get residuals," Randi said. "There's no greater thing for me now, me being this old, I go to the post office box, and there's a check. You can't make a living from it, but it sure as hell helps your income out."

A full list of sessions Leon worked from his arrival in LA until around 1968 would itself take up a hefty book. His schedule in 1963 shows an unrelenting pace that resulted in hundreds of released recordings: the Everly Brothers, Nino Tempo & April Stevens, Dean Martin, Bobby "Blue" Bland, and Sam Cooke. Cooke and Bland were heroes of Leon as a teenager. Now, the twenty-year-old young man was on the piano for Bland's great *Call on Me/That's the Way Love Is* LP, a February 7 session. The album's final track, "Queen for a Day," features young Leon burning up the keys with confident ad-libs, slipped in perfectly alongside Bland's gorgeous vocal, sounding like a pianist who had been accompanying Bland for years.

Few stars impressed Leon more than Aretha Franklin on her fourth album, before she left Columbia for Atlantic and blossomed into the Queen of Soul, on her breathtaking "Say It Isn't So." "I worked with Aretha at Columbia, there was one session when she cut with a big string section, and at the end of the song, they all tapped their bows on the music stand," he marveled. "I wasn't used to seeing that much excitement from a string section."

Spector provided more work for Leon than any other producer in 1963. Recorded in March and released the next month, "Da Doo Ron Ron (When He Walked Me Home)" blasted from radios across the country that summer, hitting number three in June. The Crystals' Dolores "LaLa" Brooks sang the lead and, right from the top, hammering right-hand piano figures pop to the front of the Wall of Sound mix. "I was one of the piano players of 'Da Doo Ron Ron,'" said Ellie Greenwich, also one of the songwriters. "We had to play this part over and over and over again of constant triplets. The constant repetition without any breaks made it really difficult. Your arm got very tired and your fingers started cramping." Leon's piano might not sound complicated, but seek out the instrumental master take of "Da Doo Ron Ron" to appreciate the demanding part that he sustains flawlessly through the song.

"There's a picture, somebody's got it, of how intense it was," Don Randi said. "Leon was playing my piano, and at the same time, I was playing his piano. He put his left hand over onto mine, and I'd put my right hand over onto his while the session was going on. You've got to realize the cacophony of sound with four pianos. That makes the wall of sound."

The singers and players for the productions were essentially interchangeable. Still, the theme of longing—for sex, marriage, liberty, and control—was a constant and would continue to dominate Spector's records. Atlantic Records icon Ahmet Ertegun was awestruck that Spector was "the *only* producer who could create a hit record without a hit artist."

It is easy to see where Leon was learning to be a brilliant arranger, pinballing from sessions with Jimmie Haskell (Sam Cooke and Wayne Newton) and Robert Mersey (Aretha Franklin) to Jack Nitzsche and Phil Spector. "They liked me because they didn't have to write the piano parts out," Leon said. "They just wrote chord sheets and said, 'Play classical,' 'Play country,' 'Play rock 'n' roll.'"

Though he was getting an increasing amount of work on the Spector sessions, Leon's calendar filled up with sessions for other star producers, including Lou Adler, who coproduced Jan and Dean with Jan Berry. The same month as the "Da Doo Ron Ron" session, Leon worked on tracks for the duo's *Surf City* LP, including the title track, cowritten by Brian Wilson, a number one record.

"Brian gave us 'Surf City' half-finished," Torrence said. "And just said, 'If you want to finish it, be my guests.' We took it and finished it . . . and Jan recorded the track that was one of the best tracks we ever cut. And so we took the track and called Brian and said, 'If you want to come in and help us with some vocals, we'd love to have ya.' Brian heard it and he was almost speechless, because he couldn't believe—it was such a good track." Brian asked, "So, how'd you do that?" Jan said, "Brian, these are studio guys; they're the best in the world. They're two hundred bucks, and you'll have the best players in the United States, if not the world." As Randi put it, "We were the studio musicians that you'd better get because we were making hit records."

June brought sessions for the Ventures' *Let's Go!* and the Everly Brothers' *The Everly Brothers Sing Great Country Hits* LP. Leon is prominently featured on the latter. The arrangements are sparse, allowing him to shine through the open spaces on the album. His licks are never hurried; he settles himself right in the pocket. This delightful and overlooked album was a blueprint for the Flying Burrito Brothers and Gram Parsons solo records that came at the decade's end.

Randi said that he and Leon, seated next to each other for hours at a time, shared a sense of humor that helped them cope with Spector. That July, Randi said, "It might have been 'Be My Baby.' We had been in there seven and a half hours or eight hours or something, doing that same song over and over and over again. . . . We went in and listened. As we're listening back, it was a stone-cold hit. We were sitting in the booth, and everybody's packing up, ready to go home. I think Larry Levine was the engineer, and he left the record button on. It erased the tape! We had to go back in for another two hours."

"Be My Baby" was recorded in July 1963 and took thirty five hours. Michael Spenser was one of the four keyboardists, each on a different instrument. "On my left was this fellow in a three-piece suit and a DA [ducktail] hairstyle," he said. "That was Leon Russell before he took acid." What makes it one of the most distinguished *records* of sixties rock 'n' roll is Phil Spector's production, which features Leon playing eighth-note chords to propel the verses, the piano parts popping from the mix. "I figured out early on that if I wanted to be heard on a record I had to play high," Leon said, referring to the upper octaves. "If you don't do that, you'd get lost in the Wall [of Sound] so to speak."

Hal Blaine launches the song on the finished version with one of the most famous beats in rock 'n' roll, a pattern that has been lifted for countless recordings. But he laughed about how he faked his way into that one. "The beat I used on the Ronettes' 'Be My Baby' was actually a mistake," Blaine said. "I was supposed to play more of a *boom-chicky-boom* beat, but my stick got stuck and it came out *boom, boom-boom chick*. I just made sure to make the same mistake every few bars." When it was finished, Spector did what he would always do, checked the mix on tiny and tinny speakers to approximate the sound through a car radio before blasting everyone's ears out on the big speakers in the control room.

As July flipped to August, as the weather got even hotter, the room more crowded and sweltering, Spector, a twenty-three-year-old Jew who loved Christmas (and was born on Christmas Day 1940), decided it was time to make a Christmas album. He had booked Gold Star twenty-four hours a day. Ronnie Spector of the Ronettes said, "Phil started recording in the summer and he didn't leave the studio for about two months. We'd start recording early in the evening, and we'd work until late in the night, sometimes even into the next morning."

A Christmas Gift for You from Phil Spector is one of the only long-playing albums Spector made during this era. Brian Wilson claimed it's his favorite record. It didn't perform very well when it went on sale on November 22, 1963, the day that President John F. Kennedy was assassinated. But the album has become a standard over the intervening decades, particularly the one original song, Darlene Love's "Christmas (Baby Please Come Home)." Written by Ellie Greenwich, Jeff Barry, and Phil Spector, the track is glorious, peak Spector, with Love singing to beat the band.

It is also the apex of Leon's contributions to Spector records. Starting around the 2:00 mark, the man *goes off* at the end. The arrangement pauses, building tension, before hitting that heavenly release, Leon climbing higher and higher on the keyboard. "Everybody had this feeling of grandeur," Love remembered. "We called it Leon's little concerto. He just went wild on the piano and, when he was finished, he fell right off the stool." Spector himself was so excited with the piano climax that he whipped off a bonus check and presented it to Leon as soon as the take was over.

"He really did a lot on those Spector records," said Randy Newman. "He did the top, and he did the bottom with a fast tremolando."

The Christmas album took six weeks. "I never wanted to work with Phil again after that," Levine remembers. "My nerves were shattered, and everyone was exhausted." Although he had been seeing a psychiatrist in New York and would often call him from the studio in LA, Spector's mental illness had been written off as eccentricity, mitigated by his charisma and sheer vision. Randi explained, "He could be very rude. We put up with it because we realized what a great talent he was. Phil Spector was always eccentric, let's put it that way."

There are several stories about Spector the gun nut emptying rounds into the ceiling of a studio on more than one occasion. Eventually, everyone's patience wore thin, even the taciturn Leon Russell, whose MO was to keep his mouth shut and play. "Leon never said boo to anyone," Cher said. (She'd sung on several Spector sessions, including "Be My Baby.") "He would just come in and play his piano." That is, until one day when he reached his limit. Spector's recording dates were "interesting at first," Leon wrote. "But most of the sessions ran seven to eight hours, with the same mundane figures played again and again, except for minor changes or attempted improvements. One day in particular it was starting to drive me crazy! Unfortunately, I followed the lead of my friend and copyist, Roy Caton, who was playing trumpet on the session, and went next door to the liquor store, where I bought a pint of peach-flavored vodka. It was a mistake. About two or three hours and eighty takes later, I was standing on top of the Steinway, doing a pretty good impression of A. A. Allen [one of Leon's favorite televangelists]. That's about all I remember, except for an exchange with Phillip, which started when he said through the talkback mic, 'Leon, don't you know what teamwork means?' 'Phil, do you know what "fuck you" means?' I returned."

Cher remembered that the word Spector asked about was *respect*. "And Leon jumped up on the piano and said, 'Phil, have you ever heard of the word FUCK YOU?' And that was it, people were . . . They couldn't get it together for a half an hour. People were dying on the floor. I mean, tears rolling in the studio because it was the weirdest thing you ever saw." He took on the character of a fire-and-brimstone preacher while yelling at Spector.

"The next day, I didn't recall too much about the whole incident," Leon confessed, "but Tommy Tedesco . . . came over to my apartment and offered to finance a religious tour for me in exchange for half the profits. 'I'm serious about this, now, Leon; I'm not kidding. I'll put up the money for a big tent and trucks and whatever we need. We'll make millions.'" It was another significant step in his development into the charismatic preacher-like rock star who arrived fully formed in the early 1970s.

"I think Leon and I stopped working for [Spector] around the same time," said Don Randi. "Leon was just becoming too big. He was approaching stardom at that point."

This was around the time that Mac Rebennack, soon to be known as Dr. John the Night Tripper, came from New Orleans and started playing piano parts for Spector. Dr. John and Leon were often compared throughout their careers: both amazingly accomplished pianists with Southern-tinged honks when they sang and funky appearances.

Leon did not make a clean break from Spector. Even into the 1970s, he professed his admiration, noting in a 1970 *Rolling Stone* interview, "Some of those people I really studied—like with Phil Spector, with Terry Melcher. I studied their style just because it was so amazing. The main thing, I believe, was to act like I knew how to do it. And that's really true; I was so impressed with his confidence, his apparent awareness of what's going on." Leon and Spector would even work together again in 1973 on John Lennon's *Rock 'n' Roll* LP.

Leon continued laying the groundwork for his solo career. Using the handle "C. J. Russell," he sang lead on a single, "The Girl I Lost in the Rain" b/w "She's the One That Got Away," both written by David Gates, which were recorded at the end of 1962 but not released until July 1963 on Mercury. Leon brings a rocking flair to the latter, a typical upbeat pop number of the era. "The Girl I Lost in the Rain" is a moody baroque-pop number, covered, fittingly, by the Walker Brothers on their first album.

In September 1963, Leon was enlisted to play on "Sugar Dumpling" and "I'm Just a Country Boy" with Sam Cooke, one of his earliest idols. Leon provides some basic rhythm stuff on "Sugar Dumpling," a confection as saccharine as its title. But "I'm Just a Country Boy" is a soulfully sung ballad that features the light touch of Leon's right hand. The session, held at United Recording in Hollywood, was arranged by Jimmie Haskell, who worked on hits for Ricky Nelson. Al Schmitt was coproducer alongside Cooke. Leon would work with Schmitt throughout the sixties, and the pair were reunited when Schmitt engineered *Life Journey*. The engineer for the Cooke session, Bones Howe, who produced everyone from the 5th Dimension to Tom Waits, would help Leon set up his Skyhill Drive home studio in the following year.

Leon and Gates were also hustling songs for other artists to record. The infamous Kim Fowley said in a 1972 interview that Gates picked him up hitchhiking one day in '63 and sang him a new song he'd written called "Popsicles and Icicles." It seems apocryphal. The two had likely met back at Gary Paxton's studio. Nevertheless, as Fowley tells it, he found a girl group called the Murmaids—Terry and Carol Fischer and Sally Gordon—to record it. The Fischers' mother had taken all three girls, who had grown up together, to Chattahoochee Records, which Fowley managed, and he furnished them with the number. It was a smash hit for Metric Music in October 1963.

It was another brick in the wall between Gates and Leon. There was a distrust that went back to their high school days. "Popsicles and Icicles," a cloying song but a big hit, eventually did in their friendship and partnership. Kim Fowley had called, "looking for songs for a new group he was producing," Leon said. "David said, 'I don't want to have anything to do with that guy.' So I ended up playing some of the demos we'd done for him." "Popsicles and Icicles," recorded by the female trio the Murmaids, hit number three on the *Billboard* Top 100 in early January '64. "When David and I were dissolving our fledgling publishing association for the last time, we signed a contract listing all the copyrights we owned together. They included 'Popsicles and Icicles,' but David admitted that I didn't really own half of the song because he had 'removed' my copy of the contract and I couldn't possibly prove my co-ownership."

"Leon was incensed," said Jim Karstein. "I wouldn't even ask Leon about it. I just knew that David took all the money."

Another collaborator of Gates, who wished to remain anonymous on the matter, offered: "David wouldn't give Leon his share. They had an agreement that whoever got the first song would put that song with the company, and they were to share it together. Leon was absolutely furious at David. And I do remember Leon's exact quote: 'Well, he's had his third strike with me.'"

Gates went on to found the soft rock mega-selling band Bread, "whose first album cover featured many pictures of money in various denominations," observed Leon.

Chapter 6

Playboys, Beach Boys, and Byrds

LEON'S CONFIDENCE AS A PLAYER increased as he realized he was bringing a certain mojo to sessions. Yet he continued struggling with insecurities about his limitations, dismissing his dazzling skills as "an illusion" and begging off when some session leader or another wanted something he felt outside his lane. Mel Tormé came to Leon. "He said, 'I want you to play on this record, it's gonna be great.' He'd taken a lot of the stuff that I play and written it down and he wanted me to play it on Hammond organ," Leon recalled. His previous parts on organ had been limited to primarily garage-band-type stuff, like the Ventures' version of "Telstar." "Fucking nightmare. I mean, I don't play Hammond organ. Billy Preston is who you want, you don't want me."

On more than one occasion, Leon felt producers overestimated his skills. Take *The Beatles Song Book* by the Hollyridge Strings: "I ran into this guy and he said, 'I'm so glad I saw you; I need you to play this sixty-strings session tomorrow. You play just the right stuff.' I said, 'Wait a minute. That's an illusion. Don't think you can write a bunch of stuff down, and I can read it; I can't read it well. . . . I'm not your guy.'" Because his colleague was insistent, Leon went in anyway and tanked it. "The contractor came in and yelled at me and said, 'How dare you take a session you can't play.' That was the most embarrassing moment of my life."

We think of Leon as the flamboyant risk-taking bandleader he became in the late sixties. But his fear of embarrassment, which was connected to the stage fright that never left him, would later manifest as stubborn pride, self-defeat, and reticence, if not outright detachment. But Leon began to recognize that his ambition was only restricted by whatever limitations he placed on himself. He wasn't just a pianist; he could also arrange and produce other artists. He looked around at guys leading his sessions, like Snuff Garrett and Phil Spector, and realized their vision and confidence were what was important. The producers left the nuts and bolts of it all to the team they assembled: the best arrangers, top studio musicians, and ace engineers.

As 1964 began, though, Leon was "making a lot of money" and "you know, doing sometimes four sessions a day for six or eight days in a row, I'd forget to eat, I'd come home and realize I hadn't eaten all day. . . . It's sort of a mindless existence." But studio work was so lucrative that he was able to buy a Cadillac and a house in the Hollywood Hills.

Saxophonist Jim Horn, a mainstay in the Wrecking Crew, recalled the Caddy: "We were driving along, and I said, 'Man, that's a really great car,' and he said, 'You want to use my phone there and check in with your answering service, and see if you got any work waiting for you, or any messages?' And I said, 'A phone?' And I looked down and there was the phone between our seats."

In May 1964, Leon bought 7709 Skyhill Drive, a raised ranch house in North Hollywood, on the San Fernando Valley side of the Hills, near Mulholland Drive and Universal Studios. It quickly became a flophouse for his musician pals, mostly the Tulsa Mafia. "We used to call it the Sky-hill Home for Unwed Musicians," Karstein said. Fellow musician and Tulsa buddy Larry Bell described Skyhill right after Leon moved in. The living room was "furnished with a lawn chair, a huge TV set, and two or three buckets of Kentucky Fried Chicken setting out for us. And that was about all that was in the house." Within a year, Leon built the home studio there, back in a time when it was still unusual for someone to have a studio in their home, but Leon had been inspired by those who did it before him, including Gary Paxton, Les Paul, Joe Osborn, and Ernie Kovacs.

In the meantime, though, Leon kept the bucks rolling in with session work. He kicked off 1964 with his first session for the Beach Boys, on their cover of the Frankie Lymon and the Teenagers' "Why Do Fools Fall in Love." The same month, Brian Wilson, inspired by "Be My Baby" and in the thrall of Phil Spector, recorded the Beach Boys' "Don't Worry Baby," with Leon again contributing.

Leon recorded with the Everly Brothers again on January 16, 1964. Although the Beatles' game-changing appearance on the *Ed Sullivan Show* was still a few weeks away, the Fabs had already started to become popular stateside. "I Want to Hold Your Hand" hit number one in January. The Beatles took the Everly Brothers harmonies as a foundational influence and added a harder-driving attack. This sort of edge was folded back into the Everlys' sound and can be detected on a track Leon contributes to on the Everly Brothers' *Gone, Gone, Gone* LP, "The Facts of Life." Written by Don and Phil, "The Facts of Life" rides in on a martial drum tattoo, with horns blaring and a strumming electric guitar at the forefront of a mix decidedly denser than that of the *Sing Great Country Hits* LP. Leon uses his usual technique to cut through the din, his right hand climbing the high octaves.

During his session work, Leon's ambition to become a recording artist himself only increased. He had been gaining valuable lessons in what worked in creating hits, plus the ins and outs of composing, arranging, and producing. Running through hundreds of takes while recording hundreds of backing tracks before any vocals were added gave him space to imagine his own melodies and words to go along with the changes. His first release under the name Leon Russell came in 1964, when he sold two recordings, "Cindy" and "Misty," to Herb Alpert for $500. Alpert had skyrocketed to success in 1962 on the back of his "Lonely Bull" record and formed A&M Records with his partner Jerry Moss. Leon had started to work on sessions Alpert produced. The tracks were recorded at Gold Star on February 13 with regulars Steve Douglas, Glen Campbell, Hal Blaine, Tommy Tedesco, Billy Strange, and Alpert himself.

"Cindy" is a bluesy rockabilly stomp, an arrangement of a traditional North Carolina folk song that offered an early indication of the direction Leon would take with his first 1970s records. Asked in 1970 about the novel reinvention of the standard "Misty," Leon said, "That was back in the days of my more obvious satire. I think what moved me to do that was I'd just heard John Lee Hooker's version of 'I Left My Heart in San Francisco.' It was so funny I decided to do one, too. But I think Herb Alpert . . . bought the record from me 'cause he thought I needed the money—which I probably did. . . . I just did them after a session—I think it was a Bobby Darin session, and everybody was just hanging around, so we cut this record."

The following year, Leon would play piano on the mammoth hit album by Herb Alpert and Tijuana Brass, *Whipped Cream & Other Delights*, including the tracks "A Taste of Honey" and "Whipped Cream." "Leon played on quite a few Tijuana Brass records," Alpert said. "There are a couple that he just laid a special little groove on, 'Green Peppers,' is probably the one." Leon can be heard on the left speaker, first adding a bluesy riff, then subtle, anticipatory four-note climbs between sections.

"When I saw him the first session, he came in with a suit and tie, short hair, you know, like a choirboy, just about," Alpert recalled. "He'd look at me and say, 'Herbie, I don't know what to play.' I said, 'Well, if you don't feel anything, don't play anything, just see what happens.' So I'd get the thing started churning, and he's tinkling, he's playing something, and all of a sudden, the thing goes in his direction. He has his undeniable way of playing. And there was this unique conversation he would have with musicians, musically. He started playing something that you'd say, 'Wow, how do you come up with that? I never would have thought of that!'" Alpert would not be the last to observe how Leon would wordlessly steer the direction of a track.

"His time was something special," Alpert said in another interview. "This was before click tracks. He was a human click track."

Leon lent his "special little grooves" to tracks featuring some of the biggest names in showbiz in 1964, including Pat Boone, Duane Eddy, Johnny Mathis, Connie Francis, Julie London, Johnny Rivers, and Jewel Akens, on the oldies radio station staple, "The Bird and the Bees." Most of the material was middle of the road, but there are many highlights. He played on sessions for Ike and Tina Turner, including "Finger Poppin'." Leon also played on sessions for Irma Thomas's *Wish Someone Would Care* and *Take a Look* albums, including her original vocal version of "Time Is on My Side." He added a Latin vibe to Ann-Margret's saucy "Someday Soon." The prior year he'd also played on her movie soundtrack recording of "Bye Bye Birdie."

"Because of his session work—and I did lots of sessions as well—you adapt yourself to play in many, many styles," said Elton John. "He could play any kind of music you wanted."

Even though a player of his caliber was overkill for unsophisticated material, Leon was still the main guy such successful producers as Gary Usher and Joe Saraceno would call for surf/hot rod rock. His piano is there as a quiet rhythm instrument on Jan and Dean's "Surf City," as well as on "Little Old Lady from Pasadena," recorded on March 21, 1964, for Liberty Records. They almost overlooked the latter at a recording session where the duo cranked out five tracks with session guys to flesh out their album. With a title taken from an old Jack Benny bit about a used car salesman, the artists and their assembled personnel didn't give the novelty song much thought and recorded it last. But as is often the case in pop music, it is just those sorts of weirdo throwaways that hit squarely with the zeitgeist. It reached number three on *Billboard*.

While the Beach Boys and Jan and Dean were actual acts, Leon continued to work on genre knockoffs, a lucrative specialty of Liberty Records. "They did this album called *Liverpool, Dragsters, Cycles & Surfing*, and they made this phony group called the Eliminators." Keith Allison laughed, recalling how they managed to merge four fads into one album.

Through Jack Nitzsche, Leon met hotshot twenty-one-year-old producer Terry Melcher, the youngest staff producer at Columbia. He had been part of a surf duo called Bruce and Terry with Bruce Johnston, who went on to join the Beach Boys. Near the end of 1963, Leon worked a session Melcher produced for the Rip Chords, "Hey Little Cobra." Melcher was born into Hollywood royalty as the son of actress Doris Day and would play an indirect role in Hollywood tragedy as a producer who passed on signing Charles Manson to a recording contract.

Leon worked with Melcher throughout the 1960s, most notably in 1965 on the Byrds' "Mr. Tambourine Man." Before that, Melcher worked with Leon and some of his session buddies, with Bruce Johnston on vocals, on the faux surf/hot rod band the Vettes' 1964 LP *Rev-Up!* And Melcher brought in Leon on a recording with his mom, on her version of the Weil/Mann song "Oo-Wee Baby." "I've always felt I struck out with Doris Day," Leon said. "I couldn't play the song she wanted me to very well, but she couldn't stop raving about the car I was driving at the time, a beige Cadillac convertible."

Looking suave on October 21, 1964, Leon appeared, wailing on a white grand piano as Donna Loren sang "Down the Line" and danced around him in the opening sequence of one of the first episodes of the new ABC prime-time show *Shindig!* It was produced by Jack Good, an English, Oxford-educated TV and film producer who had been hanging down at the Palomino Club around 1962, where he rounded up musicians from that scene, including Delaney Bramlett.

It took almost two years to get the show on the air. "We did a pilot with Roy Clark for a show called *Shindig!*," Jim Halsey, Clark's manager, said. "It was going to be a country music show, a variety show, kind of rock 'n' roll style. So when we went to California for Roy to do the pilot, the bandleader at that time was Leon Russell."

But ABC decided to go in the rock 'n' roll direction. Leon had come recommended by record producers and Jackie DeShannon and stayed on to help assemble the band and produce the backing tracks for the various featured performers. Bassist Ray Pohlman was tapped as musical director, and he and Leon hired the musicians for the two bands that would be part of the show: the Shindogs, and a second nameless band that backed many of the guest performers.

James Burton was still working for Ricky Nelson when Johnny Cash asked him to play dobro for him on the pilot for the show. Good invited him to be in the house band every week. Burton also helped put the Shindogs together. Good, he said, "also wanted to have a smaller group to do all the rock 'n' roll tunes on the show, so he called me up and asked if Glen D. Hardin and I could put together a band, which he called the Shindogs. We actually ended up doing 75 percent of the music in the show, while the orchestra [the house band] did the other 25 percent."

Russ Titelman, who became a three-time-Grammy-winning record producer, got the call from Pohlman to come join the show as a guitarist in the house band. "The Shindogs was their little Beatles. The house band was just the house band. We didn't have a name," Titelman said. Donna Loren and Bobby Sherman would sing with the Shindogs, and the band recorded some and even toured a little. Burton explained, "They tried to keep us separate from the house band."

Leon and Billy Preston would sit in as featured performers with the house band. Leon can be seen in tails, his coif, by Hollywood stylist Jay Sebring, expertly in place, playing a white grand piano and singing "Roll Over Beethoven" on the November 18, 1964, episode. A month later, he's shown backing Aretha Franklin. On February 3, 1965, he was in a western saloon tableau, wearing a vest, sitting at an upright piano, singing "Jambalaya," with Glen Campbell on banjo, Titelman on rhythm guitar, and Jerry Cole tearing it up on the lead guitar. By that point, the back of Leon's hair was down to his shoulders.

Shindig! was just one of the latest vehicles to capitalize on the potential of rock 'n' roll's visual and visceral appeal. The *T.A.M.I. Show* was another. Released in December of 1964, the concert movie brought a jaw-dropping dream bill of acts to teenagers in big cities and small towns alike.

On October 28–29, 1964, two electrifying concerts held at the Santa Monica Civic Auditorium, with an audience mostly of high school kids, were captured on a new high-definition video technology called Electronovision. It seems as if they came up with the acronym T.A.M.I. first; its definitions—either "Teenage Awards Music International" or "Teen Age Music International"—changed depending on whom or when you asked. Jack Nitzsche was hired to put together the house band, including himself as conductor. The supercharged young dancers from *Shindig!*, including Teri Garr and Toni Basil, weaved frenetically around the stage throughout the exhilarating presentation. Jan and Dean emceed, introducing acts that were topping the charts, including the Beach Boys, Marvin Gaye, the Supremes, Chuck Berry, Smokey Robinson and the Miracles, James Brown, and the Rolling Stones. The exuberant pacing is unrelenting, and watching the film leaves viewers breathless and giddy.

Who's there in the shadows behind the Stones? Why, it's Leon Russell, seated on his piano bench among his fellow session musicians, bearing witness to the beginning of the end of their gravy train. Jack Nitzsche started working with the Stones just a few days later, on November 2, at RCA Studios and found working with the band liberating. "The Stones stood for something," said Nitzsche. "I thought they were going to be leaders of change. They were telling record executives to go fuck themselves . . . and not cracking under any of the social pressure and not doing it the way other people would have done it. . . . When they first breezed in, everybody in the studio stopped what they were doing and stared."

For the time being, Leon was too busy, so after the first season, he mostly left the weekly *Shindig!* gig to his friends in the house bands. In 1964, much of his work still came from Liberty. But that was also the year that Leon started to blossom as a producer, arranger, and recording artist himself.

Though he would end up on thousands of sessions, Leon did not stick around the Wrecking Crew as long as Hal Blaine, Carol Kaye, Tommy Tedesco, or Don Randi did, all of whom remained session players well into the 1970s. "I wasn't one of the main guys," Leon said. "But I played on enough of it that it, you know, I got to experience the section; that was quite something." He estimated "90 percent of the records that I did were bullshit. I mean, I didn't play on any Ray Charles records. Didn't play on any Mancini records." Henry Mancini was a figure Leon held in great esteem. "Come on, Karstein," he said to his friend when they were hanging around the Skyhill house one day. Leon took him out in the Cadillac to Wallichs Music City store and bought Mancini's book on arranging.

By the fall of '64, Leon was working with Snuff Garrett on a new project, Gary Lewis and the Playboys. According to Lewis, Garrett discovered him and his band when they were playing a regular summer gig at Disneyland. After the show, Snuff handed Lewis his card and said, "Hi, I'm head of A&R at Liberty Records, and I'd like to talk to you about doing some recording." Lewis deadpanned, "Now, isn't that the way everybody wishes it would happen?"

Garrett remembered it differently. He had been a lifelong fan of Gary's father, Jerry Lewis, and Jerry's pianist Lou Brown told Snuff about Gary's group playing Disneyland. Snuff caught the band rehearsing at Paramount Studios. Lewis was on drums, so Garrett moved him up front. "I always told the artists, 'Look, what you're getting into is a totalitarian dictatorship,'" Garrett said.

Here, Gary Lewis agreed. "The first thing is that Snuffy let us all know first, right off the bat, that he was in total charge, total control. That was great because we were all nineteen. We didn't know what we were doing. Leon was the arranger." They met in January 1964. By the end of the year, their first single would be a number one smash.

In 1964, Al Kooper was a hustling twenty-year-old songwriter in New York. He and his lyricist partners, Bob Brass and Irwin Levine, wrote "This Diamond Ring" with the Drifters in mind, but that group turned it down. Garrett first offered the song to his proven star Bobby Vee, who also passed. Then he brought in the new act and the new arranger. "Here comes this nineteen-year-old kid, knows nothing about the recording business," said Lewis. "I listened to everything he said." Garrett himself was only twenty-five.

Nonetheless, Lewis harbored some skepticism. "The demo was much slower" and sung in a baritone. "I didn't care for it at all. That's where Leon Russell came in. Leon told me, he said, 'Don't judge anything by the demo. I'm going to work real hard on that arrangement.' We used to call him 'the Thinker' because he would just sit in the studio sometimes, and he would be holding a piece of sheet music, and he'd be looking up at the ceiling. He always spent about twenty minutes just sitting in the booth, thinking." Lewis laughed. "And what came out of it was always just great, all those Leon arrangements."

He continued: "When I heard the finished product, 'This Diamond Ring,' I was really excited about it. Not only did he arrange it, but he played some instruments on everything we ever did. Sometimes he'd play piano. Sometimes he'd play guitar. Sometimes he'd play the tack piano. Sometimes he played a bass trumpet. It was just amazing, the amount of instruments that he could play."

Once Kooper and his partners heard it, "we were revolted," he wrote. "They'd removed the soul from our R&B song and made a teenage milkshake out of it." The dismay of Kooper and his partners ebbed as they watched the song rising up the charts, eventually unseating Phil Spector's production of "You've Lost That Loving Feeling" by the Righteous Brothers as number one.

Within three months, Kooper's attitude changed from "I don't even want to hear shit like this" to walking around boasting "I wrote that!" But Leon later distanced himself from the record. "I said, 'Oh, my God. I hate this shit.' Two weeks later, it was number ten or something." Still, it was the beginning of a partnership between Snuff and Leon that would last until around 1967.

Gary Lewis was never going to win any vocal prizes. On this and other records, Leon had Lewis sing over and match guide vocal tracks by Leon or other singers, like Ron Hicklin, and he even kept a bit of that in the final mixes. "Gary would copy my vocal one line at a time," Leon said. "It was tough, boy."

But the track is an effervescent no-doubt hit from needle drop to fade-out. Obviously, that upbeat approach is the main point of contention for those who knew the more deliberate and haunting original recording. But the basic components are all there, taken from the demo: the opening riff, the modulations from minor-key verses to major key choruses, and the melody and structure. The original has more soul; that's an understatement. But Leon's arrangement demonstrates more craft, necessitated by the complete absence of soul. The Lewis version jettisons the pain and does not approach the depth of the original. It's the kiddie end of the pool. The arrangement is more about the hooks of the song.

"This Diamond Ring" was the first of seven top tens in a row that

Garrett and Leon produced for Gary Lewis. "I don't need anybody to make a hit record except a song," Garrett would say.

The original band Lewis "rounded up from Theater Arts College" was deemed good enough by Leon to lay down the basic tracks. Lewis himself still played drums. He had lessons from a friend of his dad. "I got like five years of lessons from Buddy Rich for nothing." While at college, Lewis also took lessons from Jim Keltner, who would later join the Playboys.

Lewis said, "It was me and the original Playboys who did all the basic tracks. The overdubbing, that was a different story. That required a lot more musicianship than we had. Most of the solos and the overdubs were done by Leon Russell alone."

In 1965, Garrett quit Liberty as a house producer and went independent, forming Snuff Garrett Productions and hiring Russell as a "junior partner." They bought publishing rights on songs, scouted new artists, and conceptualized new projects. But they primarily focused on Lewis and the Playboys. Leon and Snuff would often track the band doing basics at Western Studios, and then Leon would bring them back to his recently completed home studio at Skyhill, where he would work on the arrangements. "As time went on, we'd be excited to get there to see what Leon came up with," Lewis said. "He had everything. He had it all."

Sonny Curtis of the Crickets was there for the recording of the Playboys' "She's All Woman" and "Little Miss Go-Go." "That was before Leon grew his hair and wore a long, long beard," Curtis said. "I remember he was really clean-cut in those days." Curtis wrote such classics as "I Fought the Law," "Walk Right Back," and later "Love Is All Around," the theme for the *Mary Tyler Moore Show*.

The next single Gary Lewis and the Playboys released was "Count Me In" in March. It is a perfectly framed song, with an opening glockenspiel riff that recurs thematically throughout the arrangement. Each chorus is punctuated by an elegant piano flourish, played by Leon, presaging ABBA's "Dancing Queen" and "Oliver's Army" by Elvis Costello & the Attractions. Glen D. Hardin wrote the song. "He came in, and he started playing it on piano," said Lewis. "Evidently, Leon wasn't that thrilled with what he was playing. Leon sat down and said, 'Let me see. Let me think.' . . . We ended up doing Leon's part."

Across 1965, the Tulsa Mafia took over the Playboys. Bassist Allan Ramsay was first to leave. "He got drafted, poor guy," Lewis said. Leon called up his old high school bandmate, the quiet and unassuming Carl Radle, who joined the band.

Next came Lewis's drum teacher, Jim Keltner. Though he was originally from Tulsa, his family had moved to California when he was thirteen and he only met the rest of Leon's Okie gang in LA. At the music store where Keltner gave lessons, Lewis also met John West, who played the Cordovox (an electric accordion) and organ in the Playboys. On the *Ed Sullivan Show*, Lewis was still seated behind the drums, alongside West playing the Cordovox.

Keltner was a jazz player. He was playing gigs with Don Randi, the first of those close to Leon to employ Keltner. "I gave [Leon] the first drummer that he fell in love with," Randi said.

Lewis was chiefly looking for a drummer for the live band and invited Keltner down to the studio to listen to what they were working on. "Leon had him play drums on a tune that I couldn't really get," he recalled. "He had Jim sit in and play this tune, and it just happened to be 'She's Just My Style,' one of the big hits. I couldn't play a very good shuffle, so Jim sat in and played it real good. That's how Leon heard him."

Leon implied that it was Lewis who brought Keltner in. "So he started playing, Jimmy sounded like jazz to the max, I mean there was no afterbeat," Leon recalled. "I sang all the fills to him, and he says, 'You want me to play [*sings beat*]' and I said, 'Yeah. We're making rock and roll records. That's a rock and roll fill.' . . . I said, 'Jimmy if you ever learned anything about the genre, you could make a lot of money.'" Decades later, Leon would tell the story with a bit more piss and vinegar. After Keltner told him the part sounded "stupid," Leon summed it up for Keltner: "Well, either you're gonna play that or I'm gonna get another fuckin' drummer!"

"Just My Style" was Keltner's first serious recording session. "I had done some other recording prior to that, but it was demo stuff. I didn't know what Leon's background was at that point. All I knew was that he was from Tulsa. . . . The time that I spent with Leon in the studio doing that, I got hooked. I knew I wanted to make more records."

This Gary Lewis song, this bubble of froth, was a pivotal point in rock 'n' roll. It turned on an erstwhile jazz snob to the musical and financial rewards of rock 'n' roll. That jazzer became one of the most in-demand drummers in rock 'n' roll history.

Lewis had ego clashes with Keltner, who lasted less than a year as a

Playboy before being replaced by Karstein (keeping it a Tulsa-heavy crew). "I was just having too much fun thinking that I was the cutest and the funniest of the Playboys," Keltner admitted. "I was getting a lot of attention from girls, and we would do press conferences. . . . I had no clue that, 'Wait, this is not your show. You're supposed to help your friend to look good.'"

Karstein's stint lasted eight months or so before Lewis was drafted. Another Tulsan, Tommy Tripplehorn (father of actress Jeanne Tripplehorn), had also joined the band. Radle and Karstein had been almost inseparable since the early days in LA, even sharing a bed at Leon's apartment during the summer of the Pandora's Box gig. "Carl, he was always the most practical of the bunch," Karstein said. "Carl was the guy whose shoes were always shined. He always had gas in his car. He always had a clean shirt to put on. He always had money in the bank."

As with Keltner's, Karstein's role in the band was for live performances, while Lewis and Hal Blaine handled recording sessions. But Lewis and Leon arranged for Karstein to be credited on sessions so he would get paid. "Hal Blaine was there with his drums all set up," Karstein explained. "I went, 'Well, all right.' What I did is pulled up a chair, sat there, and got a free lesson from Hal on how to cut records."

While the Playboys were out on the road supporting their seemingly endless stream of hits, Leon was back in the studio. On January 20, 1965, Terry Melcher brought him in to play electric piano on one of the most celebrated singles of the 1960s, "Mr. Tambourine Man," by the Byrds.

The band had just been formed the year before (and had adopted the name only two months before the recording) by folkies turned on by the Beatles who electrified the strumming and arpeggios of their acoustic folk guitars. Written by Bob Dylan, the lyric "jingle jangle morning" is as accurate a description as any for the sound that Melcher captured. Roger McGuinn was the only member of the band with recording experience, having played on sessions for Judy Collins and others, and his chiming Rickenbacker twelve-string guitar was the keystone of their arrangement. So Melcher surrounded McGuinn with the studio musicians his friend Brian Wilson had used on hit records.

Unlike on tracks that featured his high-octave flourishes on acoustic piano, Leon is not easily discernible on the recording. The best way to hear him is to seek out online the various takes without vocals. There he is, just filling out the midrange on the Wurlitzer electric piano, which he also did on the Gene Clark–penned B-side "I Knew I'd Want You." Hal Blaine played drums while Bill Pitman and Jerry Cole played guitars. Melcher asked Cole to replicate the staccato "chick-chick" rhythm part that he had played on "Be My Baby." Larry Knechtel was on bass, playing that hooky sliding line during the introduction and ending. "I didn't start playing keys until Leon quit doing sessions," Knechtel said. "He was the number one piano player—he had a great feel. I'll tell you what, at a certain point I thought I was a pretty good piano player, and when I heard him it scared the shit out of me."

The record was revolutionary. Dylan himself, upon hearing his song electrified, evidently enthused, "Wow, you can dance to that!" and went electric himself.

Leon was not aware the session was for an actual band. With an infamously arrogant personality like David Crosby and an imperious drummer Michael Clarke, the Byrds were livid at being replaced by session musicians. The record, which went to number one, is widely considered ground zero for folk rock, a pivotal gateway to the late sixties. In a 1970 *Rolling Stone* interview, by which time he was a superstar himself, Crosby allowed, "So, those cats were good, but there were some stupendous musicians amongst the studio cats. And Leon, I guess, would be the most highly developed of all of them. He's a stone fucking genius."

With popular music growing more serious in lyrical content and musical scope, even the master chronicler of the Southern California teenage beach culture, Brian Wilson, would soon take giant steps into increasingly ambitious projects, reaching his creative peak on the *Pet Sounds* (1966) and unfinished *Smile* (1967) albums. Leon was already too busy arranging and producing to contribute to those sessions, but he did play on such towering numbers as "California Girls" and "Help Me Rhonda," though it was the *Today!* album version of the latter. The single was a completely different session. Don Randi and Leon each spent much of their respective lives believing they had played on the only version of "Help Me Rhonda," but Randi explained: "[Leon] did the first [album] version, and I did the second [single] version, which was the big hit."

Brian Wilson directed everything exactingly. "He normally told me what to play," said Leon, who was always impressed with how Wilson arranged in his head. In a variation of a story he told often, Leon said, "In Western Studio, there was probably fifteen, twenty guys in that studio.

He'd start with the first guy; he's singing their part until they got it, then the second guys sing their part, and third guy, all the way around the room. Then he'd go back to the first guy, well, the first guy had forgot his part, and he'd sing it again. Sing the second. Taught the whole thing by rote. And all of a sudden, that whole band could play that shit. I mean, Brian is, when you want to talk about genius, there's not any like him that I know of. He's unbelievable."

Leon worked with the most legendary singer of them all, Frank Sinatra, in 1964 on the "Softly as I Leave You" session, which resulted in a few other tracks. On April 14, 1965, he worked again with Sinatra, on tracks released as two singles and both released on the *Sinatra '65* album. "When Somebody Loves You" is an up-tempo pop song (not to be confused with the standard "All the Way," which begins with the same lyric). The Sinatra track follows a similar template to Dean Martin's hit "Everybody Loves Somebody," with Leon hammering out triplet riffs in his high-octave wheelhouse. He takes the same approach on "Tell Her (You Love Her Each Day)," which would also be included on the *That's Life* LP in 1966. This track blasts in with the big bang of Hal Blaine's tom-toms in a wonderful arrangement from Ernie Freeman. Leon would work with the crooner again in May 1965 on "Let's Forget About Domani." Later, Leon told his collaborator A. J. Croce, "All I could think about was trying to play like [Count] Basie. And I used every single riff and trick that I knew of Basie's to back Frank Sinatra."

Leon would tell this story about Sinatra for the rest of his life: He caused the Chairman of the Board to walk into a pole. By this time, the regular group of session people were well known for dressing casually hip yet sharp, and Leon was no exception, cutting a slick presence into whichever room he would strut. After hearing raves about Jay Sebring's salon on Fairfax and Melrose, Leon made an appointment at what he described, in trademark understatement, as the "expensive barbershop." When men's haircuts topped out around five dollars, Sebring charged fifty-five bucks for his mod coifs for such stars as Warren Beatty, Steve McQueen, and Sinatra himself. Sadly, the innovative stylist and entrepreneur was later murdered alongside his friend, the actress Sharon Tate, and others at Terry Melcher's former home on Cielo Drive by the Manson Family on August 8, 1969.

Leon recalled how he "went to the shop with hair that looked vaguely like that of the *Little Rascals'* Alfalfa and came out looking, in my own estimation at least, like a movie star. I remember gazing at myself in the rearview for all of half an hour, ecstatic that I was finally and forever divorced from the chronic rooster tail that had plagued me for my entire life." He later said his hair was "lacquered, like a helmet almost." It looked so good that he felt compelled to up his game on the clothes front and wear tailor-made suits from "Harvey Krantz, 'tailor for the stars.' It was the first time in my life that I'd had the least interest in clothes."

By the time of the Sinatra session, Leon had let his hair go a bit, having been too busy to get back to Sebring's. He was running late the day of the session and, though he was able to slip into his Krantz suit, he did not have time to devote attention and ozone-layer-destroying amounts of hairspray to keep his swept-up hairdo molded in place. Instead, it was hanging down close to his shoulders when he arrived at the studio, and some of his embarrassed colleagues scolded him as a slob. Didn't he know who this session was for? Frank *Fucking* Sinatra! "Frank himself honored me with an icy stare that resulted in a minor collision between Mr. S. and an unfortunately placed post in his path. I wondered if that might end up being my major contribution to pop music."

Leon would point to this incident as making him aware of the undue importance placed on surface appearances. More profoundly, it provided him with a small but galvanizing look at how prejudice forms. Like Johnny Cash singing about his emblematic all-black wardrobe or David Crosby singing "Almost Cut My Hair," Leon explained, "I decided right then and there that no matter how uncomfortable or inconvenient it might be, I was never going to cut my hair again."

In 2000, reflecting on this same sort of awakening, he told a story to some fans: "Me and Rita Coolidge was coming back one day from Memphis, Tennessee, I was bringing a car back. I was in Oklahoma, in one of those places that was in the middle of the country someplace, and there was a gas station. I used the restroom and as we were getting ready to leave, a little Black family . . . wanted to use the restroom. And the guy said, 'Oh, you can't use our restroom; it's broken.' And I just thought, you know, I just always want to look this way [indicating his appearance] to see who my friends are."

Like many of his generation, by 1965 Leon was increasingly withdrawing from anything resembling straight society, letting his hair down figuratively as well as literally, a shaggy Okie floating between sessions at the wheel of a yacht-like Cadillac. He was too busy, too young, and too libertine to be held down by any steady romantic relationship. At least two people interviewed for this book spoke about him briefly dating a prostitute around this time.

Leon's style would slide from playboy to beatnik to hippie in a few short years. "I remember we were on a lunch break from a Beach Boys gig," said bassist Carol Kaye. "Leon Russell had been out in his new Cadillac with that long beard of his, and his robes and cowboy hat; even back in the sixties he dressed pretty out-there. The cops stopped him and thought that he'd stolen the car. He'd left his wallet at the studio, so the cops followed him back. After Leon showed them his license, one cop looks at all of us: 'Why the hell don't y'all get a real job? You guys can't be makin' more than twenty bucks!' Everybody was real quiet, and as soon as they left, we all started laughing, 'cause we were making about $400!"

Kaye and Leon play together on a killer version of "Lipstick Traces (on a Cigarette)" by the O'Jays. These 1970s hitmakers had been releasing music since the early 1960s. Leon had played on "You're on Top" in 1964. Released in April 1965, the recording of Allen Toussaint's "Lipstick Traces (on a Cigarette)" was the first production hit for erstwhile promo man Tommy LiPuma, who had recognized Leon's talents back in '62 at Pandora's Box. LiPuma would champion Leon for decades, producing his song "This Masquerade" as George Benson's overdue breakthrough and producing Leon's own final album, *Life Journey*. On the O'Jays recording, Leon's cascading piano flows through the slippery New Orleans groove laid down by Kaye (her first session with a Fender Precision bass) and Earl Palmer on drums.

His partnership with Snuff Garrett represented a significant stepping-stone for Leon. He was no longer just another ace session musician playing on hits for other artists and producers; now he was part of a highly successful production team. But Garrett increasingly pressed Leon's patience.

"He actually drove me nuts," Leon told the *LA Record*. Talking in an interview with Denny Tedesco, Leon reflected on the collaboration with Garrett. "I often wondered how my life would have been different if Snuff Garrett wasn't the first big music producer that I met when I came to California. If I'd met, oh, somebody like Lou Adler. I mean, he was kind of a Beverly Hills version of Snuffy. He made better records than Tommy."

And Leon wanted to make better records.

Chapter 7

High on Skyhill Drive

BY THE FALL OF 1965, Leon had transformed his 1960-built four-bedroom, three-bath suburban two-story home near Universal Studios, north of Mulholland Drive, into a home studio. Inside, Leon was freeing himself from the straits of straight society, becoming a vampire, living nocturnally, covering the windows in tinfoil, and blacking out the day.

The Caddy was parked in the driveway and the garage was turned into studio space. Leon installed double walls, added soundproofing, and upgraded the electrical wiring to support the equipment. A bedroom was converted into a control room and a den into the live studio room. A grand piano sat in a corner of the living room, all miked up. Bathrooms were used as vocal booths and echo chambers.

"The whole house is a studio," Leon said in 1971. "The money in the two rooms is worth thirty or forty percent more than the rest of the whole house. I like to record all the time. I can do a whole record myself—starting with a metronome, working my way through all the keyboards, guitar, bass, valve trombone, bass trumpet, baritone horn, and percussion. But I can't play all the drums at once. I have to bang them one at a time."

Leon's house became a place where musicians reported to work. The Knickerbockers, whom Leon arranged for, recut vocals and blistering guitar there on "Lies," the fabulously shameless Beatles pastiche, with Jerry Fuller producing, after they failed to attain the edgy sound they were looking for at Western Studios. T Bone Burnett, who would produce Leon's 2010 comeback record *The Union*, said in the sixties he went to Skyhill to work on recordings, sometimes with Jim Keltner, without ever meeting Leon.

Johnny Cale, who had studied electronics in the Air Force, went back and forth on the well-worn Route 66 path, making a living working day jobs and painting houses in LA. He became "J. J." when he got a regular gig at the famous Whisky a Go Go. The promoter Elmer Valentine told him, "There's a John Cale, a viola player in the Velvet Underground. I want to change your name."

Leon gave Cale a job as an engineer at Skyhill Studio, the name they started using for the semiprofessional space in his house. "We played around in there every day," Cale said. "There was a bunch of guys we all knew and there was nothing to do in LA. So everybody just hung out in Leon's house, and if you hung out there, you might as well go down and play some music and turn the tape recorders on. We cut an awful lot of stuff there that nobody ever heard."

Cale said, "The neighbors thought the Hells Angels lived at Skyhill because of all the cars, motorcycles, and loud music at all hours of the day and night." But the musicians did their best to be professional when needed, at least before the place became "psychedelic": "The first legitimate union sessions done here in this house were the Glen Campbell sessions," Cale told Diane Sullivan, who became Leon's assistant and the eventual owner of Skyhill. "I came at eight in the morning and started sweeping out the butts, beer cans, and everything. Leon wanted everything real straight."

It was an open-door policy. "It was just like a Greyhound bus station," Karstein said. "I mean, it was a twenty-four-hour-a-day deal there." Songwriter Bobby Hart said, "There were plenty of girls around."

Two of the central women, also from Tulsa, Francine Brockey and Kay Poorboy, popped into LA in the later sixties and would continue to be a part of the Leon scene into the 1970s and beyond. Each of them was working at the Classic Cat, a topless joint on the Strip with valet parking and a well-heeled celebrity clientele. Brockey was a cocktail waitress, Poorboy a dancer, and both partied seriously hard. "I met [Brockey] at a nightclub," Hart said. "She was staying at Leon's at the time. I just got to know her through the nightclub and then got a call from her maybe three or four months later, she needed to get out of the Home for Unwed Musicians. I don't know why she needed to get out, but she ended up staying with me for a year, a year and a half or so. I don't think [Leon] was even living there at the time." By the late sixties, Leon was renting an apartment to escape the crowd at his house.

In 1965–1966, Leon took his work—mainly Gary Lewis and the Playboys—home to Skyhill. Snuff Garrett also started bringing more projects to Skyhill, and the two collaborated on Leon's subsequent solo work. In September 1965, Leon played most of the instruments on a song he cowrote with Cale and Garrett. "Everybody's Talking 'Bout the Young" is a Dylan-meets-Stones protest song, perfectly in tune with the times, with a wailing, reverberating guitar riff set to a slinky country/R&B groove, in the vein of "It's All Over Now." The lyric takes on the generation gap, the Cuban Missile Crisis, the KKK, and the war in Vietnam, packing an enormous punch in an economical one minute and forty-eight seconds. Leon spits out a lyric that challenges rednecks and oldsters, "Who's a-gonna bury all our young?"

Leon said he hadn't been aware of Bob Dylan until he played on the Byrds' "Mr. Tambourine Man," but it is likely he had heard Dylan earlier because Jackie DeShannon evangelized about Dylan in the early sixties. Perhaps it was the recently electrified Dylan that was an epiphany for Leon, because '65 brought the half-electric *Bringing It All Back Home* in March and the fully electric *Highway 61 Revisited* in August, one month before Leon's session.

The B-side of Leon's record, "It's Alright with Me," is even more Stonesy. A cowrite with Chuck Blackwell (Snuff is also credited again), who pounds out the same 4/4 snare beat heard all summer in "(I Can't Get No) Satisfaction," in Roy Orbison's "(Oh) Pretty Woman" the year prior, and again in Stevie Wonder's 1965 "Uptight (Everything's Alright)." "It's Alright with Me" takes the fuzzed-out glory of Keith Richards's guitar riff on "Satisfaction" and amps it higher, on a double-tracked boogie lick, likely played by Cale. There's also a Beach Boys–inspired "Oo-diddy-diddy" post-chorus vocal refrain, a remnant of the doo-wop era.

The tracks served as an exercise in learning how to record at home, which allowed Leon to work at a relaxed pace. "I wanted to build my own studio and practice being in there so I wouldn't be so nervous," Leon said. "I was still nervous when I went down there and the red light was on."

Leon spent most of his time in 1965–1966 working on Lewis's records. Right out of the gate, Lewis was a wholesome, geeky, good-natured, and lovable star. His nonthreatening charm won over teens and their parents alike with a well-chosen and impeccably produced repertoire. As the conformity and postwar prosperity of the 1950s churned into the political assassinations and protests of the sixties, Lewis was a throwback to the teen heartthrobs of earlier years.

The Gary Lewis records brought Leon to the attention of other musicians. Don Nix had become buddies with Leon, Cale, Markham, Karstein, Radle, and Blackwell when his Memphis-based Stax group, the Mar-Keys, played shows at the Peppermint Lounge in Tulsa in 1961–1962. From Memphis, he would travel back and forth to the LA apartments of Leon, Markham, and other Tulsa guys. Three or four years later, Nix went back to LA with some of his Memphis friends, including Duck Dunn and Steve Cropper, who had been in the Mar-Keys and then the Stax house band, Booker T. & the MG's.

"Don Nix said, 'You gotta come out and meet Leon,'" said Cropper. "I'm a radio person, and to hear 'This Diamond Ring,' and think, 'Man that's a hit' . . . That was a big hit in Memphis. I knew how great he was."

It's amusing that the record Al Kooper bemoaned as devoid of soul was so popular among the guys who played on records at Stax, ground zero for Southern soul and home of Otis Redding, Sam and Dave, William Bell, Isaac Hayes, and Carla Thomas. The respect flowed both ways. "We were hearing some of the first Stax stuff up at Leon Russell's house," said Bobby Keys. "Steve Cropper and Duck Dunn had come from Memphis to Los Angeles to do some overdubs. So I heard some of that stuff before it came out. And I was thinking, 'This is definitely the wave of the future.'"

Keys had quickly latched onto gigs with Markham and Gram Parsons's International Submarine Band, who had recently arrived in town. "Leon was the only guy who had a steady gig," Keys said. "The goal back then for most of us was just to survive. We were havin' fun. I mean, we weren't striving for any record deal or anything like that. . . . As musicians, we all thought we were pretty good, but everybody knew Leon was superior. He was a phenomenal pianist and stylist. Leon was what all the other Okies and Texans were aspiring to be: he had a black Cadillac, he had his own house in the hills, he had a studio in his house, and he had chicks up there day and night."

"Most of all those people either drank or they were smoking pot, and this and that," Gary Lewis said. "Everybody knew that I didn't. Whenever I would come over, Leon would say real loud, 'Hi, Gary!' That was to alert everybody in the house. I'd hear all these doors slamming. They didn't want me to know about that stuff. If I would have found out, I probably would have fired everybody."

Jimmy Karstein lived in a closet, a topic laughed about by each person familiar with the arrangement, including Karstein himself, who declared, with mock pride, "I was the one that *designed* it." It was a big closet, but a closet, nevertheless. He had a portable KLH record player. "And we'd get in that closet and drink wine, smoke joints, and we'd put on 'The Last Time' [by the Rolling Stones] and sniff amyl nitrite. . . . Between the Stones and Jr. Walker & the All Stars, you know? Yeah, we just used to *get in there*, man."

Karstein's collection of blues 45s, a selection of which he would bring on tour with the Playboys, was legendary among fellow musicians. While with the Yardbirds, Jimmy Page could often be found in Karstein's hotel room, enjoying his tantalizing combo of amyl nitrite poppers and 45s. Nix said, "Page didn't know whether to kiss him or kill him, but he always came back for more."

In late '65, Leon and Snuff Garrett produced J. J. Cale's first record since arriving in LA the year before. Cale held down the regular gig at the Whisky, worked day jobs, and helped Leon with the studio. He recorded a track called "Dick Tracy," about the comic strip character and released as a single in October on Liberty. The novelty track is backed with the curiously slinky "It's a Go-Go Place" about a groovy sort of establishment down on the Sunset Strip and sounds like a jingle for the Whisky. And it seems to nod to the girls at the Classic Cat. Either way, Cale forewarns, over blues changes, "We're going out to the edge of your mind / It's only ten blocks west of mine." The adolescent boys at whom "Dick Tracy" was aimed must have found the B-side tantalizing.

With the success of "Dick Tracy," Snuff and Leon produced a whole album of songs based on popular comic book characters. The band for the album was billed as the Spotlights and featured Gregg and Duane Allman, who had previously been known as the Allman Joys.

Leon also recorded Cale performing a song that would eventually make Cale a great deal of money. "I can remember several times during breaks from the Gary Lewis tour," recalled Tommy Tripplehorn, "that Carl [Radle] and I would go out clubbing in Hollywood, come home to Leon's house at two or three in the morning, and there would be Cale in Leon's studio writing new music at Leon's grand piano. I can remember him working on 'After Midnight' at Leon's mixing board during one of those late-night sessions, recording on four tracks."

This early-1966 version of "After Midnight" is surprisingly fleshed out. There are horns (trumpet played by Jimmy Markham), a backward guitar track (the Beatles influence seeping in), and background singers. Though Cale perversely buried it as a B-side, it eventually found its way into the hands of Eric Clapton a few years later via Delaney Bramlett. Clapton recorded a hit version that hewed closely to this original 1966 demo recording. Cale finally released his own on the 1972 *Naturally* LP on Leon's Shelter Records label, reinventing it with the restrained-but-intense style that became his trademark. Clapton would in turn soak up the laid-back Cale style as the 1970s rolled on.

Skyhill became an experimental laboratory for Leon, the mad scientist. On a trip back to Tulsa, Leon had met drummer David Teegarden. "I had befriended J. J. Cale a few years prior to actually meeting Leon," said Teegarden. "Cale was quite into recording. And I was too, for some reason, but being a kid, I couldn't afford any equipment. I did finally acquire an old two-track recorder, a reel-to-reel recorder. And so, word kind of got around our circles that I might have been some kind of electronic prodigy, which I was *not*," he said with a laugh. "He [Leon] called me a couple of weeks later, after he got back out to LA, and asked me if I wanted to come out there and live in his house and work in the studio. Of course, I said, 'Yeah! My flight arrives at . . .' So I was quite charged up about that. I get to the airport in LA and look outside. Leon had a four-door black Cadillac. . . . And my idol was drummer Chuck Blackwell. He had a chauffeur's cap on and was driving the Cadillac. I was seventeen, maybe eighteen." Teegarden moved into the Karstein Closet while Karstein was on the road with Gary Lewis.

Teegarden was one in a line of technically advanced people Leon would tap to help translate his inventive ideas into reality. "I was just amazed with Leon's talent," said Teegarden. "But he was always trying to get me to put together electronic stuff he was dreaming up. I said, 'I can hook stuff up, but I can't write circuitry or invent circuitry.'" One such idea was for something similar to the Mellotron. "He bought an old upright piano, and he wanted to—instead of having strings in it—have tape loop players," Teegarden said. "He kept at it. It was *serious*. He was really trying to get it done, but I had no idea how to hook all that stuff up and to make it work off the keyboard."

Leon would eventually get a Chamberlin—which became the Mellotron when manufactured and marketed in England—from Harry Chamberlin himself. Chamberlins and Mellotrons were essentially analog sampler playbacks, using tape loops—of string sections, voices, flutes— playing the notes that correspond with each key on a keyboard, each with individual playback heads. (The opening of the Beatles' "Strawberry Fields Forever" is one prominent example of the Mellotron flute sound.) Chamberlin was an engineer at Universal Studios. "He invented the laugh-track machine they use on situation comedies, where you press a key and it produces any one of sixty different types of audience laughter," Leon said. "The Chamberlin is the musical version of that. I have one with four manuals, the biggest he made."

Cale had a motorcycle at Skyhill that was just one of the vehicles for a transformative experience Leon had. "I would have to say that my first acid trip was the single most important event in my life," he wrote. "My vision and awareness were immediately expanded to 70 mm Cinemascope and revelations were made to me that I previously hadn't even imagined. Many charades of my own and others' manufacturing were stripped away at the speed of light, leaving a panic and fear that I am incapable of describing. . . . It materially affected the course of my future life."

Markham recalled, "We were living at Skyhill when acid came around. A lot of people we knew had taken it. We hadn't, but we kept talking about it, and he [Leon] wanted to do it. . . . So he took [the LSD], and it started taking effect, and he was enjoying it. There was never any bad trip involved. He was laughing and singing and doing the things you experience with acid."

After this epiphany, Leon decided he had to ride J. J. Cale's motorcycle, the first time he had ever been on one. Markham said, "I kind of freaked out. I said, 'I'm not so sure that's a good idea.' I mean, that was so unlike Leon. He'd never ridden a motorcycle in his life." He did not go very fast or far, but he flipped over the bike while taking it up a hill. Markham and Nix helped Leon up the stairs to his house. "He had hurt his leg and his hip, and he wouldn't go to the hospital. I tried to put him to bed," said Nix. "I'll never forget, his long hair was in my face." Leon went into shock. "When I went to the hospital the next day, they discovered I had not only broken my hip, but also that it had reset itself during my walk up the hill," Leon wrote.

The emergence of psychedelic drugs in the mid-1960s served as a de-marcation in the decade. The first half of the sixties was a carryover from the fifties, just as the sixties lingered into the hangover of the early seventies. Music changed as a result. Bob Dylan had already been influencing rock 'n' roll musicians to write their own songs with more profound lyrics than the teeny-bopper stuff that had been monopolizing the airwaves. Psychedelic drugs accelerated the process, as did the general maturing of baby boomers writing the material. Tumultuous current events were inspiring songwriters to go beyond love songs.

Leon felt the pull of his own ambition. Recognizing the trends early on, as self-contained bands were becoming more of the norm, his timing was right to begin stepping away from sessions. "It's an exotic factory job," he said in 1971. "You can get trapped. I see a lot of people now who are just starting to do the number of sessions that is necessary to make big money. If they would devote time with a group playing the music they want to, they would be further ahead. It's a cycle you have to go through before you can see it."

Teegarden recalled one incident that fed Leon's insecurity and fueled his ambition to move beyond the hit-making assembly line. Teegarden drove Leon and Snuff to RCA Studios so they could make a copy of a tape. They told David to wait in the car while they went in. "They took the tape in, and they weren't gone maybe twenty minutes, max." When they came back out, Leon was visibly upset. The Rolling Stones were there recording at the time (probably sessions for the *Aftermath* album) and teased Leon as the lightweight pop guy, Snuff's boy. "They were really putting him down."

Garrett kept Leon employed, though, and offered his young charge valuable production and arranging experience. But even arranging wasn't enough to keep Leon interested. "He was always into his thing," said Lou Adler, the producer of the Mamas & the Papas, Carole King's *Tapestry*, and founder of Dunhill Records. "I remember the first time I used Leon as an arranger, and I never used him again because he spent all his time in the booth telling me what to do. He'd tell me, 'This piano part calls for a lot of highs,' and I'd say, 'Leon, you're just arranging it.'"

Bobby Hart and Tommy Boyce wrote and produced demos for the new concocted-for-television band the Monkees, "an American Beatles on television sitcom" produced by Don Kirshner and Lester Sill of Screen Gems. Hart explained, "Once it sold to NBC and then got a couple of sponsors, [Kirshner] said, 'We need to bring in the big guns. In other words, you're off the project as producers.'" Kirshner selected Snuff Garrett and Leon. Though Garrett was not enthusiastic about the project, the money was too good to pass up. But the Monkees did not gel with the brash Garrett, and Kirshner and Sill had to buy out Garrett's contract. The original producers Boyce and Hart were back at the helm for what became a massive success.

This detour did not slow Snuff and Leon's roll. But their so-called partnership amounted to Garrett making out like a bandit while Leon remained his faithful but much-lower-paid sidekick who did most of the heavy lifting. More than compensated for their time on the ill-fated Monkees sessions, Snuff received an additional $250,000 from Dot Records owner Randy Wood for Garrett to start his own label, Viva Records. For the new company's first project, Garrett said, "I told Leon, 'I want you to arrange these twelve songs for string quartet.' Leon looked at me like I'd lost my fucking mind. I made up a name—the Midnight String Quartet. We sold three hundred thousand of that album [*Rhapsodies for Young Lovers*]. We did follow-up albums. We cut the whole album in an hour and forty-five minutes."

Leon recalled things differently: "One day, I told Snuff that I would like to do something as an artist. He suggested a string quartet, with piano and harpsichord, playing standards. He gave me a list of songs and I picked out the ones I knew and went to work on the arrangements, which took about two weeks. It was very stressful because I had never written for a string quartet before and didn't have a piano in my office. When I was finished, I went to Western Studios and recorded the album in two days. . . . I played the harpsichord. I was well pleased with the album, as it was my first attempt at writing for a string quartet, so you can imagine my surprise when Snuff informed me that instead of using my name, as had been originally proposed, he was going to call the group the Midnight String Quartet. I was shocked and disappointed at this development. . . . The album stayed on the charts for fifty-nine weeks and spawned a whole series of Midnight String Quartet discs—none of which I had anything to do with."

Leon met folk singer Donna Washburn through David Teegarden, who was dating her. It was not long before Leon and Donna became a couple, though. He cowrote a song called "Raspberry Rug" with Donna, and they landed it on the debut album of a new sunshine pop group called Harpers Bizarre, produced by Lenny Waronker. Waronker had escaped his ill-fitting role as a promo man at his family's Liberty Records and gladly filled a newly opened position in the publishing side, at Metric, then as an A&R man with Reprise/Warner Bros. "I was into songs and had spent an enormous amount of time with Snuff Garrett, who was an unbelievable A&R producer," Waronker said. "He was a great pop song evaluator. I learned a hell of a lot from him."

One of Waronker's earliest projects as a producer was Harpers Bizarre, which featured a young Ted Templeman, who would go on to legendary status as the producer of both Vans—Van Morrison and Van Halen. Waronker called several whip-smart young lions like Leon and Van Dyke Parks. When he met Leon, Parks was still at the beginning of a long and distinguished career, a singular path that included scoring works for Disney, writing lyrics for Brian Wilson's *Smile* project, recording critically acclaimed solo records, founding Warner Bros.' audiovisual department, and producing records by compelling acts like Ry Cooder, Little Feat, Joanna Newsom, and Rufus Wainwright.

The task at hand was a song written by Paul Simon, "The 59th Street Bridge Song (Feelin' Groovy)." The Simon and Garfunkel version, Waronker explained, "was only an album cut. I'd heard it as a commercial. It's when record companies started to play music in their time-buys. I heard a little snippet of it, and I just thought, 'Boy, that sounds good.' I got the album. It was great, but it was only one minute and thirty-two seconds."

Leon was initially not on board. "He said, 'No. I don't want to do that anymore.' He was becoming Leon Russell," Waronker said. "He was just going through that transition where he stopped working with Snuff.

He didn't want to do pop stuff anymore. He liked producing to some extent. He just didn't want to do anything like that. I said, 'Leon, we could do whatever we want. It's a good song. The problem is that it's only one minute thirty-three seconds. If we repeated the first verse at the end and add a Beach Boys kind of break in between where they're doing an a cappella thing, I bet you we could get close to three minutes.' I think he liked the spirit of that, having things go out, and then the voices keep doing stuff. There's a bit of psychedelia going on. I said, 'Have you been thinking about anything musically that you'd like to try or whatever?' He said, 'Yeah. I've been thinking about writing eight flutes and try the voice in strings.'"

Waronker laughed. "I looked at him and said, 'That's a great idea.' About three days later, he called me up and said, 'I changed it around. The flutes, I don't think it was going to work, so I got us a bassoon.' Every time he mentioned an instrument, it actually got me excited."

They assembled at Western Studio on November 25, 1966. J. J. Cale is listed as conductor, with Jim Gordon on drums, Larry Knechtel, Plas Johnson, Al Casey, Jay Migliori, and other A-listers. "Glen Campbell was on it, along with James Burton, a bunch of string players and an orchestra that went all the way to the back of the room," Cale said. "I didn't know it was that song we were playing on until later on. That was in the three-track recording day and the singers weren't around, but we had Leon's lead sheets and cut all that stuff that Leon had arranged. He had a real knack for arranging."

Parks was impressed. "This is at the apogee, at the gilded age of analog recording. Leon had a great sensibility about sound, how things within a room would sound. And he never lost that because he was enough of a performer to know that."

On the session, Waronker was amazed with the result. "I actually called Randy [Newman]! Randy was astonished. He said, 'You've got to understand something; writing for woodwinds is as hard as it gets. This guy just did something that's absolutely over the top great.'"

It's a sweet haiku of a song, a simple short shot, with a sunny veneer, combined with Simon's lyric capturing an eyes-wide-open sense of Zen. It emotes on a deeper level than its compellingly shimmering surface. The arrangement takes the Phil Spector concept of "little symphonies for the kids" to a more crisp and vividly heightened level, stripping away anything unnecessary. No murky Wall of Sound here, just a white picket fence with a few American Beauty roses poking through. It's a great one to listen to on headphones. As the music fades around 1:26 (of the overall 2:39), there's slight letdown at what seems to be the cruelly short tease of this gorgeous melody. But there's barely a breath before cascading, and overlapping voices enter high in the mix. The already effervescent song opens like the flowers of the lyric. Waronker's idea for a Beach Boys vocal break in Leon's hands became something more like a Bach chorale from madrigal singers. Waronker confirmed that another inspiration was an early-1960s group from Paris called the Swingle Singers.

Purely as a musical arrangement, it stands with some of the great moments of *Pet Sounds*. "It was something," Waronker said admiringly even decades later. "The instrumentation suddenly got used a lot. Almost every commercial started using woodwinds and stuff. It was interesting. It actually had an effect." It was recorded days before the Beatles did something very similar with woodwinds, "When I'm 64," recorded in December. Something was in the zeitgeist, because the Harpers Bizarre single did not break the *Billboard* Hot 100 until February 1967, and the Beatles were already on the same road. It's quite a presentation of a song that Simon has repeatedly claimed he "loathes." Harpers Bizarre's version of "The 59th Street Bridge Song" reached number thirteen on the pop chart.

Another landmark arrangement of Leon's came that same autumn. Gene Clark left the Byrds in the spring and recorded a solo album at the Columbia Recording Studio. The country-flavored *Gene Clark with the Gosdin Brothers*, Clark told journalist Bruce Elder, "was all very intense. I remember telling people I was doing an album with Leon, Clarence White, Glen Campbell, Chris Hillman, Chip Douglas, and Vern and Rex Gosdin and they thought I was crazy. It was like, 'You're going to make a record with them? What a weird combination of people.'"

Leon's contributions include a string arrangement on "So You Say You Lost Your Baby" and the gobsmacking "Echoes." Leon used a thirty-two-piece orchestra to provide a bed of woodwinds and strings for a song that so betrays the influence of Dylan that it is practically a pastiche. Leon's arrangement frames the piece, perhaps with his own homage, to Stravinsky via Gershwin. The song dawns a bit like "Rhapsody in Blue" and

"The Rite of Spring, Part One: The Adoration of Earth." It's an audacious arrangement. It's not as if the strings are just there to provide a lush pad. The dynamism could easily distract from the vocal, and the level of the orchestration in the mix would overwhelm a weaker singer than Clark.

Astonishingly, the entire arrangement was written in one day. "Those sessions were unbelievably creative," Clark told Bruce Elder. "I remember going to Leon two days before the first session with 'Echoes,' with nothing but my voice on a demo, I left it with him, came back the next day and found him passed out next to a stack of thirty-two lead sheets—in one day, he'd written out the parts for each member of a thirty-two-piece orchestra. It was that kind of time."

Leon closed out 1966 with his final Gary Lewis session. They had spent much of the prior two years working together, with Leon even conscripted into the recording of Gary's dad's musical endeavor, the Jerry Lewis Singers, which is as awful as one would imagine. According to Marc Benno, who had just drifted into Leon's orbit as a valuable collaborator and catalyst, Jerry bullied Leon into doing this last Gary Lewis session. But, in January 1967, Gary received his draft notice. "It put a sudden halt to the whole thing," Lewis said. "Things work out. I even got out of music because when I got out of the service, there were these new people like Jimi Hendrix and Janis Joplin, and harder rock and all that. I said, 'I don't feel that.' It's just not me."

Leon and Gary met again at Western in December and recorded a Leon/Don Nix song, "The Loser (With a Broken Heart)." Andrew Sandoval, a producer, author, and musician, pointed out that the record "is an important transitional single for both of them," Lewis and Russell. "I think that was Leon pushing forward," Sandoval said. Indeed, it is a driving arrangement along the lines of the Monkees' "Last Train to Clarksville" with a touch of Paul Revere and the Raiders' 1966 recording of Boyce and Hart's "(I'm Not Your) Stepping Stone." It also leans toward the bass-and-drum-heavy rock/soul groove that Leon would help usher into the late 1960s. The horns, B3 organ, and overall production point the way for such brassy groups like Blood, Sweat & Tears (formed by Al Kooper in 1967), Ides of March ("Vehicle," 1970), and Chicago. Horns bleat, background singers (the Blossoms) answer, and there's even a Harpers Bizarre–like psychedelic breakdown for a bridge.

Lewis hated it: "That spacey, slow interlude, whatever that was . . . That's not happening. That's not Gary Lewis and the Playboys." But when I suggested that maybe it was more Leon anticipating and pushing where Lewis might have gone, Lewis replied, "I never thought about that either, that maybe Leon realized the music was going to progress into something else, and maybe he was trying to set me up for it."

Chapter 8

Asylum Choir

THE OUTCASTS WERE A TEXAS teenage garage band who had tracked down Snuff Garrett and presented him with a demo when he visited Dallas in 1966. When Garrett returned to the city, he told the band, "I've got my arranger with me." Lead Outcast Wally Wilson recalled first meeting Leon this way: "It was like Jesus Christ walking in the room. . . . I've just never seen anybody look like that in my life."

By the time they were ready for their recording session for a third single with Snuff and Leon, the band was eager to leave the lightweight pop stuff behind. "Now we're going to be kind of psychedelic," Wally Wilson said. "This is 1967, the Summer of Love. Leon said, 'Come on out.' So we all drove out there."

Like the Tulsa Mafia six or seven years earlier, the erstwhile Outcasts headed to Hollywood, six guys with no money in a '63 Chevy. "We drove twenty-three hours and we got out to LA and went to Leon's, and he let us do a record," Wilson said.

By the time they returned, Leon was in full hippie mode. "That was the first time I had seen Leon, when we went to Skyhill," said Marc Benno, a recent recruit to the band. "When we got there, he opened the door, and we were all completely freaked out because he already had the beard, the long hair. He was way ahead of the Beatles. Even *our* hair wasn't over our ears, but we were *trying* to get it to grow over our ears. . . . He intimidated the hell out of us by being so calm. He was on a different plateau. And we couldn't reach him."

They recorded a remarkable track written by Leon and Bill Boatman called "Land of Oz," a psychedelic soul-pop blast that indicated the direction of Leon and Benno's future collaboration over the next year or so. There are backward-tracked instruments and manipulated vocals describing a quest for a magical world set to heavy bass-and-drums groove, in the vein of the Beatles' "Rain" or "I Am the Walrus." It was released on the delightful Buddah Records under the band name Le Cirque in October 1967, just after the Summer of Love. At the time, the airwaves were infused with incense and peppermints and rocking horse people eating marshmallow pies.

On July 31, 1967, a combination of Skyhill regulars recorded the backing tracks at RCA Studios for Le Cirque's single. There were also three Leon-arranged backing tracks recorded for Delaney & Bonnie at this same session. On the "Land of Oz," Benno's boyish voice floats in harmony over the groove of Boatman on drums and Carl Radle on bass. Jesse Ed Davis plays guitar. Benno gushed that Leon "was the greatest musician I had ever encountered. A lot of people I knew, including myself, were kind of garage band guys. We were self-taught, so we could do one thing pretty well, but Leon was so much more expansive. . . . He could play every instrument, and he knew the entire board, how to create records completely from scratch. This was totally magical to me."

As with other emerging artists who entered his lair, Leon encouraged the Outcasts to write their own songs. "He was asking if anybody had any songs [for the B-side]," Benno recalled. "And I said, 'I've got some songs.'"

They recorded Benno's "I'll Be Thinking of You." Chuck Blackwell played drums. "It was, like, very light, like almost brushes or something, but he played perfectly on it." Leon played Hammond B-3 organ. Wilson added, "Leon went to the piano and said, 'Look, let's do this. It sounds a little bit like ["Pomp and Circumstance"], so let's really make it like the graduation song.'" Benno provides all the vocals, and his backing parts are so high they sound as if a young woman did them. "I sound like a little boys' choir," Benno said. Le Cirque made one more trip into the studio and recorded "Icicle Startree," written by Leon, Wilson, and Benno. Intended as a Le Cirque single or B-side, it was released on the first Asylum Choir album instead. The band went back to Dallas and broke up. But Benno would be back.

The partnership between Leon and Snuff burned out in 1967. "I found myself wondering why I was associated with my then-current business partner," Leon wrote. "He was putting his name on every song I wrote, even though he didn't help write most of them. He reveled in psychologically debilitating would-be writers by listening to five or six seconds of their songs and saying, 'No, that's not a hit.' . . . When I dissolved my association with Snuff Garrett, I was paid the equivalent of union scale for all the records I had made during the two years I was with him. . . . I think it cost me between seven and eight hundred thousand dollars."

So he struck out on his own. "Leon and I got a little production company together," Don Nix said. "He had run out of everybody else in the house. It was just me and him living there at Skyhill. There was a guy named Bob Skaff who was a big shot at Liberty Records. He started a label called Independence." Singles by Don Preston, Delaney Bramlett, and Joey Cooper fizzled, as did a pair of Preston LPs. But it was a start.

Back in Texas, Benno wrote a letter to Leon. He knew Leon had a publishing company, which he pictured as an actual, fully staffed company in an office building. "I told my mother, 'I'm going to get a job at a publishing company.'"

When Benno arrived back at Leon's, the maestro wasn't there. "The front door was unlocked, and there was music blaring. I went in, and no one noticed a thing. There were several musicians there. An Indian guy playing guitar while sitting on the couch, with a Fender Telecaster. His name was Jesse Ed Davis. They were actually recording while eating hamburgers."

By now, Skyhill was a three-ring circus presided over by Leon, already the ringleader he would become famous for being. "He was a rock star before he was a rock star," Nix said. "He was the guy that walked in the room, and everybody noticed. You felt it."

But starting around 1967, he would naturally need respite from the chaos. "He was generous to a fault, and it really kind of messed him up," Nix said. "He had horrible depression, and nobody ever knew. He had that his whole life. It'd be a house full of people. He'd go sit in the car all day. I hated that for him."

Karstein explained: "Leon, I think, in this day and age, people would tend to call it bipolar. Some days you could tell: 'Just give him his space. Don't mess with him,' because he'd be down. But it wouldn't last."

Leon would usually crash at Donna Washburn's house. She was wealthy, and her house in the hills of Burbank, just across the 101 freeway from Skyhill, was clean, comfortable, and well appointed. It would have seemed luxurious in comparison to the crash pad on Skyhill. Teegarden had returned to Tulsa, and Benno had taken his place in the closet for about a week by the time Leon came back to Skyhill. Leon had no idea Benno was living there. "'What do you want?' That was his favorite line," Benno recalled. "I said, 'Well, I want to make a record or something.' He said, 'Okay. Okay.'"

Leon brought Benno to a session he was arranging. Glen Campbell, who would have been voted most likely to succeed as a genuine recording artist by everyone in the Wrecking Crew, was finally on the precipice of stardom. Campbell brought in his buddy Leon to arrange a song, "My Baby's Gone," for the breakthrough *By the Time I Get to Phoenix* LP. "I went to one session at Capitol Records," Benno said. "The big room. [Leon] had the rhythm section. He also had a room full of strings . . . thirty or forty players. That's when I realized how great he really was. He stood up there and conducted all of these players. He would stop it and turn the music page, and he would say, 'OK, page thirty-four, bar eight. That's a dotted eighth on that. You're not playing that.'"

Leon was not taking many drugs, but he enjoyed a few beers and a joint regularly. Acid was an occasional experience. But with all the freaks coming and going, he started to get concerned about the police showing up. He still remembered working with Sinatra, who had been accompanied by "eight or ten Highway Patrolmen at his sessions, and it scared the shit out of me."

Karstein recalled: "He said, 'No more smoking dope,' to anybody that was there. You couldn't smoke dope in the house. Well, it got to where you weren't supposed to smoke dope at all. That was Leon's rule."

Breaking that rule led to Karstein's exile from Skyhill. From there, he went to "another house, known as the Plantation, where Southern musicians hung out and lived," as Benno described it. The Plantation was a house at 4504 Mammoth Avenue, Sherman Oaks, in the San Fernando Valley, where most of the guys in this circle of musicians lived at various points.

Drummer Gary Sanders had found the spot after returning from the road with J. J. Cale. "Sanders and his wife went out about five miles to Sherman Oaks," Karstein explained. "He found this two-story house; it was set right on the corner. It was perfect for musicians." There was also a guesthouse that had been the service quarters. Various musicians cycled in and out of the property, while others rented places within walking distance.

Karstein "took over operations of the Plantation for about a year," he said. "That's when I'd say the Tulsa nucleus expanded. We kept sucking all these other guys in." Cale, Bobby Keys, actor and musician Edward James Olmos, Taj Mahal, Bobby Whitlock, and Levon Helm of The Band all lived at or near the Plantation. Whitlock said that by the time he moved in, the house had thirteen people living there.

Fresh from Texas, T Bone Burnett came through as well: "That's the first place I went. . . . I walked into a jam session with Taj Mahal and Delaney and Bonnie—Bonnie and Delaney, as they were called in those days—Eddie Davis, Bill Boatman, Carl Radle, and Chuck Blackwell. It was an amazing introduction to the Los Angeles music scene, much of which came from Texas and Oklahoma."

Benno managed to stick around Skyhill for more than a year, long enough to make two albums in full collaboration with Leon, both under the name of Asylum Choir.

Benno could not believe Leon, with his immense talent, was not already a solo star. "He liked talking to me, and I was building his ego up. I would say, 'Leon, I think that you're as good as Bob Dylan. I can't believe you don't have any records out. You should put a record out under your name.'" Benno was bold. He asked, "'What about if I wrote a song with you?' [Leon] said, 'Yeah, well, maybe.' I don't know if it was the next day or that night, we wrote a song. He said, 'That's pretty good, let's write some more.'" Benno was impressed with how engaged Leon was with current events, so he encouraged him to look there for inspiration. "We came up with some war songs like 'Down on the Base' and stuff." The two would often sit around the house with acoustic guitars writing together.

"When I left the studios, I started blowing my own horn," Leon said. "I didn't miss the studio stuff because I didn't really get to express myself like I did on my own records."

Gordon Rudd came to Skyhill to engineer. As a student at UCLA, he was looking for a job and saw Leon's ad on the bulletin board of the job placement center. Skyhill was not what he expected. "I was told that Leon had a recording studio in his house, but I didn't expect a full-blown professional setup. That was very rare in those days. It was not fancy, but it was as good as most any serious studio in Hollywood at that time.

The décor in the house was 'early hippie.' Bare linoleum floors with no rugs, various walls spray-painted black or neon green. Nothing was ever finished."

Rudd studied physics and had accumulated some minor audio engineering experience. But Leon wanted someone he could mold to fit his idiosyncrasies. Rudd, laughing, said, "I think it's fair to say that *everything* was unorthodox. He took me to sessions at RCA and Capitol Records to show me what *not* to do."

Rudd's hours were one p.m. to one a.m., and he made seventy-five dollars a week. "After a while, Leon invited me to come live at Skyhill. I accepted and moved in. Poor Marc Benno had to [go back to] live in a closet." Rudd moved in and dropped out of school.

Benno recalled that the Asylum Choir recordings came together effortlessly. "Nobody had the technology that he [Leon] had, and he was buying a lot of equipment." Benno remembered going out with Leon to buy a Chamberlin, the Mellotron prototype, from Harry Chamberlin himself. "He wanted to make a record that was as good as *Sgt. Pepper's.*"

You never knew who you'd run into at Skyhill. Don Preston said, "I went up there one night, and Pat Boone was doing commercials." Don Nix said, "Glen Campbell, of course, was up there all the time. Keltner was up there all the time." Keltner recalled, "It was pretty much always crazy. Leon had these big, big wild parties. We did some real fun stuff in there."

"Leon was very kind to me, and at one time, we were like best friends," Rudd said. "But I do have to explain that, at that time, I was very shy and had no social skills whatsoever (and still don't)." He has Asperger's syndrome, "a condition that prevents me from having relationships with people." Leon probably saw some of himself in Rudd or, on some level, identified with Rudd's difficulties with socializing. He just didn't have a diagnosis for it yet.

While sessions were underway with Benno, Greg Dempsey, whom Leon had met while scouting talent with Snuff, came to Skyhill with a new psychedelic project called Daughters of Albion. "Greg Dempsey, he was a guy about six foot three, skinny as a green bean. And he had a girlfriend and Kathy [Yesse] was absolutely beautiful," Benno said. "I didn't know what the hell they were doing," he confessed. "I didn't get it. I mean, I liked him personally. But I thought, 'What is this stuff?' you know?"

The resulting album was what some refer to as a "kitchen sink" record, woven with pretty much everything you might hear from various pop, folk, and rock music trends of the time. Leon's innovative and crystal-line production drops out instruments, rides up the levels of effects, like echo, and loops playbacks from different tracks. It's a little-known gem. Dempsey was a pivotal influence on Leon's evolution as a songwriter, and he and Yesse formed an extraordinarily close relationship with Leon, mov-ing into Skyhill.

The Asylum Choir recordings began in the fall of 1967, and they worked on them throughout the winter of 1967 into the summer of '68, overlapping in timeline, personnel, and approach with the Daughters of Albion sessions. "I recall spending a lot of time" on it, Rudd said. "As Leon played all the parts himself (except drums), it involved a lot of over-dubbing. I thought the music was pretty weird, considering what I knew he could do."

Comfort food and the places that served it, be they family-style buffets out on a highway or little holes in the wall, all washed down with iced tea would be a theme throughout Leon's life, to the point of impacting his health. Not coincidentally, "Soul Food" is the name of the second track on *Look Inside the Asylum Choir*, and the album's back cover credits include "Soul Food: Olivia's." Olivia's was in the Ocean Park neighborhood of Santa Monica and also inspired "Soul Kitchen" by The Doors (of whom Leon was not a fan, calling them "the Doors to nowhere").

Though Benno, Boatman, and Markham also get songwriting credit, "Soul Food" is arguably the first real "Leon Russell" song on record, the one that doesn't sound like him trying to be anyone other than himself. Leon boogies into "Soul Food" on a Wurlitzer electric piano and adds a B-3 organ. Boatman adds understated stops and accents, a kind of groove that smacks of Tulsa drummers. The case can be made that "Soul Food" is the first Southern rock song. Leon was ushering in a new funky rock 'n' roll blend of gospel, soul, country, and blues with a nod to the lingering psychedelic zeitgeist. But he was listening to a lot of blues, Junior Wells's *It's My Life, Baby!* and *The Greatest Hits of Howlin' Wolf* among them.

Leon was also listening to a lot of Rolling Stones. "He changed," Wally Wilson recalled. "He started saying, 'Well, Mick Jagger would do this, and we should do it like that.' He would sing more." Leon had been naturally inclined to pretty things up with overdubs and arrangements. "But he kind of pulled all that away. And then we'd do the 'blues nights' [weekly blues jams at Skyhill], and whenever we did, he got deep into that in a really basic way, which became who he was when he made the two or three records that put him on the pinnacle."

The first Asylum Choir album vacillates between traditional American-roots earthiness and the more airy and experimental intellectualizations of the psychedelic era. "I lit him on fire," Benno said. "I was like, 'Why are you worried about the Beatles and Bob Dylan for? You're more talented than both of them!'" Answering Ben Fong-Torres in *Rolling Stone* about the influences on the album, Leon replied, "Beatles, yes, the Beach Boys, yes, Frank Zappa, yes"—even though, Wilson said, "Leon did not like Frank Zappa. He would always talk bad about him."

Benno looked up to Leon as a big-brother type and valued the collaboration. The duo recorded more than enough tracks for an album. In 1971, when Leon was a big star and had his own label, he released *Asylum Choir II* on his Shelter Records. They finished one project and started work on the second, with a few songs remaining from the sessions for the first album. "I was there at the time they were cutting the records," Don Nix said. "I thought that the first Asylum Choir LP was a hit album because it was so ahead of its time."

Benno said a "strange guy" came to Skyhill to begin working on the art for the *Look Inside the Asylum Choir* cover. Lou Kimzey, a forty-year-old biker, had produced a couple of hot rod/rock 'n' roll B movies in the fifties, *Hot Rod Gang* and *High School Hellcats*. Kimzey also published magazines covering hot rods, martial arts, and pop music. Leon even contributed some record reviews for Kimzey's *Paperbag* magazine, giving decent marks to the Jimi Hendrix Experience's debut but a low grade to the Grateful Dead's.

Leon had arranged for Kimzey to use Skyhill for filming in exchange for a sweetheart rate on art direction for the album cover. "One morning at about nine, the doorbell rang," Benno wrote. "I put my jeans on and went to answer the door. There was a girl standing there, with long black hair and a little night case. She looked pretty good but made me nervous. . . . She was saying she was there to do a movie and that [Kimzey] sent her."

Soon, another young woman showed up, followed by the big, bearded Kimzey, with movie and still camera equipment. The two women followed him up to Leon's bedroom. "Leon walked in. He was in a good mood but didn't want them in his bedroom. There was a quick meeting in the upstairs hall, and Leon came back in smiling and grabbing the camera. The girls were called upstairs. They walked in, jumped in bed, and started making out! Cameras rolling, our album playing full blast, lights blaring, a porno flick was in the works! This was my first encounter with the movie business." He said Leon got in on the action briefly before leaving the women to get to work.

After they finished the scene, Leon had a burst of inspiration. Beckoning Benno and the brunette woman to follow, he went down to the studio control room. Leon "sat at the board in his swivel mixing chair," said Benno. "She spontaneously sat on his lap, and I picked up the guitar and aimed it up her crotch while she spread-eagled, completely nude! The shoot was over, and everybody left happy!" They were so pleased when the resulting shot came back that Leon had it printed up on glossy eight by tens with the phrase, "The Asylum Choir is Coming," a takeoff on the 1964 Capitol Records promotional campaign for the Beatles. He took it down to run as an ad in the underground paper *Open City*. The ad caused quite a stir, the desired effect. But it landed an obscenity prosecution on the publisher, John Bryan, in March 1968. The $100,000 fine bankrupted the paper, and Bryan moved on to work at *Los Angeles Free Press*.

Leon was asked about it in *Rolling Stone* a few years later. "That's when that stuff had just been declared legal—that the human body wasn't obscene—so they were driven out of business on an illegal premise."

Look Inside the Asylum Choir was released in October 1968 on Mercury subsidiary Smash, along with a single of "Welcome to Hollywood," a satire of commercialized hippie culture, backed with "Soul Food." In addition to the controversial ad, the cover of the album—a roll of toilet paper—also caused some trouble. *Asylum Choir II* would be a more streamlined and straightforward collection that would be recorded mainly over the course of 1969 but that would not appear until November 1971.

Benno said, "The first album we completed it, and he [Leon] said, 'I'm going to take this album to Bob Krasnow, my buddy at Mercury Records.'" They cut a deal. "Leon gave me a lot of money. We came back, I didn't know how much money we had. Krasnow had given us a deal and [Leon] just threw the money on the bed. I thought, 'Wow, look at all this money, man. What are we going to do with this?' He said, 'That over there is your money.' . . . I bought a '49 Chevy for about a hundred and seventy-five bucks."

Look Inside the Asylum Choir received a few good reviews, including in *Rolling Stone* and *Hit Parader*. But not much more attention was paid to it, and Leon and Benno did little to help the cause. "Leon didn't want to go on the road" to promote the first album, Benno said. "He didn't want to do any radio interviews. Nothing." So they went back to work. "Leon told me, 'I will go make another album.'"

Chapter 9

Accept No Substitute

LEON RUSSELL WROTE A FUNKY rock 'n' roll song called "Shoot Out on the Plantation," which he included on his 1970 solo debut album. The chorus goes, in part, "Yeah, the last one to kiss is the first to shoot / And stabbing your friends is such a drag to boot."

Trying to nail down what actually happened at the Plantation the first week of January 1968 is a little like watching *Rashomon*. Don Nix got there a day after New Year's Day, when the house was at its apex as a party headquarters. Various unemployed Tulsan and Texan musicians were living there or hanging around, including Gram Parsons, Taj Mahal's band members (Taj had recorded his 1968 debut at Skyhill), Delaney & Bonnie and Friends (including Bobby Whitlock and Bobby Keys), and a few nightclub dancers. The vibe was predominantly mellow, but things got combustible one night when booze and speed fueled jealousy among musicians over some of the women guests.

Chuck Blackwell, a renowned lothario from his earliest days, lived there. "Chuck Blackwell was running women in and out of there on a daily basis," Bobby Whitlock said. "In one door and out the window. Three in one afternoon." One of the women was dancer Kay Poorboy. This particular night at the Plantation, she was in bed with Blackwell. At the time, Jimmy "Junior" Markham still considered Poorboy his girlfriend.

Jim Karstein and Markham were together earlier that night at a gig. It was a good forty-minute drive back from the show. "Of course, we were all drinking. I said, 'I tell you what, let's go to the Plantation and write a song,'" said Karstein. "Before that, for a month or two, Chuck Blackwell had absconded with Kay Poorboy. She'd moved from Markham over to the Plantation and was staying with Chuck. Markham said, [grumbling] 'I don't want to go over there,' and I said, 'To hell with it.' I drove straight over there. Then he came over, and the fireworks started. It pissed me off so bad that I just got in the car and drove up the hills and slept in the car. I just didn't want to be there. I thought it was childish bullshit."

Markham arrived drunk and angry, and Gary "Colonel" Sanders, who was still living at the Plantation, was awakened by Markham's ranting. He warned Junior to pipe down. But Markham continued, threatening everyone in the house. Sanders then reappeared brandishing a .38 but otherwise nude. Markham hid behind one of Jim Karstein's conga drums. Nix, who was present, said Sanders shot six times as Markham darted out the back door. Four bullet holes would later be discovered in the drum.

Karstein recalled: "I wake up about noon the next day, naturally with a hangover. I drive back to the Plantation, and there's a TV that'd been thrown out the window, and the phone was hanging out the upstairs bathroom, down on the cord. The you-know-what had hit the fan after I left. The rest of the story is written in the song. I guess the real action went down in the kitchen, and Markham grabbed a knife.

"In my songwriting aspirations, besides just being a drummer, I had adopted a nom de plume of James Swann. I stole that name from a rhythm and blues artist named Bettye Swann . . . and so everybody called me Swann." Hence the lyric, "Heaven help Mr. Swann."

Whitlock, remembering the events differently, said that Markham did not even make it into the house because Sanders stopped him outside. "Somebody had a .22 pistol. It was stupid. At the back door, and it went off. You know, it just accidentally went off and went through a trashcan next door at J. J. Cale's. So I mean, it was not a *gun battle*. There was no .38 or .45 drawn."

Leon tried to press Whitlock and others to tell him what really happened. "Leon being a songwriter could elaborate and make it like this thing was some kind of something. It was nothing."

Markham himself weighed in sometime before his passing in 2018. Responding to the account in Nix's memoir, Markham said, "Well, that's all greatly exaggerated. First of all, I wasn't drunk, and Nix wasn't even there at the time. Bobby Whitlock tells a story about it in his book, and it's even farther off the mark, and he wasn't there either." He concluded, though, by pointing to the only guy who said he *wasn't* there. "I don't really remember. I know Nix and Whitlock weren't, but I think Karstein was."

If nothing else, the incident illustrates the collaborative and communal—some might say incestuous—web of musicians that formed around Leon and Delaney and Bonnie Bramlett. Delaney and Leon went all the way back to the Palomino scene. Nix knew Delaney from Mississippi. "I was with him on the night he met Bonnie, and she was singing with a band," Nix said. Bonnie was from Illinois, outside of St. Louis, and had begun doing gigs as a singer in her teens, including three days subbing with Ike & Tina Turner as the only-ever white Ikette. She met Delaney when he was performing with the Shindogs at the Geisha Room, a cocktail lounge by LAX airport, in 1967. "He said, 'I'm going to marry her,' and two weeks later, he did," Nix said.

In a whirlwind, two of rock 'n' roll's greatest singers got together in what would prove to be an explosive, abusive, and toxic marriage. "Delaney was a real jackass, but he sure could sing," said Karstein. They formed a duo called Bonnie & Delaney before changing the name to suit Delaney's ego and expanding to Delaney & Bonnie and Friends, a magnet of a revolving-door band that attracted superb musicians, including Leon, who had been producing recordings of Delaney for years.

As 1968 wound down, Leon was still working selective sessions as a player and arranger, including recording with the Everly Brothers and arranging for Tom Northcutt (a sweeping Michel Legrand–like treatment of "Sunny Goodge Street" is one highlight). He kicked off 1969 playing on a January session for Glen Campbell's hit recording of the Jimmy Webb composition "Galveston." But from about '68 on, he focused on being an artist.

In January of 1969, a second single was issued from *Look Inside the Asylum Choir*, "Icicle Startree/Indian Style." By then, Leon was peeling back much of the experimentation and ornamentation on the first Asylum Choir record, as he and Marc Benno continued to record the tracks that would make up the *Asylum Choir II* album. Almost every track is rooted in straightforward blues or rock 'n' roll, and more than half of them feature sharp political or social commentary, including the standout "Ballad for a Soldier." Set to a primitive drum machine beat, this bluesy lament is narrated by a serviceman set up by commanding officers to take the fall for a Mai Lai Massacre type of event.

"Sweet Home Chicago" is one of the early examples of Leon writing new songs with existing titles. In this case, it's a jab of irony, a satirical reaction to the police brutality on nightly display during the Democratic National Convention that previous summer. "Tryin' to Stay Alive" would no doubt have resonated for almost any young man in 1968, whether a soldier or a hippie. But Leon takes the point of view of a Black man trying to get by in his own country.

The music was a good indication of Leon's direction as he embarked on his solo career. The piano work is stellar. The often loose but sophisticated vocal arrangements and production techniques indicate a seasoned pro at the controls. But there's a natural cohesive rock 'n' roll band feel to the set, with prominent electric guitar.

While Leon was finishing up the first Asylum Choir record, he was also helping his old pal Delaney in his new duo with Bonnie. As one of their songs would go, they were trying to get themselves together when Leon brought Duck Dunn to see them. Dunn was so impressed that he encouraged them to come to Memphis to meet with Jim Stewart, head of Stax. At the time, the label was in the midst of an ill-fated attempt to broaden beyond its bread-and-butter soul 45s into the white pop and rock album market.

In Memphis, Dunn brought the Bramletts to see Bobby Whitlock's combo at a nightclub. Whitlock was about eighteen, singing soul songs and playing organ. The Bramletts told him they were forming a band in California and invited him to join them. He moved in with the couple and their extended family in Hawthorne. "I had never been west of the Arkansas line, and I knew there had to be a better life waiting for me," Whitlock said. "Little did I know what was in store for me."

In addition to their newborn daughter, Bekka, Bonnie had another daughter, Susanne, and Delaney had his parents, Mamaw and Preston, living out in the garage. "We were packed in there like sardines. . . . I swear it was *The Beverly Hillbillies* all over, and those two couldn't last a day without having it out. . . . I had left Duck and my solo deal at Stax to come out to California to sing third-part harmony with two people who were at each other's throats from the moment I walked through the front door."

Early in his LA days, Whitlock met Benno and went up to Skyhill to sing on the Asylum Choir stuff. It gave Whitlock an early glimpse of Delaney's controlling mien. Leon and Benno dug the way Whitlock sang, so they recorded something called "So Long for My Baby," with him singing lead. "When Delaney found out about it, he nearly lost it," Whitlock said. "If he hadn't been in such a bind with me being such an important part of the sound, I'm sure that he would have fired me. I probably would have been real happy if he had. I always had a gut feeling that Marc and Leon had been talking about me joining them. He was thinking that they were gonna try to nab me, man. And he got all upset about it."

Bonnie said that by that time, "Leon was head guru." In addition to the solo single Leon and Don Nix produced for Delaney for the Independence label, Leon did another on Delaney & Bonnie as a duo on the same label before the Stax deal. Their version of "You've Lost That Lovin' Feelin'" was their first release and gives a magnificent early example of their vocal power. They sound like a male-female Sam & Dave. Each was an awe-inspiring singer on their own, but together they were staggering.

The band that coalesced around them was an extraordinary group of musicians attracted like moths to the duo's burning flame. After Whitlock, Jim Karstein became the first "Friend" in Delaney & Bonnie and Friends. Leon and the Shindogs guys were usually close at hand. Karstein said, "Everybody had known Delaney, of course, then it was a Gary Lewis deal, and then Taj Mahal . . . everything was interchangeable parts" revolving about the Plantation–Skyhill axis.

Around the summer of 1967, Leon and Jim Horn worked on a concept called the New Electric Horn Band. It included players that would soon fill out the rosters of Taj Mahal's band, Delaney & Bonnie and Friends, Mad Dogs & Englishmen, and Leon Russell and the Shelter People. Asked about it in *Rolling Stone* in 1971, Leon said it was "Delaney and Bonnie Bramlett . . . Don Preston, Don Nix, Chuck Blackwell, Carl Radle, John Gallie [organ player], Jim Horn, and a guy who's playing with Ike and Tina now. But it really wasn't that much of a deal." Nix listed Jim Keltner, Jim Gordon, and Sandy Konikoff, also, as those who passed through the group. Konikoff had subbed for Levon Helm in the Hawks and then backing Dylan after Helm got tired of being booed during Dylan's first electric shows. Sandy spent much time at Skyhill and would end up on Joe Cocker's Mad Dogs & Englishmen tour.

"I was going to do a group with Jim Gordon, and that's the time that Delaney first met him," Leon explained. "Carl Radle was playing with Delaney at the time. Jimmy Keltner was playing. . . . But the people that were involved with that band were already working with Delaney—it was like an organized thing, they'd been working for a month or so at a club in town." Leon considered the Electric Horn Band his first attempt at forming a performing group, noting that the Asylum Choir was a studio project. But he was also wary of having live arrangements being dictated by horn parts. "It takes a certain amount of spontaneity out of it when you have a horn section to deal with, in front," he said.

Leon and Jim Horn "came up with it together," Nix said. "There were just big Sunday afternoon jam sessions. It was the start of the Mad Dogs arrangement. Leon got it all together. He landed some big place. I guess it'd be fifteen, twenty people show up on a Sunday. We got [Don] Preston and Joey [Cooper] to play. It was the greatest time." Almost all of these people would end up in the Mad Dogs band or Delaney & Bonnie and Friends, and most were in both groups.

But before they had fleshed out their band, Delaney, Bonnie, Bobby Whitlock, and Leon began sessions in February 1968 in Memphis at the Stax studio for the *Home* LP for the Stax label (sessions were sporadic, finishing in November 1968). Although this was the first album recorded, it was not released in most markets until after *The Original Delaney & Bonnie & Friends: Accept No Substitute* album on Elektra. Don Nix and Duck Dunn produced the Stax session, and the backing band, for the most part, is Booker T. & the MG's, with Whitlock on backing vocals and Leon on piano. It features Stax all-stars Isaac Hayes, the Memphis Horns, William Bell, and others playing and contributing. The instinct to go to Memphis to record with the killer Stax house band was spot-on. The results are top-notch blue-eyed soul. Radle and Karstein are also on some *Home* tracks recorded at Skyhill. "I worked on the Delaney & Bonnie *Home* album but didn't get any credit," Gordon Rudd said. "I remember that one well, especially 'Piece of My Heart.'" Never mind the Janis Joplin version; Bonnie's take is far superior.

While in Memphis for one of the sessions, Leon met Rita Coolidge, a stunning folk singer of Cherokee Scottish heritage with a gorgeous voice. Coolidge grew up outside of Nashville and had recently moved to Memphis and become entrenched with the scene around Stax. She introduced her sister Priscilla to Booker T. Jones, and the two were later married.

Around the time that Leon arrived in Memphis for the Stax sessions, Coolidge was living with Leon's pal, Nix. "Don was friends with all of these California musicians, and the California musicians all worshipped the Memphis musicians," Coolidge said. "Don knew everybody in California, so I knew about all these people, Delaney and Bonnie, Carl Radle, and Whitlock, and all those people from Tulsa. Don let me know when they were coming, and he said Leon Russell's coming to town."

Coolidge felt like she already knew the California people before they even arrived because of Nix's passionate descriptions of them. Still, meeting them exceeded her expectations. "I just fell in love with all of them, with the music, and the people, and the energy, and just at the strength of their sound, and how unlike it was with everything else that was going on. When I first met Leon, he was so charming and so soft-spoken and just easygoing. He was wonderful. I pretty much was drawn to him as well. . . . Those eyes would just go right through."

Don Nix said, "I think he fell in love the first time he saw her. And before he left town, he said, 'If you ever break up with Rita, let me know.' I broke up with Rita after about six months. . . . I called Leon. He said, 'I'll be down there tomorrow.' Now, he was living with Donna Washburn at the time. He said, 'Don't you worry about Donna, I'll be down there tomorrow.'

"So the next morning, I found out that Rita and her sister Priscilla were doing a background vocal session at Sam Phillips Recording. So I picked him up at the airport, and I took him straight to the studio, and I said, 'Leon, Rita. Rita, Leon,' and that was it. They moved in down the hall and didn't come out for a long time. So I thought things were going good. . . . And Leon went and bought a '60 Ford Thunderbird at Earl Dobbs motors. And they jumped in the car and drove back to California." They struck out of Memphis in November 1968, just before Thanksgiving. "By the time the Delaney & Bonnie album was done, he asked me if I would drive this Thunderbird he'd gotten," Rita said. "So I drove the Thunderbird to California with him. I knew that there were some ulterior motives. I had no idea how tough the journey might be because he never got out of the car."

In her memoir, Rita recalled: "Leon never dealt with a single human being except me on the whole trip. I did all the checking of us into the motel after dark so they couldn't see who was in the car. Leon never got out of the car, especially in Texas. He was so paranoid about the way he looked—in the late 1960s, longhairs were still openly harassed outside of the big cities."

When they reached Skyhill, Leon got out of the car and walked into the house, leaving Coolidge behind. "I just assumed that I was expected to get the bags, which, of course, I'd been doing along with everything else." When asked if he was thoughtless or entitled, Rita explained, "I think it was just Leon being Leon and having tunnel vision around him. And by the time we got home, I don't know what had gone through his head on those long drives, and driving across Texas, and just been scared for a few days. So we got home, he just went into the house. And I'm schlepping the bags in, and once you're in the front door, another flight of stairs up to the bedrooms." Once inside, she introduced herself to a man she was passing in the hall. "There's this stranger in the hall, and I introduce myself. He said, 'Rita, it's me. It's Leon.' It was just like, 'Oh my God.'" He had shaved off his beard as soon as he went inside. "It was so strange—he would have been fine with a beard in California. I thought to myself, If you were going to do that, why didn't you do it in Memphis?

"I didn't say it, but I thought, 'If I had known you had no chin, I'm not sure that I'd be here.'" She laughed at the recollection. But as Rita described Leon, a picture of someone with a possible bipolar disorder emerged, consistent with similar descriptions by other friends. "I was beginning to get a sense of who Leon really was," she wrote. "He wasn't the guy prancing around the studio in control of the session and being adored by fellow musicians. He seemed terrified of the world. And that gave me a different perspective from the one I'd had getting to know him in Memphis. . . . I think Leon had some really deep, deep issues, which unfolded over the next year."

She explained, "I do think Leon was bipolar. It was never confirmed [to me], obviously. I don't know if that was even something that people were aware of at that time. But now, over the years, and knowing people that were bipolar, that explains so much about Leon, because he would be just over the moon, Mr. Personality, or totally, totally shut down. Manic periods of activity and not sleeping, in the studio, and just nonstop, just screaming, 'Make us some tea! We need some more tea!'" But he was not a teetotaler. "Oh, he loved to take some LSD. And when he took the LSD, he would literally look like Quasimodo. He would drag his leg. It was just amazing. And he couldn't control that. I would know if he'd been dipping in the acid because I could see him dragging that leg. And his [piano] hand wouldn't work as well."

She was ambivalent from the get-go with Leon but was thrilled to arrive in California and find that a single she had recorded back home, "Turn Around and Love You," was the number one song on the radio in LA. "I thought it was love. I was infatuated with Leon."

Home would not be released until May 1969, but in the meantime, Bonnie and Delaney began filling out a band and gigging around LA. The initial core was Coolidge, Whitlock, Karstein, Radle, J. J. Cale, and Bobby Keys. Radle played the Stax recordings for Karstein, who'd been on tour with the Everly Brothers. "Everybody knew that Delaney and Bonnie were going to be a hit. Carl played it for me, and he just got this shit-eating grin on his face. And he said, 'Look out Peaches & Herb!'"

Over the next few years, Delaney & Bonnie and Friends would pick up and drop off icons like Leon, George Harrison, Eric Clapton, Dave Mason, Gram Parsons, and Duane Allman, who was introduced to them by Jerry Wexler and who played on one of their albums. Even Jimi Hendrix sat in.

The band was explosive on- and offstage. As bandleaders, Delaney and Bonnie were manipulative at best and tyrannical at worst, and few in their orbit could deal with their poisonous atmosphere for long, mitigated, as it was, only by the amazing music they produced and the foxhole camaraderie the various bandmates forged. Karstein said, "I mean, they were a tour de force. And I knew it was such a neighborhood deal. We were all such a clan, more or less."

But for a while, the music was sustaining enough for all involved. They would assemble in different combinations for gigs around the Valley and Topanga Canyon, in venues like the Brass Rail, Snoopy's Opera House, and the Topanga Corral. They were gigging six nights a week, with jam sessions on Friday and Saturday nights, with Leon sitting in fairly regularly.

Bobby Keys recalled, "Gram Parsons played out there in the International Submarine Band. And I played with them, too. . . . I played a lot with [Junior] Markham at Snoopy's Opera House, and Delaney's band at the time played there, too. There were so many good musicians, so when a band finished playing, there was always another band playing down the road. That's when it was really fun for me."

The players were all grateful to be part of something they all knew was exceptional. Karstein said, "We could've gone onstage either before or after Sly and the Family Stone; that's how good a band that was."

Gram Parsons was enamored of this circle of musicians around Leon. Parsons, already a country rock pioneer, was in the midst of a brief but potent stint in the Byrds, providing the direction for their groundbreaking *Sweetheart of the Rodeo* album that was recorded in the spring of 1968. But he was only on the precipice of realizing a concept he called Cosmic American Music, a synthesis of blues, country, soul, gospel, R&B, and folk—the great American-roots vernacular—in one satisfying stew; music without boundaries. In other words, music like what Leon and his buddies were already up to.

By 1967, Parsons's International Submarine Band had broken up, but some of the erstwhile members were jamming out in the Valley and Topanga under Flying Burrito Brothers, a joke name. Leon joined them onstage occasionally, which impressed Parsons, who was also sitting in regularly and singing with the loose collective. They had various guests from the Plantation–Skyhill scene and regulars like Barry Tashian, who as leader of the Remains had supported the Beatles on their 1966 US tour. Parsons put together a new band, including Skyhill resident Chris Ethridge on bass, and adopted the Flying Burrito Brothers name. But he was a big fan of Leon's in particular.

Dave Mason had already racked up an impressive history when Parsons, whom he'd met during the recording of the Rolling Stones' 1968 album *Beggars Banquet*, brought him to see Delaney & Bonnie. Before he turned twenty, Mason had sung backing vocals on "I'm a Man" and "Gimme Some Lovin'" by the Spencer Davis Group, formed Traffic with Jim Capaldi and the Spencer Davis Group's hotshot singer and organist Steve Winwood, and had written the song "Feelin' Alright?" "They'd play regularly out at the Palomino Club in San Fernando Valley," Mason said. "So I sort of got to know all those guys, a lot of Tulsa people. And Traffic, for me, was done. I didn't see much point in staying in England. . . . Here was a great band, and I just became friendly with them."

Mason would join Delaney & Bonnie and Friends in 1969 as a guitar player for their big tour opening for Blind Faith, a band that included his ex-bandmate Winwood. "I didn't know Leon very well at all," Mason said. "I actually had been hanging out or had been to his house a couple of times back then, but Leon was very much a recluse. It was a time when he had a band called the Asylum Choir." Mason was writing songs for his landmark debut album *Alone Together*, recorded in 1970, with contributions from Leon and many of these folks.

Leon did not appear at all of the Delaney & Bonnie gigs; he was an occasional featured guest. He primarily helped them in the studio. "I used to produce some records with Delaney and Bonnie," he said. "That was before I was together or Delaney was together—the records really weren't that good, and it certainly lacked any kind of a business organization." Parsons brought a wealthy friend, Alan Pariser, to see an early iteration of the band. Pariser, a coproducer of the Monterey International Pop Festival in June 1967, was suitably impressed and "offered [Delaney] the organizational capability he was lacking, and gave Delaney the confidence that he really did have something to say," Leon said.

"Had it not been for Gram Parsons, the phone wouldn't be ringing," Whitlock said. "Gram was totally responsible for the discovery of Delaney & Bonnie and Friends." Pariser spread the word, which quickly caught on overseas. "Alan knew every producer, musician, every movie star, anybody of any standing at all that passed through Los Angeles, Hollywood, because he had the best drugs in the city. He had the best cocaine, the best pot that there was available."

Pariser sent Eric Clapton an acetate of Delaney & Bonnie. "I first met Alan when I went to LA with Cream, and we became buddies," Clapton said. "When Cream dissolved and I was starting Blind Faith with Steve Winwood, [Pariser] knew we were coming to America, and he asked me if I would like to have Delaney & Bonnie open the shows on our tour, and I thought that was a fantastic idea. Little did I know how that would play out. I should have known, really, because that was an incredible band."

"They were the talk of the town," Karstein said of Delaney & Bonnie getting noticed by Pariser. "The first deal was a showcase at some big house up in the Hollywood Hills, and we went up there and loaded in through the kitchen and set up in the dining room. And I had set up a bunch of folding chairs, and all of a sudden, the house just got packed. And Clapton and George Harrison were in there. . . . And we played our set and just blew everybody out the front door." Leon met Harrison for the first time while Harrison was spending about two months in America at the end of 1968.

Pariser worked out a new deal for the band with Elektra Records. Things were off to a great start. There was a big Thanksgiving gathering at Skyhill, with Rita, the Bramletts, Jesse Ed Davis, and the usual Tulsa folks.

"The next thing you know, it's Christmas," Karstein says. Delaney wanted to take a break for the holidays. "So Cale and I, we drive back to Tulsa for Christmas. And a day or two after Christmas, we decided to drive down to Memphis to visit with Don Nix, and we drive down there, and I get a call one night from Bobby Whitlock. 'Delaney didn't think you were going to come back, so you're fired.' Fired me and Cale. And I was just absolutely crushed." But they begged Karstein to come back, and he agreed, even though Cale never did go back. He said, "Delaney always wanted to pay me in cocaine." Cale would respond, "Delaney, my landlord won't take cocaine for the rent."

Jim Price was the trumpeter who joined Bobby Keys to form a two-man horn section that was with the band on *Accept No Substitute*. Price came to town from Texas looking for gigs. "One night, I went to a club in the Valley. Onstage was a guitar band with a tenor sax player. I went up to the tenor player and said, 'I'm a trumpet player. I'd like to sit in.' He asked, 'Where are you from?' I replied, 'Texas.' 'Come on up here, boy!' I played the rest of the night, about five hours. That was the happy beginning of my long friendship with Bobby Keys. He was working on an album with Delaney and Bonnie and invited me to come down the next afternoon to record some horn overdubs. I quickly became a member of the band."

Price joined Leon, Radle, Whitlock, Karstein, Bobby Keys, Rita Coolidge, and guitarist Gerry McGee for the *Accept No Substitute* sessions at Elektra Sound Recorders Studio. McGee had been kicking around the session scene in LA—that's his opening chord on the "(Theme from) The Monkees."

Jim Keltner replaced Karstein after Delaney fired Karstein for the last time in response to his bringing nothing more than a minimalist drum kit, inspired by the MGs' Al Jackson Jr., to a gig. "Leon was in the studio when they asked me," said Keltner. "I was just really knocked out by playing with Leon. Leon was so much fun to play with." But he ran into a trait of Leon's that would negatively affect his direction in later years. "I always felt that had Leon not been so stubborn . . . He had ways about him that you couldn't get into. He was like a mule. He wouldn't move."

"When he wasn't playing, [Leon] sat at the piano with his hands in his lap, and his eyes closed," Jim Price recalled, "as if in some deep meditative state, remaining motionless for fifteen to twenty minutes at a time. He didn't wish to be thought of as enigmatic, but he was. His deep psyche and sharp wit made him a very interesting person to me. He was a respectful and loyal friend to those around him. I don't believe that many people saw those qualities in Leon because on occasion, a harsh exterior would form, and some tended to see only that. Leon was a very private person; he didn't care to join in much of anything, nor did he care about getting to know anybody."

Jim Gordon joined Keltner for double drums on the road. "You couldn't have asked for nicer people," Whitlock said. "The only person that ever caused any discord was Delaney. His ego was massive, and it ruled every decision he ever made." The album was produced by Delaney and David Anderle, with Leon credited for the arrangements. "Delaney would acquiesce to Leon musically," Keys said. "He was the kingpin of our Okie/Texas/Southern bunch of good ol' boys out there. Leon had the big, long, black Cadillac and the rest of us didn't."

Leon said, "I think the first record experience where I really did just what came off the top of my head was that Delaney and Bonnie album. We just all got around and had a party. That's what it sounds like."

It was a welcome step out of the claustrophobic two-person, overdub-heavy, nocturnal Asylum Choir sessions. It must have felt liberating to leave the heady experimentation behind and get back to soulful rock 'n' roll roots, particularly earthy, Ray Charles–like R&B. Perhaps the most prominent influence on the album overall would be Aretha Franklin's 1967 Atlantic landmark *I Never Loved a Man the Way I Love You*, not just on Bonnie's vocals and the brilliant cover of Dan Penn and Chips Moman's song "Do Right Woman, Do Right Man" but also on Leon's piano work. He displays a distinct attention to Franklin's gospel pacing and dynamics.

Jimmie Haskell arranged strings on a drop-dead version of "Do Right Woman" and the album's centerpiece, "The Ghetto." The latter is the standout track for Leon, one that features him prominently and made ears prick up across the Atlantic.

The Original Delaney & Bonnie & Friends: Accept No Substitute helped change the trajectory of rock music. In England, it had a pivotal impact on such artists as the Beatles, Traffic, and the Rolling Stones. Dylan, The Band, Van Morrison, and others were all looking back to earlier traditional music forms, taking a step back to move forward two.

As it did many others, "The Ghetto" captured Clapton's attention, and he saw Leon as a link. "By the time I heard Leon, I already knew Little Richard and Ray Charles and all those people from New Orleans, and I wanted to hear anything like that. So, the chance of being around someone who was still kind of young that I could play with was incredible."

If there is one key to understanding Leon's particular sound, it's his specific interpretation of gospel piano. There's a myth that Leon came from a Southern Pentecostal or Baptist tradition. But Tulsa was more of a Western than a Southern town, and Leon's people were white-bread Protestant. "Those Methodists are a bit starchy," Leon said. He heard Black music on a crystal radio set he had as a kid. "I started playing some of that in the Methodist church, and they ran me off," he said. "So that's where that comes from—the radio." He also noted that "Delaney was actually involved in that kind of church, and he told me a lot of his stories about his experiences, and because I was interested in him, a lot of it seeped through."

Whitlock also came from an actual Southern gospel tradition. His father was a fire-and-brimstone preacher. Whitlock, though, emphasized the difference between Leon's interpretation and the real deal. "'The Ghetto' is a perfect example of what I'm talking about," he said. "That's what it was, a gospel *feel*. It wasn't gospel playing; it was gospel *feel*."

Leon doesn't do anything flashy on the song. It's about the touch. Rock 'n' roll piano players have a general reputation for rushing, playing on top of the beat. Leon's playing is relaxed, in the pocket, unhurried. He enters "The Ghetto" as support for Delaney's soul-stirring vocal. His left hand holds down the bottom end with bass-line runs, even after Radle enters on the bass guitar. The string arrangement takes its cue from Leon's playing. Each musician stays out of the way of the others as the performance builds upward. For an example of the kind of riff that Elton John would incorporate into his work, listen as Leon spikes up to the high octaves around the 2:45 mark with a lick that stabs right into the heart.

Leon said later, "I never had thought of playing that way before. I mean, I just played it. That was the thing that Denny Cordell heard that ultimately made him form Shelter Records with me. That's what he did; he listened to records all the time. He'd hear this guy play something he'd like, and this guy, and he'd put all those guys together on a record for somebody that he was producing, and it was kind of his trick."

"I was so in awe of Delaney and Bonnie and, and the band," Coolidge said. "That band was one of the best bands ever. I think that they raised the bar for everybody, all over the world. Bonnie was the powerhouse singer, but Delaney was just adamant about being the boss and the king. At that time, he hadn't really turned into *such* an asshole yet, or at least it wasn't showing, but it wasn't long before it did."

Leon was back to working on his own recordings through the summer of 1969. "Intro to Rita" offers a halfway candid slice of the domestic life Rita and Leon had. Leon and Benno left the tape rolling while she strolled down to inquire about dinner plans. "One morning, while Rita was out shopping for groceries, we got an idea," Benno said. "We would leave the tape running, wait until she walked in, and record our conversation to use for the intro. . . . Having no idea it was being recorded, she might say something that would be funny and entertaining, as she usually did."

"Marc said something about making a lasagna or something," she drawls in her honeyed Southern accent. While he is chewing gum, Leon asks, "Hey, which one of these do you like better?" He proceeds to play her two versions of an intro he was ostensibly considering as an introduction to "Straight Brother." The first is sort of a New Orleans slant on the "(I Can't Get No) Satisfaction" or "Jumpin' Jack Flash" riffs. The second choice is a bouncing eight-note piece that presages the Mad Dogs arrangement of "The Letter." "What is it for? Is it for something new?" Rita asks. "That second one sounds like 'Straight Brother.'" They flip a coin, and apparently it indicates the second choice. "Which one is it?" she asks. "It's this one," Leon replies, and then they cut into "Straight Brother," an evisceration of Leon's older brother Jerry, who in Leon's estimation chose a bourgeois path.

The target of the song does not realize or care that he's being used up and spit out by corporate America. The song name-checks General Hershey, who was virtually synonymous with the Selective Service, setting up and enforcing the draft. "And deal out artificial skin and bones," Leon sings. Jerry Bridges was a prosthetist.

It's the album's hookiest song. Shelter Records issued it as a single when the album was finally released in 1971 (contractual and Leon's changing business arrangements held it up until then).

"He didn't think [Jerry] was cool at all," Benno said. "You had all the straights, and then you had the guys who were getting high. You remember, if you were straight, you were like, 'Not a part of my generation, dear. You're out.'" "The Gulf" in the song also stood in as a metaphor for the fundamental gap between straights and hippies, young and old, liberals and conservatives. It really came down to civil rights, the Vietnam War, and all the social upheaval.

Almost all of the lyrics on *Asylum Choir II* were Leon's. Benno and Leon shared a sense of insecurity. "We both covered up good—the drugs and alcohol helped," Benno said. "The more talented you are sometimes, the deeper the act is, and in Leon's case, it was as deep as the ocean. He really could mystify you when he wanted to see who could go to the deepest. He could quiet you to death, stare you down, just look at you and you'd be intimidated."

The time came to finish mixing and mastering the second record. "Leon was all about going to Memphis to mix it," Benno said. Leon was, by this point, very close with Don Nix, who had been going back and forth from Skyhill to Memphis. "Rita said that me and Duck Dunn were the first two bicoastal people," Nix noted wryly. "Leon and I got to be brothers. I mean, we were so close. We lived there at Skyhill. Every night, he had this big old Hollywood bed, huge bed. He'd lay up on the pillows, and I'd lay at the foot of the bed, across the bed, and we would talk all night until the sun came up. I'd go sleep like that. We told each other everything in our lives. Every secret, everything."

Back home in Memphis, Nix met John Fry, who in 1966 built the renowned Ardent Studios, still in operation over half a century later. "I was learning not only how to engineer from John, but how to produce from Leon," Nix said, noting that at Stax, "production" had been a matter of whoever was in the control room at the time, a group effort. Nix recommended that Leon mix the Asylum Choir at Ardent. "I was always like, 'I want to go, too,'" Benno said. "I'd never been outside of Dallas much, and now I was traveling like a rock star!" They flew to Memphis and stayed at a spare apartment Nix had because rent was so cheap there. "Don Nix's whole floor smelled like a marijuana den," Benno said. "He was chain-smoking weed."

Leon mostly let John Fry and Terry Manning work the controls. "He would comment if there were things he wanted to change but most of the time, he liked everything," said Manning, another who fell under the sway of Leon's charisma. "He was such a presence. He was so distinctive. And one of those people that immediately stood out, that you knew—even if you didn't know who he was, or what was going on—if he came in the room, just one of those commanding people, incredibly intelligent." He remembered Leon as an entertaining storyteller.

On the back cover of *Asylum Choir II*, there's a dreamy candid photo taken by Carl Radle of Leon and Benno working in the dimly lit control room at Skyhill. Above the photo, it reads, "Produced by Leon Russell and Marc Benno, April 1969." Their fruitful collaboration was coming to an end as they finished the Asylum Choir recordings.

Benno was already playing with various combos of the people in the Leon/Delaney & Bonnie orbit. He would later go on tour in Rita's band. But before he left the scene at Skyhill, he was playing in a band with Jesse Ed Davis. "One night, [Davis] showed up with a monkey in his car," Benno said. "I was like, 'What is that doin' in your car?' He said, 'Oh, well, I had to get a monkey.' He ended up giving the monkey to Leon, and Leon gave it to Rita for her birthday present. I thought, 'How romantic.'"

Benno recalled a moment of awakening. "I was standing at the [kitchen breakfast] bar and eating something," Benno said. "Rita walked in. She said, 'What are you doing?' I said, 'I don't know. I'm eating a grilled cheese.' She said, 'Don't you know what today is? It's Thanksgiving. I'm getting ready to go over to my family's.'

"I said, 'Do you know what? I'm going home for good. I don't like this. With Leon, we don't know what day it is. We don't celebrate holidays. We just keep recording. We don't talk to our family anymore.' These were known rules that Leon had set up for creativity. He was becoming more and more extinct from society. Leon was a hypnotizer. He could look at you, and it was like, 'Whoa.' He was hypnotic because I think he was trying to create something weird, but everybody knew he was the leader of the whole thing."

But not far from the Hollywood Hills, another magnetic long-haired leader, the manipulative ex-con and wannabe rock star Charles Manson, had a harem of acid-damaged hippies and dune-buggy-driving outcasts hanging on his every line of jailbird gibberish. It was mere weeks until they invaded the former home of Leon's colleague Terry Melcher and slaughtered Leon's former stylist Jay Sebring, movie star Sharon Tate, and their friends. "I actually put [Beach Boys drummer] Dennis Wilson together with Melcher when Dennis was looking for somebody to listen to this hippie [Manson]; we didn't even know the guy's name," said Dean Torrence, who also knew Sebring. Melcher never got over it. "Oh God, he was spooked. Yes, he moved and made sure he was hidden."

Glen Campbell, Neil Young, Stephen Stills, and others all met Manson at Dennis Wilson's house. "The Manson factor in rock music was a horror story to every working musician, producer, studio engineer, studio manager, or owners who lived northwest and northeast of Sunset Boulevard just after the Family's rampages," said singer Claudia Lennear, who was about to walk into Leon's life. "Most people began to lock their doors and beef up security, especially in the Canyon areas like Nichols, Laurel, Benedict, and Coldwater."

Leon was attracted to self-formed communal families of friends and collaborators. He brought out the best in others, encouraging them to head off on their own paths. He was conscious of the responsibility of his powerful magnetism and his success in the music business. But it's not likely a coincidence that Dave Mason, who met him around this time, said Leon seemed like a recluse. As Byrd and Flying Burrito Brother Chris Hillman put it, "It suddenly seemed crazy to have unknown people coming and going from your house."

Chapter 10

Hello Little Friend

THE ORIGINAL DELANEY & BONNIE & Friends: Accept No Substitute was released in July 1969. The influence cast by Delaney & Bonnie and Friends as a band is immeasurable. With a big push from Leon, these world-class musicians injected a huge dose of soul and gospel into white rock 'n' roll. Other artists took up this post-psychedelic, back-to-the-roots trail after *Music from Big Pink*, The Band's 1968 breakthrough. But the musicians bopping between Skyhill and the Plantation were a dominant force in advancing rock 'n' roll into the 1970s.

Fellow musicians took notice, particularly overseas. "Best white gospel sound I have ever heard," said Mick Jagger around that time. Keith Richards said decades later, "There was something about the feel of that band that really interested all of us in the Stones. The band impressed us as a unit, with the horns on top, just at the time we were beginning [to use] horns."

"Best band in the *world*," proclaimed Eric Clapton. Clapton was the musician most directly influenced by the band, and he adopted a newly impassioned singing style lifted specifically from Delaney. He even co-opted the band itself for his 1970 eponymous debut solo LP. "[Delaney] taught Eric Clapton to sing," Jim Keltner said. "[Delaney] was just a killer singer and a killer rhythm guitar player. But the more high he got, the more screwed up he got, and he wanted to *be* Eric Clapton. So he would take off his rhythm guitar, put on a Strat, and try to play like Eric, and it was terrible."

Hiring the band for his solo debut was not enough. Clapton stated bluntly, "I stole [Derek and] the Dominos from Delaney Bramlett. I left

Blind Faith and moved in with Delaney and his family" after a tour the two bands did together. Most of the band formed the core of the Mad Dogs & Englishmen band that backed Joe Cocker's 1970 tour.

Meanwhile, Peter Nicholls had dropped out of university in England and joined as a roadie with a band he had booked there, Cocker and the Grease Band. "The Grease Band, we were just driving up and down the M1 in England, you know, doing eight gigs a week," Nicholls said. "And then [Cocker] had a big hit record with 'A Little Help from My Friends.' Fantastic! Then we were invited to go to America to do a tour." On the eve of their flight in early 1969, Cocker went record shopping and came back with *Accept No Substitute*. According to Nicholls, Cocker bought it on the advice of Reg Dwight—before he took the name Elton John—a story Elton refutes. "But I first heard [Leon] on the Delaney & Bonnie sessions, not knowing at that time that he played on all those great Beach Boys records and all that," Elton said. "He was the most soulful piano player. He combined gospel and soul with blues rock 'n' roll, and he made it his own. And I hadn't heard anyone who played quite like that, ever. . . . He had everything that I wanted in a piano player. He was the person that I wanted to play like more than anybody else. He was my number one."

Nicholls continued, "Joe put it on the record player, and we all went, 'Holy shit. What is this?' We listened to that record all night long. 'The Ghetto' was the one that knocked us out." It was Leon's piano playing on the song that stood out for these Englishmen. "So we made a pact then, and said, 'All right, we're gonna fly to America in the morning. We'll go do the tour. Denny Cordell, you get on a plane to Los Angeles and go find this guy [Leon] because we want to meet him.'"

In September 1968, Cocker had recorded the hit "Feelin' Alright" at A&M Studios. As with his recording of "With a Little Help from My Friends," it was more than an interpretation; it was a reinvention of the song Dave Mason had penned while in Traffic. "'Feelin' Alright?' is a question," Mason said. "The song is about 'not feeling too good myself.'" But Mason feels like he owes Cocker because Cocker inverted it. "It was the version I wished I'd done myself." The experience of recording it at A&M opened Cocker up to the benefits of working with American session musicians. In August 1969, Cocker made his career-making appearance at Woodstock. At the end of that summer tour, he and the band finally reached Los Angeles.

Leon wrote about being asked to play with Cocker in the studio. "It was an exciting prospect for me, as I very much liked 'With a Little Help from My Friends,' the title track of Joe's first album, which Denny had produced. Joe's Grease Band, with Chris Stainton on keyboards, was scheduled to record with him, so I wasn't quite sure why they needed me. Still, I was excited at the invitation."

When Leon "first dropped by Sunset Sound, where the Cocker sessions were to take place," he recalled, "I found much sitting around going on, the studio liberally sprinkled with ganja and prime hash in huge blocks. After I had been there for about two hours . . . I started to get a little nervous. I was from the Hollywood school of union record-making, where you were expected to cut three songs in the allotted three-hour session, no matter what." According to Cordell, Leon and Rita hung out, but "didn't say anything to anybody for three hours. Then about two o'clock in the morning they got up, said, 'Thank you very much, very nice,' and left."

The next day, the Grease Band got a call to come to Skyhill. Leon, recognizing it as a good opportunity to pitch some of his songs, wanted to play them a song he thought they might like. "So after the session I played a couple of tunes for Denny Cordell and he was quite taken by the different persona that I exhibited when I was [performing] than when I was playing on the records. I always kept my mouth shut when I was playing on the records, and when I was playing songs it was a different feeling."

"I was in total awe of him," Stainton said. "I was just sitting there watching Leon play, being totally amazed by his playing. He was at the height; it was the complete height of his powers then."

Nicholls recalled, "Leon said, 'Um, I've got this one song. Maybe you'd like to hear it.' So he sat down and honked out 'Delta Lady' for us. We said, 'Great, let's cut that one now.' Then he played one more for us. It was a ballad, 'Hello Little Friend.' So we did those two, and that was the end of that."

"Leon song number one," Cordell announces on the demo tape. Leon performs "Hello Little Friend" and is already clicking the back of his tongue between lines to keep time, a habit he continued through his career. Stainton noodles around on the bass, trying to follow the chord changes. Then Leon confidently runs through "Delta Lady." Cordell chuckles on the talkback at the silly, abrupt vaudeville ending Leon tags it with. "Shoot Out on the Plantation" is particularly great, with a perfect tempo and Leon's clarion vocals allowing the lyrics to come through. Cordell applauds over the talkback mic. This is essentially the audition that launched Leon Russell's solo career.

"I was stunned by how brilliant [Leon] was," Cocker said. "He sat down and played 'Delta Lady.' Game over." Subsequent renditions—Leon's solo version and especially the Cocker-sung live recording on *Mad Dogs & Englishmen*—bettered this comparatively tame studio version, but it was a fine launching point for the song.

Written for Rita, "Delta Lady" is a carnal romp, with "delta" serving as an evocative double entendre. Though Coolidge, from the Mississippi delta, protested that she never stood "wet and naked in the garden," she was flattered, nevertheless. "I was deeply honored, of course," Rita said. "No one had ever written a song about me." Leon had been helping Rita advance her career as an artist. "Leon introduced me to the cream of the LA recording scene—many of them among the most accomplished players in the world who at the moment were emerging from session work and, like Leon, beginning to carve out careers as solo artists," Coolidge wrote. "Since I'd been validated by my own hit, I was confident enough to lie back and take it all in and not worry about being tagged as Leon's 'old lady,' the preposterous, sexist catchall that male rock-and-roll musicians, supposedly so enlightened, affixed to any attractive female."

Released in the fall of 1969, Leon is in elite company as a songwriter on the *Joe Cocker!* album, with its repertoire of Dylan, Lennon/McCartney, Leonard Cohen, Lloyd Price, John Sebastian, and George Harrison. But Leon is the only writer represented with two numbers. The Asylum Choir song "Hello, Little Friend" follows "Delta Lady" on side two, and Cocker vastly improves upon the Asylum Choir version.

Leon also ended up as coproducer and arranger on the album. He recorded many of the tracks for Cocker's version of "Delta Lady" at Skyhill. They had run out of time at A&M, so he brought the tapes home, along with Cordell, Cocker, and Merry Clayton. Bonnie Bramlett and Eric Clapton were also at the house that night. "It seems like they were [recording] it in the bedroom or something," Clapton said. "It was such a weird—that was Leon's house. It was the studio, and there were people getting stoned everywhere, lying on the beds." He laughed at the recollection. "At the same time, there is Joe singing 'Delta Lady.' And I thought, 'What is *happening*? This is a movie. I'm in a movie.'"

But Rita said she was not there for all of it. "I just would get out of the house when stuff was going on because I had to," she said with a laugh. "All I did was make tea and cook, and I was like the housemaid." She had misgivings about dealing with Leon's mood swings. "He was either introverted or Mr. Entertainment. There was just no in-between. And when he would shut down, there was just no communicating."

But it was Leon's libidinous appetites that would prove to be the undoing of his relationship with Rita. "One night, out of the blue, Leon asked me how I would feel if we had a threesome. I told him, 'Well, I don't know, really, I'm not sure what you mean.' Then he said, 'Maybe if we had Carl Radle come over, 'cause I know you like Carl.' Carl and I had become good friends through Leon. And I said, 'And what?' He said, 'We'll all get naked.' I was mortified. I said, 'Wow, you're serious.' I felt like Carl would be as mortified as I was. It was just so strange, and I don't know where it came from except that it was apparently something that Leon fantasized about. That was the turning point in our relationship."

Soon after the sessions with Joe Cocker, she decided to leave Leon. "I realized that I was probably not going to be sticking around much longer, so I got my plan together," Coolidge continued. "Leon had a white van that had the LAPD insignia painted on the side, yet another of his eccentricities, which I drove on house errands, and I borrowed it when I decided that I was moving out. I couldn't tell Leon that I was moving because I knew there would be a campaign to keep me from going.

"It got so that it just felt so uncomfortable at that house," she said. "I was just looking for a way out. And I had met the twins, Terry and Annie Rodgers [Marc Benno's girlfriend], and they said, 'If you need a place to stay, come stay with us.'"

Don Nix said Rita's leaving devastated Leon. Nix was back in Memphis at the time. "He always *loved* Rita Coolidge. And when she left him, he called me, and I had to go out there. I had to fly out there the next day. He picked me up from the airport. We stopped up on Sunset at a pizzeria. He sat there and cried like a baby. I'd never seen Leon cry. It hurt him." Another friend said Leon told him he didn't eat for three months. "It broke his heart."

Nix explained: "He didn't like to be left alone in that house by himself. He told me one time I could live there. He'd pay me a hundred bucks a week if I'd stay and write with him for a while. And I did for a while, but man, it got so crazy. I had to get out of there."

During the Cocker sessions, Leon forged a life-changing bond with Denny Cordell. The well-educated English producer with an elite upbringing had already scored international smash hits with Moody Blues and Procol Harum. Cordell's taste was impeccable. In 1964, he convinced the Moody Blues to cover the Bessie Banks heartbreaker "Go Now," a top ten in America and number one in the UK. He was also an astute businessman, having begun his career in music managing jazz trumpeter (and Oklahoman) Chet Baker in the mid-1960s. He also worked in the Beatles merchandising office and went on to help his old schoolmate, Chris Blackwell, run Island Records. Cordell soon formed a production/management company that got a substantial slice of royalties on Procol Harum's 1967 worldwide smash "A Whiter Shade of Pale." That alone earned him millions of pounds.

After the Cocker sessions at Skyhill, Leon wrote, "The next day we met at A&M and discussed starting Shelter Records. I told Denny my ideas about label identification, in the style of the early Atlantic Records, where you knew that if you bought anything with that label on it you would get good music. . . . I had spent time making overtures to Herb Alpert, Bobby Darin, and others I'd worked with, trying to get them to recognize my potential as a solo artist, but for some reason they all seemed to be on a different wavelength. Cordell, who was a fan of mine, reckoned they were just not rock 'n' rollers. (Who would have thought?)" In fact, Alpert credited Leon with turning him on to hard rock 'n' roll in 1970.

Leon was poised to become the solo artist that Marc Benno had encouraged him he could be. In the future, when Leon appeared on someone else's record, it would be as a featured special guest, not a nameless hired hand.

"[Leon] took off after that," Benno said. "He took off once he started to be a solo artist. He didn't even start to be; he was a solo artist from the second I met him."

Chapter 11

A Song for You

IN DECEMBER 1969, THE LEGENDARY Atlantic record man Jerry Wexler wrote a *Billboard* article headlined "What It Is—Is Swamp Music—Is What It Is," which surveyed the new roots music scenes in Muscle Shoals, Memphis, and LA. "It is the Southern sound! R&B played by Southern whites! . . . It's country funk. The Byrds put something in it, Ray Charles added a lot. It's a pound of R&B, and an ounce or three of country." The month before, Jerry Hopkins had written about the LA roots movement in *Rolling Stone.*

No longer would this scene remain regional or even national; now, the world was about to discover Leon Russell and his coterie. Delaney & Bonnie and Friends had hit the road the previous summer with Blind Faith on a US tour, with Leon sitting in on a few key dates. "Eric [Clapton] was caught in a quandary or a crossroads of his life," Bobby Whitlock said. "He didn't know what he was gonna do. And George [Harrison] turned him on to Delaney & Bonnie and Friends. That's when he got us to open for him." Dave Mason sat in with the band for the whole US tour, as well as some dates overseas. "You know, actually, those are some of the first big arena concerts," he pointed out, with Madison Square Garden and the Philly Spectrum as two notables. Mason was happy to play sideman. "I mean, they were so fucking good live."

Then, for the overseas part, Clapton left the ill-fated supergroup headlining the tour and took up with the opening act. Blind Faith were feeling their way through a druggy fog. Steve Winwood referred to the tour as "one of the tackiest rock circuses of all time . . . vulgar, crude, disgusting . . . and lacking in any integrity at all." Clapton admitted,

"I thought we were pretty boring. Delaney and Bonnie Bramlett were miles better than us." So he joined them, along with Mason, for the UK and European legs, where his pal George Harrison hitched onto the caravan, giving the "and Friends" part of the band name a hint of understatement. Leon was not on any overseas dates. *On Tour with Eric Clapton*, a scalding live album, was issued in 1970.

In early September 1969, Denny Cordell took Leon Russell and the Joe Cocker tapes back to London. Cordell introduced Leon to the engineer Glyn Johns, who had already recorded the Rolling Stones, Led Zeppelin, the Small Faces, Traffic, and the Steve Miller Band. He was working with the Beatles and would soon add the Who and Eagles to his peerless résumé. Johns had seen Leon in action when he'd sat in with Delaney & Bonnie at the Whisky. Johns recalled, "I had never heard anyone play like that." David Anderle had given Johns a preview of the *Accept No Substitute* album at Elektra Studios. "It absolutely blew me away, as I'm sure it did everyone else who's heard it," he said. "That whole Tulsa rhythm section was so different from anything I've heard—obviously, Leon's influence. Leon was like a bloody rhythm section on his own. You don't really need anyone else. It blew my socks off completely. It turned my head."

Leon was well into his songwriting groove after working with Marc Benno and Greg Dempsey and had been digging the channels, imagining his own melodies and words while playing along for hours to backing tracks.

For over five years, he'd been honing the skills and assembling the equipment to record his ideas. He had a batch of them on tape when he got to London, under the joke working title of *Can a Blue Man Sing the Whites*. "Denny was a client of mine," Johns said. "He turned up with Leon when I was mixing the Joe Cocker record. Leon had already started making the record at his home studio in Los Angeles. For some reason, they decided to do some sessions in London with me. I'm pretty sure we re-recorded everything."

Leon and Cordell had also used a few American studios, including a live-sounding session at Ardent in Memphis, where Delaney and Bonnie sang along to "Give Peace a Chance." Bonnie got a cowrite credit on the song. Terry Manning of Ardent remembered, "It was sort of loosey-goosey."

An incredible roster of talent came in to play on Leon's debut album while he was in London: two Rolling Stones, Bill Wyman and Charlie

Watts (Mick and Keith also turned up); two Beatles, George Harrison and Ringo Starr (John Lennon also came to hang out); Clapton and Steve Winwood of Blind Faith; Joe Cocker, Chris Stainton, and Alan Spenner of the Grease Band; and bassist and old Beatles pal Klaus Voorman, who'd played on Lennon's solo debut. Leon's reputation, reinforced by the connections with Cordell and now Glyn Johns, opened doors all around London his first trip there. "Glyn Johns was responsible for that," Leon said. "He was engineering for me over at Olympic Studios in England. I had this song that I liked, and I played it for him. I said as a joke, 'Boy, Eric Clapton would sure sound good on this.' He just said, very matter-of-factly, 'Well, let me call him up and ask him.' Before I knew it, Eric and the rest of them ended up playing on my album."

Johns said, "George was well into [Delaney & Bonnie]. In fact, George wanted to release the album on Apple in England. Obviously, he couldn't because it was owned by Elektra."

Cordell brought Leon to the Beatles' Apple offices and introduced him to a twenty-one-year-old Oklahoman-via-LA go-getter, Chris O'Dell. "Standing there, staring at me, was a man with long salt-and-pepper hair, dark mustache and beard, and deep-set eyes that seemed to look right through my clothes, my skin, even my bones, deep into my heart, maybe even my soul," O'Dell recalled in her memoir. She felt her knees buckle. "His eyes were scary. They could be scary if he was looking right through, and they could also draw you in." She recognized him from his photo on the back of the Delaney & Bonnie record. But that whole LA scene had blossomed only after she had arrived in London, where as a young American working for the Beatles, she felt set apart from the kids back home. Anyone who remembers their first time abroad can identify with her desire to avoid another American, never mind another Okie who had played music as a young man at her church in the tiny town of Owasso. Leon was literally too close to home. "I was in London in '68. I'd left LA," she told me. "There wasn't a lot of the LA scene I was aware of after a year in London."

She fumbled for words, and Leon was content to just stare at her, his lips sealed. "I was so flustered by his silence," she said. She felt as if she were on display and was intimidated by his manner, which she described as "brooding." As she chattered, Leon just regarded her with a sideways glance and a crooked smile, as if bemused. She was also aware of how well regarded Leon was. "For me, the Beatles were . . . the top of the ladder. They adored him and thought he was wonderful. That made him OK, too." Though she was not initially attracted to him sexually, she was drawn in by his magnetism.

Cordell explained to O'Dell that Leon was in town working on his record and divulged that he and Leon were planning on starting a label together. They checked out the troubled and balky new Apple studio and left unimpressed.

Later the same afternoon, George Harrison showed up at the Apple offices and complained that he would have to delay sessions he was producing that coming weekend for Jackie Lomax, because Nicky Hopkins, the in-demand pianist he'd planned to use, was in America. O'Dell quickly made the connection, telling Harrison that Leon Russell had been there earlier that day checking out the studio. Harrison, who had met Leon back in LA with Delaney & Bonnie, was genuinely excited. O'Dell offered to ask Leon if he was available, and Harrison told her, "But look, even if he has something else to do, let him know I'd like to see him while he's here."

Leon agreed, of course. But Harrison's mother fell ill, and they had to postpone the Lomax session, but O'Dell forgot to inform Leon. Because he suddenly had an open night, he invited her out to dinner. She agreed to go, primarily out of a sense of duty to the Beatles organization. That evening, they discovered just how close their Oklahoma connections were. As they said their goodbyes, O'Dell recalled with a chuckle, "He told me that he was falling in love. I said, 'With who?'"

She was not ready to fall in love with anyone, but Leon persisted. A few days later, he invited her to Eric Clapton's home in Surrey as his date. "I said, 'No, I can't. I've got to work.' I felt really guilty."

"I remember him coming to England," Clapton said. "He came to visit me where I lived, out in the country, on his own. And he sat, and he sang 'A Song for You,' looking at me. It felt like he had written this song [to me]. It was so personal. And he got a real kick out of doing that; I'm sure he did that wherever he went, sit down with the person that he wanted to sing it to and make it about them. He was a very powerful presence. I was overwhelmed."

O'Dell said, "About a week or so later, I called Denny and said, 'I feel really bad. I should probably talk to him.' Denny said, 'He's still at Eric's.' I thought, 'Well, good thing I didn't go.' Anyway, he called me when he got back in town and said he was leaving and this was his last night of recording. . . . That's why I went to the studio."

When she arrived at Olympic Sound Studios, Glyn Johns and Denny Cordell were there in the control room, while Leon was on the other side of the glass, in the live room, at the piano. She was struck first by the intensity of his performance, playing and singing live, his hair hanging down in curtains around his face, baring his soul, awakening those same passions in her. She described the performance as "an aphrodisiac." It was only after he finished and they exchanged smiles that she noticed a sickly looking Clapton and his ghostly girlfriend, Alice Ormsby-Gore, present there in the shadows of the control room.

As Leon continued to perform, O'Dell noticed the lyrics revealing something familiar. First, she heard the word "Apple," followed by "Pisces." She and Leon had discussed their astrological signs at dinner. She asked Cordell the name of the song. "Pisces Apple Lady," he said. It was a song for her.

"It certainly did change me to a degree," she remembered. "I had avoided him and stood him up a few times, literally, because I was into the English. There was something definitely dynamic about him. . . . Of course, that's the way he operated. He let the song tell what he was feeling [in a way] he couldn't do himself."

She said he had written all the lyrics except the last verse. He needed to know how the story ended before completing the song. When Leon came into the control room, he asked O'Dell, "What do you think of your song?" She asked if it really was for her, and he nodded. "His eyes, formerly so dark and penetrating, now looked warm and gentle," she explained. "I could melt into those eyes." Leon told her he wasn't sure if he would see her again and that he wrote that song hoping that one day she would hear it.

His sessions at Olympic with the upper echelon of English rock stars continued, with Clapton playing on "Prince of Peace." "Oddly enough, they all agreed," Leon recalled. "Bill Wyman and Charlie Watts played on 'Roll Away the Stone,' with Stevie [Winwood] on organ." Even decades later, perhaps still feeling the sting of the Stones insulting him in LA back in '66, Leon described his lingering insecurity. "I remember at one point I said to Bill, 'I want you to play that thing you do that goes da-da-da-da-dah,' and Bill looked over at Stevie and said, 'Do you know who we are?'"

Wyman and Watts positively swing. "Glyn Johns used to get me these great sessions at Olympic," Watts recalled. "I'd never heard of Leon. And I remember he sat down and started 'Roll Away the Stone,' and he sat down with this intro, and I just remember sitting there and thinking, 'Where the bloody hell is he going with this intro?' I thought it was all over the place, and then he came in, and Wyman, and it suddenly. . . . It took me a couple of run-throughs for me to realize how great he was."

That piano intro made its way into the Mott the Hoople song "All the Way from Memphis," and Mott's Ian Hunter also used the title for another song. "My thing was Leon," Hunter said. "Most rockers run round the tree. Only a few are the tree and Leon was one of the select few. God knows how many keyboard players I've pissed off (Chris Stainton, especially) begging them to 'do a Leon'!"

All these guests were not just on board as a promotional device, though Leon was certainly savvy enough to understand the value of that. He took advantage of their specific musical strengths. "I was interested in making a Rolling Stones–type record of that song," he recalled. "And those were just the guys to do it." Leon knew exactly what he was looking for in "Roll Away the Stone." "I'd had an awareness of all those guys, their licks, and how they played," Leon said. "Bill plays on the front part of the beat and Charlie plays on the back."

But Leon had to leave town and return to LA to finish the album. When Chris O'Dell asked why he couldn't finish it there in London, he told her he could not find "the right kind of drummer." Like who? "Well, someone like Ringo."

As luck would have it, George Harrison showed back up at the office the next day and inquired whether Leon was still in town and available for the Lomax sessions. O'Dell explained to Harrison that he could probably convince Leon to stay longer if Ringo agreed to drum for Leon's session. "I'll get ahold of Ringo," George had said. "But only if I can play, too." She remembered something their press officer Derek Taylor had once told her: "The Beatles are generous with fun."

Leon played on Lomax's recording, and sure enough, George, Ringo, and Leon were back in the studio recutting "Pisces Apple Lady." Graham

Nash and David Crosby were also hanging around that session. "George was such a pleasure," Leon recalled fondly, "constantly lending support and enjoying the whole event so much." Even John and Yoko attended. "They were sitting in the control room and listening," O'Dell said. "Then they went outside and sat outside the door of the control room at one point. That's when I said, 'Well, do you want to play?'" John replied, "No, I wasn't asked to do it." Later, after the session, when Leon was back at Chris's apartment, he found out that John would have played on his record, too, if he'd been asked. "Really?" Leon looked stunned. Leon mitigated his own disappointment by noting what he had accomplished. "Imagine having two Beatles on your song," he said to Chris. "And another Beatle sitting in the studio, listening." The Beatles were the kings of the mountain, and all bowed to them. "[Ringo] amazed the shit out of me," Leon had said. "That New Orleans syncopation on 'Shoot Out on the Plantation.'"

Leon was not cocky, but neither was he intimidated by fame. He knew his talent placed him among this elite group. He appreciated how the English guys played American music that he folded back into his take on Americana. Chris Stainton cowrote "Dixie Lullaby" with Leon at Skyhill. "I just came up with some chords, and he wrote some words," Stainton said. He was inspired by the surroundings. "He had a great studio at his house. The most fantastic sounding piano, really bright, and he had, like, microphones hanging from the ceiling that you could pull down."

Leon's album has that loose-but-locked-in rhythm section, funky bottom, and ragged marble-mouthed soul singing that were hallmarks of Leon's peak years. A few habits and artistic conceits that Leon would employ throughout his career are displayed as well. "I Put a Spell on You" alone is an example of two. First is his penchant for recycling titles of existing songs (he'd done it previously with the Asylum Choir's "Sweet Home Chicago"). Second, he leaves in count-offs, false starts, and studio chatter—the sort of reflexive audio vérité that runs as a theme throughout the record, peeling back the curtain to offer a glimpse of the recording process. "I like to put the whole thing out," Leon said at the time. "You need mistakes, it helps the first time we play it."

A rave-up gospel blues, "I Put a Spell on You," also lifts elements from the Rolling Stones. With a call-and-response vocal arrangement, Leon adds some Jagger-like vocals, elongating vowels, to a raunchy lyric that could have been ripped from Mick's notebook. It would be at home on the Rolling Stones' masterpiece *Exile on Main Street*, and Leon in turn served as some direct inspiration for *Exile*.

At one of the sessions at Olympic, Leon played a run-through of "(Can't Seem to) Get a Line on You," an embryonic version of "Shine a Light," released in 1972 on *Exile on Main Street*. Mick Jagger sings, with a lineup purported to have included Ringo Starr, Paul McCartney, and Keith Richards, as noted by Cordell on the tape box. Leon's on piano—we can hear his characteristic count-off—and it's likely Starr on drums. The bass and guitar credits are dubious. It sounds like Richards on bass (playing like a guitar player would—busily); it is almost certainly not McCartney. If it had been, Leon and O'Dell would have mentioned his presence. The halting slide guitar part sounds like someone just learning how to use a slide, which was the case with both Harrison (who started learning while playing with Delaney & Bonnie) and Richards at the time. So it might be someone else on bass. "That was quite nice," Jagger says as they end the take. The outtake was eventually released in 1993 as a bonus track on the DCC reissue of Leon's debut album. It has been credited under both titles, and some list Leon as a songwriter. But the Stones had apparently been kicking this one around since the preceding March.

"Leon really liked 'Shine a Light' because of its bent towards the sound of gospel music," said Claudia Lennear, who became friends with and a collaborator of Leon in 1970. It would seem that Leon might have deserved an arranging credit, at the least, for his contribution to the fledgling version of "Shine a Light," but the Stones were infamously stingy with songwriting credit.

On the album, we hear the tape roll up to full speed on "Shoot Out on the Plantation." Over Ringo's drums, Leon starts in on that sort of insistent rhythm he liked so much that he used it on "Straight Brother" and that would begin his arrangement of "The Letter" a few months later with Mad Dogs & Englishmen. "Shoot Out on the Plantation" remained a staple of Leon's live shows, stretching to around five minutes, even at the faster live tempo. But the slower tempo of the album track serves the funky gospel-soul-pop mélange well and was an influence on Elton John's "Ballad of a Well-Known Gun." "If you listen to *Tumbleweed*, it's a mixture of Leon Russell and The Band," Elton acknowledged. Leon "managed to synthesize all the music I loved—rock 'n' roll, blues, gospel, country—into one, perfectly natural style. Listen, when you're English, the only decent music you could hear was American music. Leon was everything I wanted to be."

Leon's own cut of "Delta Lady" adds an introduction that isn't on the Joe Cocker version. Leon brings it back after the first chorus and the bridge, a trumpet, slide guitar, and organ, all playing a regal figure—it sounds like it was inspired by New Orleans producer/songwriter Allen Toussaint. As with the rest of the album, Leon brings a soulful commitment to the lead vocal.

"Prince of Peace" is another blues, but typifies Leon's inventive streak, with nontraditional percussion in place of a predictable drum part. The treble end of the recording sparkles with a flossy acoustic slide guitar by George Harrison. Clapton is on a Stratocaster. Leon said, "He showed up and played the shit out of it."

Clapton identified with the lyric of "Prince of Peace." "I was very, very pleased and excited that he gave me that song to play on because he knew I had—I was having kind of Christian moments," he said. "Every three or four years, I'd had some kind of revelation, or little weird coincidences would happen; would bring up my childhood religious roots, being a country boy, you know; going to Sunday school and going to church on Sundays. And that would all come up around Leon. And when I talked to Delaney about it, 'Oh,' he said, 'Oh yeah, Leon's a preacher.' You know, back here [in England], you don't say that. Unless someone is ordained, it's not something you say in a loose way.

"But then, I came from working with Delaney during that period, and a couple of times, Leon would come and play onstage with us. I saw that happen. I [also] saw Delaney preaching. We were in the Fillmore in San Francisco, and this weird dialogue started up between someone in the crowd, who I think was having a bad trip, and he was shouting at Delaney: 'What about Hitler? Did God make Hitler?' and this kind of stuff. Delaney seemed to bring this stuff out. They would come, and he would deliver; he would get on the pulpit, figuratively speaking. And we'd stand there watching and thinking, 'Well, when are we going to do the next number?' And Delaney would be on fire. I'd heard, too, that Leon could do it; they were lay preachers."

Despite the potential pitfalls of writing enlightened lyrics, this one rises to the challenge. One of two songs on the album written with Greg Dempsey ("Roll Away the Stone" being the other), the lyric of "Prince of

Peace" offers a sample of the hippie consciousness that lingered from the Daughters of Albion project. A guy who grew up in a self-described racist milieu, Leon sings with undeniable conviction, "I choose the friends with love and not by color."

"The first three or four days of recording with the stars went all right, mainly because I was able to get into the studio session-player mode I was very familiar with," Leon wrote. "I steamrolled my way through it without much thought beyond trying to keep it interesting for everyone and designing arrangements that would best spotlight the individual players. But after it was all over, I was in a state of complete disorientation and literally had to be led from the studio because I couldn't find my way out—even though I had been in and out of that very studio at least twenty times before. It took several hours to recover my senses. . . . I was higher than the proverbial kite at the prospect of playing with these great artists I had admired so much from a distance. After about five days, we returned to Wally Heider Studios in the States to finish and dub down." He also did overdub and alternate take sessions at Gold Star and Crystal Sound with Jim Gordon, Chris Ethridge, Jim Karstein, Jim Keltner, and Jim Horn.

When the London sessions were over, Leon convinced Chris O'Dell to come back to LA with him. Notorious accountant and manager Allen Klein was in the midst of overhauling (vandalizing, by most accounts) Apple, so O'Dell figured her days were numbered anyway. She was flying back with a man who, she said, "in a few short weeks, had become the love of my life." He sang in "Pisces Apple Lady" that he wanted to stay with O'Dell "for the rest of my natural life." O'Dell said, "He's like, 'Okay. I'll make this work.'"

Leon had intended on bringing Chris back in high style, but the premium seats were all taken by the Rolling Stones. "You have to imagine how funny that was," O'Dell said. "He wanted to get first-class tickets. That was his thing, to take me back first class. It was pretty interesting when [Bill Wyman and Charlie Watts] came back to coach to talk to us. We were in the forward section of coach, so they didn't have to walk through the whole plane. They were just, 'Hi. How are you? Where are you going?' I believe that was when it struck, the idea of him playing on their [*Let It Bleed*] album in Los Angeles."

When Leon and Chris got to Skyhill, she was disappointed that it was more of a studio than a home—and a filthy one to boot. No one seemed to take any responsibility for keeping the place up. There was a motorcycle parked in the upstairs hallway, probably J. J. Cale's. "I'm not even sure if Leon knew whose motorcycle it was," she recalled, "but there it was. How it got upstairs and why it was there, I never knew. I'm like, 'This isn't the white picket fence I was thinking about.'"

The usual crash-pad arrangements were still in full effect, affording little or no privacy. "He had all these people hanging around his house all the time. It was like a cult leader, in a way," she said. Karstein was back in his closet and hardly ever came out. Flying Burrito Brother Chris Ethridge and his wife had taken one of the bedrooms. Greg Dempsey and Kathy Yesse were also living there, and O'Dell felt like they perceived her as a threat: "They were a weird couple. They felt like part of a cult, 'Leon is everything.' It felt like that. It was almost like interrupting a romantic relationship," she said, laughing.

"There was some weird, interesting sexual [experimentation]. I can't go too far with that because I wasn't going along with it." When Chris was informed that Rita Coolidge had said in her book that the turning point for her was when Leon proposed a ménage à trois, O'Dell replied, "Well, he did the same to me. As a rebound of his and Rita's relationship, he said to me, 'If ever we decide to sleep with someone else, we have to be sure and tell each other.' I wasn't that secure. My little antennas went up, and I went, 'Uh oh, who's going to get there first?' He proposed that [group sex] to me, with [Dempsey and Yesse]. There were things going on. Some of it, I don't think I even noticed. It was very uncomfortable for me."

Soon after arriving in LA, O'Dell accompanied Leon to outside studios for a few sessions, including one for Rita. Though Chris felt insecure there, Leon assured her that he was over Rita. O'Dell was also a fly on the wall at overdub sessions for the Stones' *Let It Bleed* album. Glyn Johns was engineering with American producer Jimmy Miller. Leon barrels in with a propulsive second piano part on "Live with Me," weaving around the one that Nicky Hopkins had already laid down. Mick's lyric must have resonated with Leon, and Chris as well, as it comically described a rock star's idea of domesticity. Leon is also credited with arranging the horns on the same track. There is only a tenor sax solo from Bobby Keys on the album, but the session contract confirms that there had been a whole horn section, some of Leon's regulars from the Wrecking Crew days. Leon recalled, "Mick Jagger said, 'That sounds like "Harlem Shuffle" [a 1963

R&B single by Bob and Earl].' I said, 'I thought that's what you guys did.'" The Stones scrapped the section and just left Bobby's solo. Decades later, they released a cover of "Harlem Shuffle."

"It was nerve-racking," O'Dell said. "Leon was pretty nervous about it. Even though he didn't show stuff like that, these were the big-time musicians; this was the English set." But now, he was regarded as a peer. "I remember it was a pretty light atmosphere, believe it or not. . . . He liked it. He was impressed that he got invited to that."

Back on Skyhill, Chris and Leon got a couple of puppies they named Sam and Dave. She tried to convince Leon to get a separate place for just the two of them, even managing to get him out to look at houses. But Chris wasn't exactly settling down herself. "I would sit around and just get absolutely schnockered, sitting at the table downstairs while they were all in the recording studio. He didn't drink like that. That was not my memory of him. I abused alcohol for years. I didn't necessarily see that with him. I don't mean he didn't drink. He used drugs, but it wasn't on the same level I was abusing. We'd had pot around. We smoked joints, but I don't remember it being that drugs were such a big part of it. I had come from a lot of drugs. There were always drugs back then. Everybody was doing something." Leon would get into angel dust (PCP) within the year, though. "That was partly Jesse Ed Davis's fault," said O'Dell, who later in life became a substance abuse counselor. "By '73, I remember there was a lot of angel dust around. Jesse Ed always had it."

After one particularly booze-soaked night with Davis and Jim Price, O'Dell woke up with a vicious hangover. Leon leaned up in bed with a look of loving concern. He told her that, the night before, she'd kept coming back into the studio while he was recording and drunkenly announcing she wanted to go back to London. Then he played her a rough mix of a new song he had written for her, "Hummingbird." He explained that he wrote the words after watching her sleep.

Recorded at Wally Heider Recording, Los Angeles, on December 29, the track begins with an acoustic slide guitar and what sounds to be tabla drums. It sounds like something the Stones did in 1968 on *Beggars Banquet*, similar to the beginnings of "Prodigal Son" and "Parachute Woman." Leon enters with some relatively sparse piano. "I thought my life had ended / And I've found that it's just begun / 'Cause she gets me where I live," he sings in the first verse. The arrangement leads into an ecstatic coda, dark dawning into light, with Jim Horn wailing a sax part over backing vocalists Merry Clayton, Bobby Whitlock, Clydie King, and Delaney and Bonnie singing, "Don't fly away." Such stars as Bob Seger and B. B. King would also record it—the latter twice, once with Leon and many years later with John Mayer.

In January 1970, Leon entered A&M Studios and laid down the song that would remain his signature. A haunting piano cascade falls into "A Song for You," the opening song of Leon's eponymous debut album. It's the kind of musical figure a film might use to introduce a dream or a flashback sequence. "I had never played it that way before," he said. "All off the top of my head, which is the story of my life, really."

Though Leon had been fooling around with the song at home, the grand piano at A&M Studios brought out something magic. "Herb Alpert had bought that grand from Western Studio 3," he recalled decades later. "It was my favorite grand piano in Los Angeles." This was very likely the same piano also heard on Carole King's *Tapestry* and Joni Mitchell's *Blue*. In her memoir, King talks about scheming to use that piano while Mitchell had the studio booked. Imagine this same instrument when you listen to "River" from *Blue*, "I Feel the Earth Move" from *Tapestry*, and "A Song for You."

After the classically tinged introduction (Elton described it as "Nina Simone–type chords") of "A Song for You," Leon's distinctive voice comes in, singing what he described as "kind of a study in blues standards." But it has the slow piano cadence of a gospel number. "I've been so many places in my life and time," he begins, with a slow vibrato on the last word.

Actor and friend Stuart Margolin (who'd contributed a voiceover to the Asylum Choir) recalled Leon telling him, "When I was a kid in Tulsa, I used to play on the piano and sing and pretend there were ten thousand people. I would look at the wall and pretend there were ten thousand people. Now I find myself playing, looking at ten thousand people pretending they're the wall."

The mix of self-awareness and intimacy, coupled with the overall musical approach of "A Song for You," mapped the way for Elton John's "Your Song," released later the same year. "I can't remember, but 'Your Song' probably was written before 'A Song for You,'" Elton said. "'A Song for You' is one of the top five songs I wish I'd written. And, yeah, they are very, very similar songs—lyrically anyway, not melodically. 'Your Song' is a much more gentle song."

"A Song for You" opens austerely, with the piano and Leon's voice. The mix is so sparse and clear that you can hear what sounds to be the studio door closing (about two seconds in). For the back half of the verse, a French horn enters as a bed of support. Leon reaches for the uppermost region of his singing range. When he performed the song in later years, he would adopt an alternative melody that did not require him to strain on those lines. He arguably does not quite get there on the original version. It's enough to make you wonder if he considered a lower key for the song. But thankfully he kept it; the emotion of it is raw and honest. "Basically, I was trying to sing like Bonnie Bramlett," Leon explained decades later. "At that time, we was *all* trying to sing like Bonnie Bramlett."

"He apparently didn't like his own voice, so he started using other singers," Ian Hunter said. "I remember Steve Winwood saying that Leon couldn't stand his own voice, and Steve—a great singer himself—had tried to persuade him otherwise!"

Leon's voice was a unique instrument, to be sure. In later years he described it as a cross between the mush-mouthed comic Moms Mabley and gravel-gargling Tom Waits. One apparent similarity is Mac Rebennack, who already had a couple of solo records out under his Dr. John moniker by that point. The two overlapped as pianists for Phil Spector and other Hollywood sessions. "Never did work very much with Mac Rebennack," Leon said. "I always admired him and went to see him at shows when I could. I went to one of his sessions that he was doing that the guy from Atlantic, Jerry Wexler [was producing]. But I was just kind of listening."

"I went to [a 1972] session with Leon Russell," Jerry Wexler recalled, when Leon was nearing the height of his fame and Rebennack was struggling. "I don't think most people realize how much Leon took from Mac, the way he plays piano, the way he sings, even the top hat."

Though there was a mutual appreciation, and influence flowed both ways, Rebennack's influential *Gris-Gris* album appeared in 1968, recorded at Gold Star Studios in 1967. Leon Russell was using his stage name before Rebennack adopted the Dr. John images, and then Leon's outward appearance began adding to an already distinct persona. It's little surprise that about five years later, the two, plus Elton John, served as composite inspiration for the groovy Muppets character Dr. Teeth. Both were too freaky and talented to play it straight in the Hollywood hit-making factory scene, especially after bands and singer-songwriters began to dominate rock 'n' roll.

An accomplished pianist and a scholar of those who came before him, A. J. Croce pointed to "A Song for You" as a perfect example of what distinguished Leon from Dr. John. "I think of them as being very different. Mac was probably the cleanest, most proficient New Orleans piano player in that sort of style that may have ever been. He executed it in such a clean way. Leon hit these more dynamic, more thought-out chords that build, more from like an arranger's perspective than a pure math game. His left hand was more inclined to play the octave, an octave of the third or the fifth or some harmony of it, whereas Mac is probably on the root." Croce emphasized Leon's versatility and ability to play a diverse range of styles, skills which he developed acutely over his session years.

When Leon talked about his session days, he would claim that much of what he did was an illusion, a little bit of trickery. Not that he did not have a broad musical vocabulary, but he felt he had to play a shell game to cover his limitations, especially with his right hand, because he was left-handed in addition to the birth injury that affected his right side. Being able to play dazzling-sounding stuff was, in his mind, a bit of a trick.

"A Song for You" is a perfect song. The lyric, melody, and arrangement—any songwriter would envy it. And most would identify with the pivotal lines in the bridge: "If my words don't come together / Just listen to the melody for my love's in there hiding." This is the very reason that music exists: to express the ineffable. Leon makes clear he is the kind of man who has a difficult time expressing such emotions in words. "Words have been the most difficult thing for me," he said later that year. "Melodies have been the easiest for me; I have more than enough melodies to go around."

Steve Winwood pointed out that Leon tapped into a tradition going back to songs of the antebellum South. "We [Traffic] used to have a cottage. . . . Leon came up to the cottage, and he said, 'I've just written this song, and I want to play it for you.' And he sat down and—we had this rather nice Bechstein upright piano up there—and played 'A Song for You.' It's a lovely song. It has a sort of slightly old-fashioned Southern thing, the chord changes, and it suited his piano. Sometimes when songs are written, everything just sort of falls together, and I think it certainly did there. Stephen Foster sort of invented or was the one who popularized those sorts of harmonies from the old South."

The song's emotional impact is knee-buckling. Leon captures a precious sense of vulnerability, not just in the lyric but also in the performance. He gives rare expression to a "truth, withholding nothing," a holy revelation of human connection that unfolds over four minutes. It's a standard that will resonate forever.

"A Song for You" was one of two songs on the album commonly thought to be at least partially inspired by Rita Coolidge. "Everyone told me that it was," she said. "I think, by that time, Leon was so angry with me for leaving that maybe [he] put his heart and soul in that song, but the anger was definitely directed at me. I mean, we would walk into a room, and after I left, if we happened to be in the same room, he would literally pretend like I was not even there. He just would look right past me, right through me. I could say something to him [and] he wouldn't acknowledge it. He was just horrible to me."

But, in 2015, Leon said, "I saw where she said in an interview that I wrote the 'Delta Lady' for her, which is true. She also said I wrote 'A Song for You' and 'Hummingbird' for her, which is absolutely not true."

She titled her 2016 memoir *Delta Lady* after the song definitely written for her, but other songs were written about her. "Hurtsome Body" and "Roll Away the Stone" lament their breakup. Even "Pisces Apple Lady" references getting away from "the Delta girl and the painful situation." Roughly half the album references Rita. "Indian Girl"—one of the outtakes, later included in the 1993 CD reissue of the album—describes falling in love with Rita in Memphis. "He loved Indian women," she said.

Leon never publicly divulged the inspiration for "A Song for You." Don Williams, who became head of music publishing at Shelter Records that year, theorized that it was Greg Dempsey who was the subject in "A Song for You": "I honestly believe that it has to do with the songwriting relationship between Leon and Greg."

Leon gave credence to this idea when he hinted, years later, "I wrote that song in ten minutes. I wrote it for somebody that I had an argument with, that I didn't want to have an argument with. I wrote that song so I could sing it for him. The person was very instrumental in teaching me about songwriting and writing in general." Leon gave the biggest hint publicly by using the word *him*.

Leon's son-in-law, friend, and collaborator, Matt Harris, said that Leon told him privately that Dempsey was the inspiration. "Leon said, 'I was living with my friends. They were a couple [Dempsey and Yesse]. They were fighting, and I was sleeping on the couch. I was a third wheel. . . . I wrote it to both of them. When I talk about the bridge, "You taught me precious secrets of a truth withholding nothing," that's about songwriting. He taught me how to write a song. He taught me how to put it together, to talk about the truth. And to be honest, this was my love letter to them as a couple of how much I loved them. It's not about a girl.'"

As with many songs, the truth is that it probably was a composite of a few people who impacted Leon at the time. Songs, like dreams, follow their own logic.

When he wrote "A Song for You," he was setting out to write a standard, something he imagined one of his biggest influences, Ray Charles, singing. "When you first hear a standard, it sounds just like a shitty little tune," Leon said with a laugh decades later. "And then you come back later, and you hear it twenty years later, they're different. . . . I still try to write standards. I don't try to write hits." In this instance, a very personal song was crafted so perfectly that it did become a standard.

Eventually, Ray Charles recorded his own definitive interpretation of "A Song for You," a song that had already been recorded hundreds of times by such world-class singers as Donny Hathaway and Karen Carpenter. (Charles's version won the 1994 Grammy for Best Male R&B Vocal.)

Many years later, when asked if he had a favorite version of "A Song for You," Leon pointed to Hathaway's version, from 1971. "He was gone too soon," Leon lamented. "A lot of people think he wrote it," Leon acknowledged. "Yeah, I always enjoy that on *American Idol*, someone will say, 'Here's Donny Hathaway's "A Song for You,"' and somebody else will get berserk and it's kind of fun." Leon told a story about how he'd met a limousine driver in New York who had once driven Aretha Franklin, and when "A Song for You" came on the car's tape player, it was the first time she'd heard it. Aretha sat in that car and made the driver replay the song twenty times. "She listened to it over and over again," Leon marveled.

Chapter 12

Shelter in Place

DENNY CORDELL RELOCATED TO LOS Angeles in January 1970, bought out Leon's contract from Mercury, and formed Shelter Records with Leon, making it official in March. Its name inspired by a line in "Delta Lady," the label was set up to "shelter" developing artists from the shark-infested waters of the major label music biz. "It's an attempt to try and give artists the vital things they need," Leon said that year. "It's different to other record companies because we're a small company who can devote time to each individual artist."

The two enlisted attorney Owen Sloane to help form the company and work out distribution deals. Sloane said Shelter was "sort of my first clients in the business. I got started, and it was like trial by fire." He admired the two visionary partners. The label was set up as a subsidiary of Tommy LiPuma's Blue Thumb Records, which was distributed by Capitol in 1970.

Shelter shared office space with Blue Thumb in Beverly Hills and brought in Ellen Basich as Denny's secretary to help them get up and running. Soon, Chris O'Dell found the company a new headquarters at 5112 Hollywood Boulevard. "I had that Oklahoma taste deep down inside me," she said. She had come across a "funky old Hollywood house in the 'less desirable' part of Hollywood Boulevard, definitely in need of repairs," she wrote. "It had a 'down home' feel, which Denny and Leon loved." Denny installed a barber's chair in his office. Don Williams was brought in to run the music publishing division.

There was a good buzz about the start-up company and about Leon as a star. "He'd be around other women, and they'd go, 'Oh, you're so wonderful!' He told me that," O'Dell said. "He said, 'I'm getting a lot of attention.' He realized that suddenly he'd become a little bit of a sex symbol. He really liked that." It was a manic period, not one of the low times when he could not get out of bed. O'Dell said his ego at this point was "soaring," and this was still months before *Mad Dogs & Englishmen* thrust him into the worldwide spotlight. Some of Leon's friends from Tulsa gave Chris a little insight into Leon's personality. "They said he was one of those guys who wasn't really popular [when he was younger] and put everything into the piano."

It was an observation shared by Marc Benno. "You've got to remember in his beginnings how nerdy he [Leon] was. And then he became a little bit better looking, in the hair and the beard; it helped. A lot of people developed their looks like that, that you go back and find that they were real nerdy. You can't believe it because you're thinking, 'This guy is so cool, so good looking.' Also, it forms a real humility when they're young, and everything. They carry that through their lives, even if they try to get rid of that, of being cool."

As self-focused as he was, Leon was attuned to the feelings of others. "'Hummingbird' is about me leaving, really, before it happened," O'Dell said. Leon had to know it was doomed. As Shelter ramped up, the whirlwind romance between O'Dell and Leon rapidly disintegrated. "He flew first," she said, wryly referring to the conclusion of "Hummingbird."

They were star-crossed from the start. "I couldn't see us sitting on the porch in old age; let me put it that way." But she did want to give it a good shot. "I was looking for a happy home; he was just looking for an 'old lady.'"

Here she was in a filthy crash pad, with nothing to do but party, attend to the puppies, and tidy up. There was nowhere near enough stimulation for a twenty-one-year-old who had been in the eye of the Beatles hurricane. She tried to mitigate the comedown with booze and drugs. One particular night, while so high on amphetamines that she could not speak, Leon hung out with her, watching television for a while. "Remember, no matter what happens, I love you," he said, leaving the room. After a while, Chris, wobbly, got up and eventually found him in the living room, "up against the wall, kissing one of the Oklahoma girls who was always hanging around." Leon and the girl stopped and turned to see Chris, who went back to the bedroom. He came in and said, "It was nothing."

She got away from him, but not over him. Not knowing many people in LA, she moved into a house in Laurel Canyon with Basich, Denny's secretary. This did not make for a clean break. In February, after only four months, she headed back to London.

As the relationship was breaking up, Leon had an impossibly busy first quarter in 1970, which set a breakneck pace for the next few years. Between January and March, he helped set up the label and began promoting his debut. Along with Eric Clapton, Leon sat in with Delaney & Bonnie and Friends for a hot show at the Fillmore West in San Francisco on February 22, the same one Clapton mentioned when discussing Delaney and Leon as "lay preachers."

Somehow, Leon managed to carve out time to work on sessions for such classics as the Flying Burrito Brothers' second LP, *Burrito Deluxe*, and the solo debuts of Dave Mason and Clapton. Clapton had fallen in love with Delaney & Bonnie and Friends. Parties would carry over from stages into hotel rooms, with boozy all-night sing-alongs. Clapton was attracted to this new rootsy and collaborative-ensemble vibe and bonded particularly with Delaney, who encouraged Clapton to sing and write more.

By November, Clapton had flown Delaney & Bonnie and Friends over to stay at his estate in England, where they began rehearsing for a European and UK tour for which he intended to simply be part of the ensemble. But, of course, his presence meant promoters emphasized his name on the billings, and a few shows devolved into open hostility from angry attendees who, expecting Clapton's wailing psych-blues excess, instead found him in the background, playing second guitar in the shadows.

Then Clapton followed the band back to California. "I actually joined Delaney & Bonnie, and we did a lot of touring around America," he said. "I moved in with Delaney. I became part of his family for quite a while. I met all the musicians from Tulsa, or most of them. Yeah, it was culture shock, it was. It was a bit like *The Beverly Hillbillies*, just straight out of Mississippi.

"I was loose. I didn't have anywhere else I wanted to be, having left Cream and not really settling down as a family man or a married man. It was so obvious, just a treat. I was on the loose. I was in my ideal state. . . . These people all hung out every day, and they went and played clubs, and I just suddenly felt at home."

In January, Leon joined the whole cast of characters at Village Recorders to work on *Eric Clapton*. It is essentially a Delaney & Bonnie and Friends album, with Clapton playing the part of Delaney—and doing a pretty good job emulating him. Clapton would later do something similar, lifting a musical approach from another of Leon's friends, J. J. Cale. Though a musical sponge, Clapton is the first to acknowledge his influences, noting he even tried imitating Leon's vocal style on eighties songs like "Pretending."

In addition to playing piano on the Clapton album, Leon cowrote two tracks, the Southern-soul-inspired "Lonesome and a Long Way from Home" with Delaney and "Blues Power" with Clapton. "['Blues Power'] is a song that Leon wrote," Clapton said. "The words are really applicable to me." Cale wrote the album's biggest and most lasting track, "After Midnight."

"Blues Power" is a misnomer; it is not a blues. For all its dad-rock bluster, it's a catchy rock 'n' roll number, elevated by the groove from the players themselves. Leon shines, opening the song with a mournful, minor-key head fake before the song snaps to attention with Jim Gordon's downbeat on the snare.

"It seemed to be a very quick record to make," Clapton said. "Leon would say, 'I've got one,' and he would sing, [*sings*] 'Bet you didn't think I knew how to rock and roll.' He would have two lines. Leon said that, and I thought, 'Oh, he's just thought this up in his head as we're standing here. I've never seen anyone do that before.'"

Clapton observed that, "from what I could see, everybody had something to say, I mean everybody in that room, maybe with the exception of Bobby [Whitlock], because Bobby was a good deal younger than those guys. I never saw a kind of friction or any dominance. It would just seem to go back and forth. I mean, when Leon called ['Blues Power'], Delaney just followed it. I'll tell you what, it was one of the most loving environments I've ever been in. Musically, it was kind of odd, I never saw a hint of jealousy or rivalry, those kinds of things. Maybe it was because I'd come from that [Cream and Blind Faith] kind of experience, but it felt like home. It felt great."

Around the same time as Clapton's sessions, Leon reunited in the studio with his pal Tommy LiPuma, a producer and partner with Bob Krasnow at Blue Thumb Records, the parent company of Leon and Denny's

Shelter Records. LiPuma signed Dave Mason to a solo deal and was producing his debut record with engineer Bruce Botnick. "When I did *Alone Together*," Mason said, "Tommy LiPuma sort of brought in most of the players. I added Leon to two songs, 'Shouldn't Have Took More Than You Gave,' and 'Look at You Look at Me.' His piano style is so cool. That syncopated sort of style is just so, so cool."

One of Leon's last outside projects before the Mad Dogs & Englishmen tour was the Flying Burrito Brothers' second album. Gram Parsons had been a fan of Leon since arriving in Los Angeles in the mid-1960s. Leon had already achieved pretty much everything Parsons wanted to do musically. Musicians like Parsons understood that Leon was not only a dazzling technician but brought with him a deep reservoir of soul.

Leon was called in to contribute to "The Train Song," which Parsons and bandmate Chris Hillman wrote; Hillman called it "another semi-gospel song." Seeking some authenticity, they also hired two well-known figures from the Hollywood R&B scene, Larry Williams and Johnny "Guitar" Watson, to produce. Hotshot guitar player Clarence White was also on the session, which devolved into a coke-fueled debacle until Leon took over the controls and brought it in for a landing. The resulting track is a hoot that listeners would not be surprised to discover was fueled by booze and blow.

By this point, Denny Cordell has started introducing his partner as "the Master of Space and Time," a nickname taken from a line in "A Song for You." One day in January 1970, he and Leon were at A&M making plans to head out to Joshua Tree in the California high desert, where Parsons would meet them. Cordell had rented out the whole Joshua Tree Inn for the weekend. Parsons had been making regular treks there—bringing such friends as Mick Jagger, Keith Richards, and Marianne Faithfull—and did so until the end of his life, which was just a few years later via overdose at the same motel to which they were heading.

The party continued all weekend at the Joshua Tree Inn, with musicians in every room, including some of Delaney & Bonnie and Friends, everyone singing songs. One person there characterized it as a rock 'n' roll convention. Parsons was in heaven.

Angel dust was featured on this trip to the desert and Leon enjoyed the drug. "In further experimentation with elephant tranquilizer, commonly called angel dust or moon dust on the street, I had many mystical

revelations and visions of a previous life," he wrote. "I experienced a tremendous feeling of well-being from these visions, which lasted for several
weeks. It was unlike anything else that was happening in my life."

"That was one of the worst things ever invented for anybody to take,"
Jim Keltner said. "It was unspeakable how horrible it was. He fell for it.
He liked it, which tells you something about Leon. Leon was a strange
guy. It wasn't like he smoked a little bit of it once in a while; he got
hooked on it." Keltner, who is open about his personal struggles with
heroin and other substance abuse, continued, "There were many nights
when he would throw big parties up at his house. A lot of people would be
smoking it. I got smart; I only did it the one time. I realized that it was too
destructive. He liked it, I think because it did take him completely away
from who he was. That's the sad thing; Leon had health problems early on
in life. . . . That's why he strengthened his left hand so much. His left hand
was killer. All of those things turned out to be the thing that shaped Leon's
music and his playing, for certain. It's too bad that that wasn't enough.
There was nobody else like him."

On the heels of the trip to Joshua Tree, Leon took twelve people to
see Elvis Presley at the Las Vegas Hilton. Among them were Cordell and
Parsons, along with Tulsa friends Kay Poorboy and Emily Smith, who had
just walked into Leon's life and would remain a friend and confidante for
years. "A friend of mine was going to the West Coast, and I said that I
would go too," Smith said. "Somehow I wind up at Skyhill and [another
guest] walks in and says, 'Take a puff off of this.' Well, it was like *Alice in
Wonderland*. Next thing I know, Leon's got on his white suit and snakeskin
boots, and we are in his Thunderbird on our way to the airport. We ended
up in a suite with Ike and Tina Turner getting higher than kites. They were
in the lounge and Elvis was in the big room. So we went to see Elvis and
then went and saw Ike and Tina's show."

Leon wrote, "When we first entered the [hotel], a little tourist man
looked forlornly at his wife and said, 'Jesus,' whereupon I raced over and
said, 'Yes! It's Me! You've found me!' Placing my hands on his head and
shoulder, I entreated, loudly, 'Heal him! Heal him!' Then, as he was melting into a heap of shock, I whispered, 'Go in peace and tell no one you've
seen me.'"

Dressed from head to toe in white, including his patent leather shoes,
Leon had a photo taken of himself with the eleven others at their table,

which he entitled "The First Supper." Swept up in the spirit of the events, and at the sight of women approaching the stage to receive scarves and kisses from The King, Leon shouted, "in the Pentecostal style . . . 'Touch the people, Elvis! Touch the people!'" The energy so overtook Leon, he noted wryly, that the security guards at the show had to repeatedly request he calm down. But it carried over to the Ike & Tina Turner Revue show in the lounge, "running up to the front of the stage and screaming answer notes to Tina as she sang." Leon acknowledged, with a touch of embarrassment, "I have never done anything like that before or since, as that kind of behavior is completely outside my normal reality." Those who got to witness his full-on preacher mode in concerts from 1971 to 1974 might beg to differ.

Leon continued to help out his friend Parsons. Gram and the Flying Burrito Brothers were back at A&M around February–March to record their follow-up album *Burrito Deluxe*. Leon contributed piano to the Tex-Mex rave-up "Man in the Fog" and their version of "Wild Horses," recorded before the Rolling Stones themselves did. Parsons and company had to steal Leon from the big soundstage next door, where he was rehearsing with about two dozen of the greatest musicians in town.

Chapter 13

Meet the Mad Dogs & Englishmen

THE FILLMORE EAST IN MANHATTAN was packed on March 27, 1970. The audience filled the hall right to the lip of the stage—they were there to see Joe Cocker, who'd recently skyrocketed from obscurity to stardom on both sides of the Atlantic, in large part due to his knockout performance at Woodstock the previous August: a blue-eyed soul singer for the rock set. The documentary film of that festival had just been released the day before the Fillmore show, but his definitive version of the Beatles' "With a Little Help from My Friends," a number one single for Cocker in the UK, was making waves in the States.

"'Delta Lady'!" yelled a woman in the crowd.

"'Delta Lady' it is, my love," purred Cocker.

The drums rumbled in, syncopated with the horns, bass, and Leon's hard-driving piano. Even in a band of hippie gypsies, he stood out with his long hair and Old Testament beard, bedroom eyes peering out from under a green felt top hat, tank top basketball jersey emblazoned with HOLY TRINITY across his chest, and tight striped bell bottoms. Here was the prototype for 1970s rockers. Take Leon Russell Wilkeson (his real name) of Lynyrd Skynyrd; he would cop his namesake's look wholesale.

Leon was *the* man; the man who counted this number off; the man who wrote and arranged the song. He was the man who put together the musicians, a dream band of ace Americans, for an English guy who, as a kid, grew up listening to Ray Charles, soul, and blues on the radio back home in industrial Sheffield, fantasizing about how to get *that sound*. Leon wrote all of the arrangements of the songs he helped select for this tour—the tour that was saving Joe Cocker's ass, whether he appreciated it or not.

Relatively few in the audience had yet seen Cocker in action. His now-familiar jerking, twitching, writhing locomotion—playing air guitar while his eyes bulge out from under his sweaty, matted hair—is an iconic rock image, parodied in the late seventies by John Belushi on *Saturday Night Live*. But in 1970, it was a striking novelty. Even fewer knew who Leon was.

Cocker was center stage, under a white spotlight, fronting a twenty-two-piece big band Leon had whipped together—a soul-rock revue with a choir of hippies; two drummers on full kits plus another on congas; two *more* drummers relegated to tambourine; bass; multiple guitars; two keyboardists; and a horn section the Rolling Stones would soon scoop up and a rhythm section that would soon be the backbone of Derek and the Dominos. Various hangers-on filled the stage's wings; an actual dog or two wandered around. All but Cocker were lit in smoky auburn or were hidden in the shadows, and the trippy Joshua Light Show projected on the massive screen behind them, while a film crew captured the spectacle.

It had all been put together in mere days.

"Immediately after the Elvis trip to the Vegas Hilton," Leon wrote, "Denny Cordell arrived at my house on Skyhill Drive, with a very dismal Joe Cocker in tow." But Cocker was troubled from the get-go. Though he was electrified in performance, offstage he was a taciturn man, self-medicating with booze and whatever else he got his hands on. From Woodstock to the Isle of Wight festival and a tour that lasted until early 1970, with his face on the cover of *Rolling Stone*, Cocker had then fled to Los Angeles. He was exhausted and needed a vacation. As far as he was concerned, the Grease Band was done. He'd used LA studio session pros to make his records and no longer felt the need to carry a band. "By the end of '69, I'd done Woodstock, and the Grease Band and I weren't getting along well," recalled Cocker. "Chris Stainton and I stuck it out for the most part. . . . I stayed at Leon's house in LA, 7709 Skyhill Drive. People were very naked. I got the clap there."

They arrived on March 11. Cocker's respite would not last long. His manager Dee Anthony in New York had booked an American tour of forty-eight cities in fifty-six days. Cocker, aware of this, commenced to engage in a game of chicken. "The more Joe said, 'No,' the more Dee was becoming ominous," said Alan Spenner, bassist in the Grease Band. "The rest of us, we more or less caved in and said, 'Well, it looks like we're doing it anyway,' but Joe stuck to his guns and it built up. . . . But by this time it had turned into something more—I think he could see that his life was just being taken over by people."

"Joe would say, 'All this star business is rubbish,'" Denny explained. "He wanted to go back to the old days, in Sheffield pubs, with people enjoying themselves. He said people make better music that way. Leon thought Joe was the voice of the common man, the guy who could get up and sing at the end of a hard day's work."

Ignoring Joe's refusals and pleas that he no longer had a band, an irate Anthony had called Cordell, who was in LA setting up Shelter, to try to get him to persuade Cocker. "I put the phone down," Cordell recalled. "Eight hours later there's a pounding on the door. I open the door of the motel—it's Dee Anthony. We're in Hollywood and Dee's flown across from New York—and he's getting really heavy. . . . I hated him. I never approved of him handling Joe, as his management, because as far as I was concerned he did not really know where Joe was coming from. He'd been handling Tony Bennett." Anthony had put in seventeen years with Bennett by that point.

Anthony's appearance in LA convinced Cocker. The singer quickly realized that he had little say in the matter—upon receiving warnings of lawsuits, musicians' union bans, visa revocation, and explicit threats of bodily injury. He simply did not have a choice. So he turned to Denny Cordell, and they both looked to their host at Skyhill for an answer on how to conquer this tour.

Leon and Denny were at that very moment plotting out the best way to launch the promotion of the upcoming *Leon Russell* album, because, despite Leon's reputation in musician circles, this would nevertheless be the debut of a relatively unknown artist. "After thinking about it [Joe's plight] for a minute or two, I realized it wouldn't be that difficult to do," Leon explained. "Most of the musicians I'd played with in one configuration or another were available and would be happy to go on the road. So I said yes. . . . Those calls took all of fifteen minutes, after which time I reported to Joe that the principal rhythm section was in place and that I had some other ideas about the tour, if he was interested. Starting to get a little color back, he asked me to continue." Cocker would have been happy to keep the band at just that size. But Leon had grander concepts.

Delaney & Bonnie and Friends had recently arrived home and were without future work. Their recent tour had ended in rancor over money and the general malevolent cloud that followed the Bramletts. Leon wrote that Bobby Keys and Jim Price "begged to be in the horn section, but I was reluctant to use them because they were, I thought, playing at the time with Delaney & Bonnie. They assured me that they had just quit and it wouldn't interfere with anything if they were on the tour."

About Delaney & Bonnie and Friends, "Things went sour fast," Bobby Keys wrote. "It culminated in a gig in San Diego in which Delaney threw something at Keltner and Keltner threw his sticks at Delaney and we rode back to L.A. in just awful silence. . . . I think *we* fired *Delaney*."

"Drugs were dominating, and Delaney didn't do it well," Keltner said. "The drugs and the drinks destroyed Delaney, which is one of the crimes in the rock 'n' roll world because he was gifted."

"We came back from the tour and there weren't [any] other things booked," Rita, also on the Delaney & Bonnie tour, said. "There was a window that we could jump in and do this thing with and for Joe. And I think everybody did it thinking that we would do the Mad Dogs & Englishmen and then when that was over, we'd go back to Delaney & Bonnie. But as it turns out, Delaney and Bonnie both felt like the band had been stolen from them."

Keys, Price, Keltner, Coolidge, Jim Gordon, Jim Price, and Carl Radle all jumped ship to form the core of Mad Dogs, leaving Delaney and Bonnie with their original and only remaining friend, Bobby Whitlock. "When they left," said Bonnie Bramlett, "we were the last to know, and it broke our hearts."

Later Delaney would be angry with Leon for "stealing" his band. Bonnie declined to be interviewed but said in an email, "I love Leon, and I respect his family, and it's a pity how we all just fell apart!"

On March 13, two days after Cocker had arrived in LA, Leon was making phone calls for people to assemble at the A&M soundstage to start working as the band to back Cocker. By that night, already a core of ten musicians had formed at the rehearsal. Chris Stainton and Peter Nicholls had flown into New York the same day Cocker had flown to LA. The two had picked up a van in New York and drove it to LA. "We arrived at Leon's house up on Skyhill Drive," Stainton remembered. "He had this huge living room with a parachute in it, tacked to the ceiling, and all this weird music going on." They learned of the newly developing tour. "I didn't know what was going on, really, I just did as I was told," Stainton said with a laugh. Nicholls would be the tour's sound engineer, and Stainton played organ, switching over to piano when Leon was on guitar.

Don Preston was working on becoming a singer-songwriter. He went out for a drive that week with Leon and Denny. When they invited him on the tour, Preston answered, "I've always said that if a spaceship landed, I would get on it—and this sounds like it."

Leon had seen that his new partner needed help—there was no way Denny could have whipped together a band, never mind the repertoire, arrangements, and a whole show. Leon had been destined for this moment, after putting in all of the years of practice, observing the great bands of the past and present, and attuning to, even anticipating, the zeitgeist. The timing was perfect for him personally, with a new record and his own label due to launch. It's like all roads in his life led to this. He saw a vacuum in leadership and slipped in to fill the space, living up to the new nickname his partner had bestowed upon him.

"He worked with all the great producers, all the great arrangers," Keltner observed. "He became a great arranger and producer himself. If he's on the scene, why shouldn't he be in control?"

Meanwhile, Joe Cocker was more or less alone, in his own world. No one would tell him when he'd had too much or not to take that extra pill or pull from a bottle. "Did Leon have a plan? Probably," Peter Nicholls said. "Did Joe go along with the plan? Definitely not. The poor guy was so fucked up, you know? The one thing he had was an abundance of common sense, but he had nothing much else. He intellectually couldn't grasp situations. He had no business sense. And Denny was a nasty businessman. . . . Anyone who could read the tea leaves could see that Leon and Denny already got it figured out."

Claudia Lennear, coming from the exacting discipline of Ike & Tina Turner, happened upon the Mad Dogs rehearsal. A Catholic kid from Providence, who grew up on rock 'n' roll and show tunes, Lennear had relocated to LA with her family when she was a teen and sang with the Superbs there. In 1967, she had learned about an opening in the Ike & Tina Turner Revue for an Ikette. She stayed with them a couple of years during which she also supported the Rolling Stones on their 1969 US tour, where she became romantically involved with Mick Jagger, possibly inspiring "Brown Sugar" (other theories point to actress Marsha Hunt as inspiration). In outtake clips from the *Gimme Shelter* documentary, Mick is seen playing and singing a rough draft of it in a dressing room for Ike and Tina, with Claudia getting ready for the show in the background.

Lennear recalled, "Somebody told me, 'Mick is pitching a song to Ike.' So I kind of slid in the background. But the picture itself is really dark, and then I'm dark, so you can hardly see me. I look like a shadow."

Claudia had met Gram Parsons the year before, in 1969, through the Stones. While Mad Dogs was coming together, she was with Parsons next door at A&M, on a session for the song "She." "This was the week after I had left Ike and Tina," she said.

On a break, Gram told her, "'Let me take you over and introduce you to some more friends of mine.' Gram went up onstage and said something to Leon. Then, he invited me to come up and meet him, so I did. I met Joe as well. Leon's words were, 'You were an Ikette?' I was like, 'Yeah, well, as of one week ago.' He said, 'Well, would you like to sing something?'" She chose "Let It Be." "The only reason I picked that was because Aretha Franklin had a hit with 'Let It Be' at that time. I liked the way she did it. I gave them the key. After the song was finished, they both asked me if I'd like to join their tour.

"I was looking around," Lennear elaborated. "The stage had a setup of two drummers, a bass player, about three guitar players, two keyboardists. I had never seen a rhythm section put together like that. I was a little wary because I wasn't sure I would know what to do. I decided, 'Okay, look, just be fearless and just go for it, and whatever.'"

Recalling some of the first shows he'd attended as a kid, Leon said, "One of them was the Alan Freed *Show of Stars*. They had like fifteen or twenty acts on it. Little Richard, Chuck Berry, Fats Domino, Jerry Lee Lewis, with the Lloyd Price Show of Stars Orchestra, which was about [a] twenty-five-piece horn band. . . . That's actually where I got the idea for Mad Dogs & Englishman."

"One of the things that I've found out is that bigger bands are easier, especially in rock 'n' roll," Leon said. "It's much tougher to form a band like the Beatles than it is to make a band like the Mad Dogs & Englishman. That's why I use three drummers and a big chorus and a lot of people because it kind of averaged out." Mad Dogs, though, grew exponentially larger than what even Leon had envisioned. "I originally wanted two drummers, but for every person we asked to play, two more asked to play with us," he said. "There were about twenty-one people playing and singing on most of the dates, and the other twenty-five were family and friends."

One of those friends was Carla Brown. Another Tulsa kid, she had moved to LA and met Kay Poorboy, who invited her to a party at Skyhill but never showed up herself. As Brown explained in an interview with Teresa Knox, she told Leon, "I think you're the guy I'm supposed to meet. But [Kay's] not here, so I'm gonna leave."

A couple days later, Leon called to take her out. She declined again. But he was persistent. "I had a piano in my living room," Brown said. "The doorbell rang. I went to the door, and there was all these flowers. And I couldn't see anybody. And all of a sudden, these flowers come in, and there's this guy, Leon Russell, and there's Kay, and then there's a guy over at my piano—Chris Stainton. And then there's a guy singing—Joe Cocker. And they're singing 'Happy Birthday,' in a real groovy way. And I'm pissed because nobody better step on my kitchen floor I just mopped. And where in the hell am I gonna put all those damn flowers? . . . Kay said, 'Come here, I want to talk to you.' She said, 'Let's get Shawn dressed,' which was my boy. She said, 'We're going to A&M Records. And they're going to be putting a group together called Joe Cocker Mad Dogs & Englishmen. And I want you to go with us.' And I said, 'You know, what room am I supposed to be in?' Leon Russell said, 'You're gonna be in my room.' I thought, 'I don't even know you. I'm not gonna have my kid around somebody I don't know.' He said, 'You can trust me.'"

Many of those who went along on the Mad Dogs tour were part of the Space Choir. Though some were amateurs, the choir included such experienced young pros as Coolidge, Lennear, Pamela Polland, Donna Washburn, Donna Weiss, Bobby Jones, and brothers Daniel and Matthew Moore. The Moores were songwriters and had heard that Leon and Denny were looking for material for the tour.

"I had just shown [Daniel] my song ['Space Captain'] the day before," Matthew said. They took a copy of it to Joe, and he liked it, as did Denny and Leon, who started arranging it. "I wrote that in January or the beginning of February of 1970, and almost immediately, there was word put out in the songwriting community here in Los Angeles that Leon Russell was looking for songs for this guy named Joe Cocker.

"Right away—I mean a few days—we were invited down to the A&M soundstage for rehearsals," Matthew remembered. "I guess there was some really short timeline on getting things together and out on the road. That's where Leon started working on the arrangement. From my little song he turned that into a real production. They got set up in the studio, and we recorded it, and they decided to release it as a single as the launch of the tour."

Daniel Moore, seven years older than Matthew, had known Leon for years already. Daniel had come from the folk scene, putting out his first album in 1962. "I got really into producing records in about 1965 and produced a lot of stuff," Daniel said. "I was hiring the same musicians that Leon Russell was hiring." Radle, Blackwell, and Karstein had played on his *Colours* album in 1968. "All of a sudden, out of the blue, the Mad Dogs thing popped up. Leon called me and said he wanted me to come and be in charge of the choir."

Coolidge had been working at A&M on her debut solo album and was just getting over her bitter breakup with Leon. According to Leon, Jim Gordon and Coolidge had come down to watch the rehearsals and asked to join the show. Donna Weiss, who wrote "Turn Around and Love You," a hit for Coolidge, also joined the choir at Coolidge's behest. They had known each other back in Memphis. "She was very Southern," Coolidge said, describing Weiss. "She was such a dedicated songwriter. Donna's hair was rock 'n' roll black, and her skin was pasty white, and she wore a black trench coat and kind of hunched over. That was kind of her image. And I would call Donna, and I would say, 'Donna, let's go to lunch.' She'd say, 'I got no business traipsing around in the sunshine.'" She was an early goth. "Yes, she was a vampire." Coolidge explained, "I didn't want Leon to be able to pick everybody. He would just be picking his own girlfriends," she said, laughing. As it was, Coolidge and Donna Washburn were two of Leon's exes on the tour. Weiss would go on to cowrite Kim Carnes's giant eighties hit "Bette Davis Eyes" with Jackie DeShannon.

Space Choir member Pamela Polland's marriage had just ended. "A girlfriend of mine said, 'Hey, come with me; we're gonna do something fun tonight. It will help you to take your mind off this thing.' That was the first of ten nights of rehearsals on the A&M soundstage." Leon approached her during a break. He said, "I was a huge fan of the Gentle Soul [Polland's earlier band]. After the break, why don't you get up and sing with us?" An offer to join followed. "I said, 'The first thing, if I do, I'll have to bring my dog.' And he was like, 'Oh, no problem!'" Polland said with a laugh. "And that kind of sealed that right there. . . . We were off and running, me and my dog [Canina] for two and a half months on the road."

Polland roomed with Donna Washburn on tour. "She was so sweet, and she was kind of a refuge for me because some of the other people on the tour were just a little bit—the word that comes to my mind is 'hard-core.'"

Daniel Moore said, "It was so great because nobody really had to tell me what to do. On that first rehearsal, I remember Leon saying, 'Daniel, you're in charge of the choir.' And I turned around and looked at this motley crew, and I said, 'There's three good notes. Nail one of them!' I never told anybody anything else on that tour."

The rehearsals at A&M are the stuff of legend. Over a few days, hundreds of people from around LA heard about it and came down to check out the show. Jim Dickson, who was producing the Flying Burrito Brothers in the studio next door to the soundstage, said it was tough to get anyone in the Burrito session to concentrate. About Leon's ensemble, Dickson said, "They sucked up all the energy. It was a whole lot more fun to watch them rehearse with Leon than it was to be in our session. It was like having Barnum and Bailey's circus next door when you're trying to put on a puppet show. It was overwhelming." Word had it that even Bob Dylan lurked in the corners, enjoying the proceedings. He did come to at least two New York shows on the tour. A few years later, Dylan adopted a similar traveling circus idea for his Rolling Thunder Revue tour.

A few of the usual suspects, including Jim Karstein, pointed out the increasing drug intake as one reason they did *not* go on the tour. "I was in the closet the night that Leon and Denny cooked up Mad Dogs. And of course, they threw a wide net, and anyone that was moving, they conscripted to go on the road. I had committed to a tour with Taj Mahal about two weeks before. . . . Mad Dogs was a little over the top. They started smoking angel dust and doing a lot of acid, and I think cocaine started filtering in."

Karstein would have had difficulty finding a role anyway. "Leon," protested Denny Cordell during the rehearsals, "we can't have three drummers!" (They ended up with five.) "Well," Leon replied to Cordell, "who's gonna tell the other two they can't come?"

Keltner and Jim Gordon did most of the double drumming on the kits. "I was the drummer," Keltner said, "until Jimmy Gordon expressed interest and wanted to play too. Then they asked me, 'Do you mind if Jimmy Gordon plays double drums with you?' I said, 'No. Absolutely.' At around that time, he was one of my heroes. It was always just going to be me and Jimmy. Chuck Blackwell sat in some nights and played percussion the other nights."

Blackwell and Sandy Konikoff each played congas and percussion. Bobby Torres joined the tour in New York, displacing Konikoff from congas to tambourine. Konikoff, who had hung out at Skyhill in 1966, had moved around LA to various places and played in the Gentle Soul with Polland. Along with Blackwell, Konikoff had played drums on Taj Mahal's first album in 1968.

At Leon's invitation, Konikoff came to the rehearsals with Linda Wolf, who had been his girlfriend a couple of years earlier. Wolf said that on March 13, 1970, the day Leon started putting the tour band together, Konikoff called the "Fanny Hill House," home of the all-female band Fanny. "My sorority was Fanny," Wolf said. "That was where I lived prior to the Cocker tour." Fanny member Nickey Barclay was one of the choir members to drop out shortly after the Cocker tour started. Wolf convinced Denny Cordell to hire her as one of the two tour photographers, alongside Andee Nathanson. Leon and Denny also gave cameras, but not film, to other women, she said. They wanted it to look like the press was always covering them to help create more of a scene, as if this traveling hippie circus would not draw enough attention.

Leon's scope on this project went beyond rock 'n' roll. "I had this religious notion in my mind that everybody should eat together, so I was making huge trash cans of potato salad, macaroni salad, egg salad," which his pals would bring down to the soundstage, he said.

After rehearsals ended each night, everyone would go back to Skyhill and party, crashing wherever, and with whomever, they fell. "It was an anything-goes sort of scene, with girls around, and Leon was very permissive; let's put it that way," Stainton said.

Day turned into night, with the windows blotted out with tinfoil, lava lamps for lighting, car seats used as furniture. At the same time, Denny and Leon conducted business meetings. One friend later likened it to *Boogie Nights*. Leon envisioned the group as a family and tried to make everyone feel welcome and safe.

"I recall jam sessions," Wolf said. "I recall a lot of pot. I recall acid. . . . I recall nights of bed-hopping, myself." In a log entry in *Tribute: Cocker Power*—her book of photography from Mad Dogs and the 2015 reunion show at the Lockn' Festival—Wolf wrote, "What's happening in the world disappears for me. I lay under Leon's grand piano one night while he's playing. All I hear are cascading notes falling around me like a rainbow."

On March 17, two days before the tour started, the band recorded the whole rehearsal live on the A&M soundstage. "I was a staff engineer at A&M," said Grammy and Emmy Award–winning producer Tommy Vicari. "Before they went on the road, Henry Lewy, who was an engineer who did Joni Mitchell, set up Mad Dogs in Studio A like it was a concert—facing the control room. We recorded the entire show, from start to finish. And it was unbelievable. It was like a train. It was so tight and so exciting, and Leon was like Duke Ellington. I mean, Leon was the leader of the band. Joe was the star, but Leon was in control of the whole thing."

A&M cofounder Herb Alpert recalled stopping in to hear what was going down: "I was kind of a stuffed shirt when it came to rock 'n' roll. I used to audition and listen to music with my eyes closed; I learned this from Sam Cooke. Sam used to say, 'Hey, man, don't be intimidated by the way somebody looks, or if they can dance, or if they're handsome or beautiful, you know? Just listen to it.'

"I walked onto the soundstage while they were rehearsing—this is prior to me getting any feeling from rock 'n' roll—and I slowly opened my eyes, and I was looking at Joe Cocker, and he was gesticulating like he was playing a guitar and I said, 'Holy shit, man, this is good.' It's that the whole band was, like, *vibrating*. . . . It was tightly arranged, but it was loose at the same time. Leon wouldn't just read the music off the page; he would interpret it every time he played. He was basically a jazz musician; he was very spontaneous. And I think he was greatly responsible for that sound and the feeling because when you played with him, you just got into this motion that really touched you. That was an amazing, eye-opening experience for me."

"It was one of the most spectacular nights I've ever witnessed," Vicari said. "I mean, as far as energy, pure energy, and pure talent, I've never seen anything like that. You had them all in this room, so there wasn't much separation; it was just this wall of sound, and it all worked because the arrangements were so good. I thought it was better than the album."

Recorded during the rehearsals, "The Letter" was released as a single in April, backed with "Space Captain," a number seven, Cocker's first top ten hit in America. The credits list "Joe Cocker with Leon Russell & the Shelter People." This is the version of "The Letter" in Quentin Tarantino's *Once Upon a Time in Hollywood*, which visually captures this trippy-era Los Angeles, the mixture of the burgeoning hippie scene with rock 'n' rollers and movie stars in a still-kinda-small-town Hollywood, in a retro saturated-film presentation.

On the last night of rehearsal, Denny, Leon, and Jerry Moss decided the show had to be filmed for a movie. "Because of the enlarged production cost, the tour wouldn't make much by itself, but it would finance the movie, which had a chance of making a lot of money," Leon wrote. "I wanted a private airplane for the concert and movie crew, who would film everything that happened both on and off the stage, giving an insight into the hippie culture that was flourishing in America at the time. . . . It was the first time in my life that I had laid out an idea with all the components, documented by a secretary, who sat quietly taking notes in the corner." Leon said that after the documentary *Woodstock*, and with *T.A.M.I. Show* still fresh in mind, it was "obvious that films have a far-reaching effect for a longer period of time than a single concert or a series of concerts."

"There was such an energy force about the whole thing, such an aura about the band, that a film seemed a logical extension of what they were doing musically," Moss said when the movie was being released. Later, he would remember the tour fondly. "From the rehearsals, you could hear Joe's singing dominated the band. No matter how many people were on that stage, nobody could outshine him. . . . But unfortunately, by the time he was on the tour, he was drunk most of the time, and you couldn't really talk to him. . . . Denny was a friend of mine, and Leon was somebody I knew from his piano-playing days in the studio. I had no idea Leon played guitar so beautifully."

Moss hired Pierre Adidge, who had formed Creative Film Associates (CFA) after working on documentaries with the CBS News Department. He directed television specials for artists like Creedence Clearwater Revival. Adidge put together a five-person crew to follow the tour with

16 mm cameras and expanded to ten camera operators for the concerts at the Fillmore East and Santa Monica Civic Auditorium.

The day before leaving, the group headed over en masse to the Plantation to jam. Everyone was in sync, a band that was grooving, firing on all cylinders. "Jim Gordon was knocked out," Konikoff said. "He said, 'Man, looks like we got a band here.'"

Emily Smith viewed the tour as a continuation of the trip Leon and everyone took to Joshua Tree and then to Vegas. "Out of that little angel dust roll came *Mad Dogs & Englishmen*," she said. "Gram Parsons was there and was supposed to go on the tour, but jumped off the bus at the last minute."

A photo taken by Jim McCrary shows everyone on the bus on the way to the airport to board a chartered plane. It's smiles all around, and there's the look of happy anticipation on everyone's faces, like middle school kids embarking on a field trip. Leon is seated next to Andee Nathanson. Parsons is in the aisle seat in front of Leon, craning his head back, wearing the top hat he gave to Leon. That hat became Leon's trademark on this tour.

But at least two top hats made their way onto the stage. "I was out at Burbank airport . . . and Gram came out there and gave me this green top hat," Leon said. "I was fond of 'em at the time," he continued. "I took it on the road, wore it, played catch with it, somebody sat on it, and the inside started coming out. And inside it said, 'MGM 1938, Al Jolson, the Jazz Singer.'" From Al Jolson to Gram Parsons to Leon is mythical enough. But Leon claimed that the hat had been given to Gram by Keith Richards.

The circus metaphor is impossible to avoid when discussing this tour—like an old medicine show, it was modeled on a combination of circuses, carnivals, and tent revivals. A publicity packet for the film described Leon as "The flamboyant warlock/ringmaster who led the magic music circus of whirling dervishes, genies, sprites, and minstrels." Journalist Jacoba Atlas likened Leon to a lion tamer, with Cocker the beast in the center ring. Cordell compared it to "*Alice in Wonderland*, a kind of flying *Easy Rider*."

"After the band got to be four or five people, I tuned out for the rest of it," Peter Nicholls said. "'Who are all these people?' All I needed to do was make sure that the core band had a good sound and we could take it on the road and make it work. All the kids, all the dogs, and the space captains, and all that stuff didn't matter a damn thing; that was just production. Sandy Konikoff, when he showed up, I remember Denny Cordell asked him, 'So what do you do?' because, by this time, it's a freak show. And [Konikoff] says, 'Well, I play the sphincter phone.' They said, 'Okay, demonstrate it.' So he did. Yeah, he blew a fart through a trumpet and he was hired."

Karstein explained the genesis of the sphincter phone: Jackson Browne had witnessed Konikoff inserting a slim condenser microphone up his ass and playing percussion on his belly in a recording studio. It led to a banner under Konikoff's photo on the *Mad Dogs & Englishmen* album: "Purveyor of the Sphincter Phone."

For eight weeks on the road, Leon juggled personalities, performances, arrangements, and logistics. The power dynamic between Leon and Joe was the heart of the tour. Neither was hot-tempered, but the tension was an undercurrent that most in the traveling party detected. Leon told Alanna Nash, "The closest we came to a blowup was when we were rehearsing at A&M. . . . I was acting like the bandleader, which I was." Leon, under the gun to flesh out a two-and-a-half-hour show around Cocker's hits, had to quickly assemble and arrange a bunch of other songs. Each time he had an idea, he would run it by Cocker, who would not offer an opinion. The band would run it down. "And I said to Joe, 'Does that sound OK to you?' And he said, 'It never sounds OK to me.'" Leon concluded that Joe's passivity gave Leon the freedom to do what he wanted.

"Denny Cordell was a businessman," Peter Nicholls explained. "Leon was an opportunist. You know, he'd been around for a long time in the music business. He wants to make it work. Joe didn't get it. He just was fucked up, so what were Denny and Leon to do? Their plans never excluded Joe, but Joe didn't want to be included."

As much a traveling tribal commune as a rock tour, the backstage reality of Mad Dogs & Englishmen, though, got much darker, with an excess of hard drugs, ego clashes, and a violent assault by someone battling genuine madness.

Chapter 14

Learning to Live Together

ON MARCH 19, 1970, FORTY-THREE hippies crowded into a 1950s Lockheed Super Constellation propeller-engine plane, newly emblazoned with "Cocker Power," and winged into Detroit. "The pilot was an elderly gentleman. He really probably would have been a pilot of some sort in the Second World War," Sandy Konikoff said. The Constellation, he added, had "three tails, four prop engines. I says, 'How fast is this plane flying? How did we do?' He says, 'Son, we're lucky we made it off the ground.'"

Some passengers freaked out as nuts and bolts occasionally fell into the cabin. But with Carl Radle playing mandolin, Leon and others playing guitars, wine bottles popping open, and joints getting passed, frayed nerves were usually soothed. Jim Keltner remembered waking up and watching a red pill rolling down the aisle. Cordell coolly informed him that it was a Seconal, another way to calm the jitters. "I remember when we were in Texas, in Dallas," Daniel Moore said. "And the laws in Texas were really strict about drugs, marijuana, that kind of stuff. I remember when we landed in Dallas, Denny Cordell said to Smitty [Sherman Jones], 'I want you to gather up all the marijuana, all the drugs from everybody, and put 'em in a bag, and be in charge of that.' And Smitty [a Black man] said 'Forget it!' He could have ended up with a life sentence."

Jones was on the tour as the logistics guy. He was the adult nanny and the chief cat herder, charged with rounding up this ragtag group and getting them from the plane to the hotels and to the gigs. After the shows, he had to get them fed and back on the plane to the next city. In one scene in the film, the group arrives late at night at a Holiday Inn in

Plattsburgh, New York. Jones is seen politely and patiently cajoling a full meal for forty-some people from a surly cook in horn-rimmed glasses who seems like he was minutes away from closing the kitchen. The guy, who is middle-aged and white, acts like he can't even hear Jones, who never loses his diplomatic cool.

Leon described Jones as "a very colorful procurer of female entertainment, who was forever reciting Shakespeare and recounting stories of his adventures with Frank Sinatra." Later he was more blunt. "Sherman was a pimp," he said. Jones apparently ran with Sinatra and Tony Bennett. Daniel Moore explained, "He was a Shakespearean actor. He was a New York guy. Dee Anthony got him. He babysat everybody."

Peter Nicholls and the technical crew attempted to travel with the musicians and friends, but it was too much equipment and too many party people. "We did the plane for day one," Nicholls said. "It was a joke. It didn't work, so we traveled on commercial airlines." It was a time where you could just roll eighty pieces of gear and load it into a commercial jet, no questions asked. They missed out on the partying on the plane but had to make sure the shows were up and running.

"There's a lovely scene in the [*Mad Dogs & Englishmen*] movie, one of my favorites, about Denny pitching up in the afternoon talking to me," Nicholls said. This was shot in Minneapolis on April 3, about two weeks into the tour. It was the grand opening of The Depot, which had just been converted from a Greyhound bus station. Later, the venue became the legendary First Avenue club, seen in Prince's *Purple Rain*. "I'm pointing out lighting positions, and so on," Nicholls said, and "Denny says, 'As long as there are follow-spots on Joe and Leon.'"

Someone from Dee Anthony's Bandana Management allegedly shook down the local show promoter at The Depot, threatening that Cocker would not take the stage for the second of two nights if he was not immediately paid more. By that point, fans were already lined up around the block. The promoters got the impression that the management was caught off guard by the success of the *Woodstock* movie, which had just been released on March 26, quickly vaulting Cocker to a new level of fame. There were about two thousand people present for the only true club date in a tour of mostly theaters and ballrooms. "Allan Fingerhut, the principal owner and investor in The Depot, was obviously perplexed in a satisfied sort of way," read the review of night one in the *Minneapolis Star Tribune*. "'I don't know what's going on here anymore. . . . We ran out of booze at eight o'clock and had to send out for more.'"

The tour was in full stride by Minneapolis, but it had commenced in Detroit's Eastown Theatre, where Leon was reunited with his buddies David Teegarden and Skip Knape, who were performing there under the name Teegarden & Van Winkle. "I went over there, and so many people in that band were guys from Tulsa," remembered Teegarden. "So, it was like old home week to see all of them. It was a hell of a weekend, for sure." Seeing the Mad Dogs show was life-changing for Teegarden and Knape. "We were inspired," Teegarden recalled. "We thought, 'Leon likes that gospel sound, so let's write our own gospel tune." They wrote and recorded "God, Love and Rock 'n' Roll," a Top 40 hit in 1970. Teegarden and Knape soon joined Bob Seger's band and convinced Seger to cover Leon's "Hummingbird."

The Detroit crowd ate it up. But Peter Nicholls and crew were having a baptism by fire. "We played our first gig at the ballroom in Detroit. And I was, I swear, the first person to put the mixing console out front in the crowd. And I had this long wire of [a snake] of thirty cables, where the wires came out to the mixing console. About thirty minutes before the show went on, some kid cut it because it was in his way."

The tour reached New York City for two nights at Bill Graham's Fillmore East. These shows were recorded for a live album and make up a large portion of the film. By the time the tour got to New York, Leon's debut album had already been released on March 23. But no one interviewed seems to recall being aware of the release of Leon's album, never mind whether it distracted him from the Mad Dogs shows, which speaks to his concentration on the gigs at hand. While at the Fillmore, he did sing two of his new songs, "Hummingbird" and "Dixie Lullaby."

Backstage before the shows at the Fillmore, Leon formed a prayer circle, as usual, which Carla Brown insisted on. "She was very Christian," her and Leon's daughter Blue Bridges-Fox said. "The whole praying-in-the-circle, that is all on my mom. My dad told me that. My mom would shoot heroin and read the Bible. I mean, she'd shoot heroin, drink a fifth of tequila, and walk straight into the middle of the church."

Bobby Keys offered his own benediction, "Every night's a Saturday night and every day's a Sunday." Then everyone joined as the choir sang

"Will the Circle Be Unbroken," with Cordell's kids, Barney and Tarka, playing tambourines. They were ever present on the tour. In one photo, they can be seen playing with toy trucks at Cocker's feet while he is singing to the crowd at The Depot. Cocker noted that it "was the closest [he] ever came to beating up a kid."

One of rock music's most soulful (if underappreciated) lead guitarists, Don Preston, was mostly relegated to rhythm, as Leon strutted the stage with a black Gibson Les Paul to open the show. Along with the horns, Leon and Don played harmony lines on the soul-revue overture. In the film, which opens with the show at Santa Monica Civic Auditorium on April 18, Leon is in one of the top hats (Pamela Polland wears another), the HOLY TRINITY tank top over a long-sleeved multicolored jersey in a Mondrian-like pattern, and tight white bell bottoms with flowers embroidered across his ass. He bought this new stage outfit from a used clothing store in Hollywood before hitting the road. Rita Coolidge recalled first seeing him wearing it at the rehearsals at A&M. "I had lived with him for a year and never seen that side of him," she said. "He got out of the car, strutted across the parking lot, and that was the persona that lasted through the tour. His way of overcoming stage fright was to be bigger than life."

"I was just trying to make a show," Leon explained. "When I was living in Skyhill, there was a little store right down right off Lankershim that sold used clothes. So I knew this tour was coming up. I'm not much of a clothes person, actually. So I went into that store, and they had all these used clothes, pants with flowers on, just all kinds of different clothes. I just bought a whole bunch of that stuff. They had that Holy Trinity T-shirt, and had LDS shirts, which I thought was close enough to LSD to be interesting; Latter-Day Saints, which is Sixth Day Adventist [*sic*]." Either of his jerseys would match the occasion of Easter weekend at the Fillmore East. "Don't get hung up about Easter," Leon deadpans on the live album.

During the intro on the live album, there's an almost immediate drum break, with Jim Gordon and Jim Keltner cooking, joined by conga player Bobby Torres, who had just come down to the Fillmore to join the tour.

Torres had first come to see Cocker and the Grease Band open for the Jeff Beck Group (with Rod Stewart on lead vocals) for multiple shows at the Fillmore East in 1969. Torres recalled, "When I saw them at the Fillmore, they didn't have a conga player for 'Feelin' Alright.' So, I asked if I could sit in. He says, 'Yeah.' I said, 'You don't want to hear me play first?' He said, 'Okay.' I played a little, he says, 'Okay.' And I came back every night and sat in with them for one song." Torres showed up the next time they came to New York and headlined the Fillmore. Then he flew to Chicago to join them at a gig on his own dime. "I went to Kinetic Playground, and they were so happy to see me they made me a permanent member."

Paul McCartney issued a press release announcing the end of the Beatles on April 10, while the Mad Dogs tour was working its way along the Eastern Seaboard. Early in the show was "She Came in Through the Bathroom Window." A lot is going on in the Mad Dogs arrangement of the song—listen to the intricate horn parts, and Carl Radle's bass groove. Leon provides a mediocre guitar solo. He was a fine guitarist for a piano maestro. He had a deft touch, impressive vibrato, and he knew how to bend the strings smoothly. But he still had only a limited vocabulary on the instrument, and he runs out of gas for the second half of the solo.

Glyn Johns minced no words: "I think he was a *terrible* guitar player," he said, laughing. "He shouldn't have been allowed anywhere *near* a guitar. Absolutely fucking awful, but showing off."

Leon knew that putting on a spectacle trumped impeccably executing musical performances. Since his tutelage under Jerry Lee Lewis, Leon understood how to work a crowd. "Once they were all worked up anyway, then it would be these moments that were highly choreographed where he would strap on a guitar and get up on the piano, and people would go insane," said one observer. Like James Brown, these types of performers were showmen mixed with a little bit of Southern going-to-church.

"It was brilliant some nights," Jim Keltner said. "The recording itself, I've always maintained, that wasn't the very best that it was. There were some nights that didn't get recorded. First of all, those shows that got recorded, I can tell you right now that most of us were on MDA [a forerunner of MDMA/Molly/Ecstasy] at the time. You get really high on that. There were some that had smoked some angel dust. We were all drunk. It was a mess."

"Generally speaking, we did okay," said Chris Stainton. "Because there were enough people in the band that were together, like say, Jim Keltner, Jim Gordon, they always seemed to hold things together. And, of course, Carl Radle was always good. He was Mr. Clean at that time. Healthy, so he held everything together. And Bobby Keys and Jim Price always held it together."

While the influence of Ray Charles on the tour was most obvious in Joe Cocker's singing style and the inclusion of three songs from Brother Ray's repertoire—"Sticks and Stones," "I'll Drown in My Own Tears," and "Let's Go Get Stoned"—his spirit infused the whole show, in the arrangements and in the disregard for genre distinctions.

Claudia Lennear recognized Leon in that tradition. "I think Leon was one of the best exponents of that music. I really can't find any precedent of Leon's music. He takes snippets from Black gospel; yes, that's obvious. He also does a lot of things from white gospel music, if you want to see it in a Black–white way. To me, people just waste so much time over silly things like what's white and what's not, what's from the South, and what's not. It really should boil down to what you like. All of us were the same age group. We all grew up with the same kind of music. We all liked the Everly Brothers. We all liked Bo Diddley. We all liked Chuck Berry. We all loved Little Richard. We all adored James Brown. I mean, what difference does it make, you know?" Bobby Keys turned Lennear on to Bob Dylan on the plane trips.

The Mad Dogs version of "Sticks and Stones" is fiery, with Stainton ably handling a subtle Charles-like rhythm, accented by flashy glissandos on the piano. When Leon was on guitar, Stainton generally took over piano. When Leon moved back to piano, Stainton shifted to organ. He got a nightly lesson from Leon, whose "really fast octave playing" was striking to Stainton: "It was the gospel feel that I loved about him."

The Ray Charles numbers of the set are among the most gratifying. On "Let's Go Get Stoned"—a Nickolas Ashford–Valerie Simpson composition Charles first heard via a recording by Ronnie Milsap—Leon and Don Preston launch into a killer two-guitar attack, with Chris Stainton peeling off inspired runs on the piano. Keys reaches deep for his fiery sax solo. Leon is brilliant on piano for the gospel arrangement of Leonard Cohen's "Bird on the Wire." The original solemn composition was already hymnlike in tone and its chord changes; here, the stirring choir delivers it straight to church. Don Preston's guitar was fed through a Fender Vibratone Leslie revolving speaker for an organ-like texture.

Rita Coolidge stepped into the smoky spotlight for a riveting rendition of another new song, "Superstar." Who, exactly, wrote the song is

controversial in the Delaney & Bonnie/Rita/Leon world. No one disputes the fact that Rita inspired the title. The first recording came as a
Delaney & Bonnie and Friends B-side in 1969, under the title "Groupie
(Superstar)." Coolidge said she wrote it with Bonnie Bramlett on the road
with Eric Clapton. "Delaney and Leon came in, heard what we were doing, and went into the other room and finished it. But when the song
came out as the B-side, my name wasn't on it. And, God, that really, really
hurt. Because Bonnie was one of my closest friends."

Not in dispute is Leon's role in the composition. A close friend who
requested anonymity said Leon admitted that "Rita wrote that chorus, not
Bonnie Bramlett. And Leon was so pissed off at Rita that he didn't give her
credit; he gave it to Bonnie Bramlett." This explanation makes the most
sense. Rita is seen in the *Mad Dogs* film on the plane guiding others in the
harmonies of the chorus.

While the lyric might seem uncharacteristic of Leon, the chords,
melody, and arrangement fall squarely into his wheelhouse. It became a
monster hit for the Carpenters.

The mournful melody and pleading emotion of "Superstar" are heart-
rending. Coolidge gives a devastating reading of it on the *Mad Dogs* recording, with Leon spiking breathtaking piano runs around her vocal line.
The anguish Rita tapped into was informed by horrifyingly real physical
and emotional trauma.

It happened at the Hotel President in New York. Leon was treating
Coolidge like a persona non grata, simply ignoring her. Reflecting on his
threesome proposal the previous year, she recalled, "That was like, 'No,
this, this is definitely not my direction. And if this is just the beginning,
I can't imagine what life is gonna be like.' Of course, on the Mad Dogs
and Englishmen tour, I could see it; everything unfolded there, with the
orgies."

Moreover, Rita was performing the song with a black eye from her
current partner, drummer Jim Gordon. She was absorbed in the tour's
camaraderie and the warmth and comfort she felt with Gordon, but it all
changed with a shocking assault. "After each show on the Mad Dogs tour,"
explained Coolidge, "a lot of the nights the people who were not participating in the orgies, or whatever else was going on, would still be so full
of music that we would go to somebody's room and pull out guitars and
sing for another hour, or smoke a joint and watch Johnny Carson." One

night in New York, "Jim said very quietly, so only I could hear, 'Can I talk to you for just a minute?' He meant he wanted to talk alone. And I said, just as quietly, 'Yeah, sure.' So we walked out of the room together—it was late at night, the hallway was deserted—and he closed the door." Because he was such a romantic, she said she would not have been surprised if he proposed marriage in that intimate moment. "And then he hit me so hard that I was lifted off the floor and slammed against the wall on the other side of the hallway."

"Jim went out in the hallway for a few minutes, and then he came in," Jim Price said. "Three of us were just sitting there, and he came back in, sat down, and said, 'I just hit Rita.' And nobody said anything—we just stopped, and our little pow-wow split up. We didn't want to talk to him about it then, but we should have. That's something that you just didn't do. To think someone on the tour would hit a woman."

By that point, Gordon had shown few, if any, outward signs of a creeping mental illness to his friends and collaborators. He had heard voices even as a small child, though. Jim Keltner was seemingly the only person on the tour who knew about it. "This is what blows my mind. Jimmy Gordon was actually insane," Keltner said. "He had severe schizophrenia, and he was an outpatient at UCLA Medical Center. There was one night that I had messed up. I had taken acid with Jimmy Gordon a night on the tour. I couldn't play. . . . Years later, I realized that the reason Jimmy could do it was because he wasn't normal. He was insane."

Keltner continued: "The way it was explained to me was that there was nothing they could do until somebody does something violent. Normally, the schizophrenic doesn't do anything violent unless he stops his medication. Then the voices that you hear take over. If they're violent, then that's what happens. That's exactly what happened with Jimmy. He was an outpatient the whole time that we all knew him. [Rita] didn't know what was going on. . . . I remember her having one of the biggest, boldest, baddest, purple-blue-black eyes I've ever seen on somebody. He must have hit her so hard. She's a proud Indian woman. She didn't even try to cover it up. She was pissed. I think that was it." Rita confirmed she was unaware of Gordon's previous treatment for mental illness. "I didn't know that until right this second," she said.

Asked if Gordon was somehow self-medicating with acid, Keltner answered, "Yeah. We were all crazy. We were just kids. We were doing every dumb thing you could do and still being able to hang in there a little bit. I was hard-core enough to be able to do most of it and still play and make it work. The acid thing was too much then. It wasn't just acid that I had taken that night. I was doing my normal thing, drinking champagne, and smoking, and snorting. It was too much. The acid, it sent me over the top. I grabbed Chuck [Blackwell] off of the conga and said, 'You gotta play.' He said, 'Wait a minute. I'm not playing on this one.' I said, 'You've got to play.' I set him at the drums. I went down and sat at the edge of the stage in the back with my head between my knees. There's video of Chuck playing on the drums. I think they [filmed] it on that night because he played the rest of the night."

Gordon never stopped dropping acid, snorting coke, or drinking. "He was trying to keep the demons at bay," wrote Barry Rehfeld in a 1985 *Rolling Stone* profile of Gordon. "'I had a feeling I was being watched,' he says, 'but it was all in the background.'" It got to be too much for Gordon to handle. He has been in prison since 1983 for bludgeoning and stabbing his mother to death after the voices commanded him to do so.

"It came from nowhere. I'm sure his mother felt the same way before she died," Rita said. Increasingly on the tour, a coked-up Gordon exhibited an empty stare. "Jim didn't have any problem getting whatever he wanted," Rita said. "He was the golden boy. He had plenty of money. He could charm the pants off of anybody. He was an amazing guy, just really so charismatic. And that smile, but, man, those . . ." Her voice trailed off. "Again, after everything happened, I started to recognize that look in his eye and knew that he was not playing with a full deck."

Gordon did acknowledge his guilt. He was apologetic and left books of poetry for Coolidge, even after the tour. But she was understandably done with him. "I would come out of a session, or walk out of my house, and there would be, like, a present on my car, or flowers by the front door," she said. "And I would just throw them in the trash and never even looked at them."

Everyone else tried to move on as best they could, a bunch of twenty-somethings out for a rolling peace-and-love fest all of a sudden faced with a brutal dose of reality. "It devastated me that she was my friend, and this violent assault happened to her," said Claudia Lennear. "I think everybody did sweep it under the rug. I think everybody came to Rita's side, to help her, to do her makeup, or kind of fix the blemishes on her face that happened from this or tried to control her, because she was ready to leave the tour when that incident happened. And, of course, nobody wanted her to go."

"Joe begged me not to leave," Rita said. "I wanted to leave so many times, but Smitty looked out for me. Everybody did. I always had an escort. People would come to my room and take me to soundcheck or wherever we were going. I was never by myself. Thank God [Smitty] was there."

Coolidge did not press charges but did sign a restraining order. She said the band "formed a wall around" her. She concluded, perhaps too pragmatically, "It wouldn't have benefited anybody to have a lot of people taking sides." Smitty escorted Rita to and from her hotel rooms, shows, and the plane and kept Jim away from her.

Though he was looked to as the leader, Leon was not one Rita could turn to for help. "We didn't have a lot of communication," she said. "He was always, you know, at some party or some orgy, or with everybody going to get shots for VD or something. I hung out with Donna Weiss and Pamela Polland, some of those people. I didn't spend a lot of time with him. And then, of course, after the crap happened with Jim Gordon, I pretty much was stuck in my room because I was afraid of being attacked if I walked out."

"The Mad Dogs and Englishmen thing was cultural," Claudia explained. "Most of us—myself, Donna Washburn, Rita—none of us had lived that way. We weren't taught to live in communal circumstances, which is what Mad Dogs and Englishmen was all about . . . where you do what you want, and when you change, you go naked if you want to, or you have free love and sex, and blah blah blah. That's what that period was all about in the seventies. . . . Lifestyle-wise, it was a bit of a clash."

All the sunny vibes built up on the tour were now overshadowed by a dark cloud. "The Happy Hippies story was nothing like the tour," Price said. "I was perhaps the tamest member of the entourage, never participating much in the wild side of things. We were about forty people who split into numerous small groups. The film's flavor was concocted. There was less and less social unity as we went."

Looking back, Coolidge was struck by how young they all were. "Everyone was in their twenties: men, women, children, girls, boys. Pamela's little dog. We were kids. Even Leon, though he didn't look like it, was in his twenties."

As usual, Leon was the calm eye of the storm, never losing control of himself. Linda Wolf said she knows Leon "drank quite a lot," but she never witnessed him drunk or out of control. As one of the youngest, she felt Leon looked out for her especially. She took too much acid at one of the San Francisco shows and thought she was losing control while dancing onstage. "He did have his eye on me because he pulled me back that night. . . . He had his eyes on everybody, I believe. . . . I was falling backwards on stage, and he lifted me back up with this tractor beam in his eyes. He was very devoted, it seemed, to Carla." Carla was getting into a level of drug and alcohol abuse that would eventually lead her to bottom out, clean up, get sober, and find a vocation as a substance abuse counselor. "She had a small son on the tour. [Leon] seemed to be very fatherly to Shawn."

All the participants observed Leon's guiding hand. His concerns were the music, the shows, and the communal spirit. The business-minded people on tour—Cordell, management, label execs, et al.—had their eyes on different things, especially the money. The rest of the troupe weren't thinking that way. They thought they were going to change the world through music.

Matthew Moore's song "Space Captain" captured the ideals, if not the realities, of the tour: "Learning to live together." With a tiptoe beat, set by Leon's solo piano intro, a burlesque bump-and-grind "Ooh! Ahh" part from the choir, all released on an uplifting chorus, the song served as the anthem for the tour.

For Leon, Mad Dogs was not an empty libertine mission, though a good time was undoubtedly a benefit. "I thought it was important that all the cast and crew eat at least one meal together each day, to have an opportunity to discuss the latest events and, in general, to weld the consciousness of all concerned into one common awareness," he wrote.

One person described Leon and Emily Smith's behavior as being like a couple of faith-healing evangelists. No one could get on the plane until Emily went through it with a giant cross to clear the energy to keep it airborne. "I think she was there protecting Leon. She was like his consigliere."

The tour stopped in New York twice. Given the amount of time spent in the city, a lot of action happened there. "I had met this girl in Chicago called Gail a few months before," Stainton said. "I had lost contact with her." At the hotel, "Peter Nicholls came rushing over and said, 'Gail's here,' and I said, 'What?!' And so, we did the Mad Dogs tour together, and we got married after that. And I'm still married to Gail fifty years later. . . . At the end of the tour, Gail got pregnant with our daughter, Jenny . . . and we had this lovely big house [in Laurel Canyon], and then, it was just the three of us and a couple of dogs—one of them was Canina's puppies." Pamela Polland did not know that Canina was pregnant when she took her out on the road. "I think we figured it out maybe halfway through the tour," Polland said. "She just kept getting fatter and fatter."

"Me and Joe decided one day to take a walk down to Central Park," Brown recalled. "And we were walking through Central Park. And this guy said, 'Hey, Joe!' So we stopped, [thinking it was] somebody maybe we knew. He comes over and puts a gun in me says, 'Give me all your money.' And Joe says, 'Man, you're gonna have some bad karma.' I said, 'Fuck the karma! Give him the damn money! The gun's on me, Joe!' So he gives him the money, and the guy takes off. And I said, 'I need to go home.' And then Denny Cordell said, 'No. You got to be here for Leon. He needs you. You're the only one that could talk him into doing anything.'"

Leon and Carla's daughter Blue explained, "Denny called and asked her to come back out because I guess [Leon] was having some mental health issues." Leon's depression would set in, and he would lie down for hours. "He would get into his depression or his anxiety," Blue said. "He would lay in bed in the hotel and hide out, and she had to go in there and scream and yell and try to get him up. She'd tell him, 'You know, those people paid good motherfucking money! You're not gonna lay here and not go out there and put on a show!'"

Bob Dylan showed up on Friday for the first show at the Fillmore East. On the recording, Leon announces, "There's a guy in the house tonight that I know that you all have watched for a long time. Me and Joe have watched him for a long time. We love him. We're gonna do one of his songs cuz we love him, that's why." Leon sings the first verse of "Girl from the North Country." Joe takes the next, and they trade off, accompanied by Leon's uncharacteristically clunky piano. It would seem nerves got in the way.

They filmed night two at the Fillmore East. The actor Michael J. Pollard got onstage and played the tambourine on "Feelin' Alright," off-tempo and loudly. "One tambourine will shake musicians up pretty good," noted Jerry Moss. "I was sitting in the audience with Quincy Jones and he said to me, 'You can't hear a thing because of that tambourine.' Finally, Leon threw his hat at the guy and two hands miraculously came out from backstage and took him off and they finally got in the groove." As seen in the film, after he throws his hat, leonine Leon and roaring Joe meet at the center of the stage and play off each other, Joe responding with facial expressions to everything Leon plays.

The show featured individual spotlight moments—which can be heard on expanded versions of the album—for Leon (duetting with Cocker on "Girl from the North Country" and his solo takes on "Hummingbird" and "Dixie Lullaby"); Claudia ("Let It Be"); Rita ("Superstar"); and Bobby Jones (who takes over for Cocker on "When Something Is Wrong with My Baby"). Don Preston steps right up with lead vocals and scorching lead guitar on "Further Up the Road."

"As far as artistic direction was concerned, that was 100 percent Leon," Polland observed. "Now, of course, the rub was Joe, in the end, he felt usurped, basically, which I never thought was the case. He was the lead singer. If anything, it was Joe that was the one that became the most famous. But it was absolutely Leon's show; there's just no getting around it." Like most involved, she only heard about the rumblings about negative feelings after the tour was over.

Keltner said, "Leon was in his element when he was reading a bunch of people and playing at the same time. Joe was like a machine. Not sure how he survived the abuse. When you listen to the record, [you can hear] the abuse he put himself through." In the film, a wasted Cocker waxes philosophical about rising above illness and other physical challenges in performance. "You should be able to work hard up there for seven hours and feel okay," he slurs. Singing is a release, he notes.

Joe would not say much in front of the camera. "For the first week, all Joe would do is smile," said Pierre Adidge, who directed the movie. "I don't think he said more than five words. It took quite a while for him to open up. The tour was a tremendous strain on him. I've never seen anybody go at it like Joe. At one point, he lost his voice and the next performances were really like gravel, but he wouldn't give up on one single song." The film shows Cocker, in stockinged feet, uncharacteristically gaunt, furry mutton chops framing his face, eyes bulging, glaring comically at Leon as the bandleader counts off multiple reprises of the definitive version of "Delta Lady," one of the standouts on a consistently excellent album.

When Leon starts the song up again, pounding out the song's three-chord coda on the piano, the crowd goes nuts. It's a gospel trick.

The ecstatic Pentecostal frenzy that Leon conjured was just part of the act, like the Holy Trinity shirt. "I believe that organized Christianity has done more harm than any other single force I can think of in the world," he said in 1971. In response, Ben Fong-Torres asked him, "What's the alternative for that kind of organization and that kind of religion?"

"Rock and roll," Leon answered.

Chapter 15

I'm Coming Home

THERE ARE FEW BETTER SOUNDTRACKS for highway driving than the Mad Dogs & Englishmen version of "The Letter." Leon's arrangement of the 1967 Box Tops song is an inspired recasting of an already great number. Leon kicks it off with a repeating minor-key blues riff on the piano, like a chant. The drummers step in with a tom-tom tattoo, like a Cherokee war dance, the song building in tension and anticipation.

In the *Mad Dogs & Englishmen* film, Leon's eyes are half-lidded in an almost sexual tension as he plays sixteenth notes while Cocker sings the refrain. Release comes in the form of an explosive post-chorus horn-driven riff that settles into a funky swing. The drums break down near the end of the arrangement, with Cocker ad-libbing over the outro. It wraps up in a tightly syncopated ending.

"Leon surprised me with his arrangements of some of those songs," Cocker recalled. "I mean, one day he came up to me with 'The Letter'—he just said, 'Hey, Joe, what do you think about this?' It clicked instantly."

With the New York shows over, the tour still had about a month and a half to go. Though everyone in the group was young, energy levels were depleted by the exhausting itinerary, the demanding performances, and the substances; good nights of sleep were few and far between. Toward the end, "We all got worn out about six weeks, and it was an eight-week adventure," Daniel Moore said. "It's like Sisyphus, pushing that rock up the hill," Pamela Polland said.

One moment of relaxation is shown in the film: a gauzy and blissful-looking picnic outside of Tulsa, with Emily Smith serving up tantalizing barbecue followed by Smitty Jones reciting the poem "The Face on the

Barroom Floor" while Joe and Carla Brown hold hands. As the scene progresses, all of the participants join hands and run in a circle. The punch was spiked with mescaline. For Rita Coolidge, the day was a chance to relax and not be "messed up," she wrote. "It was dreamlike to have that in the middle of this tour," a tour that, for her, was "not lovely. I did the last part of that tour with a black eye. . . . That tour has haunted me for my life, and not all of it good. I had a bad experience, and by the time it was over, I was just pathetic," she said. "But I'm very grateful for the experience. I learned an awful lot. It almost broke me, but it didn't."

Polland said, "I'm pretty sure I'm the only person that didn't sleep with anybody on the tour. Several people slept with several others, but everybody slept with *somebody*. You heard about the Butter Queen?" The Butter Queen was a notorious groupie in Dallas named Barbara Cope whose preferred lubricant was butter. She is seen in the film and even gets a shout-out in the Rolling Stones' song "Rip This Joint." "Women were lined up outside the hotel room doors of the big male players, like Joe and Leon, every night," Polland continued. "There was a line of women just waiting to be able to say that they fucked Joe Cocker." And it wasn't just groupies. "At the Fillmore West," Carla Brown said, "Janis Joplin said she wanted to suck Leon's dick until his head fell off."

Jim Horn popped onto a few select dates to add another sax to the horn section with Bobby Keys and Jim Price. Horn was in the band in Santa Monica on April 18 for the stirring performance of "With a Little Help from My Friends" shown in the film. The whole stage is taken up by people, including Mama Cass Elliot, lining the wings, dancing along the rear perimeter behind the drummers, and augmenting the choir. Joe is in a glittery Shelter Records T-shirt. Donna Washburn and Pamela Polland hold hands as they hum the quiet vamp before the song builds to a crescendo. Arguably, it tops the version from Woodstock. Joe was in better voice at Woodstock, but for the call-and-response arrangement, the Mad Dogs choir and horn section set the bar high.

The LA crowd went nuts, chanting, "We want Joe!" The band returned, and Leon launched into his song "Give Peace a Chance," with a very pregnant Canina at the lip of the stage. In a few measures, Leon takes us on an adventurous musical journey, beginning with a quote of "The Star-Spangled Banner" into a Liberace-like flourish, adding a tinge of easy listening, slipping in some jazzy chords, turning it around with a hint of ragtime, blues, and minor-key balladry, before bringing it back to gospel. It all flashes by in a head-spinning forty-five seconds.

The tour crisscrossed the continent. In the audience in Boston was a young Jon Landau, who wrote for *Crawdaddy* and *Rolling Stone*. He would go on to produce and manage Bruce Springsteen, Jackson Browne, and others. "I saw Mad Dogs at Symphony Hall in Boston, and I was sitting in the front row," he said. "And in the *Mad Dogs & Englishmen* package, there is a bunch of all these little mini pictures on the tour. And there's a picture where I recognize myself. That was one of the greatest things I've ever seen to this day. Joe was just at his absolute peak. They were clicking on all cylinders, and Leon was just this unforgettable presence."

By the time they reached the end of four nights in San Francisco, just the husk of Cocker's voice remained, leaving him sounding more like Howlin' Wolf than Ray Charles. They had four shows in the city, two at Winterland on April 24 and 25, bookended by two more at the Fillmore West on the twenty-third and twenty-sixth. Van Morrison opened the shows, a perfect pairing—he was already into his horn-tinged Celtic soul period. Within a few years, the Belfast Cowboy would assemble his Mad Dogs–like eleven-piece Caledonia Soul Orchestra.

The final show was in San Bernardino on May 17, with Nils Lofgren's band Grin opening the show. They had arrived back in LA and everyone went their separate ways before regrouping for that last show. Leon recalled it being the worst of the tour, ascribing the poor quality to the break disrupting the cocoon-like tribal feel of the tour. "When we were all together and eating together, the music was incredible."

Lofgren went on to a long-running tenure playing guitar for Bruce Springsteen and the E Street Band. Springsteen himself was inspired by the *Mad Dogs* album and the large-band format. "I was listening to Van Morrison and Joe Cocker's *Mad Dogs & Englishmen* and was interested in returning to my soul roots," he wrote.

Springsteen expanded on that for this book: "Me and Stevie Van Zandt went and saw the movie. The film got everywhere. It came to our little town, and we went and saw it. And all I remember was leaving going, 'I want a band *just like that*.' And I went about, shortly thereafter, putting together locally—which was hard to do—a ten-piece band that was really based on Mad Dogs and Englishmen. We had singers and horn players. You know, it was a big, big band that was dedicated to primarily soul music and rhythm and blues. And I played with that band for a while until I couldn't afford it anymore, and that slowly broke down.

"But Leon, as a bandleader, was very, very impactful to me as a twenty-one-year-old kid," Springsteen continued. "He was the music director, and I was interested in musicians who played that role because I was studying my craft and learning how to do that from my own bands, and he was a unique figure, also. He was charismatic and colorful and was very talented on his own. His own singing and playing was really stellar, and he was just somebody I admired greatly at that moment, particularly. I had no awareness of his role previous to *Mad Dogs & Englishmen*. And then I went back and saw how all these great sessions he'd been on, and how he'd been at the birth of a lot of incredible records that I loved."

Leon's soul preacher/ringleader persona also influenced Springsteen. "I picked a little bit of that up and used it in my show," he said. "And I picked it up from other places, also; all the great soul front men all had a little bit of that. But it was just a fascinating blend of music and people, and it was so colorful and had that circus atmosphere, and the great, the great vocalist in Joe."

But by tour's end, Cocker was just barely functioning. He had been in a fragile state to begin with. "Joe was hurting because he really was not in control of what was going on," Rita Coolidge said. "It was set up that way. Leon said, 'Basically, you show up, and I'll do everything else.' That might be a good thing, but that's not who Joe *was*. So he was not happy with it." Along the way, people would hand him pills, tabs, whatever, and, Coolidge said, he wouldn't even look at what they had given him; it would all go straight into his mouth. "The only difference between one tab and ten tabs of acid," Cocker told her, "is the pain in the back of me neck."

He came back from the tour a shell of a human being. Footage shot of him in the following year shows him hollowed out, eyes glassy, unable to put together a sentence. "That's when I ended up in a heap at Denny's place," he said. "He had this little place in LA I was curled up in a ball for a year, and I didn't want to know the world. That's when Dee [Anthony] was screaming at me about, why didn't I just listen to him. So I ended up giving him all my money to say good night. The frustration coming out of that was that I had no musical direction left in my mind at all. You know, we thought, we honestly thought, that a flying saucer was going to come down, pick us all up, and send us off to heaven."

Cocker was smarting in larger part from, to his mind, Leon's betrayal. "I knew he was an incredible talent, and it started like he was a big brother to me," Cocker said in 1992. "As the tour progressed and all the attention was on me, he got a little envious. . . . But he took over the whole show. . . . It just ended up bitterly, which is a shame."

As witnessed by the movie, the album, and the radio broadcasts, Mad Dogs & Englishmen was one of the greatest bands during a magical time for rock. Leon didn't think it had to end. But by the tour's finish, Leon realized that the large format of Mad Dogs was not what Cocker wanted. "I don't think Joe likes working with a big band," Leon said. "He prefers a smaller group, where he gets more of a chance to sing and improvise. With a big band the arrangements are tight, and you only improvise when you come to an improvisation part."

It ultimately boiled down to money. Leon and Denny profited, and Joe was broke. "Joe had no more money. That was the bitter end," Linda Wolf said. "They had to add a few shows in order to try to make him some money at the end. He came back with, I thought, $700 in the bank. . . . I know he was so angry."

"I think [Joe] was happy with the music and the results, but it wasn't his," Rita said. "He was center stage, he was the star, but he came away penniless. A lot of people came away with a future. Joe kind of came away just damaged. And I don't think that Leon—I think he was aware of it. I just don't think he gave a shit."

"It was very expensive," Leon said at the end of the tour. "If we had not traveled by private plane, and had flown everywhere by commercial airlines, it would have cost us at least three or four times more. But then Joe is not interested in money." Since the tour expenses were fronted by A&M, Cocker would have to recoup them against future royalties. "Joe was not getting a real high artist percentage," Daniel Moore said. "Leon and Denny were getting the high producers' percentage, and none of the expenses from the tour went against their royalties. They made millions of dollars. Joe Cocker broke even. Joe just went and lived on a farm in England for a couple of years and drank his head off. I thought Leon saved Joe's ass. But also, at the same time, Joe's situation kind of made Leon a star."

Much of the tension and fallout originated from the fact that two unusual guys in their twenties were unable to communicate. Joe and Leon each felt betrayed by the other and would never have a substantial talk about their feelings about the tour.

"Within the next couple of months, I started getting a lot of bad press about how I had taken advantage of him," Leon said in one of his final interviews, with Alanna Nash for *Penthouse*. "As a matter of fact, when we were doing the show, Denny came up to me one day and said, 'You know, you're going to be accused of career profiteering.' I said, 'What the hell is that?' He said, 'Where an unknown guy takes advantage of somebody's fame for his own use.' I said, 'Oh wow, complicated.' I just kept thinking that Joe was going to step forward and say, 'All the stuff that they say in the press isn't true. That's not what happened.' But he never did. So maybe he thought that too."

"People said [Leon] was trying to upstage Joe and take over the show," said Leon's widow, Jan Bridges. "That wasn't where he was coming from at all. It hurt him until the day he died. . . . People were mad at Leon because they were thinking that he was this big badass guy. Leon was just so excited to be playing with Joe. He wanted to do his best. He wanted the band to do their best. He wanted Joe to have a great show."

"[Joe] started off okay; the tour started off okay," said Chris Stainton. "There were so many drugs being taken. They gave him cocaine and all sorts of stuff, all this weird stuff. And he seemed, to me, like he was losing his mind a bit. He was losing it in those days, and I don't know how he persevered, but he did somehow. It was a shame, really. People were just giving him anything. And Grandmaster Leon didn't really take anything. He was always well together. We had some cocaine, and I offered him some, and he said, 'No, thanks. It gums up my works.'"

Hot off the Mad Dogs tour, Eric Clapton snatched up the killer rhythm section of Jim Gordon and Carl Radle for Derek and the Dominos, the new band he formed with Bobby Whitlock; the one album they produced, *Layla and Other Assorted Love Songs*, marked Clapton's artistic apex. Bobby Keys and Jim Price became adjunct members of the Rolling Stones from 1970 to 1973. They all contributed to George Harrison's magnum opus, *All Things Must Pass*, released in the fall of 1970.

"[Keys] got the job with the Rolling Stones—him and Jim Price—primarily 'cause Jagger saw him in the *Mad Dogs & Englishmen* movie," Leon said years later.

Already an in-demand session player when he joined the Mad Dogs tour, Jim Keltner's calendar in 1971 alone included records for John Lennon, George Harrison, the Everly Brothers, Barbra Streisand, Albert King, Sergio Mendes, Bill Withers, and Leon's own *Shelter People* LP. Keltner said, "I remember thinking, 'Oh, I wish that night had been recorded or that [show].' They were just magical. Of course, that didn't happen. That's the main thing. We were so young. I came away from that tour thinking, 'Oh, my God. We escaped with our lives.' It was crazy. We were all just way too out of control."

Keltner also played drums on the debut album for Rita Coolidge. Understandably, Rita was the one least prone to nostalgia when recalling the tour: "What became evident was that the friendship, and the camaraderie, and sheer tightness of Delaney & Bonnie and Friends was unique because the Mad Dogs tour was nothing like that. We didn't choose to be together; we were thrown together for the tour. Everything about it was kind of upside down, with everybody competing to take over the stage."

The comedown was harder for some than for others. Keltner battled substances for a while. Jim Gordon continued his singular drug-fueled descent into madness. While living in London with the Dominos, he became romantically involved with Chris O'Dell. "The minute we met, we already knew about each other because of Leon and Rita," O'Dell said. "In some ways, it was a total rebound. It was like, 'Oh, I'll get back at them.'" But then he chased after her through an apartment with a knife and likely would have killed her if she hadn't escaped. "He was such a nutcase," she said.

During and after Mad Dogs, Carla Brown was in a relationship with Jimmy Markham while also intermittently with Leon. Brown was dancing at the Classic Cat with Kay Poorboy and Francine Brockey and soon went off the deep end with drugs. "[Leon] really thought she had a good ear, and he would send her to go listen to people," said Blue Bridges-Fox. Leon asked her to attend a Dr. John recording session and report back what she heard. Blue continued, "Mac Rebbenack, Dr. John, was shooting up, and she walked in on him and a bunch of people, and she said, 'What are y'all doing?' and he said, 'You don't want any of this.' And she pulled a hundred bucks out of a pocket and said, 'Yes, I do.' She wasn't going to be not cool. He shot her up, and she used, for four or five years."

"I remember when everybody started using, [Leon] was so disappointed," Brown herself recalled. "And I knew it broke his heart when I did. He went over to Europe, and they were all using." She shook her head. Even Carl "Mr. Clean" Radle later developed a drug habit.

But the Mad Dogs tour launched successful careers for nearly the entire band. "[Mad Dogs] has been a calling card for me ever since," Polland said. "I was in a much better position to get a solo record deal. . . . Being handpicked by Leon gave me a kind of sense of confidence."

Matthew Moore had some of his songs recorded by Cocker, Yvonne Elliman, and other big stars. But it was all anticlimactic. He eventually left the business and managed a taxi company in Orange County. "I will always remember I loved that tour," he said. "That was one of the biggest things that ever happened to me in my life, and it kind of wrecked me because everything else kind of seemed smaller in comparison. That was quite an ordeal."

Despite more decades of harrowing abuse and self-sabotage that would normally kill a career, if not the person himself, Cocker later ascended to worldwide superstardom, in fits and starts, with a little help from his friends, indeed. During the singer's post–Mad Dogs self-imposed exile, Jim Price tracked down Cocker in England and brought the hollowed-out singer back to Los Angeles and into a studio. One song they recorded was Billy Preston's "You Are So Beautiful," a *Billboard* Top 5 hit for Cocker.

But in the immediate wake of the tour, Leon became the biggest star. "It was just that persona that showed up at A&M the day that we started rehearsals and did our photograph for the album," Rita said. "He was not, you know, he just didn't *do* that. He wasn't a strutter. The outfit was holding him together." Like Superman's cape.

Chapter 16

Shelter People

LEON ARRIVED HOME IN THE spring of 1970 as a bona fide rock star. His debut album was in the midst of a nineteen-week run on the *Billboard* Top 200, peaking at number sixty on May 2, and he was receiving rave reviews. "Until the release of this first disk on the new Shelter label . . . Russell's work was familiar only to music business insiders," wrote Don Heckman in the *New York Times*. "Leon Russell's first solo outing represents the belated debut of a major talent."

The coverage was not limited to American publications. "This is Russell's first album and it runs the risk of being regarded merely for the number of 'super-stars' assembled on the various tracks," wrote Rob Partridge in the British weekly *Record Mirror*. "Which would be a great pity. More than anyone, the album belongs to Russell. . . . Not one dud track—a happy, beautiful album."

Leon's new band, the Shelter People, took some of the Mad Dogs & Englishmen players and added others, like his friend John Gallie on organ. Gallie also played bass on a Fender Rhodes bass keyboard. Joey Cooper, from the Shindogs, was on rhythm guitar, and Don Preston played lead guitar, and both sang backup. Jim Horn played sax on some of the early gigs, and Kathi McDonald, another former Ikette, joined Claudia Lennear on backing vocals. Lennear and McDonald became fast friends, and Claudia credits Kathi with inspiring Claudia's hippie-chic style on the Mad Dogs & Englishmen tour. "She lived in Marin in a hippie commune, which was fine with me because I was making a transition from R&B," Lennear said.

"The deal," said Don Preston, "was [that] the seven of us would get 5 percent apiece. All the money would go into a pile, minus hotels, flights, roadies, and so forth. Until we made some money, Leon would front us a hundred dollars a week, with the understanding that when we started making money, Leon would be recompensated. It was totally based on trust. There was also an agreement that when we had enough money, there would be a trust fund set up. In the event someone quit, you would get the money, but you had to sign an agreement that you no longer had a part of the band's business, such as record royalties."

Though scaled back from the rock orchestra of Mad Dogs & Englishmen, Leon kept the big ensemble concept rolling, a revue format where he'd give individual members their moments in the spotlight. He was the preacher, they the choir.

"I remember him telling me why he picked the guys for that band that he did," Peter Nicholls said. "I said, 'Why not Jim Keltner on drums?' He said, 'Wait till you've worked with Chuck Blackwell for six months, and you'll see why these guys are in the band.' He wanted a band that would be the most *smoking* band of all time. And he was right—*live*. They couldn't play worth a damn in the studio, but live, it was a whole other thing."

After Mad Dogs, many of the hangers-on crashed at Leon's, including the "Tulsa girls," Francine Brockey and Kay Poorboy, and their friends. By now, Emily Smith was a constant presence. By the end of the Mad Dogs tour, Claudia Lennear and Leon had become romantically involved. His relationship with Carla Brown was hot and cold. Claudia moved into Skyhill. But she was not used to the sort of lifestyle that the domicile was known for. "By the time Carla moved in, I had moved out because it kind of wasn't quite the values I had been brought up with," Claudia said. "I'm not saying it was bad, and I'm not saying I'm a prude, either. I'm just saying I like my privacy in my house, and I don't want to be living with twenty other people going to my closet trying to find some shoes to wear."

Claudia stayed at Skyhill a month or two. "When the Tulsa people started moving in, I went and got my hat and coat. . . . I got along with everybody. I never had any disagreements with anyone. I didn't have any disagreements with Leon. Actually, I just let him know that that wasn't quite my cup of chamomile. So, I just found my own apartment, that's all. Leon and I always had a relationship, I think since we first met. But during those days, we were in the hippie days, when things were open, relationships were open. That's another thing I didn't like. I was always worried about having relationships with somebody, and they were having relationships with two or three other people. I'm not trying to sound all proper, but I'm just saying that it was always a worry for me."

Lennear, who was said to have inspired "Brown Sugar" and who would stir David Bowie to write "Lady Grinning Soul" for her, was also a muse for Leon. "Of course, during the seventies," she said, "it was common for rock star girlfriends to have songs written about them. Leon and I shared literature, culture, and music respectfully. He was such a great person in terms of his musical intellect and social wit. It was always amazing and whimsical to me how, in private, he would refer to himself as being a self-professed hillbilly, as if that wasn't good enough. I loved him musically, at any rate."

His workload was tremendous. In addition to working on his follow-up album, Leon was still promoting his debut and mixing the Joe Cocker *Mad Dogs & Englishmen* live LP with Glyn Johns and Denny Cordell. "Jerry Moss had a meeting with Denny and Leon," Johns said. "They said, 'We don't have an album; it's all rubbish.' Obviously, Jerry had invested a substantial amount of money into shooting the film. Without the album, there was no film. Jerry, he's got a bit of a situation and says, 'If I was to bring someone else in that we all agreed to, would you give it a shot to save the album?' They said, 'Who?' He said me, and they both agreed. I trotted over to LA. The whole thing about my involvement [is that it] was done as a favor to Jerry."

Johns mixed the record for a flat fee. "I delivered the album, and Jerry said, 'Well, I'd love to give you a royalty, but I can't because there are too many people already on Joe's contract that have to be paid a royalty. The list is as long as your bloody arm.'"

The two recorded shows that were under consideration were the New York Fillmore East and Santa Monica. "For some reason, the concert in LA [Santa Monica] wasn't very good at all," Johns said. However, Johns thought the New York show was extraordinary, bursting with fresh energy and gusto. "Obviously, in the interim, they'd done loads of other concerts, perhaps where they'd felt they played better, or the concert had been better. Joe, Denny, and Leon decided they didn't think they had an album at all, but it was good enough. They were wrong, basically. They were too close [to it]."

Johns continued: "The biggest problem was the choir. They had every hanger-on in the industry onstage with them, who were not singers, of course. They were all stoners, and bloody hell, none of them could sing. It was awful, the racket that crowd made. It was an obvious thing for me to get the original core of the choir, who were all really good singers, to come back in and help it up on their own, which is what I did." Daniel Moore, Rita Coolidge, Claudia Lennear, and a few others came in to overdub new vocals to mix with the live choir.

Johns had worked with Leon on his solo debut album and, though taken by his musical skills, became disenchanted by Leon's personality by the end of mixing *Mad Dogs*. "Leon, without any question—and Denny probably, to a degree—used the Joe Cocker tour to promote Leon. Big time, which I found a little distasteful. . . . No one had taken Joe into consideration at all in this whole process. Nobody! I said, when I finished mixing, 'I'm not going to give anyone these tapes until Joe's heard them and approved of it.' I got hold of Joe, and he came in and listened—rather sadly—but it was OK, and he left. Then I released the tapes. He could have been perfectly fit and well, and it wouldn't have made any difference."

But of course Leon benefited; this wasn't an act of charity. "Both are true," Johns acknowledged. "The band that Leon put together, and the arrangements, and everything else, were phenomenal. It was a great show, without any question, slightly put in danger by the drug abuse. But I'll admit he did a brilliant job. But not quite to the extent that he shoved himself in the front all the time."

Johns is also credited on the second Leon album, *Leon Russell and the Shelter People*. This was tied to the *Mad Dogs* film soundtrack via the gorgeous postmortem "The Ballad of Mad Dogs and Englishmen." "I got him to write for the credits of the film," Johns said. "We did that specifically for the film, and they also used it on the [*Leon Russell and the Shelter People*] album." Johns would not work again with Leon. "He was not a nice bloke. I think as he got on, he got more and more unpleasant."

"That 'Ballad of Mad Dogs and Englishmen' was written originally from a poem that I wrote for the program," Leon said. "And they wanted me to turn it into the song. So there was a guy called Nick DeCaro who was gonna be the string writer. And so I actually sang the poem with three different melodies and let him pick out the one he liked. And that's the one we used."

A melancholy goodbye to that momentous tour, "The Ballad of Mad Dogs and Englishmen" suffers not at all separated from the film. Leon's romantic lyric effectively distills two months into four leisurely minutes, peppered with just enough in-jokes to bring us along for the ride. Leon balances it with nostalgic notes of confusion, aching regret, and ultimate acceptance. The recording is lushly orchestrated with strings arranged by DeCaro, Leon's colleague from his session days.

Peter Nicholls was quickly learning how to engineer recordings at Leon's home studio for his second album. Nicholls hoped to stay in America permanently and work with Denny and Leon. The album's sessions were recorded at Skyhill, Muscle Shoals, Island Studios in London, and a session at A&M with Glyn Johns. Recordings started in earnest at the end of summer 1970.

The Shelter People band rehearsed for two weeks at Skyhill before their first gig at Anaheim Stadium on June 14, opening for the Who, John Sebastian, and Blues Image. "What I remembered most was Leon and Denny hustling to get that gig," Lennear said. The poster for the show reads: INTRODUCING HIS FIRST SOLO APPEARANCE: LEON RUSSELL.

Ann Moses wrote in the British *New Musical Express*, "Leon Russell . . . had the audience dancing from the time he walked onstage, underneath an enormous top hat encircled with roses."

It was a time when ballrooms and arenas were dominated by the likes of Led Zeppelin, the Who, and the Stones, all notable for loose performances of loud, blues-based rock. As with his blueprints for the Mad Dogs tour, Leon's shows in the early 1970s retained a loose feel, but with deceivingly meticulous arrangements, more choreographed performance components, precisely executed parts, and tight harmonies. Still, there was reasonable room for spontaneity. "He did not tell you what to do," Lennear said. "You had the framework of the song, and then whatever you did within that, that was free rein. He never admonished anyone. He always accepted what they contributed."

He followed up the Anaheim show by opening for Traffic for three nights at the Fillmore West on June 30 through July 2. In addition to Blackwell the band had a second drummer, Bob Lanning. "He played three or four gigs with us," Don Preston said. "He was literally very stiff. I think we were playing at the Fillmore West. He hurt his back so bad that he couldn't play. We were all worried about the gig that night. Someone said they thought Keltner was in town. KSAN broadcast an alert; if anyone knew where Keltner was, tell him to call Leon. No such luck. The band was so hot with just Chuck, everyone just went, 'Chuck is all the drummer we need.'"

Leon joined Delaney & Bonnie for *Motel Shot*, released in June. Before Mad Dogs, he and others—including Joe Cocker, Duane Allman, Dave Mason, and Gram Parsons—helped re-create the informal sing-alongs that Delaney & Bonnie and Friends were known for on the road. The music would carry over from the stage into motel rooms, buses, and even commercial flights. They eventually realized they had to bring the project into a proper recording studio, where they managed to re-create the same down-home essence by taking a live approach: various voices and instruments in one room, little or no isolation, few overdubs. The resulting album is a joy.

Leon's piano work is typically stellar, especially on a divine gospel arrangement of "Faded Love," the Bob Wills song Patsy Cline made famous, on which Delaney demonstrates why he was one of the great blue-eyed soul singers. Leon cowrote the LP's final track, "Lonesome and a Long Way from Home," from Eric Clapton's solo debut.

In July, Leon and the Shelter People hit the road, headlining the Eastown Theatre in Detroit on the eleventh and twelfth. On July 18, they played at Soldier Field in Chicago on a festival lineup that included the MC5, the Stooges, Funkadelic, and headliners Chicago (the band). Lynn Van Matre wrote in a *Chicago Tribune* review, "Until Russell's group enlivened things, the all-day rock concert . . . had been a festival of lethargy rather than life. . . . Russell had stirred the crowd."

On August 1, Leon played the Swing Auditorium in San Bernardino (where the Mad Dogs tour had ended a few months before) for Denny Cordell's birthday. Joe Cocker came along to help celebrate but did not perform. *LA Times* pop critic Robert Hilburn called Leon "something of an underground musical legend in Los Angeles for years . . . his hair well down past his shoulders and a long beard that gives him something of a Rasputin appearance, is the hottest thing to hit rock since, well, Cocker himself. He's actually playing second on the bill on this particular evening (to Procol Harum), but he has been stealing almost every show he has done (including, some feel, the recent Who concert in Anaheim) since he hit the concert trail a few weeks ago."

"It is really amazing to me to have played all those clubs where people came to drink and didn't care about your music," Leon says in the article, "and now have thousands of people come to listen to what you are playing."

In August, the *Mad Dogs & Englishmen* LP was released. *Rolling Stone* gave it a ho-hum review. But in 2021, Jon Landau recalled, "I always thought that was just a great live album. That incredible 'Honky Tonk Women' into 'Cry Me a River' just blew me away because I had no interest in standards. I was much more interested in those as I grew up. When it goes to a dead stop, and Leon does the count, and they come back in—my head was spinning. Certain things stay very vividly in mind. That's one of them."

Leon headed to England later that month for an action-packed few weeks. Many of the erstwhile Mad Dogs were there, working on records with George Harrison, Dr. John, and Eric Clapton. In London, Leon laid down two new tracks at Island Studios with Andy Johns, Glyn's younger brother. Credited on the album as "Friends in England," the backing band was Carl Radle, Jim Gordon, Jim Price (on organ), and Chris Stainton (guitar). They recorded one of Leon's early standout rockers, "Alcatraz."

The song was inspired by current events. The previous year, seventy-eight Native Americans, calling themselves Indians of All Tribes, took over Alcatraz Island and occupied it for nineteen months to protest against the government's illegal theft of Native lands. Leon takes the voice of a young Native American who "used to dance for ABC" (on a show like *Shindig!*) but is now homeless on the streets of San Francisco.

Leon visited George Harrison at Friar Park, where he was reunited with Chris O'Dell (for whom Harrison would name a 1973 B-side, "Miss O'Dell," also the name of her memoir). She was not yet over their relationship and hoped it could be rekindled, but Leon had moved on. "George played his new album, which was *All Things Must Pass*," O'Dell said. Like a middle schooler passing notes between two shy friends, O'Dell helped facilitate Leon's early recording of the then-new Harrison song "Beware of Darkness," which he also recorded with the Friends in England. "We were all sitting around in a room with no furniture in it. Leon went, 'I would love to record that.' I said, 'Well, why don't you ask him?' He didn't feel comfortable. I went across the room and whispered to George, 'Leon would really like to record that.' He went, 'That would be great.'"

Leon's cover of "Beware of Darkness" is an inventive recasting that would have suited Harrison himself. Harrison's own Phil Spector–produced version is a relaxed ballad in the same groove as "Something." But Leon's is an intense, multitempo, richly textured recording, with Indian-inspired tabla drum and sitar-like sounds. "That was an illusion," Leon said. "I was playing that on a thumbtack piano and Jim Gordon was playing tablas. He's an amazing player." His approach on the verses is in the same ballpark as Harrison's, but Leon frames them with a rapidly strummed and hammered drone. Gordon kicks into a backbeat for the bridge. As the drone builds to a crescendo, Leon takes Eastern spirituality to a double-time American gospel realm.

At Friar Park, Leon had something like a spiritual awakening. "After we 'just said yes' to a Jamaican-sized portion of the Holy Moroccan Ganja," Leon wrote, "George treated us to a tour of the quasi-dungeons that ran for about a mile underneath the house . . . the tunnels deepened until they held four or five feet of water. Originally, they had supported small boats in a sort of tunnel-of-love motif. Wearing galoshes, we waded through the water and mud to a point where the tunnels opened onto a pristine lake. George walked out across it, on top of the water, in the style of Peter Sellers's character in the movie *Being There*. Given the state I was in, I was convinced I was with a true extraterrestrial. As it turned out the lake was made of concrete and the water was only one and a half inches deep." He explained, "I thought, 'Oh, my God—George Harrison really is a religious figure!'"

But spiritual experiences, real or imagined, did not wash the materialism away from our budding rock star. In England, Leon bought a Rolls-Royce Silver Cloud and shipped it back to LA. His main ride into the mid-seventies, this acquisition was mentioned in "Leon Russell: King of the Delta Rockers," an interview he did with *Melody Maker*. In the article, Leon also describes a recording he made during his visit, with Harrison and Ringo, which consisted of loose jamming that he hoped to be able to build into a song. Most of the recording for *Leon Russell and the Shelter People* would be done over September and the winter.

Back in California at the end of the summer, Leon met his fan Elton

John at Elton's storied debut at the Troubadour. Hollywood was accustomed to hype, but rarely had there been such a buildup for a new performer. The twenty-three-year-old Englishman came in with his small backing band on August 25 to commence an eight-show, six-night run. He had just signed with UNI Records, the home of Neil Diamond, which partially explains why Diamond introduced Elton onstage. The audience on night one included such celebrities as Quincy Jones, Peggy Lipton, Linda Ronstadt, Randy Newman, Brian Wilson and Mike Love of the Beach Boys, and Crosby, Stills & Nash. Robert Hilburn penned a famously glowing *LA Times* review that was syndicated nationally, breaking the star across America almost overnight.

Leon came down the second night. Elton spotted him near the end of the set—he could not mistake the distinctive figure his hero cut. "Second night at the Troubadour in August 1970. I'm playing 'Burn Down the Mission' and I open my eyes, and I see him in the second row; how can you miss him? That hair! And I kind of temporarily—I kind of froze for a nanosecond. It was quite a menacing look. And he was so sweet and so nice. He couldn't have been more encouraging to me. He took me on the road, and I played gigs with him. When you're an emerging artist and someone you idolize pays you compliments when you're beginning, it gives you that feeling of validation, which is so important."

In a 1973 interview with *Rolling Stone*, Elton said, "At that time I slept and drank Leon Russell. I mean I still really like him, but at that time I regarded him as some kind of a god. And I saw him and I just stopped. He said, 'Keep on,' and he shouted something, and I said, 'Oh fuck,' and he said, 'Come up to the house tomorrow.'" In an interview for this book, Elton said, "I never went up to his house in LA, never. And it's probably good because it was a big druggie house. I went to his house in Tulsa after we played there once. I think that's when my drummer, Nigel, started going out with Claudia Lennear. He went out with Claudia for quite a while. But I really didn't do drugs until I started the *Caribou* album, in '73."

The day after Elton's first Troubadour show, Bill Graham offered him the highest amount ($5,000) ever to a new artist to play his Fillmore East. Hilburn, who had anointed Elton in his concert review, followed up with, in the September 13 Sunday Arts section, a piece calling Elton "a superstar." Elton is quoted in the piece: "I was really excited when people like Leon Russell started coming by."

In September 1970, Leon led the Shelter People to Muscle Shoals Sound Studio in Sheffield, Alabama. It was the facility that the renegade house band from Jim Hall's Fame Studios—Jimmy Johnson, David Hood, Roger Hawkins, and Barry Beckett—had opened in 1969. Within a year, it was *the* place for rock 'n' roll pilgrims to trek in hopes of capturing some of that mojo that the house band had provided to soul artists like Percy Sledge, Arthur Alexander, James Carr, Wilson Pickett, Etta James, the Staple Singers, and Aretha Franklin. A converted coffin-maker's shop across from a graveyard, this unassuming place was where some of the greatest rock 'n' roll of the 1970s was created, including one-third of the Rolling Stones' *Sticky Fingers* and classics by Willie Nelson, Lynyrd Skynyrd, Jimmy Cliff, Bob Seger, Paul Simon, and dozens more.

Don Nix had been working on his solo record there when he brought Joe Cocker home to Memphis to recuperate after Mad Dogs. "I brought [Cocker] to my little hippie apartment here in Memphis for a couple of weeks, and then that's when I was working at Muscle Shoals." In November, Cocker worked there on tracks, including the excellent "High Time We Went," shortly after Leon's sessions.

Leon and Denny somehow squeezed in time at Muscle Shoals during a very busy September, bringing the whole band, and Emily Smith as a chef. "I remember when they came in here, they had been out on the Mad Dogs & Englishmen tour, and so it was like a real freak-show circus coming through our studio," said Hood. "I mean, they were crazy!"

They partied, jammed, and fished for a couple of days before the sessions. "He [Leon] rented this house on the Tennessee River, a big old house," Nix said. Hood said, "There were some houses that the guys would rent and stay in for a while. Jimmy Johnson and another friend bought a house on the Tennessee River for musicians to come stay. There were several different houses." Duane Allman had a place there as well.

"I don't know *what* Muscle Shoals was all about," Lennear said, laughing. "There were a lot of trees and a lot of white people. I don't want to get vulgar, but I remember one of the guys in the rhythm section telling me, 'Claudia, all we have to do down here is fish and fuck.'"

The house on the river was about four or five miles from the studio, and Leon wrote some songs out there late at night. Once in the studio, he set up the band as if they were performing, with PA speakers as monitors instead of headphones. They recorded everything live. "No one had seen that much energy released in such a small space before," Nix observed. "And that, mixed with some strange pills Kay Poorboy had flown in from New Orleans, made it almost more than one could stand."

"At Muscle Shoals, everybody was so on top of what they were doing," said Lennear. "We were so impressed with those guys. If anyone ever asks me, what was the best studio I ever had the fortune to play in, I would always say Muscle Shoals. I love that rhythm section. When you know somebody, you can finish their sentences. They had that same sort of ESP when they played together. Somebody just kicked off with whatever the rhythm was gonna be, whatever the tempo was gonna be, and everybody just fell in place. They usually got it on the first or second take, at least no more than three times. And so humble, these Southern guys, you know; take life easy; nobody gets nervous. They talk slow."

"The magic takes place anytime that you have a group of people that are together every day and that share a common frame of reference," Leon said. "The fact that it's in Miami or Alabama—I think it's just where those people are from."

But it wasn't until Denny Cordell came in with Leon that the studio's house band came to be known as the Muscle Shoals Swampers. Denny had heard Leon describe the ensemble's "funky, soulful, Southern swamp sound," and that's how he credited their contributions to *Leon Russell and the Shelter People*, bestowing the nickname in the credits on the LP sleeve. "Denny took the notes of what musicians played on which songs," said David Hood, bass player and co-owner of the studio. "He had the Tulsa crew, and then he listed 'the Muscle Shoals Swampers.' And we got a gold record for that record, and it said on there, 'For the Muscle shoals swampers,' or something like that. And the guys from Lynyrd Skynyrd saw it on our wall, and that's why they put us in their 'Sweet Home Alabama.'" The famous lyric goes, "In Muscle Shoals they have the Swampers / And they've been known to pick a song or two."

Wayne Perkins was a Muscle Shoals session player who had contributed to Bob Marley & the Wailers' *Catch a Fire* album and would do the same for the Rolling Stones a couple of years later, on *Black and Blue*. He would join Leon's bands in 1973–1974. Perkins said, "Leon came up with a term 'Swampers' for the Muscle Shoals rhythm section. I was sitting next to him when he did that. He said, 'That's what we'll call you!' 'Well,

Okay.' But that was like Leon; he was that way. He named something; he could call it, and boom, that was it." He dubbed the non-Swamper musicians "The Tulsa Tops."

"Shortly after that," Perkins continued, "Ronnie Van Zant and them were in Muscle Shoals recording Skynyrd's first album, and I had a copy of Leon's album. I showed it to Ronnie. Leon had a song on there called 'Home Sweet Oklahoma,' which is where Ronnie got the idea for 'Sweet Home Alabama.'" (Though Perkins would tour with Leon, he never contributed to any of his studio albums.)

The Shelter People were in Muscle Shoals about a week. "I fell asleep in the studio on a couch during an all-night session while Leon continued to work, and when I woke up, he said he'd been working on a couple of songs that he proceeded to play for me," said Emily Smith. "The first one was 'Sweet Emily' and the second was 'She Smiles Like a River.' He had written both songs about me, and at first, I was mortified that he spent the whole night writing these songs about me, but then I realized this was Leon's way to tell me what I meant to him, and I was touched and honored beyond words."

"She had fallen asleep in the control room and was snoring," Leon said. "We had an idea to write a song about her and have it playing when she woke up," he said. "Sweet Emily" is a loping Ray Charles–via–New Orleans ballad, an ode to his friend, the rock he could always depend on.

But "She Smiles Like a River" offers a glimpse into Leon's depression, described in starkly poetic terms. Contrary to Smith's assertion, Lennear said it was she who was the main inspiration for "She Smiles Like a River." Claudia and Leon were involved at this time, while he was on a break with Carla. And several lines suggest something more romantic than the deep friendship, even sibling-like relationship, Leon had with Emily.

Nevertheless, Lennear explained, "Emily, especially, *really* got Leon through a lot of his emotional problems. Emily always had the right words to say. She always had a great perspective on life, on the band, on the music we were doing. Between her and Carla, they would really keep Leon's spirits up."

Some of the tracks were recorded with the Swampers rhythm section: the country-flavored "She Smiles Like a River" and "Home Sweet Oklahoma," the latter the most plainly autobiographical of Leon's songs to that point. The first verse is the lament of a somewhat provincial young man, still wet behind the ears, making his way to Hollywood, only to get wrapped up in and let down by the fast life. Then it snaps into a strut for the chorus, where Leon sings, "Well, I'm going back to Tulsa just a-one more time," which he, in fact, would soon do.

"That second album was a weird one," said Peter Nicholls, who had never engineered or produced a record before. "A lot of basic tracks for that were done down in Muscle Shoals, which was a huge eye-opener for me. I loved it there. Yeah, serious business. But we didn't really get anything serious going."

Nicholls explained further: "We took those tapes [back to Skyhill], but then we realized that they were quality, but they had no fire. There was nothing in it. Those guys [the Swampers] were pickers, you know, they just played. It was okay. 'What are we playing today, Leon?' They just played, and they played it brilliantly, but it didn't have any soul at all." Not many have returned from a session at Muscle Shoals with anything less than soulful. But sometimes things don't quite click on tape. "So we took it back to Skyhill and stuck on some soul, and that's when I became a proper recording engineer because it was just me and Leon. The rap in 'Stranger in a Strange Land' was recorded in the toilet because I couldn't get a proper echo anyplace else. And afterwards I said, 'That's pretty good, Leon. You want to try it again, for real?' He said, 'Fuck no, I can't speak.'"

Written with Don Preston, "Stranger in a Strange Land" was inspired by the 1961 science fiction novel of the same name by Robert A. Heinlein. The book, which has not held up well over the intervening decades, is a tedious *Playboy*-era lampoon of religion, politics, and sexual mores. But it's easy to see how it would appeal to someone who straddled particular subcultures of the early sixties—the Hollywood lounge scene, hip Lenny Bruce fans, futurists, and erstwhile beatniks ready to embrace the post-Pill hedonism and free-love aspects of hippie culture—guys like Leon.

Heinlein had taken the title from a Bible passage: "When a stranger resides with you in your land, you shall not do him wrong. The stranger who resides with you shall be to you as the native among you, and you shall love him as yourself, for you were strangers in the land of Egypt." The song's lyric is more in line with this biblical inspiration. Don Preston said he and Leon wrote it while staying at the house of "some benefactor" on Grand Lake in Oklahoma.

The Shelter People excel on the track, with Blackwell and Radle particularly locked in. Leon's voice is distorted on this gospel-like arrangement, which is also peppered with Moog synth lines and Mellotron (or Chamberlin) strings. He added those extras when he took the record down to Ardent Studios in Memphis to mix, with John Fry and Terry Manning. "I was very into the Moog synthesizer at that point," said Manning, who had traveled to Trumansburg, New York, to study with Bob Moog on how to operate the device. "I used it on the Big Star record, the first album, and I think it was on the second album as well. I was putting it on the Staple Singers, all sorts of stuff. I was explaining it to Leon, and he hadn't had one yet. He was into new things like the Chamberlin, so he really wanted to know about it. He wanted it on 'Stranger in a Strange Land.' It took both of us, because of changing things and playing it, and got it on that before we mixed it."

The "rap," as Nicholls described it, has Leon up on the secular pulpit, speak-singing to his congregation. It's inspired, stirring, and another big step in creating Leon's rock star preacher persona. Heinlein's novel "was the first science fiction book I ever read," Leon said. "A lot of times my songs are tributes; they're based on other songs, or on books, or on other things I've heard in my life that mean something to me, and I actually thought that was a pretty astonishing take on religion, actually . . . religious industrialism. My hometown of Tulsa is a sort of a Mecca of religious industrialism, TV preachers, that sort of thing. I've always been vaguely interested in those guys."

"He was going onstage doing that preacher thing, that evangelical rock 'n' roll," Nicholls said. "The funny thing was, where that came from was, when he first started out as Leon Russell, he was really boring onstage. He was *so* boring. He used to play a song, 'Thank you very much [long pause]. My next song will be called blah blah.' It was *so* boring. Little Richard opened for Leon at the Fillmore West, and it was ridiculous. You know, Leon was so boring, but Richard, what can you say? Richard was Richard. One day, at some arena in Baltimore, we were walking up the ramp and there's a wild-eyed acid kid who came up to Leon and said, 'Man, you're the Prince of Peace! It's so cool, man!' And Leon *got* it."

Leon described a separate similar incident: "Some guy came up to me in San Francisco and asked—he told me that he'd quit turning on because he'd heard 'Roll Away the Stone.' 'Is that what that meant?' And I told him 'If that's what it means to you, then that's fine, but that's not what it means to me.' And he said, 'What does it mean to you?' That's not the reason that I do it, so I can go out and explain."

"Leon suddenly figured, 'Maybe if I do the evangelical thing, they'll like it.' And it transformed it," Nicholls said. "Suddenly we stopped playing to two hundred people in some stupid club. We're playing fifteen thousand, twenty thousand people in a basketball arena anywhere in the South. . . . It was that transformation, that's when it all turned around, was he suddenly decided, 'I'm just gonna do what I knew when I was growing up as a kid in Oklahoma, you know? Bible-thumping gospel guys, and I'll just take that and do rock 'n' roll.'"

It *was* just an act. Leon was agnostic. Answering an interviewer about his religious background in the Protestant Church, he said, "I make it a habit of trying to be really aware of the things I love and the things I hate, and I use them all equally."

Bobby Whitlock said that Leon was conscious about crafting his persona. "He asked me, when he was putting this thing together; you know, he's kind of finding himself, starting his solo role, he asked me about it. My dad was a Southern Baptist preacher and [Leon] asked me about it, how he preached, and I said, 'I can't do that; that's not what I do. But just look at these hellfire brimstone preachers. That's what my dad did. That's how he did it.'"

Leon had *duende*—a Spanish term often used to describe flamenco performers with an almost supernatural power to draw in audiences. "I was in the Forum one night with a full house, and I got into one of those call-and-answer-responses things, where I'd say something, and the audience would do whatever I told them to do. I'd say something else, and they'd do that. In a moment of silence, I said, 'You guys gotta be careful with this stuff because Adolf Hitler did it too. He did it the same way I'm doing it. So you just have to be careful when you get caught up in the frenzy of it, that someone's not giving you a load of bullshit.'"

Lennear noted: "He was, in many ways, very shy. On the other hand, he was very outgoing. When he was on that stage, it was like egomania. There was no way he was not in charge, did not love what he was doing, and playing to the best of his ability, and knew what everybody was doing, and had the whole show in control."

Fourth song on the A-side, warming up with Kathi McDonald's bluesy melisma and the sound of the tape swooping up to speed, "Crystal Closet Queen" is an amped-up, grinding throwback boogie, an homage to one of Leon's heroes, Little Richard. "All I got with me is my faith in Jesus to show me every step of the way / Sticks can't burn me, fire can't turn me away from my rock and roll road." Like Jerry Lee Lewis, another pillar of Leon's foundation, Little Richard struggled with the tension between the secular and the sacred, swearing off rock 'n' roll more than once before returning to the music. "Christ-haunted," as Flannery O'Connor so eloquently put it.

The Pixies' leader, Black Francis (aka Charles Thompson), grew up as a big fan of Leon and took some influence in some of his vocalizing. "The tempo is just so good, so magical, and so right," he said. "There's a lot of love in that song for Little Richard."

On the breakneck-tempo "Of Thee I Sing," Leon sings a tormented lyric, a brilliantly patriotic critique of America. While Mad Dogs was out on the road, four students had been shot dead by their own government at Kent State in Ohio. "Mad Dogs was an actual planeload of hippies flying around the country doing gigs almost every night," Don Preston said. There were a few incidents between Mad Dogs shows when they were harassed, even threatened with violence. "Joe and Leon were careful to emphasize that [the tour] was not political at all." Leon did not shy away from current affairs on his own record, though. "Of Thee I Sing" would prove a potent live staple.

The cover of Dylan's "A Hard Rain's A-Gonna Fall" also doesn't shrink from politics, though as with much Dylan, most of the message is cloaked in allegory. Leon's arrangement is what some started to call the "Tulsa Sound," a vaguely defined, relaxed, blues-and-country-informed groove.

Leon also included a cover of Dylan's "It Takes a Lot to Laugh, It Takes a Train to Cry." "I did some songs for him, for his birthday," he said. "I did 'It's All Over Now, Baby Blue,' 'Hard Rain,' and a couple more." There were five Dylan songs altogether; the others were released on the Right Stuff CD reissue of *Leon Russell and the Shelter People.*

Nicholls said the session of covers was not for Dylan's birthday but as a Christmas present. The tape is dated "1/2/1971" with "Tulsa Tops" listed as the artists. They started at two a.m. and finished at six a.m. At the top of the tape box, in big letters, it reads FOR DYLAN. Nicholls recalled, "Carl, myself, Leon, Keltner, Don Preston, we're up at Skyhill, and Leon says,

'Let's make a Christmas record for Bob Dylan.' Why? I don't know. . . . We did 'Hard Rain's A-Gonna Fall,' which, to me, is still as good a track as he ever laid down. That was take two. So we sent that tape to Bob, and Bob comes back and said, 'Come to New York and make a record with us.'" And they would, the following March.

Leon Russell and the Shelter People was mixed at Ardent. Terry Manning said, "Leon loved the way the mixes sounded. He said they sounded louder over the radio."

In October, the *Mad Dogs* album peaked at number two on the album charts in the United States and would be certified gold, both tougher achievements for a double live album than for a standard single studio record. The Shelter People headed out to do a few showcase gigs around LA, mostly in clubs, at the behest of Capitol Records, Shelter's distributor. "Leon didn't want to do that," Nicholls explained. "It was old hat to him. What he wanted was to get out and play on the road. So we got a van and I got some equipment together and we drove mostly up and down the West Coast, to start with."

Leon headlined a bill with Miles Davis at the Fillmore West on October 15, and another over Pink Floyd and Hot Tuna on the eighteenth at the University of California San Diego. Also that month, B. B. King released *Indianola Mississippi Seeds*, recorded with some illustrious rock and pop musicians, including Leon, Carole King, Russ Kunkel, and others. King had recently had crossover success with "The Thrill Is Gone." B. B. included Leon's "Hummingbird" on the album, having been introduced to the song by producer Bill Szymczyk. We hear Leon (who else?) count it off. There is a great jam with Leon, as the two answer each other's parts, on the instrumental "King's Special," over Joe Walsh's funky rhythm guitar. Released as a single from the album, "Hummingbird" made it to twenty-five on the R&B chart and thirty-eight on the pop chart. "We got to the end of the song, played the ending, B. B. started crying," Leon recalled in 2014. "He said, 'Leon, I ain't never had that before.' I said, 'B. B., I ain't never had it either.'"

From one King to another, Leon went into the studio in October with a newly signed artist to Shelter Records, Freddie King. Freddie was already a legend among blues aficionados—his instrumental "Hideaway" was a standard. Likely observing the crossover success of B. B. King (no relation), Freddie's manager, Jack Calmes, recognized his client's appeal to a generation of white kids raised on blues rock and agreed to a multirecord deal with Shelter. Freddie King was one of the primary artists Leon and Denny had set their sights on when forming Shelter.

Rather than record King in LA, Leon and band blocked off time from the road to hop into the blues Mecca, Chess Records studio in Chicago. "This is where all the big blues hits were cut," says Don Nix, who coproduced King's album. "Muddy Waters. Howlin' Wolf. Everybody had cut hits in the studio." But this was not the more famous original studio at 2120 South Michigan Avenue; Chess had moved to 320 East 21st Street in the mid-1960s.

Don Preston noticed on the tour itinerary that they had almost a full week off scheduled in Chicago. "That's good—just lie around and smoke. We were in a hotel corridor, and Leon says, 'We're cutting an album with Freddie King, and I want you to play on it.' I said something like, 'Aw, man,' and Leon says, 'Come on, it'll be good for you.' He was right. We cut *Getting Ready* in four or five days at Chess."

"I was just walking on air," Nix recalled. "I couldn't believe this. It was on the fifth floor. So we go in, we start on Monday. And we're all sitting there, waiting. Freddie's coming up on the elevator. We didn't know what was going to happen, who he was or what he was going to be like; he walked in, this big old guy [King was only thirty-six at the time], with this biggest-ass grin on his face. And he was wonderful. He was just one of the best artists I've ever had anything to do [with]."

Duck Dunn came in to play bass with the Shelter People, and King brought in his touring drummer, Charles "Sugar Boy" Myers. "Freddie was the most aggressive and confident guitar player I had ever heard," Preston recalled. "And it was so much fun working out parts with my good old friend Duck Dunn."

They started the sessions on a Monday, with Leon and Don Nix producing. But the former Chess Records studio was, Leon recalled later, "a substandard studio compared to the one I had in my house. Chess was antiquated and difficult to work in, that's what I remember about that studio the most."

King brought in some ideas for songs, as did Leon and Nix. Everybody clicked, and they almost finished the record in just a few days. They ordered hot chicken every night and had a ball. "It got down to about four days. I said, 'Man, let's all go on the road. We're having so much fun,'"

Nix said. "We're getting the tracks one after the other. 'This is too much fun; let's drag this out as long as we can.'" Nix had produced a song of his, "Going Down," with the Memphis group Moloch. "I wanted to cut it on Freddie, but Leon said, 'Nah, no, that's not good.'"

The Moloch version is sludgy Cream-style blues rock typical of the era—no wonder Leon felt it unsuitable for Freddie King. But Nix was determined: "I got Freddie aside, and I said, 'What do you think about?' I got my guitar, and I played 'Going Down.' But it was a slower version. He said, 'I like that.' So Leon had no choice. But he double-timed it. And it made it a whole different song. And that turned out to be the big hit. That's where 'Going Down' started, it's been recorded over a hundred times, but Freddie started it."

The Freddie King recording is scorching. Leon sets it off hammering a sixteenth-note riff. The flat, dry, and crisp sound of the rhythm track is lacerated with King's treble-heavy lead lines. Gallie's organ pipes through the spaces like shafts of summer evening light in a smoky room. Both drummers set up and played together, locked into an unrelenting mechanical-but-sexy groove. "It's Chuck, and then [King] brought a drummer, Charles Myers, from Dallas," Nix said. "We set them up drum to bass drum, facing each other, and put a mic in the middle. Yeah, it was wonderful. Man, to be in that studio live and to hear that!"

After recording King, Leon and the Shelter People got back on the road through the autumn. Stops included Salt Lake City with Poco; Austin with the Allman Brothers and Chicago; Procol Harum and Ten Years After at the Philadelphia Spectrum; and Boston with Elvin Bishop, a Tulsan who started his career in Chicago. "For the whole first year, it was like they would go on and play for about an hour," Nicholls said. "I mean, the band was just *too* good; you couldn't believe how good they were."

In November, Leon and the Shelter People played a few shows with Elton John, including two nights at the Fillmore East. A few days before, Elton had recorded a live radio set from a studio, later released as *17-11-70* (in America, *11-17-70*). They played two nights together on November 20 and 21. "I went out to watch one of [Elton's sets at the Fillmore East] and said, 'My career's over. This guy is so much better than me,'" Leon said in 2010. "We had tried to get Elton for Shelter Records, but we missed him by a couple of weeks."

Leon came out during Elton's set on the twenty-first and played guitar on a nearly ten-minute version of "Burn Down the Mission." Elton repaid the favor by jamming on "Roll Away the Stone" during Leon's encore. "Fasten your seatbelts," Leon warns as the latter revs up. Elton takes over the piano during the coda while Leon straps on a guitar to take the song home.

While in New York, Leon had an accident and called Don Nix and asked, "Can you come to New York to play the Fillmore for three days? I fell on the street today and cracked a couple of ribs, and I need you to come and take care of me." Nix, who always felt a debt to Leon, caught the next flight out of Memphis. When he got there, he said Leon just "sat, smoked dope, and watched *The Price Is Right*." Seeing Leon so depressed, he felt the need "to call in reinforcements. Duck Dunn arrived the next morning, and his presence seemed to do the trick."

During this tour, Leon would usually start austerely, just himself at the piano for a couple of solo numbers. In New York, he began with his soulful rendition of Bob Dylan's mournful "Girl from the North Country" and "A Song for You." Dylan himself was at one of the Fillmore shows and went backstage. Nix was there and always carried a camera. "Here comes Bob Dylan, and Levon Helm, and Donald Sutherland, four or five people, and they come in and, oh my, it's a big deal now," Nix said. "On the tours we had been playing, like with all these other people, I'd been taking pictures of Leon with them. . . . And at his Skyhill home, he had a wall with all these pictures. He called it his 'star wall.' I wish I had all those pictures now. But [Dylan and entourage] are all in a group in the middle of the room. Everybody else is sitting around. Claudia Lennear's got these cutoff jeans and this halter, you know, I mean, hot as a firecracker. Leon [whispers], 'This should be a good shot for the star wall.' I said, 'All right.' So I took my camera, pulled it up to take the pictures in this group. And Dylan was carrying an umbrella with a sharp tip on it. And he saw me he said, 'Hey, man!' and he almost stuck me . . . went right by my head. And I was so embarrassed. Bless Claudia Lennear." He laughed, remembering. "She stood up, she had her little Daisy Duke cutoff jeans on, and she stuck her butt out and said, 'Fuck Bob Dylan. You can take my picture anytime.'"

"I was just trying to make Don not feel bad," Lennear said. "Because, you know, Bob Dylan is—as much as the world loves him and his music—he's a very difficult personality."

After one of the shows, Nix recalled, "Denny came back and said, 'Paul

Simon wants to meet you.' So he got me, him, and Claudia Lennear, and we went over to Paul Simon's house." On the way over, Nix said a cab driver pulled out a joint and passed it around. Arriving after midnight, Nix said there was just a bit of small talk before Leon and Paul were trading licks on guitars. "The trouble was, Leon was high, and Paul wasn't, and the whole thing turned out to be a wash. They had nothing in common. Nothing. Simon was nice, though, and he even called a limo to take us back to the hotel."

Nicholls said, "Leon could be very smart. He could really have a sharp, smart-ass tongue. I don't think of Leon being academically intelligent, but he knows what the hell's going on. He knows how to converse with anybody if he needs to. But he knows when to play dumb and when to play smart. But Paul Simon was just trying to be *too* cool, right? He was very patronizing with us, and Leon wasn't going for it."

The Shelter People band on these dates was still hot from working together on Mad Dogs. On the radio broadcast recordings, Don Preston sings backups with Claudia and Kathi. Preston seamlessly harmonizes with Leon, even mirroring his vibrato assiduously on "Delta Lady." Leon was still promoting his debut record and riding great reviews. He appeared on the *David Frost Show* in New York in November (broadcast in December). In addition to the Fillmore East radio broadcast, two other long-form recordings capture Leon Russell and the Shelter People as a live band. One is a bootleg album captured by an audience member at the Anaheim Convention Center on December 11, where they performed again with Elton John. And the other was a live in-studio *Homewood Sessions* performance for television.

Jim Horn was with them in Anaheim. "Leon asked me to join the band and be a Shelter Person," Horn said. He was too busy with recording work to accept the full-time touring position, but he did certain gigs as an adjunct member. "I turned down sessions because it was fun to play live with him. There was nothing better than playing live with Leon. Elton opened up for us at a gig that we had outside of Los Angeles. Everybody loved Leon by then. He was already starting to get a big name. And I asked him, 'Who's that guy out there opening up for you?' And he said, 'Oh, his name's Elton John, he's from England.'"

Horn recalled Leon being in a near-meditative state before the show. "He would sit real quiet in his dressing room before each show and not say a word. So I just sat there, didn't say anything either much, and then we got out there and got ready for him, all the Shelter People. When he sat down at his piano, he laid into this music so well that you felt like he was in his own church, preaching."

Leon opened the show with an ironic take on Merle Haggard's "Okie from Muskogee," evoking multilayered interpretations. Haggard's parents had migrated to the Bakersfield area from rural Oklahoma during the Dust Bowl. He recorded his song in character, empathizing with the narrator, but he would later distance himself from the lyric. It wasn't an either-or situation for Haggard; he played it both ways. The character is expertly drawn with some nuance. And, of course, there were also commercial considerations; Haggard knew who was buttering his bread.

In the live recording, Leon gets a rise from the audience with the song. "We don't smoke marijuana in Muskogee," he sings. "We don't make a party out of loving." It's satire, but Leon, an Okie like Haggard, was intimate with this sort of character and would later be an invaluable lieutenant in Willie Nelson's effort to bridge the gap between rock 'n' rollers and country music fans. Lest we forget, this was the same year Leon declared he was going back to "Home Sweet Oklahoma."

The Anaheim show also featured drop-dead versions of songs by Little Richard and Jerry Lee Lewis. On this recording, Leon blends "Great Balls of Fire" into "Of Thee I Sing." While the crowd is at a fever pitch, clapping on every beat of the bar, Leon has the aplomb to stop the band and ad-lib, "It's so strange," before launching into the riff that starts "Of Thee I Sing." He has them right where he wants them, working the audience like an old pro. At the end, there's an early example of his charismatic preaching. "There are too-oo many people in the world today," he sings in a blues style, at which point the crowd erupts. But Leon quiets them, "[*speaking*] Listen to me—[*resuming singing*] that are afraid of each other . . . when too many people stand up and start having a good time," and the crowd responds even more exuberantly. "They're good people, but they just don't understand," he sings. "I want you to keep that in mind." Then they hit the chorus of the song again, repeating it, before Leon stops again, "Oh, it's so strange," with the band punctuating the line, repeating it a couple of times. "But with the help of an artificially induced religious experience," he sings, finishing the song and the set in a crescendo.

It was Leon's biggest show as a headliner. "While Russell has been something of an underground legend in Los Angeles for some time, his work with Joe Cocker . . . and his own Shelter album established him this year as one of rock's top attractions," Robert Hilburn wrote in his review of the Anaheim concert. "Since [Leon and Elton] are both big enough to headline any rock concert in the nation, it is unlikely that they will be on the same program again." Hilburn described the "theatrics" that Elton was quickly becoming famous for and wrote, "There aren't a half dozen people in rock that could successfully follow Elton John. . . . For the next hour, [Leon] brought the audience to its feet time after time with some of the tightest, hardest rock 'n' roll Anaheim has ever heard. . . . It is pointless to try and determine who won. . . . The fact is the audience won."

Another recording from the same month captured video along with audio. The band convened for about six hours at the KCET Homewood Studios at the Vine Street Theater in Hollywood. Produced by Alan Baker and directed by Allan Muir, the show also had an associate producer, Taylor Hackford, who became a Hollywood film director (*An Officer and a Gentleman* and *Ray*). "I'm kind of a child of rock 'n' roll," Hackford said. "Alan Baker liked to do music. So I became his associate producer, and we did a whole series of popular music. It was really eclectic, from flamenco guitar to Lightnin' Hopkins."

Hackford was a fan of the Dave Mason record *Alone Together*, so he decided to try to book Mason for *Homewood Sessions*. "I called Denny Cordell, who was managing Leon, *kind* of," he said, laughing. "I said, 'It would be great if Leon could play in the band, like he did on Dave Mason's album.' Denny went, 'Well, why don't you have Dave *and* Leon? That would be a really cool combo.' And I said, 'Hell, that sounds great to me.' So, I then went to Alan Baker, and I said, 'Listen, if we can do this, we should do something that's longer than a half hour.' Our regular shows were half an hour, and Alan had the ability to go and talk to his executive producer and convince them to do something more."

Meanwhile, Hackford said, "I continued to have this conversation with Denny Cordell. We went back and forth, and we set the date for the recording of it at KCET. Well, just a few days before, Cordell says, 'Oh, Dave's not going to be able to make it.'" He chuckled again. "I was putting together the show, and it happened so suddenly. 'He's got another gig, but Leon can come.' Cordell was so slick; I'm sure he never even mentioned it to Dave Mason. Denny was very smart, because people weren't doing rock 'n' roll on television at the time. This is before *Midnight Special*. It was before *In Concert*. You know, this is a local show in Los Angeles, on a UHF station." But Cordell sensed television could be important to building Leon's groundswell. "So, he played me pretty good," Hackford concluded with a laugh.

AFTER AN HOUR WITH LEON RUSSELL, YOU MAY UNDERSTAND YOUR KIDS' MUSIC was the headline over an iconic photo of Leon wearing mirrored aviator shades in an *LA Times* ad. The first local screening was simulcast in stereo on KPPC FM, and the newspaper ad includes a helpful chart of how to position your speakers. Leon had resisted invitations to appear on television until he was assured control over every aspect of the production. Getting the sound right was paramount.

"Allan Muir [the director] was good enough to respond to whatever was happening," Hackford said. "He was a very good video director. So we put this thing together. Nobody had done it before. Leon said, 'Don't worry; this is my family. We'll all be here.' All these people, we put them in a circle, with Leon at the grand piano, facing them. And he just took over. He knew what he was doing. I've got to say that, artistically, the conception of the show was Leon Russell's. Because normally, what we would do is, we'd put a band on a kind of stage to perform, and the cameras moved around, and we'd have an audience. No audience for this, although we did have friends. Like, a friend of mine from college came and he thought he died and gone to heaven."

Don Nix recalled Leon saying, "We need somebody else." They decided to fly in the elderly Memphis-based country blues hero Furry Lewis. "Leon, when he had come to visit me in Memphis, we always hung out at Furry's a little bit," Nix said.

Nix was dispatched back home to try to find his friend Lewis. He also had to get Lewis's guitar out of hock at a pawnshop. "I called Furry. Furry was seventy-eight years old. I asked him if he would come out there and do this TV show. We were going to give him some money for it. He didn't like to fly. He said, 'But I'll come, if you come get me.' I realized he couldn't see, and I flew to Memphis. I spent the night with my folks. I went and got Furry." Nix said that tracking down Lewis and getting his guitar were the easy parts. Convincing him to get on a plane was more challenging. Although Lewis had lost most of his sight by then, Nix prevailed.

This show has an intimate behind-the-scenes feel that was intentionally

informal, with some contrived "down home with the folks" elements, like
Lewis sitting in a rocking chair and Emily Smith baking a pie while the
musicians play their songs and kids cavort among them on beanbag chairs.
But as with the "understand your kids' music" newspaper ad, it's as if Leon
set out to consciously present himself and his band of freaky longhairs in
a way that would extend a hand to an older generation who might have
been understandably alarmed by the darker events that marked the end of
the sixties. This was Los Angeles in December 1970, the month Hells Angels stabbed a man to death at the Rolling Stones' Altamont concert. The
Manson trials were happening in LA. "And the Vietnam War, that was
really dividing the country," said Baker. He pointed out that the older PBS
audience were "the ones who funded PBS when they held the fundraisers."

The bad vibes of the era were hard to avoid. But this impressive show
could make a person forget the heaviness, even if for only an hour. It
opens with a stilted, era-specific introduction that will feel familiar to fans
of Martin Mull's *Fernwood 2 Night* or Albert Brooks's *Real Life*, both sat-
ires of this sort of presentation. The host, Charles Champlin, sits in a
wood-paneled control room on the edge of a mixing console in a brown
suit and tie, wearing oversized eyeglasses, acting relaxed. You know, *letting
his hair down* and ready to have a *rap session* with the *kids* but also reassur-
ing their parents and the public station's financial supporters ("You may or
may not regard this kind of music as your bag," he warns).

Leon and friends march into the sparse studio in a procession, carrying tambourines, drums, guitars, cigarettes, and babies, singing "Will
the Circle Be Unbroken." Here come the Shelter People: Don Preston,
Chuck Blackwell, Joey Cooper, Claudia Lennear, Kathi McDonald, John
Gallie, and Jim Horn. Gallie handles the bass lines with a dedicated
Fender Rhodes keyboard atop his B-3 organ. "He'd play the bass lines
with his left hand and the organ with his right hand," said Jim Karstein,
who had played drums in bands with Gallie in the mid-sixties. "That was
one of the real early challenges for me, keeping up with Johnny playing
that thing."

Ken Burns opened episode six of his 2019 PBS documentary *Country Music* with this clip of "Will the Circle Be Unbroken," also the episode's title. Burns grew up in Ann Arbor and saw Leon come through the
Eastown Theatre on the Shelter People tour. "God, he was the bee's knees.
If you take 'Will the Circle' from Leon, just the idea that I could put that

in my film—and it wasn't me; it was somebody else who worked with me not knowing of my number one status as a Leon Russell fan," said Burns. "I was trying to say, 'Look, the reach of country music is so great. This is not going; this is staying. This is how we're opening.' [Leon] doesn't yet look like anybody else in country music. Pretty soon, the country rock stuff will have that, but he doesn't look like anybody there."

We see Don Nix and Furry Lewis in the Homewood recording as well. The latter is seated in the rocking chair with dark glasses on, sipping whiskey, as he would for most of the six hours. They launch into an instrumental version of Van Morrison's "Caravan," featuring Horn taking the lead on alto sax. Horn said the session "was another loose thing, you know, just play a little bit, and talk."

"Caravan" is followed by two aborted starts of "Delta Lady" before Leon counts it off again, clucking his tongue like a drum in the count-off. The band slides into a rollicking version, with exuberant whoops from Leon and bluesy shouts from the backing singers. As she did in most live performances, McDonald, in particular, offers spirited ad-libs as punctuation between Leon's lines throughout the show and dances and waves her arms wildly on every number. Lennear, looking stunning in painted-on jeans and a little leather jacket open to a bikini top, loses the jacket as she gets warmed up. "Everybody was looking mostly at Claudia Lennear," Baker said with a laugh.

There are several instances when the backing vocals were dubbed in, out of sync to the point of vocals being audible even when mouths are closed. But they all look cool, and none more than Leon, who wears the multicolored shirt he sported in *Mad Dogs* and mirrored aviator shades that repeatedly catch both the piano keyboard below and the studio lights above, shooting off gleaming rays. "One of our camera people had gotten a 16-point star filter, which had never been used before then," Baker remembered. A freeze frame of one of these instances was used for the iconic cover of *Leon Russell and the Shelter People*.

Leon ends a definitive version of "A Song for You" with a flourishing arpeggio. Horn said, "One time I heard that, I said, 'Man, where'd you learn to play the arpeggios?' And he said, 'I took lessons when I was younger, and my teacher taught me how to play an arpeggio.' She said to him, 'You might need this someday,' and he said, 'Nah, I don't think so.' But, man, he played so much of that with the Shelter People on the ends of the songs, and when he wrote a song about a lady, he always had a long arpeggio."

"We edited it, and then I took the audiotapes to his house he was living in, up in the Hollywood Hills," Baker said. "He had a recording studio. And I remember when I went up there, I knocked on the door, and a nine-months' pregnant woman, naked, answered. And the question is, where do you look?"

They had to recut the backing vocals, hence the dubbed look on those parts. Hackford spent a good deal of time at Skyhill as Leon repaired, edited, and mixed the music. "It was a bit of a commune-type situation. . . . I'd spent a fair bit of time with rock 'n' rollers, so it was a free-for-all. He had a studio there, and it went twenty-four hours. I wasn't shocked or surprised by what I saw, but it was rock 'n' roll." Hackford's passion for music remained, and he directed *Hail! Hail! Rock 'n' Roll*, the seminal 1987 documentary about Chuck Berry.

A few days later, on December 10, 1970, Leon made the cover of *Rolling Stone*, giving an in-depth interview to Ben Fong-Torres. In the same issue, a long four years before he saw "rock and roll's future" in Bruce Springsteen's performance at the Harvard Square Theater in Cambridge, Jon Landau declared, "There is a lack of excitement in the air—it's like the days before the Beatles." Landau offered a summary report of the popular music scene, and in his estimation, it wasn't pretty. Rock 'n' roll was going through a growth spurt, and the baby boomers who had grown up with the music were no longer kids. Many were starting careers and families. Others, including many of their favorite musicians, had fallen into drugs, which had gotten heavier, with casualties more numerous.

Landau pointed to Joe Cocker as an anomaly among the current crop of mostly mellow performers and singer-songwriters, "a storm in the middle of this new sea of tranquility. . . . His tour last spring with the Leon Russell group of musicians was an exciting and sometimes spectacular event, as it matched one of the fine vocalists of the moment with what was at the time the best performing band in rock. . . . The Cocker tour not only had musicianship and artistry, but a grapes and wine decadence and glamor that was inspiring in itself."

Reflecting in 2020 on his 1970 assessment, Landau said, "That was me. That was my taste. And as a critic, one of the reasons I became so well known was that I was a bit of a maverick taste-wise. I hated The

Doors, and I loved Sam & Dave. I was sort of on a mission to really bring Motown and Stax into the forefront and for people to understand that this music was worth as much as English rock 'n' roll, as defined by the Stones and the Beatles, who I loved. It's not like one or the other. But Leon was obviously American music; all-American music was where he was coming from, and he was just great at it.

"Leon brought to the foreground a lot of great talent. To play in a band Leon was organizing, you had to be A-plus in your spot. He didn't get onstage with B players. That's why Mad Dogs was so great. Everybody in it was great."

The *Shelter People* record was mostly in the can by the time Fong-Torres caught up to Leon in Denver, where Leon performed in "a Malcolm X shirt, violet jeans, and a feathered cap provided backstage by a lady fan, Tinker Bell." The interview with Fong-Torres is the most valuable in understanding Leon's early history. It captured him on the precipice of worldwide rock stardom. Their discussion was wide-ranging. Leon was not immune from political observations and opinions, and astute ones at that. He offered opinions on the profiteering from the war in Vietnam, tribal aspects of rock music, capitalism, religion, movies, pop art, and his own manic pace.

He talked movingly about having played a hospital in Tulsa for developmentally challenged children in the early fall just before going to Muscle Shoals. Dressed in a pirate outfit, Leon had fronted the band at the Hissom Center on September 9. He admitted, "It started out as a publicity stunt—and I'm not above stunts because that's what I'm in—public relations and communications." He thought that doing a good deed would get him on the front pages of the local paper and on the evening television news. "I figured out that since my physical image is not in context with Tulsa acceptance, that it should be something of a public service nature and be unquestionable as far as service to the community was concerned." Leon worried about the effect his music would have, noting that the kids would not have the same defenses as his usual audience. "I mean, normal people can be moved to riot by rock 'n' roll music," he observed. He had given the event a considerable amount of forethought and called the performance "one of the most profound experiences of my life. It was all I could do to keep from crying long enough to sing the songs. I finally quit singing and just said the words."

Chapter 17

On the Road to Bangladesh

HAVING SEEN HOW THE HOUSE bands operated at Muscle Shoals in rural Alabama and Stax in Memphis, Leon conceived of creating something similar back home in Tulsa, which he did throughout 1971– 1972. Leon explained why he recorded at Muscle Shoals: "It's mainly the musicians. They have that unique experience of playing together for quite some different artists, and they really are easy to work with." Along with Denny Cordell and Peter Nicholls, he had scouted Memphis first. But with its wellspring of talented homegrown musicians, cheap real estate, and home cooking, why not keep it in Tulsa? "It was really an interesting experience because we went to Tulsa, Oklahoma, and spent a week on a lake there laying around, then went down to Muscle Shoals for a week, where we were on a lake as well, so the music [on *Leon Russell and the Shelter People*] is considerably more laid-back than in the first album."

Don Williams was running Shelter's publishing companies. He had started his career in music publishing in the mid-sixties working for the estimable Don Costa, an in-house producer and arranger for ABC Records. At the end of the decade, Williams was a manager at MCA Records. When he heard the *Mad Dogs & Englishmen* version of "The Letter" on the radio, "I said, 'I've gotta find out who those guys are.'" Williams was already a fan of the first Asylum Choir record, so it did not surprise him when he found out Leon was behind *Mad Dogs*. "So the guys [Denny and Leon] were just starting. They were barely off the road."

Cordell and Ellen Basich started building out the office while Leon concentrated on music. "When I joined Shelter," Williams said, "there were about five people in the office. As I recall, there was Denny and Leon.

There was Dino [Airali], who was doing promotion, and his assistant. Then there was the general manager, Joel [Maiman], and his assistant. When I went down to the meeting, I didn't actually meet with Denny; I met with Joel. I hadn't met Denny at that point, but the thing that was odd, which I didn't find out until after the meeting, was that it was Denny sitting in the room during the interview. He just sat there quietly and listened to the interview."

Williams continued: "One of the reasons that I was able to move up the ranks at Shelter is because, aside from Leon and Denny, I was one of the few employees that actually brought money into the company. I had raised some money somehow to run the publishing companies at Shelter. It was really divided into two separate operations because both Leon and Denny clearly knew the value of music rights, the rights that are attached to the ownership of a recording and the separate rights that are attached to the song or the composition. By that time, we were in our thirties, and that was pretty much second nature."

Music publishing spurred Shelter's relatively sharp growth. Publishing is one of the least understood aspects of the music business, and countless songwriters have signed away the rights to their compositions in ignorance. Savvy songwriters set up their own publishing companies and generally have some larger company administer and collect those royalties for them for a fee. This is the type of arrangement that Leon and Denny had, both via A&M (which Williams consolidated under Shelter).

The publishing arm brought in revenue to compensate musicians and pay studio expenses on the Shelter Records side. "And that was the time when there were a lot of musicians hanging around," Williams said. "You can imagine when there was a new [company] in town, owned by Leon Russell, everybody that was anybody in town certainly wanted to be connected." Leon and Denny would sign new artists for recording contracts; for those who wrote their own songs, they'd try to get the publishing deals as well. However, two of the first significant artists to sign to Shelter in 1971–1972 were J. J. Cale and Willis Alan Ramsey, but they formed their own publishing companies and kept that revenue.

Ramsey met Leon at a show in Austin. "I was playing the UT coffee house, and I heard that Leon and Gregg Allman were in town playing a festival and staying at the same hotel," Ramsey said. "So I told them I thought they should give me a listen. It was a pretty asinine thing to do back then, and I guess they thought I was so cocky they gave me the chance. I played my songs for Leon and his roadie, and then for Gregg and [Allman Brothers guitarist] Dickey Betts, right there in their rooms."

"He was a very strange guy, a beautiful singer and guitar player and writer," Leon recalled about Ramsey. "I was down in Austin playing a show and he came in my motel room, pulled out this beautiful custom Martin guitar, and played these incredible songs. I signed him right on the spot, took him up to my studio in Hollywood, brought Jimmy Keltner and Carl Radle and some others over to play, and he didn't like that. He said, 'You've got all these studio musicians messing up my music.' He was a troubled soul, and I think that early in the game he developed a strong aversion to the possibility of being famous. He did that one record [*Willis Alan Ramsey*], had a huge success, really, but never did another. He comes from money, though: that might have something to do with it. He likes to think of himself as a Woody Guthrie figure, but I think he's more of a Donald Trump! He was always talking about 'hard hats' and 'real people.' I never could understand what he was going on about."

"Leon went on a world tour and let me stay in his house in Los Angeles with his recording studio," Ramsey said. "I got to hang with all these incredible Tulsa musicians but started getting discouraged. I couldn't get a good sound and became convinced his studio wasn't that great. Then one night Phil Spector and George Harrison came by to play one of George's old master tapes. It just sounded so unbelievably good that after they left I remember thinking, 'Okay, well, it's not the studio.'"

Ramsey performs at the end of the film *A Poem Is a Naked Person*, a long-shelved project that documented Leon from 1972 to 1973. The album *Willis Alan Ramsey*, the only one Ramsey has released, is regarded as a cult classic. A charming collection of songs in a warm 1970s country-folk singer-songwriter mold, it contained "Muskrat Candlelight," later covered under the title "Muskrat Love" by Captain & Tennille, whose version went to number four.

Ramsey's refusal to sign a publishing deal with Shelter "turned into a really big fight," Williams said. "He had chosen an attorney in LA that was very pro-artist. And so he felt that the record deal and the publishing deal should be completely separate; they shouldn't be tied together. And so Shelter actually ended up with what's called an administration deal [collecting publishing monies for a fee; not owning any percentage] for the Ramsey copyrights, which Denny was always pissed off about because of the fact that that song earned millions."

In addition to running the label and his role as a record producer, Cordell was also managing Leon's career. He and Maiman set up 360 Degrees, Inc., described in the trade magazine *Record World* as "a full-service management company whose initial client was Russell." This was another industry innovation, for better or worse. So-called 360 deals gained more attention in the mid-2000s as record and CD sales fell. Record companies, artist management, and live promoters would make a deal with artists for a percentage of all revenue—from music releases to T-shirts and other merchandise sales. Perhaps the best-known example was Madonna's all-in deal with the concert promotion company Live Nation. Such arrangements were controversial by the 2000s, but in 1971, this was a novelty. The *Record World* article stated, "Cordell is account executive for this firm, which handles all agency contracts, production pacts and sets up everything for concert tours. The firm is also geared to handle merchandising, recording and publishing of artists and groups."

Under Cordell's advice, Leon set up a corporation called Scissor-Tail, Inc., through which flowed all of Leon's revenue. Cordell was to be paid a commission: 20 percent of everything. Acting as a record label partner, talent agent, and personal manager surely raised several conflicts of interest and would now probably violate portions of the California Labor Code relating to talent agencies. "Denny did most of the business in terms of the day-to-day business, and the signings and the deals, and all that," said Owen Sloane, their attorney at the time. "Leon really wasn't involved much in that." Shelter started off distributed by Blue Thumb, but from 1970 through 1973 the label went through Capitol Records.

Leon had yet to experience any downside of working with Cordell and was impressed with his new partner's business acumen. "When he found out I had an Asylum Choir record [*Asylum Choir II*] in the can at Mercury, he borrowed the necessary money and bought the master with cash," Leon wrote. "I will never forget the nervous expression on the Mercury man's face as Cordell laid out two hundred one-hundred-dollar bills on the desk, picked up the tape, and left the office. . . . Denny's ability to communicate his past achievements was a delight and a wonder to behold. Many times I saw and heard him relate sales figures to a potential investor or distributor without missing a beat, recalling the chart positions for perhaps twenty singles and ten albums with all the attendant accounting that is of interest to people of that type."

By 1971, Leon was a cottage industry in and of himself. Peter Nicholls was his road manager, sound engineer, and aide-de-camp. "I'm a young English boy living in America," Nicholls recalled. "What am I going to do? Joe had no idea for me. But Leon and Denny said, 'Come work with us. We're going to make this company, Shelter Records.' I did A&R, cleaned the coffee cups, ran the tours. So we've done Mad Dogs. Hugely successful. Thank you, Denny, you did a great job. Denny starts Shelter. Slow start, then it starts to take off. J. J. Cale comes in, some other people, and things are moving nicely now. Now we got a business. Leon is out there touring America. We're cleaning up."

After the fall 1970 tour of the States, the band went over to the UK and Europe to start the new year, adding Carl Radle into the fold. Derek and the Dominos had released *Layla and Other Assorted Love Songs* the previous November. Rita Coolidge asked me, "When you talked to Eric, did you mention anything about 'Layla'?" The title track of the Clapton album includes the famous piano coda that was cowritten by Jim Gordon and Rita, the latter of whom was not credited, which still understandably irks her. Gordon was her second consecutive boyfriend to deny her credit on a song that would have paid her significant lifetime residuals after Leon did the same with "Superstar."

Though it eventually was certified as a gold album, and it's now re-garded as a classic—with torrid guitar interplay between Clapton and Duane Allman, and impassioned vocals from Clapton and Bobby Whit-lock—the *Layla* album was a commercial disappointment when it was released. Clapton was heavily into heroin, Jim Gordon descending deeper into mental illness, and the band dissolved over the first half of 1971. Even Carl Radle fell victim to rock's trappings.

"I think when I first met Carl with Delaney, we all liked to drink," Clapton said. "And we liked to do a little bit of weed, and then a little bit of coke. It seemed that we were moving through the time when stuff was becoming available, and people were turning you on. I remember one party we had that Leon threw, a big birthday party at Sunset Sound. There was a very famous lady from Tulsa. Not Emily [Smith], but some-one else [likely Kay Poorboy], who liked to look after you, you know, when you were on a gig or something; come and bring something for you. And she was handing out, we all took PCP, I think, for the first time. Whoa."

Emily Smith described what seemed to be the same party, but it was at Gold Star, right before Joe Cocker arrived in LA to start the Mad Dogs tour. "Denny and Leon's idea was to get everybody high in the studio and see what would 'happen.' Everyone got so high that nothing happened." She recalled Dave Mason, Jim Keltner, Delaney Bramlett, Carl Radle, Chuck Blackwell, and about "forty or fifty people writhing on angel dust." Apparently even John Lennon popped in. They recorded music, but "when they played the tapes back, they couldn't make sense of any of it."

Clapton continued, "What I'm trying to say is that it was all uncharted territory. Everyone was like, 'Let's try some of this.' And I don't remember anyone being more adept than anyone else. Carl was just, 'I'll just go with the flow.' He wasn't a party animal, but he saw the sense in it. He was actually the root of any band that we were in together. He was the driving force. He didn't like it when people were just goofing off."

Radle said, "I split up Derek and the Dominos—I was the one that quit that. We were just a mismatch of personalities and lifestyles. So I quit and went back home and started playing with Leon again." Coming back into Leon's fold, he added extra grease to the Shelter People. Despite Leon's deteriorating voice, they sound exceptionally on point in a recorded show broadcast on Dutch radio from the Castle Groeneveld in Baarn, Netherlands, on February 5, 1971. "Carl made us just a little bit more professional because he came from Eric's band," Nicholls said. John Gallie could concentrate on organ, while Radle took over the Fender bass. Even though Gallie was adept at the Fender Rhodes keyboard bass, Don Preston emphasized the difference Radle—one of rock music's most underappreciated musicians—made to the show: "It was good, but when Carl joined us, it was one of my happiest days ever," he said.

To have two keyboardists in a rock 'n' roll band was still relatively uncommon during the era (Sly and the Family Stone was already there). Gallie complemented Leon well. They'd known each other since the mid-1960s. There's a photo of Leon during the Snuff Garrett years, his hair growing out, a goateed chin, in a short-sleeved Oxford shirt, sitting at an organ or piano bench alongside a very young Gallie, who looks like Chip Douglas in *My Three Sons*, with horn-rimmed glasses and dark bangs. "I used to room with John Gallie," Nicholls said. "He was such a funny guy.

He was wacky as can be, but a good player," Nicholls said with a chuckle. Jim Karstein said Gallie is "a very intelligent guy. Helluva keyboard player. But you start talking to him, you'll know what I mean about him." Patrick Henderson, who would join the second phase of the Shelter People in '72, added: "He was such an odd guy, John. I wouldn't say he was autistic, but there was something very nerdy about him in the way he looked, and the way he carried himself. But, man, he could make that organ scream. What a musician!"

"The only thing I last heard about John Gallie is he's in an old folks' home in Oklahoma," Preston said. That's where I reached Gallie on a shared hallway phone, just months before he passed away. He spoke in a halting voice, his Texas drawl slowed by age. It was hard to connect it with the one-time wiry "Jumpin' John," as he was nicknamed. But he came across as a sweet and grateful person. "It was great being in his band, nice to work for, and paid me well," Gallie said about Leon. "I always loved the organ as much as the piano. Leon felt more at home on piano." Besides, he added, "Being in a rock star's band, even if you're not a rock star yourself, is a great way to meet girls. There wasn't a lot of drugs; the music was our drug."

Nicholls explained, "A lot of people have asked me, 'Did Leon do a lot of drugs? I mean, he must have done . . .' But in reality, two Coors, and he was off. He would sit down with me, when we were really close, and have one hit of hash. And one hit and he'd be raving all over the house. . . . The guy was a total wimp when it came to that stuff. Everyone *around* him— now that was something else."

Gallie was a mainstay in Leon's bands through the 1970s. About the experience, Gallie said, "He [Leon] was a great musician and a great band-leader. I didn't get very close to him. I was kind of scared of him cuz he was rich and famous, and I was just a poor struggling musician. But it wasn't a struggle working for him. I always thought he was a nice guy."

"The band was a bunch of adults," Preston said. "No one ever missed gigs. Offstage, it was relaxed because we all knew it was good." They met Ahmet Ertegun at a club in London on that first tour. "He said something like, we were 'bluesologists with a touch of vaudeville.'" Preston continued, "I met Joey [Cooper] when I joined the Shindogs. Chuck Blackwell got me that gig." Cooper had come to LA from Kentucky. "Joey [had] quit the business in '67 or '68 and went to work for an oil company, but when

Leon started the Shelter People, we all wanted Joey to be in it. He was the rhythm guitar player who just wanted to play rhythm."

Claudia Lennear spoke with a fondness for her bandmates. "Kathi [McDonald] would sing melody, Don the fifth below, and me the top. To me, Don Preston was the top rung of the ladder," she said. "He had such a great voice. He had such great musicianship. He had such a command of understanding blues. . . . I don't want to be so, maybe childish, that I'm thinking, 'This is magic.' On the other hand, it actually was." Lennear reserved her highest praise for the Master of Space and Time, Leon. "He was absolutely amazing," she raved. "To appreciate it, you would have had to have been there to make that hit home."

Leon was brimming with raw talent, evident as far back as the high school records he made with David Gates. His piano playing on those earliest of records in the late 1950s was almost fully formed. Then, he accumulated all those years in the studio learning from the great arrangers and peers. By the time Lennear met him, Leon Russell was complete, though not in his own estimation. "One of the things I admired most about him was that, although he had all of that talent and had it intact, there was not one day that he would not go down to the studio in his house on Skyhill and practice. He never gave that up. He always prepared, always," said Lennear.

The band did twenty-four gigs in twenty-eight days, including February 2 at the Royal Albert Hall. While the band was in England, the San Fernando Earthquake struck on February 9. Before they got back from tour, Leon had decided to leave LA. "Leon freaked out and moved lock, stock, and barrel to Tulsa," Preston said. "I no longer had anything keeping me in LA. I moved to Tulsa. Leon had rented a little house in North Tulsa, across the street from a cemetery [on Sandusky Avenue]."

The Shelter People were back in the States by March 5, when they started a two-night stand at the Capitol Theatre in Port Chester, New York, with Freddie King in support.

Leon returned to New York on March 16, invited by Bob Dylan to produce a few tracks. That past December, Ben Fong-Torres had asked Leon if he had ever worked with Dylan. "No, but I hope to sometime, because I've always thought—and this may be purely my own fantasy—but I've always thought he was making musical constructions that were far beneath his actual awareness, just so they could be assimilated by a lot of people. . . . He's been a great inspiration. The first time I ever heard him, I was amazed at how much he sounded like me—this is from my point of view."

Leon had sent the cover versions to Dylan for Christmas and told Dylan that he wanted to hear Bob with a band and a proper rhythm section. Dylan responded, "You know, I don't get it—you walk out on stage and play [with] 14 or 15 people, and it sounds great. But if I get up there with one [other] guy, it always sounds awful." Leon replied, "Well, how about I bring a little rhythm section up to you? And what I'd like to do is, I'll give them the changes. And then I wanna watch you write the songs to those changes." Leon had heard that Dylan would write songs between takes in the studio when he was recording in Nashville in the sixties, and he wanted to learn how to write on the fly like that. Dylan agreed and booked three sessions at Blue Rock Studios in Greenwich Village, with Leon as his first independent producer.

"So, I took Jim Keltner and Carl Radle and Eddie [Jesse Ed] Davis up to New York. And I gave them some changes to a song, and we cut this track. And Bob listened to it, and he walked around with his [note] pad in the studio and allowed me to walk around and look over his shoulder, and he wrote 'Watching the River Flow,' was the first one. And the second one was 'When I Paint My Masterpiece.' I constructed the changes in this track, and then he listened to the track and wrote those songs. And he allowed me to watch him do that, which is what I wanted to do. It was great."

Leon's descriptions of the session make it sound like he had written the music, and Dylan wrote lyrics over it. But Keltner described Leon's part as something more like arranging, and no one had Leon's expertise in arranging rock 'n' roll. "I always assumed that it was Bob's changes, and Leon put his spell on it, put the groove together," Keltner said. "It's just shuffles, all this, but it was a shuffle played by Leon, and Carl, and Jesse. All I had to do was hook my wagon. ['Watching the River Flow'] is one of my favorite shuffles. It's fantastic. It was just so easy to play. That's the perfect example of what I'm talking about. I always assumed that it was Bob's song, but he hadn't completed writing it. For instance, I have very distinct memories of sitting at the drums, sometimes playing and sometimes not, and watching Bob—most of the time we were playing the groove—and Bob was standing right up against the wall as if to have the words bounce back into his ears, and he was singing, or at least his mouth is moving. He had a tablet, and he was writing. I have a feeling that he probably had those songs fleshed out, mostly, and just honed in on them when we got there. 'Masterpiece' was really quick, as I recall. 'Watching the River Flow' was probably several takes, but not many."

Recalled Peter Nicholls, who was there as well: "The way Bob wrote in those days was he came in with a pad of lyrics and started singing, and the musicians would kind of start to play along with him and put the song together. . . . Bob—and also Leon—was so fast musically, so quick, that as soon as Bob sang the song once, Leon had gotten it. But Bob really hadn't figured out the song yet. Leon was lapping up Bob. Bob would start something off, and then Leon would come in with his chords on the piano, and that would get Bob going. But there was no organization at all."

Leon became "totally submissive" to Dylan, said Nicholls, who could not believe his luck to be a fly on the wall. Dylan did not even allow Denny to come to the sessions. "We were just amazed having made that Christmas record at Skyhill and sent it off to Bob, that he actually invited us to go to New York."

The exuberance of the two tracks fit the lighter-and-brighter mood Dylan was mining during this era. Although his mythical stature had only heightened during his self-imposed absence from the public eye, his work largely reflected his domestic life this time, for example, the 1970 *New Morning* album. The Leon-produced tracks were included on *Bob Dylan's Greatest Hits Vol. II*. "I remember around that time Leon told me that him and Dylan had agreed to coproduce that [session]. When it came out, Leon's name was nowhere to be seen," said Don Preston.

"What's the matter with me? I don't have much to say," Dylan sings to open "Watching the River Flow," probably referring to the writer's block he had been experiencing around the time. He sounds like he had a cold during recording and his vocal tone is not far from Randy Newman's. Leon and the band's backing is buoyant.

The tracks Leon produced sounded unlike anything Dylan had done before. And though Leon stamped his particular flavor and energy on the arrangements, as soon as Dylan starts singing, there is no doubt whose songs these are. Still, though Leon did not seek a writer's credit, all of the descriptions of the sessions sound like he had a hand in the songwriting for each of these tracks.

"Leon and I, we didn't do that much," Dylan said in 1974. "It went fine, it was as good as it could've been expected to be." Leon came to accept that Dylan was not an ensemble player. He was essentially an old folkie who played well solo but who did not feel comfortable within the strictures of band arrangements. And Leon was, by nature, a bandleader. But there was no one Leon admired more than Dylan. "I was excited to be that close to him," Leon said. He would tell the story of how Dylan took him out on the streets of the Village and showed him what inspired certain songs. "'You see that statue over there? I wrote this song about that. See that building? I wrote this song about that.' He told me everything I wanted to know; I was so grateful for that." The experience reminded Leon to stop talking, be the observer and listener he was in his sessions days, find inspiration in his surroundings, and write about what he knew.

With Carla Brown keeping Leon company, Leon and the band did a string of dates through Texas in April, with Poco, Badfinger, and Lee Michaels. In Springfield, Massachusetts, May 14, they played a festival with this mind-boggling lineup: the Allman Brothers Band; the J. Geils Band; Taj Mahal; Humble Pie; Frank Zappa and the Mothers of Invention; Laura Nyro; Alice Cooper; B. B. King; and Johnny and Edgar Winter. This was followed by four consecutive nights headlining the Fillmore East, with Donny Hathaway opening three shows. The band headed back to California for shows at the Forum in LA and the San Diego Sports Arena, with Freddie King and Buddy Miles (who had recorded at Skyhill) opening.

In April, the *Mad Dogs & Englishmen* film was released. It captured the joy, some of the fatigue, the chaos, and the skin-of-the-teeth looseness of a rock 'n' roll tour just as the idealistic potential of the sixties gave way to the cashing-in of the seventies. It's a movie that influenced generations of musicians who harbored rock 'n' roll fantasies, from Bruce Springsteen, who reacted by forming a prototype of the E Street Band, to the Tedeschi Trucks Band, who formed after seeing it decades later. Sixty-two hours of footage filmed over the course of eight weeks had been edited down to 117 minutes. "I thought it would be more interesting to see all the trials that went on behind the concerts, so that people could understand that it's not just one big, continuous party," Leon said. "If I'd edited it, it would've been X-rated. It was an adult event." The mind reels at what was left on the cutting room floor.

It accelerated Leon's fame. "I sort of gained quite a lot of profile from that Mad Dogs & Englishmen tour," he reflected later. "I think, then, that when my album came out, I was known from that [tour] already in some way. . . . The audience is about forty times bigger for movies, it seems like. You're dealing with forty million rather than . . . whatever. So, in fact, there were a lot of people that saw that movie. I know that it was an unusual experience because I went to the premiere over in London. And when I walked in, I was one of a crowd of a thousand people. It was a rather large theater. When we came out, all the eyes were looking at me."

"It's such a wonderful film," said Taylor Hackford. "It's so cool to have Joe Cocker, but the way the camera went, you just all of a sudden realized that Leon was the leader of that band, which was playing incredible stuff."

In his contemporaneous review, illustrious film critic Roger Ebert wrote, "One of the wonders of *Mad Dogs* is the radical difference in the personalities of Joe Cocker and his chief guitarist, piano-player, and leader, Leon Russell. Cocker throws himself into his highly mannered, almost spastic onstage style, and then simply leaves it behind when he gets offstage. He raps with some friends, and he's thoughtful, quietly humorous, almost shy. Russell, inarticulate offstage, becomes almost catatonic while performing. Everybody onstage [is] whipping himself into a frenzy, and he maintains such stony-faced control that you can only speculate what fearsome energies are churning underneath."

Richard Cromelin dissented in *Creem*: He didn't enjoy the film, and he especially didn't like the bandleader: "Unfortunately, the whole thing is under the direction of Leon Russell (whose overbearing, evil presence tarnishes the silver screen every time the camera lingers on him)."

The overbearing evil genius was about to strike again. *Leon Russell and the Shelter People* dropped in May 1971. It would peak at seventeen on the *Billboard* Top 200, stay on the charts for twenty-nine weeks, and be certified gold in February 1972. The competition in 1971 was fierce. It turned out Jon Landau's concerns at the end of '70 about the future of popular music had been misplaced. In 1971, the Rolling Stones released what many consider their best album, *Sticky Fingers* (which had a few tracks recorded at Muscle Shoals and featured the Mad Dogs horn section, Jim Price and Bobby Keys). Rod Stewart's *Every Picture Tells a Story*; The Who's *Who's Next*; Carole King's *Tapestry*; Marvin Gaye's *What's Going On*; John Lennon's *Imagine*; Elton John's *Madman Across the Water*; Joni

Mitchell's *Blue*; *Led Zeppelin IV*; and Van Morrison's *Tupelo Honey* are just a few of the classics released that year.

Along with nationally distributed magazines like *Rolling Stone* and *Creem*, freeform FM radio was rising to prominence and spinning it all. "People were experimenting with different sorts of music," Elton John said. "They were playing with other people. There was fusions going on. There were no rules. What was so important was the advent of stereo radio, of FM radio, because on AM radio, you just heard the hits for two minutes and thirty seconds. Then when the FM radio came in, you can hit everything you wanted to hear that you couldn't hear on the radio before and in *stereo*. So I was just like a kid in a candy store. Stereo FM radio in America pushed music forward so much because people who beforehand had just got a reputation by playing live and getting an audience—like the Grateful Dead, Jefferson Airplane, and all those people—suddenly had a means of getting their records played, and in stereo. You could play anything; you could play Jefferson Airplane next to Aretha, next to Leon, next to Ray Charles, next to the Mothers of Invention. It didn't matter."

Playboy pronounced *Leon Russell and the Shelter People* "one of the best rock albums so far this year. Russell practically invented what might as well be called Okie rock—with that shit-kicker Gospel sound heavy on Baptist-revival piano and chorus—and it gets as good on this album as you'll ever hear."

Leon left such rumination to the critics; he barely had time to think. He was on the road through the summer. Soon after hometown LA shows in June, Leon received a call from George Harrison asking if he'd play a benefit concert on August 1 at Madison Square Garden. Harrison's friend, Ravi Shankar, the master Bengali sitarist, had described an increasingly dire catastrophe taking place in his country. A revolutionary war had displaced refugees, a tragedy exacerbated by a cyclone, and Pakistan's army was committing mass atrocities and war crimes.

George had learned from John Lennon to use the power of the Beatles as a force for good beyond music, so he picked up the phone and spent twelve hours a day, for three weeks in June and July, appealing to friends for help. "There were certain people I knew I could rely on," he told VH1 interviewer John Fugelsang. "I was hanging a lot at the time with Leon Russell. Leon said he would come and brought Don Preston." Harrison had consulted with an Indian astrologer in LA who advised him the ideal date would be August 1, which just so happened to be available at Madison Square Garden. Before long, he had commitments from Ringo Starr, Eric Clapton, Billy Preston, Jim Keltner, Klaus Voorman, Badfinger, and Leon, plus a semi-commitment from Bob Dylan, the best anyone could hope for. In the end, Dylan showed up.

It would be the first superstar benefit rock concert. "George was a little apprehensive about appearing in public again," Leon wrote. "I told him I felt that his fans were still out there, dying for a glimpse of him and a chance to hear his voice. I had no doubt that the audience response would be incredible, especially after he told me that Eric Clapton was set for the event and Ringo had committed. He was trying to get Bob Dylan to appear, and he wanted me to put the band together. That night, he wrote the ballad 'Bangla Desh.'"

"Leon was very helpful in the song itself, 'Bangla Desh,'" George said. "He suggested to me to write that intro, where it kind of sets up the story." The intro is very similar to that on Leon's "Home Sweet Oklahoma." "Leon played on the single. We did it in one night, I think." With that, Harrison penned and recorded the first charity single in pop music. Leon joined Keltner, Billy Preston, Ringo, Jim Horn, and Voorman at Record Plant West on June 4 and 5 with Phil Spector producing "Bangla Desh"; it had been a few years since Leon had worked with his old boss, Spector. "Leon's the one that got me on the recording," Jim Horn said. "That's how my relationship started with George. Leon was always saying, 'We've gotta call Jim Horn.' He did so much for me with my music career there."

The resulting track is an impassioned plea within an insistent, catchy rock song. Purpose-written message songs often get bogged down in earnest platitudes. That is thankfully not the case here. Despite its quick gestation, "Bangla Desh" set the standard for all that followed. "Leon played, and he helped arrange the song," Keltner said. "The concert sort of started with this single."

About a week out from the show, the band assembled in New York for rehearsals in a Carnegie Hall rehearsal room and then onstage at the Garden itself, during soundcheck and staging for the concert film. Leon and the Shelter People canceled a gig in Chicago to facilitate it. "The third week into the tour, we were each earning about seventy-five dollars a week," Nicholls said. "We were all earning no money, and Leon, Carl, Don Preston, and I flew to New York to do the Bangladesh benefit, and they put us up at the Park Lane Hotel. We had to eat at the Star Deli because we couldn't afford to eat at the hotel."

The ensemble was principally picked from Leon's stable: Shelter People Don Preston, Carl Radle, Jim Horn, and Claudia Lennear. Don Nix assembled more vocalists for a Mad Dogs–like group of backing singers, dubbed "the Soul Choir." "I went back to Memphis," Nix said, "and George called me and said, 'Why don't you come up, too, and sing?' The best week I've ever spent in my life. George had rented two floors of the Park Lane Hotel. I stayed between Klaus and Keltner. We just kept the doors open." Billy Preston also brought some singers.

The rehearsals lasted two and a half days, with Dylan arriving in the last moments of the second day. "He watched the rehearsals for a good while, appearing to be uncertain about whether to play solo or with the large band," Leon said. "After much coaxing from George, he finally got on the stage and sang a song or two by himself. Then, he asked George and me to join him. George, of course, played electric guitar, and I played bass. . . . We tried a song or two, then I suggested that Ringo join us on tambourine."

A report from the scene in *Rolling Stone* at the time said: "Leon seemed to be suggesting songs for Bob to do and they tried them out. 'They'd just all walk back from the mikes for a minute and talk and then they'd come back and they'd have it all worked out, doing harmony, and then they'd go out and talk and in another few minutes they'd come back with another one,' Tom [Evans, of Badfinger] said. 'That really blew my mind.'"

Voorman handled the bass for most of the show, with Radle subbing in for the Leon-led number. Jim Keltner and Ringo played double drums. Billy Preston was on the organ; Leon played piano. Horn brought along a six-man horn section culled from LA session cats dubbed the Hollywood Horns, who were decked out in fabulous matching blue-and-white wide-collared print shirts and bell-bottom jeans. The guys from Badfinger played three acoustic guitars, while Clapton and Jesse Ed Davis played electric. More than even the Mad Dogs had been, it was Spector's Wall of Sound brought to a live stage, and Spector himself was credited as the music producer. "Spector was the X factor," Keltner observed. "Spector being in the control room, in the recording truck made the difference. Spector was a monster, just ears, as producer. He basically produced the sound of that whole thing." They would play two shows, an afternoon matinee and an evening concert.

Clapton was in the midst of one of his lowest druggy ebbs. "After the Dominos had broken up, and I was deep into hard drugs—just snorting loads of smack—and everyone was worried, I had gone off and shut the door I wasn't letting anyone in," Clapton said. "I spent about two to three years in isolation, really, just throwing money at Chinatown. And at one point, George and Leon came over. [Leon] took me aside and said, 'What are you doing? This is pretty dark stuff. Why are you doing this?' And I was really moved. I've never forgotten that. It's one of those instances in my life where I felt like someone really, really cared. For Leon to come all this way, and there was even a spark of curiosity in the question. And all I remember saying is, 'I don't know what I'm doing, but I know I've got to go through this, for some reason, to see because maybe there's something to learn. I know I'm going to be alright, but I've got to go through it.'

"It was a big moment for me; for him to come and knock on my door. I never let anyone in for a long time. On that visit, he gave me a book written by Stanislavski, *An Actor Prepares*. He was a big fan of Stanislavski. It was a very deep moment."

Chris O'Dell recalled, "Pattie [Boyd Harrison] couldn't understand why George had asked [Clapton] to join the concert when he was so desperately ill with his addiction. I think she was afraid he might go into withdrawal and die right there on the stage, although we had talked about the need to get drugs for him to make sure he could make it through the concert safely and get back on the plane without going into full-blown withdrawal."

"I just didn't want to go," Clapton said. "I didn't want to go because I knew I'd be stretched. There would be a period of cold turkey. I wasn't sure if I could handle it. Anyone who's been an addict has got to go through that. If I got on a plane, I knew before I would land in America, I'd already be going into withdrawals. I really didn't see if it was feasible to be able to play, or show up for rehearsals, and then do my best. But people in the production company were saying, 'We can take care of that when you get there. There'll be someone there with some stuff for you to get straight on.' And there wasn't; they didn't materialize.

"I wanted to go, but I knew it would be catastrophic. And in a way, it was. It's one of those times when I dropped the ball really badly. Someone had gotten some kind of painkiller for the gut, which I think came from Allen Klein—for his ulcers, or something. And I remember seeing everybody in the dressing rooms in the locker rooms in the Garden, Bob and Leon and Jesse. I could barely make conversation, and here's all these luminaries. I just thought, 'You shouldn't have gone there.'"

For four days, Harrison booked flights out of London for Clapton, and Clapton failed to arrive each time. Jesse Ed Davis had been hanging around the hotel hoping to get invited to join the show, and when Harrison finally got tired of waiting for Clapton to appear, he asked Davis to join. When Clapton did show up, he was not in his best form, so it was a welcome consolation to have Davis. Though he would eventually succumb to his own drug abuse, Davis played exceptionally well.

Keltner said Davis was the magic mojo. "Without Jesse, I don't think that would have happened that well," Keltner said. "I just don't think that the groove would have been there like that. Ringo and I together was pretty strong. I gave Ringo a sense of security that he wouldn't have had on his own because he wasn't used to playing live. He hadn't done that in years. We locked. We became fast friends."

Keltner added: "We gave the guitar player something to play to. The guitar player happened to be Jesse. Eric was there, but Eric was sick. He was still fighting, coming back, and getting himself back on his feet. George was always great, but he wasn't carrying the show, as far as rhythm goes. It had to be somebody. Jesse just nailed it."

Originally from Oklahoma City, Jesse Ed Davis had been introduced to Leon and the Tulsans in LA by Levon Helm in the late sixties. He made his mark with Taj Mahal and was a beloved team player, which allowed him to excel as a session guy. "On sessions, he'd come in for thirty minutes and play a solo on your record, and it'd be a big hit record, maybe not because of his solo, but people of that caliber would always want him there to play," Keltner said. "He could knock your socks off."

In a 1974 interview with *Guitar Player* magazine, Davis recalled how Leon helped him develop. One drunken night, Leon told him: "If you want to be a musician-turned-singer like me and Dr. John, but you don't think you can sing, then just sing as loud as you can. Just turn it up as loud as you can stand it."

At the benefit concert, prior to the first audience coming in, a jittery Leon disappeared to be by himself, perched high up in the nosebleed seats. Harrison, meanwhile, said before the show, "Just thinking about it makes me shake." In the documentary film of the concerts, an Indian music section starts the program with Ravi Shankar, Ali Akbar Khan, Alla Rakha, and Kamala Chakravarty setting an intense and sacred tone. The next scene shows Spector walking out from the dressing room area wearing an impressive wig and shades. He's followed by Ringo in a snazzy suit, who is walking along with Leon, who is in white flared pants and a reddish-orange tank top that matches the collared shirt Harrison wears under his striking white suit. Leon is smoking and already the early stages of a pot belly are showing. They lead the procession of musicians to stage and launch into Harrison's new and most raucous solo song, "Wah Wah," a swipe at Paul McCartney. Leon's glissandos brighten the joyful racket, like the high filigrees he used to embellish the Ronettes and Darlene Love records eight long years ago.

This was the first time most of the crowd got to see a live Beatle. The band had famously stopped touring in 1966. Here, concertgoers were getting to see half of the Fab Four. Harrison is in great voice, and his cool demeanor belied his nerves.

Clapton, though dealing with the monkey on his back, in the film manages a fine slide part on a Stratocaster for "My Sweet Lord." After the two Harrison songs, Billy Preston gets the spotlight for "That's the Way God Planned It." The clip in the film is from the second of the two shows, and after getting the nerves of the first one out of the way, Preston lets the spirit overtake him. As the choir and band vamp on the chorus, he comes out to the lip of the stage and does a Holy Ghost church dance, flapping his arms and dazzling all with stagger steps. Even the band seems overjoyed, with Harrison shaking loose from his immobile stance to rock himself with a back-and-forth sidestep, a wide grin plastered across his face.

After a solid "It Don't Come Easy" from Ringo, bravely singing while playing drums, sneaking peeks at a cheat sheet of the lyrics, the band floats into a spacy "Beware of Darkness." After the song's bridge, the voice of Leon, semi-obscured behind the wall of amps, emerges from the shifting shadows and takes the lead for the third verse. The crowd responds with knowing applause for this newly minted rock star perfectly at home alongside Harrison, Starr, and Clapton. "It was the birth of Leon as an absolute superstar because the crowd went absolutely fucking nuts," Peter Nicholls said. "The sound of his voice! To this day, I get chills when I hear it." Band introductions follow this, and Leon gets virtually the same level of applause as the established stars. He follows the ovation for Ringo with a playful snippet of "Yellow Submarine" on the piano.

Next up is "While My Guitar Gently Weeps." Clapton inexplicably plays a semi-hollow-body guitar to reprise the lead parts he played on the original Beatles White Album recording. These parts require a certain level of sustain associated with solid-body electric guitars. As a result, Clapton's part comes off as inadequately plinky. At the end, Harrison needs to step in on the lead, while Clapton offers sheepish half-smiles and shrugs.

Clapton acknowledged, "That was not the right guitar for that song. I should've used a Fender or a solid-body Gibson. But that's because I was in another world," he said. "I don't remember much about it in terms of recollection, but I remember watching the film when it came out and thinking, 'You weren't there, actually.' I did it for George. I did it for George, and I did it for Ravi. He and I had become friends, and I really respected him."

For many observers, Leon's turn in the spotlight was the highlight of the show. "Somebody you all know by now—Leon," Harrison says by way of introduction. Carl Radle takes over from Klaus Voorman on bass, and Don Preston steps out from the choir and straps on an electric guitar to help Leon lash into "Jumpin' Jack Flash." It's invigorating. Leon trades banshee yowls with the choir and frames the arrangement with blistering double-lead-guitar riffs.

Leon detours the band into a breakdown, with Don Preston skidding into the space with a wailing blues run. Leon testifies, with Billy Preston answering on the organ, and guides everyone into a sultry version of the Leiber/Stoller-penned Coasters song "Young Blood," Don Preston taking the lead vocal on the bridge. It goes on like this for more than nine minutes—rock, pause, testify, rebuild, climax, repeat, Leon shouting like a tormented bluesman seeking redemption on a Sunday morning after a devilish Saturday night.

Fresh from the sting of accusations of spotlight-stealing on the Mad Dogs tour, Leon displays unshrinking audacity to frame a ten-minute medley within a Stones song in the middle of a charity show by half of the Beatles in front of a sold-out Madison Square Garden. And though the focus of the event was to benefit a nation in the throes of a humanitarian catastrophe, Leon felt no compunction to keep the show solemn; this was a rock 'n' roll audience, who had waited in line, some overnight. The best way to respond to a grim situation is with fervor, love, empowerment, righteous anger, and shining blinding light in the face of the daunting darkness. Billy Preston had shown the way, singing the joyful Good News.

Leon finishes. The crowd roars their approval as he coolly takes a sip of the Coca-Cola atop his piano. It was a momentous career highlight, the point of discovery for many lifelong fans. "He turned 'Jumpin' Jack Flash' into a tent revival," Nicholls said, laughing. Keltner added, "That performance of his, man, that night, was incredible. It was like falling off a log, playing with him."

Leon later explained, "I thought I was gonna be real nervous." But the presence of "all those stars" made him relaxed; the pressure was on them. "All I had to do was show up and sing. . . . In the rehearsal, it was just a matter of picking out stuff that people knew." Speaking of stars, "Mick [Jagger] was quite taken with that 'Jumpin' Jack Flash' performance on that Bangladesh concert," Leon recalled. "He called me up and told me about that."

It was a perfect way to end the main set, which is followed by an acoustic segment. Peter Ham of Badfinger joins Harrison for a duet on "Here Comes the Sun." In the film, musicians cast glances around the stage's wings checking whether Bob Dylan would appear. It was not a certainty. There was a question mark on George's setlist on the back of his guitar where Dylan's slot was. Harrison glimpsed Dylan rear stage with a guitar, took the leap of faith, and introduced him. It was just Bob, George, and Leon at the lip of the stage, with Leon on bass guitar, at Dylan's request.

"I have never seen such a complete metamorphosis take place in any other human being," Leon wrote. "When Bob Dylan was offstage, he looked like an ordinary guy. But as soon as he reached the back of the stage, he changed drastically . . . his presence became all-powerful."

Bob runs through inspired versions of "A Hard Rain's A-Gonna Fall," "It Takes a Lot to Laugh, It Takes a Train to Cry" (two that Leon had covered), "Blowin' in the Wind," and "Just Like a Woman." The latter features three-part harmony, with Leon taking the high part.

Leon said Dylan relaxed markedly after the first show. He noticed Dylan sitting alone backstage between shows, holding his guitar. No one approached him, so Leon just strode up. "I took the opportunity to request all my favorite Dylan songs. He played about twenty of them in a row for me." Leon said that Dylan also answered every question he asked about the music business and songwriting. "He'd been off for two years since his motorcycle accident, and he wasn't sure we'd sell out the second show. But we did," Leon said in an interview. In his memoir, Leon wrote, "Before the evening concert started, he called me over and asked if I thought the second audience would be like the first. 'In what way?' I asked. 'In any way,' he replied. 'Well,' I said, 'there will be 20,000 people again, and they will all know who you are and know all your songs. I guess from that standpoint they will be pretty much the same.'"

It was only Dylan's fourth public performance since his 1966 motorcycle accident. In *Rolling Stone*, Jonathan Cott warned, "Anyone who thinks that Dylan will now start writing more 'protest' songs had better wait and see what self-portrait he draws next. Behind all his protean changes and disguises, it's possible that Dylan, as one person commented, was singing his older songs because Leon Russell just happened to like them."

The film wraps up with an enchanting version of "Something." George flubs some of the lyrics and looks back to his old mate Ringo to share a self-deprecating laugh. It's a beautiful moment of humility.

"It was just one of those angelical, celestial, cosmic things that came along when the Big Bang happened and just developed the way it did," said Lennear. "We were all just there trying to make a really good show. Nobody ever thought that fifty years later, people would still be asking about it."

"We [the Shelter People] were out on the road on a big, big tour, trying to be a famous band, but we're still struggling," Nicholls explained. "I mean, I think the gig we did before that [Bangladesh concert] was in Winnebago, Wisconsin, or somewhere. Some joke place where I don't even remember if we got paid. There were about two hundred or three hundred people packed up in front of the stage. The next day, we fly up to New York: limos, the Park Lane Hotel. When Leon comes in on the bridge [of 'Beware of Darkness'], I mean his voice hit that microphone, and the fucking crowd just lifted off. The show took off right at that point. Within two weeks, it was all over the press. The recordings were around, and the word was out: Leon was red hot. The funny thing was that Bangladesh, in fact, kicked his career off. People always say Mad Dogs, but he struggled. Within two weeks, we were selling out everywhere."

The sales of the resulting film and triple live album from the Concert for Bangladesh made a significant impact financially and by raising awareness of the tragedy. After initial hold-ups over petty disputes between labels regarding contracts of the individual artists and over which label would release it, the album was released in the States on December 20, 1971. It won the Grammy for Album of the Year.

The Shelter People stuck around New York, playing August 10 at Hammerstein Ballroom, before working their way to Wildwood, New Jersey. On August 12, the Carpenters released their Grammy-winning version of "Superstar." What it lacks in the rawness of Rita Coolidge's *Mad Dogs* version or Delaney & Bonnie's original it makes up for with Richard Carpenter's brilliant arrangement. Karen Carpenter's flawless vocal conveys both a woman's mature emotional control on the minor-key verses, cradled in the lush sonics, and a more adolescent edge with double-tracked vocals and blaring horns on the choruses. It went to number two on the Hot 100, and number one on the Easy Listening chart.

"I never met Leon," Richard Carpenter said. "I just believed that with the correct arrangements vis-à-vis the Carpenters, the songs of his I selected would work well for Karen and me. They have memorable melodies and melody to me is of primary importance." The Carpenters also recorded "A Song for You" and "This Masquerade."

Helen Reddy recorded a Leon composition, "I Don't Remember My Childhood," for her 1971 self-titled album. He gave her the exclusive rights to it. "He really didn't have to do that at all," she said. "He hasn't even recorded it himself. I was recording 'I Don't Know How to Love Him' at A&M, which was the first and only time we used the studio, and Leon was next door working and came in to talk and ended up giving me the song, which was really unbelievable." The introspective lyric and minor-key verses offer a preview of themes on Leon's next album, *Carney*.

The Concert for Bangladesh was not Leon's first connection to Badfinger. By that point, the band had already opened shows in the States for Leon. George Harrison had started producing their album *Straight Up* around June but had to halt in order to make preparations for the concert, only working on a handful of songs. One was the yearning ballad "Day After Day," which he elevated by having Leon overdub a crucial piano part. Todd Rundgren, brought in to finish the album, featured Leon prominently in his final mix. He provides just the right amount of varied fills between vocal lines on successive verses, building his part along with the arrangement. It ranks among his finest moments as a contributor to someone else's session. The single was released in the States in November and climbed to number four on the Hot 100.

Also that summer, Leon learned that Carla was pregnant with his first child, adding incentive for them to nest in Tulsa, where her family would offer support. The balance of 1971 was spent on the road in the United States, but Leon went back to New York to work on one more Dylan session, for the recently written "George Jackson," an ode to the Black Panther leader killed by prison guards at San Quentin. Leon played a muted thumping bass guitar line, his second time on bass for Dylan in a few months. Leon also added a little piano part, which sounds out of tune. "Now, Bob Dylan is known for having little patience for multiple takes. That's true," Leon said. "When we were listening to the playback for 'George Jackson,' I said, 'Bob, that last take had a little clam [mistake] in it. Do you want to do it again?' He said, 'Nah, because if we do that, it'll just have another mistake in it.'"

Meanwhile, the Shelter People was ending phase one. The first to leave were Kathi and Claudia. "We were at Duke University in a half-full basketball arena, and we had about three dates left on the tour," Nicholls recalled. "Leon had been in a pretty funky mood the last few days. He was snapping at people and he was doing some unusual things onstage." When they were all back at their hotel, Leon called a meeting. "We're sitting there for about fifteen minutes. Finally, he says, 'OK, here's the deal. It's not easy for me to go onstage and do this shit. Some people think I'm this and I'm that, but I'll tell you, it's an act,'" Nicholls said, noting that he was paraphrasing Leon. "He was trying to say that 'This is a show. For me to get up there and act this part, I need your support 100 percent all the time. And you two,' he pointed at Claudia and Kathi, 'are standing up there laughing and making fun of me while I'm standing up front. You're fired.' That was the end of that. They were on a plane the next morning."

Lennear did not recall the incident but added: "Leon was really a nice guy, but it kind of broke off when he wanted me to come to Tulsa. I'm not a Southerner. I declined." He had been talking up Shelter Records to her since the Mad Dogs tour. "He would always say to me, 'When this is over, I'm gonna put the record company together, would you like to create an album?' You're not gonna say no. I wasn't Leon's live-in girlfriend, or whatever, at this time."

As for the reasons that Leon and Claudia ended their personal and music relationships, Lennear said, "It was a myriad of things. Why does any relationship not work out? . . . The bottom line was that I was not going to sign with Shelter. I'm sure I broke Leon's heart. I begged him to forgive me because there's no one I've ever admired more than him. I had to say, 'OK, if I'm going to go with Warner Bros., then I have to break off my relationship with you and Denny,' although it broke my heart because they had brought me that far."

Lennear—a highly talented, glamorous, and sexy singer on high-profile tours, films, and television appearances—would not stay in the background for long. On September 26, she had a fashion spread in the Sunday *LA Times*. "The publicity for that shoot was arranged by yet another friend, Gary Stromberg, who went on to produce blaxploitation films like *Car Wash*," she said. The following year, Claudia did a nude spread for *Playboy*. Lennear released her only solo album *Phew!* in 1973.

Claudia revealed that she and Leon were briefly engaged to be married (though no one else interviewed for this book knew of it). "As far as I know, Carla and Leon were together while we were on the road," Claudia explained. "Carla got pregnant. She had the baby, Blue [born February 1972], who is Leon's child. After I moved to Hollywood, I was engaged to Leon for about a year. He was so generous to me and gave me this beautiful two-carat marquise diamond. There were two packages in the little bag that he gave me. The other one was a gold Mickey Mouse watch. That was the initiation of our relationship." She laughed, then said, "Maybe the culmination of our relationship."

She continued: "I adored Leon. He was into that hippie, communal thing. That wasn't my schtick, as you might say. Those were steps leading up to, probably, why we wouldn't have ever made it as a married couple. I moved on to David Bowie!" By that time, there were photos of Claudia with Andy Warhol at Studio 54. Eventually, though, she quit the music biz and pursued her other passion, teaching languages.

"As for Claudia and Kathi," Preston said, "what I know for sure about them leaving is, one day they were there, the next day they were gone. . . .

There is a clip on YouTube of us in Sweden, just the band, no girls. No offense, to me, that was the heart of it all."

The band is shown on the television program *North Country Fair* before a live audience in Stockholm on November 26 playing a raging set, including a version of Dylan's "George Jackson." Leon had gained weight, quite evident in his cheeks with his beard shaved off, and wore a layered hair style in a shag more like Kenny Rogers's. He's wearing a suede or velvet jacket featuring wide lapels trimmed with white piping over a red-and-blue horizontal-striped crewneck shirt. In the few short months after the Concert for Bangladesh, he had changed his look significantly.

While Leon was overseas, *Asylum Choir II* was finally released. He and Denny recognized it was time to capitalize on Leon's fame with more product. The album cover has an unfortunate sketch of Leon and Marc Benno with pouty expressions and a whole lot of hair, like it's a soft rock album by Seals & Crofts or Dan Fogelberg instead of the scorching rock 'n' roll record contained therein.

The band was at London's Rainbow Theatre for two nights, December 3 and 4, with Freddie King and the Grease Band, who had signed to Shelter Records sans Joe Cocker. Eric Clapton came down both nights and joined Leon and the band onstage after the first song and stayed for the rest of the set. Freddie King joined in as well.

Not a bad way to end a remarkable year. But the pressures were getting to Leon. Shelter's Ellen Basich said, "Leon was on top of the world, but he didn't like what went with it: having to schmooze, the interviews, record executives, radio promotion. He moved back to Tulsa to get away from the hype."

Chapter 18

Going Back to Tulsa

BY THE MIDDLE OF 1971, Leon had decided to transition to Oklahoma full-time. In addition to the small rental in Tulsa, when summer of '71 came around, he started living in what he described as a "small fishing cabin on Grand Lake O' the Cherokees, about seventy miles northeast of Tulsa," which he'd bought earlier that year. "It was part of a picturesque and primitive resort that featured floating motel rooms with boat parking right inside." This description barely scratches the surface. In addition to a few cabins at Pappy Reeve's Floating Motel and Fish Camp, the five-room "floating motel" was basically a shed over a long dock, like a boathouse. As shown in *A Poem Is a Naked Person*, the Les Blank documentary that began filming around May 1972, there were boat slips in the rooms themselves and metal counters for gutting fish. "I used to get periods of deep depression," Leon said. "I'd tell friends someday I'm gonna go back to Oklahoma and get me a bait shop. Here I am in Oklahoma with a bait shop."

He moved a piano into one of the concrete-floor, one-room cabins, located up by the ruddy dirt area that had served as the parking lot for the camp. It was otherwise furnished with only an old refrigerator, a big metal-framed bed, and a Sony television. On the walls were a framed gold record for "This Diamond Ring," a photo of himself with Ricky Nelson in their short-haired days, and a poster of Albert Einstein. Leon was interviewed there by *Rolling Stone* for a November 1971 profile. "The cities are marked," Leon told Jerry Hopkins. "You get out here and you have to learn how to take care of yourself. If you don't do it, it doesn't get done. In town, there's always some specialist around the corner who'll come charge you ten times what it's worth to make it look like everybody else's. . . . The city is so impersonal. And the earthquake [in San Fernando]—I wasn't prepared to handle that."

The simple shelter of the cabin on the land would serve as a retreat from the increasing demands Leon's skyrocketing fame put on him. "At some point in '71, Dad comes, and he tells my mom he's officially a multimillionaire," Blue Bridges-Fox said with a laugh. "And she said, 'Oh . . . cool.' And he was like, 'That's really underwhelming. Come on!' It became a running joke. 'Cool.' Yeah, anytime there was some kind of big money to-do: 'Cool.' But he was quite excited. And he got on one of his highs, and it was one of the longest highs she'd ever seen for him. It really taught her something about him. There was something that money really did to him, and she didn't necessarily like it. And I can tell you from my experience, money's one of those things that really also kind of broke my heart about my daddy. He can be very stingy with it to the people around him . . . [but] he'll give a $10,000 keyboard to a stranger he met that day."

Leon often trusted the wrong people. Blue explained: "Mom said, in Tulsa, he would have accounts at places. And people would just go in and say they were with Leon Russell and sign it, like credit, not even a card used. It was like, 'Oh, we're with Leon.' And they'd just send a bill, and they'd just get paid, no matter what it was, who it was for. . . . And I do think it changed him in his later years."

Leon, uninterested in the business aspect of Shelter, left Denny behind in Los Angeles to deal with the day-to-day operations as well as Leon's publicity and went back to Oklahoma. While still living in LA, Leon had only rarely popped into the office anyway.

"He bought the Grand Lake property as a romantic gesture for [Carla]," said Blue. Leon was determined to win Carla's love. They had not been communicating much from around May to November of 1970. She worked as a dancer and was trying to make a go of it with Jimmy Markham. But, since Leon had first met Carla, "he just was like, 'You'll learn to love me,'" Blue said. "And she absolutely did. But my parents didn't have a run-with-love-with-a-passion kind of thing. He liked her, and they would say, 'Oh, we're good friends.' My mom was probably the best friend he ever really had because she wasn't out for anything."

Leon had hired Diane Sullivan, a personal assistant/secretary who would remain with him for the rest of the 1970s and who would remain in California, eventually taking ownership of the Skyhill house. Blue continued, "Diane calls [Carla] and says, 'What would it take to get you to come back to Oklahoma?' And my mom said, 'An open-ended round-trip ticket and a black Ford truck,' because she didn't want to get stuck. Because on the [Mad Dogs] tour, especially, she had to crash with Carl and Kay while Dad was fucking somebody else. . . . Dad could be really romantic and sweet, but he was not that sweet gentleman who worried about your well-being. He's all about a grand gesture. They moved there while it [the house at Grand Lake] was being built. She never lived in the house, though. After Mad Dogs, she stayed in California, and he kept asking her to come to him in Tulsa. And she finally said yes."

Because Carla was non-materialistic, Leon conceived of just the right "grand gesture." In California and Oklahoma both, the couple would take long, aimless drives. One day in Oklahoma, Carla took Leon for a ride and showed him a special place to her, a spot with deep personal significance. "Her dad used to take her fishing at that cove," Blue said. "Her father passed away when she was only fifteen. An electric company truck hit her father's truck, and he died immediately. A lot of money was thrown at her, but it never would bring her daddy back."

But Carla and Leon's relationship was rocky and non-monogamous. He was on the road for most of 1970 and 1971, and also involved with Claudia Lennear, while Carla was working in LA. Before that, when he and Carla had shared a room on the Mad Dogs tour, Carla's only criteria were that he not flaunt his dalliances and that he not give gifts to other women while they were together.

Sometime in 1970 or 1971, when they were both back home in Oklahoma, Leon asked Carla to go for a ride with him in his truck. "As they drove that long drive from Tulsa, things seemed familiar, and she was asking where they were going and why," Blue explained. "He wouldn't tell her at all. Finally, she realized exactly where they were. He had bought the cove and all the property around it. She was really shocked." Leon told *Rolling Stone*, "I couldn't resist the charm of this place." He had likely already set his sights on Grand Lake because Don Preston and Leon had been up there about a year prior for a visit when they wrote "Stranger in a Strange Land." Much of the property can be seen in *A Poem Is a Naked Person*.

Leon pegged J. J. Cale's young neighbor Harold Thompson to draw up some plans for the lake building projects. "My brother knew Leon from Tulsa and stayed with him briefly in California," Thompson said. "But there were specifics of studio design that were not in my wheelhouse. Emily Smith knew John Judd, who was part of a homebuilding company known as Busch, Bartlett, and Judd. . . . My initial association with BBJ was getting the studio and associated buildings designed and built." Leon's friend, architect Steve Busch, designed a $500,000 complex on over seven acres on the lake. "It all started as a remodel of the buildings associated with Pappy Reeve's Floating Motel, [including] a studio, cottages, an enclosed swimming pool, and a thirty-five-hundred-square-foot house, with a fifty-foot-wide living room, cantilevered over the lake," Leon wrote. "Walls of glass overlooked the water."

He brought in a red U-shaped Helios mixing console, custom-made for him in England by legendary audio engineer Dick Swettenham. It was all well underway by May 1972. The house and studio came together at the same time and were still being built while Les Blank and his assistant, Maureen Gosling, were filming *A Poem Is a Naked Person*. "The night the studio opened," Don Preston recalled, "I was sitting by Leon, and he strangely said that he would like to run as fast as he could into the wall on the other side of the room. Leon wasn't all that happy at the time because the local workers weren't moving all that fast. It did get built, though."

"It's important to understand the overall mood of this time," Thompson said. "I asked Leon one day, 'How's it going?' His reply was, 'Rollin' and tumblin'.' Everything was being done bespoke; there were no grand, detailed plans or contracts. From my perspective, it was pretty much seat-of-the-pants."

"The towns of Disney and Tia Juana were a couple of miles away by dirt road, for food and staples," Preston explained. Leon got a forty-year-old, forty-foot boat, a cabin cruiser named *Under Aries*—his astrological sign. "One day, me and Leon got in it and started it up and set out to go across the lake to Disney," Preston said. "There were gas fumes. We were lucky it didn't blow up. They hauled it back to the property and set it among the trees, and there, I guess, it finally rotted."

Setting a pattern that he would follow through three different states and about a dozen properties, Leon worked on his new record while simultaneously building and developing a place to do that comfortably.

"What we've got here is a place where we can relax," Leon said in 1971. "When we're not touring, we can come here, fish, play music, sing, sit around, do nothing, read, drive into Lela's Café, relax between the fast moving. Eventually I want to build a studio so we can do our recording here, too. I'm thinking of putting a geodesic dome [another recurring obsession of his] up in back of the bait shop. Nobody's ever used a dome to record in that I know of. I'd like to try it. Although Denny's looking for a house and studio in Memphis now." Peter Nicholls said the plan was to try to buy Ardent Studios and base Shelter in Memphis before they decided Tulsa made more sense. Leon continued, "We'll keep the studio in Los Angeles, the one in my old house on Skyhill . . . use it for a place to stay when we're out there . . . and Denny's gonna keep the office open in Hollywood . . . but we're trying to get away from all that." At night, when everyone was finished swimming, fishing, and doing their own thing, they gathered around the piano and would sing standards like "Alfie" and "It Was a Very Good Year."

The lake complex was the beginning of a real estate buying spree in Oklahoma. Shelter was growing rapidly and needed more space. The label hit big in 1971 with J. J. Cale's *Naturally* album. After working with Leon at Skyhill in the mid-sixties, Cale helped Snuff Garrett get Amigo Studios up and running before he played in the original Delaney & Bonnie and Friends. But Cale wouldn't last long under the tyranny of Delaney Bramlett. After Cale split Delaney & Bonnie and Friends, Bobby Keys recalled, "I thought he was nuts. I remember I called him up and said, 'Johnny, you're crazy, man, this is a golden fucking opportunity!' But he stuck to his guns. A couple years later I remember calling him up when Eric Clapton recorded 'After Midnight,' which J. J.'d written. I held the phone up to the playback speaker and said, 'Listen to this, you son of a bitch!' He'd been right." Cale found out about Clapton's recording when it was a Top 20 hit on the radio. In fact, he had sold his Gibson Les Paul to Marc Benno for cash to move back to Tulsa. *Naturally* had started out as demos, set to a primitive Acetone drum machine. Carl Radle got involved, and they ended up keeping much of that flat and dry demo sound.

Cale had recorded most of the songs with Audie Ashworth in Nashville in the fall of 1970. Cale had met Ashworth via Snuff Garrett around 1967–1968, and it was Ashworth who encouraged Cale to record the album, even financing it personally. Cale recalled, "I said, 'Try to get it to a major label.' He said, 'John, I've had five record companies turn us down, but Denny Cordell, who has Shelter with Leon, will put it out.'" Radle encouraged Leon to listen to the tape, but Leon had been unenthusiastic. In 2003, Cale said, "Denny Cordell was the businessman; Leon, the musician. I loved Denny; he was like a musician. . . . Leon wasn't crazy about the first album. Then Denny said, 'I like it.' If it hadn't been for Denny and Leon, the album would have never come out." "Crazy Mama," a sleepy blues, was an unlikely Top 40 hit, climbing to number twenty-eight. Cale was told he could very likely goose it into the Top 10 with an appearance on *American Bandstand*, but Cale refused to lip-sync.

Unfortunately, Don Nix's 1971 record *In God We Trust*, the second album issued by the Shelter label, did not achieve a similar level of success. The little publicity Nix did receive was double-edged, coming as it did because of his association with Leon Russell. Nix decided he had to detach his career from that of his friend. "I looked at it as a business decision, and he looked at it as me doubting him. . . . We stayed friends. We weren't as close. Then he . . . moved back to Tulsa. We lost contact there."

Shelter Records juggled releases like the Freddie King album *Getting Ready* and the Cocker-less Grease Band's eponymous albums, both of which came out in 1971. Most intriguing, Bob Marley and the Wailers' first American release, the single "Duppy Conqueror," was released by Shelter in October 1971 (misspelled "Doppy Conqueror" on the label). Chris Blackwell, who was raised in Jamaica, established Island Records in 1958, and Cordell had started there. Island had long been a home for Jamaican music, issuing records by Toots and the Maytals, Jimmy Cliff, and Bob Marley and the Wailers.

"One day [Denny] comes into the office," Don Williams remembered. "Within two or three minutes, I hear this record coming out of his office. I said, 'What the *fuck* is that?' It was the first time I heard a reggae record: Toots and the Maytals, produced by Sir Coxsone Dodd, 'I'll Never Grow Old.' I just went wacky for this stuff. I persuaded the management of EMI to get to cut me a check for twenty grand so I could go down to Jamaica and see if I could sign Jamaican songwriters. There was nothing on American labels that had anything to do with reggae." (In fact, Desmond Dekker's "Israelites" had been a Top 10 US hit for UNI Records in 1969.)

Fortuitously, the first musician he met was Bob Marley himself. "Chris and Denny want to release reggae in the US, so they set up Mango Records. I kinda remember when Denny came back from the lunch with Chris where he had drawn the record deal on the back of the lunch napkin." In a few years, Wailer Peter Tosh would make his way into Leon and Denny's studio in Tulsa to work on his *Legalize It* album.

Peter Nicholls was doing a bit of A&R but mostly ran Leon's tours. "For the first few months when we got to Tulsa, we had an office in the architectural firm Busch, Bartlett and Judd," he said. Dewey Bartlett Jr. would become the Republican mayor of Tulsa in 2009. "The three of them in there—a lot of cocaine, a lot of bullshit."

Tulsa musician and Shelter songwriter Richard Feldman said there was trouble with the lake house: "Part of it fell into the lake. [Busch] was a brilliant architect, but as a contractor told me, 'He draws pretty pictures.'"

Leon and Denny wanted to create a studio in Tulsa in addition to the one out on the lake. In February 1972, Carla was with them at the Ranch House, a greasy spoon diner, when she noticed that a church was for sale across the street, on 3rd Street and Trenton Avenue. As they were walking up the steps, Carla said, "This is perfect, Leon. Because you love gospel, you love Jesus, and you love music. Church Studio! You can't get any better than that!" So they bought it. They envisioned a sanctuary for Tulsa and Oklahoma musicians to have the freedom to make their music on their terms, in direct contrast to the strictures of the LA recording scene. He wanted to foster a local recording scene with house bands, like Muscle Shoals, Motown, and Memphis.

Work on the Church began even before the place on the lake was finished. In addition to the Church, they bought up a bunch of houses and buildings nearby for offices and to house employees. By 1973, Leon and Shelter would own "fifty-four different pieces of property" in Tulsa, according to *Tulsa World*.

Transforming the church into the Church—a studio—required significant renovation and demolition, which they were sensitive about, given its last sacred incarnation. Carla encouraged Leon to pick up a sledgehammer himself. After he demurred, she called him a "wuss." So he picked one up and "he didn't have a lot of strength," she said, "but he hit it. And then he just got with it, got to hittin' it, and hittin' it. He came over, with his laugh, and said, 'That was *fun!*'"

Carla gave birth to Baby Blueagle Bridges on February 20, 1972. "I was full-on heroin baby," Blue said. "She's in labor; he starts driving her. He's mad because she wants to go to the Claremore. He wants to go to a regular hospital; she says no, it's free at the Claremore Indian Hospital," which is about forty-five minutes away from Tulsa. "So she's kicking him, telling him to drive her out there. And he's driving all over the damn road and then gets on, going the wrong way. Now, keep in mind, this is the highway. I don't think he was ever there for any of his children's births because he just can't handle that kind of shit."

Mary Jones, Steve Busch's girlfriend at the time, said, "Leon drove off the road. He couldn't do it. And Carla said, 'You're gonna kill everybody!' So Carla said to Leon, 'Leave! Go on the road! Go somewhere, leave town, go to LA,' you know. So they asked me to drive her." But it was a false alarm. The second labor about a week later was for real. Leon was in California, and Carla's friends took her to the hospital to deliver. On the way, she shot up.

"Emily [Smith] was the first person at the hospital when I was born," Blue said. "I was named in Emily's living room. "'Baby' is because I was the firstborn, his first kid, and then 'Blueagle' after Acee Blue Eagle, the Native American artist." Blue said a family DNA test revealed Leon was one-sixteenth Cherokee. "Anytime Daddy would be out at the antique shops, anytime he ever came across something by Acee Blue Eagle, he bought it for me."

Leon's return to Oklahoma was "a big damn deal," said Larry Shaeffer, who would be known for booking the Sex Pistols at Tulsa's Cain's Ballroom on their first US tour. In 1971, Shaeffer started Little Wing Promotions to book shows around Tulsa. "I mean, he was our rock 'n' roll star. You'd hear stories, 'Hey, we saw Leon driving his Rolls-Royce down Peoria yesterday, and we waved at him. I think we saw George Harrison in there with him.'"

Chapter 19

Carney

THE SHELTER PEOPLE BAND WAS about to enter phase two, as they worked on what would become the *Carney* record. Peter Nicholls had started engineering the sessions at Skyhill, and the recording continued as the new facility at the lake—christened Paradise Studios—was completed, with engineer John LeMay. Leon wanted to take the band in an even more gospel-oriented direction. His first step was to hire new backing singers, so he and Don Preston went to Dallas, where they auditioned Patrick Henderson, Nawasa "Wacy" Crowder, and sisters Mary Ann and Phyllis Lindsey. They were put together by Showco, one of the first big road production companies in rock music, owned by Freddie King's manager, Jack Calmes. Henderson originally intended to be the singers' roadie, but then, he said, "I got on the piano. Leon asked, 'Is he included in this group?'" Now the band had two pianists *plus* an organ player.

Another addition was made: conga player Ambrose Campbell brought the number of band members to eleven. Ambrose would become like a brother to Leon.

Born Oladipupo Adekoya Campbell and raised in Nigeria, Campbell had started singing in the choir of his father's church in Lagos. But his pious Christian father had rejected his son once Ambrose became enamored with the mixture of secular folk music that sailors and travelers introduced to the Lagos waterfront. After a brief stint as an apprentice printer, Campbell signed on as a merchant marine and settled in London in 1945.

In England, Campbell hooked up and traveled with Ballet Nègres, Britain's first Black ballet company, formed the West African Rhythm Brothers, the country's first Black band, and brought his version of West

African highlife music to the nightclub scene in Soho, where Denny
Cordell saw him. Ambrose was a bona fide legend back home in Nigeria.
The renowned Fela Kuti called Campbell "the father of modern Nigerian
music." Ambrose's son Danny added: "When he used to go back to Nigeria, he was getting mobbed like Beatles were here when they used to arrive
at Heathrow."

He was also venerated in England. Danny—who enjoyed a long career
in music himself, working with Tom Jones, Dido, and others—said it
was common for, say, Ringo Starr to come by the family's place in Isling-
ton, London. Ambrose collaborated with West Indian immigrants, who
brought their music, like calypso, mento, and Bluebeat ska, which melted
in with the West African stuff. Jazz musicians from nearby Ronnie Scott's
club would swing by and jam. He met Bohemians, artists, and aristocrats.
Ambrose was the inspiration for a character in Colin MacInnes's novel
Absolute Beginners.

Ambrose was already fifty-three by the time he became a member of
the Shelter People. "Ambrose Campbell was introduced to me by Denny
Cordell, in response to a comment I had made about how I'd like to
meet an African drummer," Leon wrote. "He is that and much more. . . .
Ambrose comes from a well-known family in Lagos, Nigeria. The city has
a prominent park named Campbell Square which was named after his
grandfather, who was what might be called a witch doctor by 'civilized'
society." Campbell would remain with Leon until 2004, when Campbell
then returned to England. "He said he followed Hinduism, Buddhism,
Catholicism, Anglicanism, Jehovah, you know," Danny said. "And I was
like, 'Dad, how can you support them all?' He said, 'Son, when I arrive
upstairs, I'm covered.' He was placing bets," his son said, laughing.

Leon's spiritual curiosity grew more intense with each year. But, as with
many musicians, it was not about specific dogma for him. "He referred to
it as an 'artificially induced religious experience,'" Henderson said. "We
authenticated it with the gospel music show." Asked if he thought Leon
had any religious beliefs, Henderson was quick to answer "None. None
whatsoever. But he was spiritual. I think he was a mystic. He was beyond
the trappings of religion."

Leon's practice regimen allowed him to harness mystic energy as a
source of inspiration. Henderson said, "He had the most amazing fingers,
and he had [palsy]. It was therapeutic. Leon believed that people worship

music. He didn't believe they worship God. . . . The only thing that makes a song a gospel song is the lyric. I took Leon to James Cleveland's church with me. He said to me, after the services, he said, 'Shit, I'd rather put fifty dollars in the offering and scream and howl and roll on the floor like everybody else than give that fifty dollars to a shrink.'"

But Leon was also wary of charlatans. As he told *Rolling Stone*, he was fascinated by what he called "the mass manipulators, people like Elvis Presley, Oral Roberts, Adolf Hitler." During his freewheeling conversation with Jerry Hopkins, Leon talked about "how people preferred martyrdom to leadership." Much of the ideas stemmed from the book Leon was reading at the time, *The Morning of the Magicians*, a 1960 cult classic written by French journalists Louis Pauwels and Jacques Bergier that helped fuel several conspiracy theories.

Leon bestowed the honorific "Reverend" on Henderson, who was not an actual minister. ("Leon ordained me as such," Henderson said.) As a fellow pianist who started in his father's ministry at the age of four, Henderson sat across from Leon, center stage on tour, in awe of Leon's skills: "Not only octaves, but he was left-handed. If he started the solo, he started with his left hand and finished with his right."

The house at the lake was not yet completed, but people were staying there when Henderson and the women backing singers, who collectively became Black Grass, arrived. "We all had our own private rooms," Henderson said. "The guys, their girls, and their wives would end up there, so it was like a huge family. I did a lot of the cooking because Leon loved my cooking. Once he found that I could cook, he just gave me a credit card and said, 'Feed me.' We had a great vibe, lots of liberty: just freedom to live, freedom to be yourself, freedom of curiosity, freedom to inquire. There was no subject that was taboo. Members in the band had their little hangout buddies. Me and Chuck Blackwell, we were always really close. We got into some devilment. They didn't put us in jail, but we had some fun."

Leon Russell and the Shelter People was an integrated band, almost equally balanced between white and Black musicians. Sly and the Family Stone had set an example, but this was uncommon in early 1970s rock 'n' roll, especially for a bandleader who made a significant share of his performance fees in the American South.

"[Leon] was really into politics," Henderson said. "I got into politics from watching the Watergate hearings. I sat down with him every day, man. He would watch it till it came on or it went off. That's where I really got to know who he was as a human being. In some ways, he was really like the father that I've never had. [To him], all people are created equal. He hated crackers. He hated Confederate flags, and he hated all that bullshit."

Unfortunately, Leon had many racists in his fanbase. "To find out that a lot of the people that were following him . . ." Henderson's voice trailed off sadly. "I told him the Confederate flag was to Black people what the Nazi flag was to the Jews. There was no in-between. It was the same thing, and he totally agreed." When Leon saw people show up to his shows with the symbol, "he would tell them to go somewhere else, 'I ain't got time for you.'"

While at the lake, the band rehearsed for the upcoming tour while putting the finishing touches on *Carney*. Filmmaker Les Blank and his assistant Maureen Gosling arrived in the spring, and Gosling said work was still ongoing for the album, which would be released in July, rushing to meet a deadline for an album that Leon had started working on almost a year before.

Blank was an art-house documentarian whose 1969 short film *The Blues Accordin' to Lightnin' Hopkins* came to Leon's and Denny's attention. They invited Blank to the lake to discuss making a verité-style profile of Leon for television. Blank and Gosling stopped by Oklahoma on their drive back to California from Louisiana, where they had been working on *Dry Wood* and *Hot Pepper*, two companion pieces about Cajun musicians, the latter spotlighting Clifton Chenier.

The documentarians did not make it to California. Blank was hired by Denny and Leon and put on the payroll. In other words, this was not to be a Les Blank film, per se. While Leon and Denny gave the director free rein to film as he saw fit, the parties operated without a contract for months.

A treatment was put together that gave biographical sketches of Leon, Denny, and others. Leon's reads, "Russell's favorite movie is *Mondo Cane*; he also likes the movies of Andy Warhol and Dennis Hopper." *Mondo Cane* is a 1962 Italian exploitation film known for its shock value.

They did agree that Blank and Gosling would stay at the lake compound and edit their Louisiana films while they filmed the new project. "Les was trying to decide whether to do it or not, and he got excited about the lake because it's nature," Gosling said. "And so he proposed to Leon and Denny that he would like to edit there and do the film there because it would give him a chance to be in nature." Blank sent for the editing machine, and he and Gosling remained in Grand Lake about two years. What they ultimately finished was a feature-length film intended for theatrical release. "Les wanted to do theatrical *and* TV," Gosling said.

"We were living in the floating motel," Gosling explained. "One of the Black Grass girls was smoking, and the mattress caught on fire. So we had to have a bucket brigade to put the fire out."

Steve Busch's girlfriend, Mary Jones, first met Leon up at the lake. She said, "They rehearsed all night, and they slept all day. Some of them slept in the studio because it was air-conditioned and nothing else was, and it was always really dark and really nicely cold. It was hot and humid at Grand Lake." A scene in the DVD extras of the film shows everyone sharing a meal at a big table in the main house. "The table was built by Anthony, who was one of the carpenters, and was there for a while," Gosling said. The wood for the table came from the pews taken out of the Church. The table was still the heart of the house when I visited it in the summer of 2021.

When Leon first found the lake property in the spring of 1971, he had been on the way to Muscle Shoals to record some of the *Carney* tracks there. But Peter Nicholls said about half the album was recorded at the lake, though Leon wrote that he "recorded most of *Carney* there." Gosling recalled "Magic Mirror," "Cajun Love Song," and "Queen of the Roller Derby" being worked on at the lake studio.

"They were just still finishing [the studio]," Gosling said. "And it was really beautiful. It had a blue carpet and was full of instruments. Leon eventually brought a Mellotron there. He brought his forty-track tape recorder there. And when Ambrose joined in, he brought a shipment—two crates from Nigeria—of his drums, and I think we filmed that, opening up the crates of all of his beautiful drums."

Henderson shook a tambourine on "Out in the Woods" in spring of '72. Probably the closest Leon came to showing the influence of Dr. John, "Out in the Woods" is the definition of "swampy." It was inspired by, if not pulled together at, Muscle Shoals, where the band returned. "For *Carney*, we all went to Muscle Shoals," Preston said. "Someone rented us a house by the Tennessee River in the country. When we went into the studio, Leon had a hymnal on the piano and kept pulling all these songs out."

"The most important thing was, with the tracks on the *Carney*, half of them were laid down by the Muscle Shoals guys," Peter Nicholls said. "It was the drums and bass more than anything else that Leon loved. Don Preston played a few things, I played a couple of things. He loved the feel of what [the Swampers] did. We took it back to the lake studio and finished it off. . . . The second side of *Carney* was all done at Grand Lake. [Leon] was all fired up about it. Until then, we'd use that primarily as a rehearsal studio. We were rehearsing the big tour of 1972."

Marvelous tapes of these rehearsals demonstrate just how impressive a bandleader Leon was. They quickly dispel any question about whether the subsequent *Leon Live* album might have been edited to make it seem as though the show was more seamless than reality. The running order of the songs, the medleys, the arrangements of parts, the spaces created for improvisation—they rehearsed meticulously. And though they were only rehearsing, they pulled no punches—Leon screaming just like he did in actual shows, and the fire catches all the other members, who blaze alongside him.

Nicholls had been learning how to engineer and produce with Leon when they were recording at Skyhill. "One night I made a comment; it was right before the *Carney* tour: [a take] wasn't as good as it could be, why don't we do it again? I remember he was loose enough to say what he felt: 'You know, man, you were a much better engineer before you knew what you were doing.' That was such a tremendous shock to me, who had put in, like, thousands of hours for no money working with this guy, thinking I was learning. Then he tells me I should never had done it. . . . It almost made me cry."

Inevitably and appropriately compared to Federico Fellini's 1963 film *8½*, *Carney* is Leon's surrealistic journey out in the woods of his newfound fame. His narrator on the record veers from ambivalence to outright rejection of that celebrity. At times, the album sounds like a demented circus stranded in a gnarled swamp. But it's mostly a collection of sedate and reflective songs. (Claudia Lennear recalled Leon as "a film buff . . . he and I spoke occasionally about Fellini's films.")

The Band's 1970 *Stage Fright* would have also served as thematic inspiration, employing similar metaphors for the pitfalls of being famous traveling musicians. Leon was no stranger to actual stage fright.

In a scene in *A Poem Is a Naked Person*, filmed within a year or so of recording *Carney*, Leon reveals his disquietude: off camera, Blank, sensing his ambivalence, asks Leon probing questions about why he is pursuing his path as a rock star: "If you don't know what you're doing, then why do you do it?" Leon replies, "Because I'm supposed to. It's what I'm supposed to do. It's the only thing I've been able to figure out that means anything, that I'm supposed to be myself and trust that it's not ugly."

Carney does not shrink from ugliness. The leadoff song, "Tight Rope," tiptoes along the high wire as Leon struggles to maintain balance. His only top ten single (in *Cash Box*; it stalled at number eleven in *Billboard*) is a cry for help, as he describes his struggle: "You look into my past / Well, maybe you're just too blind to see."

The track, with influences of vaudeville and music hall traditions, is packed with hooks. If you listen closely, you can even hear Leon's tongue clicks, keeping time on breaks. But the arrangement remains uncluttered. A dobro is layered in, and an electric guitar swirls in a revolving Leslie organ speaker. The melodicism veers into dissonance on the bridge before the person teetering on the wire rights himself. The song came to Leon in a flash as he was leaving Muscle Shoals with Jim Keltner after a session. They turned around, went back in, and recorded it.

Leon's voice on "Tight Rope" sounds almost boyish in contrast to the gritty Howlin' Wolf–via–Captain Beefheart creature emerging from the muck of "Out of the Woods" and feeding lines to his alter ego in a duet with himself. The low voice, panned to one side of the stereo mix, is an inner voice that feeds the worst fears of the singer.

It's a percussion-forward mix, with two drum parts panned hard right and left in the stereo. At the end, a choir enters to brighten the mood. Introducing the song in concert, Leon would explain that the choir's lyric is in Zulu. In Muscle Shoals, he had befriended Billy Crauser, an African artist, singer, and poet. Crauser followed Percy Sledge to the Muscle Shoals area after Sledge's tour of Swaziland in 1971, a tour captured in a documentary, *Soul Africa*. "I was on that trip," said Marlin Greene, who engineered the sessions at Muscle Shoals. Greene had played guitar on Sledge's masterpiece "When a Man Loves a Woman." "['Out in the

Woods'] was a result of discussing with Leon some of our experiences we had in South Africa."

Leon asked Crauser to translate "I'm lost in the jungle" into Zulu. Crauser answered that "Zulu people don't get lost in the jungle because they're out there every day." So Leon asked for a similar metaphor; Crauser offered, "I'm a man that's gone crazy and wandering around the bush without a purpose."

Against a doleful piano and pump organ, "Me and Baby Jane" is about a hometown school sweetheart who dies from a heroin overdose, the title inspired by the movie *Whatever Happened to Baby Jane?* Leon's voice is pregnant with emotion, cracking with sorrow at the end of the first chorus. "I was told it was about my mom," Blue Bridges-Fox said. The song is more a cautionary tale, an imagined tragedy that might have felt like a very real outcome to Leon as he watched the mother of his child descend into the throes of addiction. Carla always believed the song was about her. Leon intimated later to people close to him that Carla and Francine Brockey were inspirations, but Blue explained that Brockey had not yet started to use heroin at the time the song was recorded.

The next song, "Manhattan Island Serenade," does little to lighten the mood. A masterful ballad with a wistful melody right out of Paul McCartney's songbook, it opens with the sound of tires swishing across wet pavement during a rainstorm. "There was a really intense Southern Alabama thunderstorm going on," Greene said. "It actually kicked the power off in the studio a couple of times. So Leon sent everybody home except me. He said, 'Can we record some of this thundercloud?' So I put a couple of mics up. Got great stereo thunderclaps. 'Manhattan Island Serenade,' he sat at the piano and composed that spontaneously. He got the whole thing together in about five minutes. That thunderclap in the middle is natural. That stop in the middle, where he's just vamping on the piano, and you hear, 'Boom!' He looked around, and grinned when that happened, and kept right on playing."

There is a direct Native American spiritual connection between Muscle Shoals and Tulsa via the Trail of Tears. Greene explained how attuned Leon was to such forces: "He was very careful about who he would allow in the studio. He was cognizant of their attitude about a song. When we were mixing, he would sit at the control board, and without any noise being made, he could tell when somebody walked in the studio behind him. He detected their presence. He believed that their attitude about the music would influence how it was being heard by other people."

Side one of *Carney* finishes with two upbeat tracks, "Cajun Love Song" and "Roller Derby." The latter is the one straight-up rock 'n' roll rave-up on this moody album, and it's a satisfying one. Leon sets a New Orleans boogie groove with his acoustic piano. It is complemented by a Moog synth beefing up the low and middle frequencies, much like Stevie Wonder was doing. The depiction of a roller derby queen knocking out a trucker from Dallas with a right cross is consistent with the LP's grotesque sideshow motif.

Side two opens with the full-on Fellini-esque "Carney," a comic wheezing-waterlogged calliope, like the Kurt Weill *Threepenny Opera*–inspired sounds that Tom Waits would adopt on *Swordfishtrombones*. If that wasn't creepy enough, track two is the avant-garde sound collage "Acid Annapolis," which opens with tormented ghostly moans sliding into a Zappa-warped doo-wop section set against Chamberlin tape loops of voices. Leon sent the musicians into the studio at various times to play anything they wanted, only allowing them to hear sample snippets of what else was on the track. It was a way to keep the salaried band members occupied, as he could not churn out songs quickly enough to keep them busy. "One night, I went up to the studio, probably to practice," recalled Preston. "Leon was in there, and he said something like, 'Let's make a radio show.' He started the tape, we went in and started playing around, doing odd voices and such. He had a Chamberlin machine that had all kinds of stuff on it. Dog barking, opera singing, horns, on and on."

Leon's album's sequencing is a bit perverse, starting side two with two experimental tracks. But the final four songs are all brilliant. It's not a surprise, though, that some fans got turned off considering it the "psychedelic side," and rarely bothered to flip the record over to listen to side two—a pity.

A toe-tapping country song, "If the Shoe Fits," is a gleefully cutting satire of how people react to rock stars. The lyric is a litany of impudent things Leon would hear from fans, as shown in *A Poem Is a Naked Person*. He saves the punchline for entitled rock journalists: "Can we crash here for just a few days / We're from *Rolling Stone* so it's okay." That line would be thrown back in his face by those who felt suitably scorned.

"My Cricket" is an emotional 6/8 country-soul ballad, with an un-reliable narrator denying his loneliness. It's framed with an inventive complementary piano figure. It's another number that would be at home in the repertoire of Ray Charles, taking that super-slow cadence that Charles's band would refer to as "the death tempo." Leon's early mentor, Jerry Lee Lewis, ratcheted up the tempo on a cover he recorded in 1973, a feather in Leon's top hat. Willie Nelson said, "That's one of my all-time favorites."

Inspired by the chord progression of the haunting standard "Angel Eyes," Leon crafted the bossa nova–flavored "This Masquerade." "It was one or two songs he did like that. He totally transformed them into his own," Maureen Gosling said. "He wrote words for them, but he borrowed the [chords] and just morphed it." Preston explained: "The chords to any song is up for grabs as long as the melody is changed." He pointed to other borrowings on the album: "Cajun Love Song" comes from "Standing on the Promises of God," "My Cricket" from "Tennessee Waltz."

Leon begins his recording of "This Masquerade" with eerie Chamberlin vibraphone, string, and guitar echoes swimming deeply in distant reverb. Those who remember home organs will recall the bossa nova setting on the built-in drum machine, and that's similar to what we get here. Leon constructs a lush pad of strings, flutes, organ, and a lightly strummed Spanish guitar atop that skeletal beat. It's easy to understand the appeal a tool like the Chamberlin held for Leon, allowing him to create a whole ensemble with organic sounds at his fingertips while on a lake in the mid-dle of nowhere.

As with "A Song for You," Leon said, "When I wrote 'Masquerade' I was trying to write a standard." Leon's original recording has an enig-matic quality to it, in a similar lo-fi way to J. J. Cale's *Naturally* album. In going for an almost easy-listening kind of jazz piece, Leon produced something cooler, more compelling, with some raw edges showing. It's dreamily detached.

With a few notable exceptions, it was becoming less common for song-writers who developed after the late sixties—the singer-songwriter era—to write what would be considered standards. The times were more about a personal, even confessional point of view, and less about whether others would record the song. Though Leon wrote some specifically personal lyr-ics, his most-covered songs are unsurprisingly those with his most universal messages. Even the groupie's plea, "Superstar," is left open enough that it can be interpreted as a lovelorn lament from any singer.

Leon was listening to Randy Newman's records at the time of recording *Carney*. Newman was used to having his idiosyncratic compositions picked up by other artists like Dusty Springfield and Harry Nilsson. But when it came to setting out to write a standard consciously, Newman said, "We thought that fifty years down the line, merit would be rewarded, but it's been mainly the hits that are around. If 'Downtown' was a hit with Pet Clark fifty years ago, it might still be around, and it is." Newman took the idea of the unreliable narrator to intrepid extremes—for example, singing in character as an ignorant racist who unflinchingly uses the n-word on the song "Rednecks."

Leon didn't necessarily sit down to write commercial songs, but neither did he often write in character. He usually kept his point of view central to the song. "This Masquerade" was sort of buried as the penultimate song on the album, then chosen as a B-side for "Tight Rope." The Carpenters released it the following year on *Now and Then* and as a B-side for their single version of "Please Mr. Postman." It would be cut about forty-two more times before George Benson finally had a hit with it in 1976.

On the front cover of *Carney* is our man, in a close-up, face smeared with greasepaint, staring grimly into the camera, no shades or top hat, a lighted dressing room mirror just over his shoulder. The back cover is a pulled-back wide shot, with a tiny camper trailer hitched to his blue Rolls-Royce. Leon is like the successful director Guido in *8½*, who, feeling like a fraud having an existential crisis, voices frustration via an internal monologue: "I thought my ideas were so clear. I wanted to make an honest film with no lies of any kind . . . that would help us to bury all that is dead inside us."

Leon, reflected back from others in the distorted funhouse "Magic Mirror," an eye-of-the-beholder number, is not sure who he is. The only consistent take is that Leon is an outsider who reflects the needs of those who encounter him. He's a number, a son, a bandit, a teacher, etcetera. Each line in the song distills several of Leon's ongoing concerns: prejudice, religion, politics, censorship, materialism, war, justice. But the song is neither didactic nor weighed down by the multitude of perspectives.

One line in particular cut close to home: "The sellers think I'm merchandise, they'll have me for a song." Fractures were beginning to show between Leon, the artist, and Denny, the businessman. "They were drifting apart," said Ellen Basich. "Leon felt Denny wasn't focused enough on his career."

"I played *Carney* for Denny, and he didn't like it," Leon said. "It actually was the biggest record I ever had." The album would hit number two on the *Billboard* album chart. But the partners found themselves dealing with the inevitable tension between art and commerce.

"Leon always liked a bit of the vaudeville," said Denny's son, Barney Cordell. "Dad hated it. He liked pure rock 'n' roll. *Carney*'s got that vaudeville thing. And then he started doing that stuff onstage—[it] got a bit showy, and Denny loathed it. He always liked it pure. They had a big fight over *Carney*."

It is curious that Denny envisioned Leon simply as "pure rock 'n' roll." It meant ignoring, or at least discounting, Leon's Hollywood sessions, playing, producing, writing, and arranging all manner of pop, from Herb Alpert's ersatz mariachi-tinged instrumentals to rococo Phil Spector Christmas productions. His old pals Johnny Cale and Jimmy Karstein had assumed Leon was on the path to becoming a new Henry Mancini or Nelson Riddle. His deeply engaging psychedelic records with Daughters of Albion and Asylum Choir had plenty of "vaudeville" influence. Moreover, Leon's showman schtick was there from day one on the Mad Dogs stage.

Maybe Denny thought he could keep Leon focused on one narrow lane. If so, he was just one of many who would find themselves frustrated in their attempts to box in Leon Russell.

Chapter 20

Leon's Live

BY THE TIME *CARNEY* WAS released in July 1972, it had been six months since Leon's last concert at the Rainbow in London. To some, it seemed like he reemerged after a long exile, even though his schedule had been nonstop. Pop stars today might not make music for a year or more, but that would have seemed like a lifetime in 1971–1972.

Nineteen seventy-two was another incredible year in popular music. In the run-up to the June release of *Carney*, Elton John released *Honky Château*; Aretha Franklin issued her live *Amazing Grace* (her second release in 1972, following *Young, Gifted and Black*); and the Rolling Stones, their double-LP masterpiece, *Exile on Main St.* Those three albums all trod similar ground as Leon Russell's first few records, with plenty of gospel-informed piano on each.

Leon was on the vanguard of white rockers infusing their music with Black church music. On the *Carney* tour, Leon cranked up the gospel quotient, not merely incorporating the influence but also performing actual spirituals like "Great Day" and "Sweeping Through the City." He accomplished this with help from four members of the Church of God in Christ, a Southern Pentecostal denomination: Patrick Henderson, Wacy Crowder, and Mary Ann and Phyllis Lindsey—now collectively known as Black Grass—had never performed outside a church. In *A Poem Is a Naked Person*, Les Blank and Maureen Gosling went down to Denton, Texas, to Henderson's Church of God in Christ to film a remarkable scene of a service.

"I went from church to arenas with twenty, thirty, forty thousand people in them," Henderson said. "First-class flights, private jets; it was amazing. I was eighteen years old; it was quite a life-changing deal, of course. [The women] were swept up in it all. Of course, they could buy anything they wanted, they could go anywhere they wanted. They had money, real money. He paid us pretty well, it's more than I could ever have made in a week."

A breakdown of what it took to put on a Leon Russell show appeared in the *New Mexico Daily Lobo* on September 1, 1972. Leon's fee was $15,000—plus 60 percent of the gross receipts over $27,000—for his show on August 30 at the University of New Mexico. "Leon Russell's favorite drink is Jose Cuervo Gold tequila," wrote Aaron Howard. "He will not do a concert unless there are several bottles of Jose Cuervo in his dressing room before the show." Beyond the booze, though, the article, titled "How to Gross $30G and Lose Money," does a thorough job of explaining the costs and risks associated with promoting large-scale rock concerts during the era when those shows graduated from ballrooms and theaters to arenas and stadiums. The promoter in New Mexico, Leonard Levy, lost money on the show, selling only 6,100 tickets. The show grossed $29,800. The Rolling Stones had recently played there and grossed $87,000, netting the band and their production company $63,000. In the interview, Peter Nicholls explained that Leon and the band were touring with their own sound, stage, and lighting gear carried in two trucks, one of which was owned by Showco. Leon's fee was relatively modest, and he was traveling with an eleven-piece band. Joe Cocker was receiving $25,000 a night, as were Jefferson Airplane.

Marjoe Gortner appeared onstage with Leon at this New Mexico show as well as at least one other on the tour. Marjoe had been a tent revival preacher at the age of four, preternaturally charismatic, with curly golden locks and a bow tie. He was the subject of the 1972 documentary *Marjoe*, which won the Academy Award for Best Documentary. Evangelism was the family business, and business was good. But his father flew the coop, taking much of the fortune that Marjoe had accrued. Gortner had abandoned the holy-roller circuit as a teenager, taking up with beatniks and beach bums, only to return to his calling when money ran low. The film covered his last tour as a Pentecostal preacher, when he pulled the veil back on the tricks of the trade and confessed it was always all about the dough-re-me. Still blessed with golden-boy looks, Gortner went into acting, appearing on seventies and eighties TV shows like *Kojak*, *Falcon Crest*, and *Circus of the Stars*.

In the film about him, Gortner discusses how he incorporated rock 'n' roll elements into his shows and points out the specific move he lifted from Mick Jagger: one hand on hip, the other holding the microphone, prancing back and forth. Jagger swiped the move from Tina Turner, who was raised singing in the choir of her Baptist church. The documentary serves as a vivid reminder of the inexorable circular influence of the Black gospel and tent-revival Pentecostal traditions on rock 'n' roll. As the faithful approach Marjoe to be healed with a laying-on-of-hands, their knees buckle, and they are caught by an assistant and patted down or draped with "prayer cloths" from the preacher himself, the supply replenished by another assistant. The scene will be familiar to anyone who recalls Elvis Presley's seventies ritual of bestowing sweat-laced scarves on his adoring public.

Leon and Gortner shared a mutual fascination with one another. Leon made the same proposal to Marjoe that Tommy Tedesco had made to Leon back in 1963. "He had this grand idea," Gortner said. "He got a hold of me through my agent at the William Morris office. And he was staying up at the Chateau Marmont, down on Sunset Boulevard. And he called me up and he said, 'Marjoe, I want to be your musical director. We're gonna get tents and trailers and tractors. You'll do the preaching and I'll do the music, we'll get a big Black choir, and we're going to go on the road.' I said, 'Who's going to finance that, the Lord Himself?!' That's where it all started." But the idea of a full-scale tent revival produced by Leon did not get past the idea stage. Instead, Leon had Marjoe make appearances during his sets on the *Carney* tour. Marjoe continued, "He was playing at the Forum at that time, a twenty-thousand-seat arena, packed. And he asked me to introduce it. And I did. I jumped up on top of the grand piano and I did one of my hallelujah speeches."

Leon's sets became even more well-oiled. The setlists were consistent, and though spontaneity and improvisation were built-in elements, the performers watched Leon closely as he dictated the dynamics and energy. The loose-limbed feel of the grooves belied the band's precision. The intense pacing was carefully choreographed and the shared spotlight-featured vocal performances from Don Preston and the other singers partially allowed Leon to catch a breath.

"Everything was original unless we did something by Dylan or the Stones," Henderson said. "Everything was really set in stone, and people still came back year after year; they didn't care. He would have people take something of value from their purse or their bodies and ask them to give it to somebody they didn't know, to show real love." In *Marjoe*, Gortner and other preachers ask the gathered to dig deep for their monetary contributions, to make it hurt as a "sacrifice."

Leon explained this practice: "One time on Long Island, I suggested that everybody in the audience take their clothes off and put them on-stage so we can send them to some relief effort that was going on in South America. That was an interesting concert." Henderson, laughing, remembered, "Oh God, I remember Long Island! I remember people would throw their clothes on the stage, especially the women. They would throw stuff, but that was their offering. That's the way he looked at [it]. It wasn't just enough that they bought the ticket; they wanted to give more."

The first show of the *Carney* tour was at the Tulsa Fairground Speedway on June 18—a Shelter festival of sorts, with Freddie King, J. J. Cale, and Willis Ramsey on the bill. Kay Poorboy had dressed Carla in white to match Leon, who wore a loose-fitting, open-collared white shirt, mirrored shades, with his long, flowing hair topped with a white fedora. Carla, who had given birth five months earlier, looked ravishing in white Daisy Duke cut-offs and a puffy white halter top. She joined the singers in throwing tambourines emblazoned with the original Shelter logo from the stage (Shelter's first logo was an upside-down Superman insignia; it was redone after DC Comics filed a copyright-infringement suit).

Good vibes between Carla and Leon were short-lived, however, because Leon began a fling with Phyllis Lindsey. Carla noticed Phyllis wearing one of Leon's jackets at the lake house. "So Phyllis walks in with the jacket on, and she looks at my mom," said Blue. "She walks right up to my mom—my mom's nursing me—and says, 'He's gonna buy me a Mercedes,' with just *all* the swag and attitude. And my mom, she got pissed off. She walks into the bedroom, and he's laying on the bed—and their mattress was on the floor—and she stood up on the bed and pulled up her dress. She said, 'Do you see this? Take a good look. Because this is the last motherfuckin' time you're gonna see or get any of this pussy.' And she went to the house on Sandusky [in Tulsa]."

Carla and Leon split for the last time. "She was really strung out on heroin," Blue said. "Carla was *crazy*. Cray. Zee." He kept trying to get her to come back. Blue said that Leon turned off the electricity at the rental house on Sandusky. Carla's family was furious and tried to get her to go after some of his money. "She's like, 'No, no, it's his money. He's worked hard for his money. He earned that money.' It's when he bought a Mercedes for Phyllis, and it was in the news somewhere, that's when my mom got upset.

"Keep in mind, the attorney at the time was Dad's attorney, and he was the attorney of attorneys for the state of Oklahoma. Mom walked in there, no shoes, tiny little shorts, and a cutoff buckskin little leather top, no bra, and puts her feet up on the desk. She didn't have an appointment or nothing. She leans forward, taps her finger on his desk, and she says, 'I just want whatever a Mercedes costs. That's what I want for my daughter. And you make that happen.' And he's just [*stammering*]. And she kept tapping the top of that desk with her finger, 'Whatever a Mercedes costs.' He picked up the phone and made a call." Message and money received.

It is natural to wonder whether such stories have been exaggerated over the intervening decades. But all accounts agree that Carla was independent, strong-willed—her larger-than-life personality shines through in a 2020 video interview she granted Teresa Knox (who bought and restored Leon's Church Studio)—and a serious addict. But she straightened out in a big way.

"Years later, my mom becomes a drug and alcohol counselor for the Native American community," Blue said. "She became the director of a facility. She really worked hard and busted her ass, carrying nineteen-plus hours, full-time. She went on to really do great things. She was one of the people that started NA [Narcotics Anonymous] in Tulsa, and she's helped thousands of people." One day years afterward in a Tulsa courtroom, Carla "was standing in the hallway, and this man came up and tapped her on the shoulder: 'Carla Brown?' And she's like, 'I used to be; my new name is McHenry.' She's all prim and proper by this point. And he said, 'I'm that attorney, you came in and put your feet up on my desk, tapped your fingers.' She's like, 'Oh my God, I'm so sorry.' He's like, 'No, no, no!'"

Before the band left Oklahoma for the tour, Bob Dylan came to the lake for the first time, and brought his family. "In the middle of the night, this camper truck arrived," Peter Nicholls said. "We were all sitting around doing acid or something, and all of a sudden, there's Dylan getting out of this camper."

Dylan recorded roughly an album's worth of material there, and then scrapped it, making sure John LeMay erased it entirely. "I think he was planning to stay a week, but he only stayed a couple days, because there were too many people around," Maureen Gosling said. "He was feeling intimidated or shy, and everybody was walking on eggshells around him, not wanting to bother him. We probably seemed like we were ignoring him, too, just to give him some space. But he and Leon took a boat out, and that was the time when they talked to each other. And they might have played some music out there, but nobody went with them. I remember Les being excited, thinking he might be able to film and Leon thinking he might jam. It didn't happen. Les said it felt like he had a butterfly on his tripod. He couldn't shoot, you know?"

"Lola [one of the caretakers] was quite a talker and storyteller in her own right," Leon wrote. "One day, when I was returning home from a speedboat cruise with Bob Dylan, Lola came up with glasses of iced tea and spoke to Bob: 'You know,' she said, pointing at me, 'this guy here is famous all over the world.' Bob smiled and shared her enthusiastic astonishment at this fact." Dylan would soon return to the lake again on his way back from shooting *Pat Garrett and Billy the Kid* in Mexico, bringing along Harry Dean Stanton and a few other friends.

There must be Blank-shot footage of the Tulsa Fairgrounds show because the filmmaker can be seen in a photo, onstage with a film camera shooting Leon from below, from the stage floor. But the first live concert footage to make it into the finished film is from the Warehouse in New Orleans on July 28 and 29. The band had been on the road for about a month already and were cooking. The venue was raw and intimate, a nineteenth-century cotton warehouse with exposed rafters and brick walls and a small stage. But they could fit thirty-five hundred people, standing cheek by jowl. One of the film's best scenes shows Leon coming out from backstage and setting a plate of jambalaya atop the grand piano, eating it as he sits down, before launching into a scorching version of Hank Williams's "Jambalaya."

"Les was very excited because Leon actually introduced him onstage with the band because Les was up there with his camera," Gosling recalled. "Things were good in the beginning, in terms of Leon and Les's relationship. Leon gave him a T-shirt from the Warehouse as a gift. And then Les gave him a bottle of rum."

Artist Jim Franklin also showed up at the lake that summer before the band got on the road. Leon and Denny had met him at the Armadillo World Headquarters, the Austin rock 'n' roll venue, where Franklin was artist in residence, designing distinctive posters and murals to promote the shows. Leon and Denny were there for a Freddie King show and were blown away by a poster Franklin had painted of King in mid-note-bend, an armadillo bursting from his heart. They commissioned a version of the painting for King's next album cover, *Texas Cannonball* (1972), yet another stellar record produced by the Shelter pair and featuring the cream of Leon's players, including himself.

"I was up on the scaffold working on that, and they come walking in," Franklin recalled. "First thing that Cordell said was, 'That painting is a *mawn-stah*. We want to use it for the *covuh*.' Leon then invited me to come to Oklahoma and paint his recording studio and cabins. And when I got up there, I actually saw the pool had just been plastered. I said, 'I want to paint the pool.' So that chewed up a year."

Franklin is a central figure in *A Poem Is a Naked Person*. The camera ran out of film during a crucial early scene in which country music titan George Jones casually tosses off a devastating solo version of "Take Me" (cowritten with Leon Payne and first recorded in 1966) filmed at Bradley's Barn near Nashville during Leon's *Hank Wilson's Back* sessions. Despite running out of film, we can still hear the exquisite intimacy of the performance on the soundtrack. Here is a rarely offered glimpse of Jones, in a wide-lapeled brown leisure suit, drinking Budweiser from a can, as casual as if he were quietly singing it to himself driving down some late-night back road. The film's final cut continues the audio track of Jones's performance while Franklin scoops scorpions out of the pool, plopping them into a mason jar. It was a daily ritual: Franklin liked to paint in his bare feet and did not want to get stung.

Franklin recalled a couple of recording sessions while he was at the lake for his roughly year-long residency. "Their plan was to have a nice comfortable place far away from the city, so they wouldn't be distracted, but it turns out that Tulsa was not far enough away, so maybe they can run into

Tulsa instead of spending the night out at the lake. So, that didn't really quite work out that way."

Franklin didn't become friends with Leon, per se, though they remained in touch over the years. "He was always a little bit distant, you know? Part of the project was the paintings on the wall [in a cottage], and he was explaining to me why he wasn't gonna pay me. 'So this painting is going to be more famous than anything you do.' You know, my fame was going to be greatly boosted by doing this work for him for free. And he agreed to pay my expenses, but he didn't offer any kind of chunk, you know? I know that Leon puts a price on each concert he does; he's got a price. 'Why couldn't you do that for me?' Why is it that he treats fellow artists in such a way?"

Harold Thompson recalled a similar issue about Leon and Denny holding back payments. "As I was about to leave one evening, John LeMay, the studio engineer, made the remark that he was going to pull all the wiring out that he had so painstakingly installed, allegedly because he hadn't been paid." Les Blank asked if he could film it. "Nothing happened, but it added to the drama."

Jim Franklin stuck around, but he did not feel he was treated fairly. They used the Freddie King painting, paying Franklin "maybe less than $1,000, and they kept the painting. Cordell was—those guys were just screwing every musician out of whatever they could because they'd been screwed out on their rise to fame by record companies. So they were gonna turn around and screw other people who are trying to get their names out there, you know, and it's like, 'Come on, man! Whose side are you on, motherfuckers?'"

Buddy Jones, a drummer friend of Leon, had gone to Hollywood in the sixties, but then returned to Tulsa. David Teegarden, who played drums for Bob Seger (who'd recorded *Back in '72* at Leon's lake studio), explained, "At that point, he [Jones] had quit playing drums. He was a full-fledged entrepreneur." Jones had gotten into retail businesses, including carpet remnants. Leon began partnering with Jones on show promotion, including for the Tulsa Fairgrounds show in June 1972. They formed Cowboy Carnival Productions. Bob Morris, Jones's brother-in-law, said, "It wasn't a management deal as much as it was a partnership in projects." Cordell had acted as Leon's manager. Peter Nicholls said, "He didn't need one. His erstwhile childhood friends—quote, *friends*—wanted to be his personal managers. They did not serve him well."

Even more than at Skyhill, Leon had created a welcoming, relaxed, and creative gathering spot at the lake. Franklin brought some other friends up from Austin to work on building out the Grand Lake compound. He also was accompanied by his boa constrictor, Chula, whom Blank filmed eating a baby chicken. "Denny said something like he didn't care how long we would take; he was totally open to us staying," Gosling said. But things got rocky fairly early on the *Carney* tour. Blank was drinking heavily, using cocaine when it was available, and partying backstage. He can be seen in one such scene, shot backstage at an August show in Anaheim, guzzling down a can of beer and then making out with a young woman. He quickly became overly familiar with Leon, who concluded Blank was abusing the access.

The Anaheim show was one of Leon's four LA-area concerts, all sold out in under four days, about one hundred thousand tickets total, with scalpers asking twenty dollars for tickets with a face value of five dollars. On August 28, a show at the Long Beach Arena was recorded for the *Leon Live* album, mixed at Ardent, and released in 1973. Some of the concert footage from Blank's film was shot there too. The LA-area shows also constitute much of *Leon Russell: The Best of the Leon Russell Festivals* DVD, another project that would take decades to see the light of day. Instead of film, *The Best of the Leon Russell Festivals* was shot on videotapes that were intended to be transferred to film for theatrical release, similar to the *T.A.M.I. Show*. While video was still a primitive technology, expensive and cumbersome, Leon and Denny were attracted to its potential.

The director of this project was Robert Stone Jordan, later described as "criminally insane" by his son, Jordan Roberts, who wrote and directed *Around the Bend*, a 2004 drama based on his father. "Leon's really lucky that he got any video at all because, as it turns out, Robert Stone Jordan's chief vocation was being a master con man," explained Jeffrey Haas, who finally shepherded the video to release decades later. "His usual modus operandi was to get a large deposit from his victims, then change his identity and run off into the hinterlands, buy a bunch of dope and party with his friends. . . . But the only reason he actually did step up and do an actual production instead of skipping town was because he idolized Leon

Russell, and it was his dream to actually do a concert film with the Master of Space and Time." Unsurprisingly, the quality control was lacking, and the resulting videotape was mangled. Leon took one look at the glitchy result and canned it.

Robert Jordan went to Tulsa a year or so later. "People were not happy with that video shoot," Gosling said. "And when [Jordan] came to visit Leon, there was one night when he talked fourteen hours straight with Leon," some of which is shown in *A Poem Is a Naked Person*. "[Jordan] was kind of obnoxious. I mean, he was just super egotistical."

Jordan's shoddy video work remained in a nonfunctioning freezer for years until Haas and associates finally and painstakingly rescued it. Unlike the Les Blank footage, the Leon video has the barely acceptable quality of a bootleg. But it captures Leon at his pinnacle as a performer.

In *The Best of the Leon Russell Festivals*, the band launches into the up-tempo two-chord back-and-forth vamp from Bobby "Blue" Bland's "Turn On Your Love Light." Leon comes on like a guru wrapped in Wrangler denim and rolls into a gospel preacher overture. He quotes "Tight Rope" over the Staples Singers' "I'll Take You There," released that year. The eclectic medley also includes "Idol with the Golden Head," a lesser-known track from the Coasters; "I Serve a Living Savior," a gospel song by Betty Watson sung in a rich bellow by Patrick Henderson; and Bob Dylan's "Quinn the Eskimo (The Mighty Quinn)."

With a wave of the maestro's hand, the band stops on a dime. Leon promises, "If you leave this place and you don't feel like you've had a religious experience, you go and ask for your money back because *I don't need it*." He jumps on the piano, takes solos on the guitar, strutting in desert boots, a rainbow patch on the ass of his jeans. He sits back down at the piano and swigs a can of Bud.

Chuck Blackwell's fiery talent is on full display. The pacing is relentless, and the drummer has to do the most work in pretty much any rock 'n' roll setting. Chuck is a crackerjack force on these shows, in perpetual motion, drenched with sweat. In one scene of *A Poem Is a Naked Person*, Leon signals for a stop during "Amazing Grace," and Blackwell writhes and rolls his head in ecstasy, feeling Leon's every drawn-out note. He buries his face in his hands, still clutching his drumsticks. As Marjoe said, "If you can't feel the Holy Spirit here tonight, you must be dead." Blackwell is the engine for this integrated band, helping deliver gospel music to an arena of white kids (there's not a person of color visible in the audience).

Throughout the filmed shows, which unfold almost without pauses, cameramen dance onstage. There's a claustrophobic intimacy of onlookers crowding the wings of the stage while the band lays into a particularly funky version of "Young Blood," during the medley with "Jumpin' Jack Flash." The sustained intensity for these shows rivals that of the Stones at their 1972–1973 live peak.

The Shelter People maintain an exquisite balance for such a sprawling band, heard in fine detail (if suffering from a thin-sounding mix) on *Leon Live*. Henderson intuitively understood how to play around Leon. "I knew what he wanted," Henderson explained. "I am a rhythm player. And John Gallie was really one of the best organists I've ever played with." As with Mad Dogs, various members of the band get spotlight moments.

Leon gives a shout-out to Macon, Georgia, "home of some of my favorite singers." He lists off Otis Redding, James Brown, the Mighty Hannibal (whose 1966 record "Hymn No. 5" Leon and Elton would revisit in 2010), and the Allman Brothers, before paying tribute to Little Richard with "Crystal Closet Queen."

Leon sings a Ray Charles–inspired version of "A Song for You" in Long Beach. During the instrumental interlude, he explains, "I write these little songs from time to time, and every once in a while, I run into someone who knows how to sing 'em." He brings out D. J. Rogers, a recent Shelter Records signing. Whereas Leon had whipped up the crowd response for over an hour, Rogers, who grew up in the church around Los Angeles, slowly brings the place to a rolling boil.

While out on the road, Leon met a couple who would become his lifelong friends. "It was the summer of 1972," said Connie Nelson, "and this car dealer friend of Willie's and mine had a car dealership in Big Spring, Texas. He offered to give us a new car to drive for a year, free of charge, just to advertise it. He was a big fan of Willie's. So I flew up to Big Spring, one way so that I could drive the car back. There was nothing between Big Spring and Austin; all you had was limited radio. So I stopped at this record store to get some music for the trip. As soon as I opened the door, this music was playing. It was haunting music. I asked the guy, 'Who is that playing over the speaker?' And he said, 'Well, it's new music by Leon

Russell, and the album is called *Carney*.' And so I said, 'Okay, I want that, *immediately*.'

"I pulled up to [a] phone booth. I wanted Willie to know I was on my way back anyway, but I said, 'Oh my God, you have got to hear this new music!' I literally pulled the car right up by the phone booth, and I blasted it so that he could hear it. By the time I got back to Austin, I just couldn't talk about anything else. I played it for Willie, and he was as amazed as I was."

The Nelsons saw Leon in Texas that August. "I told Connie, 'This man is one of the greatest entertainers I've ever seen,'" Willie recalled. "I understood how his image—with his crazy stovepipe hat and dark aviator glasses—added to his mysterious allure."

"From that time on, pretty much," Connie said, "is when Willie started letting his hair grow and his beard."

"He was incredible," Willie said. "He had them on their feet, yelling all the way through the show. I remember when he had them just really yelling and screaming for him, at a fever pitch, he said, 'Stop right here. I want you to remember who put you here and make sure you don't let anybody get you in a state of mind because now you'd do anything I said. So just be careful who you let take you to this point.' So that was pretty incredible for him to say that."

"My job at that time," Peter Nicholls said, "was to deal with the police and security and to encourage two things. 'One is, let him do what he does. He will control them; you won't.' And then I had to persuade Leon: 'Leon, for your encore, please do "A Song for You." Calm it the fuck down.'" Leon and the authorities both understood that someone who can stop a riot could also start one. "In fact, I'd turn it around," Nicholls said. "Only the person who starts it can finish it. He and I used to have long conversations about it. How closely do you allow them to come? Basically, '72 to '73, that was what it was all about, crowd control. They got it, the crowds. They loved him; they got it."

After the show, Willie "came backstage with some truly Jamaican-sized joints for my approval," Leon recalled. Connie said it was a lovefest from the start, adding: "I was so intimidated by Leon because it was like he could see right through every thought you had. I wasn't scared of him, but I was just *intimidated*."

"Leon and I laughed and joked a lot and he was an incredible musician and an incredible person to go along with it," Willie said. "I'm lucky to have known him."

At the end of August 1972, Leon bought a brick Georgian mansion built by the Aaronson family at 1151 East 24th Place in the tony Maple Ridge section on Tulsa's south side, near Woodward Park. Emily Smith had discovered it for sale just as Leon was about to head out on tour and told him it was "one of a kind." It was a depressed time for real estate in the city, and the house had been on the market a while. Without touring the property, Leon made an offer. The listing price was $295,000, and his offer of $75,000 was accepted. Leon was on the road at the time and could not get back to see it until he had a day off in Texas a couple of months later. He wrote, "I rented a plane and flew through the worst storm I had ever experienced. . . . It was well worth the trouble. After being inside the house for about ten minutes, I was standing in the ballroom when I suddenly remembered that I had played a graduation party there for [the house's previous owner] Trish McClintock when I was in high school. . . . When I was a teenager, my family lived on Tulsa's north side in a considerably more modest housing addition; the home I was standing in was the only house on the more expensive south side that I had ever been in at that time."

He continued, "Fifteen years later, the home was in quite a different condition. The magnificent wood paneling, as I later found out, was covered in eleven coats of paint of various garish colors. All the paint was removed, back down to the original wood, with a little trouble, except for the fire that started when one of the workers dragged his steel wool over a live electrical outlet." Thankfully, he added, "the insurance provided enough funds to completely redecorate the entire smoke-damaged house."

Gosling said she and Les came to visit soon after Leon bought the place. "We were sitting on the front porch of the front steps of the mansion," Gosling said. She and Blank were still operating on only a handshake deal with Denny and Leon. "Les said, 'Leon, we really need to get a contract worked out.' And Leon says, 'Okay, but just give me a minute, I gotta go take a shit.' We didn't see him for three more months." Gosling and Blank did not see Leon again until January 1973.

While the mansion was being renovated, Leon lived with his friends Larry and Ann Bell and their twin children when he was back in Tulsa (the Grand Lake property was over an hour's drive from the city). Some days

Ann would wake up and find a bunch of teenage girls camped out on the lawn waiting to get a glimpse of Leon. She would go out and feed the fans, paying forward the support she'd received from Leon. "He was with me when I was in the hospital and gave birth to my twin daughters," she continued. "That was in 1971. Of course, the first day that Leon came into the hallway where my room was, some of the nurses and the little candy stripers recognized who he was. Well, they started screaming like the Beatles had walked in. 'I didn't mean to bring the circus with me,' he said." After expressing dismay that Ann would be transporting her newborns around in a Volkswagen Bug, Leon bought her a Cadillac Fleetwood and told her not to allow Larry to drive it.

Leon gave Emily Smith carte blanche to take a trip to England to buy him antiques to furnish the new house. He installed a studio in the basement, installing a forty-track Stephens tape machine in the basement studio. At that time, a twenty-four-track was the pinnacle of recording technology. They had to dig down to create enough height but failed to consider drainage. "And then one of those good Tulsa thunderstorms flooded the basement," Bob Morris said. "They had to completely rip out all the wiring they put in and put it back in, put in French drains, and rewire the whole control room again."

Jim Karstein said, "There was a concrete pillar right in the middle of the room. Well, it was made of bricks. It was important to the integrity of the structure. But Leon told [Steve Busch] to get rid of it because he couldn't see past it."

It would get even worse, Morris recalled. "Leon said, 'I want a big brick oven in the kitchen.' Steve said, 'Sure.' So on top of this studio that had been dug out, with supports taken out, they put in this big kitchen, and slowly the center of the house starts [sagging]." When the house was sold years later, the assessment was that it was caving in from the middle down and could not be saved. "They razed it and put in four or five small McMansions," Morris said.

Leon and the band had been on the road all summer and would continue through the fall and winter. *Carney* was certified gold in September and hit number two on the *Billboard* Top 200. There was a slate of glowing reviews of the live shows, including the *New York Times*'s notice of Leon's concert at Nassau Coliseum in September: "One of the great rock concerts of this or any other year. . . . Constantly surprising, ever-changing, coming out at the audience with the fleet, sudden movements of a professional football halfback, his music was dramatic in the best sense of the word."

Renovations at the mansion were coming along by November 1972. Leon camped out there for Thanksgiving week. "He hadn't moved anything in except this grand piano. And it was down on the ground floor, and there was a ballroom in that house," Jim Franklin said. "I had the pleasure of hearing him rock the entire house. It was just amazing what power that guy had. Leon woke me up at like four in the morning, and he said, 'Franklin, let's drive to Austin. The Grateful Dead are playing there, and I've never seen 'em.' So we get in his Mercedes, and we stopped in Enid, Oklahoma, where his parents lived. I got to meet them. And we had a brief hour or so there and then drove on into Austin from there."

The Dead were at Municipal Auditorium on November 22. The hippie staff at the Armadillo World Headquarters fed the band before the show—beef tenderloins with bowls of joints as centerpieces. Jerry Garcia took in the surroundings and announced that he would love to play at the Armadillo. He asked if it was open the next day, Thanksgiving. The Armadillo's owner, Eddie Wilson, said he would be glad to open the venue and quickly spread the word via a local radio station that there would be a holiday performance by some friends. After the Dead's show, Wilson was backstage. "I was standing there with Leon Russell when Jerry walked in," Wilson said. "He goes, 'We're gonna jam tomorrow at the Armadillo; why don't you come over?' Leon says, 'Fine, what time?' And Garcia looks over at me, and I say, 'How about three o'clock?'"

Franklin said Leon had not arranged for a place to stay that night. "He didn't book a motel or hotel or anything, but he said, 'Well, where am I going to stay?' I said, 'Well, the Armadillo's got several beautiful great ladies that are there and ready to take care of you,' which they did. So he spent the first night there. And then the next night, Willie had gotten an apartment on Riverside Drive, where he was staying at the time, so the next morning, we drifted over to Willie's place."

The Austin singer-songwriter Doug Sahm and Willie's drummer Paul English also came by to hang out. "It was there that Leon wrote 'You Look Like the Devil' [from *Shotgun Willie*] about Paul English," Franklin said. Willie also covered "A Song for You" on *Shotgun Willie*.

Willie recalled the first time Leon and English met. "I was sitting at a table with Leon, and Paul English came by, and he had his red cape on.

And I remember Leon said, 'Who is that?' I said, 'That's Paul English.' And he said, 'He better be good.'"

People started to filter into the Armadillo Thanksgiving afternoon, unsure of what to expect. "Garcia wouldn't go on," Wilson said. "He said, 'Let's just wait till Doug [Sahm] gets here. He's the bandleader; he knows a thousand songs.'" Sahm led a rambling jam that tightened up over the course of two sets, with Garcia on guitar and pedal steel, Leon, and Dead bassist Phil Lesh. Local musicians joined, and about a thousand people enjoyed twenty-nine songs, mostly covers.

On "Wild Side of Life," Leon takes over lead vocals from Sahm and trades licks with Garcia and the fiddlers. He duets with Garcia on Dylan's "It Takes a Lot to Laugh, It Takes a Train to Cry," takes the lead on such others as "Wild Horses," and offers a sneak peek of his own "Slipping into Christmas." "I wrote this song the other day," he says, introducing it. "It's a Christmas song. I think everyone should have a Christmas song." He also plays a sweet guitar solo on Merle Haggard's "Today I Started Loving You Again."

Eddie Wilson said, "Leon Russell later told me, 'It may have been my worst performance ever.' He's not a jam musician. He's an arranged guy." He was also not a fan of the Dead. But watching a bunch of tripping Texas hippies enjoying two sets that consisted of about half country covers may have served as partial inspiration for Leon to do a whole album of country songs for his next project.

Chapter 21

Hank Wilson's Back

BY THE 1970S, TULSA'S MUSIC scene was thriving. Don Preston took up residence in the city, first at Leon's mansion, then bought his own house, where he lived for another six years or so, before returning to Los Angeles. Even Gary Lewis was living in town, working on a new band called Medicine. "The entire atmosphere of Tulsa was musicians," said Lewis, who was happy to escape the sprawling LA megalopolis. "Go to different clubs and hear the different musicians all the time. It was great. There was room enough for everybody."

Tulsa also struggled with the sort of cultural tension that would have been expected in a southwestern American city in the early seventies. Leon was a big silver-maned target caught up in that cultural upheaval. The December 8, 1972, *Tulsa World* reported: "Internationally known hard rock recording star Leon Russell of Tulsa is among sixty-two persons named in subpoenas issued here as the Tulsa County Grand Jury launched a probe into the Tulsa drug scene." Leon was on the road at the time. The article continues, "When in Tulsa, Russell has been known to frequent the Brookside area along South Peoria Avenue where some local teen-agers often congregate and where some drug activity has been the target of arrests in the past. There is also speculation the grand jury is interested in what Russell might know about drug abuse among various musicians of his acquaintance." The possibility that he was in Brookside to grab a snack at Claud's Hamburgers was not mentioned in the article, but neither was the fact that one of Leon's roadies was busted for possession of narcotics when the band played in Louisville on September 29, 1972.

The subpoena was one of the first indications that "going back to Tulsa" would not help Leon escape public scrutiny. But he was mainly on the road. "In '72 we did 265 one-nighters," Don Preston said. "In America, we all flew together most of the time. We flew first class—so much fun."

The lucrative touring continued into the new year. Tour manager Peter Nicholls said, "All of '73, we were grossing a hundred and fifty grand a week, easy. The two top-grossing traveling bands in America were Led Zeppelin and Leon Russell. Here's the numbers: Led Zeppelin had a 25 percent margin. Okay, so twenty-five cents of that gross revenue went into profit. Leon Russell had a 55 percent gross margin. We were a money machine. We decided to move the operation from Los Angeles to Tulsa. We used to go out and play four days a week, and we absolutely cleaned up. We worked with the same promoter as Led Zeppelin. But it was this phenomenally efficient touring organization. We could go into any basketball arena in the South, East, Southeast."

They had a formula for keeping expenses low. They traveled with their own sound, lights, and crew, and they prioritized smaller cities, which had fewer shows to compete with and were cheaper to play. The contracts called for each party being responsible for their own costs and splitting the net receipts. Nicholls claims he wrote the first concert contract rider (Johnny Cash had one as early as 1972 as well). "It was what we required in order that we could come and do our show. You know, stuff like, 'Don't give away tickets unless *we* tell you to,' because we were very strict about that. Leon used to throw a fit if there were any people sitting down, 'stuffed suits,' in the first twenty-five rows."

But Leon was personally beating a retreat. December saw a seven-page spread in *Creem* that examined Leon's increasing elusiveness. The writer J. R. Young lamented the run-around he was taken on by Dino Airali, who was described as a hip three-hundred-pound bearded promo man who'd smoke and snort you under the table. Airali took the writer for barbecue and club-hopping. They spilled into the next day, attending the Tulsa Fairgrounds show. The article ended with everyone up at the Grand Lake house, seven pages in, and no interview. "'Leon doesn't give interviews,' [Airali] laughed quite matter-of-factly."

By the following June, a *Hit Parader* article written by Mark David Schwartz suggested, "Maybe it is Leon's combination of musical talent and personal magnetism that make him the only candidate in the musical field that can fill the void left by the Beatles. There have been no superstars since them really—with the exception of Leon coming right up there on the inside track. He seems, like them, to be able to exert some philosophical influence as well as a musical one." It's less a profile than a caution to cultish followers who may fall under his sway, like a religious pamphlet warning against the devil in disguise.

No wonder Leon was fed up with the publicity machine. "I remember his amazement after the Bangladesh concert when the first hippie freaks started knocking on his door to tell him he was the new Jesus," wrote journalist Al Aronowitz. "Dylan and the Beatles had already gone through ten years of that kind of adulatory crap and Leon said he would try not to let it twist his head."

Groupies started showing up at the Church as soon as word got out it was Leon's. He erected a ten-foot brick wall around the Tulsa estate, with an intercom at the motorized gate. He sank into a prolonged depression after a sustained manic period. Meanwhile, he was trying to get Carla back, or at the very least, he wanted to see Blue. "[Carla] came over in her little Karmann Ghia, and she was buzzing the buzzer, and nobody was answering," said Blue. "So she rammed her car into that gate."

Leon's relationship with Phyllis Lindsey didn't last long. After the 1972 tour, the three women of Black Grass were gone, and Leon sent Patrick Henderson back to Dallas for more backing singers. He would return with four new women. "From late '72 to '73, my dad had many, many, *many* girlfriends," Blue said. "Emily [Smith] said, 'He was fucking all of Tulsa.'" Carla and her family brought legal action against Leon, who set up a trust for Blue. He also bought Carla's mother's house for them to stay in, as part of a settlement.

Then it all came crashing down. On "Christmas in Chicago," the B-side of his 1972 single "Slipping into Christmas," he sings, with a little levity, "If they find me in a snowdrift with a bottle in my hand / 'Cause my baby left with Santa when he put that diamond on her hand." "Slipping" rose to number four on the *Billboard* Christmas chart, but Leon was barely getting out of bed.

"Mom said every time she showed up, he would want her to come up to the bedroom," Blue said. "He would just be lying in his bed up there all the time. He was kind of crying out. But she was having none of it. Growing up, I always heard that he was agoraphobic, and then that kind of talk changed and became 'manic-depressive.' And then, as my mom became educated, it became, 'He's been bipolar all the time.'"

He began reemerging in early 1973. Musician Richard Feldman remembered Peter Nicholls had the keys to Leon's house and studio, and they would record there. In Feldman's own words, he was on the "B team" for the house band at the Church. He said Leon did his best to make him feel comfortable, but "he was intense, man. When he looked at you, it was no joke."

Feldman was among Leon's extended entourage as he started to venture out occasionally to Tulsa clubs. Once, they went to the International Club to catch the GAP Band, from the Greenwood section of town, site of the Tulsa race massacre fifty-two years prior. "GAP" stood for the neighborhood streets Greenwood, Archer, and Pine, "Black Wall Street." "They were absolutely amazing," Feldman said. "They would literally be thirty minutes on one chord." (The band would soon drop the all-caps spelling, to the Gap Band.)

"When you're from Tulsa, you go to all the clubs," said Ann Bell. "Like, if you had a weekend that you weren't playing, we would go support whoever was. And of course, North Tulsa at the time was predominantly the Black community back in those years. And there were some clubs over in North Tulsa where the Gap Band were playing, and . . . they blew us away because they had the horns, they dressed like Sly and the Family Stone."

The band's core was three brothers who had grown up in the musical hotbed of the Church of God in Christ: Charlie, Ronnie, and Robert Wilson. The group was fleshed out by seasoned Tulsa pros like guitarist O'Dell Stokes, who had played with Bobby "Blue" Bland, Ike & Tina Turner, and Flash Terry; Stokes's brother, Rowe; bassist Leon Rollerson; and drummer Roscoe James Smith. The group was a discovery of Buddy Jones. "One evening, I was in a club in North Tulsa with some people, which was near the Church Studio, and the band that was playing absolutely had that entire joint rocking," Jones told author Teb Blackwell. "I thought to myself, I gotta get these guys into the studio!"

Jones brought the band into the Church. "Leon Russell wasn't there, so I thought it was a bullshit deal at the time," said Charlie Wilson. "But two hours later, here comes this long-bearded, silver-haired white man. 'Is these supposed to be the bad n****rs that you brought down here for me to see? Ha, ha, ha.' That's a direct quote. I said, 'Yeah, we the bad n****rs that came here for you to see.' But we played, and he got serious. We played for two hours without stopping. When he got off that piano, he stood there and said, 'Boy, you guys can play!'" They jammed with Leon all night and half of the next day. This chemistry would lead to a collaboration with Leon on his *Stop All That Jazz* album and subsequent tour.

Guitarist and engineer Roger Linn was about to walk into Leon's world. He recalled the Gap Band "were a very powerful band; the very talented Wilson brothers, and some other guys in there. I think [Leon] liked this big band sound. The Gap Band's drummer, they referred to him as 'Toast,' because he had been in a fire and got his face burned." Smith had "suffered second- and third-degree burns over 65 percent of his body" in a gasoline fire at the age of fifteen, according to his December 2010 obituary.

You can see a glimpse of the magic that attracted Leon to them in a video online, with him leading the band through a scorching little set at the Church for an episode of *Midnight Special*. Chuck Blackwell was the one carryover from the Shelter People, drumming alongside the Gap Band's Smith. Ann Bell, Marcy Levy, Lena Lucky, and Pam Thompson sing backup, and Wayne Perkins plays guitar. "The music had a certain attitude to it," Bell said. "When we did it live, it was just his spontaneous response to the music, to the song itself, and to him because he would always set his piano where we would be around him. And we would feed off of Leon. Leon was a genius."

Bell was rebounding from her split with her husband, Leon's close friend Larry. She said Leon—always her mentor—rescued her. "In '72, I had some problems arise in our marriage, and Larry was struggling with heavy drug use. Smoking weed was one thing to me back then, but he began to deal with things like heroin," she said. "I had the twins; they were a few months old. I just didn't want to raise them around that. Within a week or two after we broke up, Leon said, 'Come over to the house.' I went over, and he said, 'You know I love your husband; he's like my brother. But I'm so glad that you're free from that because I didn't want that for you and those little babies,' and he hired me right then to sing with him. I was with Leon from about '73 to probably '77."

Buddy Jones said, "So we got them [the Gap Band] into the Church Studio and started recording them, but they had no original music. So I told them they needed original material. It turned out that they were good at writing the music but hadn't learned to write lyrics. So, I produced their first album and Charlie Wilson and I wrote most of the songs. After we started the sessions, Leon got interested in them and took them on the road to open for him." Jones wrote eight of the ten songs on the band's 1974 deep-funk debut, *Magician's Holiday*. One song, "Easy Life," also credits Kay Poorboy.

The Church was initially only the nickname given to the Shelter Records studio. Tom Russell (no relation to Leon), who was engineering down in Muscle Shoals, got a call one day from Denny Cordell asking him if he was interested in being the chief engineer at the Church. "I had mixed emotions," Russell said. "I didn't know anything about Tulsa other than it was out there somewhere." Russell came to town with Jeanie Greene, who had been married to Marlin Greene, the Muscle Shoals engineer on *Carney* and *Leon Russell and the Shelter People*. Marlin and Jeanie were among the singers Don Nix brought up for the Concert for Bangladesh; Jeanie went on to sing with Elvis Presley.

Tom and Jeanie arrived during an ice storm in November 1972. As Tom remembered, "It wasn't the best part of town. Leon had bought the whole block, except for one house. . . . These were little white frame houses. We used to call them shotgun shacks in the South. Leon's taste was never what I considered *up-to-date*, and he had gone in and remodeled all these things, and his idea of remodeling was going down to the local carpet outlet and picking out all the segments that he could get a good deal on, which turned out to be this long shag, neon-colored green and blue carpet. Each house had a different color. He recarpeted the whole thing, which was in keeping with the studio that he had in the mansion, down in the basement, which was completely covered with blue fur. You felt like you were swimming in a fishbowl."

Ron Henry, who would soon be brought in to manage Shelter Records, said, "He was known as the slumlord in Tulsa. He's the only one who bought apartment complexes that lost value. There were flunkies, or whatever you want to call them, roadies, whatever, they needed to be there. There were a lot of hangers-on. Leon attracted a lot of hangers-on, not necessarily positive."

Ambrose Campbell had one of the houses, as did J. J. Cale, right next door to Ambrose. "Ambrose was very strange," said Tom Russell. "If you went in his house, it was feathers and drums hanging everywhere. Plus, he wore a lot of traditional attire, which added to the mystique. And he had a couch on the front porch that was facing *into* the wall, not out. We never did understand that until one night, we happened to pass by, and we heard the sounds of what was going on. Ambrose attracted a lot of young girls from the town and guys too. He ended up in the backyard and had these old séances where they'd all gather. He was like a guru."

"I loved Ambrose; he was a character beyond belief," said Julie Chapman. "He knew how to charm the ladies and the Tulsa ladies particularly." Ambrose married his third wife, Antoinette, in Tulsa, and they had two daughters. Before marrying Danny's mother, he had been married to a woman in Plymouth, England.

Chapman was a freewheeling young woman from London. After a short stint in LA, Denny invited her to work in Tulsa. "I don't know much about Tulsa, but it was a job, and it's always interesting when you're young enough to keep moving." As it always was with Shelter, job titles were fluid. "I was called the office manager, but I thought of myself as a therapist because we had people that worked there from all parts of the country. You kept calm. But it was an incredibly fun time. There were so many interesting people."

Leon made relatively little use of the studio himself, as he had a great one with forty tracks in his own house. Tom Russell said, "I think that Leon had a real desire to try to give back to the local musicians, but from a business standpoint, I think the whole thing might have been a tax write-off."

Leon left all three of his Oklahoma studios behind and went to Nashville for his next project. He was burned out on touring, and the high level of energy he needed to sustain his legendary shows was in shorter supply. In early 1973, at the height of his popularity, he literally turned his back on rock 'n' roll, recording an album of country standards called *Hank Wilson's Back*, under the pseudonym Hank Wilson. Leon appears on the album's cover, with his back to the viewer, in a white suit and cowboy hat, like a hippie Hank Williams. Some money is sticking out of his back pocket as he stands onstage facing an audience—a vintage photo of a square dance.

The project was a labor of love, a luxury he could indulge. Contrary to mythology, Leon had not grown up listening to, never mind playing, country music. The Hank Wilson repertoire came from Leon selecting from hundreds of dollars' worth of trucker cassettes he bought at a truck stop on one of his countless drives between Los Angeles and Tulsa. "I just wanted to make a record that sounded like the radio the day before Elvis Presley came out," he said. In another interview, he stated, "I'd never been in a country band, and I lived in Tulsa. It wasn't until I got to California that I got in one. There are actually more hillbillies in California than there are in Oklahoma."

His friend Gram Parsons was already playing primarily country music, and the Rolling Stones, Grateful Dead, Creedence Clearwater Revival, and dozens of others were incorporating country twang into their own songs. But Leon was setting out to cover a slate of traditional country selections reverentially. His fast friendship with Willie Nelson was further evidence that rock 'n' rollers and country fans were not independent nations.

"I met Willie at a time when my profile was somewhat higher than his," Leon said later. "He said to me one day, 'You know, we ought to make records. We'd be the biggest thing in country music.' I thought he must have been kidding."

"Beyond [Leon's] mystery," Willie recalled, "I heard that his musical roots and mine were the same: Hank Williams, Bob Wills, country Black blues. To me, it felt as familiar as an old pair of jeans."

Willie and Connie Nelson had visited Leon at the Tulsa house and came away impressed. "We stayed a couple of nights with Leon," Connie said. "The bathroom was drums. His whole house was a recording studio. There were *big* wires, triple the size of garden hoses, running all through the house. You had to watch where you put your feet and where you walked."

"Leon was a major influence," Willie said. "I had gone to Tulsa and seen how he had built his homegrown kingdom," he wrote. "He had a recording studio, his own label, and his own elaborate roadshow. If Jerry Wexler had given me the confidence to be in control of my recordings, Leon showed me how to be in control of everything else, my musical universe."

Leon's attraction to Nashville had as much to do with shaking up his routines as with repertoire. "When I was playing in the section in LA, they were talking about how Nashville guys are always ready to play," Leon said. "I'm very fast myself. . . . I got to thinking, 'If those guys are that quick and that ready to play, I'm ready to play.'"

Bob Dylan had opened the door for rock 'n' roll artists to work with

Nashville cats as far back as 1965, when first-call Nashville session man Charlie McCoy, visiting New York as a tourist, was enlisted by Nashville-based producer Bob Johnston to play on *Highway 61 Revisited*. The sessions, though, were in New York. McCoy picked up a nylon-string classical guitar and added lyrical weaving lines to the album's closing track, "Desolation Row." Dylan came to Nashville to record most of the double album *Blonde on Blonde* in 1966.

"After Dylan came, oh my gosh, the floodgates opened," said McCoy. "The Byrds, Leonard Cohen, Peter, Paul and Mary, Simon and Garfunkel, Buffy Sainte-Marie, Joan Baez, Dan Fogelberg, Gordon Lightfoot—it just exploded the recording here." Neil Young recorded much of *Harvest* there in 1972. But unlike Dylan and Young, and other fellow singer-songwriters, Leon worked with material that was in the players' wheelhouse for three days in February. Many of the players he hired had played on the original recordings.

Les Blank and Maureen Gosling were at the sessions on February 26 to 28 at Bradley's Barn in Mount Juliet, Tennessee, about twenty miles outside of Nashville. It's where Owen Bradley moved operations after selling his renowned Quonset Hut Studio in the city to Columbia Records.

George Jones's understated but potent performance of "Take Me" at Bradley's Barn during the Hank Wilson sessions (glimpsed in *A Poem Is a Naked Person*) would certainly have set a high bar for Leon, who included Jones's "She Thinks I Still Care" and "The Window up Above" in the nearly thirty tracks he recorded. For many, Leon's voice is an acquired taste, limited in range and honky in tone. Leon himself admitted his limitations on many occasions. But Leon's voice arguably may have been more suited for country music than any other kind, and when he opens "She Thinks I Still Care," there's a line or two when he actually sounds a bit like his pal Gram Parsons, who in turn had a bit of Hank Williams's nasal tone.

Nevertheless, it's fair to ask what new perspective Leon brings to these songs. Take the example of Jones's songs: What's the point of swapping out one of the world's greatest singers on a track he made famous with many of the same musicians? It's not like this is one of Leon's clever interpretations, with inventive arrangements, varied tempos, and unexpected instrumentation. "Sometimes when I'd heard several different versions of [the songs], slipping from one track to another is really kind of embarrassing," he admitted years later.

It's helpful to consider the era in which this came out; the context partially explains Leon's impetus for the project. Country music had always been a significant part of rock 'n' roll, like gospel and blues. Artists like Ray Charles, Elvis Presley, and the Beatles approached all popular music—country, gospel, blues, jazz, Tin Pan Alley—as a melting pot. But radio programmers, record labels, and journalists increasingly categorized music into different silos. Country rock became a popular subgenre, as played by the Eagles, New Riders of the Purple Sage, and Poco. But the conservative Grand Ole Opry stalwarts looked down on the hippie off-shoots. "Some people, for example, program directors, are much more aware of genres than people like me," said Leon. "I'm not much on French words anyway."

But Leon digs deep into these songs. He was going through a dark period himself, romantically adrift, and the crying-in-your-beer songs were a welcome outlet. His version of Hank Williams's masterpiece "I'm So Lonesome I Could Cry" is particularly plaintive. Leon brings a distinctive and tender reading, with swelling Mellotron strings employed judiciously.

Leon mostly stuck to singing, not piano, as the musicians accompanied him live. "Everybody was all together. Studios didn't even own headphones," McCoy said. "Everyone played very soft, so you can hear. You listen to the quality of those records, it's amazing."

Decades later, Leon reflected, "Those guys, they didn't know me from Adam, I didn't play piano till the third day, they didn't even know that I played piano, they'd never heard any of my records." But many of these musicians did know his records, including McCoy. Nashville luminaries Pig Robbins and David Briggs played most of the piano. Briggs needled Leon about it over a few beers. A clearly tipsy Leon, shirt undone to let his growing potbelly hang out, tells Briggs and pedal steel guitar player Pete Drake about how his "Daddy played the left end" of the piano keyboard while his mother played the upper octaves. Leon and Briggs fool around with a bit of "Lady Madonna," and Leon jokingly asks Briggs what he is getting paid. Briggs retorts, "Triple scale. . . . I just play for guys who can't play piano on their own songs. They only call me when a guy can't do his own fucking piano work."

The joking came from mutual respect. Here were the cream-of-the-crop musicians from two of the epicenters of American music recordings.

"Leon didn't know how the country-western musicians were going to react to him," Gosling said. "A hippie coming in, right? That was really interesting because they ended up loving him and really had fun with him." But then, Briggs, like many of these musicians, got his start playing something other than country music. He started at Muscle Shoals playing R&B and moved into rock 'n' roll behind Elvis Presley.

Reflecting with Harrod Blank (Les's son) when *A Poem Is a Naked Person* was finally released, Leon said of the Nashville cats, "They look out for who's going to play what fills and are very aware of staying out of each other's way. I like Dixieland where everyone's playing at the same time . . . but it sounded good to me." Leon said, "'Okay, guys, that's fine. Let's go to the next one,' and the next one is gonna be 'A Six Pack to Go,' it was a Hank Thompson song. I said, 'I don't want you to be this polite. This is a beer joint song, and people gonna be listening to this in beer joints and throwing beer cans at the band and shit. And so, you know, just kind of play as if you were playing in a nightclub, and don't try to be so polite,' which they did. They played it exactly that way, so, from then on, we just flew through those songs."

Leon came away with a lifelong fondness for the small-town feel of Nashville. He was struck by the energy and the spirit of the players and "people lining up to bring [him] songs." The Hank Wilson records (he ended up releasing four) were a particularly inspired creative vein for him. "I think there's, like, seventeen unreleased tracks from *Hank Wilson's Back*," said Charlene Ripley. She, along with her late husband, Steve Ripley of the Tractors, salvaged and archived much of Leon's audio and video libraries. A couple were included on the CD reissue in 1995: "Hey Good Lookin'" and "In the Jailhouse Now." "It's the best thing I've ever heard," Ripley said of the unreleased tracks. "J. J. Cale's on it, plus all the Nashville players, the legends." Cale coproduced *Hank Wilson's Back* along with Leon, Denny Cordell, and Audie Ashworth, the Nashville producer and A&R man who had worked on Cale's *Naturally* album. One of the tracks that was not released is a great duet with Willie Nelson on "Blue Moon of Kentucky."

Charlene said that Steve Ripley had later written to Leon: "Leon, I've always wondered if the name Hank Wilson was a merger of Hank Williams and Hank Thompson." Leon wrote back and confirmed.

After the sessions, Blank and Gosling stayed in Nashville four extra days. At Tut Taylor's Old Time Pickin' Parlor, a gathering spot for
bluegrass musicians, the filmmakers caught New Grass Revival, a young
progressive bluegrass band formed in Louisville. The band bucked many
country music traditions, electrifying their instruments and incorporating
pop, rock, and even reggae into their repertoire. "Les recommended them
to Leon," Gosling said. "Les told Leon they would be a great opening
band for him, and Leon listened."

"We had literally just walked in the door from our first tour, opening
for John Hartford," said Sam Bush of New Grass Revival. "It was probably
four a.m. and I get a call from a friend, Butch Robins, a *great* banjo player.
He had played five-string dobro on the *Hank Wilson's Back* sessions. Leon
was jazzed about the idea of opening for himself under the name Hank
Wilson, with him just standing there with an acoustic guitar, and the
original thought was some of the session players in Nashville backing him.

"So, I get a call from Butch, and he put me on the phone with Les
Blank: 'Would you want to open for and back Leon on these country
songs?' Now, it's crazy, because when we first started our band, we had
a cassette tape. On one side was *Leon Russell and the Shelter People*, and
the other was John Hartford *Aereo-Plain*. So, we had literally gone from
opening for John Hartford to getting a call from Leon Russell. Later that
afternoon, we found ourselves at Leon's house in Tulsa. It was that fast;
they got tickets, boom! We went to Tulsa."

The band arrived at the Maple Ridge mansion. "All of a sudden, a
large lady with red hair appears. It was the lady I'd seen in the *Mad Dogs
& Englishmen* movie, Emily Smith." Emily drove them up to Grand Lake,
where the Shelter People, with Black Grass, were rehearsing, while friends
milled about. "I'm totally freaking out. I don't understand why we're there
or how it even happened." Bush was only twenty.

The New Grass guys played their version of "Prince of Peace" for Leon.
"He kind of nods his head, and he goes, 'Well, that's pretty good,' which
was high praise coming from Leon." The band stayed the night. Next day,
they tried joining Leon on some of the songs from *Hank Wilson's Back*.
But it became evident that the initial idea of backing Leon on his country
songs to open his own show wasn't going to work. "He was really nice
about it. He didn't cut us loose at all. He said, 'You know, I'm not ready

to go out there and stand there with acoustic guitar,' because there weren't really good pickups on instruments, and we were totally acoustic. 'Why don't you guys just open the tour?'"

Billboard profiled Denny Cordell and Shelter Records. "Part of Cordell's willingness to experiment resulted in the latest Leon Russell LP, a country disk," it read. But Denny's openness to Leon's artistic explorations was limited. "The vibes between Les and Denny were starting to strain in Nashville," Gosling said. "I loved Denny," Peter Nicholls said. "But Denny was getting jealous. I almost got in a bar fight one night in New York defending Denny because I loved the guy. But he was a manipulator. Does anybody get to that position, particularly back then, without being one? He got very nervous when Leon became too big and started to drift."

There was also strain between Leon and Les Blank. "Right after Nashville, we jumped right into the tour in Florida where we got kicked off the bus," Gosling said. "I remember us all having dinner together at a long table after the show, and Les got really drunk. And he was sitting next to Ambrose. Les started complaining about how Leon hadn't done an encore, and all those fans had been waiting for him, and why didn't he do an encore? He got really obnoxious, and he was even standing up, shaking his finger. And Ambrose was saying, 'Calm down, my brother, calm down.'"

In his hotel room, Blank's phone rang. "Denny said, 'You've got to go back to Tulsa. This is not working out,'" said Gosling. "We used to say you were either on the bus or off the bus. The next morning, literally, we were off the bus. We were standing on the side of the road. The band got on the bus, and we were left off. We were standing there with all our equipment. We had no idea where we were gonna go." They stayed with a family friend of Gosling. "When we went back [to the lake house], we thought we were maybe canned for good."

An interview with Blank appears in the August 2, 1973, issue of *Rolling Stone* where he presents his side of the story to Chet Flippo. Describing Leon's original concept for the film, Blank tells Flippo, "Leon and I are still playing poker about that. . . . Like I do in all my movies, I try to get my vibrations or feelings circulating at the same rate as other people. Except with Leon, it's *total* madness, chaos. Weird, crazy people. I'm *very* capable of being crazy, so I began to be as crazy as they were, *more* crazy. It freaked 'em."

Leon thrived on the chaos he surrounded himself with. Recalling this time, Leon later asked a few different people, "Have you ever spent a month in a house with thirty naked people? I have, and it's awesome."

Blank acknowledged that much of the tension came as a result of his antagonizing Denny and Leon at the rained-out gig in Gainesville, as they "stood the people up in the rain for two hours." He needled them about the cancellation, while rolling film. "How much money are you losing?" It was about $40,000. Blank finished the interview by noting he was thirteen months into the film project and still had no contract. This interview was a curious way to negotiate and did not endear him further to Denny or Leon, who were already at odds with each other.

Blank and Gosling had shot sixty to eighty hours of film already. "We were pretty much on tenterhooks for several months; we didn't know what was happening," Gosling said. "They didn't just say, 'You're fired.'"

Meanwhile, Leon was still on tour. "It was two and a half months," Bush said. "And we had an experience that [support] bands just don't have: we were paid by Shelter . . . we traveled in Leon's plane—a thirty-six-passenger prop plane—we stayed in the same hotels. . . . We went everywhere they did; we were just like members of the band. And of course, that's not how it works! . . . It was 'rock 'n' roll hysteria,' as Leon would say. We'd, of course, never seen anything like this before or since, where people were camped out in the halls of the hotels, waiting for Leon to walk by. Some people in the band would take a different girl [to] their room every night. Just rock 'n' roll, and groupies abounded."

Bush also remembered various examples of the power of Leon's mystique: "We were in Memphis. There was some violence in the audience, and the cops busted a few heads." Leon left the stage earlier than expected and one of Leon's crew got on the mic to try to calm the crowd, saying something like, "Let the cops earn their buck-seventy-five an hour." That did not go over well with the police, who surrounded the band's bus afterward, demanding an apology. Bush recalled, "We all sang 'Amazing Grace,' and the police literally took a step back from there."

It was neither the first nor last time Leon would defuse a situation with religious music. "We were in Springfield, Illinois, and a big fight broke out on the floor of the auditorium," Ann Bell said. "It was starting to get a little crazy. And he turns to the band, and he started playing a gospel song. And I'm not kidding; it stopped that fight. The next morning, the bands were down in the hotel having breakfast, and somebody brought a newspaper over. Some music critic for that local Springfield paper had come to write a piece about the concert. And towards the end, he goes, 'And it was the first time I'd ever seen women in the bedazzled bras and hot pants and fishnet stockings singing about Jesus.'"

"The last show was in Long Beach, and that was the only night on the tour we didn't get to stand wherever we wanted to because George Harrison had come to see Leon, and they didn't want anybody onstage," Bush said. "And José Feliciano sat in with Leon that night and tried to burn Leon musically, and it certainly did not happen. Leon just lowered the hammer. He later said, 'I believe he was trying to burn me out there.'"

The tour ended glamorously. "The after-hours party that we all got to go to was on the docked *Queen Mary*," Bush said. "Leon introduced me to George Harrison. George was sitting at a table, and I literally fell to my knees, dropped to my knees, and I got to talk to him [for] a couple of minutes." Leon's ex Chris O'Dell was there with George and Pattie.

"For two and a half months, we got treated like rock stars," Bush said with a laugh. "We had bag tag numbers, right? Put 'em outside the door, crew gathers and puts 'em on the plane for you. And so, the day after we got home from that tour, we immediately started a three-week engagement at Arnie's Pizza, six nights a week. 'Coffee break's over, boys.'"

Post-tour, Leon was back and forth between the lake property and the Tulsa house. Emily Smith and Buddy Jones were managing the Tulsa house. "Leon started buying all the furniture and antiques, going wild," Gosling recalled. "By April, Leon's money handlers were already trying to rein him in."

A number of sessions were underway at the lake. Patrick Henderson and Black Grass were making an album, which featured cover art by Jim Franklin. By the time he finished the record, Henderson had hired new women backing singers, Delores Allen, Nettie Davenport, Charlene Foster, and Carolyn Cook. Leon became romantically involved with Cook, his third successive liaison with a background singer.

Freddie King also worked there on his *Woman Across the River* LP, with Jim Keltner coming out to lend his drums alongside Chuck Blackwell. Emily Smith stayed in a walk-in closet with a twin bed off of Leon's suite at the lake house. While King was there, he would sometimes bunk up with Emily in that cozy makeshift bedroom.

Most of the musicians chipped in on a record by the O'Neal Twins, a gospel duo Leon produced. Their self-titled vinyl album (unavailable digitally at publication time) is worth seeking out for fans of gospel or anyone who loves the classic Leon rhythm section—Keltner, Blackwell, and Radle—joined by the mighty Henderson, who had known the twins since childhood. Leon was not happy when Chuck Blackwell was disrupted while receiving a blowjob in a small room behind the studio's control room, staining the sacred with the profane.

"Those sessions with Freddie King doing his album and the O'Neal Twins doing theirs was fantastic," Gosling recalled. But she remembers one excruciating moment: engineer John LeMay "accidentally erased the most fantastic performance of 'It's Gonna Rain,' and he was mortified beyond belief," Gosling said. "He just could not get over it." One can only imagine a version of the song that is better than the one that made the record.

"When he [Leon] was doing the O'Neal Twins record, Larry Bell and I went up there with him because Larry was gonna play some organ," Ann Bell said. "One night, everybody had gone to bed, and it was about four o'clock in the morning. All of a sudden, I woke up; I could hear him playing. It was a classical piece; he's in the living room, where he had a piano, and he's playing this piece that was forty minutes long, from memory. There was no sheet music. I sat down on the bench, and I didn't say a word. I just thought, 'They didn't understand the depth of his well.' And when he was done, I was crying. He goes, 'Girl, what's wrong witchoo?'"

Gosling captured the mélange of people at the lake that spring in her letters home: "The mixture of subcultures here is curious too: Okie workman; Texas and Okie hippies; Black church-going gospel singers; California sophisticates and artists; British freaks. The new Black women singers from Dallas, one of whom is Leon's new girlfriend, are really small-town compared with Black Grass, who were coming from more of a middle-class background. The difference is amazing. Where the other women were sassy, presumptuous, and cliquey, these women make their beds, are neat, and are shy. And they're not afraid to make their faces crinkle when they sing."

In a syndicated newspaper article in March, Leon listed "My Ten Favorite Records":

1. *King of the Delta Blues Singers* by Robert Johnson
2. *Eat a Peach* by the Allman Brothers
3. *Aretha Now* by Aretha Franklin
4. *Sail Away* by Randy Newman
5. *Sometimes I Just Feel Like Smilin'* by Paul Butterfield Blues Band
6. *Cheech & Chong*
7. *J. Geils Band*
8. *Giant Step* by Taj Mahal
9. *Only the Lonely* by Frank Sinatra
10. *St. Dominic's Preview* by Van Morrison

Denny would have been dismayed to see no Shelter Records artists on the list, but the label was rolling. They had signed Phoebe Snow. Freddie King had recorded at Skyhill. The label also had groundbreaking singles from Jamaican reggae artists, including the Toots and the Maytals scorcher "Funky Kingston" (backed with "Pressure Drop"). And there were about a half a dozen newer, lesser-known artists.

One of the first Shelter albums recorded at the Church was by Leon's future wife. Mary McCreary's *Butterflies in Heaven* was produced by D. J. Rogers. McCreary and Rogers were from the same tight-knit Church of God in Christ network as Patrick Henderson and the Gap Band. "She was good friends with Edwin and Walter Hawkins," Henderson said. (The Edwin Hawkins Singers had a Top 5 hit in 1969 with "Oh, Happy Day" and are seen performing in the 2021 documentary *Summer of Soul*). "And she also sang background for Sly Stone. I knew her first husband, Gentry, from the Church, and that's how I met Mary." Gentry McCreary had been shopping around for a label to sign Mary.

McCreary (née Rand) had gone to high school with Vaetta "Vet" Stewart, the sister of Sly Stone (whose birth surname is Stewart), and formed a gospel group called the Heavenly Tones in Berkeley, California. The young women started singing backup with Sly and the Family Stone (including on the recordings of "Everyday People" and "Stand!") and became Little Sister. Stone released a few records by them on his label. They were managed by Gentry McCreary, whom Mary married. D. J. Rogers and McCreary both signed solo deals with Shelter, releasing their debuts in 1973. McCreary's first album is serious business, with such top players as drummer Andy Newmark and bassist Chuck Rainey.

"[Leon] told me he found a Church of God in Christ radio station when he was a kid, heard the music as a piano player, and it just knocked him out," Bill Maxwell said. "He loved it, so he always had one of those kinds of keyboard players around him. Patrick Henderson's a Church of God in Christ keyboard player, and D. J. Rogers, who's Church of God in Christ, and they were all a part of Billy Preston's group." Maxwell, who'd met Leon in the late sixties, started out playing drums as a high school freshman in Oklahoma City with Jesse Ed Davis. Maxwell eventually ended up with a job playing and producing Grammy-winning records for gospel titan Andraé Crouch, a mentor also to Patrick Henderson. Maxwell would remain close friends with Leon until he passed away.

Some of these musicians performed on a soundstage at a rehearsal studio in Hollywood organized by Shelter. Gram Parsons and Joni Mitchell were in the audience. Leon introduced Joni to Patrick Henderson, who said she and Leon were like "a brother and sister who idolized each other."

Film director Taylor Hackford was also at the D. J. Rogers gospel event. Having met him at the *Homewood Sessions*, Denny and Leon hired him for the taping. "They were just interested in capturing things to do. I shot it. They had in their minds that they would be able to break artists that way."

Though not great with managing money, Leon was entrepreneurial and a visionary, especially regarding technology. "His limp, you know, that had an effect on him," Hackford observed. "You gotta figure he was making up for that his entire life. He had done, and he tried, a lot of things. It was a rock 'n' roll world. They were pioneers. They were good businessmen to a degree, but they weren't like Bob Krasnow. Krasnow was a record man, he went on and headed up Elektra. He was a strict executive. Certainly, Leon was not an executive. Denny was, I wouldn't call him an executive, but he was a very interesting entrepreneur."

Leon and Denny launched ShelterVision as the video arm of the company. They bought a truck and equipped it with four cameras and four one-inch recorders. "That was the high-quality standard at the time," Gosling said. "[Leon] wanted to get a foothold in the video revolution."

Video technology had been an interest of Leon's since at least 1970. "Videocassettes are going to do the same thing to television that television did to movies," he said that year. "The medium itself will eclipse the musical aspect of it, but this is a logical transformation to go from records to video. I think I might be more of a film director than anything else. I've never directed one, but it's something I can get into."

"There was tension that started to happen between Leon and Denny about [*A Poem Is a Naked Person*]," Gosling said. "Leon wanted to direct the film, and Les basically said, 'If we can't direct it, I'm going to Austin.' And I said, 'We know we have a film potentially better than any rock film done so far.' We just wanted to reassure Leon that we didn't want to do the film to blemish his reputation. But we didn't want them breathing down our necks." Denny agreed with the filmmakers.

In June, *Leon Live* was released, a triple album with an hour and forty-seven minutes of intense performances from Leon's peak. "I never thought much of that album," said Don Preston. "Compared to *Mad Dogs* it sounded tinny to me. It felt like they just threw it out there." Preston was accurate in his assessment of the thin sound. But the performances are stunning.

Much of the listening public had gotten to know Leon through three live albums in as many years: *Mad Dogs & Englishmen*, *Concert for Bangladesh*, and now *Leon Live*. It went to number nine on the *Billboard* Top 200, spending twenty-six weeks on the chart. It was his third solo album in a row to go gold. So did *Mad Dogs* and *Concert for Bangladesh*—five gold albums in three years. Ladies and gentlemen, King Midas on the piano!

The band members were getting royalties from *Carney* and *Leon Live*, in addition to whatever their financial arrangements were as performers. Gallie, Cooper, and Radle would each get $34,052.44 from Leon for the fiscal year ending May 1974. Blackwell received $38,552.44 and Henderson made $23,758.23. Leon would receive reported wages (independent of royalties) of $803,426.12 in 1974. Adjusted for inflation, Leon's compensation would be $5,039,447.24 in 2022 dollars, while his bandmates would be around $212,000 for the year; handsome wages for sidemen. The touring company even set up profit-sharing and pension plans.

All of this was changing as Leon's finances were being analyzed. He was running a rock star empire. Along with his big spending spree on real estate, studios, and video trucks, he had a payroll to make, with a record label and employees, a film crew, studio staff, a band, and various hangers-on. "As far as record royalties, by the time I quit, the royalties weren't that much anyway," said Don Preston, who would leave the band in 1973.

Leon hosted the wedding of Emily Smith and Simon Miller-Mundy, an aristocratic chum of Denny from back home, at his house in June, a mash-up of costumed hippies and buttoned-down Tulsa society types seen in *A Poem Is a Naked Person*. Leon played the "Bridal Chorus" in the ballroom. Several folks characterized it as a wedding of convenience, a way for Miller-Mundy to obtain a visa. "It was a hoot, and it was a lot of fun, and it was all a big sham," Tom Russell said. "But it did keep Simon in the country."

"I brought [Simon] out on the last year of touring," said Peter Nicholls, referring to his own last year working with Leon. "I said, 'Why don't you come out and corral these sons of bitches so I don't have to.'"

The ShelterVision video truck recorded a bunch of shows in Austin just as the outlaw country movement was taking hold. In March of 1972, Willie Nelson put together the Dripping Springs Reunion, a three-day music festival outside of Austin, the genesis of his annual Fourth of July Picnics. "When we moved from Nashville, when our house burned down, we moved here to Austin," Connie Nelson said. The rednecks and the hippies were commingling. "I remember Willie telling Waylon [Jennings] 'Oh my God, there's a whole thing going on down here, where everybody's playing music together, and nobody's fighting,'" said Connie.

Held in a dry county and poorly promoted, the Dripping Springs Reunion was a commercial flop. But Willie had grand visions. "When Woodstock happened, I saw all those folks come together to listen to all kinds of music," he said. "I decided that would be a good thing to do around Austin. . . . The following year I put on the first Fourth of July Picnic in the same place, and we got fifty thousand people."

Austin writer Bill Bentley said, "Leon really hung out in Austin quite a bit, even though he was never part of the outlaw scene, because Leon wasn't a country singer. . . . I felt like he didn't want to be confined in an outlaw crowd." "Outlaw" was not hyperbole. This was still Texas. Guys with long hair would still regularly get pulled over by cops when they weren't getting beaten up by rednecks who picked them up hitchhiking. Promoters and road managers carried guns. "If you didn't have a gun, we'd give you a gun," Willie said.

Ray Benson of the band Asleep at the Wheel was in Leon's video bus once when it took a bullet during the filming of a show at a nightclub. Kirk Bressler, who engineered at the Church, had installed the soundboard in the video bus and was operating it in Texas, sponsored by Lone Star Beer for a number of months. "We were staying in Leon's GMC mobile home at the time, and there was a gunfight at one of the clubs one night. Willie Nelson and his band and sister were playing the Alliance Wagon Yard in downtown Austin. This guy was in there, and I could see him off to my left, and all of a sudden, he went 'OW!' and grabbed his right leg. There had been a gunfight right outside on the sidewalk, and the bullet came through the wall and struck the guy in his right calf."

"I'm in the video truck with a guy from CBS Records named Herschel," Benson said. "One of Willie's guys had shot at [musician] Joe Gracey's brother with a .22, and the bullet went through the side of the van, grazed my left hand, and then went into Herschel's leg. But when CBS found out who shot him, they decided not to press charges. They didn't want to alienate Willie."

"I figured that if you send your million-dollar truck down to Austin, you've got to expect to get a bullet hole or two in it," Leon deadpanned.

Leon had the distinct honor of being the first person to sign Trigger, Willie's storied Martin N-20 classical guitar. First, Leon asked Willie to sign Leon's guitar. When Willie reached for a marker, Leon told him to scratch it in instead. Willie asked Leon to do the same, so Leon's inscription on Trigger was made with a knife. "I had him sign it and he first signed it with a pen," Willie said. "I said, 'No, I want you to scratch it in there . . . where everybody will know it,' and he did. He was the first."

Both Leon and Willie saw the potential in joining the tribes. Willie wrote: "He said, 'You bring the rednecks, Willie, and I'll bring the hippies.' . . . We were convinced that those two worlds weren't that far apart."

The first Fourth of July Picnic was a multiday party for "ropers and dopers," in Austin vernacular. "Leon and I stayed up all night before the first picnic," Willie recalled. "We smoked a little bit. And next thing you know, it's daylight, and we go out, and people are coming into the picnic in Dripping Springs. They're carrying their beer or whatever; they're carrying sandwiches, and they're coming in by the thousand." As Willie and Leon got more jittery, they decided to calm their nerves with music. They turned the sound system on. "We go up at daylight and start singing gospel songs to them as they're coming in. And I'll never forget that. That was a great, great time for me."

"Although the show wasn't scheduled to start for seven hours," Leon wrote, "the crowd was already streaming through the many tall rock for-mations that surrounded the back of the natural amphitheater. I was sit-ting with Willie, watching this rather inspiring scene unfold, when he said, 'I've just figured it out. You're Jesus and I'm John the Baptist.' I was a little shocked at the prospect, and I said, 'No, no, not this time. *You* be Jesus this time.'"

Leon was referring back to first being called Jesus in Vegas in 1970. When he had returned to see Elvis at MGM in August 1972, The King called his name from the stage. "At the end of the show, Elvis stops the band dead," Nicholls said. "'There's a young gennamen, a famous song-writer, in the back I'd like to introduce you to, Leon Russuh. Stand up, Leon.' All of a sudden, the whole table is illuminated by a spotlight, BAM! Elvis really admired Leon."

"He said I was one of the best songwriters in the world and sent word for me to come backstage for a meeting," Leon recalled. "After we were introduced by his piano player, Glen D. Hardin, I heard myself saying, 'Elvis, how did you end up in all those horrible movies?' You can imagine my horror. Yikes! Was that mild-mannered me saying that shit? I couldn't believe it. He responded with much grace and without a moment's hes-itation: 'I don't know, man. The last thing I remember I was driving a truck.'" Now Leon discovered what it was like as the target of his own song "If the Shoe Fits." He could now wear the shoe—in his mouth.

What Leon did not write or talk much about was that his faux pas when he met Elvis sent him into a serious depression. He later confided in his son-in-law/friend/musical collaborator Matt Harris, who paraphrased Leon: "Here's the hero of my life. Here's the guy—between him and Jerry Lee Lewis—who made me want to do what I do and made me know I could, and touched my soul. And I'm trying to be cool. I'm trying to be a rock star. I'm fucking Leon Russell, instead of just Russell Bridges. . . . And Elvis had this look on his face . . . and his handshake. . . . I didn't talk for three days after that. . . . I went to bed for three days. I was so embarrassed because I was trying to be so fucking cool. And all this is just false pretense. I'm not even who they think I am. . . . Man, I felt like such an asshole."

Willie's first Fourth of July Picnic lineup included Waylon Jennings, Tom T. Hall, Loretta Lynn, Hank Snow, Tex Ritter, and Bill Monroe. Kris Kristofferson came up from Durango, Mexico—where he was filming

(*Below*) The Accents promo photo, 1957. *Left to right*: Chuck Blackwell, David Gates, Russell Bridges (aka Leon Russell). All three would move to Los Angeles by 1960. Blackwell would drum for the Everly Brothers and Taj Mahal before rejoining Leon in 1970 for Joe Cocker's Mad Dogs & Englishmen and Leon Russell and the Shelter People. Leon had formed a publishing company in the early 1960s with Gates before they had a falling out over money. Gates went on to found the soft rock mega-selling band Bread, "whose first album cover featured many pictures of money in various denominations," Leon observed. *Courtesy of the OKPOP Museum*

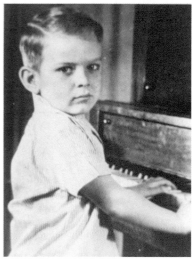

(*Above*) Claude Russell Bridges (aka Leon Russell), piano prodigy, circa 1946.

Courtesy of the OKPOP Museum

The Starlighters at the Tropicana Club, 1959. *Left to right*: Leo Feathers, Chuck Blackwell, Ron Ryan, Johnny Williams, Russell Bridges (aka Leon Russell). A promoter at Cain's Ballroom hired the Starlighters to back Jerry Lee Lewis at a show there. After the Starlighters' first warm-up set, Lewis came up onto the bandstand, pointed at

seventeen-year-old Leon, and declared, "I'm not gonna set down at that piano. He plays a lot better piano than I do!" Lewis immediately hired the band to back him on a tour.

Courtesy of the OKPOP Museum

Left to right: Jim Karstein, Leon Russell, and Carl Radle, Hollywood, 1962. Leon encouraged his other Tulsa musician friends to come out to Los Angeles in the early 1960s and connected them with various gigs, sessions, and bands. He hooked up Karstein and Radle as members of Gary Lewis and the Playboys. Karstein, Radle, and Leon would all play with Delaney & Bonnie and Friends later in the decade. Radle would also be a member of Mad Dogs & Englishmen, Derek and the Dominos, and the Shelter People, and a longtime sideman for Eric Clapton.

Courtesy of the OKPOP Museum

Leon was established as a first-call session pianist by the time he was hired to put together music for the television show *Shindig!* and the *T.A.M.I. Show* movie. Here he is rehearsing with Marvin Gaye and the Blossoms for the *T.A.M.I. Show*, Los Angeles in 1964. *Left to right*: Marvin Gaye, Darlene Love, Jean King, Fanita James.

Photo by Michael Ochs Archives/ Getty Images

Leon was a regular member of the LA-based session group of musicians known as the Wrecking Crew. The group started to come together regularly for Jan and Dean sessions, but they really gelled to form Phil Spector's so-called Wall of Sound productions in Gold Star Recording Studios circa 1963. *Left to right*: Don Randi, Leon Russell, and Al DeLory. Most likely on a Phil Spector session.

Photo by Ray Avery/Michael Ochs Archive/Getty Images

Leon and Snuff Garrett, Liberty Records office, Los Angeles, circa 1967. Garrett was a classic record man, an A&R guy with golden ears who could identify hit songs. He gave Leon some of his first big breaks. Leon became Snuff's secret weapon as a talented arranger, instrumentalist, and producer. Snuff called Leon his junior partner. Together they were responsible for a remarkable string of hits for Gary Lewis and the Playboys.

Photo by Michael Ochs Archives/Getty Images

Marc Benno and Leon Russell, Los Angeles, circa 1968. Eventually, Leon tired of the light pop music that Snuff Garrett produced. By 1965, Bob Dylan, the Beatles, the Rolling Stones, and other artists who wrote their own songs with greater depth were taking rock 'n' roll in exciting new directions. Inspired, Leon formed the Asylum Choir, a collaboration with Marc Benno. The two albums they recorded are essentially the first Leon Russell albums as an artist. Leon "took off once he started to be a solo artist," Benno said. "He was a solo artist from the second I met him."

Photo by Don Nix, courtesy of the OKPOP Museum

An all-star cast assembled for Eric Clapton's 1970 solo debut album. He basically hired Delaney & Bonnie and Friends and *more* friends, including some of Buddy Holly's band, the Crickets. This is an outtake from the photo shot for the album. *Front row, left to right*: Eric Clapton, Rita Coolidge, Jim Price, Bobby Keys, Bobby Whitlock, "Clark—Equipment" [per credit on the LP sleeve], Leon Russell, Sonny Curtis. *Back row, left to right*: "Eddie—Friend" [per credit on the LP sleeve], Jim Gordon, Bruce McCaskill [obscured], Bonnie Bramlett, Bill Reed, Delaney Bramlett, Carl Radle, J. I. Allison, and Bill Haverson.

Photo courtesy of the Barry Feinstein Estate, barryfeinsteinphotography.com

"The First Supper," Las Vegas Hilton, 1970. Waiting to see Elvis Presley. *Left to right:* Joe Massot, Sandy Krasnow, Jim Gordon, Shady Adams, Mia Cordell, Emily Smith (in sunglasses), Leon, Kay Poorboy, Gram Parsons, Theodora Brinckman, Denny Cordell, Clare Massot. Emily Smith, who had just met Leon, recalled, "Somehow I wind up at Skyhill [Leon's house and studio] and [another guest] walks in and says, 'Take a puff off of this.' Well, it was like *Alice in Wonderland*. Next thing I know, Leon's got on his white suit and snakeskin boots, and we are in his Thunderbird on our way to the airport. We ended up in a suite with Ike and Tina Turner getting higher than kites. They were in the lounge and Elvis was in the big room."

Las Vegas staff photographer, unknown, courtesy of Barney Cordell

Soon after the Las Vegas trip, Leon assembled the band for Joe Cocker's Mad Dogs & Englishmen tour. "Out of that little angel dust roll came Mad Dogs & Englishmen," Emily Smith said. "Gram Parsons was there and was supposed to go on the tour, but jumped off the bus at the last minute." Leaving the A&M soundstage for the airport to begin the Mad Dogs & Englishmen tour, 1970. Leon seated next to Andee Cohen (now Nathanson). Gram Parsons seated in front of Leon with the famous top hat.

Photo by Jim McCrary for Metro-Goldwyn-Mayer/Getty Images

Cocker Power! Leon leading the band on guitar while Joe Cocker fronts the legendary Mad Dogs & Englishmen, Fillmore East, New York City, 1970, one of the shows recorded for the soundtrack album.

Photo © Amalie R. Rothschild

(*Right*) Leon and his most famous acolyte, Elton John, soon after they first met in Los Angeles, 1970. Elton said Leon "was everything I wanted to be as a pianist, vocalist, and writer. His music has helped me and millions of others in the best and worst of times."

Photo by Don Nix, courtesy of the OKPOP Museum

(*Left*) Staged promo shot for Shelter Records signing Don Nix to a recording contract, 1970. *Left to right*: Denny Cordell, Don Nix, and Leon.

Courtesy the OKPOP Museum

(*Below*) "Somebody you all know by now—Leon," George Harrison said by way of introducing Leon at the 1971 Concert for Bangladesh. Harrison had befriended Leon a few years prior and played on Leon's solo debut album, while Leon arranged George's "Bangla Desh" single to promote this show, the first all-star benefit rock concert. Dylan had recently called on Leon as Dylan's first independent producer to record "Watching the River Flow" and "When I Paint My Masterpiece." *Left to right*: George Harrison, Bob Dylan, and Leon.

Photo by GAB Archive/Redferns/Getty Images

Les Blank filming Leon for *A Poem Is a Naked Person* at the Tulsa Fairground Speedway, 1972. Though the two men would have conflicts that resulted in Leon shelving the film, Blank's son Harrod convinced Leon to finally agree to release the film in 2015, soon after Les Blank's death. Les regarded the critically acclaimed film as his masterpiece.

Photo © Les Blank, www.lesblank.com, courtesy of Harrod Blank/Les Blank Films

Left to right: Roy Acuff, Ernest Tubb, and Leon filming at the House of Cash, Johnny Cash's studio, 1974. Leon had moved into country music with his 1973 album, *Hank Wilson's Back*, recorded with Nashville's A-team of session players. He returned to Nashville a year later to produce a video production with his new friend, Willie Nelson, and some of country music's elder statesmen and stateswomen. The video suffered from technical problems and was never released.

Photo © Les Blank, www.lesblank.com, courtesy of Harrod Blank/Les Blank Films

The newly married couple, Mary Russell and Leon Russell, 1976. Tina Rose Bridges, Leon and Mary's daughter, said that Leon was struck dumb by Mary the first time he saw her, at an audition for Shelter. "He said that she was so beautiful that he had to walk *out* of the room."

Photo by Gilles Petard/Redferns/ Getty Images

After his marriage with Mary ended, Leon met Jan Constantine (later Bridges) while she was working for the Jim Halsey Agency in Tulsa. "Out of the blue, I said, 'Yep, Leon's going to fall madly in love with me and want to marry me.'" Jan and Leon on tour with New Grass Revival, circa 1981.

Photo by Diane Sullivan, courtesy of Jan Bridges

Left to right: Sam Bush, Bill Kenner, and Leon. On tour with New Grass Revival, 1981. "For two years, we would open the show, and then we would back him, so it was strenuous work. I mean, it *wore our ass down*," Bush said.

Photo by Diane Sullivan, courtesy Jan Bridges

Leon met Willie Nelson in 1972 and they became lifelong friends. Willie said, "We always had a good time together. Leon and I laughed, talked, and joked a lot. He was an incredible musician and an incredible person to go along with it, and I'm lucky to have known him." Leon and Willie Nelson at Willie's seventieth birthday celebration at the Beacon Theater, New York City, 2003.

Photo by Stephen Lovekin/FilmMagic/Getty Images

"If you're in Oklahoma, the amount of real legends that you can just reach across, just bump into and touch, there's not that many," said Taylor Hanson of the band Hanson. "But Leon was one where, all of a sudden, it was a relationship." *Left to right*: Leon, Steve Ripley, and Taylor Hanson. Tulsa Mayfest, 2005.

Photo by Kelly Kerr

Getting the old band back together! Claudia Lennear, Leon, and Rita Coolidge. Mad Dogs & Englishmen reunion concert at the 2015 Lockn' Festival. "Although I'm heartbroken that Joe is gone, I had loved the song 'Girl from the North Country' so much that when I was asked which songs would I like to sing, that was one of the first ones," said Claudia. "If I could sing one song with Leon, that would be it. And Leon welcomed me to do it. That was one of the greatest points in my musical career."

Photo © Linda Wolf, www.lindawolf.net

Leon "was one of the first musicians I ever saw who just had that presence where you were like, 'Who the fuck is that?'" Derek Trucks explained. "Whenever [Leon's] name was brought up, or people talked about him, there was a certain reverence in their voices—he wasn't just another musician." Leon, Derek Trucks, and Susan Tedeschi. Mad Dogs & Englishmen reunion concert at the 2015 Lockn' Festival.

Photo © Linda Wolf, www.lindawolf.net

Pat Garrett and Billy the Kid—to perform. He was joined by his new girl-friend, Rita Coolidge.

"I was really pregnant," Connie Nelson said. "It was *hot*. All I could do was eat ice chips. It was a mile-and-a-half dirt road—one way in, one way out—to the picnic. I was horrified, thinking, 'Oh God, oh God, oh God, if I go into labor . . .' And there was a helicopter that just kept circling, and I kept thinking, 'That's probably the only way out.' Leon would look at me onstage, and then he'd immediately look away. I bet he did that fifteen times, and finally, he came up to me, and he said, 'I'm sorry, but I'm so afraid I'm going to be the one that sees when you go into labor, and I'm going to have to deal with it,' he said. 'I just don't know how.'

"Every time I've ever heard him described as the Master of Space and Time, I swear to God, whoever coined that phrase nailed it. Because he just had that otherworldly, seriously, otherworldly way of looking at you."

Those who say the fewest words often possess the most perceived power. "Willie was that way for a long time," said Connie. "He picked his words carefully. I think that's one reason they bonded as much as they did; they both had that way about them. But I never saw him be an asshole or mean-spirited. I know there's stories. I know there were times that he didn't get along with certain producers or whatever, but honestly I don't know, he may have been an asshole at some times."

Connie met Rita Coolidge that day, and they remain lifelong friends. Rita might be the first person who told her about Leon's capability of being an asshole. "I remember seeing him at Willie's Picnic, and I was with Kris [Kristofferson] by then, and we were a couple," Rita said. "We walked offstage, and Leon was standing there. I go, 'Leon! So . . .' He looked at me, and the first words that he said in years: [*affecting a contemptuous sneer*] 'So, what?' I said, 'Ohhh-kay then.'"

Offstage, hippies and rednecks were shoulder to shoulder, guzzling Lone Stars in the sun. Cowboys held cowgirls on their shoulders. Old folks sat in folding lawn chairs. "Leon had as much to do with making that picnic a success as anything," said Willie afterward. "He brought the rock 'n' roll crowd. It was about everybody coming together to listen to music—country, rock, blues, gospel, jazz, everything."

Chapter 22

Factions

LEON AND DENNY, WE LUV U, PLEASE CALL, AHMET read the banner trailing a plane circling the Ontario Motor Speedway in Ontario, California, on July 29, 1973, where Leon was making an appearance. Ahmet Ertegun was pleading for Shelter Records to make a distribution deal with Atlantic when its contract with Capitol expired that month. Leon was headlining Bill Graham's A Day on the Green, joined by Mary McCreary and Loggins and Messina. Leon also headlined another concert by that name, also promoted by Graham, on August 10 at Oakland Coliseum, with McCreary and Elvin Bishop. In Ontario, Leon helicoptered in to the dusty speedway for a two-and-a-half-hour set. Potential gross receipts for Ontario were estimated at $450,000, and Oakland could have brought $390,000. Scissor-Tail, Leon's company, was to receive 85 percent of the net profits (gross receipts less expenses and taxes).

Ontario had gross receipts of $173,000, with expenses of $236,000, but Oakland turned a profit. Graham argued over who should pay for expenses and whether the profit of Oakland could be used to offset Ontario and stiffed Leon for over $53,000. In accordance with American Federation of Musicians rules, the contract dispute was mediated by the union, which judged fully in favor of Scissor-Tail and threatened to add Graham to their "defaulters list" if he did not pay up, which would have prohibited him from future business with any union members. The resulting litigation continued until 1982, eventually reaching the California Supreme Court. Graham's side offered to settle for most of the money, but Leon's side declined. The Supreme Court ultimately kicked it back to a neutral arbitrator, where they agreed to a settlement.

Don Preston had been replaced by Wayne Perkins, the guitarist Leon had met in Muscle Shoals. Perkins was hot from Bob Marley and the Wailers' *Catch a Fire*. Chris Blackwell had taken the original tapes of the album, overdubbed Americans Perkins and John "Rabbit" Bundrick, and remixed the tracks to make them sound more like the American and English rock on the radio. This blend of influences helped break Marley and the Wailers into the big time, thus opening the door for reggae in general. "All you have to do is listen to Wayne Perkins's guitar solo on 'Concrete Jungle' and you'll understand why that record made it in the United States," Don Williams said.

Perkins laughed. "When I was doing the overdub on 'Concrete Jungle,' Clapton showed up, and [Jimmy] Page, and [Jeff] Beck—all three of the Yardbirds! Oh my God! They were in the control room, and the lights are all turned out. So I couldn't see nobody. I burned 'em a new one, I think. Bob Marley came right out of the control room with this joint about— looked like a damn circus cigar, you know those big old fat bastards? I can say I smoked a joint with Bob Marley; how about that?"

On the strength of the Marley record, as well as the Muscle Shoals connections, Leon hired Perkins to join the Shelter People after Don Preston left the group amicably to pursue his own career. Perkins was home in Birmingham, Alabama, for about a week when he got the offer. "There was a first-class airline ticket to Tulsa waiting for me, and the tour was starting within weeks," Perkins recalled. "Leon picked me up in this Rolls-Royce Silver Cloud in Tulsa, with a couple of chicks, and we go out for steaks bigger than our heads.

"They raked me over the coals, boy. Buddy Jones gave me Leon's triple live album and says, 'Here you go; you got three days to learn this.' I go, 'What?! Are you out of your damn mind?!' He goes, 'You want the gig?' I said, 'Well, what's it worth?' '$650 to $800 a night,'" Perkins recalled. He responded, "That ain't a hell of a lot of time, Leon." He didn't sleep for three or four days and listened to the triple album on repeat.

Onstage, Leon kept the band on its toes. Perkins said, "When I got there to the first rehearsal, he said, 'If you don't watch me every second, I'm gonna do my best to fuck you up.' Really? So he was watching me like a hawk. He saw me and [Joey] Cooper laughing one time. He stopped the band. He pointed at me. He's like, '[pause] Whatcha got?' A fifteen-piece band stops on a dime in front of seventy-five thousand people out there. He points, 'Okay, whatcha got?' I just had to burn something until I could bring him back in. I think the favorite thing to bring him back was, I just started going [*sings the riff to 'Jumpin' Jack Flash'*]. He laughed, shook his head, 'Yeah, you got me,' put his thumb up. I mean, we rocked the house. I've never seen anybody with hands like that on the keyboard. He looked like a damn octopus. He did things that make your jaw drop. He could sound like Little Richard one minute and Liberace the next."

The aerial Ertegun message indicated the high regard that high-flying Shelter was held in at the time. Denny—who took his Ferrari for a spin around the race track after the show—did not want to deal with the day-to-day administration of the business and instead wanted to focus on the creative side, developing artists. They had been without a label manager for about a year after Joel Maiman left. In August 1973, they hired Ron Henry to run the label. Cordell said, "Perhaps some of these problems require my personal attention, but a number can be handled by a competent person who can grasp the problem and solve it. Fortunately, I found this in Ron."

Henry said, "I was just a college guy who went up to New York and got a job at the RCA Corporation." Henry got involved with Shelter via attorney Owen Sloane. "I get a phone call: 'Hey, this is Denny Cordell. I'm here in New York. Can we meet?' I happened to have a meeting at corporate [HQ], so I'm wearing a suit. And he shows up in a work shirt and jeans. A week later, he offers me a job. I met Leon on August 12. He was playing at Nassau Coliseum. That was the first time I'd ever heard Leon perform live. I didn't even know his music.

"I arrived at the hotel, and there's this man running up and down the hall handing out half tabs of acid. I go into Leon's room, and he's just drinking iced tea. He goes, 'Denny tells me you're a marketing guy. So, what are you gonna do to make me successful?' That was Leon, right to the point."

Henry was not impressed with the label's roster at the time. "Other than J. J. Cale, they really didn't have any other artists on the label, per se. They had just signed Phoebe Snow. [The others] were left over from Leon's bands. Initially, Jackson Browne was supposed to be on Shelter, because Jackson Browne wanted Denny to produce him. Denny didn't produce him because he went with Asylum."

Peter Nicholls said, "We wanted that bad. I actually recorded some demos with Jackson to show to Denny. 'Jamaica Say You Will.' I was a huge fan." The demos were recorded while Browne was on tour in England with Laura Nyro. Denny was producing, and Leon played on "Jamaica Say You Will." Other players included Jim Keltner, Chris Stainton, and guitarist Albert Lee.

With his MBA from the Wharton School, Henry was even less impressed with Shelter Records' business side: "We had that funky house in East Hollywood. We had some girl responsible for international but [who] would do tarot card readings all day. I got in a lot of trouble with everyone in the first couple of months because I said, 'You can't do drugs in the house between nine and six.'"

However, Henry was struck by the visionary creativity of the partners. "The mobile video van; another brilliant creation that Leon was part of: the first mobile video van ever in the music industry."

Leon was trying to get Les Blank to run the video truck and take it around the country. But the filmmakers were still operating with no contract for *A Poem Is a Naked Person*. They were alone at the lake complex. By the middle of the summer of '73, it appeared as though they would have to shut down the Paradise Studio at the lake. "Leon was sinking thousands into it and was going into debt. It was just going to be a cottage at the lake or a rehearsal space," Gosling said. But this was a temporary situation, and everything seemed to be in flux, including whether he would pull the plug on Blank's film. "We were really hanging in the balance for quite a while, and what tipped the balance was, we finally showed Leon dailies," Gosling said. "This is August 17. [*Reading from her letters home*] 'Close to leaving, but didn't. We showed Leon six hours' worth of films, including *Dry Wood and Hot Pepper*. He said *Dry Wood and Hot Pepper* was the best of Les's films and to go ahead and finish ours. Leon said he would talk to Denny about it.'"

Leon's summer tour began. Mary McCreary and her band were the opening act. Black Oak Arkansas followed McCreary's set at Schaefer Stadium in Foxborough, Massachusetts. In a *Boston Globe* article about that show, McCreary complained that her sets were getting shorter and shorter as the tour progressed, from an hour down to thirty minutes. Leon would arrive at his concerts in a motorcade of limousines (Leon being driven in his own, naturally) after the opening bands had started. In his review,

Glenn Alberich wrote, "The problem with excellence, as Leon Russell has no doubt learned, that once achieved, it is more difficult to sustain—particularly during a grueling concert tour. Leon came. . . . But he was tired. Not bad, just tired."

New Grass Revival was on the bill for one or two of the shows on this tour. "I think it was Charlotte," Sam Bush recalled. "His girlfriend, when we were on the tour, was one of the backup singers, named Carolyn Cook. Well, he stopped being with Carolyn and fell in love with Mary."

The revenue from the summer tour did not yield the usual high margins Leon was accustomed to. Back off the road, he started to record new material at the lake in September. Part of the idea was that he could charge Shelter for the expenses and help offset his hemorrhaging cash situation. But he got sick and returned to Tulsa.

Also in September, *Hank Wilson's Back* was released and rose to number twenty-eight on the *Billboard* Top 200 pop albums chart. The single "Roll in My Sweet Baby's Arms" barely dented the charts, rising higher on country (57) than the Hot 100 (78).

Leon was on board for another project of cover songs. That fall, John Lennon hired Phil Spector to produce an album of classic oldies to satisfy a settlement with infamous record "hit man" Morris Levy over Lennon's infringement of a Chuck Berry copyright that Levy owned. Lennon quoted some lines from Berry's "You Can't Catch Me" in "Come Together." The resulting covers album from Lennon would finally be released in 1975 as *Rock 'n' Roll*.

In the middle of October 1973, Spector and Lennon came together during Lennon's notorious "Lost Weekend" estrangement from Yoko Ono, when he spent about a year and a half gallivanting around LA with drinking/drug buddy Harry Nilsson, damaging their bodies and their reputations. Still, session musicians in LA wanted to participate, so it became a class reunion of sorts for various bricks in the old Wall of Sound and others from the Leon/Delaney & Bonnie gang. Spector's right-hand man, Larry Levine, engineered, while Leon, Hal Blaine, Jim Keltner, Bobby Keys, Jesse Ed Davis, Nino Tempo, Steve Cropper, Mike Melvoin, Barry Mann, Larry Carlton, and others came in. Lennon had specifically requested Keltner and Davis.

Spector was deep into his lunacy by this point, drunk, high, and armed. "Oh, Phil," Keltner sighed. "He never did the drugs that everybody else was doing. He was old school; he took pills and drank. He was fine until the end of the night. The only time that he went really off was on John's *Rock 'n' Roll* record. That's why there's only a couple of tracks used on the record from those [LA] sessions. The rest of it, John had us all go up to New York upstate, rehearse up there, and then we came back down to the Record Plant and redid the record."

Spector had developed a habit of sniffing amyl nitrite poppers. He was drinking Manischewitz wine while Lennon was swigging vodka straight from the bottle. Inevitably, drunken egos clashed. Spector, dressed in a white doctor's coat and stethoscope, fired one of his two guns into the studio ceiling, damaging Lennon's hearing. Booze was spilled into the mixing console, as was, apparently, urine. In a handwritten note, Lennon scrawled in red marker:

Matter of Pee

Phil—See ye around 12:30!

Should you not yet know, it was Harry [Nilsson] and Keith [Moon] who pissed on the console! . . . I can't be expected to mind adult rock stars. . . . P.S. Why does Leon's people not get shit?

The comedy duo Cheech & Chong was at A&M around the same time, recording their "Basketball Jones" single, produced by Lou Adler and featuring such impressive personnel as Carole King, Billy Preston, George Harrison, Jim Karstein, Nicky Hopkins, and Klaus Voorman.

Cheech Marin met Leon at A&M. "I took him to have sushi for the first time," Marin said. "I grew up with it because I lived right in downtown LA, in South Central. My dad was a cop, and Little Tokyo was part of his beat. [Leon] fell in love with sushi, so every time he was in town, he would call me the night before, 'Let's go have some of that sushi.'

"He got up at seven o'clock, eight o'clock at night. We'd go down and have sushi and then spend the rest of the night picking up musicians and singers around town and taking them back to his suite at the Chateau Marmont." Leon had musical gear set up and would bring musicians by there to play. "He was a stone-cold musician. He could do anything."

Like many in comedy, Tommy Chong and Cheech Marin were also

musicians. "Musicians were the first ones to pick up on us with Cheech & Chong because we are doing musician's humor." The duo had a house in the Hollywood Hills. "We'd have little parties. I remember one time [Leon] came over one night, and it was Joni Mitchell, Hoyt Axton, and Kris Kristofferson. Everybody jammed and talked. The only time I ever saw him—not intimidated by—but in a state of awe, was Joni Mitchell. He says, 'I played with a lot of musicians, but she's in another category,'" Marin said.

"We would go to dinner five or six nights in a row. We took him to sushi, and he took leftovers, doggy bag. He had this brand new Rolls-Royce, a Silver Cloud. Then he went on the road for two weeks. They came back, and he forgot he had left the sushi in the car." Marin laughed. "What a mess."

That autumn, Leon was back in Tulsa, and the city was being taken so seriously as a music hub that *Billboard* dedicated a pullout section of the November 10, 1973, issue to the scene. The central feature was headlined TULSA HAS JIM HALSEY, LEO SABELIN, LEON RUSSELL, AND ORAL ROBERTS: TALENT AND THE LORD ARE ON ITS SIDE. The biggest agent in country music, Halsey had brought his operations to Tulsa, which he considered home, having grown up in nearby Independence, Kansas. He also owned radio stations, a publishing company, a production company, recording studios, and commercial and residential real estate. Halsey would work closely with Leon in the late seventies, and their families became very close.

Billboard dedicated a piece to Shelter. Denny described the Tulsa branch as a place to breed homegrown talent. "We also have complete video facilities in the studio with the control booth located above the audio booth. . . . We hope the video will add an extra dimension to all we do." The foresight of the partners is evident with Cordell's explanation that, "meanwhile, it's all going into the vault so that when videodisc or videotape comes along at the consumer level, we will have a complete history of all our artists. Imagine being able to buy a history of Bob Dylan, for example, from the early folk days to what he's into now. This is what we want to have with our people. We've already got 40 hours of Leon's Hank Wilson sessions in the can on film."

He compared Tulsa to the then-burgeoning Austin, explaining you could see J. J. Cale, who did not go on tour often, two nights a week in town. And he emphasized the homey and relaxed atmosphere of not only the lake compound, but Tulsa proper as well. Artists could stay in one house, have their publishing administrated in another house next door, and walk down the block to record at the Church. The Church and Leon's home studios were hives of activity, though. Leon did not record much at the Church himself.

"We worked every day," said head engineer Tom Russell. "But it was usually pretty self-contained. And we used lots of locals. We would let them come in and play around when there wasn't something Shelter-related going on. And that sort of filtered down to a group that repeatedly jelled good together, and I ended up using them on nearly all my sessions: Walter Richman [keyboards], Jamie Oldaker on drums, and Jimmy Byfield [bass]."

A few fans found out and would show up in hopes of getting some attention from their favorite rock star, and a few were successful. Russell described nights when the Church was more like a clubhouse for Leon when he was off the road. "One night, probably three in the morning, Leon came in with his driver and man Friday, Ricky Hill. Ricky was a strange little guy. When he'd come to the studio, Leon would send him out to get some beer." At one all-nighter, Leon walked out in the morning and had Russell run him a long cable to his microphone and did some "man-on-the-street" interviews with drivers as they waited at the traffic light.

Russell remembered some actual Leon music happening as well. "As soon as he opened that control room door, I'd go start the tape," he said. "Sometimes a whole reel or two reels would spin, and nothing would be on it. But sooner or later, he'd usually get up, walk out into the studio, and he'd sit down at the piano and start doing his thing.

"One night I was there by myself, and he came in, and we talked a little while, and he went out in the studio and wandered around doing something. I turned my back, and I heard that piano, so I started the tape. He sat down, he played his song and sang it, just like that, and I'd never heard it. He came back in and said, 'Yeah, it just came to me.' I said, 'Man, that's one of the best songs I've ever heard you do.' And that was the last of it. The name of it was 'The Whores of Babylon.' And never touched it after that. I never heard of it or saw it again."

Whenever Leon's friends came to town, they'd stop by the Church or his home studio. Patrick Henderson said, "That's when I first met Stevie

Wonder. Stevie came to the studio and hung out." Did Stevie and Leon play together? "Leon, whenever somebody was in there, there was a tape rolling, okay? I'm kind of surprised that we haven't heard the *Church Basement Tapes* yet. He liked to show us off to his friends. I had the song called 'Sinner Man,' and Leon knew it, and he asked me to play it for Stevie, and Stevie just loved it." The song appeared on the *O'Neal Twins* album.

There's a significant amount of creative overlap between Leon and Stevie. They were both young piano prodigies who could play multiple instruments, though few commanded Stevie's level of proficiency on each. Leon, for example, could not really play drums, and Stevie was an expert drummer. But this is partially what drove Leon in his pursuit of a satisfying drum machine. He would later serve as the creative spark behind Roger Linn's revolutionary LinnDrum, and Stevie would be one of the machine's first buyers. "Leon had all these incredible synthesizers, and Stevie was just getting there," Henderson said.

Elton John and his band came by Leon's house after playing in Tulsa one night. By then, his star had begun to eclipse Leon's. Leon was about to beat a retreat, equal parts design and negligence. "I'm not as suited for [fame] as someone like Elton, who seems to really thrive on it," he said many years later. "I like to go to Walmart, and there was a period of time when I couldn't get out of the car in Manhattan and walk down the street. . . . I used to have to have my staff lay stuff out in advance if I was going to be in a public place."

The last hurrah of the Shelter People band came via a tour of Asia and Australia, including four dates in Japan, in November 1973, producing a great concert album from Budokan, *In Japan*, released in 1974 only in Japan. In 2011, Omnivore Recordings coupled it on a CD with a storming 1971 set from Houston. Wayne Perkins stands out on the Tokyo show, with a barrage of impressive solos on "Alcatraz" in particular.

TOKYO FANS GO WILD OVER LEON RUSSELL proclaimed the headline over the review in the Pacific *Stars and Stripes* on November 10. "Before the night was over, Russell turned a typically staid Japan audience into an emotionally charged mass." As he had been doing in the States, Leon had asked the audience to place any offerings they had on the stage. "When we did it in Japan, it was surreal," Patrick Henderson said. "I had chills. Man, they were dancing in the aisles."

They played the Randwick Racecourse in Sydney on November 11. Twenty thousand fans were expected. "Leon Russell considers himself more of a magician than a musician," the article said. "People in Jamaica had regarded him as a conman, and Africans had called him a witch doctor, he said last night. 'I create illusions,' he said, 'and I know the ease with which they are created. . . . I admit I'm a bit of a racist, though I prefer black to white anytime, whether it's music or people.'" Leon went on to claim he was "ordained as an honorary Baptist minister with the black church in Dallas, Texas about three months ago." The article states, "He said racism in America had developed into a very ugly problem, although he was not much involved in it. 'I'm not much of a fighter.'"

"The pace was pretty intense," Perkins said of the tour. Don Preston realized he got out just in time. "Oddly enough, I was in Tokyo for a song contest [at the same time], and I talked with Leon," Preston said. "He was very tired sounding."

In 1973, *Billboard* listed Leon Russell as the "top concert attraction in the world." But Peter Nicholls was burned out, and this Asia tour would be his last with Leon. Even when they were off the road, the advancing for upcoming tours and accounting for past dates kept Nicholls busy seven days a week. These were the days well before faxing, never mind the internet, email, or cell phones. "Everything was difficult. There was never, never a relaxing moment in the day." But Asia was the tour that broke his back, and it was the last for the Shelter People.

"I remember walking away from a cricket stadium somewhere in Australia about halfway through the show, thinking, 'This is bullshit. The band doesn't give a shit anymore, Leon doesn't give a shit anymore, and we're not even making good money. Leon's not making good records, I mean, nothing's happening.' I took a cab back to the hotel right in the middle of the show and sat in my room, thinking, 'This is ridiculous.' So when Leon returned after the show, I said, 'I don't know if you noticed, but I wasn't around after the show. I've had enough; I'm out. I'll do this tour, and the two dates we've got at Christmas, and I'm gone.' Leon says, 'Great, that's fine because we were going to fire all you guys anyway.'"

Back in the States, Leon called Nicholls. "He said, 'Well, I don't know what you English people do. And I can get a bunch of players on the north side of Tulsa [the Gap Band] for cheap. I don't need you guys.' The local people, who didn't respect him when he was a kid, when he became a superstar, wanted to be part of his circle, and they convinced him that we 'English people' were taking his money. He literally, in one day, shut it down. He just destroyed it."

Factions had formed between the Okies and the Brits. Mary Jones (who had moved on from Steve Busch) said, "The LA people didn't like Leon's Tulsa people. The English group didn't like the Tulsa group. I was in all three. Then I left to marry Otto Elliott, who was a friend of Denny's. This placed me in Denny's group, but disliked by the LA people, because I was in Leon's personal group."

The Tulsa faction moved Nicholls's stuff out of his house and turned it into an office. "That's when the bust-up occurred. I got out real quick. And I took some time off. I was only twenty-seven years old. I was physically very ill. And I just got out, just completely shut down. I came back and didn't have a place to live.

"What happened to the Shelter People if it was this phenomenally successful operation? And I'm telling you, it was *phenomenally* successful. We were bringing home a hundred grand a week in the early seventies." Nicholls reckoned the problems could be traced back to Leon's youth. "Leon, growing up as a kid, he was afflicted [his limp]. As a teenager in Oklahoma at that time, you were a nerd, or a jock, or whatever, and he was not a popular guy at all; he was a nerdy musician. He left as a late teenager to go to Los Angeles." These old acquaintances showed up out of the woodwork when Leon returned to Tulsa as a star. "I think it's a psychological cycle. If you were [picked on] as a kid, and now you're an adult, you're susceptible to people coming to you and telling you you're great." Leon began to question his own judgment. His uncanny habit of trusting the wrong people would be an Achilles' heel his entire life.

Buddy Jones became the loudest voice in Leon's ear. "When I met [Jones], I just thought, 'So what exactly do you bring to the equation?' But Leon believed him," Nicholls said. "He sold Leon on this idea. At the end of the day, he bought the Buddy Jones story. And I don't think his career ever was the same again."

Jones's proposition—which was paraphrased by various parties—was: "Why do you need this expensive band and a crew of English people, when I can hire a whole band of Black guys for a lot less money?" Emily Smith, as a Tulsa native married (at least on paper) to one of the "English people," Simon Miller-Mundy, seemed predictably torn. But she also felt the changes were a mistake. And in a 1989 interview, she gave her frank opinion. She said that when the *Carney* tour happened, "I had gotten 'haughty' [Leon's term for her] and run off, because I had decided that I was better than all that cheap trash anyhow."

Leon, though, was genuinely inspired by collaborating with the brilliant musicians in the Gap Band and would use them on his next record, *Stop All That Jazz.*

Some of Leon's Tulsa friends questioned Leon's business arrangements with Denny as well. Leon, relying more on Jones as his personal manager, was pursuing his artistic impulses and increasingly ignoring Cordell. But the professional end of their relationship stayed together until 1976 because of their business entanglements. Nicholls explained, "The money all went back into the Shelter account. I think that's probably where they [the Tulsa contingent] got it; they convinced him that he didn't know where the money was going. They told Leon that he was getting screwed, and he wasn't. And as a result, it changed his career trajectory."

For Nicholls, it was an awakening of what such relationships meant long term. "For three or four years, Leon and I were tight. I mean, we did everything together, you know, but I never knew him as a person. I don't think we ever really enjoyed each other at all. We didn't ever have any fun. When the split came with Leon, it was a big split. That was it."

"I spoke to him fifteen years later," Nicholls recalled. "I was helping a friend of mine that was a big concert promoter in the Tulsa area, Larry Shaeffer. Shaeffer asked me to go down and take care of the show that he had with Leon Russell. I said, 'Yeah! Of course.' So I went down there. The road manager comes in. 'Lovely show,' I said to him. 'You know, I do *know* Leon Russell.' So he went and got Leon, and they brought him in, and he hobbled in the room. And he looked at me and said, 'So, you got the money?' I said, 'Yeah, I do.' And he said, 'Good.' That was the last thing he said to me.

"It's weird to work so closely with somebody for three or four or five years, doing amazing stuff, and then never speak again. That's the weird thing about this stuff. You can go through these amazing years together, but at the end of the day, it doesn't actually mean anything, you know?"

Chapter 23

Stop All That Jazz

MARY JONES WALKED ONTO A plane in Tulsa with precious cargo: a Gibson Hummingbird acoustic guitar Bob Dylan had given Leon Russell. Leon had asked her to fly it down to Dallas, where he was performing a New Year's Eve show at Market Hall with Willie Nelson and Kinky Friedman. Jones joined them, Emily Smith, and the Tulsa crew for the final night of 1973. Leon's foray into country music and his collaboration with Willie had been accepted as relatively novel and innovative, if not a giant step, by his audience of rock 'n' rollers. But he was about to go in an altogether different, perplexing direction.

Though he looked even older than he was, in the early 1970s, Leon's actual age of thirty-one was considered old by rock 'n' roll standards. Impressed by the young musicians in the Gap Band, he not only would release their debut album *Magician's Holiday* on Shelter in 1974, but he would virtually adopt the group as his own for his next album, *Stop All That Jazz*, and they would be his backing band for all of his touring in '74. In keeping with the Shelter philosophy of having a Shelter act gain exposure on their lodestar's tour, the Gap Band would also open the shows.

Coproduced by Buddy Jones (who also cowrote some songs) and Gap Band leader Charlie Wilson, *Magician's Holiday* glides through a constellation of funk, pop, and soul, with references to Sly and the Family Stone, Stevie Wonder, Billy Preston, and New Orleans artists like Allen Toussaint and the Meters. Though markedly different from their breakthrough in the eighties—with such synth-funk hits as "Burn Rubber on Me" and "You Dropped a Bomb on Me (Why You Wanna Hurt Me)"—their debut album displays a command that belies their rookie status. Leon contributes a repeating guitar riff on "Fontessa Fame," and Wayne Perkins plays solos on "Bad Girl" with fuzzy phased lead guitar inspired by Ernie Isley's distinctive tone on "That Lady." Leon returns on synth for the title track, which closes the album and is the song that owes the most to Stevie Wonder's influence, specifically reminiscent of "You and I," from Wonder's *Talking Book*. The Gap Band even had help on the album from Malcolm Cecil and Robert Margouleff, the same synth pioneers who worked with Wonder.

Stop All That Jazz was recorded in Leon's home studio, the lake studio, and the Church. There was also one track recorded earlier in Nashville with Willie Nelson at Pete's Place (Pete Drake's studio). J. J. Cale, drummer Karl Himmel, and steel guitar player Pete Drake joined other Nashville studio luminaries to rework the Tim Hardin song "If I Were a Carpenter." Leon managed to make an already cloying song worse. "I think Bobby Darin had just died," Himmel said. Darin, who died December 20, 1973, had a hit with the song in 1966. A couple of weeks later, Tex Ritter died and Leon (who had played on a session or two for Tex in the early sixties) recorded a fantastic but unreleased song called "The Day Tex Ritter Died." Himmel recalled, "We did 'If I Were a Carpenter' and 'Wild Horses.' That was something. 'Meet me in the studio. Now!'"

Leon wallows in the mawkishness of the Hardin song, but it was apparently not yet insipid enough for him, so he added: "If I was a rock star / Would you be my groupie?" Amid the ham-handed parody, though, he reveals an autobiographical glimpse of his personal crisis with yet even more supplemental lines: "Well, I get so mean sometimes / When the spirit's on me."

Personal revelations aside, it did not augur well for the rest of the album as the leadoff track. But before even listening, record buyers had to first get past the atrocious *Spinal Tap*–like sight gag on the album's cover: Black members of the Gap Band and Ambrose Campbell dressed in native African costumes, holding spears and a human skull, surrounding a kettle containing Leon in a pith helmet. (Like cannibals, get it?)

Poor taste and terrible judgment permeate the album. There's a topical stab with a novelty track, "Streaker's Ball," the boring filler of an easy-listening version of "Spanish Harlem," and a Holiday Inn–lounge band arrangement of a forgettable original, a blues-jazz number called "Mona Lisa Please." The title track is interrupted by numerous breakdowns that serve to disrupt the flow, as if Leon himself—his vocal drenched in gobs of echo—cannot bring himself to play any more "jazz." It's a shame, as it could have been a welcome opportunity to hear him redouble his dedication to such jazz/R&B/pop crossover influences as Nat King Cole, Charles Brown, and Ray Charles. But any sense of serious commitment is hard to discover in these tracks.

There are exceptions, though, moments of genuine inspiration. He offers an intense reinvention of Dylan's "The Ballad of Hollis Brown," making the already dark and claustrophobic murder ballad sound apocalyptic. The band—including Jamie Oldaker joining Roscoe Smith on drums—and Leon start the track with howls that continue throughout the song in a call-and-response blues, as the synths throb in a stereo spread, hammering one monotonous chord. The stark rural folk song is transformed into a dense urban-industrial nightmare. It's ahead of its time, as if the synth-punk duo Suicide collaborated with Giorgio Moroder with backing vocals from a chain gang. Here's a gray-bearded Okie hippie conjuring up dark new wave aesthetics in the basement of a Tulsa mansion in 1974. Engineer John LeMay claimed the house was haunted. The ghoulish moans and dusky low crunch emanating from these sound machines make it easier to believe.

The Leon composition "Leaving Whipporwhill" [sic] returns to piano-driven pop. The song is a lovely tribute to Hank Williams, with Leon singing, "A song for the back of a blue Cadillac." Featuring Don Preston on guitar and dobro, Joey Cooper on guitar, Chuck Blackwell and Jim Keltner on drums, and John Gallie on organ, it was an earlier recording, done up at the lake. A wistful song is made that much more so when you know that this was one of the last songs to feature most members of the classic Shelter People lineup.

Leon handles the warmly intimate ballad "Time for Love" on his own with piano and synths, and it is one of the few tracks that demonstrate an audible emotional presence from him vocally. But aside from a handful of tracks, the record is a disappointing listen. The repertoire, with four covers out of ten songs, indicates Leon was running out of songwriting steam. He offers nothing new to the Mose Allison song "Smashed."

Leon reflected, "I only wrote it if I had a reason. I've had houses with studios in them for forty-five years, and I'd sit in those studios and wait for inspiration. I'd wait for a reason to write the song and I'd end up writing one or two songs a year." He found it challenging to write on the road, in particular, and he had spent virtually three years touring more often than not. So it is not surprising to look back and see such a shortage of compelling original material coming in 1973–1974: six new songs total on two albums. While the ambitious artistic reach found on *Hank Wilson's Back* and *Stop All That Jazz* was admirable, the results were middling at best. Even the most forgiving fans would have to acknowledge a drop-off from the first three albums.

Stop All That Jazz was released in May 1974 and the tour with the Gap Band began that spring. Before that, Leon was in Nashville in January 1974 with the video bus for a four-camera shoot at Johnny Cash's studio, the House of Cash, with Willie as his cohost. Cash was not around, but the list of performers who did appear is jaw-dropping: Jeanne Pruett, who sang "Satin Sheets"; Bill Monroe, the father of bluegrass music; Ernest Tubb; Earl Scruggs, of Flatt and Scruggs, and his sons; and Roy Acuff. Maureen Gosling read from her old notes: "Many of the musicians who played on *Hank Wilson's Back* and who we see in our movie [*A Poem*] all the time showed up. It was like seeing old friends."

Leon and Willie joined in, with musicians calling out for solos from one another. Leon did some of the Hank Wilson numbers. "Many stories were told about the early days of country music," Leon wrote in his memoir. "This came along sometime after my Hank Wilson album, and I think many of the country stars were curious to see this rock 'n' roll guy who had made a country record."

"Unfortunately, we had some audio problems, and the show was never completed or edited," Leon wrote of the aborted show. Bob Morris, who had started off in cable television and who worked with Leon before continuing a long career in television, said Leon would throw tons of money into projects like the video van but was shortsighted and cut corners. This is a recurring theme in the conversations with those who knew Leon at various points in his life. In this case, the van did not have a tool it needed to sync the audio with the video.

Leon had still not learned his lesson after the Nashville debacle. Later in 1974, Morris said, "Kirk Bressler and I went down to ShelterVision in Texas. We put together a wish list of equipment that they needed to buy.

One of the major items that Kirk and I listed was called a mag sync. And these guys at ShelterVision there decided they didn't need that. It was a total nightmare. There was really nothing salvageable out of it."

Les Blank made a rough video edit of the House of Cash session, but Leon was unsatisfied and wanted to edit it himself, "which made us worry about our film," Gosling said.

Leon was in St. Louis on February 4 for a concert with Bob Dylan and The Band. Leon walked on during "Rainy Day Women" during the first of two sets. "As Dylan entered the last verse, a familiar figure walked onto the stage," read the review in the *Alton* (IL) *Telegraph*. "Old Dylan friend, and great artist in his own right, Leon Russell brought the crowd to their feet as he danced to the music of The Band." He returned for "Like a Rolling Stone" and sang the chorus with Rick Danko and Robbie Robertson. Blurry audience video clips show Leon, in a big old cowboy hat, sidling up to Dylan and mussing his hair. He was one of the few people confident enough to get that close to the bard, never mind audaciously touch his hair as he sang his signature song.

Also in February, Leon managed to find some time to slip over to play on Bill Wyman's album *Monkey Grip*, the first solo album from any Rolling Stone, repaying the favor of Wyman playing on Leon's solo debut back in '69. Leon's featured on "Mighty Fine Time." Wyman told *Rolling Stone*: "I thought of Leon [Russell] because the way I play piano has a vague Leon style, only very mediocre, and I like the way he turns chords around. But I'd heard how he takes things over and I was scared of that."

Leon flew in the Nitty Gritty Dirt Band's John McEuen from an off day on tour, and also brought along Wayne Perkins. "We went over to Ike Turner's studio," Perkins recalled. "Bill Wyman says, 'Here, Perkins, you play bass.' He wanted to play guitar on his record." Perkins would reunite with Wyman on the Stones' *Black and Blue* a couple of years later when the band auditioned guitar players to replace Mick Taylor. Leon would also play on Wyman's 1975 *Stone Alone*.

Planning began in earnest for the upcoming Leon spring tour. Though both were on their way to successful careers in broadcasting and film, Bob Morris and Tim Harkin were detoured, lured away from the nascent Tulsa Cable company by Buddy Jones. Jones was actually filling a vacuum created when Leon lost his longtime and loyal road crew to Eric Clapton. "Later in April came major firings and quitting, including the roadies, who were Leon's most loyal, hard-working folks," Gosling said. "[Leon] fired them because they had been invited to be roadies for Eric Clapton on their off-season. When they weren't working with Leon, Eric Clapton said, 'Well, if you're not working, why don't you work for me?' But Leon said, 'It's either him or me.'"

Clapton had been hanging around Tulsa on and off over a couple of years. "I went up there with my first wife [Pattie Boyd], and we stayed in Claremont," he said. "I met all kinds of crazy people and had a great time." Over the next year, as Clapton filled out his band with players and singers from Leon's band and the Church scene, Leon would half-joke that Clapton "stole" his band after having done the same with his crew. "Oh, for crying out loud!" Clapton laughed in response. "This goes on *all the time*," he said, laughing. "It was the same with Delaney. I got it in the neck from Delaney, that I stole his band. I mean, these guys came knocking at my door!"

Marcy Levy, another musician who would jump from ship *Leon* to SS *Clapton*, had come to the lake with Bob Seger when he recorded there in '72. She relocated from Detroit to Tulsa in '73. Carl Radle brought Clapton to see her perform. But singing with Leon was her main goal, so she was understandably happy when he and J. J. Cale would drop by and sit in with her band, which at times included Jamie Oldaker and Radle. Ten years younger than Leon, she had idolized him as a teenager at home in Detroit. She particularly admired how he worked with his backing singers.

"Jamie and I were both asked to join Leon Russell's band, but Jamie went off to join Eric Clapton," said Levy (who now is known as Marcella Detroit). "I was asked to join Eric Clapton as well, but because of my desire to work with Leon and my love for him, I chose to work with him and joined everyone else with Eric Clapton after my tour and my relationship ended with Leon." Leon was seeing a number of women during this time.

Levy sang on *Stop All That Jazz* and the subsequent tour. When that ended, Clapton recorded with Levy as well, memorably featuring her voice on such songs as "The Core," "Wonderful Tonight," and "Lay Down Sally." As a result, she is one that Leon included when charging Clapton with musician poaching. "Time for me to set the record straight," Clapton said with a laugh. "I think this wasn't even my idea. I was so stoned at that point in time." Clapton would be arrested at the Tulsa airport for drunken behavior in 1975. "I don't think I knew the couple of tracks that

she was on. I didn't play on half that album; I was so out of it. This was
something to do with the Tulsa team. It would have been Carl and Dickie
up to no good. I take no responsibility."

Ann Bell said that tension lingered in Tulsa. "Marcy did one tour
with Leon, but then she left Leon and went to go with Clapton, but I
stayed. . . . In Tulsa, you were either Team Leon, or you were Team Clapton. Well, I was Team Leon, yeah. Hats off to Eric, but Eric's not Leon."

Clapton hung around Oklahoma long enough to jam at the basement
studio with Leon, Mary McCreary (Clavinet and vocals), Oldaker, Radle,
and George Terry (guitar). There's a recording of this online referred to as
"Eric Clapton and Leon Russell: Apartment Jam, 1974." He also recalls
going up to the lake, but not recording there. Clapton said that at the
Tulsa house, Leon "was going through a period, [*laughing*] where he had
a panel of TV screens, you know, how you see in a science fiction movie,"
Clapton said. "I think he actually had that in the studio and [I remember]
thinking, 'What is *happening* with Leon? Leon has gone completely out
of a door.'"

Jim Karstein, who had returned to Oklahoma, said it was around that
fall and winter of 1973–1974 that Leon pretty much abandoned Grand
Lake, allowing Karstein to stay there. "That was the story of Leon's life.
He'd get these *big* nuclear ideas, and he'd just go off the high dive and
do a triple gainer right into the middle of 'em and, you know, sink God-
knows-how-many dollars into it. It'd be the biggest and the greatest deal,
and then he'd lose interest in it, and then he'd just walk away." Gosling
said that staying at the lake house for too long was "conducive to madness." The dark Tulsa house cluttered with antiques, though, was "gloomy
and depressing."

In 1974, Peter Tosh of the Wailers came to Tulsa with his band to work
on sessions at the Church for *Legalize It*. "Carl Radle brought him in and
was pretty much producing it," said Tom Russell, who engineered the
sessions. "They were rolling these joints that looked like a snow cone. The
session starts and less than fifteen minutes in, it was like close to a total
fog." Kirk Bressler also engineered. "I remember them telling me, 'More
bass, mon, more bass.'"

The band stayed with Peter Nicholls while in town. "Rastas in Tulsa,
it was completely ridiculous," Nicholls said. "It was bizarre. Nobody had
any idea what was going on." Shelter was instrumental in popularizing

reggae in the States. "Jamie [Oldaker] and Carl were terribly influential with regards to Eric Clapton getting into the whole reggae thing," Don Williams said. "Clapton made a huge hit record with Marley's 'I Shot the Sheriff.' That breaks the ground for Marley." Radle and Oldaker's stellar groove is what makes Clapton's cover so effective.

Also coming through the Church in 1974 was Tom Petty. He and his pre-Heartbreakers band, Mudcrutch, had driven a van from their home state of Florida to Hollywood, demo tape in hand, intending to land a record deal. "We drove down the streets and everywhere you looked were signs for record companies. MGM, RCA, Capitol, A&M," Petty said. "We could just walk into these places, and a lot of the time, someone would listen. It certainly doesn't happen like that anymore."

London Records bit first and sent Petty back to Florida to retrieve the rest of the band on a handshake deal. Before leaving town, he had also handed off his tape to someone at Shelter in East Hollywood. Back home, Petty got a call from Denny Cordell, who had heard the tape via Simon Miller-Mundy. "We went home [to Florida] and sold everything we owned, and got ready to come to California," Petty said. "And literally, in a rehearsal, the phone rang and I answered it, and it was Denny Cordell. I thought he was calling about a car we had for sale. And he said, 'I really want to sign your group.' I was like, 'What is this?' But we knew who Denny Cordell was. We knew he had done 'A Whiter Shade of Pale' and the Joe Cocker stuff. We knew that he was a real guy we were talking to on the phone. But I had to say, 'Well, I'm really sorry, but we already promised London Records we would sign with them.' And he said, 'I've got a studio in Tulsa, Oklahoma. And that's going to be not far out of your way. Why don't you stop in Tulsa and meet with me, and then you can see if you like us.'"

Cordell met them at the Ranch House diner, and the band was instantly charmed. "We had never met anyone who was English," Petty said. When Cordell realized they were short on dough, he also gave them a few thousand dollars in cash and took them across the street to the studio.

"Leon Russell had a place in Tulsa, and Shelter was built around Leon," Petty said. "[Cordell] said, 'Spend the night, and tomorrow we'll go in and do a session.' And we were like, 'Wow, we get to do a session in a studio! Hell yeah, we'll spend the night.' . . . We spent the next day recording, and he went, 'That's it. I'm sold. I want to sign your band.' And we liked him a lot, much better than the guy at London, who was an executive type. So we said, 'Okay, we'll go with you.'"

Mudcrutch continued on to LA and soon settled into the Shelter scene out there. Denny mentored Petty, playing him old R&B and new reggae records, and the band cut a reggae-informed track called "Depot Street" at Village Recorders. During the take that ended up released as a single, the only Mudcrutch record Shelter released, Joe Cocker walked in. Petty called it "a novelty record," too much under Cordell's sway: "I was hearing reggae for the first time."

While Denny was involved with Mudcrutch out in LA, Leon started rehearsing the fifteen-piece touring band for the 1974 summer tour in the arena at the Tulsa Fairgrounds. In her notes from the time, Gosling described the band "doing new and old Leon songs, Gap Band songs, country & western, soul, rock, gospel, nightclub, Leon's revival of some of his Tijuana Brass links. Horn players surprised Leon by yodeling on 'Truck Driving Man.' Leon is far away from his blue-jeans-and-blue-jean-jacket attire of the last year. This year, it's cosmic cowboys; ten suits made by a seamstress who put rhinestones on them. I said he will lose weight carrying around all those rhinestones." And Leon had started to become better acquainted, musically and personally, with Mary McCreary.

When *Stop All That Jazz* was released in May, aside from his hometown newspaper *Lawton Sunday Constitution*, which tepidly allowed, "The new album is good Russell," the press was not kind. "This may well be his all-time low record effort," wrote his early champion, Robert Hilburn in the *LA Times* (syndicated nationally), "a virtual hodgepodge of styles (from jazz to country to cocktail lounge pop) that makes you think that Russell, in the 'big fish in a little pond' isolation of his Tulsa compound is beginning to believe all that 'master of space and time image.' . . . There's no heart or soul in the album, much less joy."

Chet Flippo penned a personal attack on Leon in the ever-important cultural arbiter *Rolling Stone*. The writer carried a chip on his shoulder regarding Leon and eyed him suspiciously as a snake oil salesman of sorts. Now he saw him as a cult leader just short of Manson-esque. "Those who visit the Leon Russell empire at Disney, Oklahoma [the lake compound], and do not succumb to Russell's dark magnetism come away muttering about mind games and mass manipulation and even 'rock evangelism.' Rita Coolidge, I know, was glad to pull herself away from the Russell influence. I have seen rock audiences who could not resist his control begin behaving just the way I have seen audiences react to another Oklahoma performer, Oral Roberts. Both Roberts and Russell offer a form of salvation and, importantly, both men appear to have been tamed by success, which led in both cases to a quest for respectability. . . . Russell [has become] musically schizoid."

Anyone who skyrockets to such dizzying heights of fame should be prepared for backlash. But Leon did himself no favors with the press. He was largely shunning interviews. One of the few he did give that year was with an architecture student named David A. Williams, who was putting together a proposal for a possible new Shelter studio and suite of offices. This academic project was not intended as something the general public would see. As such, Leon is refreshingly candid and insightful about his philosophy at that moment. "My music was rather limited in its style up until about the time *Carney* was released," he revealed. "I started experimenting then with the crew to see if we couldn't come up with something else, sort of an open season on music. I guess you would have to say *Hank Wilson's Back* was the turning point. It wasn't until *Stop All That Jazz* that a new diversity of style became apparent, though. The new one [referring to 1975's *Will O' the Wisp*] should reveal this even more. It's almost as if I have become attuned with nature." He speaks reverently, with a little awe, as if he was merely a channel for the art he produced.

Blank and Gosling were wrapping up the edit of *A Poem Is a Naked Person*. It was entered into Critics' Week at Cannes in early April but missed it because of an administrative error made by someone in Paris. It was accepted into Directors' Fortnight, though, and it was entered into the Berlin Film Festival in June. "The finishing of it was one of those mad, mad, crazy deadline kind of things, where we stayed up twenty-four hours, rushing to the airport because Les was going to LA to do the sound mix. And John LeMay was mixing all the concert sound before we went to LA." The concert mixes were being finished at Paradise Studio at the lake.

Gosling sighed, recounting the sense of melancholy she felt as the film project finished up, as the lake was being abandoned, and the old band, crew, and management were replaced. She read from her letters: "'A whole new band on the road and leaving behind his longtime friends. The Gap Band, with Buddy as manager, not Denny. Leon and Denny at odds. Long hours; not enough pay; misunderstandings.'"

When she left Oklahoma, all looked extremely promising for the film that Gosling had dedicated the better part of two years helping Blank create. But the next thing she knew, it was canned. The reason the film was so abruptly abandoned remains something of a mystery to Gosling, even after all this time. "Something happened. And I don't know if Leon finally decided he didn't want it shown [at Cannes], or whether it didn't make it in time." But it wasn't just a matter of holding the film back from imminent festivals; Leon was determined the film would not be shown. It was over. That door was slammed shut, and he was moving on.

Bob Morris said, "My sister called and said, 'Come over and watch a film.' So I go over, and it was the only showing of *A Poem Is a Naked Person*. I just happened to be there that night." At the end of it, Leon stood up. "Leon goes, 'That's it. That's the only time it'll ever be seen.' He said, 'Can it.' He told Les that night, 'We're not ever going to release it.'

"The biggest thing in the whole deal," Morris said, "was, 'Why *the fuck* did you put the chicken in there?'" This is in reference to the most controversial scene in the film, where a chick is devoured by Chula, Jim Franklin's boa constrictor. "That was Leon's whole deal: 'You had a minute or something of the chicken, and you've got musicians from around the world you can put in there, and you *chose to put a chicken in there?*' That pissed Leon off. It wasn't an argument, it was just a statement. 'This is it.' And they had an agreement that Les could show it, but Les had to be there. So anytime it was shown, Les has to be there with it." It could not be screened for profit, so it was relegated to academic, museum, and other institutional showings.

In 1974, Leon was slipping into a state of paranoia, distrusting and diminishing the influence of those who had supported him as he climbed to the point of superstardom. He had cut out Peter Nicholls, his band, and his roadies and rapidly moved away from Denny Cordell. He was listening more to Buddy Jones and his cronies. "It's possible that some people saw the film and maybe had some critique that Leon didn't like," Gosling said. "When we met up with him again and did the touring with him with the film [in 2015], he said he thought that the film was more about Les than about him." But he had seen it, and he had been seeing it in its iterations. He should have understood what they were going to get from Blank, particularly as they had been viewing dailies of the footage, and Leon had seen the director's cut. But someone got in his ear.

It was Leon who came up with the title of the film, which was lifted from Bob Dylan's liner notes on *Bringing It All Back Home*. And there is an undeniable nakedness about the film, no matter how poetic it is, that made Leon, a self-described illusionist, uncomfortable. As a master showman, he had second thoughts about showing the general public something like home movie footage of him sitting bare-chested at a kitchen table, feeling no pain, as a long night of drinking with Robert Stone Jordan carried into the wee small hours of the morning. That was perhaps too real for a guy with a lifelong fear of being called out as a fraud.

Les Blank told *Tulsa World* in 1997, "It was kind of a continuous party. There were recording sessions that would go all night long. There was a constant influx of people coming and going." Here's a question: Why is there not more of *that* stuff in the final cut?

If the final edit was not to his liking, then why didn't Leon ask for further edits? Did he offer any constructive criticism? "No," said Les Blank's son Harrod. "My father actually did not know what the problem was." And it would not have mattered. Harrod would be the one ultimately responsible for the 2015 release of the film after forty years (two years after his father's death). Leon said he had invested $660,000 in the film, but that was not enough to keep him from pulling the plug, partially out of spite. Blank had angered him several times. "There were a couple of incidents where Les actually crossed the line with Leon," Harrod said. "Leon told me, 'You know, your father got inappropriately drunk one too many times.'" And Leon was not a forgive-and-forget kind of guy; he was a confirmed grudge-holder. "He was good at what he did," Leon acknowledged about Les. "He was just kind of a jerk sometimes. But I guess I was kind of a jerk too."

When Leon hit the road in May, it would be his first tour without Peter Nicholls and the Shelter People. "We left town with the Gap Band," Morris said. "Leon also took enough rock 'n' rollers to be able to do the rock 'n' roll part, as opposed to adjusting to the Gap Band's music, Tommy Lokey, Chuck Blackwell, and Wayne Perkins."

The apex had been reached, and the descent was pronounced, if not precipitous. Now Leon was planning a tour to support two peculiar albums almost 180 degrees different from each other in style, performed by the same band. "That was kind of crazy because we came from a first-class tour on jets around the world," Wayne Perkins said. "Then Leon started wanting to cut some corners, so we went from jets to buses."

Leon and Buddy Jones had put together a partnership called Cowboy Carnival Productions to book and run his appearances. Fans would be forgiven for being confused about what exactly they were going to witness at these shows. "All of the three albums came out at the same time, so people didn't really know what to expect," Morris said, referring to *Hank Wilson's Back*, *Stop All That Jazz*, and the Gap Band's *Magician's Holiday*. "So they were sort of the combination of Leon's original music, and people expecting *Hank Wilson's Back*, and all of a sudden, here's this Black band." The Gap Band playing country tunes was quite a mash-up.

"Leon wanted to go out and get funky, put his cowboy hat on," Perkins said. As for the band, he noted, "We picked the Gap Band up, but Leon kept the Shelter People drummer, Chuck Blackwell, and me because Chuck knew where all the changes were, and Leon was always one to throw changes at you that nobody in the band had ever heard before."

"It was me and an all-Black band playing cowboy songs. It was a lot of fun," Leon said in 2001. "I have been told it was the inspiration for that band down in Florida. Who was it? KC and the Sunshine Band."

The racism that would confront Leon's bands in 1975 and 1976 had not yet become an obvious issue at the shows. "The crowds never objected; they embraced it right away," said Ann Bell. "But where we had problems was when we'd be in the hotels, would be in the restaurants, and we'd be in the bus, and we'd have to pull off to try to get food somewhere they wouldn't serve [the Black musicians]. And, oh, it just pissed me, Leon, and Chuck off." Leon was traveling separately in a camper with his cousin, Steve Marr, and had cautioned the band on the bus to avoid attracting the attention of the local authorities. Bell said they'd stop just short of causing enough trouble to get the cops called. For example, after one restaurant refused to serve the Black members of the entourage, the white members ordered dozens of hamburgers to go, prepared with various custom orders to be as difficult as possible. "And as we go up to the steps of the bus, Charlie Wilson turned around and grabbed me and just started kissing me, which just *infuriated* these racists down there," Bell chuckled.

Along the way, they played shows—headlining almost all—with the Eagles, REO Speedwagon, the Allman Brothers, ZZ Top, Billy Preston, Lynyrd Skynyrd, Santana, the Beach Boys, and dozens of others. The tour played the Midwest in early May, headed east, stopping in Albany, and worked down the Eastern Seaboard, arriving in Tampa on May 25 for the Springtime Rock Jubilee at the Old Florida State Fairgrounds. The *Tampa Bay Times* review complained about most of the acts, and the festival itself (filthy toilets, lack of shade, overpriced Cokes). But the piece reported, "Leon's show was great, though. He's been here before, but this new band of his is just as good as any of his previous collections. During this performance a lovely streaker kissed Leon and then pranced right across the stage—a Tampa first." "Streaker's Ball" was paying immediate dividends.

The promoters of the show had planned a second with the same bill, two days later, in Reading, Pennsylvania. "They had chartered an Eastern Airlines 737," Morris said. Leon, the Gap Band, Ike & Tina Turner, and the New York Dolls all flew in, but the show was rained out. "These two events were the same promoter, and we figured it was probably the mob laundering money, 'cause they spent money like it was going out of style."

Dr. John was also on the dates. "They would just have all of us on these flights, so it was just a free-for-all on the flights," Bell said. Dr. John would get up on the rolling stairway to the plane after everyone was seated. "He would make the flight crew roll him to the nose of the plane, and he throws gris-gris dust on it and did this Cajun prayer of some sort before he would let us take off. My eyes were as big as saucers when I saw the New York Dolls," Bell laughed. "Makeup and everything. 'You guys are *loud*.'"

In Brooklyn, Emily Smith showed up with Caroline Kennedy. "I have no idea how she got to know her," Ann Bell said. "But here they came. We were in an old theater that seated about five thousand. When we started doing 'Honky Tonk Woman,' she [Emily] came out on the stage, dancing. She was butt naked. She had on a dress that was made out of cellophane, carrying a dozen red roses like she was Miss America. She's got her tambourine, whackin' it on her butt, turned her back to the audience, and they could see the whole thing, and Leon *loved* it!"

They toured North America for four months, from May through August, with Leon making sure he stopped off at Willie Nelson's second annual Fourth of July Picnic. This one was filmed, and it's like a Texas Woodstock. The crowd is in various stages of suntanned/sunburned nudity, straw hats, draining cans of Lone Star, passing joints and gallon jugs of wine, kicking up dust as they dance around. It looks like a goddamned good time. The list of artists who performed over three days is mind-boggling: Randy Newman, Lefty Frizzell, Townes Van Zandt, Bill Monroe, Billy Joe Shaver.

Billed as the Master of Ceremonies on the poster, Leon himself was well lubricated by nightfall. In the film, brew and butt in hand, he joins Willie and wild-man Cajun fiddler Doug Kershaw, dancing onstage while B. W. Stevenson and his band play. Leon takes the mic, rambling wildly, and introduces Kershaw. Then he stands there, swaying, drinking beer, ostensibly singing backups but really just eyeing the velvet-clad swashbuckling Kershaw. At the end of his song, a nude young woman comes up and embraces Kershaw, before she grabs Leon and holds him in a headlock of a hug, knocking off his hat. She strides offstage without anyone escorting her. Waylon Jennings appears all of a sudden at the mic and purrs, "How about that," in his deeply resonant voice. Then he gestures toward Leon and says, "That's the most expensive harmony singer in the world, right there."

Leon confesses to the crowd, "You know, I went down to Nashville not too long ago, and I was drunk down there, too. See, it seems like I am drunk every time, everywhere I go." It seems like during a song with Waylon, Leon could not hear the acoustic piano very well, and likely realized he was not in the best condition to play. So he simply stands front-of-stage and calls for the key of D. On he rambles.

In a much smaller dose, this might have been briefly entertaining. But by this point, Leon is one of those annoying uncles who gets up with the wedding band, and no one has the heart to ask him to leave the stage. By the end of the medley, Leon is sitting between the floor monitors on the proscenium, pale beer belly hanging out, looking like he might roll over and pass out right then and there, good night Irene!

As many would attest over the years, Leon was a lightweight when it came to alcohol. It quickly turned him into a sloppy "wild man," as one put it. He also had such a reputation as a stoner that the satirical midnight movie *The Groove Tube* (1974) cast a lookalike as Leon doing a television commercial pitching a "Western Union Marijuanagram" to send to your valentine. A Bob Dylan lookalike leans in at the end to light up Leon's joint.

Later that month, Leon hosted back-to-back episodes of the weekly *Midnight Special* television program. The July 26 show featured him and the Gap Band, previously filmed at the Church. "They wanted Leon, and Leon said, 'Yeah, I'll do it, but you have to come here to do it,'" said Tom Russell. The Gap Band did three songs on their own and Leon performed nine of his own numbers with them. He returned as a host on August 2 for an episode that consisted of footage of Willie's Fourth of July, including Rick Nelson, Michael Murphey, Waylon Jennings, Bobby Bare, David Carradine, John Hartford, Doug Kershaw, and Willie himself.

Wayne Perkins was hanging out at Leon's while they were off the road. "You wanna talk about pressure? He used to love my songwriting. I wasn't writing anything really valuable back then. But I was writing pretty good, and I'm sitting down in the ballroom of that big giant monster he used to live in in Tulsa. He yelled down, 'Perkins! Get up here. I want you to meet somebody.' I was in the middle of trying to put a bridge in this thing. So I go up the stairs, and he said, 'I want you to meet this friend of mine. I want you to play him some of your songs.' It didn't really hit me who he was, you know?

"Leon gave me a guitar, that Hummingbird of his," Perkins continued. "So I'm sitting there trying to play a song or two, and I give the guitar to Leon; he strummed something out. And then Willie would play 'Angel Flying Too Close to the Ground.' You always try to outdo the other guy. Play one, give it to Leon, he does, 'Masquerade.' He gives the guitar to Willie, he goes, [*sings*] [*pauses*] 'Crazy . . .' I said, '*That's* who you are! I knew I seen you somewhere before!'"

Willie and Connie Nelson had come up to see the Tulsa show on the Leon/Gap Band tour. Connie recalled: "After the show, Leon called Willie and said, 'Hey, the guys from the Gap Band really want to smoke a joint with you.' So we agreed to go to some other hotel. Willie and I went to their suite. There was a circle of chairs, and all the Gap Band guys were sitting in the circle, and there was a place for Willie and I. We sat, and they passed this joint around. And I was never a big smoker; I was a mom. I took a hit and passed it. From then on, I don't think that I took another one. It would come to me, and I'd just pass it. And honestly, the very next thing I knew, we were in the elevator. I remember it going up and down, and people getting on and getting off, and we were still in the elevator. I just would maybe get a second of clarity, enough to think, 'Wait a minute.' And Willie was just gone. He was gone. And I remember thinking,

'Okay, this isn't our hotel, I have no idea where our hotel is. I don't know how we got here,' I mean, it was *that bad*.

"The next day, Willie called Leon and said, 'I don't know what they gave us. It might have been heroin. I don't know what it was, but we were scared. Can you find out what that was?' and Leon said, 'I'll call you back.' Leon called back after a little while and said it was angel dust. And the only way that we got through it is, I took one hit and kept passing, or we'd still be somewhere in Tulsa."

Chapter 24

Will O' the Wisp

IN *A POEM IS A NAKED PERSON*, Leon and Les Blank visit the Spooklight Museum, a roadside tourist trap down a country lane in the Missouri Ozarks, not far from Joplin. The Spooklight is an atmospheric ghost light, the kind of phenomenon described in various folklore around the world as a jack-o'-lantern or a will-o'-the-wisp. These nightly illuminations float over bogs and marshes, and for centuries have led nocturnal wayfarers astray, especially young paramours. The blame was often ascribed to malevolent fairies, or other evil spirits, who lured travelers into swamps or out to sea.

Leon titled his 1975 album *Will O' the Wisp*. Business decisions, artistic choices, romantic dead ends—was he acknowledging poor judgment in any or all of those instances? Was he blinded by the light and led astray?

As 1974 came to a close, it had become clear that Mary McCreary and Leon were a serious item, even to those not paying much attention. Though she'd recorded parts of her debut album at the Church for Leon's label and opened his 1973 summer tour, Leon did not get to know Mary very well until she came back to Tulsa to work on her follow-up, *Jezebel*. Tina Rose Bridges, Leon and Mary's daughter, said that Leon was struck dumb by Mary the first time he saw her, at an audition for Shelter. "He said that she was so beautiful that he had to walk out of the room."

"He seemed kind of strange at first," Mary said. "I never had more than three or four words to say to him." She was friends with Patrick Henderson, D. J. Rogers, the guys in the Gap Band, and Tulsa-bred singer Maxayn Lewis. They were like family. Lewis had grown up with the Wilson brothers in the Greenwood neighborhood of Tulsa. When her brother Emzie "Boonie" Parker III was just thirteen or fourteen, he started the band that became the Gap Band with Robert Wilson, before older brothers Charlie and Ronnie Wilson joined up. "D. J. was incredible," Lewis said. "He could do gospel; he could do R&B, pop. He could do everything. Then he met my mom and dad, as my mother was friends with Leon Russell [Lewis's parents were caterers who sometimes worked at Leon's studios]. The next thing I knew, he [Rogers] was acting like they were *his* mom and dad." She laughed about that.

D. J. produced Mary's first record on Shelter. McCreary recorded *Jezebel* at six different studios, including the Church, with another roster of hotshot musicians, including Jim Gordon and Carol Kaye, and Wayne Perkins. "I was with Leon," Perkins said. "We went out to hear her, and I said, 'Son of a bitch!' She was so beautiful, her voice . . ." Leon is listed as a coproducer along with Denny, but had not been hanging around the studio much, and a lot of the album was done in LA. "We were doing vocals on 'Levon,'" studio engineer Tom Russell said, referring to the cover of the Elton John song. "She was singing, and Leon just happened by and watched her for a little while. He asked who it was and he went to talk with her. They went out the front door, and the rest is history."

Well, not so fast; Mary was still married to Gentry McCreary, but there had been some rockiness. He was abusive and controlling. Mary told *Rolling Stone* in 1976, "It was a jail, a prison. He was always telling me what I should do and who I was supposed to be."

Leon was respectful of Mary's marriage. "They did not get together until she came back to town when she was leaving Gentry. In '74, she was going to Texas, and she told her mom that she was coming [home]," Blue said. But Mary had gotten the call to see whether she could sing on some tracks. Blue believes it was a session for the Gap Band while they were recording at Leon's basement studio. "She was trying to earn some money because she was leaving her husband," Blue continued. "She goes to the house to record, to earn some money. And that night, Dad said, 'You can just stay here. You don't need to go and stay at [a] hotel.' She never leaves."

Mary moved into the Tulsa house in January 1975. Friends and associates said the relationship had developed earlier, more gradually and discreetly. "[Mary] did show up at the lake to record. I seem to recall that Leon and she were already becoming involved," said Maureen Gosling.

In 1979, Mary would release a solo album called *Heart of Fire*, which contained a song she wrote called "Music Man." Ann Bell explained, "She had written it about Leon, about the beginning in the relationship when they had to keep it kind of secret because she had to divorce her husband, Gentry. They were separated but they weren't legally divorced, so they had to keep the relationship on the quiet."

Things between Leon and Carla Brown were tempestuous, though there would be moments of detente. Mary went to Carla's house, where Blue was sleeping, to bring Blue to visit Leon. "My mom really respected the way that Mary showed up and was so respectful," Blue said. Mary asked Carla, "'Can I take her?' And Mom said, 'Yeah, go ahead.' So that may have been the beginning of when [Carla and Leon] had kind of gotten okay. Mary said I had not seen him, and Daddy would tell the story of me singing, 'I'm going to see my daddy! I'm going to see my daddy!'" But when Blue was brought to see him and turned in his direction, the sight of Leon freaked her out and she ran away screaming: "He scared me, I guess all the hair."

George Harrison had gone on tour in late 1974 with saxophonist Jim Horn in tow. The tour stopped in Tulsa on November 21, and Leon joined Harrison onstage. "He said, 'When you're through with the concert, come on over, I got a song I want to put you on.' So I put the alto on 'Lady Blue'," said Horn. "He wrote that for [Mary]."

If he was looking for a hit, Leon found one with "Lady Blue," backed by Al Jackson Jr. and Steve Cropper of the MG's. (Fellow Stax session man guitarist Bobby Manuel joins them as well.) Jackson lays down the sort of beat he made famous on the classic Al Green and Ann Peebles sides. And like those steamy ballads, "Lady Blue" is a silk-sheet-sexy romantic song in the smooth mid-seventies Philly Soul style of Gamble and Huff (though without heavy orchestration), rather than the unadorned Memphis strain of R&B. The soft rock sheen of Leon's production took it to number fourteen; it spent nineteen weeks on the Hot 100.

It's curious that the effervescent "Laying Right Here in Heaven" wasn't released as a single. It starts with a light reggae lilt before striding into a Stevie Wonder–like groove, with a nod to Huey "Piano" Smith's "Rockin' Pneumonia and the Boogie Woogie Flu." It's the first (and arguably best) recorded duet from Mary and Leon, something they would do a whole lot more of over the next couple of years.

The personnel on "Laying Right Here in Heaven" helps explain why it sounds so electrifying: Carl Radle, Don Preston, Patrick Henderson on organ, Ambrose Campbell on percussion, and Jim Keltner and Karl Himmel on drums. But even the most intrepid crate-digging record geek would have had trouble in 1974 identifying the "Teddy Jack Eddy" listed on the back cover of *Will O' the Wisp*.

Gary Busey had first gone out to Hollywood in 1966 as a drummer in the Rubber Band, a frat house group from Oklahoma State. But Busey was an increasingly successful actor, not musician. He traveled back and forth between Tulsa and LA and wherever else his roles in movies and television took him.

While back in Tulsa, Busey was a recurring character, "a belligerent know-it-all," on a local television show called *The Uncanny Film Festival and Camp Meeting*, which ran in the early seventies. It was a low-budget, absurdist improvisational sketch show that framed screenings of old horror/monster movies like *Dracula*, *The Skull*, and Busby Berkeley musicals. Gailard Sartain, the show's creator, played the host, Dr. Mazeppa Pompazoidi, and area teenagers referred to the show as *Mazeppa*. Busey joined during its second year, bringing the chaotic, borderline threatening energy that would later almost consume him. He was recognized on the streets, and people would shout out his character's name, "Hey, Teddy Jack Eddy!"

One night, some friends of Leon's spotted Busey in a Tulsa bar. "Teddy Jack!" they shouted. Busey responded, "YOU GOT HIM! What do you need, baby?" They invited him to meet Leon. Busey thought it was a practical joke when he drove to a church. But inside, he was mesmerized by the atmosphere, the exotic lighting, and most of all, the wealth of musical instruments all set up. A drum set seemed to be begging him to play it, so he sat down and played a quiet beat. Leon slipped in and joined him on piano. "It was by far the most magical musical experience of my life," Busey wrote in his memoir. "'Teddy Jack, it's good to meet you,' Leon said. I laughed. . . . To Leon, I *was* Teddy Jack. He continued to call me Teddy Jack as long as I knew him. Later, he would even name his firstborn son Teddy Jack after my character on the *Mazeppa* show and name me Teddy Jack's godfather." Leon himself would even make a cameo on the program and became friends with Sartain, who was also an artist and created the cover for *Will O' the Wisp*.

Busey declined to be interviewed for this book, but when reached via phone, he briefly said that Leon was his "soulmate," a connection that was immediate, deep, and lasting. When Busey came back to Tulsa in 1974 after a couple of months of working in California, he demonstrated what he considered to be an innovative beat for Leon, something Busey called the "ham bone." "It was a powerhouse rhythm with so many different beats happening all at the same time," Busey wrote.

Leon was inspired enough that he suggested the two do some record-ing. While Busey played some beats, Leon built tracks, starting with the piano. Busey was inspired watching Leon's workflow, which seemed ef-fortless, as if the music was always there to be divined out of some organic wellspring. From that point on, Mary would call him over for playdates with Leon, and Busey would come in to play drums in the basement stu-dio. It wasn't long before Leon asked him, "How much do you make in a week?" After Busey responded with "three thousand," Leon offered five hundred, plus room and board, to be his in-house drummer. Busey agreed and brought along his young family and he started working with Leon on the songs for the new album.

Leon even had Busey play on a Nitty Gritty Dirt Band session in be-tween takes for *Will O' the Wisp*. John McEuen recalled, "The Dirt Band was playing in Tulsa, and I called him up, and I said, 'You probably don't want to come to the show, but can I come by and see ya?' He said, 'Well, why don't you bring somebody, and we'll record something?' So we did. We recorded 'Joshua Come Home,' and Teddy Jack Eddy played drums. I thought he was pretty damn good. He knew his sticks well."

Will O' the Wisp opens with the title track, a minute-long piano-and-synth instrumental overture that would be at home on a Stevie Wonder record. Busey joins in with a solid and sparse groove, an unfussy founda-tion upon which Leon constructs the minor-key "Little Hideaway." In about four minutes, he builds the song up from an earthy blues. The track spreads its wings with slashing synth arpeggios that pan across the ste-reo spread before a stop and a reintroduction reminiscent of Elton John's "Funeral for a Friend," a synth mini-symphony from *Goodbye Yellow Brick Road*. Leon plays the rest of the instruments himself.

Busey said he watched Leon write the lyrics. When Leon asked him what images and feelings the music evoked, Busey described a man and woman on camels coming upon a desert oasis scene that becomes "their little hideaway." Leon took that for the title of a song about a couple in the early stages of romance, sequestering themselves away from everyone to get to know each other better. The budding relationship with Mary served as a new source of inspiration for Leon. He layers her multitracked vocals here in an inventive choral arrangement, taking full advantage of his forty-track.

It became immediately clear from these first two tracks on *Will O' the Wisp* that Leon was reinvigorated creatively and embracing new textures to color his recordings. Given his lifelong quest for innovation, Leon was a natural early adopter of synthesizers and was aided in harnessing the technology by a young guitarist named Roger Linn. Linn had come into Mary's band through Denny Cordell.

When Linn started with Mary, they were mostly playing nightclubs. "Then we got on the bill with Leon, and he was doing one of these big concerts," Linn said. "They'd have these very large concerts where they have ten bands in the bill, and people would sit on the lawn of a football stadium and watch these shows all day long. The headliner was either Leon, or Leon and somebody else because he was big, particularly in the South. He would squeeze in Mary for twenty-minute sets before Leon went on."

Linn and Leon shared an interest in tech. "I was a real nerd; I knew about synthesizers, and I knew about the fundamentals of recording. He saw how well I worked with synthesizers, and he allowed me, at night when the studio wasn't being used, to work on my own things. He hired me to be a recording engineer for him and help him with some of this new technology that was coming out." Linn laughed describing the basement studio. "He had found this blue fur . . . all over the walls of the studio, in the ceiling. Yeah, it looked like it was decorated by a person with not the best of taste."

In high school Linn had taught himself how to play a Mini Moog synthesizer. "There was one party one night and Leon had a Mini Moog synthesizer. I'm sitting right in front of Leon, and I was just showing off and making it do a flute sound, and drum sounds, and a bass sound. And he thought, 'This is great. He can be the recording engineer, and he can make synthesis sounds.'"

Linn is credited as a recording engineer on *Will O' the Wisp*, "although I would say that I was kind of the second engineer to him because he knew

of the recording process too." Though Leon was eager to learn about synthesizers, Linn said he employed them judiciously. "He was very much into
synthesis and tried to find out what was good for the music, as opposed to
just being a solution looking for a problem." Linn recalled accompanying
Leon on shopping trips where Leon dropped $20,000 (about $119,000 in
2022) on one of the first polyphonic synths, made by E-Mu.

With Leon's inspiration, in a few years Linn would invent the first
programmable drum machine to use samples of actual drum sounds,
the groundbreaking Linn LM-1. Leon was already using primitive, non-
programmable drum machines as click tracks to build songs on top of.
"On *Will O' the Wisp* he used the drum machine solely as a click track,
and I don't think he mixed it in at all," Linn explained. "He would always
have the best drummers around."

Not always, of course. Sometimes Leon would want to create at the
moment inspiration struck. Describing something that sounds like the bipolar patterns others witnessed in Leon, Gary Busey said Leon could stay
"in bed for four weeks" at a stretch, but then find himself in the midst of a
creative flow that he would not want to interrupt. A convincing drum machine was the missing link between what Leon was aiming for and could
later achieve, capturing musical ideas as they came, arranging them on
tape with as little filtration as possible. "He was prescient," Linn observed.
"He was on the leading edge of an idea that people ended up embracing,
which is to overdub an entire record."

Until then, Leon had a resident drummer on call: Busey. "Little Hideaway" ends abruptly, and there is the bracing sound of an urgent knock
on a door, which functions like a Zen slap, introducing "Make You Feel
Good," the album's only superfluous track. Busey is also present on this
one, though his part is much more cluttered and sloppy. "Gary is one of
the most godawful drummers," said Bill Maxwell, a close friend of Leon
and a great drummer himself. "I don't know why in the world Leon would
ever want to play with him, but they did. Gary's terrible! I think it was
because of Tulsa, and he was in the movies. But Gary's the kind of guy you
see, and you try to get as far away from him as you can."

The haunting "Can't Get Over Losing You" begins with the reverber-
ant sounds of exotic Japanese instrumentation—a biwa from Masako
Hirayama, and a wooden flute from Minoru Muraoka—before it slips
into a blues in the same swampy netherworld as "Out in the Woods."

J. J. Cale lends a brilliant slide guitar part and answers the vocals while Leon handles the rest of the instruments. He multitracks Mary again in a spellbinding backing vocal arrangement. In another moment of studio reflexivity, Leon leaves in her request to hear a previously recorded vocal she is harmonizing to: "Can I hear the other part, too?"

Leon bares his psyche on the 6/8-time ballad "My Father's Shoes," with Steve Cropper and Al Jackson. The MG's appear on four of the eleven tracks on the album. Their bandmate Duck Dunn joins them on the other three.

Cropper recalled working at Leon's home studio. "We were there for about a week, and we played on a lot of things. Leon would get an idea in the middle of the night, and he'd want to wake everybody up and go cut."

Shelter manager Ron Henry was staying at Leon's house at the time of the session. "Leon was not a guy you'd sit down and just talk with. He was like many people who are creatively brilliant, but socially weak." As an artist, though, Leon could articulate complicated emotions concisely and poetically. In "My Father's Shoes," Leon sings about a son he does not yet (but soon would) have. It's poetic license, likely a stand-in for Blue, so that he could write about the continuum of three generations of fathers and sons. The bridge leads us, appropriately, to his father for the final of three verses, and it's a heartbreaker: "I'd like to say I love him, but the time has passed away." It's the emotional heart of a record that's primarily about budding romance. "He didn't see his dad as often because he was living with his mom," said Leon's widow, Jan Bridges. "They still had a relationship, long distance." One of the few friends who met Leon's father said he was cold and distant, with the demeanor of a "drill sergeant."

The blues-funk of "Stay Away from Sad Songs" spotlights the effective application of the new tech. Synths flutter, stereo Clavinets (electric harpsichord) crackle, and tack-piano pops. Leon also swoops in on a dobro to announce the chorus sections. After nodding lyrically to his immediate past about "a new girl every day," Leon sings about settling down with a Mary, who has caused him to change his ways, a development he gladly embraces.

"Back to the Island" is layered with extra cheese: the sounds of waves crashing and tropical bird calls threaten to take over the mix during the chorus. It's a little too on the nose. But it rides a soulful "Into the Mystic" sway thanks to the Stax/MG's rhythm section that keeps it from listing too far into easy listening. It's easy to understand why Jimmy Buffett would cover it in 2004. The lyric makes it one of the few romantic downers on the album that mostly celebrates new love.

"Bluebird" is a legitimate classic, a Top 40 hit in 1975 for Helen Reddy, who had also recorded his "I Don't Remember My Childhood." Leon seemingly tosses off this wide-ranging melody over distinctive changes. He makes it sound so easy, as if he could just pull out a standard at will. It begins with a moody up-and-down bossa nova piano figure that falls somewhere between Vince Guaraldi and Nick Drake's "One of These Things First," from *Bryter Later*. "He might have written 'Bluebird' for Carla," Patrick Henderson said. The lyrics support Henderson's theory, particularly the bridge about being locked away in his room "with my sorrow / No escape, no way to get away."

Trust had withered between Leon and Denny. "Denny was not involved at all with the production of *Will O' the Wisp*," said Linn. "Leon told me that the coproducer credit was an arrangement he and Denny had for all his albums." *Will O' the Wisp* would be the last Leon Russell album on Shelter. Later in life, Leon explained that Denny was always "the one behind Shelter." Leon didn't even listen to music for enjoyment: "My hobby is silence." According to his family, it was not a joke.

But Denny, a born A&R man with a golden ear, was still signing new artists: Tulsa natives the Dwight Twilley Band went to LA to try to get signed. "Leon was the curse to us," Twilley said. "When we were starting to get going in Tulsa, all everybody wanted to do was get in with Leon, and some of the real old farts around town, they were in with Leon, and they were cutting at his studio, which everybody called the Church Studio. That's all everybody was concerned with. On a typical Friday night, you just went down the street from club to club, everybody was sounding like Leon."

That gray-bearded Southern hippie image was outdated as far as these young progressive Anglophiles were concerned. Beatles fanatics Twilley and his musical partner Phil Seymour had struck upon a distinctive modern power-pop sound that linked to late-seventies new wave. They wrote economical, melodic pop songs with stripped-down instrumentation, heavy on harmonies and fluid rockabilly-inspired guitar riffs. The resulting roughed-up Beatles-influenced sound became their own. They were not interested in being identified with the "Tulsa sound." But somehow their demo ended up at Shelter. "As fate would have it, we drove all the way out to Los Angeles to get away from Shelter Records and ended up getting signed by Shelter Records," Twilley said.

Once signed, they were encouraged to work on demos at the Church with Williams. The idea was to get comfortable in a studio setting. "It was like a little sanctuary," Twilley said. "They wanted to see what you could do. Then you started working at Shelter in Hollywood."

"Dwight Twilley was originally signed as a writer," Don Williams said. "The record deal followed, after he went down to Tulsa and cut a record that everybody said, 'That's a hit!'"

Twilley had written "I'm on Fire" "right before we left to come back from LA," he said. "And when we went back to Tulsa, we had the song and, 'Here we are, and here's the studio.' A lot of the old codgers were there. They didn't like it very much when we showed up. It was their territory." The band cut "I'm on Fire," a Top 20 hit, in 1975.

Back in Tulsa, Twilley said the locals had made the logical but incorrect assumption that they knew Leon. "We had a hit record with 'I'm on Fire' long before we ever met Leon. So it was a strange turn of events." Twilley had seen Leon around town before. "He kind of scared me. You didn't know to say hello to him or if he'd attack you suddenly."

Leon slipped into the room during one of their sessions. "He was actually invisible in the back of the room, but once you notice that guy in your session, you realize, 'That's Leon Russell.' And that was, to me, when he looked most intimidating.

"But it turned out that he was just so kind and so generous. He just wanted to listen to what-all we were doing. And he invited us to his house. That was an interesting experience." The band could not believe how great his personal studio was. "We had just been promoted to sixteen-track recording [at the Church]. So, we go to Leon's house now, and here we got forty tracks, which *nobody* had. He had the Stephens machine, which was like the starship *Enterprise*, as was the whole studio. . . . Our eyes were like saucers, walking into this place and thinking about forty tracks." Leon even asked the band to show him their own studio. "Our little hole-in-the-wall studio, which we called the Shop."

With a hit single but no album, the band quickly got to work at the Church and Leon's home studio. They recorded a masterpiece, the album *Sincerely*. "I remember making a few records with him," Twilley said about

Leon, who plays bass and piano on a couple tracks. One of them, "Feeling in the Dark," could very well fit on a Leon record. It has a bit of that Freddie King "Going Down" intensity. Roger Linn engineered some of the record and added some backward guitars on the title track. Leon produced and played on an outtake, "Shark (In the Dark)."

"It was really cool," Twilley said. "There were a couple of tracks that were just me and Phil and Leon. That's the way 'Shark' was recorded; a big amount of energy in the room. When Phil would play drums, and I would do anything, and Leon would play piano, it just felt full. He could make such a big noise with just his fingers and that piano; it felt like you'd have a whole band playing." "Shark" was intended as a single but shelved after ill-placed concerns that it would seem like the band was a novelty act trying to cash in after the success of *Jaws*.

Tom Petty and his band, who were now friends with Twilley and Seymour, had been sent back to Tulsa as well. "They probably learned a lot of their beginning studio chops from having the run of [the Church]," Tom Russell said. Mudcrutch broke up after their initial single, but Shelter retained Petty as a songwriter and potential solo artist, and he recorded demos backed by such aces as Jim Gordon, Al Kooper, and Duck Dunn. He missed the camaraderie and chemistry of a band, though, and out of the ashes of Mudcrutch (Mike Campbell and Benmont Tench were members) was born the Heartbreakers, a name which Petty said Denny came up with (as did former New York Doll Johnny Thunders around the same time).

The Denny–Leon partnership was still technically together when Leon and Mary moved back to LA in March of 1975, getting a house at 4504 Woodley Avenue in Encino. They kept the Tulsa house for the time being. The new home was "just off of Ventura Boulevard," wrote Leon. "Originally built by Bud Abbott of the famed comedy team Abbott & Costello, it was a rambling ranch affair. . . . I soundproofed the living room and two bedrooms, using one bedroom for drums and the other for a control room. Most of the two duet albums I did with Mary were recorded there."

The Encino house had a pool and a cabana. Leon commandeered much of the main house as a recording studio. Mary Jones had been given the mission of bringing Blue out from Tulsa. "[Mary McCreary] gave him a wonderful birthday at the Encino house in April 1975. Everybody came: Cheech and Chong were there. I think Barry White was there. Her friend,

Donna Summer, was there. Gary Busey and Gailard Sartain were running around. . . . I made sweet tea for George [Harrison] and his wife. Leon always had big jugs of sweet tea in the fridge and glass mugs chilling in the freezer, frosted, at all times. The amount of sugar added was staggering."

Ann Bell said, "I'm out in California with him and Mary at one of the birthday parties, the doorbell rings, and Mary goes, 'Ann, go get it.' I open it, and there's Ringo and George."

Harrison had Leon working on *Extra Texture* at A&M (Leon also appeared on "Try Some Buy Some" on George's *Living in the Material World*). There are some unreleased raw recordings of "World of Stone" and other tracks as the two worked on arrangements at Leon's studio. "I was playing on one of George Harrison's records one day, and we were on take 168," Leon said. "I went up to him, and I said, 'George, do you want me to play the same thing 168 times, or do you want me to play 168 different things?' Because it was driving me crazy. I didn't like to do that."

Will O' the Wisp was released in May. The 1975 tour headed out in two buses, one for the band and crew and the other for the lovebirds. As he did on previous tours, Leon lugged around his Steinway grand, which needed careful attention and daily tuning. Subsequent concerts saw him embracing newer technology like the Yamaha CP-70 electric baby grand, which still needed tuning but was far more compact and allowed him to easily compete with other band members for stage volume.

Leon and Mary had some new musicians along, including Maxayn Lewis. As Leon was a friend of her parents, and her brother was in the Gap Band, Maxayn was like family to him, and she was close with Mary. A pro who had been an Ikette, sung with Bobby "Blue" Bland and Buddy Miles, and fronted her own hard-funk band, Maxayn was already living in LA, so she rehearsed with Leon and Mary to go out on the *Will O' the Wisp* tour.

Leon hired Gary Busey to drum on that tour. Busey was swept up in the tribal vibes of being in a touring band: jamming on the bus, hamming it up onstage, running naked through a carwash (his only "shower" of the tour). It marked the beginning of his abuse of heavy drugs like cocaine and PCP.

Mary and Leon were married at Willie and Connie Nelson's house in Texas on June 20, 1975. Connie recalled, "That might have been the time that we met Mary, when he and Mary got married at our house in Austin." The good vibes even extended to the woman who broke Leon's heart,

Rita Coolidge. "When they married, at Connie and Willie's is when Leon started to soften with me," Coolidge said. "Connie and I were best friends, and she wouldn't put up with him saying shit about me around her. After that, whenever I would see him, he would be civil."

Old flame Chris O'Dell laughed when recalling, "Don't forget, when I met him, he wrote, 'If I believed in marriage,' in 'Pisces Apple Lady.' Later, when I saw him, and he was married, obviously I thought, 'Wow, okay, *that* changed.'" Leon wrote, "I had often said I would marry a woman who was a better artist than I was but wouldn't beat me over the head with that fact."

"It was a wonderful time," Maxayn said. "It was a beautiful thing. And they loved each other. He *loved* her. She was pretty, she was talented, and they were fun, her whole family. I was at that house—and then their next house in Toluca Lake—every day."

The racism of a significant portion of Leon's fanbase, though, reared its vile head on the tours with Mary that started in 1975. They went to "places where Leon had a huge following as Leon," Lewis said. "Then when he married Mary—I remember distinctly in Houston, Texas, the place was sold out, like seventy thousand people—and they threw little tiny nooses onstage."

The bigotry backlash lasted through the years that Mary and Leon performed together. Michael Johnstone went to work for Leon as an engineer around 1977. "He told me, 'My career is stuck in the mud here, you know. Maybe I should hear from my fans and see what I'm doing wrong.' So he made this questionnaire: 'What would you like my next record to sound like? Fill in the box with your comments.' There was a lot of, 'Get rid of the n****r.'"

Johnette Napolitano started working with Leon around the same time—she later founded the rock band Concrete Blonde. Her first job with Leon was going through the questionnaires. "One of the first times I had seen some serious unbelievable racism is when Leon married Mary," she said. "And it was so devastating to him."

Maxayn said it was not just a matter of hiding behind anonymous cards. "Throwing the little tiny nooses onstage . . . I mean, tons of them. People would yell from the audience, 'Get rid of the n****rs!' *Really loud.*" None of this was surprising for Lewis, Mary, or Mary's sister, Frances (Pye), who also sang on the tour. "That's what we were telling you," they would say. "What do you think is gonna happen with this? Now you know what we go through. Everybody was just incredulous: 'What the *fuck*?!'"

"My dad didn't talk about it," Tina Rose Bridges said. "My mom was talking about it; she went through a lot of shit in Oklahoma. She told me that they were doing a show in Tulsa and someone did throw a noose up on the stage while she was playing. My dad didn't tell her until after the show was over and she said she was real pissed about it because he probably knew she would have gone up and [said], 'Let's not finish the show.'"

Leon dealt with these racists in his own indirect way. "He just let the music speak for itself," Lewis said. "Sometimes he would do this whole gospel thing, and he would say things that would have a religious connotation to it, about hate. That was his way. But just actually going toe to toe, head to head, arguing about race, no, he didn't do that."

Most of these people were cowards who lobbed their vitriol from a safe distance. But Blue Bridges-Fox remembered Mary telling her about a more immediately threatening incident. "They were backstage at a Willie show, and this man said something like, 'I'm gonna walk over there and punch her right in the fucking face,' this drunk redneck guy. He didn't say it quietly; he said it so she could hear it. And it was actually Willie that stood up, 'Of course, you'll have to fuckin' go through me first.' And the dude said, 'Oh, sorry, Willie.'"

Another legendary musician whom Leon admired was not as supportive. Napolitano and Steve Ripley went to see Jerry Lee Lewis at the Palomino. Ripley was just starting to work with Leon around the same time and would invent a mass-produced stereo guitar championed by Eddie Van Halen before going on to form the Tractors, and he became the owner of the Church for a while.

"Jerry Lee is sitting on the couch and he has two bottles of Jack in front of him, one empty and one half empty," Napolitano said. "He goes, 'You work for Leon? Well, he was all right until he married the n****r.' He gets up off the couch and he goes to walk out the door, and he reaches over and grabs my ass, and then walks out onstage. I'm just standing there in a cloud of 'What the fuck?' I saw Leon the next day and I go, 'Hey, I saw Jerry Lee last night and, look man, he said you were OK until you married the n****r.' And Leon stroked his beard and said, 'Jerry Lee said that?' And he just walked away. I never heard Leon ever say a bad word about anyone. That's why he trusted me. I wanted him to know shit."

Leon would never forget it. Tom Britt, who played with Leon in the eighties, recalled, "Leon told me, he went in to say hey to Jerry Lee and Jerry Lee goes, 'Hey Leon, I heard you married a n****r.'"

The racism on the road affected Mary. "It made her depressed," Lewis said. But back home in LA, things were good. And being back in LA was easier for an interracial couple than Tulsa. "The way she looked at it was, Leon was a very brave guy who wanted to do what he wanted to do, and he was totally unaffected by what people thought. He never gave in to it. He forged ahead because he thought the music was worth it. And he was right."

Chapter 25

Don't Fly Away

BY THE MID-SEVENTIES, ROCK 'N' roll had only been around for about twenty years. First- and second-generation rockers were trying to navigate how to age gracefully in the medium while remaining relevant. Not everyone could reinvent themselves as successfully as David Bowie. Punk rock was just rounding the corner, all riled up to kick the ass of Laurel Canyon navel gazers and indulgent prog rockers alike. But there were more immediate threats ready to take Leon's market share. The Eagles were huge already, and kids in stadiums were going apeshit for soft rock bands like Pablo Cruise and Ambrosia.

But hard rock groups like AC/DC were scratching the itch of a new generation of juvenile delinquents not overly interested in tasty piano licks or lovey-dovey duets. J. Geils Band was filling theaters and ballrooms for those who loved their good-time rock 'n' roll with a chaser of R&B. A new generation of Southern rock bands like Charlie Daniels Band, Marshall Tucker, and Lynyrd Skynyrd—all of whom were indebted to Leon, even opening for him—were filling the vacuum as Leon waded into the tepid waters of adult contemporary. Elton John would soon lighten up his own sound with AM-radio-friendly takes on the Spinners and Philly Soul, such as "Don't Go Breaking My Heart."

Then there were the heartland rockers with fresh, rootsy, urgent songs. Bruce Springsteen released his first album in 1973, influenced in part by Leon, as well as Dylan, Van Morrison, and the classic sixties groups. Bob Seger was piling up album-oriented rock (AOR) hits, and Tom Petty would soon release his debut album on Shelter. Petty told *Rolling Stone* in 1978 that the goal of the Heartbreakers was to create "the kind of rock that used to come blasting out of the AM radio when every song was a new Creedence or a new Stones, and all you wanted to do was crank it up."

Denny Cordell was smart enough to poach Petty. Cordell had even signed 100 percent of Petty's publishing for a $10,000 advance, which would later come back to haunt both men and strain their relationship. But in 1975, Petty felt like he was living the high life. While Leon was out on the road with Mary, Denny had ensconced Mudcrutch at the couple's Encino residence. Petty was dazzled to indulge in the recording equipment: "I went from this two-room place into this big mansion. . . . Not a bad gig, really."

"[Leon] had a Steinway in one of the bedrooms and just started adding to it," said Mary Jones. "Poor Mary. He took over the master suite and started running cables and wires." Petty, his wife, Jane, and their daughter took Leon and Mary's bedroom suite in the main house, while the rest of the band stayed in the pool house. "The band was wild, making a mess of everything—putting wet glasses down on wooden furniture that Mary had just bought, marking it all up," Jones said. "I told Leon, 'I can't control these guys. I can't be responsible for that.'"

Mudcrutch broke up while recording at Leon's house. Denny had been frustrated with the slow pace of the band's development and recognized Petty as the star. Moving one guy to the center spotlight was an old trick. Cordell had also persuaded the Dwight Twilley–Phil Seymour partnership to change their name from Oister to Dwight Twilley Band. Anyone in the music biz will tell you it is easier to market a solo act over a band.

Petty had to vacate the house before Leon and Mary returned, but Leon had heard "Lost in Your Eyes" circulating at Shelter. It was a song Petty had put aside as an also-ran.

When Leon returned home, Petty was staying at the Hollywood Premier, a cheap motel. He'd sent his wife and child home to Florida. "I'd gone from a rock star's mansion to a motel room, which, for some reason, didn't bother me," Petty said. In some ways, he preferred staying at the motel, as it was across the street from the recently expanded Shelter Records. The top floor of the two-level building was now a recording studio run by a couple of acid-head engineers, Noah Shark and Max Reese. "These guys took LSD every day, literally,'" said Richard Feldman. "And for like two and a half years, they'd been throwing empty bottles out there [the parking lot]. It was like ten feet of broken glass. That was my workshop."

"We were in the middle of the worst part of Hollywood at the time, and people were just sort of running in and out," said Kate Hyman, who started an enduring music-biz career at Shelter. "People were banging into walls because they were on Quaaludes." As if this scene wasn't *Boogie Nights* enough, it had its own Roller Girl. "Janet—she used to wear roller skates, and she worked for Don," said Hyman. "She roller-skated all over the office."

"We went to Shelter every day, just hung out," Petty told his biographer Warren Zanes. "We knew everybody. We hung out with them on weekends, fucked all the secretaries. It was that kind of thing, where everybody was friends and pulling for everybody else."

While in his room at the motel one evening, Petty's phone rang. It was Leon. "He didn't even know I was the guy living in his house," Petty said. "But he's like, 'I've been listening to those tapes of Mudcrutch, the stuff you did in Tulsa. There's some great songs there. I was wondering if you'd be interested in writing some songs with me.' I was like, 'Sure! I don't have much going on.' . . . Next thing I know, a white Rolls-Royce pulls up. People must have assumed it was a pimp."

They went back to Leon's place and he played Petty some new songs. "This was 1975. Leon's still a big star," Petty said. "I'm just trying to give my opinion. Why he wants it, I have no idea. But suddenly Leon had stepped into Denny territory. When I let Denny know, Denny just went, 'No shit? Great, great.'"

Don Williams said, "I never saw Leon get involved in any of the artists' careers, at the label [before this]."

Leon encouraged Petty to upgrade to a Travelodge close to the Encino house, put him on retainer, informed him he would like him to come by every day, and warned him that he kept weird hours. Petty said, "Nothing would happen until midnight. I'd be there just hanging out with this cast of characters coming through the house." It was a more upscale version of the old Skyhill scene. Leon had installed a pay phone, as he had in the basement studio in Tulsa, so everyone would stop using his personal phone line. But otherwise, Leon wanted everyone around all the time.

He explained to Petty a concept for a record with a different producer on each track: "What do you think of Brian Wilson?" The protégé answered that it sounded like a pretty good idea. "I simply don't know what to make of this," Petty explained. "Leon looks at me and says, 'Then let's go see him.' And with that, we pile into the Rolls-Royce and head for Brian's Bel Air house."

Leon brought Petty to a session with George Harrison, Ringo Starr, and Jim Keltner at Sound City Studios. Shelter general manager Ron Henry was also present. "I saw [Leon] rearrange a George Harrison song in less than ten minutes, and his session players were David Foster, Jim Keltner, and Ringo Starr. George Harrison brought in a cassette demo." Foster, a friend and neighbor of Leon, became a successful producer, winning sixteen Grammys. Ron Henry continued, "They didn't say it literally, but they addressed Leon [as] 'Mr. Russell.' That was the internal respect they had." Over the summer, Leon popped into different studios like Gold Star and Sound City with such A-list producers, arrangers, and musicians as Jesse Ed Davis, Steve Douglas, James Gadson, Ray Parker Jr., H. B. Barnum, Bobby Womack, Joe Sample, Keltner, Starr, and Harrison.

Petty remembered Leon's old colleague Terry Melcher—another producer Leon was considering for the project, and who played piano on an unreleased track called "The Wedding Song"—showing up at Leon's house with Sly Stone. "I answered the door," Petty said, "and he's there and he says to me, 'I came here with Sly, and he just got into the driver's seat and drove my car out of here.'" Within days, Petty had met Leon, half of the Beatles, the producer of the Byrds, and Brian Wilson, and *almost* met Sly Stone. Petty said, "I don't think Leon really knew what he wanted to do next, but he was great to me. I learned a lot from him. I saw a lot of things that maybe you shouldn't do, and some things you should. Cautionary tales were in every other room I passed through."

Petty said Leon taught him that, although he might have been "put there for a reason," he still had a ways to go. "So, the first session, in comes George Harrison and Ringo and Jim Keltner, and they didn't need any words. But those cats were so cool, you know? And I found myself . . . slipping my sunglasses on. Leon said, 'What the hell are you doing with the dark glasses, man?' I said, 'I don't know? It feels cool, you know, like Jimmy Keltner.' He goes, 'Wearing sunglasses at night is an honor you earn. Lou Adler had Johnny Rivers and the Mamas and Papas before he put them glasses on. Jack Nicholson made really shitty Boris Karloff movies before he put them glasses on.'"

The torch was being passed. Leon regarded Petty primarily as a songwriter signed to the Shelter publishing division. "He had heard a song of mine and wanted me to just be on call to write with him whenever he wanted to write," Petty told journalist Paul Zollo. "He was living this kind of life where he recorded a lot every day at his own studio. And I'm really grateful to him because he did give me a shot at seeing a lot. . . . I don't think I ever wrote much there. I don't think we sat down very often to work. We did sometimes. But it never really came out. It never really came to fruition."

Petty told *Musician* magazine's Bill Flanagan, "The way it worked was, I would write a song called 'Satisfy Yourself.' Leon would rewrite it as 'I Wanna Satisfy You' and I'd get no credit. . . . But I could never feel bad about Leon—it was a great learning experience." In later years, when a friend said, "Petty was pissed at Leon because he thought he ripped off a song of his," Leon had acknowledged, "Well, I kind of did."

Will O' the Wisp, which would be Leon's last exceptionally great studio record, marked the end of an era, capping his relationship with Shelter Records and Denny. "Leon came to life and woke up when he was around Denny Cordell. Everyone did," said Mary Jones. "Leon was his most normal when Denny was present. He seemed the happiest then."

This, another gold record, momentarily righted the ship, commercially speaking. But Leon was about to make a bold choice that would be the breaking point for Denny. Instead of another Leon Russell record, the next project would be a duet album co-billed as "Leon and Mary Russell." Denny, who had sunk a good deal of money and effort building up name recognition for Mary McCreary, was now tasked with starting over with her and marketing a new husband-and-wife duo, while trying to maintain Leon's fans *and* satisfy Shelter's distributor, MCA Records (which had won out over Atlantic's Ahmet Ertegun despite his airplane banner).

"Leon was committed to deliver one more solo album with MCA," said Ron Henry; then he "would be paid a million dollars. He was complaining, saying, 'I don't want to do that. I want to do a duet album with Mary.' He didn't want to be told what he had to do, even though he signed the contract. But he wanted the money. Then he met with the attorney David Braun, who said, 'Listen, you *are* Shelter Records. You deserve more than 50 percent.' And then he sued Denny Cordell, which led to the demise of Leon Russell."

Braun represented Bob Dylan, Neil Diamond, and George Harrison. He was a new breed of entertainment attorney. "In the evolution of the business in the early seventies, when Geffen was getting going and all those labels were evolving—Elektra, Asylum, A&M—it was still a very unsophisticated business," Henry explained. "In 1975, I was one of only two people in so-called executive roles at labels that had an MBA. The only other one was Al Teller at CBS Columbia. Most people thought my MBA was the name of the band I played in in high school. That changed in the late seventies and early eighties, but at that time, the business hadn't changed very much. So attorneys in the early seventies became really the deal makers; they did it all. They took control. Those are the days where you'd sit down with the attorneys, and one of the attorneys would pull out a vial of cocaine and start snorting."

Henry continued: "Leon was frustrated because he didn't want to do the solo album. He asked George Harrison, who said, 'Well, talk to my attorney, David Braun.' So he sits down with Braun, and, you know, the idea was, 'Leon, you made Shelter Records; you should have it all.' So they sued Cordell, and then once the lawsuit happens, communication just shuts down."

In November 1975, a story by Stephen Ford went out on the news syndication service NEA: "Ramshackle Shelter: Using his legal name of Claude Russell Bridges, Leon Russell has asked a Los Angeles court to dissolve his recording company, Shelter Records. Tulsa's darlin' says Shelter is losing $25,000 a month and wants an end to the red menace despite other stockholders' insistence the label continue."

Owen Sloane, the attorney who had helped form Shelter and who was still the label's counsel, was now called to dissolve the partnership. He recalled the meeting: "We were at Denny's house, meeting to try to sort out the issues. David Braun had been skiing over the weekend and dislocated his shoulder, and his left arm was in a sling. It was heavy, tense, and everybody was posturing. And at one point, we're in the heat of all this, and David Braun leans back in his chair and hits a standing floor lamp. He moves back, and the shade on it came forward and came down over his head. There he is, in the heat of the negotiations, his arm in a sling, a lampshade on his head, which he can't get off because he only has one hand, at which point, Denny Cordell gets up and screams, 'Don't move!' because he was afraid he'd get electrocuted. Denny came over and removed the shade from his head. We had to take a break. We laughed for fifteen minutes outside of the room and thinking of what the trades would say: 'What well-known music lawyer was found wearing a shade?'"

"Leon was poisoned," Henry continued. "Braun was saying, 'You shouldn't allow them to control your life; you're the star, you own it all.' I mean, it was laughable." Cordell was a partner with Leon in more than the record company; he took a commission on almost all of Leon's revenue, and they shared publishing companies.

"Denny Cordell was a good business guy," Henry said. "He was very instrumental to a lot of artists out there and helped Leon really break his career. . . . But Leon just got it into his head. It was a pity what Leon was going through because he co-owned the publishing company. And therefore, *his* copyrights were owned by that publishing company he co-owned. So he lost 50 percent of his copyrights."

Don Williams said, "The only thing that I was involved in, which was a major, major part of the deal, was actually doing the business of constructing the two song lists. When they broke up, they had a pretty substantial music publishing catalog that was earning pretty substantial money. So, rather than selling the company to one or the other, we just made a list. The idea was to be able to divide the publishing as assets equally. Leon got the first pick, then Denny got the things left over, but that was probably one of the most substantial parts of the sale."

He explained further: "Let's say there are three hundred songs in a song catalog. There were songs written by Leon, there were songs written by all the artists signed to Shelter, there were songs written by Phoebe Snow. I knew the earnings of the songs and separated all that. So, [half of] those three hundred songs are earning $10,000 a year, and these other half earn about $10,000 a year. But you can only pick one list because the catalog is being split in two. That was such a major part of the assets."

The record company was losing money and the publishing companies were making money. "We made a half million dollars from 'This Masquerade' alone. But the guys got into debt over going into the film business," Williams explained. "That's where things got squirrelly because when they bought the video truck, and they shot the [Les Blank] film, a Tulsa bank loaned the guys a million bucks or something. But the publishing company was on the hook for paying off the note. There was a lot of money being made at the very beginning, and a lot of [it] was publishing money."

Williams had been given the direction to make the lists equitable. "But there was a particular trick that we tried to pull because even though the list was to be equitable, Denny wanted certain songs," Williams said. "I said, 'Let's pick Leon's favorite song and make sure he picks that list.' He put one key song on one list with the hope that Leon would grab that list, and not the list that he wanted, and Leon did." Williams could not recall which song it was. Cordell ended up with "A Song for You," so it is more likely that Leon chose based on something else, perhaps "This Masquerade" or "Lady Blue."

But it might not have been a specific song at all. Leon gained full control over *A Poem Is a Naked Person*. Also, hard assets and real estate were divided. But the Les Blank film was included in the division of intellectual property. "I think my dad bribed him with it once," Barney Cordell said. "I think he said something like, 'If you don't do this, I'm gonna get the Les Blank film released.' I think he used it in a negotiation. Leon hated [the film] *that* much." After the split, Leon hired business manager Len Freedman, of the Jess Morgan Company, who confirmed Leon's legal ownership of the film in a 1977 letter. Leon's need to control that film factored heavily into which column of copyrights he chose.

The songs published while Denny and Leon's relationship was intact were held under various publishing companies. Cordell walked away with Tarka Music (named after another of his sons). Skyhill Music, which had roughly half of Leon's songs, was split between the two parties. Leon's songs from this point would now go to the newly created Teddy Jack Music. Cordell-Russell Music, mostly songs from the Asylum Choir and early Leon songs like "Delta Lady," became exclusively Leon's.

To this day, Don Williams does not understand the reason for the split. "I was always brokenhearted . . . just, 'Why? What happened? What the fuck happened?' You know, one day—it was like, damn, Leon was gone. And there was never any talk about what actually went on."

"I think it was artistic differences and maybe some idea that he was more important than getting only 50 percent," said Sloane. Years later, David Geffen would infamously sue Neil Young, essentially for handing over records that did not sound sufficiently Neil Young enough to Geffen. Denny had a similar sort of beef with Leon.

"Sometimes someone is so creatively brilliant that you can't put them in a box, and they struggle in a commercialized music world," Henry observed. "My opinion is, he never recovered from that, and his career never went any further after that. And he had to tour to the day of his death to make enough money to live on."

It would take years for Leon to adjust to his fall from grace, albeit cushioned by the millions he was still taking in. Wornell Jones, a bassist who would soon start working with Leon and Mary, recalled, "At one time, he just told me, 'Hey, man, I'm worth $2 million a year, just off of my catalog.'" Adjusted for inflation, that would be over $10 million today. But Leon was a profligate spender, and some of his biggest outlays of cash were still to come. His career would never recover to anywhere near his peak years of 1970–1974.

"There were a couple of really bad records in there," Leon conceded in a 1976 interview with the *New York Times*, which also pointed out that "his music lost direction, and Mr. Russell withdrew from public view, breaking off contact with the press, cutting off his touring and retiring to Oklahoma." He told *Rolling Stone*, "I was trying to collect my thoughts" during what the writer Patrick Snyder called "the slightly askew years." "Neurosis is the key word in the whole deal. Predictability is not one of my strong points," Leon said.

Roger Linn said, "There's that old joke with musicians that applies just to anybody that has a short time of career and in the public eye. That was the four phases of the musician's career. Phase one: 'Who's Leon Russell?' Phase two: 'Get me Leon Russell!' Phase three: 'Get me the *new* Leon Russell!' Phase four: 'Who's Leon Russell?' This happens over maybe around a five-year period."

Leon had been in that flow where everything seemed right, effortless, and as if it would last indefinitely. No one can sustain that forever. But he did not putter out, nor did the world simply pass him by; he jerked the car into the ditch. Pursuing a singular artistic path, following his creative inspiration, whatever the source, staying weird for better or worse, is part of what makes Leon Russell compelling. But if an artist takes hairpin turns creatively, they have to prepare for the inevitable commercial consequences.

When Leon left, Shelter started to fall apart. "Leon Russell was Shelter Records," Henry said in an article a few years after the split. The company shuffled distributors from MCA to ABC before the latter was bought out by the former. Petty was sued by Shelter. He famously held off recording what became *Damn the Torpedoes*, threatening personal bankruptcy to free himself from the previous contract. As for initially signing over 100 percent of his publishing to Shelter for $10,000, Petty said, "I thought publishing meant *songbooks*. I had no idea I'd never make any money if I did that."

Everyone who was asked offered a different viewpoint of Denny as a businessman. But they all conclude that he was not much of an executive like Clive Davis or Ahmet Ertegun. Henry said he was not even a very good marketer. Cordell was a music fan, but he was also a shark in the way an old-school A&R guy would exploit an artist's ignorance of the byzantine ins and outs of the record business. Yet he was a velvet-gloved operator. He sincerely cared about his artists as people and their growth as musicians and songwriters, even while taking them for everything he could get. "My father was extremely stubborn when it came to business," Barney Cordell said. "I saw him a couple of times lose deals. He simply wouldn't shift to what I'd consider a reasonable point."

The two strong-headed men had closed the book. The tremors were felt in Tulsa. Bob Morris said, "Leon told [engineer] John Harkin one afternoon, gave him a list, and said, 'Go get this stuff out of the Church.' We go get my dad's pickup truck, and we go down this list, and we start taking stuff out of the Church. An Echoplate, this thing's five foot by eight foot long, a big stainless steel plate, pulling this stuff out, put it in the back of my dad's truck. Peter Nicholls [who was still working for Denny] drives up, and he's fuming because we basically pulled the middle out of the control room. This young Tulsa police officer comes up, and he's asking us what we're doing. 'Well, we're just doing what our boss said.' And Peter Nicholls is going, 'This is ours.' The police officer asked, 'So, this is Leon's stuff?' And I said, 'Yeah.' He told us, 'Y'all just drive off,' so we left Peter Nicholls standing there fuming."

"Leon hardly ever recorded there [at the Church]," Charlene Ripley said. She was married to Steve Ripley. They would both go on to work for and become friends with Leon and eventually own the Church. "I think they were really generous with letting young people come and record there."

Driving by the Church as a teenager, Jamie Oldaker had dreamed of getting in those doors, drumming with the great Leon Russell. Buddy Jones finally brought Oldaker over to meet Leon at the mansion and he was in. Oldaker built a career playing with Leon, Bob Seger, Eric Clapton, and the Tractors. "Looking back at it now, he gave a bunch of nineteen-and twenty-year-old kids a first-rate high-tech studio and expected this to turn into, like, a Muscle Shoals or Stax, to make hit records. All we did was party in here, drink beer, and pick up girls and bring them down: 'We could get you into Leon Russell's studio.'"

After the settlements with Leon and Tom Petty, Denny was fed up with dealing with musicians. In 1978, he opened up an infamous roller disco nightclub in Hollywood called Flippers, with Ian "Flipper" Ross—one of the founders of British pirate station Radio Caroline—on the corner of Santa Monica Boulevard and La Cienega Boulevard. It was a cocaine palace with discreet VIP booths. Denny got into greyhound racing before heading to Ireland and becoming a horse breeder. He came back into the music biz when he worked with his son Barney and Johnny Barbis (who got his start in the record business at Shelter with his brother, Dino, and who would reconnect with Leon at the end of Leon's career) in the 1990s to sign the Cranberries, another smash success. He passed away in 1995 from lymphoma at the age of fifty-one.

Old friend Jimmy Karstein told a story about hanging out with Leon in the late 1970s. "We talked this, that, and the other. Finally, I said, 'Say, whatever happened between you and Denny?' And he was plunking on a guitar, and all of a sudden, he hit a big open chord and choked it off. And he looked at it, looked over at me, and he said, 'Well, I asked him a test question, and he failed.' I said, 'What was the question?' 'Where's the money?' And Leon just kind of chuckled and just went back to strumming the guitar. And never again was a word spoken about it."

Chapter 26

Wedding Album

GARY BUSEY HAD JUST MET Barbra Streisand as the casting began for her version of *A Star Is Born*. She asked Busey what he did. Though he was working on a film called *The Gumball Rally*, he answered that he was currently Leon Russell's drummer. She asked, "You know Leon? How can we meet him?" Within minutes, they were in Busey's customized van (naturally), driving to see Leon in Encino.

"I decided to surprise him with Barbra. When Leon opened the door and saw us, he casually said, 'Teddy Jack, whatcha got here?'" He introduced Leon to Streisand and her boyfriend, film producer Jon Peters, and they started discussing *A Star Is Born*, in which Busey got a role. They decided to use a new Leon song on the soundtrack, "Lost Inside You," cowritten with Streisand. Streisand recorded it as a duet with the film's costar, Kris Kristofferson, who was married to Rita Coolidge.

While at the house on December 2, 1975, Barbra and Mary sang an impromptu duet on "This Masquerade." There's also an unreleased recording of Barbra singing "Lady Blue," which fits her like a glove (she changes a line in the bridge to "I was a blue lady," shifting the perspective of the lyric). She is backed by the dueling pianos of Leon and Mary, with Busey on drums.

They also recorded a version of "Music Man," a new song Mary had written about the early days of her affair with Leon when it was still secret. After the kind of soaring finish that Streisand excels at, as the pianos stop sustaining, she modestly asks, "That wasn't quite together, was it?"

Busey had been hanging out most days with Leon and Mary. The couple's first child was born on New Year's Day 1976. They named him Teddy

Jack and honored Busey by making him the godfather. In 2022, Teddy
Jack said Leon later "apologized profusely every day" to him for choosing
Busey as his godfather. As Teddy explained to the *Tulsa World*, "Because
Ringo Starr asked if he could be my godfather, and he said he had already
told Gary. He told Ringo 'no' and I have never forgiven him for that."
Leon had also told his son he would be fine with Teddy changing his name.

Maxayn Lewis said the house was always filled with a kind of joyful chaos. "All the crazy bunch of famous people who just loved Leon,
they would always bring somebody to be around him, and there was always somebody who was funny, quirky, ridiculous, off-the-beaten-path."
Lewis painted a picture of a blissful, welcoming, extended family centered
around the couple.

Mary and Leon still had the house in Tulsa and the lake compound.
But they would soon be settling down more regularly in California. As
he had spent more time in LA, Leon moved away from his partnership
with Buddy Jones, who only acted as an advisor and partner more than a
manager. Most of the old hometown connections faded away. "When they
shut the Church down, of course, everybody scattered like the wind," said
Tom Russell. "I got a phone call from Leon over at his house, and he said,
'Would you like to stay and take care of the house and the studio while
we're on tour, and then we'll record stuff when I'm not on tour?' Sure."

Much of Leon and Mary's next project, the *Wedding Album*, would be
recorded at the home studios in Encino and Tulsa. Some of the personnel included Bobby Womack, Willie Weeks, Nigel Olsson, Richard Torrance, Marty Grebb, and old buddies from the sixties sessions days, like
Steve Douglas, Jim Horn, and Julius Wechter. While in Tulsa, Leon would
house the musicians and they'd record in the basement studio.

Womack had been called in as part of the concept record Leon had
been working on before Shelter imploded. As Womack explained in an
interview with the English weekly *New Musical Express*, "He came to me
and said 'George Harrison just did one half of my album, would you do
the other half? I'm only trying to compare the difference in his music and
your music, you understand.' After I'd given him about four or five songs,
I told him that's it, but he said, 'I heard something about a song you got
called "Safety Zone."' . . . That was the title track of my album! I said,
'Hey, c'mon, man, I'm doing that myself.' . . . It didn't get on the album
in the end, but his album has been held up too. I gave him 'Daylight' too,

which is the best song on my album, but he promised me he wouldn't come out with his version until mine was released."

"Daylight" is one of the better songs on the *Wedding Album*, one of the songs that survived the project with Leon wanting to use different producers. It has a little soulful grit to it, which is welcome on a glossy and mostly light album. If Leon was paying attention to Top 40 radio, he was hearing a lot of the Bee Gees' *Main Course*, released in '75. With the number one single "Jive Talkin'," the record is a landmark that bridged the pop-funk of the early seventies to the disco that would dominate the latter half of the decade.

But looking at the song titles alone set expectations low for fans who were still buzzing on "Shootout on the Plantation" or "Alcatraz." Here are the first four tracks on *Wedding Album*: "Rainbow in Your Eyes," "Like a Dream Come True," "Love's Supposed to Be That Way," and "Fantasy." The album opens up with a breathy chorus of Mary's overdubbed cascading vocals, an idea that Kenny Loggins would nick for "Whenever I Call You Friend" a couple of years later. Leon in the same lane with Loggins was indeed a highway to the danger zone.

Though the record is beloved by certain Leon fans, it has not aged well. "Like a Dream Come True" has the two vocalists singing as a duet simultaneously, but not really *together*. "Love's Supposed to Be That Way" is catchy but mediocre. While her backing vocals are dreamy, when Mary takes the lead vocal, she sounds tentative. The single "Satisfy You" sounds like a duo at a poolside tiki bar. The rest of the album suffers from the same shallow lovey-dovey sentiment and cold artificial-sounding production. Leon Russell was never just pure wild-man rock. But the material here also fails to stack up against his early ballads, which always had heft and soul. And it fails to live up to the promise of the key contributions Mary made to *Will O' the Wisp*, like "Laying Right Here in Heaven."

Though Leon is to be lauded for leaning forward, the results sound dated in a way Bee Gees and Stevie Wonder albums do not. The culprits here are an overreliance on the hot new technology of the time and, more crucially, a dearth of compelling songwriting. Having the home studios might be partially to blame. The album sounds like it was written to tape, with musical ideas getting recorded as they were conceived, half-baked.

"At a certain point, I said, 'I got to figure this out better, this is not right. I need to be able to go to work like an accountant or a bricklayer and go do my job and then come home and eat and go to bed. I can't do this waiting around for inspiration,'" Leon said. "So, about the time I was making my *Wedding Album*, I started doing some research about how to do it. I read a book, I think it was called *How to Write the Popular Song*, and I tried some of the exercises that they had to say. They talked about the blank page, how threatening the blank page was and it had to do with the writer or the singer or whatever trying to be the audience and the performer at the same. Said that doesn't work. You can't do that. You have to separate it. And they gave some suggestions about what to do about it, which I tried and it absolutely worked."

Writing on demand, like punching a clock or going to the office, does not necessarily result in great songs. The album cover tells the story: Leon in soft focus, wearing a tan three-piece suit and fedora, clutching the ravishing Mary Russell. On the back is a full-bleed black-and-white photo of them nose to nose, lips to lips. The credits for "Quiet Nights" include the sweet note, "Teddy Jack Russell: Born January 1, 1976," the first of two children the couple would have together. Few would begrudge their happiness, but domestic bliss rarely results in memorable music.

The album had been intended to be released on Shelter, but distributor MCA refused to consider it as the fulfillment of Leon's contract. By March 2, 1976, there was an agreement between Leon and Warner Bros. to release the album on his new Paradise label, an imprint under Warner Bros. "We were in Mo Ostin's office," old friend Lenny Waronker recalled. "Leon didn't have a lawyer. If he did, the lawyer wasn't there. He was negotiating his own deal. They reached an impasse on something. Mo has an enormous amount of patience. He could dig in. I remember Leon, who I always thought would never give in to anything except what he thought made sense for him, gave in. He finally said, 'OK. You're right on that one.'

"I got a phone call, maybe three months later," Waronker continued. "It was late. It was like eleven o'clock or something. He said, 'I just finished this record. I want to play it for you. Can you come to the studio?' I'm in West Los Angeles, so I had to drive all the way to Hollywood. I kept saying, 'Lenny, you've got to be honest with him,'" he remembered, laughing. "I went down and listened to it. Usually, when something's done, it's done. What good am I going to be if I add something? I just didn't believe the record. I was certainly as diplomatic as I could be, but I was also saying, you know, 'I have concerns about this. I think maybe she's singing too much.' He just sat there, nodded his head, and that was the end of it. I'd heard a couple months later, he was angry. He said, 'Lenny's too editorial.'" Lenny laughed again.

Leon was able to sign artists to Paradise, the first being Gary Ogan, who had sent a demo. "There was no better place for a new artist such as myself at the time," Ogan recalled. "I pretty much got to call my own shots. It wasn't lost on me how lucky I was to have Leon personally ushering me into the LA music scene of the late seventies. In fairly short order, I was brought into the fold, signed my contract, and moved into the guest bedroom at Leon and Mary's." Ogan appreciated and connected with Leon primarily as a fellow singer-songwriter, preferring his ballads and the *Wedding Album* to Leon's funky gospel-rock.

Leon and Mary hit the road in the spring of 1976, with Ogan and the Paradise Roadshow Band—which Ogan had helped assemble—in tow, who opened the shows and augmented the Leon and Mary band. "I loved being on the bus," Ogan said. "We'd be home, and we'd leave for two or three days and come back. I think Leon had hit the point in his traveling that he wanted to cut back. But he was really enjoying his best effort to get the Mary-Leon thing across because, as far as I could tell, they were getting along; everybody was happy."

Leon, Mary, and the band made an appearance on the first season of *Saturday Night Live* on May 15, 1976. Maxayn Lewis and Ann Bell were there, along with Mary's sister, Frances Pye. The show's first cast was legendary, including Dan Aykroyd, John Belushi, and Chevy Chase. Chase had taken part in a satire of Leon Russell in 1973 on a National Lampoon album, *Lemmings*.

Paul Shaffer was the keyboardist in the *SNL* band. He had been a fan of Leon in Delaney & Bonnie and Mad Dogs. As a fan of the classic Phil Spector sides and other sixties hits that Leon and the Wrecking Crew played on, and as a session player himself, Shaffer's appreciation of Leon grew when he became aware of that pedigree. "I certainly was there at the soundcheck and watching him like a hawk. He did Bobby Womack's 'Daylight.' We got to watch him in action; that was terrific."

The first song Leon and Mary performed was "Satisfy You." "There's a part where he looks at my mom, and you can just tell, like, oh my God, he's so madly in love with her," said Tina Rose, referring to the part around two minutes and thirty seconds in. A camera is close up on Leon as he glances in Mary's direction when she takes her next vocal line.

Maxayn Lewis said Belushi, Aykroyd, and Chase were friendly and, naturally, hilarious. Belushi came out with his Joe Cocker impression during their second song, "Daylight." "Leon didn't know he was gonna do that. So his reaction, that's authentic." Leon has an impassive facial expression watching Belushi come out, take a vocal mic center stage, and flail around, spilling a can of beer all over himself. "He didn't know that was gonna happen. None of us did."

Ann Bell said, "I remember Belushi saying, 'Would it upset you if I came out in the middle of one of your songs and acted like Joe Cocker?' Leon goes, 'I'm not really into that,' and then he came out anyway. It was awkward!" Leon casts an annoyed glare.

Bell had witnessed Cocker and Leon chatting amiably when Joe showed up at the 1974 Miami Orange Bowl show. But immediately after the *SNL* appearance almost two years later, Leon told journalist Al Aronowitz, "I would have had some reservations about the taste of that bit, except for what Joe's been saying about me in the press and the way he acted the last time he was over my house . . . saying all those horrible things." Cocker had apparently been so drunk at Leon's house that he had assumed Gary Busey was Leon's bodyguard. "You don't scare me!" Cocker shouted at Busey. According to Leon, Joe turned to him and said, "Leon, you buried me. Leon, you can't play God." Leon lamented, "Those were his parting words."

While in New York, they played at Nassau Coliseum, and Aronowitz wrote a long piece about them that gives a glimpse of Leon's rapidly descending career as a performer. "The gate at the Nassau Coliseum had been light; maybe only $35,000, with Leon's share just a little below his break-even point of $11,500," wrote Aronowitz. "It's expensive to fly a troupe of twenty-seven around the country in a private plane, even if it is just an aging putt-putt-prop job, and the box office had been down in every city except Cincinnati and Atlanta. 'I'm going to do it through August,' Leon said. 'If it doesn't get into some money by then, I'm going to have to stop. It's just too damn painful.'"

Reading the *New York Times* preview of the concert is also painful: "'I feel that the new album is the best one I've done,' Mr. Russell argues hopefully, 'and Mary has a lot to do with that.' The trouble is that though the new *Wedding Album*—on which Mrs. Russell is co-billed—may be better than some of his stylistically bizarre excursions of recent years, it doesn't come close to recapturing the ebullient, down-home white gospel of his glory years. And audiences seem to sense that. Although his record company contends that his current five-week tour has been triumphant so far, the 16,000-seat Nassau Coliseum had only sold about 6,000 tickets early in the week."

Seemingly overnight, Leon had gone from lithe hippie Master of Space and Time to paunchy "Oklahoma patriarch," in Aronowitz's words. At the time, Leon was thirty-four, and Mary was twenty-five. He was smoking Winstons, and he explained that touring had worn him down. "I became disenchanted with the road. Traveling. Hotel food. I ain't got that much strength. Also, it takes me so long to make a record, I really think I put out a couple of bad ones when I was working on the road. I found out I liked to stay at home and just overdub records. Mostly in California. Encino . . . we only spend three or four months a year in Oklahoma. We've been spending most of our time in California, finishing up the *Wedding Album* and rehearsing the live show. Mary and I worked on the *Wedding Album* for a year. It was after we got married I realized it wasn't fair for me to keep her talent hidden. You know, she is better than me. I decided I had to get her out there, and I'll be the bandleader in the family."

It's a rare interview, period. But it is particularly worthwhile, because Leon was uncharacteristically open about business with Aronowitz, with whom Leon was friendly. But Aronowitz—known as the guy who introduced the Beatles to Bob Dylan—understood the limits of this access: "Part of anybody's con is the illusion of intimacy and Leon is one of the superior con men of our time, already an old carny at his tender age. He has charm, wit, brilliance, extreme power, a fine sense of beauty and he's quick on the draw. Yeah, he's a con man but he's a con man with ideals—which, for a con man, can be a fatal flaw, unless that's part of his con, too." Leon told him, "I get a lot of shit from people. They think I'm a schemer. And I am, I'm a con artist. All musicians are, whether they know it or not. . . . But the shit that some of them get away with!"

Leon started to complain about how he got screwed by Denny Cordell, but he stopped himself, explaining, "I'm prohibited in the settlement from talking about it." The break was not a clean one. Leon hired CPAs to do forensic accounting and audits, discovering hundreds of thousands of dollars in back royalties that Shelter owed him. The litigation lasted the better part of a year. The Labor Commissioner reviewed the employment contracts between Denny and Leon to determine whether they were purposely devised to skirt the Artist's-Manager's Act, aka the Talent Agencies Act, a section of the California Labor Code. Cordell and Shelter filed restraining orders against Leon to cease further removal of equipment from Shelter property, like the Church. Shelter filed lawsuits and wrote threatening letters to prohibit Leon from recording for any other company, like Paradise/Warner Bros. The two sides finally settled in June 1976.

Even with the national exposure on this new hip TV show, *SNL*, the reception to *Wedding Album* was lukewarm. It made it to thirty-four on the Top 200 album chart. They did also hit number thirty-four on the singles chart with "Rainbow in Your Eyes." It would be the last time Leon cracked the Top 40.

Leon's profile was also kept high by George Benson's version of Leon's "This Masquerade," released in April and a number ten hit. It was also an R&B Top 10 and won the Grammy for Record of the Year in 1977, with additional nominations for Song of the Year and Best Male Pop Vocal. The Tommy LiPuma–produced album *Breezin'* with "This Masquerade" on it went triple platinum and topped the jazz, R&B, and pop charts, the first number one on all three. The record sold over four million copies worldwide. Fortunately, this was one of the songs Leon had kept in the publishing split with Denny.

Leon said that among the session musicians he cut his teeth with, Benson had long been respected. Much the same way they used to chatter about Glen Campbell, Leon said, "They'd say, 'Boy, George Benson, why isn't he a star?' . . . They talked about him for years. And then Tommy [LiPuma] cut my song with him, and it was a huge hit." Reflecting with Denny Tedesco in 2013, Leon said, "'Masquerade' was cut forty-three times before George Benson cut it."

Benson later said, "I had never heard of Leon Russell at the time. . . . I didn't know so many other people had already recorded 'This Masquerade.' If I had known that, I would never have recorded it."

A hero in the world of music production, Tommy LiPuma believed enough in Leon to pay attention to his catalog and matched a brilliant song with a long-overdue artist. "Tommy loved that song," said his longtime right-hand man, engineer Al Schmitt. "He thought it was a hit song. It sure came out that way; that album exploded."

The song illustrates Leon's timeless compositional ability, launching off from the chord pattern Matt Dennis wrote in 1946 for "Angel Eyes," adding a brand new melody and on-point lyric, while extending a bridge to twice the usual middle-eight bars, and modulating in key, and creating his own standard from the template of an existing one.

"[Leon] would show us all kinds of things, tricks for writing songs," Maxayn said. "He said, 'The trick to writing songs is to become a great thief.' All the great songwriters are excellent thieves." Great thieves know how to cover their tracks. But like an art thief who can't help but brag about his exploits, Maxayn said Leon "sat down one day at the piano, and he just showed us how he stole every song that he ever wrote that became a hit. He showed what he stole it from and how he stole it. And then how he flipped it around and incorporated it, 'And then the next part was like this.'"

After years of not doing interviews, Leon was finally availing himself of high-profile publications. But the press, sensing a dying career, hovered like vultures. An interview with *Rolling Stone* begins with a description of Leon at home in Encino. It took a bit to get Leon out of his shell. "In fact," wrote Patrick Snyder, "the day before, he'd stayed in bed, while his wife Mary kept the appointment." And then, for the kill: "Once a major force in pop music, the 34-year-old Russell has watched his record sales and popularity tumble to cult level since he stopped touring some two and a half years ago." After noting the show at the Forum in LA was only half full, Snyder concedes, "Still, it was pure Russell, and his six-piece band responded to every twitch of the master's head. And Mary, with her wailing, piercing voice, more than convinced the audience of her right to share the stage with Leon."

Back in Tulsa, Leon met a guy named George Bingham, a car dealer who bought and sold old cars at auctions. "Well, it wasn't but a few days after they'd gotten together that Leon got really interested in buying cars at auctions," Tom Russell recalled. "Before we knew it, the backyard of the mansion was starting to slowly build up with all these dumb cars. It ended up looking like a used car lot. I remember thinking, 'Where's this going? And is he ever going to sell any of these? What is he doing?'"

One late night, Tom Russell and Marty Grebb were in the basement studio. Russell recalled, "I said, 'Yeah, wouldn't it be funny if Leon had an amusement park?' Marty said, 'Yeah, that would be hilarious.' Before long, we were talking about bridges over little creeks with planks laid out like a piano. We were chatting this up something crazy, not knowing that the door had opened and Leon is standing there. He finally cleared his throat or something. He just came on in like nothing happened. We were thinking maybe he hadn't heard us.

"Two days later," Russell continued, "I was sitting up at the kitchen table. And Leon and George walk in the kitchen door from the back of the house. And Leon walked in and said, 'Didn't you have a little portable drafting board?' So I went up and got it. 'Okay,' he said, 'now, start at one side and go to the other side and draw me, to scale. Now, right in the center of it, cut that open, and put in a double gate, and make it higher, and put a square cross for a sign. Now, letter across that sign L-E-O-N L-A-N-D.' I got a pit in my stomach. Here it comes. So I do it. And Leon held it up for George. And George said, 'Yep.'

"But unbeknownst to me, George, being a used car salesman and living in Glenpool, had access to a guy that ran an amusement park," Russell said. "They had gone out and bought all the old equipment. George had land out there in Glenpool, and they were going to do Leon Land! Make an RV park with all these rides and—*Leon Land*! So, they had all these things brought from the amusement park, out there in that field, where they probably sat until they rusted because nothing ever happened. And I used to go by years later; I'd still see remnants of the Tilt-a-Whirl sitting there."

Perfect: Leon Land, where fantasies go to rust.

Leon hired a fan from upstate New York as a handyman and property manager for the Tulsa house. David Lambreth was fleeing the stress of corporate life. Russell said: "Work pressure sort of blew him out, and now he wanted to totally get off the grid." Leon brought in him and his wife, Chris. "They were really nice people, and the guy was a wonderful carpenter." Leon hired Lambreth to maintain the house and yard. Chris became the nanny for Teddy Jack.

On October 11, 1976, the temperature climbed into the eighties in Tulsa. "Leon was up at Grand Lake. Mary and the baby were there in the house," Russell said. Blue Bridges-Fox said she was also at the house at the time. "Some wasps were buzzing around. One of them got too close to Teddy Jack, and Mary freaked out. . . . So David goes and gets a long ladder. He found a very big wasp nest at the very top of the eaves. He gets up there. He's got a newspaper, and he lights it. He sticks it up there, and the nest falls down. But what he didn't know is that the eave had a little crack, and the suction from the air sucked the flames right up into the attic space there above the third floor. Mary calls up and says, 'I smell smoke.' As soon as I get out in the hall, I smell it too. I look, and I'm seeing smoke creeping out of the thing, so, of course, I call the fire department."

After the fire was extinguished, Mary and Teddy went to stay with some neighbors. "I went back up inside in my apartment to see if it had spread downstairs," Russell said. "I was doing the second-floor check, checked in Leon's suite. I go in my apartment. I don't see anything, but I'm smelling something. I opened my closet doors, and water's pouring down, and my microphone collection, that I had spent years on, was getting soaked. It hadn't done a ton of damage, but it smelled horrible, a mildewy smell, and of course, they had cut off the electricity."

Leon had told him before all this that he was expecting a phone call from LA and to let him know if that call came in. "Well, they did call and left a message that he'd been waiting on. And during the course of the excitement, I hadn't even thought to call Leon. Just about the time I was thinking, 'I should call Leon,' he called and said, 'Did my call come in?' I said, 'Well, I've got some good news, and I've got some bad.' He said, 'What's the bad news?' And I said, 'Well, the house caught on fire.' Without missing a beat, he said, 'What's the good news?' I said, 'Your call came in.' He said, 'Oh, great. What did they say?' I told him, and he said, 'Great!' Click. Uh, okay."

At dusk, Russell went out to a balcony for some air. "I happened to look down the street, and here comes Leon's Mercedes. He pulls his car up to the house, slows down—I know he was just sort of looking up at it—and zip! Then he just keep driving on."

"I had bad luck with fires at that place," Leon wrote. "The water used to put it out ran all through the house and ultimately down to the studio, completely ruining all the bottom floors. It was so depressing that we moved out. . . . We never lived in the house again."

Leon tasked George Bingham with selling off the used cars that were littering the estate grounds before the fire. He also took Bingham on tour as a road manager. That was short-lived. A lawsuit came between them. It all started with a Chinese junk.

"We had a big tornado here in the Tulsa area that year [May 1976], and it did a lot of damage around Grand Lake," Tom Russell explained. "There was a lawyer that had a big place out there, and he had a Chinese junk he had actually shipped in from Hong Kong Harbor. It got hit in the tornado and it had been breached and rolled over on its side. Somehow Leon and George got wind of it, and out they went. Well, of course, Leon immediately bought it, and they uprighted it. I said, 'Where are you gonna get it fixed? I mean, we're in the middle of Oklahoma.' Leon said, 'Oh, I found a shipbuilder. I found this guy who has impeccable credentials; he's an Indian.'" Russell laughed, remembering. "Probably six months went by, and Leon came in one day. He said, 'Well, they've finally got the junk all fixed, and we're going to take it up to the house at Grand Lake.'"

George Bingham and his wife, Pat, were going to go into business with Leon to make use of the dormant lake property. The idea was to turn the place into a bed-and-breakfast and have meals served on the boat. When the day came to launch it, though, the junk sunk, with many of the locals there to witness the christening. "The boat just went straight on down." Russell laughed. "Leon's standing up there just as deadpan as can be, and just opened the door to the Rolls and got in and just chugged off."

The team pivoted to turning the property into "Grandma Walsie's Senior Citizens Retirement Center." Pat Bingham was to develop the property, with expenditures going toward her share of the purchase price. There was no written agreement about any of this. Nothing came of it and Leon felt he could no longer afford to keep the property. In 1976, he donated it to Oral Roberts University, located in Tulsa, as a tax write-off. "I was going to give [Bingham] and his wife $12,000 for their effort and expenses," Leon wrote. "They had reported expenditures of about $5,000." Pat Bingham sued Leon for $750,000 in early 1977, saying Leon reneged on the deal. In the suit, Pat Bingham testified that she spent more than $11,000. Leon's attorneys contended that no agreement could be enforced since there was no written contract. Ultimately, a judge awarded Bingham only $1,500. They appealed and received another $1,200. "I enjoyed very much the time I lived at the lake house," Leon wrote, as if with a resigned sigh.

The Oklahoma days were pretty much over for Leon. Mary wasn't made to feel welcome in Tulsa, never mind the open hostility she was met with at Grand Lake. When Leon brought Mary up to the lake in the early days of their courtship, she was greeted with overt racism by some of the people in the area. There was little to keep him in his home state.

The Tulsa house was listed for sale in March 1977 and was sold to an attorney, who held it for about ten years. In November 1987, it was razed. "I always said Leon had the Midas touch in reverse," said Jim Karstein. "Everything he ever touched seemed to disintegrate."

Chapter 27

Paradise in Burbank

AS 1976 WAS DRAWING TO a close, rock royalty assembled at the Winterland Ballroom in San Francisco to bid farewell to The Band. Leon said he had been invited to the Last Waltz, as it is known, but must have had a scheduling conflict. Watching the Martin Scorsese film of the star-studded concert, it's remarkable that Leon was *not* there. He had been buddies with Levon Helm since the early 1960s, and the bill was filled with his friends and collaborators: Bob Dylan, Joni Mitchell, Dr. John, Ringo Starr, Eric Clapton, Neil Young. Dylan had been on his Rolling Thunder Revue tour that year, similar in presentation and approach to the Mad Dogs & Englishmen shows six years before.

The concert and film seemed to mark the end of an era. Though most of these musicians continued to create vital music for years, they were arguably all past their peaks. It was a wonderful event, but the rock stars all looked a bit too self-satisfied to some. The Ramones, Sex Pistols, The Clash, and Talking Heads all issued shots heard 'round the world in '76 and '77. The revolution would not be televised, nor would it be filmed by a coked-up Marty Scorsese.

Leon had taken notice of new aggressive rock 'n' roll being marketed as punk rock, but you wouldn't detect it in his own music. But he would soon provide an outlet for many Los Angeles bands inspired by the raw approach of punk, with a local television show and records produced at his new Paradise Studios in Burbank. The facilities grew out of a warehouse on Magnolia Boulevard in Burbank, which he rented to store the stuff he moved from Tulsa. "I had so much junk to move . . . that it made the cover of a trade magazine for household movers," Leon wrote. "The article inside was titled 'The Largest Residential Move in History.'" It took seventeen moving vans, with everything packed into crates.

His new deal with Warner Bros. funded much, if not most, of the studio's building costs. Leon placed an ad to help transform what had been an appliance warehouse into an audio and video complex. Frank Latouf had just graduated from studying record engineering and studio maintenance programs.

"I was looking for a gig, and I dreamed of working at one of the big studios in town. Opportunity presented itself in an ad in the paper. It mentioned a recording studio, and they were looking for a carpenter. I answered the ad, and Diane [Sullivan] hired me. I was a young punk, and I think Leon saw that I had the drive to get some of the things done that he wanted done. One of the first things Leon asked me to do was assemble a small mixing room. We had his API console and Stephens forty-track tape machines. And we lined the side walls with mattresses, and the back wall was nothing more than just a drape that led out into this enormous warehouse. For the front wall, he told me, 'I need you to just go down and buy me a shitload of cinder blocks,' which I did. And I built a monitor wall out of concrete cinder blocks, and in the cinder blocks was the studio monitoring system, and the room *kicked ass*, I gotta tell you, for something that we just threw together."

Leon could half-ass something like this and have it turn out nearly ideal. "He jerry-rigged everything. That was his favorite term. But he knew what he was doing in the back of his mind," said Latouf. "I learned what I know today from him, as far as acoustics and soundproofing. Leon was a pioneer, leading the way amongst recording artists with [regard to] audio equipment, design, and acoustics." Latouf eventually went on to be *the* premier studio builder in Los Angeles.

Leon also enlisted his stalwart Skyhill engineer from the late sixties, Gordon Rudd, who in the intervening years had helped the Beach Boys build their Brother Studios. Rudd designed the console the group used on their *Holland* album and did some engineering at Brother, where he worked with engineer Earle Mankey. Rudd hired Earle's brother, James, who would soon come to work for Leon at Paradise. The Mankeys had also been early members of the art-rock band Sparks.

"First thing that happened was Leon abandoned the original studio design for the Magnolia studio [the warehouse], even though a fair amount of construction was already done, and it was a good design," Rudd said. "Leon had a dislike for doing anything the usual way. Skyhill was a hippie-commune version of a recording studio, and things were no different now. . . . I guess that's the trouble with being a visionary; I don't think Leon was able to properly express his vision."

Leon was a people collector, hiring interesting and offbeat folks—some of whom brought highly developed skillsets, while others were just people he liked—and groomed them for certain roles or allowed them to find their own path. One of the highly skilled staffers, Rudd said the plan was to convert the warehouse into two spaces, the audio studio and "The Ambrose Campbell World Video Centre." "We built a stage with lights and sound system, plus a control room for recording," Rudd said. "It wasn't used much, at least in my time [from 1976 to 1979]. One problem was that the stage was too high and the ceiling too low to use the lights correctly."

With the split from Shelter, the move from Tulsa, and a growing family, Leon and Mary upgraded from Encino to a sprawling house in Toluca Lake, where their neighbors included Bob Hope, John Ritter, Henry Winkler, and Jonathan Winters, who lived next door. Maxayn Lewis described the compound as "a big huge house, a big Olympic-sized swimming pool, and an orchard of fruit trees."

Naturally, Leon would quickly construct a home studio as well, which was built as an addition to the house, as the work was happening in the warehouse on Magnolia. "We started building the 'Woodbridge Studio' in Leon's backyard in Toluca Lake," Rudd wrote in an email. The address was 10265 Woodbridge Drive. "It was a two-story addition to the house. It was a well-designed studio and where the serious recording took place (Gary Ogan, Wornell Jones, and Leon and Mary). It was more 'normal' and state of the art, but the walls of the control room were upholstered in synthetic blue fur. Blue was Leon's favorite color." Latouf said, "It didn't look like a home studio; it looked like a commercial studio."

Leon purchased a bungalow house on Ledge Avenue, across from the warehouse on Magnolia, and converted it into a studio with offices. Rudd said, "I went to Texas and bought an API console from ZZ Top, which we installed in the Ledge studio. It actually worked out pretty good because he didn't want to use it himself, so he let others use it. Leon was always very reluctant to let anyone else use the Woodbridge studio or the [video] theater because he wanted to reserve it for himself."

Michael Johnstone happened into Leon's world. A pedal steel guitar player who also became an actor (in the series *Deadwood*, among other credits), he installed and maintained mixing consoles in the home studios of rock stars around Hollywood. A true fan who had first seen Leon in Virginia in '73, Johnstone was at the home studio installing wood paneling in a chevron pattern, full 1970s chic. On the first or second night, Leon came walking through with Ambrose Campbell, showing him around, and said hello to Johnstone. "A couple of hours later, he came back in and he had Don Preston with him. I had played some steel guitar gigs around LA with Don Preston. But he didn't recognize me with a rag on my head, in bib overalls and holding a saw. Leon turned away for a few seconds, and I just took a moment to say, 'Don! It's me, Mike Johnstone, the steel player from the other night.' 'Oh yeah. What are you doing here?' I say, 'Well, this is something else that I do.' So then Leon turned back, they talked more, and then they left.

"Then about a half hour later, Leon comes back down by himself and says, 'Don says you're a steel player.' I said, 'That's right.' And so Leon says, 'Well, come up to the house; I'm going to show you something.'" Leon had a pedal steel and asked Johnstone to show him how to play certain chords on the instrument. "And he goes, 'God! It was right in front of me. Do you give lessons?' I said, 'I could.' We hit it off right away. 'Do you play around town?' By then, I had been on the road with Charley Pride. And I went up to Bakersfield and played with a lot of the Bakersfield guys. He said, 'Well, great! I want to keep you around.'"

After working at the house for a bit, Leon brought Johnstone down to Magnolia and showed him the space he wanted to convert into a video soundstage. Leon's interest in video had only intensified since the break with Shelter. His conception was a live soundstage dedicated to musical performance videos. "He didn't foresee the three-minute lip-sync video," Johnstone said.

Leon wrote, "MTV wasn't even on the drawing board at that time, and record companies were not convinced that video was very important in record merchandising. For Warner Bros. to be interested in any kind of video at that time, an act would have to sell seven hundred thousand units." He couldn't believe the pushback he got from the record industry when he participated in a conference on the future of television in promoting records.

"Leon thought that video was going to be the future of the business," Johnstone explained. "He wanted to buy some video equipment. So he hired Jack Jester. Jack had been around Hollywood since the fifties. He had worked with old-school television, Red Skelton's show, game shows; he knew his way around . . . things that nobody around there knew. We were recording studio people. That guy was a character also. He was full of himself." Video gear retailers and wholesalers set up their wares in the big space and Leon basically held auditions. He also wanted a video control room in a mobile unit. "He wanted to find out what's the latest and the greatest, what was the state of the art, and he wanted to buy that," Johnstone continued. "So we ended up buying seven one-inch reel-to-reel videotape machines, made in Germany, they were worth about a hundred grand apiece. And he bought these Hitachi Japanese cameras when they were big." Leon bought seven of the Hitachis.

Leon had still not let go of the idea behind ShelterVision. Jester got wind of a used mobile unit, a bus that had been used for sporting events. Leon bought that and parked it outside the soundstage. "After I moved to Los Angeles and went to work for Elektra, we would get together occasionally, and we'd go to lunch," recalled Marlin Greene, who had engineered *Carney* sessions at Muscle Shoals. "He had just bought one of the big TV stations' sports bus, with all the recording studio gear in it. He was all excited. I asked, 'What in the world are you gonna do with that?' He said, 'Turn it on,'" Greene said, laughing. "He had no idea what he was gonna do with it. The other thing he was trying to put together, he wanted to go on the road with the Lawrence Welk Orchestra. He was in negotiation with them. He would come up with these outlandish deals and pursue them until he hit a brick wall."

"It was sort of like the Spruce Goose," Charlene Ripley said about the video bus. "They drove it once, and then they took it back and never drove it again. It was just too heavy with this lead-lined structure." Rudd provided me a copy of a marketing brochure they had created for the video bus. It looks like a nicotine-stained Lancer's bottle on wheels, in various shades of brown, tan, and brass, with shag carpeting and wood paneling.

"Leon had the two buses," Latouf said. One was the video bus, a Golden Eagle. "He had a love affair with blue fur. Inside it looked like a pimpmobile, with blue fur on the dash, walls, blue carpet, blue everything. He also had a bobcat track, which is a Chevy 5500 with a big box on it. The box was about thirty feet long, so it was a big-ass truck, and we also built a mobile recording truck out of that. And then there was Leon's custom motorhome. He brought it on tour with them. We put multitrack recording in there. He could just take a vacation, go up to the mountains, and just write songs." Latouf said the motorhome was Leon's "mobile man cave." "It had maybe a dozen small monitors and then a large monitor, and he'd be watching the news or televangelist on one channel, anything on a multitude of those smaller TVs, and then he could just bring it up on the big screen whenever he wanted."

As with everyone on the Leon payroll, Latouf wore whatever hat was necessary at the moment. He took to the road with Leon and Mary. "I did everything for him," he said. "If we were traveling, most of the time it'd be on weekends. We'd fly out of LA. Let's say we were playing Texas. We'd play maybe Dallas first on Friday night and Saturday night, and Sunday in Austin, and then fly home. That's how he liked to tour."

"I don't know why he built so many studios," Johnstone said. "It was like, 'When are you gonna start making some records?' The joke among the staff at Paradise was, 'How do you know it's time for Leon to make a record?' 'When he starts to build another studio.'"

Jim Mankey met Johnette Napolitano at Paradise, and they would form the band Concrete Blonde together in 1982 (their name given to them by R.E.M.'s Michael Stipe). For a time, they shared a house with Michael Johnstone, who became as much of a buddy with Leon as one could be within the boss-employee dynamic. "He would call in the middle of the night, share his thoughts, and a couple of us were like that," Johnstone said. "Leon would have a persona. And then he was just a real guy in real life, with hopes and fears: 'What are we gonna do? I'm running out of money.'"

"Leon was always a presence," Jim Mankey said. "We'd have conversations with him. He was pretty friendly for a great gray god. He was comfortable being the guy in charge; you never forgot who was in charge when he was around, but he was nice. He liked to joke around with the staff—be the lord of the studio for an evening." Mankey said he had been a fan of Leon but that "I became an even bigger fan after I got to know him."

The usual suspects, like Bob Dylan, would swing by for a party or two, and George Harrison was still around a lot. Latouf remembered shaking his hand and being starstruck. "Maybe two weeks later, that same thing happened with Willie Nelson. The next week, Larry Carlton walked in with Leon. Another time, a Mercedes-Benz pulled up, and the tinted windows rolled down, and they said, 'Is the professor here?' Looking for Leon. The minute it drove off, I realized it was Tom Petty. He was like the glue that held everything together." Leon was a loyal and low-key friend to his fellow rock stars, but he had his limit. "He had a falling out with Clapton," Johnstone said. Clapton was no longer welcome to visit, because of his substance abuse, according to Mary Jones.

Steve and Charlene Ripley came out to California to work for Leon. Eventually, Johnstone would introduce Ripley to Red Rhodes, an acclaimed pedal steel guitar player from the session scene, who had opened an amp and guitar shop. Rhodes helped Ripley realize his dream: a stereo guitar with individual pickups for each string, with their own controls so that they could each be directed to different amps and/or panned across a stereo spread in recordings. Rhodes had already done a similar trick with a steel guitar. In the early eighties, the Ripley Guitar would become famous, manufactured by Kramer Guitars.

But that was still a few years away. Ripley was just entering the "school of Leon." "When we first got there, we actually lived at the house with [Leon and Mary]," Charlene Ripley recalled. Steve had been a Leon fan since first hearing Cocker's "Delta Lady" on the radio in 1970, having no idea a fellow Okie was behind it, and went to see the Mad Dogs concert in Tulsa. Ripley told *Tulsa People*, "I just became a fanatic."

Steve had gotten a gig mixing the stage monitor for Leon and Mary's 1976 tour. But being on the crew was no guarantee you'd meet Leon, particularly since he and the band were traveling separately from the crew. One night after a show, Leon called out to Ripley, "You'll get it right someday, Mickey Monitor." The second time he drew Leon's attention, he said, "Somehow a dead mic ended up front, and it really hadn't been my mistake, but what Leon saw happen made it look like I'd put the wrong mic in place. . . . Leon goes out to the front of the stage, and I'm stage right behind the girl singers and, with the music grooving, Leon squats down like a football player and he waves the girls out of the way, so he's got a clear path, and he throws that Shure SM57 right at me. It would have hit me right in the head except the cord ran out—like one of those cartoons with the dog on a chain. The mic ran out of cord and dropped at my feet."

His first face-to-face meeting with Leon happened at the end of the tour. "After the last show, I still hadn't met him. . . . One of the production guys grabs me when Leon's walking by and says, 'Leon, Steve Ripley here would like to meet you,' and fortunately there's a picture of me shaking hands with Leon, and I'm rolling my eyes because it's all kind of funny, but it documents my real first meeting with Leon." "Uneasy" describes Ripley's expression. Leon is grinning like a Cheshire Cat under a ten-gallon hat, holding a big stogie as he embraces Ripley with one arm, shaking hands with the other, in a mismatched plaid sport coat and cowboy shirt, looking like a Texas used car dealer who just closed a sale. "Well, bless your heart," he said to Ripley.

In 1977, Leon hired Ripley to be his house engineer, working alongside Rudd, getting everything built. For Ripley, working in Leon's unconventional studios was a matter of putting out fires, though, unlike the Tulsa house, these were figurative, not literal fires. "Lots of times, Leon's setups were . . . not professionally put together, is a nice way to say it," Charlene Ripley said. "The piano was actually in the house. But the old Helios mixing console was in the garage [studio addition], so it was a long way from the garage to where the piano was set up. The Helios was not in great working order, and Steve was doing all he could just to keep it going."

Steve did whatever Leon asked him to do: "Leon's always had this concept, not unlike those giant factory towns—like, where they make Steinway pianos, and the whole city and all the stores are Steinway-owned, and all their workers shop at these places—and Leon liked that concept. When you're not mixing, you're building the bus for the next tour. You're on salary, and it's the family and the team."

For all his earnest efforts, Ripley only lasted about a year before Leon sent him packing. The break came one night when Leon had his old Shelter colleague Dino Airali at the home studio. Airali had gone from Shelter to Dark Horse Records, George Harrison's imprint at A&M, then rejoined

Leon at Paradise Records. "Leon said, 'Steve, stop the tape, come in here and set up some headphones so Dino can hear,'" Charlene said. "Steve stopped the tape and went in, which was a little trek. Leon immediately started playing. Steve went back, started the tape but didn't get everything, and Leon was mad. Steve came in, and he said [to me], 'Wake up. I've been fired.' It was Dino who did the firing, for not rolling the tape. Leon always rolled the tape. I think he saw Steve as frantic. That was part of the reason he fired him. He was gonna make it work, whatever it took."

Though he would soon find his way back into Leon's good graces, it was a devastating setback for Steve, who considered himself Leon's acolyte: "Every once in a while, there's a crack in the cosmos, and somebody falls through. That's Bob Dylan or Elvis, or Hank Williams, or the Beatles, or whatever," Ripley explained. He later accompanied Dylan on guitar on the 1981 *Shot of Love* album and on the subsequent tour. Jim Keltner made the introduction, and Dylan listed Ripley among his favorite guitarists. "There's a handful of those guys that don't know what they're doing; they can't explain what they're doing. Leon is one of those guys. . . . Shaking hands with him, you knew there was something different in those hands. An acoustic piano or an electric piano, or whatever, when he, to use a biblical term, laid his hands on that keyboard, something else happened that is unexplainable."

Like Ripley, many of the employees at Paradise were musicians. Jim Mankey was between his stint with Sparks and on his way to forming Concrete Blonde. "We [Concrete Blonde] did better than I had ever dreamed or could hope, but most musicians are lucky that they're not living under the nearest overpass," he said with a laugh. "Leon was one step along the path to avoiding homelessness in the music industry. He showed me that you could rely on whatever skills you may have, and do your best, and God will provide—that was Leon's phrase, he'd leave little notes around the studio: 'God will provide.'"

Leon encouraged the musicianship of his employees and even jammed with them. Mankey said, "He just liked to play, and a couple of times I sat in on bass." The warehouse was filled with musical gear and furniture from Leon's past. Between the studios in the warehouse and the twenty-four-track one in the little house on Ledge, the employees usually had some creative space to use whenever they wished. "He was quite generous in that respect. We would record after hours. We were pretty much encouraged to use the gear. Stiv Bators [of the Dead Boys] recorded there; the Fly Boys, who I liked a lot. Johnette and I recorded a lot of stuff. It was very musician-friendly."

Though Mankey was still in his twenties, he felt like one of the old people in the scene. But he had been on the cutting edge of music since working with the innovative Sparks, starting in the early seventies. He said Leon was actively attuned to the new artists coming through his facilities. "I guess it's fair enough to call him a rootsy guy since he helped find a lot of those roots," Mankey said. "But he was always looking to be on the forefront of what was happening and was very interested in finding the weirdest stuff he could find. He could recognize the good music in whatever he heard. That was the whole basis behind the studios; he wanted to find out what's happening and new in LA and bring it forward."

While the studios on Magnolia and Toluca Lake were hopping, so was the domestic scene inside the house. Maxayn Lewis said, "When Mary had Teddy, [Leon's mother] Hester came out here and stayed at the house in Toluca. She was wonderful. She was also a painter. She was really good. I wish I had some stuff that she showed me. She was just a really nice lady.

"But now, Leon's father?" she continued. "When he came to California, Hester was already here. Maybe a couple of weeks later, he showed up. She calls him and says, 'You need to come out here and meet your grandson.' Somebody picked him up at LAX. We were like, 'Leon! We're gonna get to meet your dad? Wow, this is gonna be cool,' because his mom was so sweet." It was likely Hester's second husband, Gene Fullbright, who was that visitor: John Bridges and Hester were no longer on friendly terms.

"It was still daytime when he arrived. Everybody ran into the living room: 'Hello! Hello!' And he just froze because everybody was embracing him and hugging him and welcoming him. Mary said, 'Are you okay? Do you need something?' And she had her arm around his waist, 'Are you okay?' And he said, 'I'm just not used to a bunch of Black people touching me.' He was serious. 'I'm just not used to it. I mean no harm; I just wasn't raised this way.' And so I was like, wow, how is he gonna reconcile this little half-Black kid?" Lewis laughed. "But his wife just kind of pulled him along and finally he became more comfortable, and then I think by the time he left and went back home, he really had had an eye-opening and life-changing experience."

Jan Bridges, and others in the family, said Hester was also prejudiced.

"She told me she grew up in Apache [Oklahoma], and she was always really afraid of Indians," said Jan, a Native American. "She was overtly racist to me. She'd let me know. But then when [Leon and Jan's second child] Honey was born, she was all about Honey because Honey was white. Gene, her husband, was very clearly racist, and he made comments about her dark grandchildren."

Leon and Mary did not do much performing in 1977. They joined Willie's annual Fourth of July Picnic on July 3 at the Tulsa Fairgrounds Speedway. They put together a follow-up album together called *Make Love to the Music*, their final album as a duo. Despite some nods to his rock 'n' roll past, it was clear that Leon had transitioned into what he thought was music for grown-ups. But it didn't seem many grown-ups were interested. In the July 16 *Atlanta Journal-Constitution* that year, Scott Cain wrote an article called "Past-30 Rockers Rock On," in which he observed, "Roger Daltrey, who may come to be regarded by future generations as the perfect symbol for the rock era, shows himself fresh as a daisy and looking good to rock with the best for an indefinite future. Leon Russell, on the other hand, has moved into a specialty where no one seems willing to follow him, and Elvis Presley provides further evidence of his decline."

On the whole, *Make Love to the Music* is disappointing but also boldly experimental and compellingly weird, like most of Leon's work from roughly 1973 to 1983. But there was rarely any discernible musical chemistry between Leon and Mary. They were not George and Tammy, Marvin and Tammi, or Peaches & Herb. They were not even Elton John and Kiki Dee. Mary had a powerful voice, but it was relatively thin and sharp. Leon's twangy honk was always an acquired taste; as a partner on romantic, light pop duets, he was unconvincing. The couple's voices simply did not blend well.

Gary Ogan was enlisted to help write songs for and coproduce the album with Leon. Ogan wrote most of the music for "Now Now Boogie" and "Say You Will" to accompany Leon's lyrics. The two would each sit at typewriters tapping out stream of consciousness for thirty minutes and revisit the pages later to see whether there were any germs worthy of developing. Said Ogan, who was a big fan of the *Wedding Album*, "Comparing the two albums, the record I worked on is not nearly as magical and wonderful, even though I think it's magical and wonderful. Leon and I would spend certain parts of every day working really diligently on writing songs.

I was surprised what an effort it was for him. He was very forthcoming with wishing he could have an easier time with finishing a song. He was fretting all the time about it."

It's as if Leon was daunted by his own illustrious past. He felt like he had set the bar so high right from his first three albums that he had too much to live up to. Ogan said, "He suffered mightily, on all kinds of levels, about his stature and who he was as a songwriter. He was such a beautiful, together cat otherwise. But that was the one can of worms that would show you his humanity."

The second track, "Joyful Noise," works as an attempt to get back to Leon's blues-rock roots. But most of the material is thin. "Say You Will" is Caribbean-lite that begs to be turned off as soon as the piña coladas are done churning in the blender. The rest of the album is retreads about love (four tracks feature the word in the title), all set to busy and buzzy ticky-tack arrangements. He had started a technique of underscoring recordings with polyrhythmic percussion, like a dotted-eighth-note hi-hat sound, often on a beaded gourd, that didn't always help the groove so much as distract from it. But that sound would remain a trademark to the end.

To be fair, this was an era when the charts were often topped by highly polished soft pop and lite R&B. The top year-end single that year was Rod Stewart's "Tonight's the Night"; Rita Coolidge's smooth version of "(Your Love Has Lifted Me) Higher and Higher" finished the year at number eight. Boz Scaggs, Bob Seger, and the Steve Miller Band were also high on 1977's year-end LP chart, and Leon had more in common musically with these acts before partnering with Mary. You've got to give a guy credit for following his heart and muse, but he was ceding ground in the battle for the rock 'n' roll heartland and the FM album-oriented-rock audience. Stevie Nicks and Lindsey Buckingham had opened for Leon on some tour dates before joining Fleetwood Mac. Like many of his opening acts, they rocketed by him: *Rumours* was the year's best-selling album.

Leon worked on Ogan's self-titled album for Paradise. Leon even drew and painted the cover for the record, tracing Ogan's photographed face projected onto paper. The album has the lush and polished production that Ogan loved about the *Wedding Album*. In the hands of a major label that had a staff and clout to properly promote it, the single "The Road" might have stood a chance of being a hit. Instead, Paradise Records had only Dino Airali. "You got the sense that they were trying to keep it as

low-budget as possible," Ogan said. "Leon drew my face for my cover—
they saved some money there." Warner Bros. distributed Paradise, but
Ogan said, "I don't think Warner Brothers did anything for my record
besides put it out."

Airali was road-managing the touring Paradise Roadshow band when,
two weeks after Ogan's LP came out, Leon fired him. "I heard from somebody else in the inner touring team that he was taking all the per diems
from the band," Ogan said. "For all the magic and good fortune Leon was
to manifest throughout his life, he also managed to align himself with
more than his share of those who would hurt him in one way or another."

For all his breaks with his past, Leon still had John Gallie playing in
his bands during the Mary years. Old friend Patrick Henderson was living in LA and fit right in with the family scene in Burbank. He became
a significant figure in the gospel music. Henderson had been friends with
the gospel legend Andraé Crouch since Henderson was sixteen. Leon's
old friend from Oklahoma, Bill Maxwell—yet another in a line of killer
Oklahoma drummers—had been playing with Crouch since 1972. He
had brought Leon to play on Crouch's 1976 LP *This Is Another Day*. "Leon
immediately fell in love with Andraé," Maxwell said. "Leon played very
delicately. I think he had a birth defect, and his right hand wasn't particularly strong. So he played very light. He was heavy with his left hand.
Andraé pounded the piano, and Andraé was like a whole orchestra. Leon
just loved the way he played."

Maxwell and Leon had a lifelong friendship. Maxwell said Leon was
one of the sweetest people he knew until he wasn't. "The closest I could
describe it is like Bob Dylan; extremely friendly, extremely intelligent,
extremely kind, until they don't want to talk to you anymore, and a wall
goes up."

Chapter 28

Paradise Lost

IN 1978, PRODUCER KIM FOWLEY lurched back into Leon's life. Leon loved characters, and there were few more larger-than-life characters in Hollywood than Fowley.

Fowley and Gary Paxton had released the number one 1960 single "Alley Oop" as the Hollywood Argyles, and the two had given Leon some of his earliest session work when his clothes were not yet completely clean of the Oklahoma dust. Fowley had been around for the early days of rock 'n' roll, a genre that "is driven by revenge and sex," he proclaimed in his memoir, *Lord of Garbage*. Like Leon, Fowley had suffered childhood illness, polio in Fowley's case. Fowley had remained in the music-biz shadows, a producer, mentor, impresario, songwriter, hustler. Fowley arrived at Leon's house fresh from the sting of being fired by the Runaways, the hard rock garage band of teenage girls he had assembled, featuring fifteen-year-olds Joan Jett and Lita Ford. In 2015, Runaways member Jackie Fox alleged Fowley had raped her as a minor in 1975.

For Leon's 1978 album, *Americana*, Fowley cowrote seven of the nine originals; there's also a lackluster cover of "When a Man Loves a Woman." Leon had Lee Loughnane of the band Chicago arranging and playing horns, alongside Loughnane's bandmates, James Pankow and Walter Parazaider.

Leon and Fowley thumbed through piles of books casting for inspiration. Michael Johnstone said Fowley would shout out, "Hey, Leon, write me a song called 'Sailor on Horseback.'" Leon said, "Kim, I can't say I've ever fancied myself a sailor on horseback; not feeling it. I'm more of a midnight lover."

"Midnight Lover" is arguably the best song on this slickly produced record. Leon's voice is drenched in slap-back tape echo like Creedence Clearwater Revival. The track is all midrange rhythm, pounding bass, Clavinet, organ, electric piano, and slide guitar. The arrangement gets broken up by a recurring horn riff from Marty Grebb (the horns on the middle-eight also tip a hat to Sly and the Family Stone's "Dance to the Music" bridge). It's like Leon's back home, right in his wheelhouse. It might be the most inspired Leon vocal performance since *Will O' the Wisp*.

It would be welcome to report that the rest of the album sustains that level. Alas. "Housewife" starts as a promising R&B song, but the lyric is so ridiculous that it makes repeated listening a challenge. Critic Robert Christgau reserved particular venom for the track in his review of the album, which he characterized as "a real con artists' summit" between Fowley and Leon: "There's a soap opera called 'Housewife' that panders so ecumenically it's been covered by Wayne Newton."

The album marks the first where Leon played almost no audible acoustic piano. Most of the piano sounds come from electric keyboards, like the Yamaha CP-70. The company had provided Leon with a new one for each major tour. He had similar endorsement deals with Kustom, RMI, and other companies in exchange for thanks in his album credits and exposure at live performances. When Yamaha stopped sending him stuff in 1978, he ordered a couple of the workers at Paradise to spray paint over the logo anywhere it would be visible to an audience.

"Elvis and Marilyn" was released as a single. It's the musical equivalent of dorm room posters of Presley and Monroe as characters in Edward Hopper's *Nighthawks* painting. It qualifies as one of the worst songs to feature Leon Russell's name in the credits. "Elvis and Marilyn though they never fell in love / Elvis and Marilyn never shared the stars above," he sings on the chorus.

It was a lost opportunity to pay tribute to someone who was a significant influence on Leon. When Elvis died on August 16, 1977, *Rolling Stone* asked Leon for a statement. He wrote in part:

I was surprised at how strongly the death of Elvis Presley affected me. . . . Now I have a lingering feeling that there is a permanent void in the place and am reminded of that "above the waist only" time when ELVIS emerged. A time of Eisenhower and Nixon. A time when modern vestiges of Puritan radicalism were being tested. But Nixon came back and the puritanical potential is still with us. I have a strong concern for a future in which Anita Bryant could become president under the banner of equal employment opportunities for women. ELVIS was to love, to laugh at, to listen to with secret hearts, to imitate, to use as a comparison for the culture he created, but he wasn't supposed to die.

For the B-side, Leon wrote "Anita Bryant," a lament for his high school classmate. A Bible thumper, Bryant spent the 1970s and 1980s veering between commercials for orange juice and spewing hatred for homosexuals. But Leon's song is a compassionate plea to his ex-schoolmate over a smooth R&B backing track. His lyric is not consternation so much as solicitude; he argues for Bryant to consider the compassionate Christ, not the stern Old Testament God.

"Housewife," "It's Only Me," and "Elvis and Marilyn" were cowritten by Dyan Diamond, another underage protégé of Fowley who was in the band Venus and the Razorblades. She was fifteen or sixteen years old when she wrote with Leon and Fowley, which might explain some of the juvenile lyrics.

Fowley got a point on the record (a 1 percent royalty), which is a standard agreement for a producer, so Leon might have considered some of what Fowley did as valuable production, not just songwriting. But in the credits, Leon is the only one listed as producer, and Fowley got a thanks on the back cover. "Believe it or not, Leon Russell made me cry," Fowley said. "I was producing an album for him, and he turned to me one day and he said, 'Do you know how good you are?' He actually thought I was good in the studio. I broke down and cried in front of him and his entire band because he was the first one who had ever told me I was good."

Frank Latouf said *Americana*'s rough recordings were more satisfying before the final mix got gussied up: "Some of the raw basic tracks before it was mixed and remixed and before they came up with the final product sounded great. I think that the raw mixes was the real Leon Russell. It was like Leon's stuff, going back to *Carney* and beyond. But strings were added, and the horn sections were added, and it took away from some of those songs."

Michael Johnstone agreed. "I was mighty impressed hearing the play-back sessions, which was essentially a nine-piece band playing live and recorded at the same time. . . . Then, in the process of overdubbing the other features and finally the mix-down, somehow the finished tracks lost about 25 percent of what I really liked about them the night they were recorded. . . . Bottom line, when Denny Cordell left the picture, Leon's records started being overproduced."

As much as it's hard to give Cordell too much credit for Leon's records, it's hard to blame Fowley for anything lacking in the production of *Americana*. After all, he was mining edgier sounds at the time. But Latouf said, "Fowley had a great deal of influence on Leon at the time."

Blue Bridges-Fox said, "He'd always listen to the wrong people. You could pick two people, and whoever was the most dishonest, he would think that he was on his side. He listened to Kim Fowley!"

Americana came out in the summer of 1978, and the Russells and their band toured into the fall. Leon and Mary generally headed out on long weekends of four- or five-day legs, flying back home to reset and record. In February, they played Radio City Music Hall. The *New York Times* review was blunt: "For a man who hasn't had hits lately, the hall was remarkably well filled. Unfortunately, though, it was not a very good show, and the main reason was that neither Mr. Russell nor his wife seemed able or willing to assume the role of on-stage focus."

Rather than two forces coming together to create a more powerful entity, they weakened and almost neutralized each other. There was little musical interplay in live performances, and now the duo records were over. Mary worked on *Heart of Fire* with a usual cast of musicians and technicians. It also featured a newcomer to the Paradise Records stable, bassist and singer Wornell Jones, who would release his own record on Paradise in 1979.

Leon signed Jones to Paradise—twice. Henderson was also supposed to sign with the label. "But Leon and Patrick kind of fell apart on the publishing and the writer stuff," said Jones. "It got real tricky." In 1978, a copyright's life shifted from fifty-six years to the life of the creator plus seventy years. "I didn't know about that change," said Jones. "Leon did. So I ended up signing two contracts. One, he told me, he lost, and I went, '*Really?*' So he got my publishing. That was being in the University of Russell."

Leon nonetheless acted as a mentor to Jones. "We used to have these 'kitchen summits,' where he would cook linguine and clam sauce with butter. We would spend a couple of hours in the kitchen talking. I learned a lot." Jones worked on his own material but was on call for Mary's solo record, playing multiple instruments and singing backgrounds. "She was trying to be independent of him as a producer. I could tell there was a lot of tension going on between the two of them. There were days, he would lock himself in the room for the day. There was a little bit of friction in the air. I could feel it."

Leon's waning ticket sales intersected with the enterprising ambitions of some rookie promoters. Recognizing that Leon's audience (and the rock 'n' roll generation in general) had been settling down, with less free time, fading enthusiasm for attending cacophonous arena shows, and, most relevant, more disposable income, promoter Stan Solomon put together a show at a 1,883-seat theater in downtown Miami that was once home to the Florida Philharmonic. With a buffet, valet parking, and other big-night-out features and the ticket prices between $22.50 and $100 (in 1978 dollars), the event was a bust. Most of those who attended got their tickets free. *Miami Herald* writer John Huddy called it "an elitist event, an extravagant one, an overdue answer to those grim baseball stadium affairs, a Great Step Forward in concert promotions, a decadent excess, a potential bust—or somewhere in between."

The concept was ahead of its time: Since the nineties, deep-pocketed rock fans have been perfectly willing to pay a premium, even in those sports arenas, for VIP tickets. And a number of venues cater to older fans who seek a supper-club-like intimacy and higher-quality room. In time, Leon would become a regular on that circuit.

But in '78, this was something novel. "We're talking about an untapped market," Solomon said. "Concerts today are aimed at thirteen-, fourteen-, and fifteen-year-old kids. What about the original audience for rock 'n' roll, who want to see Leon Russell, who still like rock, and who today are successful, affluent young professionals?" The term "yuppie" (meaning "young urban professional") was on its way.

Leon was perfectly emblematic of the scenario Solomon described. Once a gritty, soulful, denim-clad rock star, who had recently filled those stadiums for the masses, now he was a married man in beige suits and a fedora making polished love ballads with his wife. The Leon and Mary

"Paradise Road Show" was a seated and refined affair, even though he was still known to strap on a guitar and get up on the piano (he also fell off once, injuring himself). Leon was now maturing alongside his audience.

On November 13, 1978, Mary and Leon welcomed their daughter, Tina Rose, into the world, but their marriage was on the rocks. One unorthodox path they took was bringing Leon's ex, Carla, to live with them and care for the kids. They paid her a stipend, along with room and board, a suite in their house. This would be a recurring theme in Leon's life: the shepherd trying to gather and keep his expanding flock together. He had always envisioned his bands and employees as sort of a family and yearned for an actual family band. His objective with bringing in Carla was twofold; he could help her get on her feet while keeping Blue—who had been there since the previous August—in his life. Carla could help watch the kids, allowing Mary to keep working. Mary was cool with it. In fact, she and Carla became friends.

"When [Carla] first came out there to California, [Leon and Carla] went outside to a little porch swing, and they sat on the porch swing," Blue said. "And he said, 'Why'd you sue me?' She said, 'Because you bought that green-eyed n-word a Mercedes-Benz and you were real showy about it.' She said he had that little Leon grin, and went, 'Okayyyy, Carlo [a nickname he had for her].' And they never spoke about that part again. He did try to tell her he didn't want her to have boyfriends when she was living out there. She was like, 'You're out of your fuckin' mind!'"

Mary longed to get out from under Leon's wing, years after being freed from the tight control of her previous husband, Gentry McCreary. "Mary was never assertive," said Blue, who is still friendly with Mary. "She didn't get paid for any of that shit she did on Shelter. She had an allowance from Dad. It's not like, 'You're married to me; you get the checkbook.'" Some characterized Mary as a devout church girl whose marriage to a rock star was a culture shock. Others said Mary was not timid about partying.

Mary also had to deal with the outwardly racist and sexist contingent among Leon's fans. It was a strain on both Mary and Leon. But they grappled with personal issues that had little to do with external factors. Mary refused to be interviewed for this book (though she was helpful in sharing chronology via Blue). But Blue said that Leon's extramarital interests became an issue. The couple decided to take a break.

Carla and Leon would take drives together, like in the old days, talking through their problems. Carla acted as something of a marriage counselor for Leon and Mary. "He loved Carla," Matt Harris said. "She was straight up. She was the only person who was like, 'Fuck this Leon shit. You're Russell Bridges, motherfucker.' The thing with Mary was, she was the one that kicked his ass. She was the one that he was in love with. Period. And that's why his pain was so extreme."

Blue said Leon had not indulged in drugs since his angel dust experiments, but "his addictions [were] straight-up food and sex." She said he would casually have porn on the television, which she said he did little to conceal. Band members in later years also noted that Leon would openly have porn playing on the television in the bus, just watching casually. And, just as in the time immediately before Mary, there was a multitude of women. Blue said that during such binges, he went for the women who made themselves available to him.

He was also a compulsive eater, and it started to show in his weight. "If you look at pictures of him, he gets the potbelly 'cause he was drinking a lot of beer in those years with Mary," Blue said. "If you look at him from . . . I'd say between '79 and '89, I bet you he gained a hundred to a hundred and fifty pounds." As with sex, Leon was not the most discerning when it came to food. Sure, he appreciated fine dining. But primarily, he was looking for quantity and comfort when satisfying both cravings. He liked greasy burgers, barbecue, soul food, and Southern all-you-can-eat buffets at truck stops.

"He got fat, and I picked at him a little bit on that," Michael Johnstone said. "I said, 'You know, it will never be easier than it is right now to get that together. Because when you get older, it's not going to be so easy. It's gonna cause other health problems.'" But nothing was quite filling the void and relieving the pain as the marriage crumbled.

Chapter 29

Life and Love

IF THE BLISS OF LEON'S good days with Mary did not yield a whole lot of stellar material, his heartbreak over the disintegration of their relationship at least inspired the classic "One More Love Song," the first track on his next solo album, *Life and Love*. The song is like a real-time bulletin from an unraveling marriage, a glimmer of hope still alive.

Life and Love is consistently inspired, but one can only imagine what the songs would sound like with more organic production. Instead, Leon burrowed deeper into one-man-band territory, working exclusively with a drum machine and other instrument sounds conjured via his keyboards. Still, the songs are top-shelf.

On *Life and Love*, the drum machine was the prototype that Leon inspired his protégé Roger Linn to develop, the first commercially available, digital and programmable drum machine, and the first using samples of real drums. "Before working with Leon, I always thought drum machines were just bad-sounding," said Linn. "They would make records sound cheaper. But Leon would always use drum machines in the recording process in order to keep the tempo steady [a click track]. And that way, if for example, he wanted to replace the drum part and record with another drummer, he could do that."

Leon started to embrace the actual sound of machines and replaced his drummers with them, starting with *Life and Love*. Now he was able to program the beats he wanted, not a factory-set loop. "We could make entirely overdubbed records and get exactly the sound he was looking for," Linn explained. "On *Life and Love*, to his credit, he used that as a featured part and a new sound, and it ended up being a sound that people would use in recordings."

The eureka moment might have come during the recording of "One More Love Song." According to Sam Bush, Leon tried to get a certain sound by banging a couple of plastic ashtrays together on the chorus. Mark Lambert, who would join Leon as a coproducer/engineer, and band member around 1988, said Leon was also tapping bottles to get percussion sounds. "According to Leon, his story was that they were breaking Coke bottles or Pepsi bottles on the backbeat of everything. He said it was so hard to punch him in and clean up the [recording], so he said to Roger [Linn], 'Why can't you just put that on some kind of chip that we can hit a button and make that happen?' And basically, that was [an] inspiration [for Linn's drum machine]."

Linn said the idea of a great drum machine had been on Leon's mind for a while, much as he had the idea of a Mellotron before those had started to be mass-produced. "What's interesting is that Leon actually had conversations with Mr. [Ikutara] Kakehashi, the founder of Roland, about making a programmable drum machine. And actually, Leon had some blueprints of a machine that Kakehashi had envisioned. And if you think about it, Roland already had programmed drum machines. They had to have a programmable drum machine somewhere in-house in order to make the programmed beats. I think there was one programmable drum machine from EKO [EKO ComputeRhythm (1972)], that used a bunch of buttons to turn on and off to program beats. So, that idea was around, but Leon, in the same way that he helped remove my negative filter on drum machines, we had some discussions about the idea of a machine where you could program the drum beats. He had a lot of ideas. Very smart guy."

Leon had fired Linn as an engineer a year or two earlier. "It was hard at the time, but largely it made sense because I was really getting sick of being the tape op behind the desk." Linn went off to work on other things, chiefly his drum machine prototype. He stuck a drummer friend of his named Art Wood in a closet and recorded each drum sound, one at a time, as samples, into an analog-to-digital converter that Linn had made. "Actually, they're very poor quality sounds, but people now associate those sounds with beautiful creativity of the early recordings that are made with them, so it's lucky for me."

Once he had the machine up and running, Linn came back to visit Leon. "He was very excited about it. It was just a prototype, and I just had one. And he said, 'I want to buy one.' And I said, 'No, I don't have one.' And he said, 'No, no—you can make one more of these.' It was hard to make a second one, but he insisted."

"It was made on these kits that you'd buy to experiment with electronics as a ten-year-old kid, which uses perf board," Michael Johnstone recalled. "He'd pull up a fader and push the button, and there was drums. And Leon was like, 'Damn, that's really drums!' The very first one was almost two feet wide, two feet deep. And then the LinnDrum, that first one he mass-produced. *Life and Love* was made on the very first one. [Leon] had two of them, and Stevie Wonder had the other two."

"I finally found a band I could get along with," Leon told Bush.

Linn continued: "He said, 'I tell you what, if you make me another drum machine just like this prototype of yours, I'll give you producer credit on the album that I'm going to make.' And on *Life and Love*, I'm listed as coproducer."

There is a handwritten note signed by Linn that reads:

—DRUM MACHINE AGREEMENT—

Roger gives Leon the Compal-80 based prototype drum machine used on the "*Life and Love*" album when Leon returns from his tour approx. May 15. Roger has the right to use it up to 2 days per month.

Leon gives Roger "Co-Producer credit," "Drums" credit, and one point on Leon's album, "*Life and Love.*"

Before April 6, 1980, Roger gives Leon one "L+M Electronic Innovations Drum Machine" (if the company has not folded) in exchange for which Leon will make sure that Roger has made $6,000.00 in royalties from his point on "*Life and Love.*"

A November 29, 1979, letter from Diane Sullivan to Leon's accountant, Bill Hoyt, reads: "Leon agreed to pay ahead of time for the balance due on the new drum machine Roger is building. Roger has said that he'll settle for $2500.00 instead of the $3000.00 that is actually due. The check must be drawn to: Linn & Moffett Electronics, Inc."

"He paid very poorly," Linn said. "But you know, it's okay. I didn't need much money, and I felt very privileged to be working with someone who was so famous, so influential, so it all worked out. Plus, I was getting to live there in his house for free, and I would have access to all these famous musicians."

Leon's was the first prototype, and *Life and Love* was the first album to use it, but one has to dig to find his name among articles and discussions of who first used the machine on a record. Herbie Hancock, Prince, and Human League were among those employing it right after Leon on *Life and Love*. But by the time these others used the LM-1, as it became known, it was commercially available. "It was in mid-to-late '79 that I introduced my drum machine," he said. "I started taking deposits for it." The LM-1 retailed for $4,995 in 1980. The LinnDrum came out in 1982 and was relatively more affordable, at $2,995, and that's what took off and is most associated with the sounds of the early 1980s.

Linn, though, was unequivocal in saying of Leon, "He had no connection with me starting my company and inventing my machine, other than he showed his interest in the idea of a drum machine where the programmer could be inferred into the machine."

"Leon felt Roger made all the money," said singer Syd Straw, who was out to dinner with Leon about ten years later. It was the first time she had met Leon, who had by then moved to Tennessee. Her manager at the time was Sherman Halsey, Jim Halsey's son, who had grown up idolizing Leon. By then, Leon had married Jan, and they were all out to dinner in a revolving restaurant atop a Nashville hotel. "We were slowly spinning when he told me about telling Roger about [his idea for a programmable drum machine], and then he was amazed because Roger went out and did it and then called it the LinnDrum. He seemed wry about it: 'Yeah, this kid, he used to follow me around like a puppy . . . and he just took all of my ideas, ran with it, and did it.' But Leon also had a prototype in his garage."

Linn explained, "Sometimes I like to say I went to the University of Russell. Leon was a very talented guy but, in my view, suffered from ego problems common to music stars who achieve success at a young age. They stay at one emotional age the rest of their life. As a result, he was sometimes prone to arrogant behavior or easily disprovable statements like, 'I was the inventor, you were the implementer.' When he told me this, I smiled and didn't contradict him, not wanting to hurt his feelings because I respected and admired him. With Leon, you tended to forgive a lot."

Linn felt it was a classic case of the protégé moving out from under the mentor's wing. "I felt quite privileged to be able to work with him. But he did have kind of a depressive leaning, so it was hard for him because when I worked with him, he was only about thirty-three, which is very young, but he looked very old, he had gray or white hair, almost, and he almost walked with a limp. That affected his health. So I think he probably felt older than his biological age. He had a sense of humor, and he had humility. But there were still times when that ego would show through in his interactions with people."

Gordon Rudd left Leon to work for Linn's first company. "At one point, I calculated that I had spent $3,000,000 of Leon's money [$14,000,000 in 2022 money] with nothing to show for it," Rudd said. "For all the work and money invested, there didn't seem to be any payoff."

Recorded chiefly in Studio C, in the house on Ledge, across from the Magnolia warehouse, *Life and Love* is a vast improvement over *Americana*—like when *Will O' the Wisp* followed *Stop All That Jazz*. The drum machine fails to swing the way a good drummer would on "Struck by Lightning." But the song betrays a welcome Mose Allison influence. Willie Nelson's longtime wingman, Mickey Raphael, wails some raunchy blues harmonica. The assertive "Strange Love" harkens back to the Asylum Choir's "Tryin' to Stay Alive" but with a New Orleans groove. The side finishes with the title track, a hopeful ballad about a faithful promise. The drum tracks are too busy and too loud in the mix. Still, it is a solid song.

The midtempo "On the First Day," which opens side two, is the most direct address to Mary on the record to that point: "Now you're laughing as you walk away / On the last day." Leon gives one of his best vocal performances, a subtle, dynamic, controlled tenderness. He lets "on the last day" lay out unresolved, as he digs more stridently into his piano part. As a track, it's ahead of its time, akin to Marvin Gaye's "Sexual Healing" three years early. The very next song, "High Horse," takes aim again at Mary. It makes you wonder what Mary's sister, Frances Pye, must have been thinking as she sang soulful backing parts on this blistering indictment.

The requiem for the marriage, "Sweet Mystery," makes a gloomy and obscure allusion. Against a 6/8-time gospel-soul ballad, Leon sings the middle-eight, "Sad lights along the Houston highway / Another man dead from the truckin' game." This refers to an incident that happened on tour with Leon and Mary a few years earlier. Leon had hired an ex-con, Mickey Crocker, to haul his gear overnight ahead to gigs in a semitruck. "It was late one night, and Mickey was coming over the hill down in Texas somewhere, and another semi had a problem, and it parked on the side of the road, just over the hill and had stopped," Tom Russell said. "And the driver was getting out to go see his truck just as Mickey topped the hill and smashed the door and driver right off. He went up on top of the truck; it killed him instantly."

On "Sweet Mystery," Leon bares his soul again in his vocal performance, a peek into an unfathomably deep vulnerability. It is so sorrowful a blues that there's an instinct to turn away: *This is just too sad.*

Tina Rose grew up not knowing her parents together. She later listened to Leon's and Mary's records. *Life and Love* was a bracing experience. "I was just like, 'Oh *my God.*' It was just so beautiful and heartbreaking at the same time. It came from a place of love, despite all of the mess. And my stepmom [Jan], it was really sweet, she really confirmed that for me. She said, 'Your dad was madly in love with your mom.'" Jan was to enter the picture that same year.

On the last track of *Life and Love*, "On the Borderline," Leon sings worryingly about his mental well-being, reeling between a "new desire" and an open contemplation of suicide. He sings harrowingly, "Think it's time for life to end." Mickey Raphael again features prominently on the track. He was in town with Willie Nelson and the rest of his band to make the album *Willie and Leon: One for the Road*, culled from sessions also recorded on video at Leon's Toluca Lake home studio. Subsequent DVD releases consist of about an hour's worth of material, with a few conversational segments and introductions from the two singers. The double live-in-studio album features twenty songs, only about a quarter of which are in the video. Each collection features several songs not on the other.

"Willie had this idea that he was going to do a string of duet records with people he admired, and the one he did with me happened to be the first one of the series," Leon said. "We cut 126 songs in five days. So, somewhere, there's about another 106 songs that didn't make it to the record."

Willie and Leon had seen a good deal of each other since first meeting in the early seventies. In addition to the high-profile Picnics, they joined on more intimate shows, such as a gig at the Troubadour in LA in 1974. Leon even wrote and recorded a tribute to his friend: "Sweet Willie," which he'd played to Nelson at the 1976 Picnic.

It's another instance in this year of Leon opening himself completely. Johnette Napolitano said that during this time, "The divorce devastated him and cost him everything. . . . We called it Leon's divorce record." She was referring to *One for the Road* but might as well have been describing *Life and Love*. The recording sessions overlapped. Indeed, the title of the latter was likely inspired by a lyric from "My Adobe Hacienda," which he and Willie recorded and includes the line "life and love are more complete."

Leon's video bus was not yet finished enough to work on the Willie project, so they had gear up in the second floor of the studio. Once Johnstone set up the audio portion, he had little else to do, so he started working on the video equipment. Johnstone soon became Leon's right-hand man for video matters. The gear was so new that they did not really have time to set it up properly, Gordon Rudd said. "We had probably the most sophisticated mobile video capability in the country, and the results I saw could have been made by a high school kid with a smartphone."

Using a blend of Leon's current sidemen and Willie's band, they plowed through acres of songs. Leon would thumb through songbooks on his piano. He had lyrics written out on cue cards, which can be seen in some of the video clips. The album consists of all covers, while the video includes some originals. Accompanied only by Leon, Willie offers a staggering version of his composition "Funny How Time Slips Away."

"I guess Willie Nelson's always been my favorite songwriter," Leon says in one of the introduction cutaways. Willie was forty-six and had finally made it as a star, not just a songwriter. His 1975 *Red Headed Stranger* had taken the music industry by surprise, the first of three straight number one albums. He was not going to take the big stages and new audiences for granted. Leon, on the other hand, had done just that with his own audience. As a result, the two men's fortunes had reversed. Leon, at age thirty-nine, was at his lowest ebb yet, surveying the ruins of his marriage and his career. Willie helped draw his friend up from the muck.

"I remember that session," Willie said. "We always had a good time together. Leon and I laughed, talked, and joked a lot. He was an incredible musician and an incredible person to go along with it, and I'm lucky to have known him. I think the good musicians know and appreciate other good musicians, no matter whether it's Tchaikovsky or Jerry Byrd. Leon played Leon. No one else could play him. No one else heard the same notes, chords, the same thing that he did. He was an individual who played his own music, and nobody else could touch it, and we didn't try. We just knew it was Leon, and that's as good as it gets."

Their version of "Heartbreak Hotel," noted Napolitano, "was a massive hit and that turned out to be Leon's divorce money." One of the highlights of the video is an appearance by Maria Muldaur and Bonnie Raitt on the 1920s blues "Trouble in Mind," another song that openly contemplates suicide. Muldaur (who had a top ten hit in 1973 with "Midnight at the Oasis") trades lead vocals with Leon and Willie, while Raitt slices through with her commanding slide solo and adds a third vocal harmony to the refrains. The title track is another that captures Leon's state of mind at the time: "One for My Baby (and One More for the Road)" was composed by Harold Arlen and Johnny Mercer in 1943, first recorded by Fred Astaire, and elevated to a torch-song standard by Frank Sinatra in 1958. In a desolate denouement, the singer opens his heart to a bartender at closing time.

Leon tried a few more video projects. He recorded a *Paradise Show* accompanied by Ambrose, and he did one with J. J. Cale that rivals the Willie Nelson episode. It includes Jim Karstein, Larry Bell, and some others from the old days in Tulsa.

"We did the Willie thing, and then we concentrated on the bus," Johnstone said. "We took it then to the big room, and we shot the J. J. Cale thing there. By then, Jack Jester was a disturbed personality," Johnstone said. "He started locking horns with Leon. So I watched him and learned everything that he did. Leon says, 'Jack is getting on my nerves. What does he do that we really need?' I said, 'Nothing. I can do everything he does.'"

"Jack was a wild man," Frank Latouf said. "He had that crazed look in his eyes. But he was a good guy. Then one day, the whole thing blew up. Jack produced a late-night video—it was like Jack was upset and had to get it out of his system, and put down everybody: 'This guy and that guy is a worthless sack of shit.' And he named everybody that worked in the company." The only person he complimented was Latouf, who didn't enjoy being singled out.

On February 26, 1979, Jester typed an eight-page single-spaced letter to Leon that began, "Dear Bozo," and only gets more entertaining from there. It's unhinged and more than a little comical, but it also is threaded with valuable and lucid insights insofar as one can navigate Jester's instability. A few highlights:

> Leon—I have no idea at all what condition or mood you may
> be in as you read this. Maybe it will be 1:00 P.M. and you'll be
> in a foul mood or perhaps you'll be loaded or shitfaced drunk
> or in agony over Mary or in ecstasy over Mary or who knows.
> And I don't think I care what condition you are in. But at least I
> finally know that I cannot take responsibility for your condition
> or your attitude or your actions or even your lack of actions. . . .
> Leon, I don't know whether you and I are still working together
> or not. As I write these pages, I believe we are. Otherwise, I am
> truly wasting even more time on your self-centered carcass than it
> deserves—at least from me.

Jester stated that Leon had asked him multiple times to tell him what Jester really thought of him. "So let us begin," he wrote. And seemingly unaware (if we're being charitable) of Leon's palsy, he immediately launched into Leon's appearance while commenting about his limp, which he implied is an affectation, calling it a "half drunken swagger—half peg leg pirate from Treasure Island walk." He continued:

> I suppose you are handsome to certain types of dissatisfied
> women. At least you always seem to have a six pack of them
> around panting to be kicked by you or at least thrown some
> sort of casual old bone. (No sexual pun intended.) Except for a
> slightly weak chin and a full rather wet lower lip that seems to
> promise sensuality but usually also seems all too ready to either
> pout or snarl.

Next, Jester threw out some severe financial warnings. "Leon trusted Jack with everything," Latouf said. "He was, in fact, super smart, brilliant, and able to communicate and take command immediately with no hesitation. Leon saw something in Jack, and that was a guy who could take control of not only the video end of the business but his personal entertainer career life also." Leon had no manager. Even Buddy Jones was well out of the picture. There was no formal executive leadership at Paradise. Jester filled that vacuum.

Jester's letter continued:

> Do you by any chance have any idea of just how much money you and your various companies own? You are approximately 2 Million dollars in debt. TWO MILLION DOLLARS.

Then he abruptly shifted gears:

> Mary called me here . . . to see if I was alright. She seemed really concerned. . . . Mary had seen that I was very upset and near exhaustion from trying to keep your leaky corporate ship afloat. . . . You have a wife smarter than you realize, Leon, and I believe she can carry her share of future company responsibility if you quit trying to control and manipulate her.

He broke down the significant components of Leon's debt, with $1,250,000 owed to Warner Bros., $250,000 under accounts payable, and $385,000 of "Long Term Liabilities as of 9/1/78," and "overhead averaging somewhere between $35,000 and $50,000 a MONTH!" He warned, "Leon, you are spending money at an excessive rate."

Jester begged Leon to sell the Willie and Leon video and beseeched, "You must do a BLOCKBUSTER album NOW for Warners."

Jester also advised Leon he needed a manager and needed to take "Mary, her sisters, and half of Toluca Lake on an extended tour now." He alluded to a "magnificent" $5,000 offer from NET [public television] to buy the Leon and Willie show. And he explicitly called out exaggerated asset values Leon used on a financial statement for a loan (there is a lot of paperwork about loans in Leon's archives). "In any serious litigation, you and Mary would come out skinned alive."

Jester mentioned a meeting in the couple's living room on February 13, when they discussed Leon's "mental health problems. . . . You agreed to seek counseling—to let Mary promote her album her way—to let me edit the video special my way. . . . But none of that happened. . . . Your whole dumb future career is in the hands of inept yes men."

Cartoonish as Jester's letter was, it was accurate about Leon's looming crises in the form of contracts, loans, and other commitments (and this was before the divorce). In August of 1977, the attorney David Braun, who had convinced Leon to break with Denny and Shelter, sent a termination letter referencing their initial agreement from September 9, 1975, that said Braun's firm was to receive 5 percent of Leon's recording agreement. Braun refers to the contract with Warner Bros.: "We believe that our participation in your gross compensation for negotiating your recording agreement and for working out your problems with Denny Cordell is a fair and reasonable fee. . . . We intend to enforce it. We hope it is not necessary to institute legal action to enforce it."

"Depending on where Leon was popular, he could sell out," Latouf continued. "But I can tell you most of Leon's live shows did not sell out, and sometimes there were only three to four hundred people at the venue, which is why he was forced to downsize to smaller venues and less money. I pretty much knew the end was in sight after Jack left. Small plastic self-adhesive signs were placed on every door of the facility that said, 'God Will Provide.' Working for the Professor [Leon] was always exciting, I was working sixteen-hour days on a fixed salary. If you expected to make money working for the guy, forget it. And never, never expect a 'thank you,' or 'great job' with a pat on the back."

"We were halfway through the J. J. Cale thing when that [Jester meltdown] happened," said Johnstone, who picked up the slack and ran the video department, such as it was. Now that the video studio was up and running, Leon would rent it out for other productions. James Taylor and J. D. Souther recorded a promotional video for their duet, "Her Town Too," a soft rock look at the aftermath of a divorce (timely enough). The singers, along with bassist Leland Sklar, guitarist Waddy Wachtel, and others, played and sang live. The video depicts the simultaneous recording of the master audio take of the single as we know it.

In a far different neighborhood from Laurel Canyon singer-songwriters singing about a divorce, the studio came to be home base for the groundbreaking *New Wave Theater*, which had started as a local access cable show spotlighting LA's rapidly booming punk rock scene. Some of the area's classic bands were showcased, like Fear, Gun Club (who were initially recorded by Noah Shark, one of the acid-eating engineers at Shelter), X, the Blasters, the Plugz, Bad Religion, Black Flag, Circle Jerks, and more. The musical acts were interspersed with absurdist comedy and satire, like an updated Hollywood version of *Mazeppa*, the underground Tulsa show featuring Gary Busey.

"It had an underground feel to it," said Johnstone, who was brought down to watch a *New Wave Theater* taping by a Paradise Studios employee. "They had this really personable, idiosyncratic host, Peter Ivers. And then behind the scenes, they had this guy who had a past. His name is David Jove. It wasn't his real name; his name was David Sniderman, alias David Jordan"—etcetera. Sniderman was the guy that Keith Richards blamed for the infamous drug bust at Richards's Redlands estate in 1967. Newspaper reports say he confessed to this on his death bed. "He had a long, illustrious past. Anyway, now he's in LA, and he's got this TV show."

The show was "starting to pick up steam because it was very interesting," Johnstone explained. "Everybody that's anybody in the punk rock scene wants to be on it. . . . I told Leon about it and brought David. Leon was fascinated by David because he was such a powerful personality. He didn't seem dark; he *was* dark. But he just seemed like a go-getter with a happening thing. We talked Leon into bringing the show over to the big room, and we shot it there a number of times. And I became the technical director for that show. I remember Ray Manzarek showing up, and David Lynch showing up, and people like that. It was a real underground LA happening thing for a while." Beverly D'Angelo and Louise Goffin were on hand to help welcome the Blasters on one episode. Debra Winger and Elvira appeared. On March 3, 1983, Ivers was found in his apartment bludgeoned to death with a hammer in an apparent robbery. "He was murdered by the producer [Jove] of the show," Johnstone said, joining others in that theory. The crime was never solved.

Though Leon made at least one cameo on the show, neither punk nor new wave held much appeal for the man. He was diving into the country and bluegrass scene again. If it wasn't a carefully considered master career move, it certainly was good timing. Where his buddy Willie had brought a little more rock 'n' roll attitude into country via Leon, now Leon was appealing again to a country audience. Specifically, he was aiming for the fans of "Outlaw Country," for whom being a grizzled middle-aged rocker wasn't necessarily a negative thing. That term crystallized in the public consciousness after the release of the 1976 album *Wanted! The Outlaws*, a compilation that included Willie, Waylon Jennings, Jessi Colter, and Tompall Glaser.

One for the Road was a resounding success. The double-record set is divided between the band playing country and blues songs on one platter and the more intimate Leon-accompanies-Willie second LP. That second disc is laden with synth strings, which does water down the direct power of when the duo just performed live for the video cameras. Still, it's a solid outing. It was released on Columbia Records in June 1979, hit number three on the Top Country Albums chart and twenty-five on the Top 200, and the single, a discordantly chipper version of the forlorn Elvis song "Heartbreak Hotel," went to number one on Hot Country Songs. It was Leon's fifth gold album, nominated as Album of the Year by the Country Music Association. The single was nominated for a Grammy for Best Country Vocal Performance by a Duo or Group. The album track "I Saw the Light" was also nominated for a Grammy as Best Inspirational Performance.

Meanwhile, *Life and Love*, released a little earlier that year, did not crack the charts at all. *One for the Road* is really more of a Willie record than a Leon one, and Willie was on a roll. *Stardust*, released the year before, had sold over five million records. The two of them started touring together that spring. On a wonderful WNEW FM broadcast recording of them together at the Capitol Theatre on April 1, 1979, Leon does a gripping version of "A Song for You" on his CP-70—one song he seldom played the same way twice. "There's healing in music, folks," Leon reports over a bluesy vamp that follows a head-spinning flight through impressionistic classical and jazz before grounding again in the blues. His voice is pure as ever. He holds a note near the end like he could sing it forever.

"Thank you very much. God bless each and every one of you," Leon intones in a preacher style over a gospel church intro, with a curious mixture of irony and sincerity, dedicating the song to Willie. Leon regarded that persona as one that he could cast off as easily as he had adapted himself to it. Now it was the less fire-and-brimstone type of preacher and more the Pat Robertson contained and assuring televangelist style.

But mostly, he was there as just one of the guys in the band. Leon was at his best when he was collaborating with and elevating others. He was too stubborn and strong-willed to be able to sustain a long-term musical collaboration, but working with Willie again rejuvenated and maybe even saved him.

Leon told the *New Mexican* of Albuquerque in November that he had grown tired of the touring circuit, calling it "grueling." He was remarkably candid in the interview, explaining he was in the process of getting divorced, "and he would like his fans to know that he is again 'single and available.'"

In May, in Tennessee, Mary had joined Leon and Willie onstage. Things were not quite finished between the couple until the summer. Marty Grebb tried to broker a reconciliation. But it fell apart irreparably soon after that point. "Things were not good," Mike Johnstone said bluntly. "It hadn't been good for a while with Mary. I remember there was this picture for the back of the *Wedding Album*, Leon and Mary nose to nose. And they had a poster of that. And this guy, Scott Goddard, he took it and sliced it down the middle." Goddard was introduced to Leon by Kim Fowley and was mostly around for his comic relief. "Instead of facing each other, he put it so they were facing away from each other and taped it together on the wall in the office. And everybody thought that was a bridge too far. Leon came in, grabbed it off the wall, and crumpled it up. Everybody knew that it was over, but nobody was talking about it until she made her own record called *Heart of Fire*. I think it was a little after that they actually split up."

"I got divorced. I didn't have a band. I was really depressed," Leon said in 2010. "I didn't picture myself as a person who got divorced. I was taking pills to sleep, pills to wake up. It's not a good thing."

Leon went back to Tulsa just a-one more time. "I've decided I like Tulsa a lot," he told the *Tulsa Tribune*. "I've got a lot more friends in Tulsa than I do in California, so I'll be spending a lot more time here."

He was about to unite with his friends in New Grass Revival. When he first met them in '73, they had just finished a tour supporting John Hartford. Now they were touring with Hartford again. The tour landed in Tulsa at the Appollo-Delman theater in September 1979, during Leon's Tulsa separated-bachelor period. Sam Bush said, "He and Steve Busch were driving by the Appollo-Delman, and he saw on the marquee, 'New Grass Revival and John Hartford,' and Leon said, 'Hey, New Grass Revival! I haven't seen those guys in years. Pull in here.' And he walked in, and we were doing our soundcheck. And he ended up setting in with us that night."

John Cowan had joined New Grass on bass in 1974. Cowan recalled, "[Leon] was really kind of listless musically at that point. He wasn't doing anything; he was not on the road. That [show] was the beginning of what came to be known as Rhythm and Bluegrass."

A reporter from the *Tulsa World* witnessed the show. "When the New Grass Revival took the stage . . . there was an unfamiliar face joining the group—unfamiliar as a New Grass member, but a very familiar to Tulsans," wrote Doug White. "Leon Russell made a triumphant return to his hometown and played a total of six tunes with New Grass as an unbelieving capacity crowd totally lost control. Russell left the stage after doing three of his songs, including 'Heartbreak Hotel,' but returned twice more during the one hour New Grass set. He finished with 'Rollin' in My Sweet Baby's Arms,' and 'Prince of Peace.'" They ended up at Steve Busch's house, jamming until the wee hours of the morning. The night revitalized Leon, sparking his creativity.

But the unwanted attention brought by being a big fish in a small pond back home in Tulsa started to annoy him. A *Tulsa World* article on October 19, 1979, was headlined TOP ROCK STAR TURNS TULSA COURTHOUSE ON. Leon was mobbed while renewing his passport. He had not traveled outside the country for years, and he was planning a trip to Nigeria with Ambrose. "No sooner had he taken off his mirror-lens sunglasses Thursday afternoon and sat down at a desk when gawkers gathered outside the glass-walled office," read the article. "Bolder ones walked in quickly, asking for autographs." Reflecting about it five years later, he told the *World*, "Tulsa wasn't used to my sort of reality. I went to the bank to borrow $50,000 and that prompted a story studying the finances of people in the music business."

He left Tulsa and would not live there again. Leon moved into the house on Ledge in Burbank. Jack Jester was not yet gone and had written a letter in September that was more professional than the February diatribe, with suggestions on some of the video productions but also advice on what to pay various employees. For example, Jester pointed out that Leon's indispensable assistant Diane Sullivan was making less than $400 a week.

"That's when they were planning to get a divorce," Mike Johnstone said. "And he moved into the house, where the Paradise offices were. You went back down the hall, and there was another half a house—two or three bedrooms down there, and the kitchen. Another door and you were in Studio C, which was a full-blown studio. It was two houses put together."

Leon sat Blue down to tell her that he and Mary were separating and that he would be living outside of the house. Along with Carla, Blue was still living with Mary, Teddy, Tina, and Mary's son Gentry at the Toluca Lake house. "We would do visitation at Daddy's," said Blue. Before Tina Rose was born, the blended family was photographed for the back cover of *Make Love to the Music*. Leon lounges on one end of a camelback sofa with Blue on his lap. Mary's on the other end, with her son Gentry between them. Toddler Teddy is standing in front of a toy piano, seemingly irritated that his half-sister Blue is leaning down to play a note on the keyboard. The depiction was one of a short-lived period of domestic tranquility.

"We'd go to the studio, the little house across from Paradise, and we had a blast! We loved going there," said Blue. "I loved going over there. He just let me run rampant. He took me to movies. Sometimes, Teddy and Tina would come, too, and sometimes they wouldn't. When he took me to see *Superman*, when we were leaving, this man says to him, 'Is that Leon?' He looked right at him and then grabs my hand and said, 'Not tonight, I'm not.' It's my favorite story because it made me feel so special and like I had him to myself—because he wasn't enough. We just had to share him. We really did."

Chapter 30

One More Love Song

WHEN NEW GRASS RETURNED FROM the tour, they got called back into battle. "I get a call from Diane Sullivan. So now we got to cut some songs in Nashville with Leon," Sam Bush recalled. "Leon got turned on to the idea of his fusion with bluegrass, because he had such a good time jamming that night [in Tulsa], and realized that our timings could match up. We played on the fast side of the beat, too, and he liked that Pentecostal feeling. We later discovered in shows when there'd just be a look in his eye, and we knew that we were going to start speeding this song up. It was never totally planned out, that we just kept speeding up, keep speeding up, keep speeding up till he stopped, bang! Pentecostal hysteria!"

They recorded in RCA Studio A on Music Row in Nashville. "Ostensibly was to be called *Hank Wilson Volume II*. I just sang on it," John Cowan said. "As a matter of fact, he used the same old legendary session guys. He said, 'Go get me some music songbooks.' I was always astounded at his ethnomusicology. He did know them, but at the same time, he didn't know the lyrics. So he knew the melodies, and he kind of knew the chords, and he just sat there with a book in front of him. And that's how we recorded."

After the Nashville sessions, Leon flew the band out to Burbank to record more songs and vocals at Paradise, putting them up at the studio-office house on Ledge, where they helped finish off the record. "When we first got there, he was splitting up with Mary, and it was painful," Bush recalled. "She stopped by to hear what he was doing, that was about it.

"We made a whole studio album that Leon was very jazzed about and wanted to put out. And in fact, Warner Brothers would *not* because they

384

already had an established star right then that had just made a bluegrass album, and it was Emmylou Harris, *Roses in the Snow*. So they didn't want to put it out." The album would finally be self-released in 2001 by Leon as *Rhythm & Bluegrass: Hank Wilson, Vol. 4*.

In July 1979, Leon wrote a letter to Warner's CEO, Mo Ostin. It read, "Dear Mo, As my reputation in the music business disintegrates, I await your reply." Cowan recalled that Leon "got crossways with Mo Ostin, who was distributing Paradise. And they had something in his contract that said, 'No live albums, no country albums.' So he intentionally turned in this record to get out of his contract." In an agreement dated November 24, 1980, between Leon and Warner, the label agreed to release a live album in exchange for Leon finishing ("rerecording portions") of a studio album for a "lump sum" recoupable advance of $125,000. An extension of the contract with Warner was being negotiated for three more albums that would include advances of $250,000 for the first LP and two more options for $275,000 and $300,000.

One studio LP from the time that wasn't released was Leon's collaboration with J. J. Cale. There are ten Leon Russell compositions listed, including "Dark Eyes," "High Life," and "In Paradise," all set to an insistent drum machine. Hearing even a handful of these songs indicates that the record would have been one of Leon's best from his middle period. The tracks overcome the drum machine and still have some hair on them.

Leon took the show on the road, calling it "Leon Russell and New Grass Revival: Rhythm and Bluegrass." They stayed out there for the better part of two years. "For two years, we would open the show, and then we would back him, so it was strenuous work, I mean, it *wore our ass down*," Bush said.

They returned to Tulsa to play the Brady Theater in November of '79. Leon surprised listeners of station KMOD with an unannounced, light-hearted appearance live on air with the band. When asked what brought him back to Tulsa, Leon joked, "I left my wallet at the Paradise Club." The club, not far from Oral Roberts University, was owned by Leon's old partner in crime—and one-time partner to Carla—Jimmy Markham. The appearance on the station was arranged by old friend Jim Halsey, who by this time had a sprawling music-biz empire in Tulsa. He was still working on and off with Leon, as he had been since 1974.

Leon met Jan Constantine in 1979, before things were finally over between him and Mary and before he left Tulsa for good. "Jan was the driver of our company limo," Jim Halsey said. "Well, part of her picking people up was Leon Russell from time to time. And, you know, I guess it just went from there to serious business. She's part of the family; she really is. She did date my son Sherman. And Sherman and Leon were the closest friends probably of any friend that either one of them had."

Sherman Halsey was fifteen years younger than Leon. "Sherman had a huge poster of Leon in his bedroom and wore a top hat all over the place," said Mary Jones, who worked for the Halsey Company. "He adored Leon. Sherman was crazy about Leon back from when he was just a little boy."

Tom Britt, who would soon play guitar on the road with Leon, said, "I knew Jan before she was with Leon, through the Halsey Company," he said. "She was just this one stunningly hot girl that would come out on the road with the Oak Ridge Boys and sit by the pool, and we'd just sit there staring at her."

Sixteen years younger than Leon, Jan came from Hugo, Oklahoma, a "blip on the map." She's half Choctaw and was raised fully in that culture. She said she didn't know much about Leon but had some intuition about her fate that she attributes to her Native American upbringing. "I had no clue about him," she replied (a few interviewed laughed off that claim). "There were things that sound silly. One night in the hot tub at Jim Halsey's house with coworkers, Terry Cline [president of the Halsey Company] said he was picking up Leon Russell, and I was picking up Gatemouth Brown." Brown was collaborating with Roy Clark, another of Halsey's clients, on the *Makin' Music* LP, produced by Steve Ripley. "Out of the blue, I said, 'Yep, Leon's going to fall madly in love with me and want to marry me.' Then I sat up, went, 'Oh, my God!' I don't know where it came from. I was happily in a relationship with Jim's son, Sherman Halsey. I was madly in love, and I didn't want to be with anyone back then. That was just one of those, to me, an Indian thing that came out that I shared with a bunch of white people. I was like, 'Oh, holy shit. That's really embarrassing.'

"My mother always told me when I dated or when I was getting married to look to the person's spirit, not to their covering. I have to say, it served me well. That became just a great love affair that we had. But he had a hard time. He chased me for several months before I finally came."

Blue said that, as with her mother, Carla, Leon approached Jan with the "In time, I'll make you love me" courtship philosophy. "Even though I said that I was still madly in love with Sherman, Leon told us flat out— Sherman and myself—that I was meant to be his wife," Jan explained. "He said, 'I'm never wrong about these things.' He had that same type of thing that I have. I blocked him for a while, but my spirit knew. I missed him. I missed someone I didn't even know. I loved someone I didn't even know. Before Sherman and I met, I vowed never to love again because my mom had recently passed. I thought, 'I'm not adding anybody else to this list because it is too painful.' He changed that. It prepared me to be with Leon."

Meeting Ambrose Campbell was a catalyst for the relationship as well. "He was a funny guy, Ambrose," Jan explained. "He had this great spiritual advisor hat, but then also he was this crazy womanizer. The first time I met him was at one of Leon's shows. . . . I finally went to get him [Leon] in Norman, Oklahoma. He was playing at Oklahoma University. So my roommate and I went because I finally realized that I was being foolish and that he was definitely my heart. It took me a while to accept that. And I'm walking down the loading area, and Ambrose is walking up. And we're both looking at each other, and then we pointed, and I said, 'You must be Ambrose,' and he said, 'Ah, you must be *the one.*'

"After the show, Ambrose took me and Leon into one of the rooms and joined our hands together, and then told me all about Leon, what kind of a person he was, told me I was going to have a hard time with him, that he was hard to understand, but he knew that I was the one that would. And then he tells Leon all about me, which was crazy because he told him that I was overly sensitive, and he was gonna have to be careful with me—all these beautiful things that were mind-blowing.

"Leon felt like home. There was just something so precious about him. He made me feel good and safe. He didn't make me feel bad about myself. Later on, he did tease me as we got comfortable, but not in a way that would hurt me."

Singer Syd Straw, who was managed by Sherman Halsey and became exceptionally close with him in the eighties, said, "Sherman told me about how his dad asked him to go pick up Leon at the airport. But he was busy, so he sent Jan. And then Jan met Leon at the airport and then never separated from him. What I took away from that story was, don't send your girlfriend to pick up somebody as amazing as Leon Russell."

After Straw and Sherman had dinner with Leon and Jan later in the eighties, they went back to Leon and Jan's house. "I felt that whole dinner was so kind of tense because of his hero worship—a father figure who ran off with [his] son's sweetheart. I felt like I was babysitting his tender heart. It might have been the first time [Sherman] had seen them in a few years. I don't think he was bitter. I think he'd had a couple of years to just go, 'Wow, what a story.' But I never knew him to be with anyone for the rest of his life."

Initially, Jan said she thought Leon "was really poor, because we were living with his friend Steve Busch. Leon had made him a bedroom up in his attic. He drove a baby blue Cadillac. I didn't know a Cadillac—I didn't know cars. It was baby blue, so in my mind, that was a poor person's idea of a nice car. I thought I was going to take care of us, that I was the one that had to make the money. It cracked him up until, up to a certain point, when he said, 'Okay, this has to stop.'" He told her, "You know, I'm pretty good at what I do."

The old Tulsa crew—Busch, Leon, Emily Smith, Gerard Campbell (one of the English cohort), and a few others—was back together. It was fun until Leon decided to go back to Burbank and took Jan with him in the winter of 1980. "In a manner of speaking, it [the move away] was just because I had too high a profile for this small of a town," he told an interviewer, then glanced into a dressing room mirror: "I don't know. Do I look like I've changed?"

His physical appearance had indeed changed. Leon was looking exponentially older than his years, as if his age were accelerating at a rapid clip. "He was old to begin with when he came on the hippie scene," said his friend Cheech Marin. "When he started growing his hair long, he went gray right away and his beard white. He was always this kind of sage-looking, mystic thing. He had those cat eyes. Almost Siberian husky eyes."

A review of a poorly attended show in Sacramento read, "If you wonder what Leon Russell has been doing these past two years, it appears eating. With a noticeable paunch and a bloated face, Leon, still in possession of his patented silver mane, long beard, and ascetic mien, looked more like Baba Ram Russell, master of fork and knife, than lean Leon Russell, once gaunt wizard of the keyboards."

Jan, though, was drawn by his magnetism. When she first met Leon,

Jan felt that he was damaged and that she had to be protective of him, something she felt until his death. "I met him right after all the big stuff had happened. He was out of place when I first met him. He always had some sort of stage fright. He was scared about going back out again because Mary had made him believe that he was horrible, that he couldn't sing, that he couldn't play, and she took his faith in himself away from him. It just damaged him because she was always making him feel less-than and laughing at him. If he would sing her something or whatever, she just laughed at him. He said it was just devastating. They were married for five years, and he realized that she was killing him because she was his dream wife in the beginning. She used to play piano, she'd sing, and he liked dark women. She was the whole package because he always wanted a family that went on the road together, just like what Willie has. All his kids do sing and play, and he did get to have Sugaree, Tina, and Teddy [Leon's kids] on the road with him. He got to experience that. That was the best part of the relationship with Teddy."

"Whenever possible, my wife was fond of turning a beautiful and moving experience into a pile of shit," Leon wrote in his memoir, referring to Mary. "I had often said I would marry a woman who was a better artist than I was but wouldn't beat me over the head with that fact. With this marriage, I was successful in doing only the former. . . . This marriage was a disaster of the first order that greatly damaged my self-esteem."

In the fall of 1979, Jan was still just learning who he was. "He wants me to come with him on a date, anywhere in the world that I want to go. I had told my sister I was coming to her house for a Halloween party, and that was in McAlester, Oklahoma. And he was like, 'What?!' He said, 'I'm offering you a place anywhere in the world.' And I said, 'Well, I have to go to my sister's Halloween party.' And he just couldn't believe it."

But Leon went along. "We went as a cowboy and Indian," Jan said. "He was wearing a cowboy hat, vest; he just went as himself. I was wearing moccasins and Choctaw shirts at the time. So *I* just went as myself. And we went to her office party, and afterwards, we were just drunk. I wanted to go dancing. There was a club, and when it's in McAlester, Oklahoma, so you know it was *really* nice." She laughed, remembering.

"We get in there, and since I don't really know who Leon is yet, we go right on the dance floor. Leon's dancing with me, and some cowboy comes in, picks me up, and throws me over his shoulder. I yell at Leon,

'Get us a pitcher of beer!' When I finally get off this guy's shoulder, I go back out looking for Leon, and he's onstage. I'm dancing to his music, and he comes off, and we leave.

"The next day we're driving home, and he says the relationship's not going to work because of the way I treated him, you know, putting him through all that, taking him to my sister's party, then to a bar, and then the cowboy, you know, the whole thing. He says nobody would ever do that to him, and that I'm not who he thought I was. And I was laying down in the seat, totally hungover, so I said, 'I don't know what you're talking about.' I said, 'I was exactly who I am. I've not tricked you in any way. How did I know you don't go dancing? That's what I thought everybody did.' Then he's like, 'Oh, you're right. It's I don't do that.' And he realized that I don't know who *he* is. I haven't even seen a show at this point. I've heard maybe two songs. I haven't even been curious enough to find out, you know?"

Leon did more to try to fit into Jan's lifestyle. She liked riding a bike, so he went out and bought one for himself, but fell off it after failing to negotiate a turn. She also had told him in passing that she wanted moccasin roller skates, something that did not exist. "I told him I wanted moccasin roller skates, not for him to *buy* me moccasin roller skates, but he goes out and buys twenty pairs of moccasins, trying to get roller skates made."

Leon had always wanted to roller-skate, it turned out. But his mother bought him those metal slide-on skates with leather straps, more akin to medieval torture devices than pleasant recreational gear. They would not stay on his feet, and he would fall, he told Jan. "That's why he always enjoyed watching me do that stuff. He saw that as being fearless. He always told me I had the balls of a high diver. That was just regular everyday stuff for me. But he didn't have the body for it."

The fact that Jan wasn't some fan pursuing him was part of what attracted him to her. "I am embarrassed about the beginning, not knowing anything. But I feel like that was a blessing because he wasn't the sort to brag. And just to say he was 'pretty good' at what he did was so small. I was just myself, which is really embarrassing. I really was this little girl from Hugo who really knew nothing and hadn't been anywhere. And he exposed me to the world, to life, and taught me so much. So I'm forever grateful."

Mike Johnstone remembered when Jan showed up. "She was a new-comer to the scene. I just figured I'd wait and see, you know? That was where things were when we left for Africa."

Just before Christmas of 1979, Leon, Ambrose, and Mike Johnstone traveled to Lagos, Nigeria. "It was truly one of the monumental experiences in my life," Leon wrote. Leon said that his intent was to find distribution there for an album Ambrose recorded at the Church. But when Johnstone asked Leon what the trip was for, he said, "Michael, I want to find the roots of rock 'n' roll." Johnstone accompanied them as videographer, taking some new tech, "a forerunner of home video."

"Dad was really, really keen for Leon to see Nigeria," Ambrose's son, Danny, reported. "It was home."

Leon and Ambrose went ahead, and Johnstone joined them about a week later, lugging a footlocker full of video gear. After an arduous journey via London, he finally made it to Lagos. "I got hustled by the cab drivers and people that were trying to jam me." It took multiple bribes for Johnstone to reach Leon and Ambrose, who had encountered similar difficulties when they tried to enter the country. Ambrose had to grease an immigration officer's palm with a five-dollar bill.

Arriving on December 23, Leon was overwhelmed by the crowds as soon as they stepped out of the airport. It became profoundly surreal as Leon was greeted as "Father Christmas" by many people. Meanwhile, Ambrose was welcomed as a returning god. Those who recognized him would fall to their hands and knees before him. He was also bitten by a mosquito almost immediately, contracted malaria, and was sick for the whole trip.

Leon was struck by the chaos and corruption, which are what kept Ambrose away for decades. "Dad was quite an intelligent guy, and he spoke five, six languages," Danny noted. "He was invited to get into politics in Nigeria in the sixties. The Nigerian secret service paid him a visit and told him that me and my brothers would be assassinated if he ever attempted to get into politics in Africa. He was very much a socialist in the true sense of the word, all about equality, fairness, and people. And he found the corruption in Nigeria really difficult to deal with because he knew the people. That's where he came from."

Leon wrote in vivid detail about the juxtaposition of elements of Lagos, from the world-class airport to teeming disorder just outside the terminals, from superhighways to "an off-ramp that seemed to take us five centuries back in time," the road changing "from concrete to dirt, with potholes that were literally larger than our taxi. . . . On this road there were no lights anywhere, except for scattered small fires burning among the thousands of residents." He described the packed buses, "passengers clinging to the tops and sides and packed inside like sardines." They stayed at a hotel that was run by a friend of Ambrose. Electricity and phones worked only sporadically.

Though they never left the hotel compound without bodyguards, the three men were able to take in some of the local culture, including a pilgrimage to the New Afrika Shrine, the world-famous nightclub owned by the legendary Fela Kuti. The Shrine can be seen in remarkable videos online. Kuti's large band, the Africa 70, wore matching, brightly colored suits; Fela was generally shirtless, with white paint lining his cheeks. Band members, playing percussion and singing, would dance out to the front of the stage and through the audience. Kuti's music, which he dubbed Afrobeat, was an intoxicating brew: jazz, Afro-Cuban music, and James Brown–style funk folding back into the source music of Ghana and Nigeria. The Africa 70 would vamp on trance-like one-chord grooves for ten plus minutes. Kuti's pointedly political lyrics and his social influence were deemed dangerous enough by the government that his commune had been raided and burned down by a military junta in 1978. The reverence for Ambrose in his home country was exemplified by the mighty Fela—nineteen years younger—who regarded Ambrose as his most significant forerunner in Nigerian music.

"I got a picture of Leon and Fela Kuti and Fela's four wives," Johnstone said. "It's a great shot. It was all done on a Polaroid. One Christmas, Leon gave everybody who worked [at Paradise] a Polaroid camera. That was the only camera I had besides the video camera. [In Lagos] every time you'd take a picture, people would crowd around going, 'Ohh, ahh.' It was juju, pictures appearing right before our eyes. And they had a weird thing about photography anyway, like, some kind of magic going on there they weren't too comfortable with."

Speaking of that same magic, Ann Bell recalled an instance backstage with Ambrose. "I looked over, and he was sitting by himself in a chair. His eyes were closed, his head was bent over. Very quietly, I took a picture of him. And when he heard it click, he goes, 'Sister Ann, that will not develop.' I asked why: 'I was praying.' And every frame developed but that one."

Leon and Johnstone were on alert not to overstep their bounds, which Johnstone nevertheless inadvertently did by videotaping compelling music from a church service from his hotel window. When he was discovered doing so, it resulted in the neighborhood protesting. Ambrose had to explain to him the reasons for the outrage that he had stirred.

The Americans also felt an ever-present threat of violence. "There was much speculation among the locals about how much my head would be worth, given that I was a white man with long white hair," Leon wrote. "A price in the neighborhood of $25,000 was finally accepted as plausible payment for getting Father Christmas' head into your house for your next ceremony. . . . When we did depart the hotel, we were stopped constantly by the police. Every time it happened, Ambrose would jump out of the car and announce, 'I am Ambrose Campbell,' which seemed to make zero impression on any of the policemen. Every time we were detained I was sure we were going to be killed on the spot. They would open our trunk, trying to take whatever was in it for 'evidence.' It was all very frightening."

They felt trapped in the village where they were staying. Leon got sick of the local cuisine and wanted a steak. They also tried to go to a music store where Leon wanted to buy some African drums, but they kept getting thwarted. It turned out that Ambrose was sabotaging the effort because the shop was run by a former rival of his from the 1950s. They tried to go to a traditional cultural festival at a sports stadium, also stymied.

"After a few days, when the temperature and unpredictable power outages became unbearable, we moved to the Lagos Holiday Inn, which had electricity all the time but water only about an hour a day," Leon wrote.

"So finally, Leon had a belly full," Johnstone said. He referred to a video he recorded in the hotel room. "Leon's on the phone talking to Diane on a transatlantic call, and he got through, and it's on the soundtrack of my video. In the background you can hear Leon saying, 'I need to get the fuck out of here, Diane. I'll pay $20,000 for a Learjet to come get me.'" They went downtown to try to book a flight. "They told us all departing flights were full for the next ten days. But when Ambrose gave the clerk five dollars he suddenly found two seats on an airliner departing the next morning. Right before we were to board, a man in a black suit approached us. He carried a sawed-off shotgun and a machine pistol, and he hit the airport floor in front of us with much clattering of armament. As he dropped down and kissed Ambrose's feet, he explained that he was head of airport security and, upon recognizing Ambrose, wanted to come over and pay his respects." Leon said he almost soiled his pants.

As soon as he returned from Africa, Leon tried again to bring Jan on a date "anywhere in the world," presumably with the exclusion of Nigeria. This time, she packed her bag for Florida. "At the last minute, he changed his mind *at the airport*, and we went to New York," she said. While in New York, Leon secretly arranged to move Jan to LA. "He had his California guys go to Steve Busch's house and get all of our stuff and our cars, and drive them to California. And then we flew from New York to California. So he moves me from Tulsa to California without me knowing what was happening. He was very bold. I have to say, that's what I liked about him, though. He knew how to make decisions. And I loved it there," at the bungalow on Ledge in Burbank. Soon Leon had an addition built on the house to accommodate them. They stayed from around mid-1980 to the middle of 1981.

But Leon didn't linger very long in his new domestic scene. He hit the ground running, with Jan along for the ride, beginning a series of tours with New Grass Revival that would continue until the band broke up the following year. Like Neil Young grabbing the already-formed Crazy Horse as his backing band, Leon absconded with NGR. "For two years, it was like being in this great ensemble," Sam Bush said. "There were certain shows, you could see him start bouncing up and down on his piano stool, like, 'Here we go. Hang on!'"

The results of this inspired collaboration are captured on the *Leon Russell and the New Grass Revival—Live and Pickling Fast* video (and heard on the audio recording *Leon Russell & New Grass Revival—The Live Album*) of a May 15, 1980, concert at Perkins Palace in Pasadena, one of the rare successes of the video arm of Paradise Studios. Leon said at the time, "Shortly, all Paradise artists will be recorded and released on video." He and the band play with ferocious energy on the recordings, with three-part vocal harmonies, as they romp through covers and songs from Leon's albums, including a great version of "One More Love Song" from *Love and Life*. Leon sounds invigorated, especially compared to the mainly stilted duo performances with Mary. "I hear that music now, and I can hear the joy in his voice and in his screams," Jan said.

He was still playing his electric Yamaha CP-70. "Leon was loud," Bush emphasized. "We literally played, many a night, at 110 decibels. He loved the dependability of the Yamaha. It was in tune, and, yes, he loved the action and just being able to control the volume so that you're not at the mercy of anybody else. Piano players are at the mercy of others with an acoustic piano on tour. When we recorded *Rhythm & Bluegrass* in LA, I got to hear him play the rock piano, and God, it was an awesome sound. But on that record, he mainly was playing the Yamaha."

In performance, he loved and eventually required the amplification. "At that point, Leon had two Peavy amps, one on either side. I mean, I stood close to him, and it was *loud*. I literally had to start setting my amp ear level on a giant road case just to hear it. So, I don't know if I had ear damage from that." Leon certainly did. But he also likely had hereditary hearing loss that had started to affect him, and it fed a vicious cycle, turning up to overcome the loss while contributing to further damage.

"I'm proud of the backup vocals John and I did with him because I love to sing baritone, and so I got to," Bush said. "At one point, Leon told us, he goes, 'I can't lose you guys; you're right on the—harmony wise—I think you're tighter with me than Mary was.'"

For an example of those tight harmonies, listen to "One More Love Song," arguably the definitive version. Bush is a natural harmony singer, which means he not only finds the perfect notes to accompany Leon but also matches his lead, bending when Leon bends, clipping the end of his words as Leon does. Bush is like white on rice with Leon's at-times idiosyncratic and improvised phrasing. And Bush knows when to diverge and then rejoin in parallel. A great harmony singer is by definition a great listener but also a great watcher. In the video version of this same show, there's Bush, shirtless under his bib overalls, glancing over at Leon in his beige sports coat, staying right with Leon as he finishes each line of the chorus.

Cowan confirmed, "Sam, especially, was like, 'If we're going to sing, you sing like you're a goddamn Okie. I want every syllable to match with him.' It wasn't a stretch for us because we listened to his music nonstop."

"Singing with Sam and John was a real treat for me," wrote Leon. "I was not used to singing in a trio, and it was completely effortless. All I had to do was sing the lead, and they would anticipate the harmony and phrasing, seemingly by intuition."

Ray Charles's "I Believe to My Soul" is one of the standouts on a consistently enjoyable album. The band relaxes for this gospel blues. As he did through much of his career, Leon follows a Mose Allison approach instead of attempting to come close to Charles's vocal. As with a number of the songs from the show, this was among the recordings they made with the intention of releasing but that were held up until *Rhythm & Bluegrass* finally came out. The arrangement leaves dramatic spaces, and the absence of drums allows for more nuanced dynamics. "One night we were cutting songs, and that's the first time I ever even heard 'I Believe to My Soul' by Ray Charles, was when Leon taught it to us when we cut it," Cowan said. "He taught me about Ray Charles."

New Grass Revival's interpretation of "Prince of Peace" is what initially brought the band to Leon's attention back in '73, so it's no surprise that he includes it here, in an inspired version, with Bush's mandolin through a phase shifter effect. And though the ensemble's lack of a drummer and electric guitar means it is far less rock than the Shelter People's versions, this reading stands on its own, as does an inventive arrangement of "Rollin' in My Sweet Baby's Arms." The record slides into the Rolling Stones' heartbreaking "Wild Horses." It's given a bouncier tempo than the original, but it still captures the composition's deep emotion.

"That version of 'Wild Horses' is unbelievable," said Eric Clapton, who, unbeknownst to the New Grass guys, was in the audience for the show. "I saw him doing it live in LA. That was a great show. That keyboard sound that he's got, and just the accompaniment, it's a perfect setting for him."

The video version includes stunning takes of "Amazing Grace," "Of Thee I Sing," and Leon's "Jesus Will Take Me Home." Leon's solo encore performance of "A Song for You" is, again, unlike any recorded version before. He improvises a new introduction, tweaking the melody and the chords, virtually rewriting the song while remaining true to the essence of the composition. He whoops up a double-time gospel breakdown for the middle-eight for a few seconds, as if launching into a different song, then seamlessly transitions back to the familiar impressionistic chords. Then he takes a bluesy turn, followed by a switch to classical. The tone and style change vocally and on piano, sometimes within the same phrases. As he takes it to the final verse, he half-times it in a slow gospel march, tying it all together as he brings it home. It's stone genius unfolding in real time.

Leon was on the road for most of 1980–1981 with a version of the New Grass Revival until the band finally broke up, partially as a result of being ridden so hard by Leon. "I think he found working with us was a great relief because we weren't anything like anybody else that he knew," Sam Bush said. "I mean, we weren't jaded, we hadn't been through everything, and everything was new for us. He was introducing us to a new world."

"It was a most enjoyable and unusual period for me," noted Leon. "I played a lot of different kinds of venues and discovered different strata of musical performance. Many times we would take out our instruments in the waiting areas of airports, or rest areas along the highway, and play for a couple of hours. Since we didn't need electricity, we could play just about anywhere."

Leon was increasingly parsimonious on the road. "He was such a penny-pincher; we used to call him 'The Miser of Space and Time.'" Cowan laughed. Tom Britt would soon join Leon's band. "We always kind of joked that he'd step over a dollar to save a nickel," Britt chuckled. "Like his buses; he had his own guy that worked on 'em. We were rolling down the road somewhere, and the welds broke on the side of the bus that was holding the generator. All of a sudden, the generator was dragging on the highway alongside us. There was always something. Consequently, I became good at fixing generators. Another time we were playing in Memphis and it took us twelve hours to get to Nashville because the bus had a flat tire, and then it ran out of fuel; just one thing after another. It was that way with Leon."

Carl Radle was along for some of the tour, but it was not a joyful reunion with the maestro. "He had just been let go by Eric [Clapton], and that was pretty crushing for him," John Cowan said. "Carl, for sure, had a bad heroin problem. Leon has this reputation that I never understood about, you know, 'he's an asshole,' or 'he's a control freak.' But I witnessed him doing some pretty darn sweet things. Carl was broke, he was depressed, he was strung out and sick, and he asked Leon if he could give him a job. We were already rehearsed [for] this big tour with Leon, and he just hired Carl. I don't know what he paid him, but Carl came along and sat on stage completely out of it. He played congas, *sort of*. He was on the bus with us. Carl had this kind of childlike quality. He would be in his bunk all the time. Now, when he was awake, we would talk to him about music. He was my personal hero. But we didn't see much of him because he was going in and out of withdrawal all the time. Occasionally he'd ask us if we had any drugs. We didn't have any heroin, that's for sure.

"The funny thing about Leon," Cowan continued, "when we played with him there was a 'no blow' rule. You were not supposed to do cocaine, but we did it all the time and thought we were hiding it from him. Of course, he probably knew."

On May 30, 1980, about two weeks after the Pasadena show, Carl Radle was found dead from an overdose in his home in Claremore, Oklahoma. He was thirty-seven.

"Carl's death will always be one of the biggest mysteries to me of all the people I've known," Jim Karstein said. "Because evidently, Carl's death was an OD. To go from Delaney & Bonnie, and then Clapton—I guess the drug culture around all that was just too much."

Via Denny Cordell and Peter Nicholls, Carl had gotten a taste for reggae, produced the Peter Tosh sessions, and inspired Clapton to cover Bob Marley's "I Shot the Sheriff." Clapton explained, "Carl's disappearance . . . I don't know because I already was in so much trouble with booze that I had to quit the band while Carl was in it. It was lethal what we were doing to one another. It was alcohol for the English guys and drugs for the Okies. I didn't know about the depth of Carl's problem until it was too late.

"Unfortunately, with Carl, we never had the chance to say goodbye. I mean, maybe it's just the times are changing now that people, the people I've said goodbye to, we've actually gone out of our way to arrange that," Clapton said. "Either a family member has called and said, you know, 'This is the time to say something to one another.' I'm really sad that I never got the chance to talk to Carl before he left. It's a lonely world for musicians of my age now; a lot of my partners have gone."

It naturally broke Leon's heart. "Daddy loved Carl. He loved him," Blue said. "When Carl died, that was a huge thing." There had been something magical about their chemistry when Carl and Leon played together.

New Grass Revival morphed while on tour with Leon, with a couple of guys burning out. Perhaps it was fueled by the New Grass guys on cocaine, but the tempos and the pacing of Leon's songs and sets got speedier and more intense as the tour rolled along. "He would just speed songs up," Cowan said. "When we started that tour, we were booked to play forty minutes. Then we'd take a break, and we'd come out and play— whatever—two hours with him. And as the tour wore on, it got down to,

'I want you boys to just play thirty minutes tonight.' And then the songs and his show would get faster, and then eventually it was like, 'Y'all just do twenty minutes.' We'd go, 'Okay.' And *that's* why Courtney [Johnson] and Curtis [Burch] left, because it finally got down, 'Tell ya what, boys, you guys are out here anyways, we'll just do a couple of your songs in my show.' Leon wanted to get the fuck out of there. He wanted to play, get paid, and get the fuck out of there. Our set got cut shorter to where we finally didn't even have one."

"Our band broke up while we were still Leon's backup band, but he still called it 'Leon Russell and New Grass Revival,'" Bush explained. "He was augmenting the band with other people as we went along. So there were a few others already who had joined us, our friend Tom Britt from Louisville, on guitar and steel, and Leon added another percussion player named Shamsi." Shamsi Sarumi had been a friend and collaborator of Ambrose and played on Ambrose's 1966 LP *High Life Today*.

Tom Britt had played with Cowan in a rock band. Britt said, "The first time I met Leon, John Cowan brought him to my house in Evansville, Indiana. I shared a house with John. All of a sudden, a motorhome pulls up out front, and Leon spends the week."

Bill Kenner was added on second mandolin. "So we had two mandolins hitting the backbeat, so there was always a mandolin chop, it's called, which Bill Monroe started," Bush said. "We called that 'Two-Grass Revival,'" John Cowan said, laughing. They recorded *Live at Gilley's*, another great record, in a different Pasadena, this one in Texas, at Mickey Gilley's famous club, on September 17, 1981. It was apparently recorded without Leon's knowledge. It was not released until 2000.

"His performance on *Gilley's* is staggering," Cowan marveled. "He was just playing and singing his ass off on that *Gilley's* thing, which I think is, for him, is even better [than the Perkins Palace recording]." Leon dips into more of his solo catalog on it, with "My Cricket" and "Lady Blue" as standouts. Again, he breathes new life into "A Song for You," tapping into profound musical depth. "Especially the *Gilley's* version of 'A Song for You,'" Cowan said. "You know, it's funny because Leon would always say, 'Aw, I can't play jazz' and 'I can't do this,' and the guy's knowledge, his chord knowledge is just unbelievable. He always encouraged us. He was like, 'Go get out on the edge of the branch and fucking go. If the branch breaks, big deal.' One day, I pulled out a Perrier bottle and started playing slide on the bass with it. And I looked at him like, 'Is this okay?' He just winked at me."

Leon brought the tour to Australia in July 1980. An announcement in the *Sydney Morning Herald* on July 20 explained that the first of two shows in the city had already sold out, and the promoters were adding a third. The article stated that Leon was divorced on June 24 and "is touring with his latest love, Janet Lee Constantine, and is in high spirits." For the Australian tour, Leon added Jim Price on synthesizers—that's right, ace trumpet player and Leon's old pal from Delaney & Bonnie and Mad Dogs & Englishmen.

Ambrose was unable to join the Australian leg because of visa complications. The Amazing Rhythm Aces had traveled from America as the support band. Bill Murray was there for that tour as well. "He was researching Hunter S. Thompson for the *Where the Buffalo Roam* movie, and Hunter S. Thompson was a huge Amazing Rhythm Aces fan," Cowan explained. "So Bill Murray made friends with Russell Smith [of the Aces]. Bill was already rich and famous in the US, but nobody knew who he was over there. Bill would rent a separate room in every hotel we went to besides the room he slept in, and that was the after-show party room. He'd order oodles of alcohol and food and have it delivered up there." Everybody went except Leon: "I think they were both intimidated by each other."

"Country music is coming out of the haystacks and into the Waldorf Astoria," Leon told the *Sydney Morning Herald* in a profile piece. "In country music and gospel, the beat induces a kind of hysteria. . . . I'm enchanted by the prospect of being able to contribute to someone going into a trance when I play. . . . For me, there has to be a Pentecostal reality in music." The article described Leon as "now close to forty and with his hair and beard shorter than in the late 1970s."

The preaching thing still had a hold on him. Leon did provide the radio preacher's voice in the 1979 movie *When You Comin' Back, Red Ryder?* Marjoe Gortner, the former child preacher that Leon had met in the early 1970s, starred in and produced it. "I just made a call to him for that scene in the trailer," Gortner recalled. "I didn't pay him a dime. I didn't send him any script whatsoever. I just said it needs to be whatever that was, thirty seconds, forty-five seconds, of: 'Just preach!'" Leon said that recording that voiceover left him completely disoriented. The only other time he had felt exactly like that was when he felt carried away to that liminal realm while making his debut album in London.

Leon continued some sort of spiritual quest, or at least still tapped that vein for inspiration. "He talked about how he remembered his grandmother singing this song—'There's power in the blood of Jesus,'" Cowan recalled. "His whole thing was Pentecostal. That's what Leon brought to rock 'n' roll—the fervor of Pentecostal music. I would never have pretended to make up what his views on that were, but a big portion of his lyrics involve the Holy Spirit, of Jesus, and he wrote that song 'Jesus Will Take Me Home.'" "Jesus Will Take Me Home" is the kind of spiritual that Elvis would have knocked out of the arena. It speaks of the ineffable spiritual aspects of faith.

While Leon and the band were on the road, Steve Ripley had been in Burbank, using the studio to work on his own record. Leon had signed Steve to Paradise, but his album was never released. Leon asked him to start packing things up at the house. "Mary was there and also Carla," Charlene Ripley recalled. "So, the two exes were there. It was a tense time because Steve would have to go back, and I think maybe Leon wanted him to make sure nothing disappeared. He went back until they moved everything from the Toluca Lake house to Paradise."

Michael Johnstone recalled the sudden shock of it all. "The divorce had been filed, and stuff was being divided up equally. Almost overnight, it was announced, 'I'm leaving town; I'm pulling up stakes; Paradise, the Ambrose Campbell Video Centre is over. We've got seventy-two hours to get the shit out of the state of California.'"

"Without Jack Jester, the company had no direction, no nothing, and Leon disappeared, and he hired this guy named Bob Grebb, who I think was Marty's brother, to run things, and Bob didn't know what the hell he was doing," Frank Latouf said. "He ran the business into the ground. I went to work for Eddie Van Halen, and I put Eddie and Steve Ripley together." Van Halen connected Ripley with Kramer Guitars to manufacture and market his stereo guitar.

It was devastating for Leon to close the video facility. He believed deeply that the medium would become the primary delivery system. "Because of my divorce and the massive [technical] problems . . . I never got the results I was after," Leon wrote in his memoir. "Disappointed, I finally gave up and moved to Nashville, Tennessee. By that time, I was tired of LA."

Chapter 31

On the Borderline

THERE'S A PERSISTENT MYTH THAT Leon became a recluse. Typical was a summary in the *Mojo* piece about his 2010 comeback. It read, "And at some point, Leon, thinking himself washed-up, went to bed and stayed there for two years."

The divorce and trip to Lagos definitely held up recording and touring dates, as did the new romance with Jan and cross-country relocation. And for a rock star, two years out of the public eye then was considered far more unusual than it is today. But as far as going to bed for two years, "That's hyperbole," Jan explained. "He was on the road all the whole time I was with him. The only time he was in bed was when he and Mary broke up. And I remember being told he thought he could never get onstage again. Because he stopped and he couldn't do it. But once I was with him, I never saw that."

David Fricke was not quite as hyperbolic, more accurate, but still blunt in his 2010 *Rolling Stone* profile: "He disappeared as abruptly as he arrived: falling out of favor in the Eighties, making records in obscurity."

"I've been playing constantly my entire life," Leon explained in another interview. "I did take off two years at the height of my success. It was getting hard on me. But in general I've been playing the whole time, just for five hundred people instead of thirty thousand."

It does not matter if he performed for big crowds or more intimate club shows; he always tried to sing for himself and an imagined single other. This is great guidance for all performers, but for a guy who battled stage fright by taking the stage nightly, trying to reach more than a couple of people at a time could be a debilitating prospect.

As for his confession about having to take pills to sleep and pills to wake up, Jan said that was before he met her. "He was also drinking before he met me. And as soon as I moved in, none of that was going on." Hearing about the pills, she added, "is shocking because he was not a drug guy. He didn't allow that kind of stuff around. I'd like to know what he was taking—unless it was, like, Benadryl. He didn't do well on pills. When they gave him pain pills, he wouldn't take them. Plus, he didn't feel pain the way most people do. He was always an alien with that stuff. He would tell people if they were giving a root canal, 'Yeah, that doesn't hurt at all!' Then he'd get a hangnail and freak out."

But he got back on the road. Leon said in 1987, "I'm probably the most pleased with the stuff I did with New Grass Revival." The guys in New Grass Revival yearned to leave the nest. "I don't know how many times he begged us not to leave," John Cowan stressed.

Cowan's replacement, Jack Wessel, knew Cowan back in Louisville. When the New Grass guys ended their tenure with Leon, he needed a new band. "Apparently John [Cowan] remembered me and put my name in the hat, and I got a call to go down to Tennessee and audition," said Wessel. "I had no idea Leon was in Tennessee. We're just about three hours away. So, I go down there, and I got the job."

Leon had fallen in love with Nashville in 1973 on the *Hank Wilson's Back* sessions. "For one thing, all the time that we were in the studio, there was no less than twenty-five or thirty people in line outside the studio to bring me songs. . . . I usually cut all my records at home, and I usually cut my own songs."

In 1981, Leon and Jan moved to Hendersonville, Tennessee, where they bought a large split-level in a log cabin style on about six acres along the Cumberland River, a spot called Old Hickory Lake. Jan said, "We both just loved the home." It had belonged to the legendary married songwriters Felice and Boudleaux Bryant, authors of the Everly Brothers evergreens "Love Hurts," "All I Have to Do Is Dream," "Bye Bye Love," and "Wake Up Little Suzie." They'd written the bluegrass/country standard (and Tennessee state song) "Rocky Top" there in 1967. Such a pedigree would naturally hold some attraction for Leon. Plus, Johnny Cash had been in Hendersonville since 1968. "When we first moved in Hendersonville, we had that grand piano in our bedroom so he could play for me," Jan said. "He played for me all the time. I could watch him play forever."

Jack Wessel sat in the kitchen waiting for Leon. "I just kept waiting for the cattle call to show up. Finally, Leon walked in there, and he had cut his hair kind of short; he called it his Kenny Rogers cut, and it still hadn't really grown out, and I didn't know that his hair was white. I always thought it was kind of blonde and brown and really long. And he walked in. I thought, 'Well, here comes another bass player.' But it was him."

Leon had bought a houseboat, which he christened the *Lady Blue*. "He had set up some gear in the living room of the boat, and we just had the audition. It was kind of easy, actually. I don't think he played any Leon Russell songs the whole day." Wessel had been a casual fan of Leon's music. "He just kind of threw out different time signatures. And we played blues stuff, you know, and just wanted to see if he could throw me. I guess he couldn't. And he had me sing something for him and sing something *with* him. He asked me to sing harmony with him on 'Yesterday,' which he was doing in the show at the time, and he hired me right then." The song that Wessel came up with to sing solo was "Stagger Lee." "I tried not to sing every verse and just get it over with."

Ambrose fixed his gaze on Jack, and he felt like Ambrose guided him through it. "You know, he was really amazing. But I noticed that he just had a bead on me, just watching me. And thought, 'OK.' I really didn't know any of those people, so you can imagine that situation, but I remember that so well, how he was just watching me the whole time."

Wessel loyally stayed in Leon's bands for about thirty-five years, until Leon passed away. Jack (or Jackie, as friends call him) was *the* mainstay and through-line for the second half of Leon's career. His role was primarily live performance, as Leon tended to play synthesizer bass on recordings. "People came and went, and I stayed, and he looked out for me, I'll tell you that," Wessel said. "The bands shifted around in different shapes and forms over the years, and sometimes it was great, and sometimes the band wasn't so great." He laughed. "I have no regrets at all about making that my career."

Leon brought Wessel out as Cowan finished the dates he had committed to, with Wessel describing his mission as "an onstage trainee. He had me set up next to John [Cowan], so there were two basses, no drums, the harmonica [Juke Logan], a steel player [Tom Britt, who stayed over from the last iteration of New Grass Revival], and two African percussionists." One of his first such gigs was the show recorded for *Live at Gilley's*. "I've learned after a while there that I wasn't really in the mix—I was just learning the show—which I was very happy to hear." He laughed again.

For the first couple of years, Wessel still lived in Louisville and would stay on the *Lady Blue* houseboat whenever he was in town. The bands would assemble and live at Leon's house while rehearsing. The first band after the New Grass Revival was an eleven-piece: Butch McDade on drums; Ambrose and Shamsi on percussion; Logan on blues harp (harmonica); Tom Britt, steel guitar and guitar; Bob Britt, guitar; Jack Myers, keyboards; Paul Brewer, trombone; and Jonathan Yudkin, violin. Almost all of them provided backing vocals. Wessel said Yudkin "was a great player, really a prodigy. He played electric violin and electric mandolin, and he was amazing but loud." They toured from October through December of 1981.

Brewer, who holds a doctorate in music, was impressed with Leon's grasp of music theory, composition, and performance skills. "With Leon, it was all the little things in his compositions that made them so great. Studying Leon's music has always fascinated me. Leon had a keen sense of what Kurt Vonnegut called 'cultural relativity.' Leon's visit to Africa had a profound effect on him in that regard." Leon's seamless assimilation of various and seemingly unrelated sources is what might have made the most significant impact on Brewer. "To me, Leon often seemed like a musical funnel through which the entire world of music from every imaginable source and culture was flowing."

On the road, Tom Britt traveled with Leon and Jan in a motorhome. "The best thing that ever happened to me in my whole career (I was pretty young then; I was twenty-five) was when we pulled over in a state park one night in the motorhome. And we got into the back, and we had a couple of acoustic guitars, and we were smoking a little marijuana, and Leon said, 'You know what your problem is?' I thought, *Fuck*. 'Musically?' I said. He goes, 'Yeah, musically.' I said, 'Please tell me.' For the next two hours, man, he raked me over the coals." Leon spoke in granular detail about Britt's tone and approach. He told him to concentrate more on melody and theory over flashy licks. "But see at the time Leon started doing all this stuff in a bluegrass style, which I felt required me to do a chicken-pickin' thing [a staccato honky-tonk style], which I wasn't really crazy about but I'll do it. And so he kind of reversed me, and he said, 'Maybe you can do this at half time, you know, it would make more sense. And that's how you need to approach this. Just concentrate on the melody which you're putting on the top there. Don't worry about the chicken-pickin' stuff.' Everything he said was right. I was upset, and then I thought, 'Man, he's right.'"

Though he started on acoustic guitar with the first New Grass tour, Tom Britt played electric and pedal steel for the bigger band until his brother, Bob, was brought in to play electric guitar. Bob is about five years younger than Tom. "Leon wanted to put a rock band together. I guess John [Cowan] told him that Tom had a brother who was kind of more of a rock-style guitar player."

The Britts had grown up listening to Leon's records. When Bob got the call, he was twenty-one and in Mexico City backing an Elvis impersonator. "I talked to my brother before I came and he said, 'Leon loves Freddie King, and just try and play like Freddie King.' So that's all I listened to till I got there, was Freddie King, and played at Leon's house. He said, 'Yeah, go get your stuff and come out.' So I flew back to the Bay Area. I had a '72 Nova, piled everything I could fit in the Nova, drove across country."

Like Tom, Bob Britt—who, at the time of writing this book, has been in Bob Dylan's live band for a few years—says Leon was a teacher. "I basically credit Leon most everything I learned," he said. "He really opened my eyes to the theory of things. His left hand was unbelievable. He had this exercise, he would play the same thing over and over for twenty minutes, just playing a groove. He explained, 'You keep doing that, and then eventually your mind starts to wander, and you get to a place where you're not even thinking about what you're playing. And all of a sudden, it's like doors open. You start playing different things that you would not ordinarily do.' When I play rhythm guitar, which is what I really like to do, I tend to play rhythms like Leon. He definitely was like a clock. His pocket was amazing. You instantly know when you hear him on piano: 'Well, that's Leon.'"

Leon called this band the Damn Boys. "That band lasted till the end of the year," Wessel said. They had a singularly elegant ensemble sound—trombone, steel guitar, violin, and harmonica blending together as a section—and tight multipart harmonies, which can be heard in recordings of rehearsals and shows that Logan made and Brewer has saved and shared. They're "such a great look at Leon the bandleader," Wessel said. "Days' long, intensive arranging rehearsals were something Leon committed to progressively seldom over the years until it was almost never."

Leon ended the big band while dressed as Santa Claus. "Paul [Brewer] and Jack [Myers], he fired them at the end of 1981," Wessel said. "It was the last show of this run. We were in San Antonio, and it was Christmastime, and Leon went out and played the show in a Santa Claus suit. After the show, Leon's still got his Santa Claus suit on and calls Jack and Paul out to the motorhome and fires them—while wearing a Santa Claus suit. It wasn't [personal]; they were just extraneous; no hard feelings."

The core of the band stayed together several years, cycling through a few drummers. "I was on the road with him the whole time with New Grass and beyond," Jan said. "And throughout the years, I homeschooled the kids." Jan and the kids traveled with him for most of the 1980s. The band itself was a family. "They were so kind," Jan added. "That was just the best experience ever. I loved every one of those guys."

Edgar Winter opened some of the shows. Leon had seen him perform with his brother, Johnny, in the 1970s. Leon wrote, "I was very impressed, as he played all the 'Fathead' Newman alto saxophone parts, sang all the Margie Hendrix parts, and played all the organ parts on their versions of the Ray Charles numbers they played that evening. . . . We later played a couple of shows together with our bands, and I took the opportunity to ask him to sit in on alto sax. He is so proficient that it was an effortless meld."

With his return to the road, relocation to Tennessee, and relationship with Jan, Leon was a new man. He was even availing himself to the press, giving more interviews than ever. To *The Tennessean* in 1982, he expressed his regret that he had not moved to the state sooner. "Nashville seems to be a village that specializes in something as oblique as music, which makes it real interesting." He also spoke to his role as a bandleader whose mission was to inspire musicians to play "outside themselves." As if counseling his younger self, he observes: "Most people try to make commercial music. And one of the factors is that there needs to be a certain similarity. You don't want to make music that sounds too different from the record that precedes it or follows it."

Leon's lessons in business had come at a steep price. While he was booked in a few sizable halls, even arenas, they tended to be sparsely attended, and by 1982, he was mostly playing nightclubs for a few thousand dollars a night. A review of a show at Mr. Pip's in Fort Lauderdale said Leon whipped "himself and the band into an absolute frenzy. The fervor seems almost religious. At any minute, they all seem about ready to start falling on the floor and speaking in tongues. . . . Whatever the reason, though, it works. It's fast, is the thing. *Fast*. Over-the-speed-limit fast. That point can't be emphasized enough. It's as if Leon has been listening to the Ramones' first album a lot lately, or been injected with a lifetime dose of some Soviet wonder-amphetamine, or is simply taxing his adrenal glands to potentially disastrous levels. . . . Most of the 85-minute set is a high-speed run on the edge of chaos—dangerously close to the edge, in fact—but the energy level, the band's impressive musicianship and Leon's spooky presence hold it all together."

The balance of Leon's life would be spent primarily on the road. He enjoyed most of it. And when he wasn't touring, he was in the studio. He needed to be working. "He felt like he needed the money," Jan said. In the later years, she would broach the idea of retirement. "I'd tell him we can have a smaller life. It seemed he just wouldn't stop because he had to, like that was impossible. You know, he was the Energizer Bunny. He had to have something to do."

His old mate from the session days, Don Randi, saw Leon perform near LA. "I said, 'Why are you on the road?' He says, 'I went through a divorce. I just got cleaned out.'"

But the road was a respite for Leon. Bobby Roberts was his agent—a talent buyer for Brassy's nightclub in Cocoa Beach, Florida, when he booked some of Leon's dates with New Grass Revival there. Leon was looking for an in-house agent to work with him out of Nashville. "The club owner had said some nice things about me to Leon," Roberts said in 1983. "Leon had recently moved to Tennessee, and he was looking for somebody to come in and help organize his office and take care of the business side of things for him in Tennessee. So, consequently, it's one of those moments that I was just in the right place at the right time.

"I came in as an in-house agent, and then my responsibilities grew to where it became very much a management situation," Roberts said. Anyone with a basic understanding of the music industry can see how this arrangement might cause some problems. For one, Leon wanted a booking agent dedicated exclusively to him. Although that might sound efficient, most performers want big-time agents with an impressive roster of artists. This gives the agent more power and leverage to bargain with talent buyers; it could also result in affinity package tours with multiple artists from the same agency's roster.

Roberts himself was aware of some of the limitations. "I would be interested in talking to one of the major booking agencies if they're interested in working with Leon in the future with some good creative booking," he said at the time. "We're not interested in a booking agency that wants to know where we played in the last two years, where all they're going to do is call the same places. I'm looking for an agency that believes Leon is going to come back bigger and better than ever. . . . Leon does not have an ego problem about opening for somebody else. In fact he enjoys it."

Another thorny issue is that often artists prefer their business agents in different columns. So, the personal manager potentially works with a business manager (like Leon had in Bill Hoyt during the Shelter years, followed by Len Freedman of the Jess Morgan Co.), who handles such quotidian concerns as the accounts payable and receivable, incorporation, insurance, payroll, and tax returns. The personal "artist manager" negotiates deals with the help of entertainment attorneys and is the connective tissue between the artists and all other team members. The personal manager also works with a separate booking agent to book tours. Though it costs more and can be more complicated, this arrangement splits up the roles and operates so that the personal manager monitors the others. And it maximizes oversight and minimizes potential conflicts of interest, such as those which arose with Denny Cordell as Leon's record producer, manager, booking agent, and business partner in Shelter.

"Leon was always independent," Roberts told me in 2021. "I think he enjoyed having that control over his whole operation. That's why he always had his own label, being partners in Shelter Records, and I think he's always kind of been an independent-thinking artist." Leon was at his low point as a draw when Roberts came on. "Which is typical," he said. "Artists do have an arc; they'll climb the ladder, they'll get to the top of the business, and then usually, after radio quits playing them, there are other artists that have come in. It's just the evolution of the business."

Roberts was listed as a point of contact for a Leon ad run in a trade magazine: THE ULTIMATE ARTIST, it read. It mentions that Leon "In '82 will be writing . . . 'hits' for other performers . . . (and a few for himself) . . . guesting on sessions, arranging and producing, and . . . in between . . . perform at over 150 concerts!" It was an attempt to put Leon's name back out there as ready, willing, and able to work.

Chapter 32

Back on the Road . . . to Obscurity

EVEN THE MOST NORMAL-SEEMING FAMILIES are complicated. But when the patriarch of the story is a rock star who ultimately fathered six (confirmed) kids with three different women, the levels of complexity start to increase. Jan gave birth to their first of three children together, Sugaree Bridges, in January 1982. Mary and Leon had been separated since November 1978 and Leon filed for divorce in October 1979, but the divorce was not yet final. And she was determined to limit his access to Teddy Jack and Tina Rose.

The divorce proceedings had begun in March of 1980. A May 15 letter from Leon's attorney, Sandra Musser, explained that there would be a court date the following month to dissolve the marriage, with bifurcation of assets and custody of the children being the matters at hand. As for joint legal custody, Mary was not going to make this easy. Musser referred the matter to a court counselor for mediation.

They requested that Mary's alimony support be reduced on a dollar-to-dollar basis in relation to her income. At the time, Mary was on tour with Bob Dylan, playing piano and singing in the extraordinary small choir of gospel-based backing singers that included Clydie King for Dylan's 1980 *Saved* tour. Musser also explained the benefits of Leon agreeing to split royalties with Mary 50-50 for the songs he wrote during the couple's marriage. It would simplify his taxes, protect against potential future audits, and provide Mary with income that would offset his alimony. But the attorney also explained the advantages should Leon choose instead to employ an appraiser to value the catalog and for Leon to keep 100 percent, which is the road he took, despite Musser's clear advice to consider the songs "community assets" and split future royalties. "We do not want to pay Mary cash if possible as you do not have it," Musser bluntly stated at the end of the letter. "We, in fact, want the [Toluca Lake] house to dwarf all other assets so that the Court feels compelled to order it sold or to allow you to buy Mary out."

The custody hearings started in early 1982. "Leon flew me out one time to show up for the child custody thing," his manager Bobby Roberts said. "I showed up for it, but the judge wouldn't hear it because he said, 'I'm not going to hear a child custody without the father being present.'"

"I didn't go into the court proceedings," Jan said. "I had Sugaree, and she was a few months old. I just stayed in one of the rooms with her and Blue because Blue was living with us at the time. I think Blue helped cement us not getting [custody of the kids]. Because she said that she saw Leon naked, and it scared her. And the deal is that she *did* see him naked, I'm sure, because she came into our bedroom. That's plausible. He never walked around the house naked, but if they saw him walking from the bed to the bathroom, it's possible. I have a feeling that's probably what happened."

Carla had stuck around the Toluca Lake house a while after Leon split and during the run-up to the divorce proceedings, but then Mary kicked Carla and Blue out of the house, leaving them homeless. "Mary accused Carla of stealing one of her rings and kicked them out," Jan said. Jan understood the unusual arrangement of having Carla live with them as something that had been convenient for Mary and Leon; Carla could watch the kids while the couple was on tour. Mary was secure with Carla, despite Mary's jealous nature. "I know she had to be not jealous *at all* of Carla for her to allow her to live with them," Jan said. "But she got rid of her right quick, as soon as they separated."

"My mom and Mary had a falling out," Blue said. "I lived with my mom in the car. She started waiting tables, and we either slept at the park, in the car, or if she made enough tips, we'd get a hotel room. I also lived with my best friend and her family." Blue later said it was about eight months, and that Leon had no idea at the time that she and Carla were homeless. "After the divorce was final, I was ten. My mom and I moved to Oklahoma, and then I went back to seeing Dad at Christmas, spring break, and summer. He was a great, great father for me and very involved."

Blue and Jan grew close over the years, becoming more like friends than stepmother and stepdaughter. But eventually, there were ruptures within the family, and the two are estranged at the time of writing and have been for over a decade. Also, Mary is estranged from her children Tina Rose and Teddy Jack. Teddy Jack is also estranged from Jan. Tina Rose eventually married Jan's nephew, and they had a child—Jan's step-grandson and grandnephew—before they divorced, and Jan and Tina remain in contact. At the time I was writing the book, Blue was in touch with Mary.

That there are several rifts is important to understand as we try to navigate the very complicated and thorny family matters going forward. Some of this family drama was aired publicly on back-and-forth social media posts after Leon's passing, so it should at least be acknowledged, inasmuch as it affected Leon Russell. Suffice it to say, there was significant family trauma for much of the last decade or two of Leon's life. He was unaware of much of it while it was happening, and that's a considerable part of the story. At times, he became more withdrawn from his family as the drama among them increased, and his own physical and mental health problems took their toll on his psyche. Though he had deep-seated issues from his upbringing—abandoned by his father, little communication with his older brother, and a complicated relationship with his mother—the split with Mary sent him reeling, and he would never really recover.

"I just know that she made him feel like he was worthless, and he just told me she was evil," said Jan. "I didn't believe him, really, because I had never met a person who I thought was evil, so I didn't think it existed. But I was from a small town and didn't know people could be *really* mean." Jan pointed to the estrangement of Mary from her kids as an indication that Mary has issues.

Tina Rose was careful not to cast any blame on any party and was particularly sensitive when talking about Mary. But the time and geographic distance between Leon and his kids had lasting damage to him and his children. "Me and my brother grew up in California, so we would sometimes go on Christmas or for the summer with my dad," she said. "And there was a long period of time that me and my brother didn't get to see my dad. And who knows what was going on behind the scenes there. I didn't see my dad from when I was five years old until I was twelve years old, which is a long fucking time. So then when we got to see him again, that was pretty exciting, and then starting to have regular visits. Me and my brother both moved to Nashville once we graduated.

"I do want to say that, even throughout whatever issues my mom and dad had, my dad never said anything negative about my mom, ever," Tina Rose said. "I mean, he may have to my brother, I'm almost positive that he did, but they had a different relationship. He never said anything negative about my mom, even when he was in the hospital before he had his surgery [at the end of his life]. He was just like, 'So, have you talked to your mom? Is your mom doing okay?' I'm just so surprised that he was just always so pleasant. He really was sensitive to that."

She continued: "She didn't ever really go into detail and tell me about their relationship. The only thing that she did that was positive—they both did this—is say, 'What I'd love right now is some chicken and dumplings. Your dad made the best chicken and dumplings.' And my dad did that too. 'Oh, your mom would have the' whatever. And I'd be like, 'You guys are weird. You both, Mom and Dad, cannot *stand* each other, and just right out the blue be like, 'Oh, your dad would have this.' 'Your mom would have this.'" Food was always a way to connect for Leon.

Leon and Mary's divorce started in 1980 but wasn't finalized until two years later, and he married Jan on February 6, 1983. Ambrose Campbell officiated, and Michael Johnstone was there to videotape the occasion. "Oddly enough, when my daughters hit twenty-one, I realized that's how old I was when I moved in with him," Jan said with a laugh. "I just saw myself as more of an adult than how I see my children now. Well, I didn't say I was mature," she said, laughing again. "We always felt we were at the same age."

Leon wanted to have all his kids under one roof, a goal he would achieve for a while a little later in the 1990s. In the meantime, Blue was shuttling back and forth between Tulsa and Tennessee in her preadolescent years. Tina and Teddy came to visit in December '83, the first of only two visits until they turned seventeen and eighteen.

Sugaree Noel was a year old, and Leon was on the road more often than he was home. He eventually had the buses moved from LA to Tennessee, added a room to the Hendersonville house, built a loading dock off on one side, and pulled up the mobile audio bus to use as a control room. "He paved the front yard, of course, which was his signature," Jack Wessel said. "So he could keep his buses. He had the band bus first, and he had an audio bus, and the video bus, which later burned sitting out in the driveway. Eventually, he built that addition onto that house, originally to put his office in there, to put his booking and management and accounting in there."

In 1982, Leon also bought two hundred acres in a rural area called Sideview, on Dry Fork Road outside of Gallatin, Tennessee. Wessel said, "He built that place for ten years before he ever moved into it. He put up a big warehouse, which eventually was his office and storage. He moved the tape and film library out there. And then he put his recording studio out there once he finally did move."

"He designed that house himself," Jan said. "They poured a slab of concrete, and he was the architect because there was nothing he couldn't do—or nothing he *wouldn't* do. Nobody helped him execute. He just did it, so there were a lot of things that weren't right. But we loved it. In fact it was our favorite home until we lived in Hermitage. It was like a painting that he kept adding on to. He put Tennessee rock on the outside, and then he put the Tennessee rock on the inside. So the walls were about four feet wide. Ambrose lived in a trailer there. It was a shabby trailer, and then Leon bought him a double-wide."

"Both trailer homes got the Ambrose treatment," Wessel explained. "Ambrose was a floor-dweller. He slept, ate, made music, and entertained company on the floor. What furnishings there were were piled high with clothes, tapes, and other various items not needed on the floor just then. Ambrose made friends with many ladies on the road, and fairly often one or more of them would make the trek to Tennessee to stay awhile with him. These visits would always begin and end with a housecleaning. They loved him, and he loved them."

"We had a little compound," Jan explained. "Leon bought my sister a double-wide, and she lived out there for a while. And Noland [O'Boyle] was working out there. Skip [Graves and wife Patsy] took care of it." O'Boyle was a friend and right-hand man for Leon. The Graves were caretakers for what Leon referred to as "the Farm" and became like family. Jan said the actual family moved out there, spending what she called "three years of heaven because that's when we had all the animals. I don't know how many cows he had—we had cows, horses, rabbits, chickens, and dogs and cats." Wessel thinks that they lived out in Sideview a few more than three years.

Real estate was an ongoing saga in the life of Leon. He would push the envelope of zoning ordinances and test the patience of homeowner associations. He paved sections of his yards, making parking lots for his musicians to leave their cars while they were on the road. He would leave noisy bus generators running overnight when between tours. The neighbors were impatient at best and openly hostile and litigious at worst. Leon and the family would end up moving over a half dozen times within Tennessee from 1982 until his death. They would ultimately settle in a 6,120-square-foot Tudor-style house with a thatched roof on over eight acres in Hermitage.

Wessel said that once Leon moved on from a place, including Los Angeles and Tulsa, he had no nostalgia for it. Leon never brought him up to see Skyhill when Diane Sullivan was living there. "We were there every year, but he was perfectly happy to stay where we needed to be. Some people would come and see him, but he laid low out there because Mary was not far, something I talked about carefully. That was the one that just went on and on."

It went on almost until the day Leon died. "He'd call me when he'd come out here [to LA]," Bill Maxwell said. "He was in town here; he'd say, 'I'm out here one day, and I get sued by Mary again.' This was maybe two years before he died."

Mary would continue filing lawsuits, "just basically nuisance suits," Wessel said. "I thought he should counter. But he wouldn't do that; he just always figured he was going to lose anyway, and ending it was the best thing. That's called the 'California divorce.' And I have a pretty funny track from a 1982 album with the Memphis Horns on it. It's called 'California Divorce.'"

Leon raves about going broke and having to leave California on the song, an upbeat twelve-bar blues. But he sings ebulliently that he got the better end of the deal by getting out from under the marriage. Juke Logan wails on harmonica, making it sound like one of the better tracks in the Huey Lewis and the News catalog.

Leon put together a whole album that included that song. "It was the first recording I'd ever done with Leon, and he didn't have his studio up and running at the time he started it," Wessel said. "So he booked studio time in town [at the Castle recording studio], and we tracked live with a rhythm section. I think for another twenty years or so, that was the last time he ever tracked live." Some of the tracks are set to a drum machine, but others are with Butch McDade of the Amazing Rhythm Aces on drums. "There aren't any great Leon Russell songs on it. There are only three or four Leon songs on it, a couple that he just kind of made up on the spot." He picked up a few more from Nashville writers. "It was just to get something out," Wessel said. "But he was in great form on that record as a singer, player, and arranger. He and the Memphis Horns were a match made in heaven."

Leon was feeling pressure from Bobby Roberts to get a new record deal and release an album. Wessel said, "Leon would say, 'Well, I don't have my studio going.' [Roberts:] 'This is Nashville. There are studios all over the place.' [Leon:] 'Well, I haven't been writing any songs.' [Roberts:] 'This is Nashville, you can buy songs at the gas station.'"

In 1983, Roberts was optimistic: "It's a shame to have to categorize a classic artist like Leon because he's experimented with every idiom. But that's the way it is, and he's willing to work a market and work it for the next few years, build that foundation, and sell a lot of records. One great record album by Leon Russell, and everything will triple. His concert price will triple, merchandising will triple or quadruple, his publishing will be worth so much more money, and he's going to make great music, but he's going to do what's necessary on his part to give us a very marketable product." Roberts explained that Leon was working an average of 175 nights a year, playing in "large showcase nightclubs" and "smaller theaters and halls up to three thousand people," with 90 or 95 percent of those selling out. "He's working to hundreds of thousands of people a year and if they'll pay $8 to $12 for a ticket they'll pay that for his new record. I feel very, very confident that this year it's going to turn around for him."

Leon self-financed the '82 album and started looking for a deal. "He pitched it to Capitol, and they didn't want the album," Wessel recalled. Capitol did consider signing Leon. "They suggested they'd find him a producer, and, 'We'll do some sides and see what happens,' which was an insult. So he said, 'Okay, thank you.' And then he sent it to Atlantic to Ahmet Ertegun, who hated it."

Bobby Roberts said, "I had the pleasure of meeting with Ahmet Ertegun for a couple of hours and played him Leon's latest music. He was very kind and very respectful of Leon. Ahmet said it was 'dated' and didn't have a clean sound. He played me Genesis's latest project to compare. I'm not an expert on studio gear, but Leon's was not up-to-date. As great as he was as an artist, he insisted on using his audio bus [set up in the warehouse] for recording at that time. It sounded awesome to my ears, but I'm not an expert in that field."

Leon accepted it. Wessel continued, "It might have hurt his feelings, but I don't think his expectations were all that high; I think he knew that he would be lucky to get signed. It was 1982, and he wasn't anywhere near classic, yet he was just recently passé. Warner Brothers had dropped him and probably talked some smack about him. So he wasn't in a good position to bargain. Plus, that was when MTV was brand new. Whatever he was doing just was not happening."

Leon had been so accustomed to being on the cutting edge until the late 1970s, but now he found himself out of step and lagging. Some of his colleagues, like Jackson Browne, Eric Clapton, and Steve Winwood, adapted and got second-wind career boosts from MTV. But Leon, who had recognized the potential of music video before most artists of his generation, was stubborn and went his own way. First, he laudably followed the inspiration he found with New Grass Revival and then the big band. But he spent years touring, mostly modest or small joints. He had no record deal in place, didn't release any new albums, and produced no music videos aimed at MTV. By the time 1983–1984 rolled around, he was no longer leading. The guy who was a primary force in alchemizing the groove-heavy, R&B-and-gospel-based American rock 'n' roll of the late sixties and early seventies was now casting around for direction.

He marched to the beat of his own drummer, only in his case, the drummer was a machine. And Leon was not Run DMC, New Order, Marvin Gaye, or Prince, embracing the sound for what it was; Leon was trying to make essentially the same kind of music he always had but with faux sounds.

"I think he became real hard-nosed about, especially with the pushback he'd get: 'Well, you need to get some real drums on that,' even going back to the Linn machine, which you can pretty much thank him for," Wessel observed. "Boy, he started using that on his records, and his label was bitching about it, you know, 'Sounds like demos, Leon.' And the more pushback he got on that, the more committed to it he became."

Leon also stopped using acoustic pianos, even in the studio. "He was a big fan of [the Yamaha CP-70]," Wessel said. "He wouldn't carry a Steinway anymore once he got the CP-70. That was very standard in the late seventies and early eighties before digital. That was the electric but real piano; it had hammers and strings, and pretty much everybody was using that, but he actually liked it and got to the point where he had it set up in the studio—he preferred to sit around and play that over his Steinway." Those Yamahas have a distinct sound that holds a nostalgic charm for those of us who saw live music in the late 1970s and early 1980s. "But once it got into good [digital] samples, he never touched it. He had the best Steinway samples, and he would use two or three at the same time. So, it's hard to argue that [a real piano] was a better way to go as far as recording goes." As with the Roger Linn shopping excursions in the seventies, Wessel said, Leon "was the king of the prototype. He went out and bought something as soon as he heard about it, and paid top dollar. Sixteen months later, he could get the same program for three hundred bucks. But he didn't care; he had to have it right now."

The 1982 album has not been heard outside of Leon's inner circle or the people associated with the Oklahoma Museum of Popular Culture (OKPOP), which has custody of Leon's audio and video library. One track, "Still Love That Girl," with the full rhythm section, steel guitar, and horns, could have been a country-pop crossover hit, like songs from the time from Ronnie Milsap and Eddie Rabbitt. It has an inspired arrangement and is undeniably hooky.

Speaking of Milsap, Leon had met him in Memphis in the mid-sixties and was reunited with his old friend on October 23, 1983, for the former's two-hour Nashville Network TV special "In Celebration." The two performed a duet of "A Song for You," facing each other at grand pianos.

Leon also played an acoustic piano in a reunion with his old pal and colleague Glen Campbell for a Canadian television program, *In Session*, on November 18, 1983. It's a freewheeling show, like the ones Leon produced with J. J. Cale and Willie Nelson. Glen does most of the talking, while Leon coolly chimes in and trades songs with his friend. One highlight is Glen reminiscing about Leon contributing a catchy riff on the "Gentle on My Mind" session.

Wessel described the unreleased Leon record: "They're not all great songs or anything, but he was in such great form I hate that nobody's ever heard that. His studio was up and running. He had discovered the Yamaha DX-7 [synth]" and would have no more need for studio musicians to help with his recordings.

After Leon decided to shelve the unreleased album, Bobby Roberts convinced him to reactivate Paradise Records as a brand. "They ended up with a mom-and-pop distributor," Wessel explained—Cue, out of Illinois.

"They borrowed some money and either leased or bought a big building in Hendersonville in an industrial park. And they put in his offices and built a nice new twenty-four-track studio upstairs and another sixteen-track studio upstairs from the big warehouse and borrowed five hundred grand and recorded *Solid State*, and he remixed and remastered *Hank Wilson Volume II*, which he had done a couple years before."

Roberts said, "I ended up hiring a fellow by the name of Richard Perna, who turned out to be an icon in the publishing business. Richard did a wonderful job doing the publishing for Leon. He organized all of Leon's publishing for him because it was pretty scattered; and then, making sure that Leon was getting paid from all the different publishing sources." One of the things Perna did was negotiate a deal for Luther Vandross to record a cover of "Superstar" in a medley with Stevie Wonder's "Until You Come Back to Me (That's What I'm Gonna Do)." It was a hit, reaching number five on the *Billboard* R&B Singles chart. "Leon and I went to Luther's concert in Chattanooga and met with him backstage, thanking him for cutting the song," Roberts recalled.

Leon and Roberts set up several publishing companies and hired a staff of songwriters. "I was one of 'em," Wessel said. "He was handing out jobs and second jobs. It was big fun starting a new company with his band and his friends, you know? It was gonna be great. And it *was* nice for a while."

They also hired an executive staff for this new company, under the banner Leon Russell Enterprises. Bruce Schindler, a record promotions guy from New York, was installed as general manager, joining Perna, who filled the position of vice president. "The fella that we put in charge of video was Bob Cummings," Roberts said. Roberts's brother Jeff was hired as a booking agent.

Bob Britt recalled the big warehouse, which had writer's rooms for the publishing company they set up. "Remember the song 'Wind Beneath My Wings' [written by Jeff Silbar and Larry Henley]? Well, we were working on a record, and Leon was looking for outside songs, and this guy came out. He played him 'Wind Beneath My Wings,' and Leon was like, 'Well, this is a good song, but it just makes my armpits tingle. I can't sing that.'" So, credit to Leon on that one. They also had signed the songwriter Nick DiStefano before he wrote "Shelter Me" for Joe Cocker's 1986 *Cocker* album.

Wessel said that Bobby Roberts somehow convinced Leon to collaborate with a guy with little songwriting or production experience, Doug Snider, on *Solid State*, Leon's next album, which Wessel said was aimed squarely at the middle-of-the-road pop market. "Bobby Roberts was concerned that Leon might still be having writer's block," Wessel explained. "Bobby proposed the idea of hiring someone to serve catalytically as a cowriter and/or coproducer to keep the ball rolling and keep Leon on track with the project between the few and brief road trips. Leon was open to the idea."

Snider hailed from Portland, Oregon, had been in some bands up there, and made his way to Nashville and became a staff writer at Warner Chappell Music. Wessel said, "What was most noticeably absent from his invisible résumé was anything of note to do with songwriting or record production. A deal was struck and for a sum, soon paid in full, Doug was contracted by Bobby Roberts to Leon Russell Enterprises to serve as cowriter and coproducer on the album to be known (though not very well) as *Solid State* and somehow get a coproducing credit for the remix and release of *Hank Wilson Vol. II*."

Wessel explained that Snider was a little unstable. "I think it was Leon's sympathetic nature that allowed him to be accepting of Doug for who he was. Leon would have been really pleased if this project had turned out to be just the break a guy like this needed. They did become truly friendly for a while." Snider would pitch song titles, and Leon would write the songs to go with them. Wessel said Leon would write everything else, increasingly ignoring Snider's suggestions, while giving him 50 percent cowriting credit. "Doug's role was meant to keep Leon focused and on track. He may have earnestly worked hard at that, but none of us thought it was necessary."

The bizarre notion of the writer of "A Song for You" and "Tight Rope" agreeing to collaborate and share any royalties with an unknown amateur illustrates Leon's self-doubt at this juncture in his career. Once the Master of Space and Time, he was now adrift and floating in orbit, unable to reenter.

"I think it could simply have been the result of a period of Leon's compliance and submissiveness to his manager, or the guy he was paying to manage him," Wessel said. "I can't recall another period of cooperation and compliance like this from Leon until decades later when the Elton project came along."

Solid State is an interesting album, even though one of the best songs, "Ain't No Love in the City," was relegated to the B-side of the "Good Time Charlie's Got the Blues" single. "Ain't No Love in the City" is a funky blues-stomp in the mold of classic Leon and has a great string arrangement. Leon wails an organ solo to end the track. It's the funkiest song—the *only* funky song—from the sessions. The slick early-eighties pop records of Billy Joel, Rod Stewart, and Joe Cocker come to mind when listening to *Solid State*.

The divorce with Mary seems to still sting in the lyric of "Lost Love," an inspired ballad with welcome gospel intonations. It would be easy to imagine Gregg Allman taking this on a few years later for his *I'm No Angel* album, which, incidentally, Allman had asked Leon to produce. Jack Wessel said, "I remember Gregg coming up to the bus, and Leon said, 'I don't know, I don't really do that anymore.'"

Much of the lush vocal tracking on the album came from Trudy Fair, who had started out touring with Lonnie Mack. She was down to her last twenty dollars when she met Leon on the last of the New Grass Revival tours. "I auditioned with Leon on a Tuesday, and our first show was Friday night in Raleigh, North Carolina," she said. "We crammed on a bus two days after we met each other, and that was our first show." She stayed on for about seven years, through the tours Leon would do with Edgar Winter. It was "intense, from Montreal to Rio de Janeiro, Key West to Seattle, constantly on the move." Fair was joined on the road by Marcia Wood, Pebble Daniel, and Do'ana Cooper.

Solid State was released in 1984, Leon's first album of original new material in five years. That year he also issued *Hank Wilson, Vol. II*, which had been recorded 1979–1980 in Burbank and included some leftover tracks from the Nashville sessions for *Hank Wilson's Back*. Leon is shown in tribal face paint on the front cover of *Solid State*, alongside a carved African statue. Inside, the dust sleeve shows a baby Sugaree, also in face paint, on her father's knee. Her dad looks more like a grandpa here.

"Good Time Charlie's Got the Blues," the single from *Solid State*, was written by Danny O'Keefe, who had released his version in 1972. O'Keefe's was an organic country-tinged singer-songwriter number, but

Leon shades it in water-colored swaths of synths. He performed it on *Late Night with David Letterman* on June 19, 1984. "Leon just didn't want to do it," Tom Britt recalled. "He hated doing stuff like that, but Letterman talked him into it." Letterman's assistant replied to an interview request, explaining, "Dave said there was a time when he was very fond of Leon Russell, and he meant a great deal to him musically, but he has no memory of making this call. He said that's not to say it didn't happen. It probably did."

That night, Letterman, by way of an introduction, reads some of Leon's credits from the cue cards. When he gets to "A Song for You," he adds, "which I was going to sing tonight, but we ran out of time." After the intro, Leon ambles out in a straw cowboy hat, white Vuarnet sunglasses, and a too-small woman's zebra print jacket over a white T-shirt with "GOY BEORGE" in basic iron-on letters.

Leon mocks surprise at his reception, tips his hat, and sits at the CP-70. He pounds out an opening figure, stops, and then looks down at his pedals and says, "We have a technical error here, just a second." This was his first national television appearance in years. There is an awkward silence; a stagehand straightens his headset and kneels under the piano as Paul Shaffer watches. Letterman comes out and looks under the piano as if he is checking a Ford Pinto for an oil leak. He cues to go to commercial "because of the danger of explosion." When they return from the break, Letterman is on one knee, clapping imaginary grime from his hands, and says, "Okay, that oughta take care of it, Leon." Big laughs, except from Leon, who plays the straight man and then launches into a New Orleans–style "Roll Over Beethoven."

Wessel was there to sing harmony. "This date was the only instance I know of where a musical guest's technical breakdown caused a cut to commercial, and I was a faithful Dave-watcher from day one till the end. After Leon's Yamaha CP-70 piano was set up, Leon cautioned a stagehand that the sustain pedal was subject to come loose and disengage unless it was securely taped down. The stage manager explained that now that the piano was set up, the show would have to pay a union stagehand for an extra hour for that bit of extra work. Leon relented, and the rehearsal went smoothly. An hour or so later, the pedal jerked loose before Leon could get through the intro to 'Roll Over Beethoven.' It was one of the greatest examples of pure Leonian tough luck."

At the end of the song, Letterman takes a seat next to Leon on the piano bench and reads from "a list of some of the songs, I didn't realize that you had played piano on." "He's a Rebel"? "You've Lost That Lovin' Feelin'"? "River Deep, Mountain High"? "No," deadpans Leon. "Where did you get that stuff?" Finally, Letterman gets a yes for "Mr. Tambourine Man."

Letterman says, "It also says here you recently had an airplane stolen." Leon, in perfect straight-man mode, responds laconically, "Yeah. It happens sometimes." Letterman: "How does somebody steal an airplane?" Leon, with impeccable timing: "I think they hot-wired it." Then he slips into "Good Time Charlie's Got the Blues." It's a better version than the album take, more straightforward, with less gloss.

There was a plane that he and Roberts co-owned. "It was stolen from the Gallatin airport," Roberts explained in 2021. "I went down and did the polygraph test with the FBI, and the pilot that we had hired did the polygraph. Of course, we all passed with flying colors because we didn't have anything to do with that. I think the final determination on that was that it was somebody that was in the drug business [who was the thief]."

"He didn't want to sit in the chair and talk to David," Jan said. "He enjoyed playing on those shows, but he didn't really care about being the one spoken to because it made him a nervous wreck." The piano malfunction didn't help: Leon maintains a very cool exterior, but it's clear he was inwardly freaking out.

For Paul Shaffer, it was an honor playing alongside Leon. Unprompted, he recalled, "The malfunction was with the sustain pedal, right? Afterwards, [Leon] said to me in a very philosophical way, 'This is sort of par for the course as far as my experience with TV.'"

Starting in 1986, Darlene Love would perform "Christmas (Baby Please Come Home)," from the Phil Spector Christmas record, on Letterman's annual Christmas episode. Shaffer discussed replicating Leon's part on that original recording. "That was an honor every year to get to do it. It's just a beautiful, classically inspired melody. It's not moving very fast or anything. But you've got to play with some feeling. It requires feeling. It elicits it, but you'd better have it, or you've got nothing."

The next day, Leon and Bobby flew down to Dallas to tape a high-budget music video for "Good Time Charlie's Got the Blues" at the Studios at Las Colinas. While in Dallas, Leon recorded the tracks for a cover of "Don't Be Cruel" he wanted to put together with Willie Nelson. Willie and Delbert McClinton appeared the next day, with Willie adding his vocal to the track. Willie also makes a cameo in the music video for "Good Time Charlie," which is set in a smoky nightclub where the denizens all appear to be middle-aged and dressed in formal attire. Leon, dressed in white tails and seated at a piano on a small stage, serves as the evening's entertainment. Willie twice peers into the window from the street. "There were two horrendous, nearly identical videos made for 'Good Time Charlie' and 'Rock and Roll Part of My Heart,' both with cameos by Willie, that MTV wouldn't run," Wessel said.

"I don't think he really liked to self-promote," Jan said of Leon. "He only cared about the music. Some people are more driven for fame and fortune. I'm not saying he didn't enjoy that also. He just wanted to sing and play and write. He did tell me how scary it was when he became famous, how scary that was to have everyone watching you." Jan said he even continued to limit the print interviews he did, for fear that "they always got him wrong."

A guy uncomfortable with self-promotion should not have been the guy releasing and promoting his own records. But here he was, in part because Leon didn't trust the right people, in part because his timing was bad. Perhaps if he had made *Solid State* in '81, he could have convinced a major label there was still some commercial potential in Leon Russell. Instead, Wessel said, "The bookings weren't coming in, but he was running up all this debt."

Did Leon have enough revenue coming in to justify the significant spending on the expansion, building a studio, hiring an executive team to run the record label and publishing companies? "Well, there certainly was some money coming in," Bobby Roberts said. "A lot of it was funded through the touring side of things. Leon had his personal expenses, and then we had the business expenses, and money was coming in from the publishing company, Leon's songwriting. We were trying to get the thing off and running, and it takes a while to get going; a pipeline of money comes in, but it'll take a while to get it generated. Was the record label profitable? At that point, it was not. It would have been, I think. With time it would have become very profitable."

Someone close to Leon who wanted to remain anonymous said, "They sold Leon's publishing for half a million dollars, which even in 1985 was *way* under the money. All the good stuff. Whatever Leon owned got sold . . . at a distressed rate to Lionel Richie, who lost it shortly thereafter in his divorce. After that, all [Leon] got was the songwriter's royalties, not the publishing royalties. I thought, 'Oh my God, what are you doing?'"

"What triggered that was his ex-wife, Mary," Bobby Roberts said. "That divorce had gone on for quite a while. There were custody problems, and she wanted a large chunk of money. There was some bitterness there."

Don Williams, who roughly ten years earlier had split the label's catalog down the middle between Denny Cordell and Leon, was once again involved in the brokering of Leon's publishing. He had left Shelter in 1979 and set up the first accounting software company for music publishing royalties. After the split at Shelter, Leon's publishing materials and royalties were administered by his business manager, Len Freedman. Now Freedman was working for Lionel Richie and he was using Williams's software. "When Leon first decided he wanted to raise some money selling the catalog, they went to a bank in Beverly Hills that was making a name for itself by taking equity in entertainment properties, film and music," Williams explained. "And the bankers gave me a telephone call and said, 'We have an evaluation of Leon's catalog, and we'd like you to take a look at it before we loan the money.'" That didn't go anywhere, but Freedman told Williams, "If you help me buy the Leon catalog, we will pay you as an agent." Lionel Richie bought Teddy Jack Music, with the copyrights reassigned on May 9, 1985.

"Richard Perna had cleaned up his publishing where we could literally sell it if need be," Roberts said. Perna said that he was not involved in the actual transaction, but explained that deals back then were based on five-to-eight-times multiples of what a catalog was earning, as opposed to today, when the multiple is more like twenty. He did believe that Richie got it at a "steal" even back then. Perna said Leon was desperate to make a deal.

Roberts continued, "Leon decided he needed to settle with Mary, and I believe she finally decided to settle for $500,000 in cash. So that's what triggered that sale of the publishing, getting that divorce behind him."

But Leon's divorce was never fully behind him. Mary received roughly half a million dollars in the initial divorce settlement and would continue filing suits until the end. Richie also got divorced in 1993, and some of those interviewed said his ex-wife Brenda would eventually come to own the Leon Russell songs in that deal. Don Williams was again consulted when Chuck Kaye of DreamWorks SKG bought the Teddy Jack Music catalog in 1997, and *Billboard* reported that the sale was between Lionel (not Brenda) and DreamWorks.

Leon concluded that he had been mismanaged. Jan said, "We got screwed when we were first together in Nashville in the 1980s by his management there that mismanaged him; that was Bobby Roberts." In 1985, Leon ordered Roberts to fire the other executives, Richard Perna et al.; and then Leon immediately fired Bobby and cleaned slate. A woman named Jerry Holliday came to work for them briefly after Roberts. In the January 5, 1985, issue of *Billboard*, Holliday was listed as a "spokesperson" in an article headlined "Leon Russell's Firm Loses More Executives."

"She kind of poisoned the situation, which happens in the business," Roberts said. "I'm not really sure what she said to Leon, but whatever was said, Leon decided that we all needed to go. I really believe in my heart that had we stayed on, we could have developed and would continue to develop a very successful situation." In fact, the men Leon fired went on to highly successful careers in the music business.

"I think Bobby might have overspent," Jan said. "That's what caused the firing." Leon was suspicious that his executive team had set him up to sell his publishing under duress, "at a distressed rate," to use his term. He also felt the executives spent too much and were not booking as many dates as he wanted.

Leon had a paranoid streak. His suspiciousness fueled his impulsive tendencies, so his decisions seemed abrupt. Wessel explained, "He could be impulsively contrary—'Just because.' Wherever he thought the consensus might be, that may be the time he would do a complete turn. His judgment could be very poor at times, I'm afraid."

He also had odd ideas, such as who should book his live appearances. Wessel said, "Leon wanted to work all the time, and he was afraid bigger agencies would just cherry-pick the big commissions, and that's as much as he would work." One of the guys he was using around this time was Brad Davis. Wessel called him "the quintessential kitchen-table booking agent. Leon used him for a punching bag; everything was Brad's fault. He was a nice guy. I got along great with him, but he wasn't very good."

Leon felt compelled to tour even more because he started to really fear his debt load, which would be the hellhound on his trail until the end of his life. But he still spent money like there was no tomorrow. Here he was in the wake of a major divorce, having pulled up stakes on his complex in Burbank, taking out loans and buying up property in Tennessee. Though the real estate was far cheaper than in LA, he might have considered diversifying into other basic investments, like mutual funds, or at least saving cash more diligently. Leon wasn't even looking at real estate as an investment so much as space to spread out.

Solid State would be the last album Leon would record for another eight years until 1992's Bruce Hornsby–produced *Anything Can Happen*. Leon struck out on the road and started his routine of playing hundreds of shows every year, almost always including Willie's Fourth of July shows (Nelson suspended them after 1980, resuming in 1983). "There was a huge change after being off for those two years," he told *Mojo* in 2010. The writer of the article, Michael Simmons, summarized 1984 to 2010: "The size of the audience had shrunk, the venues were second-tier, the self-released records sounded like home demos, he rarely appeared in the media. His hard-core fans, Leon Lifers, remain devoted to him, people under a certain age simply don't know who he is. As T Bone Burnett points out: 'It's as if he intentionally became obscure.'"

Tom Britt said Leon saw the writing on the wall about his declining career. "I could tell it bugged him. He didn't really talk about it, but he was smart enough to realize that's the way it goes. You just finally think, 'Here we go, going down.'"

Chapter 33

Going Down

LEON HAD ALWAYS GRAPPLED WITH health issues. Just walking had been a struggle since childhood. He would tell people that he spent a great deal of energy just trying to make it look like he was walking "normally." Tom Britt said Leon's father would call Leon "a cripple" when he was a kid. Steve Ripley recalled, "He said to me, 'I spent my whole life just learning how to walk to keep from making a fool of myself.'"

Things started to go downhill with his health more rapidly in the eighties. On November 8, 1985, the first night of what was to be a three-week tour, he suffered severe injuries from a fall on his way to a stage at the Tree Top Lounge in El Paso. Leon had begun to require a direct covered path to the stages he played. He voiced his frustration in a mailgram fired off to his booking agent from Virginia on June 17, 1981:

PLEASE BE ADVISED THAT IF YOU BOOK ANY FURTHER JOBS WHERE I MUST WALK THROUGH THE AUDIENCE TO GET TO THE STAGE I WILL NOT PERFORM AND I WILL HOLD YOU PERSONALLY RESPONSIBLE FOR ANY AND ALL CHARGES INCURRED AS A RESULT OF NON-PERFORMANCE.

The manager of the Tree Top Lounge, Michael Martin, said that Leon's crew requested the stage lights be turned off while he entered the show and that Leon had sunglasses on when he fell climbing the stage. "He didn't want to be seen until he walked onstage, and you had to walk through the club," Bob Britt said. "And so they had the club darkened, and there was a sunken dance floor. And we're walking down the side toward the stage, and he stepped off and went down. And I guess his wrist was broken or cracked."

Leon performed the entire show, despite an accident that also required knee surgery and scratched the cornea in his right eye. About a week later, he had developed pneumonia and needed a respirator. The rest of the band and crew had continued on to California to prepare for shows out there, while Jan and three-year-old Sugaree stayed in El Paso with Leon. He was discharged on November 19.

A significant amount of his other health problems stemmed from a bad diet and obsessive eating. Jan said he had mostly given up drinking by the time she met him, though he enjoyed the occasional piña colada. He got no kick from cocaine. "He smoked, and then one day, he just stopped," Jan said. "Then he started smoking cigars, and they tasted so horrible to him that he just quit. He knew that it was messing with his throat, so he decided that he was done with smoking. And he smoked pot until he couldn't anymore. It started making him throw up.

"But he loved every kind of food." Jan laughed. "He was crazy about sushi. Man, he could eat that every day. But on his birthday, he always wanted chicken-fried steak, mashed potatoes and gravy, and peas. I wouldn't cook it for him anymore because of his heart. I felt guilty about it. I couldn't control him."

In addition to his palsy, his hip injuries, and his weight, Leon's feet were causing him problems. It was all connected and limited his ability to exercise, even if he had the willpower, which he did not. Mike Johnstone caught up with Leon during these years. "He always had this big La-Z-Boy recliner chair beside the bus driver. I've got videos where I'm sitting right behind him. He's starting to get fat. I said, 'Why don't you get rid of that La-Z-Boy and put a stationary bicycle up there? Don't you ever feel like you should do something like that?' He goes, 'Yeah, Michael, but every time I get that feeling, I go take a nap, and that feeling goes away.' I stopped mentioning it after a while because then I just started noticing he was having to use a cane. And then pretty soon, he's got the scooter."

Along with compulsive shopping, the food obsession was a way to fill an emotional void. Jan said his struggles with depression continued throughout his life. "I have depression, and I can't function [at times]," she acknowledged. "But if he was going through it, he still wanted to be in the studio. I think he would have stayed in bed if he didn't have the studio. And if he didn't have an engineer, it was up to me to create the fun: 'What are we going to do today?' If I didn't have something, he would say, 'Well, let's go for a drive. Let's go get ice cream.' He didn't want to just be in bed."

Jan learned about autism later and realized it explained Leon's personality, including his "tired days." "I see it more as him being on the spectrum," she said. "He knew something was different about him, socially. He didn't have the social graces that most people do. He didn't pick up on social cues all the time. And as an adult, Leon barely spoke unless he had something to say, and it drove some people crazy because he just wouldn't speak."

His quiet demeanor and trouble reading social cues often gave people the wrong impression. He could be painfully blunt. Taken with his widely acknowledged genius and natural mystique, people often read it as arrogance, coldness, distance, or even mean-spiritedness. But nearly everyone who knew him well would jump to correct that misperception. "He had a great sense of humor," Bob Britt said. "And I can't really remember him ever being ugly to anybody."

Musician and engineer Mark Lambert said, "He was a really sensitive guy, really concerned about not making somebody else uncomfortable. He was always worried about that. He was very careful to not offend people. He was always serious about that. He felt really bad if somebody took offense; it really would bother him, and he would be remorseful about it."

Jan explained, "I didn't have a name for it until our girls went to a Montessori school, and they had a lot of students that had autism and Asperger's, that I finally had a name for it."

In a 2013 email to producer Tommy LiPuma, Leon wrote of this realization: "I was watching *Through the Wormhole*, Morgan Freeman's program, last night and saw a program about autism. As they described the causes and the symptoms, I realized that they were describing my life. They said it is primarily caused by damage to the left temporal lobe, that causes many brain duties to be shifted to the right temporal lobe. Apparently, autistics have limited social skills and few abilities in the real world, but in about 10 percent of the cases exhibit extraordinary talents in music, math, or art. My left brain is largely useless due to a birth injury to my 2nd and 3rd vertebrae."

Sugaree said, "I think [*Wormhole*] helped him feel a sense of belonging or fitting in, something I think he struggled with his whole life. He never received a diagnosis, but I think it's possible that he was right."

Leon and Jan's second child, Honey, was born on January 19, 1986. Leon's mother, Hester, eventually moved in with them in Tennessee after she divorced Gene Fulbright (they later reconciled). Teddy and Tina were still back and forth between Tennessee and California. "One Christmas, we had to pay Mary," Jan said. "Leon wanted his piano from her. It was the first grand piano that he ever had. And she said we could have the kids if he paid her $25,000 for that piano. So we paid her $25,000 for the piano so we could have the kids [for the holidays]." When the kids went to leave, they clung to Jan and called her Mommy, which is how they referred to Jan when they were back home.

"That was the last time that we saw our dad for a long time," Tina said. She did not have many clear memories of this event but that this level of possessiveness by Mary was consistent with how Tina knew her, especially then. "I love my mom. I don't talk to her, but I love her. . . . But it was made clear that us being able to freely talk about our dad was not a thing." Both Teddy and Tina would move to Tennessee to live with Leon and Jan once they graduated high school in the 1990s.

Some have pointed to Leon's father's abandonment of the family as the reason Leon always wanted to gather his flock. He liked having big family meals with the band. They would sit for hours at the table. "That was kind of the gathering place most of the time if we weren't in the studio in the bus," Bob Britt explained. "I think he liked having us around."

Leon took Britt under his wing. "I learned to engineer in the [home] studio. Leon always had wild ideas of how to do stuff. He loved to experiment. When all of this stuff started happening with MIDI sequencing and digital recording, Leon was naturally a very quick adopter of all that stuff." MIDI stands for Musical Instrument Digital Interface, a protocol that allows digital instruments to communicate and synchronize.

Britt said Leon's gear onstage became "over the top. He loved technology. He had these two big refrigerator-sized racks of stuff behind him and I don't know, seven, eight, stereo volume pedals down there to bring in basses, some strings, trombones, when I think everybody wished he just played the piano. Sometimes you just thought, 'Where's *Leon*?'"

In 1986, Leon joined forces with Edgar Winter for a co-headlining tour. Like Leon, Winter had been an arena star in the early 1970s with hits like "Free Ride" and "Frankenstein." But also like Leon, Winter's career dropped off dramatically. "Edgar was the opening act at a show in Florida, I think," Bob Britt said. "Leon asked him to sit in, and I just remember when Leon did 'Somewhere over the Rainbow' and Edgar took a sax solo, and everyone's jaws dropped. Right after the show, Leon asked Edgar if he wanted to join the band."

The two would end up touring on and off from 1986 to 1990, mostly in smaller clubs. Instead of Winter opening, the show paired the two together, Winter ostensibly playing as a member of the band, with featured spotlight moments. A review of a show in St. Louis said Winter "dominated the show," jumping from instrument to instrument. "I would occasionally get complaints that I was not doing enough," Leon wrote, "but it was such a pleasure to sit back, be in the band, and watch Edgar do his thing."

Leon usually complemented Winter's "psychedelic leprechaun" look (as one reviewer put it) with an ensemble that included a white wide-brimmed hat, shades, and a Hawaiian print shirt. There are clips online of a 1988 show in Murfreesboro, Tennessee, with Herb Shucher on drums, Bob Britt on guitar, Wessel on bass, and second keyboard player Flip Anderson. Leon reflected on the tour later, "Edgar Winter said three out of five notes that I sang were out of tune and I said, 'Edgar, don't hold back, tell me what you really think!'"

"Leon and Edgar were two sides of a coin," Wessel said. "Edgar was very exact. Edgar worked with every player on every part, every one of his songs. Leon's approach was approximate."

When the tour got to Long Beach, California, Leon was presented with a copy of video footage from his heyday, the shows shot in Anaheim by Robert Stone Jordan at the same shows where *Leon Live* was recorded. *A Poem Is a Naked Person* featured footage from the same shows. The videotape also had clips from Charlotte, North Carolina. Jeffrey Haas and Alan Pacella were partners who had recovered and restored the video reels that had lingered in storage for years.

The two went to Long Beach to show Leon the clips. Haas's position was that they didn't need Leon's approval to release it, as Leon had allegedly signed away any rights with the initial deal. But the pair hoped to create a deal where Leon would authorize and help promote the video on some level. Leon looked at the tape on the bus between shows, and his road manager came back out to meet Haas and Pacella. Haas recalled that they were told, "Listen, I have to tell you a couple of important things. First . . . Leon doesn't see people when he is on the road. You two will be the first people he has invited on the bus in five years. And I don't want you to get your hopes up either. What we're dealing with is a forty-eight-year-old man who probably doesn't remember all the way back to 1972, he's not in good health, and he is not beyond shooting himself in the foot over a principle."

Haas was now confronted with a much diminished older Leon. "He smiled and said it was a crazy energy back in those days," said Haas. But as with the Les Blank film, Leon did not agree to authorize the release of the video. He said he didn't like the video back in the seventies, and he purposely shelved it. As it was their opinion that they did not need Leon's blessing, they released the tapes on VHS copies. It is now available on DVD, with a misnomer title *The Best of the Leon Russell Festivals* (it's just Leon concerts, no "festivals"). The quality is fair at best, but given its journey, it's amazing to see it at all, and it is a valuable artifact that captures Leon at his peak, fronting one of the greatest bands of a golden era.

"It makes for good reading," Leon explained in 2003, referring to Haas's written account of the saga of the tapes. "Unfortunately, that's not the real story. I saw some documents that I purportedly signed, along with some documents that were signed by my partner representing Freddie King as his manager. He was never Freddie King's manager, and I didn't sign the documents."

Haas noted that at the time of his visit, Leon was already dealing with what would prove to be an ongoing issue—a leak of cerebrospinal fluid from his cranial cavity. If he leaned forward the fluid would come out of his nose. "It was some kind of malformed brainpan up in the upper sphenoid sinus," Leon explained in January 2015 to his friend, writer Alanna Nash, in *Penthouse*. "They didn't go together right, and it made a huge space. I had the first two operations done at the Mayo Clinic. The first one lasted a year or so. And the second one lasted about a week, and then it all came back and got a lot worse. . . . I'm on borrowed time."

Dr. Earl K. Miller, PhD, a professor of neuroscience at the Massachusetts Institute of Technology (and a rock 'n' roll bassist) explained, "It could have been caused by a congenital defect, head injury, or a tumor that tears the dura. Sometimes it happens for no obvious reason." It could have been related to the difficulties during Leon's birth. Miller said, "Leon must have had bad headaches and other symptoms like nausea, loss of balance, double vision. Poor guy."

It would lead to four brain surgeries over the rest of his life, the first in 1988. "We had flown from Hawaii to Jacksonville," Jan said. "He had his first two brain surgeries at the Mayo [Clinic]. The second one was in '98. The third one was in Santa Monica right at the beginning of his and Elton's collaboration [2009]. He was only about a week out of the surgery when he went in to record."

He called sixteen-year-old Blue after his first operation. "When he woke up, he said he wanted to talk to me," she recalled. "Jan gets him on the phone, and he said to me, 'Hey, Blueagle. How are you doing?' I would say, 'I'm okay.' And he said, 'How's your sex life?'" She laughed. "And I said, 'Nonexistent.' He had a lot of air on the brain.

"We left the hospital," she continued. "We're walking through the airport, and I've got my arm around him, holding on to him. He says, 'I want some ice cream.' He was talking like a baby, not like his playful little *I'm feeling insecure or vulnerable* voice, but like he was a child because of the air on his brain. It was so scary. He gets a cone, I get a cone, and I hear this guy: 'Hey, Russell!' They talk for a minute. He starts to lean, and he's physically exhausted, but he seemed different already. When we sat down, I was like, 'Who was that?' He starts playing the drums on his lap like he's a kid, the Bo Diddley beat. He said, 'That was Bo Diddley.'" Blue said she detected a pronounced change in his personality each time he had an operation. "He kind of came out of the childlike stuff, but he didn't seem to be as quick to me.'"

The Leon and Edgar tour had gone to Brazil in 1987 and then on to Russia in 1989, as part of Mikhail Gorbachev's policy of glasnost, opening up the USSR as a cultural outreach program. Russia in the 1980s proved not to be such a great time, though they did get to open for La Toya Jackson.

But Leon had lost the thread with some of his most famous peers, like Eric Clapton, George Harrison, and Bob Dylan. The latter two were joining forces in the Traveling Wilburys with two other Leon friends, Tom Petty and Jim Keltner (along with Jeff Lynne and Roy Orbison). One can only imagine how it might have helped Leon to get the call to be included in that supergroup. "Leon had long been out of touch with Dylan and had only spoken to George once that I recall, in the early eighties," Wessel said. "Leon spoke more than once of being embarrassed to reach out to some of his old, still very famous friends. After the dive his career had taken, he feared appearing to be fishing for an invite or some sort of profile boost through a new association. Leon's close friendship and complete comfort with Willie Nelson allowed him to benefit somewhat from fairly frequent bookings. Leon would refer to himself, in interviews and onstage sometimes, as 'Willie Nelson's favorite charity.'"

Larry Shaeffer had always wanted to get in with Leon's circle when he was just starting out as a promoter in Tulsa. In 1976, Shaeffer bought Cain's Ballroom. One of his first bookings there was a notorious show with the Sex Pistols. He had first promoted shows there with his company Little Wing Productions before buying the venue. He eventually booked Frank Sinatra, Willie Nelson, and other A-list headliners at venues across the Southwest and Midwest. "Leon was the model of what I wanted to do with my company," Shaeffer noted while we talked at Cain's. "I wanted to do Leon and all his dates, doing nothing else. That didn't happen."

He was finally able to work with him, but by then Leon was near his lowest draw as a performer. "He was my dream. 'I got a place. If you want five grand, I'll give you five grand.' He went from ten thousand seats to playing beer joints. He could always play here, but he never sold out here." Cain's capacity was about eighteen hundred.

Shaeffer said he was always respectful of Leon: "He was introverted and hard to know. He wanted to play, get paid, and leave. But remember, Leon was playing in the fifties, and where he played, when it was time to get paid, the club owner was like, 'Fuck you.' He was distrusting, like a guy that's been in jail in San Quentin, sitting in a corner so he can see what was coming.

"You know what would excite Leon more than music and playing a gig?" Shaeffer asked. "If you told him, 'I got a guy who runs cockfights, give me $500, and he'll give you $1,000 back.' They came out of the woodwork for him, and Leon would buy into that dumb shit. It was ground-level carnival-barker shit, and he ate it up."

Cockfights. Leon Land. Chinese junk. Televangelists. "Pure Leonia." Leon Russell was always a carny at heart.

Chapter 34

Anything Can Happen

LEON HIT THE ROAD ON and off for about a year and a half, playing one-man shows in small joints for about $3,000. Most of the deals were low guarantees with the promise to make more money from a split of the door over a certain amount of tickets sold, so Jan would sit near the entry with a clicker, keeping the promoters honest.

Through the pre-internet system of agent networking, Brad Davis enlisted the help of Jack Randall of the Concerted Efforts agency in Boston to help with bookings. He flew up to Boston and met with Randall, and they agreed to split the booking commissions fifty-fifty. "The reality, when I look back at it now—and of course I have almost thirty years more experience under my belt—Leon Russell should have been paying Brad 15, 20, 25 percent," Randall posited. "I mean, he was doing a lot of stuff for Leon above and beyond being an agent, but Leon was only paying him 10 percent. And our arrangement, for as long as it lasted, was, we were splitting 10 percent."

It was back to the small-time. Leon was booked in small dives that were really just bars with a makeshift stage. Sometimes there was just a square of carpet and a few cheap lights. Leon hadn't played joints this bad since his teenage days in Tulsa. He was willing to give it a go, attracted by the low-overhead, higher-margin prospects. But he quickly realized that it did significant harm to his value as a performer. "That's what was becoming of his market value, and it scared the hell out of him," Jack Wessel said. "So, when they struck that deal with Virgin to do the album with Bruce Hornsby, he was hoping to undo all that damage."

Hornsby had broken through in a big way, with hit records with his band the Range, cowriting and producing for Don Henley ("The End of Innocence"), moonlighting as a regular pianist with the Grateful Dead. He was determined to take full advantage of his newfound popularity. "I played enough Ramada Inns back in what we called 'the bad old days,' until things started rolling and started happening for us. In 1990, my life was crazy. I started playing two different bands; I was playing on records galore, trying to do my version of Leon, being a session guy. I just did whatever was coming up."

Hornsby had caught one of the shows with Edgar Winter. "It looked like they were up there both wearing some pajamas; it was hilarious," he said with a chuckle. "I met him on the bus. We had a nice little chat, and that was that—until the next year, '88, we got this call from *Rolling Stone* asking me to be a part of this photo essay called 'Musicians and Their Mentors.'" In the September 21, 1989, issue, the feature asked current popular artists who their mentors were. After finding out Elton John had already been claimed, Bruce Hornsby chose his other top influence, Leon Russell.

Rolling Stone paid for him to go down to Hendersonville to meet his hero. "I flew out there on *Rolling Stone*'s dime and spent two days with Leon, becoming friends with him while they took pictures of us." Bob Britt said that Hornsby visited during the rehearsal for the upcoming tour of Russia with Edgar Winter. "He was sitting there on the couch while we were working on 'Frankenstein.'"

Hornsby had ambitions for Leon. "At the end of the two-day stint, I said, 'Listen, Leon, if you have any interest in trying to get back into this game'—because at the time he was playing *regional libraries*," Hornsby said with a chuckle. "But I just threw that out to him: 'I don't know if I could help you, but I would try as hard as I can. Here's my number.' That was July or August of '88."

At midnight that Christmas Eve, Hornsby's phone rang. "It was Leon saying, 'I'd like to take you up on your offer.' I said, 'I'll do my damnedest.' The next month, I went to Virgin Records, pitched them on this, and they pretty much said, 'Okay, we love Leon, and you're kind of doing some big stuff now, what the hell.' So I called Leon and said, 'Okay, this was pretty easy; there's still a lot of fond feeling for you in this biz.'" Leon, though, wrote that he was introduced to Jeff Ayeroff at Virgin Records by "my friend Sherman Halsey and the deal was finalized with the participation of

Bruce Hornsby." It took a while for it to come together, with the two musicians getting to know each other before a record deal was in place. The
Virgin deal memo from April 22, 1991, outlining the contract stated that
advance for the record was $250,000, with options for six more records,
with minimum advances incrementally increasing in $25,000 increments.
If Leon sold enough records, the advances would increase based on a formula, up to a $600,000 ceiling on the seventh album. Such figures would
not have been offered without Hornsby's involvement.

In the meantime, Hornsby joined Leon on the road, though not onstage. "Riding around between gigs, late at night, we would talk about
music and talk about the possible record that we could make. We would
fool around with some ideas, and a couple of songs got started on the bus."

Throughout 1990 and 1991, Hornsby occasionally went down to
work at Leon's studio in Hendersonville, with Mark Lambert engineering.
He would work on the record with Leon about three days a month over
a year. They were just getting acquainted. "He called me 'Horny Man'
or 'H Man.' I eventually just became just 'H.' For a short period, I was
just Bruce. He said, 'Bruce, write me a Barry White track.' Wow, what
an assignment! Okay, well, Barry White likes minor ninth chords, minor
seventh chords, and he likes major seventh chords, too, so it's out of my
rigid harmonic aesthetic. Something I would never do on my own—it
would always sound a little loungey to me." As Hornsby said, he'd played
enough Ramada Inns.

"I put together this track," Hornsby continued. "I guess he thought it
was okay. He hands me this red notebook full of lyrics: 'Find me something to sing in here.' So I'm paging through these lyrics. I don't have
much to go on. I said, 'Hey, here's a lyric called "Anything Can Happen."
How about that?'" After listening through the track three times, Leon
called for a take. "He proceeds to deliver this ridiculous performance, just
truly fantastic. I go, 'Wow, that was just really *amazingly* great. I can't say
enough about it. But there's this *one* line where it sounds like you've got
some phlegm in your throat, a froggy sound, so maybe we can just punch
that one in.' He said, 'Well, no, no, sir. On a Picasso level, I feel like that
was my art, and I do not want to besmirch the integrity of the piece.' In
my mind, I said, 'Well, on a philosophical level, that's pretty much un-
assailable.' But in the back of my mind is, 'Try to figure out a way to get
him to do this.'"

It would take about eight months. "I found that he was always really willing to reconsider a lyric. We were working on 'Anything Can Happen' again. I said, 'Hey, Leon, do you think we can come up with a better line on this one?' Of course, there was nothing wrong with the lyric, but that was my ruse, and he pondered over that a minute and said, 'Okay.' So he sang it, and luckily he nailed the shit out of it. And then we wouldn't tell him."

"He's a great musician, and he makes great records," Leon said about Hornsby. "I think he's responsible for inventing a genre of music that I think of as Shenandoah music. 'Mandolin Rain' and stuff like that. Then he started drifting into jazz and away from that. I think he is primarily a jazz musician." In the liner notes of the album, Leon wrote, "This recording event was made possible, primarily, by Bruce taking leave of the fast lane and coming to my aid in the rest area. The Horny Man is the one out of ten who will return the favor. That's just the way it is."

Hornsby cowrote seven of the album's ten numbers. "Anything Can Happen" became the title track. Leon's vocal performance is impressive. The phrasing and meter are challenging, with a "Stranger in a Strange Land"–style rap as the coda, but there is no stumbling over the wordy lyric. For a first take, the pitch is unimpeachable. Hornsby himself recut the song in 2020, floating in Leon's voice for the chorus sections. "That was a big critics' favorite," said Hornsby. "Everyone from the *Times* of London to *Pitchfork* loved that."

Those not paying much attention at the time—who had maybe stopped listening to Leon's records around the *Wedding Album*—might naturally assume that he agreed to work with Hornsby as a producer because Hornsby had also been working with drum machines and highly stylized production. But Hornsby said this is false. "I, like probably most people, loved Leon playing an acoustic piano, but he was so into what I called 'the toys,' these piano-facsimile attempts. They still proliferate; you hardly ever see a real piano onstage anymore. There are some great versions, especially now, but back then, not so much. And he insisted on that. I said, 'Really? You don't want to play a real piano?' He says, 'Man, I haven't played a real piano in ages, and my hands are not strong enough to play the real piano.' He sat with us one time at Red Rocks Amphitheater. . . . After the gig, he says, 'Oh my God, that was so hard; that piano of yours is so stiff.' So I just let it go: 'Okay, it's gonna be machines.'"

"I asked Leon about [*Anything Can Happen*]. He said it didn't work out," remembered Michael Johnstone. "I asked why. He said, 'Well, it got kind of bloody,' so I just didn't dig into that."

"[Hornsby] wanted Leon to use a real drummer, and Leon wouldn't do that," Wessel confirmed. "I guess it was a concession that a guy come in and play like [Roland electronic] V Drums on one song, not even a regular drum kit. That's just what Leon wanted to hear."

Virgin "wanted Bruce to produce Leon and make him earthy-sounding," said musician Matt Harris, who had recently met and married Blue. Leon enlisted him to play a part on his latest album. "Leon was like, 'I can't do it,' and spent the advance for that Virgin record on a tractor. I grew up on this guy, and he was earthy and playing live. [Now] we're in the studio, and it's all being recorded to the computer. The solos that I played on ['Love Slave'] came back edited completely different."

"The Black Crowes wanted him to play on their album, and Leon wanted to bring in his keyboard rig, you know, which had really great Steinway samples on it," Wessel recalled. "He just preferred to play that keyboard. He said, 'I don't like to play wood pianos anymore.' They basically said, 'Well, thanks,' and didn't use him."

The reliance and full-on embrace of technology date *Anything Can Happen* squarely in the late 1980s and early 1990s. There's an absence of organic humanness to it, which could be okay if he were going for a robotic effect. But Leon's endearingly dusty drawl is buried under a ticky-tack synthesized sonic landscape. Leon would continue down this path after the record, with low-resolution digital production eclipsing moments of genuinely inspired songwriting.

"That was a regret for me on that record," Hornsby said. "At the same time, if you can get past the piano and drum aspect, a lot of Leon's real nutty side came out on that."

Hornsby recalled, "The main guests were his son and daughter, Tina and Teddy Jack. Tina sang a bunch of backgrounds. Teddy played the Van Halen–esque rock guitar, a ripping solo on Chuck Berry's 'Too Much Monkey Business.'" Teddy was only about fifteen at the time. Leon wrote in the liner notes, "From the start of my life, I had a vision of a family band, and it gives me great pleasure to have them appear on the record."

The inspired, personal closing ballad, "Faces of the Children," is one moment that cuts through the production. "I see you in the baby's eyes / And the faces of the children": The baby in this lyric is Coco, Jan and Leon's last child to be born, in 1990. "It's really sweet," Jan said of the song. "He knew that I love nothing more than being a mom, and he was happy to help me with that." He was, at this point, the patriarch of a sizable but scattered brood. The three girls with Jan were under one roof. Although Leon was gone for long periods, he was also home for weeks, even months at a stretch, and he made a deep impression on them as children.

Coco said, "I think we stopped going on the road with him regularly when I was three—but I still have very vivid memories of getting on the bus. My whole family has this thing; we struggle to sleep. But whenever we slept on the bus, it was the best sleep that we had. So we find that we're trying to mimic that. I'm putting up a bed tent and having a white noise machine, reminiscent of the engine."

"We traveled with him so much in my childhood; it never felt like he wasn't there," Sugaree recalled. "Even though we were always traveling with him, I still had music recitals and softball games at home, and he was there for those too. He even played catch with me on occasion. For the first nine years of my life, we traveled on the road with my dad. My mom would homeschool us, and we would visit a lot of the places we were learning about."

Blue had lived with Leon and Jan until 1989, when she essentially ran away from Tennessee, moving back to Tulsa with another friend with roots in that city. Blue wrote a letter to Leon explaining that she left because she was unhappy there, that he had changed after his brain surgeries, and that she struggled to get along with Jan. She went to see Leon again at a 1990 show in Tulsa, and they cleared the air. "I hugged him, and he said, 'I'm sorry. I love you.'"

Matt Harris grew up in Oklahoma, in a musical family, as a fan of Leon Russell, and studied music in LA. While back home in Tulsa, he met Blue at a strip club. "I was dancing at a place called Lady Godiva," Blue said. "It was my very first night dancing. I had never done it before." That was in the spring. They got married the following September, but Leon could not attend. "He couldn't give me away because he fell," Blue explained. Leon had been checking out the remodeling of his equipment truck, his pant leg got caught on something, and he fell off, breaking his femur.

Harris recalled, "From the get-go, it was, 'Ooh, be careful!' You know, 'You don't want to have too big of a wedding because Leon's gonna be there.' And it was all about, you know, 'He's this kind of strange, weird cat, and we want to accommodate because he can be overwhelmed,' and all this mythological shit, and this is from his *daughter*," Harris said with a laugh. "So, he fell off a truck and couldn't come to our wedding. The first time I met him, he drove up to our house in the bus with his family, dropped them off, and he and I went to Whataburger in Tulsa, him driving the bus. He drove off into a ditch, and we had to get some help to get out. I was twenty-four. Then we go to the Church Studio, and Steve Ripley's there. [Leon's] like, 'Cool, you're a musician; I'm a musician; let's go hang out.' I'd been around rock stars, but this is hilarious. I was a fan, for sure, and knew all of this shit—*all* of it—as a child.

"[At] the Church, he starts looking at the floor. He goes, 'I'm just looking for all my ex-bitch-wife-from-hell's heel marks on the floor from her stomping around in this room.'"

Anything Can Happen was released in 1992 and stiffed. It was a typical story for the 1990s. EMI bought Virgin, and the A&R guy who was supposed to be overseeing Leon's album got canned. He did two big-budget videos for the album, both directed by Sherman Halsey, who had become a successful music video director. "No Man's Land" is set in a vaguely postapocalyptic urban tableau, standard for the time. Leon is cast as some sort of wizard cult leader on a throne with a magical orb. A bunch of semiclad nubiles writhe around below him. He did another for "Anything Can Happen." "Such a great song," Wessel observed. "It's such a terrible video, the cows, and David Keith snapping at his woman." Leon wrote and recorded the theme song for *Flesh 'n' Blood*, a television show starring Keith that aired only eight episodes.

Leon appeared on *Letterman* again, performing the title track. But the music videos didn't get much play. "When MTV started blowing up, Leon didn't have management, and he didn't have a label when all that stuff started taking off," Wessel said. "Leon just never did partner well. Although I think in later years, he and Denny had spoken warmly a few times, maybe not in person, but wished each other well."

Hornsby said, "It was a different time in music, and so much more promotion seemed to be necessary. . . . And they're playing showcase rooms, the sort of rooms that the record company thought were key taste-making rooms, quote-unquote. I say that all cynically because Leon called me up and said, 'Man, this is ruining my pricing structure.' Meaning, 'I'm making a lot less money than I normally make, playing these gigs that the record company wants me to play.'"

Wessel said, "He put together another big band, a temporary big band for that album, with a lot of keyboards, just for the orchestral outlay. He had a guy that played nothing but string parts, and another guy who played second piano, another guy who played synth and organ parts—really quite a good band."

Reviewing one show of the *Anything Can Happen* tour, the *Hartford* (CT) *Courant* summed up Leon's career at this point: "Russell played a sparsely attended show. . . . His career struggling to rebound with a major label album co-written and co-produced by Bruce Hornsby, he's touring for the first time in years with a full band, which, in his case, means synthesizers, synthesizers, and more synthesizers."

Leon Russell, who once had the greatest drummers in the world at his disposal, continued to opt to go it alone, at least in the studio. One of the greatest, Jim Keltner, caught a Leon show around this era. "When he got to that period I figured that he was gone, because that's what happened with a lot of people," Keltner said. "I was a little resentful of that because there was nobody, nobody that you could play live with better than Leon.

"Cynthia [Keltner's wife] and I went to see him one time play live down at the beach. For me, the essence of Leon was enough. When we got back in the car, she said, 'Why did it sound so tinny?'" He laughed. "It sounded tinny, but it was $150,000 worth of gear. I said, 'You know how much money he spent to make that stuff sound like that?'"

An *LA Times* review of a show at the Coach House in San Juan Capistrano, a place Leon would play often, captures the state of Leon during this era: "Russell played digital keyboards, with a minicomputer screen staring him in the face. The ring of players around him included three others also manning synthesizers that generated almost-organ, near-guitar, and approximate saxophone. Together, they relegated Russell to the role of just another cog in his own band."

It was during a decade plus when Leon would not engage with the audience. Almost everyone who caught him during these years recalled his detachment, his robotic performances with only a few perfunctory thank-yous before launching into the next song and splitting as soon as he could, as if he didn't want to be there.

There's a conundrum with Leon starting in the 1990s—a disconnect between his past as a passionate collaborator, bandleader, and master showman, and his present as a guy walling himself off behind banks of technical gear. He had let the lean and groovy hippie-preacher persona slip away long ago. First it was usurped by Mary's suave soft rock duet partner, then by the rockin' outlaw country guy—in a leather vest over cowboy shirts, and Kenny Rogers shag under a cowboy hat—of the New Grass years. Finally, in an astonishingly short number of years, the young Leon was buried under a heavyset, surly-faced Santa Claus (he was only fifty!) in Hawaiian shirts.

"I met him, I think, when he was fifty," Matt Harris said. "And he looked the same way that he did when he was seventy-five. He had his little pocket protector and his pants that he bought ten pairs of. He was this same-thing-every-day-looking guy. He didn't move around then; he was always in a Barcalounger, so he can lay in the 'Johnny Cash position.' I guess he had some story about Johnny Cash, passed out in the studio."

The riddle is, did his dependence on technology precipitate his inward turn as a performer, or was he so tired of his act, losing the energy required to keep up this masquerade, that the tech offered him a bulwark to hide behind? The answer is a little of both. He had always embraced innovation, long fascinated by fellow visionaries, and leapt at any new gear he heard about. From his earliest days as a high school musician sticking a microphone in his acoustic piano and running it through an amp, he was looking to translate the music in his head to his audience. Leon built one of the earliest professional home studios. Before he knew someone else was creating the Chamberlin, he had a concept for the same type of instrument. He also had the idea of a programmable digital drum machine, inspiring Roger Linn to create one and become rich in the process. Leon was also at least partially responsible for the horizontal pitch lever on digital keyboards. "He was Future Man," Harris said.

The result was an eventual distancing of the artist from his audience: an almost-human facsimile that came nowhere near his down-and-dirty *Leon Live* peak. Now he was Leon Almost Live.

Harris said that Leon had described his personality transformation—from unassuming session player to Master of Space and Time—as if he were talking about someone else. "Leon took on this role as the guru, as the Master of Space, the wisdom guy—yet he was the first one to tell you, 'I don't know anything about anything.'" Leon told Harris, "All this is a false pretense." Of his fans, Leon added, "I'm not even sure who they think I am. They don't even know how scared I am and how weak I am." At various points, Leon called himself "a fraud" to others close to him. He had experienced that self-doubt all the way back and laid out such inner turmoil on *Carney*, like Guido in Fellini's *8½*.

Hornsby felt it was not his place to challenge Leon on his choice of instruments, and he feels he gets unjustly singled out as someone who overproduced Leon. But he was doing his best to puff some wind into Leon's sails. "I understand why someone would blame me. . . . Virtually all my hits were just pattern-mode Roger Linn [drum machine], so I get that. But again, they should realize that, for one thing, I'm an acoustic musician. I'm not gonna want the toy; I had disdain for it. There are people spouting off their opinions based on very little knowledge of Leon's complete corpus." Hornsby referred back to Leon's use of the Yamaha electric pianos with New Grass Revival, which he saw live at Disneyland. "That's some of the greatest music that Leon ever made. That fuckin' thing is no joke."

In 1992, Hornsby named one of his twin sons Russell in tribute to Leon (the other he named Keith, after Keith Jarrett). "I wanted it to be Leon Russell, but my wife wouldn't go for it. I thought he would be a super soul child. Jan told me later that Leon woke her up in the middle of the night, and said, 'Horny Man had his babies, and he named one of them Russell.' And Jan said, 'What did he name the other one?' He said, 'I don't know, I can't get past Russell.'"

Hornsby went back to Tennessee around 1993. By that time, Leon and Jan had moved out to the farm in Sideview, near Gallatin. Hornsby said, "He had these two big barns, massive high ceilings, large square footage. He had two or three buses, all in various states of disrepair. He was always buying and repairing buses. We walk into this big storage facility—more old studio gear, old mixing boards, old consoles from the sixties and early seventies. We're walking around his garage, and he's got some old gold record for J. J. Cale's *Naturally*, or whatever. Over there's a gold record, and a platinum record over here, some old trophy from something, a couple of old posters from gigs. I said, 'Leon, what is all this stuff?' And he goes, 'Residue from the fast lane.'"

Chapter 35

Just a Face in the Crowd

IN 1993, RAY CHARLES RELEASED *My World*, with his version of "A Song for You." "[Leon] wrote that for Ray Charles," Patrick Henderson noted. "[Producer] Richard Perry was the one that finally got Ray Charles to perform that song. It wasn't easy."

But it might have come at just the right time. The recording resulted in a Grammy for Charles for Best R&B Performance and brought him a top ten hit on the *Billboard* Adult Contemporary chart. It served as a fresh and necessary reminder of the genius of Leon Russell.

Jan said Leon was "stoked" that his hero finally recorded "A Song for You." In 2003, the two men and Willie Nelson would perform it as a trio at the Beacon Theatre in New York for Nelson's televised seventieth birthday concert. That version never gets old. Leon and then Willie take the first two verses, wisely clearing the way for Charles to bring the song home. Jack Wessel said, "Leon had pitched it to Ray before releasing his own version, but Ray passed on it at that time." Leon told Henderson that when Charles was first presented with it in 1970, Ray said, "Well, I ain't going to rip off myself."

Not only was Leon delighted when Charles finally did it, Wessel said, but he was "also excited to get a nice royalty spike." Leon could have used it right then. After the swing-and-miss of the Virgin Records deal, and after the large-band tour on *Anything Can Happen* in 1992, he was back to playing economical solo shows. Mark Lambert would stay on as an engineer and occasional guitarist for him until the end, with only one hiatus. And, of course, Jack Wessel would remain his loyal bassist, friend, aide-de-camp, and virtual family member, a guy who would help Leon in every way possible. Leon repaid the loyalty. "Towards the end of '92, he said, 'Well, I've just got a couple shows, why don't you grab your bass and play with me?'" explained Wessel. "It was fun. But he was playing tiny little joints. It was getting a little more extreme."

Wessel was by Leon's side when he returned to his old Grand Lake place around 1994. Its current owner, Rick Huskey, a chiropractor and drummer, had bought the property around 1991. Visiting the place now is like walking back in time and into *A Poem Is a Naked Person*. The buildings all look remarkably the same as they did in 1972, with the clinker-brick siding and chimneys. There have been some changes inside the main house, but the original bathrooms remain intact. The long, solid table and chairs Leon had made out of the pews taken out of the Church are still there, as are some of the doors.

On a recent visit, pop star Taylor Hanson was there with his son, working on new music, though the studio was essentially a cinder-block barn, with a control room but no permanent recording gear—a glorified rehearsal studio. The Jim Franklin murals in the pool are, of course, long faded.

Shortly after the release of *Anything Can Happen* in 1994, Huskey threw a birthday party for a friend, whose mother asked Huskey, "Do you think there's any way you could get Leon Russell to play?" He replied, "If you've got the right checkbook, I can try."

He continued: "I was treating Emily Smith at the time, [and she] helped me get connected with Leon's manager. Emily got involved, and he agreed to do it for $10,000. He came down and stayed in his old bedroom at the house one night, took a shower, and hung out."

Wessel said the place had so many photos of Leon that it felt a bit like a shrine, which made Leon uncomfortable. But he appreciated seeing the property again. Leon told Huskey, "I'm really glad somebody like you has got this place because I've often thought about what happened to it." Huskey was moved to tears.

For a while, Leon toured with just Jackie and Ambrose Campbell. "This is when 'unplugged' was all the rage," Wessel said, referring to the series *MTV Unplugged*. "And Leon had his keyboard rig set up inside of a black baby grand shell. . . . People would see what appeared to be a grand and go, 'Ooh! Unplugged.' And we'd start up, and it would be loud as hell. We were the anti-unplugged."

Leon had not toured Europe since his earliest days and would not do so again until after 2010. But he played Japan solo in 1990, and then with his bands in '93, '95, and '96, and three more times through 2013. In 1993, the band was Wessel, drummer Danny Darling, Bob Ramsey on the second keyboard, and Mark Lambert on guitar. Leon had written and performed a Japanese television commercial for Asahi Beer in 1986 (as he had for two Budweiser beers in America, in 1984 and 1987).

Wessel recalled of the 1993 tour: "The last night in Tokyo, his friend Butch Robins, the banjo player, was over there teaching banjo clinics, and he came out and played with us one night. We're all going out, and Butch came with us. Butch was buying drinks for everybody. We saw a karaoke bar, so we went in there. And by this time, we were all pretty pissed [drunk]. Leon may have had one drink that night. I knew why Leon did not drink. I saw him drunk one time, and that explained everything. Some people cannot, and he was one of those people."

The mic was eventually passed to their table. "Leon sang first, and I forget what he sang, but he did a nice honest job and got a nice hand. Then the rest of us—me and Mark [Lambert] and Bob Ramsey, the keyboard player—got ahold of the mic. All of us just went into a total Bill Murray lounge act. And we just thought we were *high*-larious. And after the last of us goes, Leon leans over to Butch and says, 'Let's go.' And we got in this van, and Leon says, 'Well, I've never been so fucking embarrassed in my whole life. I cannot believe this. My band, so-called professional musicians, all of you trying to sound like dog shit. I don't get it.' Leon was pretty good about forgiving, but he didn't forget. And for as long as I knew him—you know, twenty years later, and I'm the only one left around to take that in the face—anytime the word 'karaoke' would come up, whether it was on TV or somebody else sitting there mentioned it, if he heard that word, 'I'll never forget the time I was in Japan with my band. . . .' And he'd tell the whole thing; he'd always say, 'So-called professional musicians trying to sound like dog shit. Never been so embarrassed in my life.'"

The balance of the 1990s was a repeating cycle, touring the same circuit and recording what Wessel called the "merch records" (short for merchandise; T-shirts, CDs, and other items sold on the road). Leon created a cottage industry, forming another label, Leon Russell Records, for selling CDs from his website and at shows. He was like an indie rock or folk artist, duplicating the CDs in his studio. "He used to just make records and press 'em up and design a cover and sell them at the shows," Wessel explained. "There must be at least twenty of those things over the years."

Jan stopped touring with him during the nineties. "Leon tried so hard to get me to go back on the road," she lamented. "But I kept thinking if we were both on the road that we might both die and leave the girls without parents. He tried so hard. There was nothing stopping me. It was just me and him. But I was afraid—we'd get kind of close [to an accident] sometimes, or there were some bad bus drivers in there. . . . He worked. It was a job."

After one of those near-accidents, Leon hired a new bus driver named Michael Graham. Leon himself was driving the bus when he hired Graham. He relocated Graham and his wife, Shelley, to a trailer on his property in Gallatin, with Shelley working as an administrative assistant. He met Graham on the road after receiving his résumé as a trucker and driver on a U2 tour. But he would just as soon hire bus drivers and road managers via classified want ads as through professional networks.

The plum gigs were far and few between endless one-nighters in low-profile venues. Leon's old friend from the Nitty Gritty Dirt Band, John McEuen, was booking festival shows in between his own gigs and tours. He recalled, "I was talking to his agent once, 'Do you think he could do ninety minutes?' He said, 'Let me put it this way, I had an offer for $20,000 for ninety minutes and $10,000 for seventy-five minutes, and Leon took the $10,000.'" But Leon wanted—and was unable—to stop touring, and the choices were limited. No manager could convince him otherwise. McEuen continued. "After thirty years of assessing him, seeing him every couple of years, it didn't feel to me like he thought that much of himself. He was not a star like other people that have the right radio records."

One of the few changes in the routine was the real estate back in Tennessee. By the middle of the 1990s, Leon and Jan were living full-time on the two-hundred-acre farm in Sideview, near Gallatin. Ambrose was in his seventies and had retired to his emeritus status. Leon and Jan took care of him out on the farm, where he stayed in one of the mobile homes, along with the Grahams and Teddy Jack. A friend of Teddy's from California, Ryan Kirwan, came out to keep Teddy Jack company and stayed, playing guitar in Leon's band for a bit. Teddy took over percussion from Ambrose before moving on to drums and eventually guitar. He had moved to Leon and Jan's place as soon as he was eighteen, in 1994. "We had an unfortunate divorce in our family, and I wasn't allowed to see him for 10 years," Leon told the *LA Times* in 1999. "It was really a terrible thing. On his 18th birthday, he called me up to say, 'I'm coming.'"

"The weird thing about that is as soon as my brother turned eighteen, it was kind of like, 'Alright, bye,'" Tina Rose said, referring to Mary's attitude. "This whole time, she didn't really want to hear about my dad, but then when my brother turned eighteen, it was 'Get out of here,' basically." When asked about how home life changed once Teddy left, Tina replied, "It was horrible. Because all of the focus was on me. My mom was very controlling and hyperfocused on us as kids." Tina herself would join Teddy at Leon and Jan's about four years later.

"My dad loved his kids, and he wanted all of us together," Blue said. Blue and her young family moved out to live on the farm in Gallatin in 1995–1996.

"We went to live with them when I was about four and a half," Blue's daughter, Halen, said. "Jan and my mother became very close. And my parents split up within maybe six months of us being here. But the intent behind it was my father was a musician, and Oklahoma wasn't doing much for him."

Halen recalls the move as being less than idyllic. She was there until she was about eleven years old. The people involved have widely variable and contradicting perspectives on what life was like for the expanded family on the farm. But no one looks at it through rose-colored glasses, and each of them agrees that having all the kids—plus a grandkid—together was ultimately a failed arrangement.

Leon was away more often than not. Everyone from the family who was interviewed acknowledges his mood changes, ascribed variously as some combination of bipolar disorder, Asperger's syndrome, and the effects of his physical health. "He aged *really* fast. He had hip replacement surgery when he was forty-eight years old," Blue said. "He toured like that. Before the scooter, in the very beginning, they put him in a wheelchair. They'd have to lift a wheelchair up onto the stage, and he'd get there and play, and they'd lift him off. When he was in his forties, they said he had the body of a sixty-five-year-old. Both of his hips were bad. Even in first-class airplanes, he would be miserable and uncomfortable." That was one reason he preferred the bus, which at least had his recliner.

Wessel considered the 1991 fall from the equipment truck pivotal. "He had to have a pin. He left the pin in too long, and then he had to have the whole socket replaced. There was a time when he started using the cane—for a year or two, every time he'd walk out onstage with a cane, people who hadn't seen him would just gasp. That gave this whole notion that he was frail, and I never thought of him as frail; I thought he was pretty damn stout. He really could tough it out, no matter what. The problem he had wasn't so much his hip as his feet. There was always one orthopedic issue or another, but mostly his feet had a curvature. He could get up and walk, but it just hurt. And after he had his bypass [in 1996] it got worse and worse."

Leon's lifelong limp, the feet, the motorcycle accident when he was tripping on acid at Skyhill, the 1991 fall from the truck, and heart trouble—it all wore him down. His diet did not help. "He ate like a teenager for years," Wessel lamented. "He just didn't want to hear about it. Ridin' around the middle of the night, 'Oh, there's a Whataburger! Pull over.' He ate like a kid into his sixties and really didn't get better until a little too late."

Even when home, Leon sometimes slept on the bus parked out in the driveway, especially in later years. No matter where they lived, Leon would have a place to park the buses, and it was often a point of contention with neighbors. But with hundreds of acres out on the farm, Leon could spread out.

"When he would be home, he would often go to a dark room with the Barcalounger and watch TV," Halen said. She spent some of her formative childhood years living at the property with her half-aunts and half-uncle (Sugaree, Coco, Honey, Tina, and Teddy). Her primary memories of her grandfather from those years were of his need for quiet and solitude.

Halen's father, Matt Harris, who became a trusted friend, confidant, and collaborator of Leon, said that Leon was not one to require an inordinate amount of privacy. Harris, a self-described "type-A personality," concluded that the family often misinterpreted his demeanor. Leon didn't want people tiptoeing around him, though he did appreciate his private space and time. "Leon said to me in the early days, 'What you want to do is, you want to have a house big enough to where you could have your whole family live there, but you don't have to see them every day,'" Harris recalled. "Leon is somebody that the family feels like was disassociated and kind of shy around them and didn't show enough affection. He was actually always taking care of them financially. He actually wanted the house with everybody in it, including not only me as the ex-son-in-law, but Tina's boyfriends, Sugaree's boyfriends—that family has always taken in every boyfriend that all of those girls have ever had."

"He was sweet," Halen recalled. "He would come home and cook these big Southern meals. I mean, he always felt like he was this fluffy old man. Maybe when I was around ten it started to happen [Leon's emotional distance]. I do remember going out with him. He loved Southern food, and he would take us to these big buffets. He always liked our ears; he would be like, 'Ooh wook at your li'l ears.' He would always grab my ears. Oh man, this is going to make me cry. I'd forgotten a lot about him. . . . So many memories rush back to me."

Blue recalled a story of when Halen was about two, and Leon pulled Blue aside to seriously advise Blue to nip in the bud some trait of Halen's that he perceived. He said, "That's a character flaw." Blue laughed at him and sarcastically asked, "Oh, really?" She poked fun at her father for identifying a "character flaw" in her toddler. He admitted, "What can I say? I'll always be Hester's boy."

Harris felt no compunction to tread lightly around Leon, who marveled when Harris bought him lunch. He said, "No one ever buys *me* lunch!" Harris advised guys auditioning for a role in Leon's band to do the same; the easiest way to get into Leon's good graces was with a meal and the gesture of paying for it.

Teddy looked up to Matt, ten years his senior, a multi-instrumentalist he could hang out with. "Teddy moves out there because his mom would never let him see his dad," Harris explained. "And he meets his dad. [Mary] would hold back Christmas presents [from Leon and Jan]. Teddy gets out there, hangs with his dad; 'Oh my God, this is the greatest thing that's ever happened.' Leon was like, 'I've got a son!' And they just connected; they fell in love with each other. Teddy is super talented. When he sings, he sounds like Leon," Harris said.

"Ted was a really smart and charming and funny young guy," Wessel gushed. "Leon started showing him the studio right away. Ted started engineering Leon's merch records for him and getting coproducing credits. You know, they were mostly just merch records, but Leon was really happy in that period having Ted there." When he was home, Leon had the studio and he wanted to work. With Teddy, it became the perfect father-and-son activity, one which brought them closer; they bonded over music. The CDs were created almost exclusively to sell at the merchandise tables at gigs.

Leon and Teddy Jack recorded a new record together, *Blues*, later re-titled *Guitar Blues*. In 2022, Teddy Jack told the *Tulsa World*, "The first day I walked in the studio, he's like, 'OK, you're going to be a producer and engineer, and you're going to learn how to do this and that's the end of it.' I didn't have a choice. He just said, 'You have to know how to do this.' I'm seventeen, so I'm like, 'Cool.'" He recalled that Leon actually did offer him a choice: he would pay for Teddy Jack to go to law school at Pepperdine or record and tour with his dad. "In retrospect, I probably should have become a lawyer," Teddy Jack said, laughing.

Teddy played electronic drums, and Leon handled the rest. As with most of Leon's albums, there are at least a few good songs on *Guitar Blues*, and Leon's voice is all there, but as the label heads lamented, "Sounds like demos, Leon." For this kind of music, you need a group of people rubbing elbows in a small, preferably sweltering room, as when Leon worked with Freddie King. Instead, we have a self-released CD of digital fizz that is almost unlistenable.

The front of *Guitar Blues* features an amateurish cartoon of Leon on a city corner, neither the first nor the last bad cover, but arguably the worst to that point. Issued the same year, *Hymns of Christmas: Leon Russell, Piano & Orchestra* is even more alarming. He looks like a cult leader on a pamphlet handed out on Hollywood Boulevard. The only "orchestra" on this instrumental disc is Leon's computers and keyboards, all done up in Mannheim Steamroller style: full of excess, bereft of taste.

On the tour that followed *Blues/Guitar Blues*, Leon did not want to stand out front playing guitar because he was self-conscious about his appearance, not to mention his increasing physical challenges. He had Teddy's friend, Kirwan, learn Leon's solos on the album note for note. But it was not working out. In 1998, Leon hired John Giles at the recommendation of Matt Harris. Harris could not join the road band himself because he shared custody of Halen after he and Blue split. Leon had Giles take over solos while Kirwan took a back seat, sticking to rhythm parts. It wasn't until years later that Teddy moved from drums to guitar. "Ted didn't really bother me in the band until he started playing guitar, and he played way, *way* too loud," Wessel lamented. "There was something aggressive and hostile about it."

The next iteration of the band's involvement came with the addition of drummer Grant Whitman, who also doubled as the bus driver after Graham was fired. Leon was particularly attracted to Whitman as a drummer because he had seen him on television playing behind Dr. Gene Scott, the platinum-shag-coiffed LA-based televangelist who was the subject of Werner Herzog's 1981 documentary *God's Angry Man*. "Leon was just so tickled that he had Dr. Gene's drummer driving his bus and playing drums," Wessel laughed. Whitman took over on the drums from Teddy when Teddy switched to playing guitar, around 2000.

"By that point, Sugaree had taken over on the beaded gourd, adding some much-needed female presence in the all-dude show. Aside from obviously riveting attention to her square-foot of stage space, she is a veritable time machine on the gourd," Wessel attested in 2001. "From the time of Ambrose's entrance, the gourd has been an important component of Leon's music."

Most of the merch records were released on Leon Russell Records, but a couple were one-off indie label deals, such as his next release, in 1998, *Legend in My Time: Hank Wilson Vol. III*. This deal was with Ark 21, the label started by Miles Copeland III after he sold his pioneering I.R.S. Records label. Copeland's brother, Stewart (of the Police), was also a partner in Ark 21. Leon had bankrolled the recording himself, and Copeland heard the tapes and offered him a deal.

Once again, Leon surrounded himself with a top ensemble of A-list musicians playing acoustic and analog instruments, and the resulting record is outstanding among his 1990s catalog. Warm, soulful, collaborative, and organic; this is how Leon Russell music should be delivered. Leon covers three songs by Willie Nelson, "Night Life," "Crazy," and "Funny How Time Slips Away." Willie himself appears as a duet partner on the George Jones tearjerker, "He Stopped Loving Her Today," and he adds harmony on "Okie from Muskogee," the Merle Haggard chestnut that Leon finally recorded.

Leon also sings a duet on the Don Gibson ballad "A Legend in My Time" with T. Graham Brown, whose bruised bellow melts under Leon's raspy honk. Brown also joins Leon on "Love's Gonna Live Here," the great Buck Owens song. He also takes on Owens's "Act Naturally." Guests abound: Harold Bradley and Pat Flynn on acoustic guitar, country star Marty Stuart on mandolin, Butch Robins on banjo, Mickey Raphael on harmonica, and guest vocalists the Oak Ridge Boys—for whom Leon had recently produced a gospel record—as well as Jackie Wessel and Jimmy Snyder, whom Leon had backed in his earliest LA days. Snyder's voice, crooned from deep down inside, is as smooth as a sip of aged bourbon. As with the first Hank Wilson record, Leon recorded dozens of songs in a short period of time: twenty-four in two days. "It keeps an excitement, almost like a nightclub excitement, with these guys," Leon reasoned.

Leon saw a good amount of Willie Nelson during the 1990s, touring together in 1996, including dates on the West Coast and in Hawaii. That same year, Leon was alongside his pal for the Country Music Awards telecast. Tom Britt was there that night. He had heard that Courtney Johnson of New Grass Revival had passed away the night before. "Jan said, 'Leon's over here on Willie Nelson's bus. They're giving Willie a Lifetime Achievement Award.' So I go over to the bus to tell Leon about Courtney. I walk on the bus, and there's Leon and Willie, and they've each got their own joints, smoking. This is, you know, four in the afternoon. And so, I tell Leon. And we talked for a little bit. Each of 'em keeps handing me their joint like this [*makes the universal joint-passing motion*], and at the time, I didn't smoke. So then I drive home, about twenty minutes away. Now I thought, 'Well, I'm gonna turn this on and watch them give Willie the Lifetime Achievement Award.' So I turn it on, and I'm watching, and they go, 'Now, Willie Nelson!' The curtains open, and Willie and Leon are not there. But the band is there, and they're looking around, *well they're not here*, so they had to go to a commercial break and go find them. And they're stoned out of their gourds in the parking lot, and they get them on the stage, and they kind of hacked it in there."

The third Hank Wilson record was not Leon's only foray back into country music in the 1990s. Leon had always admired George Jones, and he contributed piano to *The Bradley Barn Sessions*, an album of Jones's collaborations with such stars as Ricky Skaggs, Mark Knopfler, Marty Stuart, Dolly Parton, and Emmylou Harris. Leon shines on "The Love Bug," playing right-hand flourishes late in the arrangement, while Vince Gill sings. Leon also contributed piano to "Golden Ring," a remake of the hit Jones had with his ex-wife, Tammy Wynette, who reprised her vocal.

Leon remembered, "First time they'd seen each other since they got divorced. Then she left [the studio], and George was fucking devastated." Leon knew firsthand the wreckage that could be wreaked by a divorce. "He went into the restroom and put a guard on the front door, and he was in there for twenty minutes. And he came out and said, 'I wanna do one with Leon.'" Though the session was well into overtime, they did "The Window Up Above." Leon rises to the occasion: "The Window Up Above" was dense with acute emotional fallout after George's encounter with Tammy. It was released on the 2008 volume *Burn Your Playhouse Down: The Unreleased Duets.*

After such satisfying collaborations, Leon retreated to his home studio with Teddy Jack and finished off the decade with the album *Face in the Crowd,* another disappointing self-production. It seems that Leon was nodding in the direction of the film that shared the album's name. *A Face in the Crowd* was a 1957 movie written by Budd Schulberg and directed by Elia Kazan that starred Andy Griffith as a drunken drifter with charisma and a little talent as a guitar player/singer. His character, Larry Rhodes, gets rechristened "Lonesome" Rhodes and ad-libs his way to fame, fortune, and political power via the mass media of radio and television.

Though there is nothing in the lyrics to suggest that Leon was using the film as a source of inspiration, he held a lifelong fascination of such shysters, conmen, carneys, televangelists, snake oil salesmen, and tent-show revivalists. Wessel pointed out that, fitting the fly-by-night shady-character theme, "*Face in the Crowd* was on some other label [Sagestone] where the guy disappeared. They told Leon he had sold fifty thousand copies, and then the guy that ran the label vanished; so, a typical Leon story. I don't know if he sold fifty thousand copies or not. All I know is they could not find the guy."

On May 19, 1999, Leon made another TV appearance with David Letterman. CBS's *The Late Show* was taped at the Ed Sullivan Theater, Letterman's new home base. Leon had his band for the show, augmented by Paul Shaffer's house band. At Letterman's request, they did "Back to the Island." This network TV appearance notwithstanding, by the end of the 1990s, Leon was so off the radar that friends sent up flares, half-hearted though they may have been.

"George [Harrison] appeared on a VH1 show hosted by John Fugelsang where George mentions, a bit pointedly, I thought, a period where he was 'quite friendly with Leon Russell,' and how he'd stopped hearing from him," Wessel recalled. Harrison made an impromptu appearance on the show, promoting a Ravi Shankar project he helped produce. It was Harrison's final public appearance. "He spoke of trying to find [Leon's] phone number in Memphis but couldn't find it." Leon never lived in Memphis.

Matt Harris said a lot of the continued career slide had to do with Leon's renegade tendency to go it alone. "He wasn't into corporate record companies." Even the press release sent by the indie label that released *Face in the Crowd* called him "the reclusive Russell, the J. D. Salinger of the music world."

The holy-rock-and-roller of the *Leon Live* era, the supple, strutting, and captivating personality, was almost impossible to locate under what he'd started calling his "Leon Russell Costume." He wore a loose-fitting Gramps-went-to-Tommy-Bahama's ensemble covering his aged and rotund frame. The swagger was gone, and now he sat hunched behind keyboards and screens, rarely engaging, barely acknowledging, never mind *saving the goddamned rock 'n' roll souls* of his audience. Leon's congregation was still there, albeit dwindled down to a cult of self-proclaimed Leon Lifers. For his whole career, Leon managed to hold on to an intensely die-hard core of supporters. They started to connect on message boards, and in 1999 co-alesced, first on a Onelist board and then on a Yahoo group for dedicated fans of Leon Russell, started by Rick Colburn and Marcia Bilynsky.

Like any online community, it started with one item of focus that brought them together, out of which a close circle started, with people spread around the world sharing their love of Leon Russell music but getting to know each other on an intimate level. There is an overlong ama-teur but poignant documentary video called *The LeonLifer Story: Anything Can Happen* made by Joe Hill in 2000, which is the year they decided to gather to meet in person. Impressively, they pooled together and hired Leon to play a show where they were meeting in Louisville, Kentucky, on September 28, 2000.

An unrecognizable, raspy-voiced Emily Smith appears in the video. She had been through decades of harrowing drug-related struggles but stuck around Leon's periphery until the end. The group managed to raise the fee to get the artist himself, Leon, to perform at Coyote's in Louisville. The assembled folks come across as a warm and welcoming community of people who already had formed deep bonds and display an intense "never treat a brother like a passing stranger" sense of care for each other, which they continue to this day. "*These* are the kinds of fans he has," says one. "These are the people *he* has brought together and created a family. This is what his life's work has done."

But Leon went far beyond the minimum. Unannounced, he comes down to this lovefest in a conference room at the hotel before his show, meeting, greeting, basking in the adulation, warmly reciprocating, and generously spending quality time with the fans who mill around in a flabbergasted frenzy. "Y'all sit down; you're making me nervous," he announces, breaking the ice. He spends over two hours with his flock, even allowing them to touch his hair. "He had time for everyone," marvels one fan. "He had a genuine interest in what each and every person had to say . . . so heartfelt," another marvels.

He offers bits of philosophical wisdom that they scoop up as precious pearls. He instructs one bearded fellow, "You need to stop and think. Trust your heart and trust your mind. Preachers and dictators will take you down if you don't watch 'em. The road to Hell is paved with lots of bad preachers." He chokes up telling the story about seeing the "little Black family" denied the restroom on a stop along that cross-country trip with Rita Coolidge. Prejudice was still very much on his mind. Leon wrote that the Lifers "treat me like a Sufi master, even though I am massively bipolar and am in constantly unexpected shape."

Leon is accompanied by some of his family: Sugaree and Teddy in his band; Halen, Blue, Jan, Coco, Honey, and Leon's mom, Hester, all in attendance. The kids and grandkids called Jan "Mimi," which Leon started to do as well, eventually shortening it to "Meems." We see starkly how badly Leon's health was failing. When he enters the poorly lit hotel conference room, he is aided by a mobility scooter and looks about twenty years older than his fifty-eight years. His pants are hiked up above his ample belly. He seems so vulnerable, so ancient. There's a good dose of "This Is Your Life" quality to the event. The Lifers arranged for Patrick Henderson to be there. Ambrose is present and explains that he has not seen Patrick since the seventies. It made for an extended family reunion. Before the performance, Patrick gives a warm speech paying tribute to Leon and the fans who brought him there. Rick Colburn, one of the earliest and most beloved of the Lifers, presents Leon with a plaque commemorating the event and thanking him for what he has given them and the world.

When he gives his acceptance speech, Leon begins to cry. He recalls an experience in Detroit with Willie Nelson and Ambrose, seated at his right hand as he recounts the memory. In his memoir, Leon described the incident, taking Willie and Ambrose to find a Church of God in Christ Easter service in the 1970s. They arrived early and the first congregants to filter in kept away from them, until Ambrose stood and bowed to an older couple, who in turn came to sit closer to them. At that point, the circle that had been left around them filled with others. Leon climaxed his speech about how he learned that day that it takes some brave people to bridge gaps: "I think we need to fill the circle."

As Leon's daughter Blue got older, she became more attuned to what she saw as a disconnect between who many of Leon's fans thought he was and reality, the same kind of phenomenon discussed by Maxayn Lewis, Ann Bell, and Patrick Henderson (who lost a lot of connections with vocal right-wing Leon fans after Obama was elected). Leon was not especially outspoken politically, but he was liberal. That much would seem obvious. But you don't get to choose your fans, and sometimes there are clashes. Tom Britt recalled that Hank Williams Jr. offered Leon fourteen gigs as the opener in the early eighties. "He wisely told Hank he will walk if things got funky," Britt said. "First gig, we walk on the stage with two Nigerian percussion players. Halfway through the opening song a whiskey bottle is thrown at the Nigerians. We all walk off. End of tour."

"I toured with him as a kid growing up," Blue said. At one show in Memphis, she recalled, "It was like, 'Oh my God,' it was just [redneck] biker people for days. I'm like, 'Do they know he married a Black woman? Did they just *forget* it?'"

But it was all love at this event, and Wessel said the good vibes from the Lifer event in Louisville sustained through the rest of Leon's life. "It's down to the loyal fans that will come see him for the rest of their lives, their lives and the artist's life, and especially in Leon's case, they didn't just come to see him. They came to see each other and be together, and that makes for a nice job. Leon appreciated it more and more. It could be kind of awkward and a pain in the ass sometimes. But he appreciated and really took the time to get to know more of those people than I realized.

If somebody approached him as *Leon Russell*, he wasn't comfortable with that. But if you just talked to him, like when we'd be out shopping in antique shops and somebody started talking about what they were shopping for, he could be really outgoing."

Leon would never lose the anxiety he felt before going onstage. "He had stage fright forever," said his daughter Coco. "I don't think it ever really went away for him." But during many if not most performances, Leon would do several songs solo, with the band leaving the stage, as they did in Louisville when he dedicated a song to a Lifer who had passed away.

That same year, Leon presented eleven of his most classic songs accompanied only by his piano on the hit-or-miss CD *Signature Songs*. Leon was both an elite songwriter and one of the greatest arrangers and bandleaders of his generation. Something like "Delta Lady" performed solo just doesn't move the needle like his original, never mind the *Mad Dogs & Englishmen* version. "This Masquerade" is the standout here, peeling back *Carney*'s esoteric dark production and revealing the song as the standard it was always intended to be. "Back to the Island" is also a discovery in this austere presentation.

Even though Leon released five new records in three years, only one (*Crazy Love*, a "merch record") featured newly written songs. Also in 2001 was the long-shelved Hank Wilson record with New Grass Revival released. Rejected by Warner Bros. more than twenty years earlier, Leon finally had a way to put it out himself, as *Rhythm & Bluegrass: Hank Wilson, Vol. 4*. The album represented the core repertoire from the tours he did with New Grass in the early 1980s.

The New Grass guys were on board with the idea of finally releasing the recordings, but Sam Bush had a spat with Leon over how it was packaged. "He said, 'You remember who played on what?' I said, 'Man, I remember everything.' So I gave him a list. And I had special-to-me pictures of us, some black-and-whites and some color. I brought them all over to Leon's house, and he never used any of them, and I never got 'em back. When the record cover came out, I just quite frankly did not like it," Bush said. Once again, Leon released a cartoon cover with embarrassing graphics and a photo of his current self, looking down at caricatures of the New Grass guys. "I love the music on that record. I just hated the record cover, and I told him, I said, 'I'm sorry, it sucks too bad for me to even have an opinion.'"

In addition to the five discs under his name, Leon collaborated with his son-in-law Matt Harris on Harris's album *Slightly Elliptical Orbit*, cowriting ten tracks and singing on one. Like the others, it was released on Leon Russell Records, which Leon had created with the vision of functioning like a fully independent Paradise or even Shelter. Leon had started working with Harris in 1998. Matt and Blue had come from Tulsa to Nashville to be close to Leon's side of Blue's family and for Harris to find work as a musician. The couple split soon after arriving, but Harris stayed in town, sharing custody of Halen. "I was thirty-two or something," Harris explained. "I wrote like a mad dog. I got a knock on my door. It's 1998, I was in Hendersonville, Tennessee, in an apartment, and it's Leon. He goes, 'I've got writer's block, and I want to know if you want to come write with me?' I said, 'Come on in.' I got him an iced tea with lots of ice. I go, 'You're just playing the same songs every night. You need to change the radio station, man.' And he goes, 'Well, that's a good way to look at it.' That's when it kicked off."

When they first sat down together, Leon asked him, "'Hey, so what do you got?' I pulled out a couple of things," Harris said. He'd come armed with demo tapes of material he had written. "He said, 'I don't like that. Write something right now. How about something in 6/8 time? Do something soul.' He put me on the fucking spot. And I just started, boom, boom; knocked it out. I laid down the track. And he goes, 'So, what are you hearing in your head?' I go, 'Like, vocally? Oh, I don't know. Let me try a couple of different things. I'll grab on to something like anybody does, right? You know, two or three different takes of different melodies, and see what we can come up with.' And he goes, 'I've never thought about it that way.' And I was like, 'Really?'" It's curious that Leon said he never thought of it that way. He had written "Ballad of Mad Dogs and Englishmen" and others with that exact technique. But as Wessel said, he had a mortal fear of being embarrassed and would rarely let anyone see him feeling around to make a song.

Harris also wondered if maybe the brain surgeries had an effect, as Leon had "recollection problems," disconnecting him from the inspiration and methods of his most creative days. Leon had lost the thread from his youth, when his stuff flowed from him. Harris said, "That's the thing; he felt like, 'This happened to me; I didn't make this happen.' He goes, 'I just thought that some kind of inspiration would come from somewhere.

I just sit there and wait for nothing.' And I go, 'Well, Leon, you quit writing about your life. Secondly, you take it too seriously.' He had that breakthrough. From my end, it was amazing, because he could pop out lyrics that were great in twenty minutes.

"He started paying me $120 a day to come down when he was off the road for about five hours, and we'd write." They generally worked Tuesday to Thursday, starting around ten a.m., smoking pot ("I brought the weed," Harris notes, "and he didn't smoke weed unless it was with me"). Leon would tell stories from the old days, and they made each other laugh, breaking for leisurely lunches. The two would come up with whimsical exercises, like Leon giving Matt assignments to write a Ricky Martin song or a Bob-Marley-meets-Foreigner song.

Much like Marc Benno almost thirty years before, Harris did what he could to rebuild Leon's confidence. Leon would even dismiss his best songs as flukes or rip-offs of other songs. "He goes, 'All that time, I was trying to write songs or just trying, to be honest, just trying to write hits. "Tight Rope" was an anomaly that I decided to stay there for a couple of hours at Muscle Shoals and knock it out. Denny told me the *Carney* record wasn't good enough, and I shouldn't put it out.' And he's like, 'So I did "Masquerade." I ripped it off "Angel Eyes."' [Later] I couldn't let him say that anymore. He needed me to go, 'Inspiration's one thing. You didn't rip it off.' He goes, 'I ripped it off. It was "Angel Eyes." That's why George Benson liked it; he knew the changes.' And 'My Cricket,' Willie's favorite song, right? 'I ripped it off from "Tennessee Waltz."' I go, 'It's not about that!'"

Leon kept up a breakneck pace that would be impressive even for a twenty-something artist. He joined a crew of all-stars backing Earl Scruggs on a 2002 revival recording of Scruggs's bluegrass standard, "Foggy Mountain Breakdown." In addition to Leon on organ, the other players include Vince Gill, Steve Martin (the actor/musician, on banjo), Albert Lee, Randy Scruggs, Marty Stuart, Jerry Douglas, Glen Duncan, Glenn Worf, Harry Stinson, and Paul Shaffer. The official video of them miming to the recording is a hoot, with Leon's solo coming near the end. Shaffer could not leave the Letterman show in New York, so they digitally inserted him into the video with the rest of the musicians. "They said, 'Be as animated as you can.' So I'm going nuts visually on camera. And then I see the final product. The rest of them are in Nashville. Nobody's moving a muscle. And they come to me, and I'm just this maniac."

Leon also reestablished a working relationship with his old pal Jim Price. "I will say that working closely together in 1999 and 2000, we did become friends. Leon was a serious guy. He wanted substance at the core of any relationships. In 2000, we put together a band made up of Nashville studio players and singers. We wrote most of the songs together. Leon's three-year-old daughter [Coco] loved to go to the zoo. Her favorite exhibit was the flamingos. She tried to say 'pink flamingo,' and it would come out 'pingo mingo.' We decided to call the band Pingo Mingo."

Price also worked with Leon on Leon's *Moonlight & Love Songs*, which was released in 2002. Again, you have to get past the cover, Leon staring into the camera with a little white lapdog up near his snowy white beard and hair against a black background. By now, you'd be forgiven if you started to wonder if Leon was just messing with his audience. But the music—a selection of romantic standards with the Nashville Symphony—is expertly arranged, produced, and performed. Leon knew the limitations of his voice. It's similar to Willie Nelson's vocals on his standards records, though not as innovative and with predictably lusher arrangements. His friends, Price, Edgar Winter, and Bruce Hornsby, all make contributions. It was an audacious project for a self-released CD.

Teddy Jack's solo record would also be released in 2002. *Signature Songs* was the last of his father's that he worked on, and he stopped playing in Leon's live band around the same time. "It didn't end well," Wessel sighed. Teddy had a grievous clash with the family that resulted in his leaving and remaining estranged. He declined multiple requests to be interviewed for this book.

The extended family started to go their own ways during the early 2000s, with Jan and Leon's three daughters staying with them. Tina Rose would come and go. She had her first child and was married to Jan's nephew: "part of the craziness," she said. They moved back to Oklahoma and had their second child there. "Then I moved back to Nashville and went on the road with my dad for about four years," starting around 2003 until the mid-2000s. A remarkably talented singer, Tina wasn't in the band the same time as Teddy, but Sugaree was still there. "When Tina came, then Sugi started singing, and it turned out she could sing great," Wessel recalled with a laugh. "I was the only one singing besides Leon. And then Tina comes, and then all of a sudden Sugi's singing, and it was great."

"That time that I spent on the road with him was one of my most memorable and favorite times in my life," Tina said. "I really got to know him, and I feel like he really got to know me too. We had two shows in one day at this venue in Canada, and we were all so tired. And my dad said, 'Boy, I sure feel like I've been rode hard and put up wet!' I had never heard that saying before, and I was like, 'What the fuck did you just say? That's so gross,'" she said, laughing. "He said, 'You know, I'm glad that you really got a chance to get to know your dear old dad like this.'

"But aside from that, I like to lay low. I have always stayed to myself, as far as family issues. It's just been the easiest for me. I love all of my siblings; I love my mom, my stepmom; I love everybody. And it's sometimes easy to remove myself. I know that my dad had the same Switzerland [neutral] stance. Seeing him as little as I did, I never did really fault him for that. I would see him when he came to town. It was the easiest way to keep things smooth."

She had to ramp up on learning her father's music because, growing up, Mary would not allow it to be played in the house. When Tina became a little older, she would do it secretly. "I listened to as much as I could until after he died. I just wanted to get as close to him as I could because, you know, you have regrets, like, 'God, I wish I just would have said this or I wish I wouldn't have cared about what somebody would have said,' or whatever. Just have my relationship with my dad.

"When I first moved to Nashville. We were next door at the studio, and he was sitting at the piano, and I sat down next to him, and he said, 'Play me something.' And I was like, 'I don't know how to play piano, Dad.' And he was like, 'Oh, come on.' And he really was expecting me to play something. And I was like, 'No, I seriously don't know how to play piano.' And he was surprised, and he said, 'You know, your mom said the same thing to me like, *Oh, I don't really know how to play.*' And then just sat down and just played the most amazing piano."

While on the road with Leon, Tina's boyfriend Cody Bailey was the drummer at the time. "One of the best drummers we ever had," Wessel said. "He was one of the few drummers who actually excited Leon onstage. Cody stayed on a while after Tina left and was replaced for a couple of years by Jaime Babbitt, a great singer and a real pro who really helped the show a lot."

Danny Eaton, who in the sixties had worked with Leon as manager of Marc Benno's band, the Outcasts, became a big-time promoter back in Texas. "He had been after Leon for years to reunite Mad Dogs & Englishmen to do a big tour," Wessel revealed. Leon's old sparring partner, Joe Cocker, had managed a career resurgence that lasted for the rest of his life. Inevitably, there were efforts to get the two back together on the same bill, if not actually staging a Mad Dogs reunion. But ill will still lingered. "The grudge," Jim Price acknowledged. "I believe Leon let it go, but Joe never did."

Wessel recalled Leon's reaction. "Leon said, 'I don't know; Joe doesn't want to do that.' Anyway, nothing came of it, but finally, we got some talks going, and they booked us to open for Joe on a few shows, you know, just to see how people would respond to a bill of Joe Cocker and Leon Russell. But when they finally got down to talking about reuniting and all that, basically all they did was offer Leon $5,000 a night to play in Joe's band and sing a couple of songs. Nothing came of it. I don't think they rekindled anything especially warm. They just really never cared for one another. They never really hit it off."

Chapter 36

I'm Broke. My Wife and Kids Are Rich

BUSES BREAKING DOWN, HIS FAMILY pulling apart, in debt, neighbors haranguing him from town to town: the 2000s began inauspiciously for Leon. But by 2010, there would be a new and welcome redemption.

Everyone, including him, understood that aside from his health issues (and even some of those), Leon was mainly responsible for the state of his own career and finances. How could the author of some of the most-recorded songs of his generation be struggling financially? How could the Master of Space and Time, who had commanded the biggest stages during rock music's golden era, end up as the "Miser of Space and Time," driving his own duct-taped bus down the highway to the next joint?

"I don't know how I managed to pull that off," Leon said. "I'm just an idiot, I guess. The fans come up to me at my shows and say, 'Thank you, Leon, for staying out here on the road and playing for us. Thank you so much.' I don't have any choice. If I had more money, I'd probably at least travel a different way. I mean, it's fun to play. I've got a good band." He concluded, "It's a rough business."

It was made rougher because his finances were never well managed and he had a shopping addiction and a penchant for antiques. As he did with kitchen-table booking agents, he employed kitchen-table bookkeepers, including his daughter Blue, who had to learn the basics, and then battle his "robbing Peter to pay Paul" approach to cash flow. In 2013, he said, "I've got three or four songs that I really make a fortune off of every year that I wrote forty years ago. That's nice. My debt package is so immense it doesn't really make that much difference."

"He had been despairing of ever getting out of debt before he died,"

Jack Wessel said. "He was sure that he was going to leave his family in ruins. He really worried about it a lot." Was it back taxes or real estate mortgages, or something else? "All the above," Wessel said. "He was in a lot of trouble with the properties and taxes and his overhead. Leon liked to say, 'I'm broke; my wife and kids are rich.'"

He was a profligate spender, which was a way for him to deal with bipolar depression. Even on a high, Leon would buy. Matt Harris recalled an interview Leon had with producer Phil Ramone at the Songwriters Hall of Fame. "Now he's talking about the thing he loves. As soon as we get done, he's feeling so happy about the interview that we're going to go buy a car with cash. And then, three days later, he called me up. 'I shouldn't have bought that car. What do I do?'"

Harrod Blank got to know Leon as he successfully lobbied Leon to eventually sign off on releasing Les Blank's *A Poem Is a Naked Person*. "One of the things that Leon would do when he'd get paid for a big contract, the first thing he'd do is go out and buy a recording studio," Blank said. "And he'd go out and buy the next greatest mixer or go out and buy the video cameras that he paid $100,000 apiece for. I think he said he bought three or five of them—and by the end of the year, they were worthless."

Harrod continued: "I said to Leon, 'Don't you ever think about investing your money and getting more money out of the money?' And he's like, 'I don't go for that. I like to get things with my money, like my new Tesla.'" On a drive one day, Blank said, "We're at a red light, and the light turned green. There were no cars in front of us, and he just gassed that accelerator. That car literally felt like a rocket ship. I got nervous: 'Oh shit! Is he gonna be able to put the brakes on in time? Leon's reflexes might not be that great in his seventies.' And sure enough, he barely stopped.

"The first thing I did when I got home was, I bought stock in Tesla. I said, 'Leon, don't you want to get some stock in Tesla? I mean, dude, that car is unbelievable.' He said, 'I don't do that, Harrod.'"

Leon's only real investments were in real estate, but those were for personal use rather than capital gains, never mind income generation. Jan said Leon had no life insurance and no investment portfolio, just tons of cash that came and went. In addition to a substantial stream of royalties, he would often play two hundred dates a year, which would gross about a million dollars in revenue. He insisted on payment in cash, which he would dump in trash bags at the feet of the in-house bookkeeper. This led to temptation for the employees to skim cash, which at least two did not resist.

Shelley Graham—not one of those accused of skimming—had been the administrative assistant, filing Leon's song publishing, copyrights, and similar tasks. She was replaced by Blue. "He made about a million dollars a year, at least," during the 1990s (the lean years), Blue said. "He would owe about three hundred grand when tax season came up, and he never had the money, and he would always have to take out a loan, every year." He would also file tax extensions every year.

After Blue, they brought in a professional business management firm. But keeping with the theme, Leon preferred in-house people, so he switched to a woman we'll call Kathy. She and her husband were friendly with Jan and Leon, and though Jan told Kathy that she preferred not to hire her so they could keep their relationship as friends, Kathy lobbied for the job. "I begged for Leon not to," Jan emphasized. "They weren't accountants or managers. They weren't in the music business at all. Leon was like a kid with the people that he loved. They did underhanded things to him, and he just didn't see it. Kathy evidently was siphoning money off for herself."

Instead of going back with a professional firm, around 2006–2007, Leon hired a young guy we'll call Rick, whose father was a music-biz exec. As with his music, Leon didn't want advice. He wanted employees to follow his instructions. But as with his predecessors, Rick allegedly wasted little time before helping himself to some cash and mismanaging finances. "This guy that they had hired really damn near ruined them," Wessel sighed. "Damn near finished them off. He was not paying bills and pocketing the money that was supposed to be going to bills. He opened up credit accounts in their name. It was several hundred thousand dollars that they were liable for. . . . At the time when they were ready to have him arrested, he was gone."

Rick split Tennessee, and they found out where he was. But Leon was self-defeating when it came time to litigate. "Leon didn't have the time and the money to have him chased around the world," Wessel affirmed. "And they were able to get enough of it straightened out through insurance that Leon just wanted to let it go. The bag he left Leon and Jan holding was in the neighborhood of $300,000 or $400,000."

Before this was discovered, Leon had given Rick a television. "He always wanted to give gifts," Jan said. "I told him that was always my first clue. He had a ton of ivory that he bought way back, probably when he first got famous or something. Every time he gave someone a piece of that ivory, they were going to harm him in some way. It happened every time; never missed. That's the closest court case we came to. We did a mediation between me and the guy. That guy, he was just a liar. The agreement for him to pay back the money didn't happen. We didn't go after him. Leon just said, 'That's it. What's done is done.'"

Rick had a role in the nadir of Leon's ill-considered real estate ventures, a project in the Nashville neighborhood of Forest Hills. After they sold the house in Hendersonville, the family mostly lived out on the farm in Sideview. But in the early 2000s, Leon decided he needed a place closer to downtown Nashville, closer to restaurants and other musicians.

Matt Harris said Leon also wanted to escape the hustle and bustle, if not chaos, of his family house. He first got a place in the chic Belle Meade golf neighborhood while holding the farm property. Harris rented in the same neighborhood, and they continued to write together. The family eventually stayed there as well. Naturally, Leon paved the front and back yards.

But in Belle Meade, as with almost every property, the neighbors complained about Leon's buses being visible from the street. His taste remained questionable. Jan chuckled and said, "When we moved into that house, he wanted to put aluminum foil on the windows because he wanted the bedroom completely black. He didn't want any light; he didn't like sunlight at all."

The front yard became a parking lot. "The Oak Ridge Boys were over there recording, so there were Cadillacs," Jan said. "So anyway, [neighbors] wrote us a letter and put it in the mailbox. It said that we were destroying the neighborhood, and we had all those horrible cars parked at our house and that we looked like *Sanford and Son*." She laughed. "And Leon's feelings were *so hurt*. I would say, 'You can't do that,' and then he would do it, and he would get busted for it, he would say, 'Well, you were right.' He thought I was being a bitch, but I was just trying to save face."

Jan and the girls would still mostly stay out on the Gallatin property, enjoying all the farm animals and many dogs that people would pawn off on them for adoption. The canine crew grew to a large pack that would follow Jan around inside and out. "He called me 'the Dog Woman' because he'd see a pack of dogs and know I was coming." But that Gallatin house was starting to have problems. They auctioned off the property in 2006, taking a loss after years of trying to sell it. "It was quite an undertaking," Wessel recalled. "There was the large warehouse structure with Leon's studios, offices, and storage, two stories' worth. There were a few other older structures, one a bus hangar never used for that purpose, for more storage. Further back on the property was Leon's bus graveyard, where three retired buses sat for years. Critters chewed through the floors and repurposed the buses as wildlife shelters. I found that out one time when I thought I'd have a sentimental look at my first tour bus. Scared the shit out of me."

Leon had to convince Ambrose to move off the Gallatin land. He had always taken care of Ambrose Campbell, since the Tulsa and Burbank days. Ambrose would usually have a car and a stipend. He was a member of the family, predating Jan by almost a decade. Ambrose's son, Danny, was by then about forty years old and a professional musician himself. "He was my dad's best mate, and he had been so for so long that he was a part of the scenery of my life," Danny said.

"When Leon had to finally let go of the property, the reality of that change shook Ambrose hard," Wessel said. "It wasn't really all that sudden because Leon had cautioned him over quite a long period of the probability of his having to sell. Ambrose just wouldn't hear it. Over time, Ambrose began protesting and arguing in a way that I thought seemed irrational and childlike." Leon and Jan wanted to pay for his rent and took him apartment shopping. Ultimately, Ambrose did not accept it, and it irreparably severed the long brotherly bond between him and Leon. "Ambrose's protests escalated, with old beefs and accusations, all but refusing to move, and Leon couldn't find the patience to deal with him," Wessel explained. "He was deeply offended and getting really pissed off."

There were problems with the singular and close relationship between Leon and Ambrose that went back decades. In notes from a July 1979 meeting, titled "Comm. w/Ambrose," Ambrose aired his grievances to Diane Sullivan. He said he "wants to put his own life together" and explained that he "doesn't take action until pushed." He saw Leon as having too much power over him. He said in Leon's attitude, he was "God" and Ambrose was "nothing." He said he was "left in [the] dark" with the Denny and Leon deals and felt he had "no one to turn to—he's too old."

Though Ambrose felt trapped as far back as 1979, his attitude would evolve to be appreciative of the support Leon gave him, before he lost faith near the end. Wessel said, "I began to wonder if maybe the onset of senility was a factor in this. I suggested this possibility to Leon, and he wasn't buying. He was offended, angry, and had no more to say other than that."

Eventually, Ambrose's son, Danny, and Danny's mother in England worked out with Wessel Ambrose's return home. Danny Campbell was about ten years old when his parents had divorced and Ambrose moved to America. In England, Ambrose had been married prior to his marriage to Danny's mother, and he also married another woman later in Tulsa and had more children. "I got a call saying that Dad wasn't well," Danny said. "I went out there, and it became pretty obvious, speaking to Skip [Gates] and Leon and everyone, that Dad couldn't cope on his own anymore. And Leon wanted to get rid of the place, and he wanted to scale down. He was really worried [about] what was going to happen with Dad. And he said, 'We can get him a place in town, but he's lived in this rural idyll for so long, I don't see how he's gonna fit on Smith Street.' And I said, 'I think he needs to come home.' I spent about six weeks there, and I convinced him to come home, and picked him up and brought him back to England.

"When I went to pick him up, Dad felt as if he had another twenty years. He was the cantankerous old bugger, but he had many, many girl-friends. When he left, this party of women just kept visiting him. I caught one of them giving him hand relief. I was packing up in the studio in the back, and we had a few beers going on. It's really hot, and I came up to ask him if he wanted to keep a particular item, and all of a sudden: 'Oops, sorry, sorry, sorry!'"

Wessel said that Ambrose was too ashamed to return to England as a "pauper." "When he finally did return to his family, it was a blessing," he said. "He only lived a couple more years, but I believe they were happy and rewarding for him."

In 2006, the news that Ambrose had passed arrived while Leon's band was on the road, naturally. "I know Leon was sad and shaken, but he said very little," Wessel recalled. "If they really did never speak again, I think that is a shame and a hell of a thing for either of them to have died with."

The move from the compound in Sideview marked the end of the sort of extended "friends and family" living situations that Leon had practiced in varying degrees since Hollywood. "I didn't know any different," said Jan. "He always wanted to live commune-style. His and my favorite thing would have been to have everybody we loved to live on our land with us." Jan had grown up with her cousins, all living in houses on her grandmother's land in Oklahoma. She said she and Leon both had a fear of abandonment stemming from childhood. Having everyone always around was a salve for such anxiety.

As the family broke apart in conflicts, including those with Blue, Harris said Leon withdrew. "He was innocent and unaware of all of the crazy shit."

Coco said, "In a lot of ways it seems like he was just very distant, kind of intimidating, maybe cold, a stoic-type person. But he was actually there. I think the core elements of his self are very soft, very emotional. If I was ever having a problem, like with my mom, if she was upset at me when I was teenager, he would always take my side, regardless of what it was. He didn't want to see you cry. There's a book about different love languages. That made sense to me. Because his way of showing love was with affection—every time we went and saw him, we'd hold hands, we'd kiss him and rub his head, he grabbed my ear, like a young child and father. And that was sort of the language of love that we had. And he would buy us stuff all the time. Every time he went on the road, he wouldn't call us often. He was on the road, and that created a lot of space between us. But we always knew when he was home, because the house would just be covered [in] all this stuff that he bought for us specifically. That was his way of saying, 'I'm thinking about you when I'm away.' Helping us with our homework, or quality time—that really wasn't his love language. Music is his first language, as opposed to English or anything else. And I think that for people who are on a spectrum, they have trouble communicating. That's a big issue. I think music is actually a much better and more accurate way to communicate."

"If you listen to, like, 'A Song for You,' you know, 'Listen to the melody / My love's in there hiding,' that speaks volumes about just him as an everyday person," said Beau Charron, who would soon join Leon's band. John Cowan added, "Physically speaking, unless he was drunk, he wasn't a hugger."

After the Belle Meade "fiasco," to use Wessel's word, Leon set about to build onto a house he bought in Forest Hills. He and architect Steve

Busch, his old friend from Tulsa, planned a twenty-five-thousand-square-foot Tudor-style house, "way more than doubling the size," Jan said. She said that the original designs were "really gorgeous. But Leon changed it because he thought *he* was the architect." Every change he proposed was shot down by the neighborhood association. "It wasn't going to be the house that Steve drew up," Jan said. "When you're in a snazzy neighborhood, you have to keep up appearances. And he just didn't understand it because he just had a different way of looking at things." He saw things as an artist, those close to him explained. He had to feel like he was making something his own.

He was turning over rocks for cash as the construction started, only to get delayed, the carrying costs accumulating, and running well over budget. Don Williams, who had run the publishing arm of Shelter Records, heard from Busch. "Busch took the position of trying to manage Leon," Williams recalled. "It was a weird conversation. Steve Busch was interested in finding a new publishing deal for Leon. He was basically looking for new money."

A new publishing deal didn't happen. The construction on the house was stalled for years, and Busch died in Jamaica. Before he absconded with bags of their cash, Rick (the bookkeeper) was still working with Leon and Jan throughout this catalog of disasters. Evidently without Leon's or Jan's knowledge, he signed off on some papers to demolish the house as a condition of a court decision won by the homeowners' association. Leon's friend and caretaker of the Sideview property, Skip Gates came to see the house being taken down, and that's when Leon and Jan learned of the sad and tragic end of that house. "Rick thought he was helping us out and doing the right thing. And Leon would say, 'I still think Rick did the right thing.' He kept believing him."

The Russells were living in Columbia, Tennessee, at the time. It was their sixth house in the state, including the Forest Hills house. They had lived in houses in Hendersonville, Sideview, the Nashville neighborhood of Belle Meade (twice, including one rental), and Columbia. Finally, in 2006, they settled into their dream house, a 6,120-square-foot thatch-roofed Tudor-style cottage that looks like something from Disney World, "our favorite," Jan said. With four bedrooms, terraces festooned with gargoyles, a koi pond, and an elevator, the house was built for Dennis Linde, the songwriter of the Elvis Presley hit "Burnin' Love." It was located in Hermitage, another Nashville neighborhood.

"That was a beautiful house," Wessel recalled. "Of course, he did pave the side yard and put in parking. He didn't put a big warehouse out there, but he managed to get two buses in there. Everybody parked. The big difference was, the neighbors over there were honored to have him, and they were great to them."

While his finances were shaky, accolades for Leon's legacy started trickling in. In 2006, he was inducted into the Oklahoma Hall of Fame. Herbie Hancock and Christina Aguilera teamed up to perform "A Song for You" at the 2006 Grammy Awards (they had released a recording of it the prior year) and Whitney Houston would do so on the platinum *I Look to You* album (she had previously performed it at her 1991 *Welcome Home Heroes with Whitney Houston* HBO concert). "He loved Whitney," Jan said.

But Leon himself wasn't doing much to burnish his own legacy. He wanted to maintain control of everything and put out more unsatisfying self-released records like the self-appraising *Bad Country*, the accurately titled all-instrumental *Almost Piano*, and the devotional *Mighty Flood*, which should have been called *Bad Almost Gospel* to accurately finish the pattern. In the wake of the latter, he heard from his old pal Johnny Williams, the sax player from his 1950s band, the Starlighters. The two had stayed in touch over the years. Williams was born again after his brother died in the early seventies. The nightlife was no good life, so Williams had turned his back on it for decades before returning to rock 'n' roll. "I figured it was the cross or the sax," he told journalist John Wooley. Williams loved *Mighty Flood* and tried to get Leon to do a tour of the religious stuff, but Leon passed.

"The great thing about dealing with all these Okies, at a certain level, they're about themselves, but also at a certain level, they're also thinking about others," said Jeff Moore, executive director of OKPOP. Steve and Charlene Ripley, who had taken ownership of the Church Studio during the 1990s after Steve's success with his band, the Tractors, had mostly stayed in touch with Leon and Jan over the years. They had an abiding respect and were stewards of the history of Oklahoma music, particularly Leon's role.

Leon's engineers constantly rolled tape in his studios, and he ended up with a warehouse full of reels of raw material. Very little of it was organized, and some had no information on it at all. Sometimes at night, after Leon would head out of his Tennessee studios, Jack Wessel, Mark Lambert, Rex Collier, and Tom and Bob Britt—whoever was around at the time—would pull out reels and listen through hours of nothing before coming across, say, George Harrison wheezing through a bad cold and suggesting he and Leon spark up a joint while working through a song for *Extra Texture*. Or they'd find a jam session with Mary, Leon, and Eric Clapton. Another tape might yield a pearl like Barbra Streisand singing "Lady Blue" accompanied only by Leon on piano.

Leon threatened over the years to trash it all, continuously warning Steve Ripley specifically. Ripley dismissed it as bluster until he got a call one day in 2008 that sounded more urgent than those in the past. Leon was fed up with carting around the library of tapes with all the real estate moves—plus all the old gear and other "residue from the fast lane." He no longer had the warehouse spaces and Jan wanted it out of the house. "I think the bluff was he started talking about disposing of them," Ripley said. "That evolved into a dialogue about Charlene and I being caretakers for his master tapes." The final call came to Ripley after he and Charlene had just relocated to his family's homestead, a farm about ninety miles outside of Tulsa. "So we dropped everything, as broke as we were, and headed to Nashville and brought back two semi-loads full of stuff," Steve said. "The tapes . . . and then why I think the other part was maybe a bit of a bluff. . . . This quote is, 'If you ever want to do anything with those tapes, you'll need the equipment that *goes with* the tapes.' Because a lot of Leon's stuff was recorded on forty-track, two-inch tape. Leon had two forty-track tape machines, but there were less than seven [manufactured]. Leon had two of them, and you can't play them on anything else. Then it became the tapes and the equipment that goes with the tapes. Then some stuff to sell. And then just stuff for the [OKPOP] museum."

Ripley brought in musician Jarrod Gollihare to help him digitize, catalog, and mix some of the tapes, which are now in the custody of OKPOP. There's also a lot of video on older obsolete formats and the raw film footage shot by Les Blank. "We saved them," Charlene said. "I think that was the last thing Steve did that he was so proud of. He spent probably five years transferring the tapes. Some of them—it's amazing." There absolutely is a great deal of breathtaking stuff that will someday be heard. Steve, sadly, passed away in 2019.

In November 2007, Moore and the director of the Oklahoma Historical Society, Dr. Bob Blackburn, visited the Ripleys' farm to discuss an upcoming exhibit on the music of the state. Steve gave them a presentation, including some audio mixes, just a tip of the Leon iceberg. He showed them a digitized clip of *A Poem Is a Naked Person*. "We were like, 'O-M-G,'" recalled Jeff Moore, executive director of OKPOP. "Leon wanted to throw it away."

Blackburn was a fan of Leon and J. J. Cale, so instead of merely an exhibit, they decided to create the OKPOP museum. Steve took them to lunch at the down-home Click's Steakhouse, not far from his farm, in the small rural town of Pawnee. "OKPOP started at Click's," Moore asserted.

The formation of OKPOP coincided with a growing newfound appreciation of Leon's place in the history of popular music. Attention also came from the 2005 DVD releases of *Mad Dogs & Englishmen* and *Concert for Bangladesh*. Leon was also included in Denny Tedesco's 2008 documentary *The Wrecking Crew* spotlighting those now-legendary studio musicians who formed the ensembles on some of the most enduring and beloved 1960s records. It came in the wake of *Standing in the Shadows of Motown*, which highlighted that record label's in-house band, informally known as the Funk Brothers. And there would soon be others of the same ilk, like the *Muscle Shoals* and *20 Feet from Stardom* docs, both from 2013, the latter of which spotlighted Claudia Lennear among an elite cadre of backing singers. All of these incremental steps toward broader and deeper recognition coincided with the formation of Leon's final core band and led to the final rewarding chapter in his life.

Chris Simmons was now playing guitar for him. He was one of a few guitarists from Alabama who cycled through Leon's band, but he stayed until 2012. Brian Lee, a Tulsa guy, was playing organ. Lee was introduced to Leon by Matt Harris. Leon stopped off to see Lee play in Seattle. The two began by writing together. "Leon was very, very generous," Lee said. "He gave me a very nice portable studio and said, 'Here, start practicing with that, start doing stuff with it.'" Lee ended up playing with Leon for about two and a half years. Leon called Lee "Soul Baby" and loved having him in the band.

In 2008, Grant Whitman had a stroke and could no longer drive or play drums. Leon drove the bus down to Oklahoma, where they hired a new driver. Lee recommended Brandon Holder, another Tulsa guy, to be the new drummer. He was thrown right in. Lee got him a CD of one of the shows, and he had to cram it in less than a week to play the show at a casino in Oklahoma. Leon arrived just at showtime and pulled up in a van, went right to the stage, and Jack Wessel said, "Go, go, go!"

"I knew 'Tight Rope' and 'Delta Lady' and some other things, but I didn't realize the scope of what he wrote, and what he did as far as the Wrecking Crew," Holder said. "I just knew he was from Tulsa and had songs on the radio." By the 1980s, Leon was getting progressively less airplay on oldies and classic rock stations in most of the country. But Tulsa stations naturally continued to play his music. "I quickly learned. I would just sit up on the bus with him almost every night, and I would never ask him anything; I would just let him talk, and he would tell me stories. We talked every night. If you were *trying* to get a story out of him, he wouldn't tell it. But if you just sat and let him talk, he would start telling you things."

An even younger group of Tulsa musicians, the family band Hanson, had scored a ten-million-selling worldwide smash in 1997 with *Middle of Nowhere*. In 2005, the band brought Leon and Steve Ripley onstage with them at the Tulsa Mayfest concert, where they tipped a cap to their hometown with a cover of Don Williams's (no relation to the Shelter executive) "Tulsa Time," made famous by Eric Clapton.

"You have Oklahoma, which is a lot of country, a lot of roots, as well as the cross section of rock 'n' roll and gospel, and some jazz," said Taylor Hanson. "And that became the Tulsa Sound, Leon's whole collection of those styles. But we were the oddballs. We grew up listening to soul records, early rock 'n' roll, Motown. I remember Ripley saying, 'You know, you guys sound like the Tulsa Sound.' It was a fusion. Leon didn't influence our initial writing, but the folklore of Leon was everywhere. But I fell in love with Leon through Ripley. I was probably sixteen, seventeen, or eighteen, really looking to be a pianist, and really write and craft songs. *That's* where I fell in love with him in a deeper way. And if you're in Oklahoma, the amount of real legends that you can just reach across, just bump into and touch, there's not that many. But Leon was one where, all of a sudden, it was a relationship, and somebody that you could catch playing at Curly's, when they were doing his birthday shows every year, down at the Brady or at Cain's. He was always trying to bring people together. He was always trying for the next thing. You saw that his entire career."

Beau Charron was in his teens when he saw the 1993 Birthday Bash (one of a series of Tulsa shows coinciding with Leon's birthdays, promoted by one of his superfans, Steve Todoroff) in Tulsa. "There was no band," he said. "It was just Leon and Jack. Jack was the constant. Never in a million years did I think, down the road, I'd be playing with him." Growing up in the city, Charron had always been a Leon fan. "His piano playing and just everything about him just sucked me in probably around fourteen years old. The first time I ever heard any of his songs, I got it, I felt it, and I loved it. People love his singing, but he's not a great singer; his voice is flawed. It's limited, certainly, but the emotion, everything that comes through that voice, makes him a *great* singer."

Charron had been in a band with Brandon Holder back in 1999. When Brian Lee was leaving Leon's band, Holder suggested Charron as a replacement. "Brandon just kept telling Leon, 'I got a guy in Tulsa, he can play guitar, he can play keys. He can play pedal steel and play mandolin.' So I'm in this mad rush to go purchase these instruments and learn the songs. March 2010, we went down to Dallas, I'm playing the show, and Leon gave me a couple solos, and they actually got some cheers. So at the end of the night the job was mine."

Leon loved his final band. "Ringo asked [Leon] to be in his [All-Starr] band," Jan recalled. "Leon was worried about his band. He didn't want to lose them or for them to struggle while he was out playing with Ringo."

It was 2010. "I couldn't have joined at a more incredible time," Charron said. Leon had just finished recording *The Union* with Elton John.

Chapter 37

The Union

LEON'S COMEBACK BEGAN WITH *THE Union*, the 2010 album he made with Elton John, and culminated in the 2011 induction into the Rock & Roll Hall of Fame, for which Elton also was largely responsible. But the machinations to make this all happen started with Steve and Charlene Ripley years before. "Steve and Charlene devised how to get Leon back, do something for Leon, and get him in the Rock & Roll Hall of Fame," Jeff Moore said. "Steve outlined a plan."

The idea was to lobby some of Leon's rock star friends. "Elton John's at the top of the list," Steve said. On Leon's trips back through Tulsa, he would regularly go out to eat with the Ripleys. When they were still trying to figure out what to do with Leon's archives, before OKPOP, they had considered starting a Leon Russell Foundation and funding it in part with a tribute record and a documentary about Leon. Elton would be a big fish to land for such a project.

Steve Ripley explained, "Charlene's done this research, and we know Elton loved him. I say to Leon, 'What about Elton John?' He says, 'He waxed me.' In Leon's mind, back then, Elton was Mr. Show Business, but Leon was dancing on the piano and stuff. But in Leon's mind, Elton sent him running to the house with his tail between his legs."

After a few dead ends, including Steve's friends at Bob Dylan's management, the Ripleys found the first successful recruits right under their noses. Serendipitously, a young friend of theirs, Bart Williams, and his partner, Dr. Greg Holt, had been invited to a once-in-a-lifetime event as the guests of John Eckel, a philanthropist and a friend of Williams who successfully bid for a fundraiser for the Elton John AIDS Foundation.

The auction item was a small dinner party for eight people on September 20, 2007, with Elton and his husband David Furnish. "I just sort of mentioned that to [the Ripleys]," Williams recalled. "I hung around their studios. I love their family."

Steve asked Bart to see if he could get the message to Elton that they wished for him to partake in a tribute documentary for Leon. Williams said, "If it comes up, of course, I will. But I don't know how much access I'm going to have. I don't know if I'm just going to shoot the shit with Elton, or if we're going to just sit there, he's going to talk a little bit, and then we're going to eat dinner, and he's going to go away. I can't make any promises, but if I do get a chance, I'll mention it."

Bart and Greg and friends were flown first class to Elton and David's house in England. "We go in, and it was really just the eight of us from the States," Williams recalled. "And we were all just meeting over there and having dinner with Elton and David. As soon as we walked in, David greeted us all. Elton walked out after everyone was there, introduced himself, and then the *first thing* he said was, 'Somebody here is from Tulsa, Oklahoma. Who is from Tulsa?' I am the person who's least shy. I've never met a stranger. So I'm like, 'We're from Tulsa!' And he said, 'Have you ever heard of Leon Russell?' I was like, 'Yeah, I've actually met him, though he wouldn't remember it. Funny you should ask because some friends of mine are making a documentary through some archival footage they came across of him and wanted me to ask you if you would just . . .' He said, '100 percent' without any hesitation. This is the first thirty seconds we've walked in the door, and he goes, 'Where are you sitting, young man?' The table had assigned seats, and it said my name on it, so I go, 'I'm sitting over here,' and he goes, 'Who's John Eckel?'" That was the name of the winning bidder who invited everyone, including Williams. "And he was sitting right next to Elton. He goes, 'Do you mind trading places?'" Eckel graciously obliged.

"I sat next to Elton John through the dinner, and we discussed Tulsa, Oklahoma, the music industry. . . . We never stopped talking. But he was like, 'How do you know Leon? Who are these people? What do they need?' And I started trying to give him the whole lowdown, everything I knew. . . . I remember Elton saying he loved Leon Russell. He thought Leon was the most underappreciated musician of his time. He talked at length about how influential he was to the music industry. And he told me so many stories about—there were songs that I heard that I did not know that Leon had taken part in. I was just like, 'Wow, you really love Leon Russell!' I was kind of feeling stupid because I just didn't know that much about somebody who was in my back yard. And I didn't *really* understand that they had such a mutual friendship and connection.

"And so as we were leaving, he said, 'Can you please give me the information?' And his assistant was there, and he said, 'Just give him all the information so I can connect with the people working on this. Is Leon in good shape? Can I speak with him?' I said, 'He hasn't been in the best of health, but I think he's actually been recovering [from a heart attack]. I don't see him a lot.' I had heard of who he was, but I did not know or really have any appreciation of who he was. I said, 'I think he could take your call.' And that was that."

"Elton's partner, David Furnish, makes a note of this," Steve Ripley said. "He knows who Leon Russell is, but not like Elton did. But he sees the affection that Elton has and has expressed in a grand manner." In December 2008, Elton appeared as a guest on the first episode of the television show he and Furnish produced, *Spectacle: Elvis Costello with . . .* Elton emphasizes Leon's influence on him: "He wrote the most incredible songs. I went to go see him in England and fell in love with the way he played piano and the way he sang. And he didn't influence me vocally because he has the most unorthodox voice. But certainly piano playing–wise, I would say he's my biggest hero." He mentions their tours together. "We were on tour in Cleveland once and staying at the same hotel. I had to go ask [Leon] what time soundcheck was, and he opened the door and was completely naked. I went, 'Oh my God.' I didn't know where to look. But I did," he says, laughing. "No, I didn't." And he finishes with a brilliant demonstration of Leon's piano style. He even gives kudos to Patrick Henderson.

Matt Harris said, "So, there's one night, I am sitting there, watching an Elvis Costello show. Elton John was the guest, and I see Elton doing his Leon shit. And I recorded it. We watched it together. I said, 'Dude, Elton's a big fucking fan of yours, man. Check this out.' After I showed him that thing with Elvis Costello, they're going off about him. I go 'Leon!'—and he was kind of making jokes—'You should work with this guy. This could be something great. I think you should have somebody call him.' And he goes, 'You think so?'"

Momentum was underway. When Elton came to play in Oklahoma City, Taylor Hanson pitched Elton on doing a project with Leon. Steve Ripley continued, "Skip ahead now, Elton and David are on safari, as Elton tells the story, in South Africa. He's shaving, and he wants to listen to something, and he doesn't have an iPod, so he borrows David's. Well, David put a bunch of Leon's stuff on his iPod." Elton had an epiphany while shaving on an African safari, hearing Leon's *Greatest Hits* on an iPod, tears streaming from his eyes. "When I was in Africa, and David played 'Back to the Island,' all those memories came flooding back to me," Elton said. "And I thought, 'God, I haven't spoken to him in years. He's been forgotten about. He should be in the Rock & Roll Hall of Fame. He should be lauded for what he did and the way he played.' And that's what started the whole process, thank God."

"I believe we finally got to Elton, but nobody knows that," Steve Ripley said. "David does, and Bart does. And it makes no difference except that then a guy named Johnny Barbis—who's Elton's guy in America, one of them, and an old Shelter guy—finds Leon."

Johnny Barbis explained how it happened from his perspective. "David [Furnish] actually suggested to Elton, 'You loved him so much, he was one of your idols. Why don't you do a record with him?' So Elton called me, knowing that I knew Leon, and I [called] Leon and said, 'Listen, would you like to do something with Elton?'"

Leon told Alanna Nash, "When [Elton] called me and asked me if I'd like to do an album, I hadn't spoken to him in thirty-five years. I was basically sitting home watching soap operas at the time. . . . I kept thinking somebody was gonna come back and get me [*laughs*], but they never did—except for Elton. That's why I tell people he came and found me in a ditch by the side of the highway of life."

Chris Simmons said Leon was actually on the road when Elton called. "One day, I was sitting there on the couch on the bus watching *Law & Order*. And his phone rings, and he goes, 'Uh-uh, yeah, alright.' He was only on there sixty seconds. He goes, 'Guess who that was? That was somebody with Elton John, and they asked me if Elton can call me.' Five minutes later, he answers the phone again: 'All right, that sounds good.' He's on *that* call two or three minutes: 'That was Elton. He wants to write a song with me for his next record.' I said, 'That is amazing.' Three or five minutes later, the phone rings again. He talks five or ten minutes and goes, 'Elton wants to do a full album.'"

Elton said Leon responded, "Thank you for the Elvis Costello show, bless your heart." The first call was just to catch up, and they decided to have dinner together as soon as they could, just like old friends who usually do not follow through on their good intentions. "When I heard that track in Africa, I thought, 'I need to rectify the wrong here,'" Elton said. "This man is so great and gave me so much. I felt really guilty." His immediate second call was to T Bone Burnett, "who I'd never met. It all came together by happenstance. I knew T Bone would know who Leon was and T Bone's history of music. I said, 'Would you be interested?' He said, 'Absolutely.' I phoned Leon back, and I said, 'Would you like to do a record?' And he said, 'Well, do you think I can?' And I said, 'Of course you can.' I said T Bone would do it, and Leon said, 'Let's do it!'"

"Leon goes, 'You called it, man. This is happening,'" Harris said.

Barbis arranged for Leon to come to Las Vegas to meet with Elton, who had a three-month residency there. First, Leon stopped in Tulsa. Charlene said the date was "April 11, 2009, we spent the day with Leon. He wanted us to drive by where he grew up, so we drove him by his old house. . . . We toured the Oklahoma Jazz Hall of Fame and ate three times."

"We had a great day," Steve said. "And then he got on the plane to go have dinner with Elton in Vegas. And truthfully, in a way, that's the last we ever saw of him. Because he hit the big time, once again."

"He really never had management," Barbis explained. "He was really self-contained. And I asked him when he came to Vegas to meet Elton, and I said, 'You want a manager in this situation?' He said, 'Yeah.' I said, 'I'd like to manage you.' He said, 'I thought you were never gonna ask.' I don't think I'd seen him for many years before I approached him. I said, 'You know, Leon, I owe you. If it wasn't for you, I wouldn't be in the business with Dino and Dino [at Shelter Records with Dino Airali and Johnny's brother Dino Barbis].' He said, 'Well, I'm going to collect.' At that time, he had a shoddy agency in Austin. I put him in [with] Steve Martin [at the powerhouse Agency Group], and I became the manager of Leon, along with Elton."

"I was introduced when the Elton John album started," Martin said. I got a call from Johnny Barbis. I'd met him a couple of times perfunctorily.

He said, 'I'm looking for a new agent for Leon. I've asked three people. Your name keeps coming up,' and I said, 'I'd be thrilled to represent Leon. It's so funny, because I'm such a fan, and not to cast aspersions, but he's been booked terribly. This guy is a legend. He's lazy, from seeing the shows, but he's a legend. I think the Elton project is going to be great. I'd be honored to do it.'"

"I loved the whole Shelter world because Tom Petty came out of that, too," T Bone noted. "And Denny Cordell was a friend. He was a very nice cat, and he seemed like a force for good. I followed all that stuff, and then I followed *Hank Wilson's Back*. I'd loved the Hank Wilson records. But I really couldn't figure it out—Leon. He could have been a huge star if he had wanted to be. But I guess he didn't want to be—every time something would be offered to him, it seemed he would go someplace else to do something else. He seemed like he was always dodging celebrity."

"I didn't really know Leon very well," Elton explained. "I got to know him much better when I did *The Union*. He was very reticent to talk about the past because I think it was very painful for him. I didn't mention his marriages. But he went through a lot. I think a lot of people he helped forgot about him, including myself. I don't think Eric Clapton or anybody else ever got in touch with him. When I broached that subject, it never seemed to go down very well, so I left it alone. I was more interested in getting him on his feet, getting him a new tour bus, getting him well. He was so ill."

Elton continued: "I think he was bad with money, and he was very stubborn. He might have been a bit bitter. Never stubborn with me, but I have the feeling that he didn't forgive people. And I think he burned a few bridges. And that just gets worse. I think he didn't want to go cap in hand to anyone. And so he ended up by playing small clubs and rattling around America just trying to get food on the table and pay the rent." Elton asserted that Leon was "not playing the sort of venues that befits the man who wrote such great songs, played on so many records, and is one of America's greatest musicians."

As for the post-hits music Leon created, Elton said, "He never really changed his style of music. But that didn't really matter because Americana music in the nineties and two-thousands started to take off again. It's a huge genre now, and Leon was one of the leaders of it." He even used

"Americana" as an album title long before it became just another marketing term.

The natural-born collaborator in Leon had been suppressed after years of frustration, and he'd become addicted to the efficiency of playing all the parts on his records, with no one else piping in with opinions. Collaborating with Elton "was violating a lot of stuff that I held to be important that turned out not to be important," Leon says in the Cameron Crowe documentary that chronicled the creation of the album. In the film, Elton explains, "Collaboration is one of the greatest gifts you can get. Not enough people are willing to give for the team, but the team gives back. I don't understand people who can't share."

Leon himself unflinchingly summarizes the state of his career. "I've been pretty much the bottom of the barrel for that whole time. I was working small places for small money. Then Elton called and said, 'I want to fix that for you.'" He never expressed bitterness or self-pity, taking the responsibility on himself. "I'm not very good at public relations, that's one of my shortcomings, so that was the missing ingredient for those. I didn't like to do interviews, and PR in general is just a little bit beyond me. I suppose I've got better and I have people working for me now who set up interviews, and before I didn't have that. So a lot of the upwards swing [for heritage artists in the eighties] I wasn't in on."

"A lot of time had gone by between Leon's last records in the early seventies and when we made that record," Elton said. "That's an awful lot of time to kind of move into an obsolete career, and his career *had* become obsolete. I only saw him in the *LA Times* when he was playing the clubs in LA. And I thought, 'Oh, Jesus, I'd love to go and see him, but I can't. I just can't go see him like that.'"

"Now they're scheduled to go," Matt Harris said. "I said, 'You've got to jump on this. If you don't do this now, man, and if you be weird and, *I don't like the manager. I don't like this shit*, like you do'—because he's been like that all his life—'you're gonna fuck up. And I'm telling you this because you're my buddy, you can't do your Leon shit, alright?' And he goes, 'Alright, I get it.'"

Elton continued, "I was more interested in the healing process, but I think there was an awful lot of pain. . . . He was very bad on his feet for a man his age. He was not in good shape. It's a miracle that we went on tour. It is a miracle we finished the album. He had brain fluid coming out of his nose when we were making it, I mean, Jesus. I didn't really want to go back into the lurid past. I wanted to concentrate on the time we had in making sure it was a good present. I didn't want to bring that pain back into the sessions. You could see there was. He never talked about it, but he carried a lot of it with him till the end. He was tightly wired, but it was like he was asleep."

The original plan was to convene in January 2010, but when some dates were freed up due to Billy Joel canceling a few tour dates he and Elton were doing, Leon and Elton started writing sessions on November 20, 2009. Leon did not exactly come in with his guard down. "I'd had an operation right before *The Union*. I was lucky to be there at all. . . . Elton had asked me to do that, and I really didn't want to get in the way. I make my own records. I'm used to running the sessions, but I didn't feel like I wanted to do that because I felt he had such specific ideas in mind." He said, "I showed up an hour late for our first recording session—I'd been in the hospital—and Elton had written four songs already! [*laughs*] So I thought, 'Well, this should be easy!'" Elton had actually arrived with five songs ready to go, and it caused some anxiety for Leon.

T Bone Burnett is the kind of producer who spends a great deal of attention on setting the right vibe in order for artists to feel creative. To set the tone for the *Union* sessions, he began the proceedings by playing a clip from *Jazz on a Summer's Day* of the Queen of Gospel, Mahalia Jackson, singing "Didn't It Rain" at the 1958 Newport Jazz Festival. It "broke the ice," Elton recalled. From there, Leon and Elton wrote "A Dream Come True," a similar gospel stomp sung by Leon and Elton as a duet.

They worked for four days and wrote ten songs, and reconvened to record in January. A week before they were due to start the January recording sessions, Leon was waylaid and had go in to have surgery for another brainpan leak, the incident Elton referred to. "He had been hit pretty hard when he finally got to the studio," Burnett said. "Just as we were going in, he had to go back into the hospital for an operation. . . . He had brain fluid coming out of his nose. He was about probably ten days late to get to the sessions. I know people kept coming to see him, and he wouldn't be there. Ringo came in one day and said, 'Where is Leon?' We said, 'He's not here yet.' He said, 'I was really horrified to hear that he was in the hospital, and I was relieved to find out that he only had brain fluid coming out of a crack in his brainpan,'" Burnett said with a laugh. "Just grim."

Jackie Wessel opined that the people in *The Union* film "melodramatized" the brain situation. "He was a little tired when he showed up, but he was fine. 'Oh, he was so frail, and every day he got stronger and stronger.' It was so cornball." Wessel said that this operation, the third and last one Leon had relating to his brainpan, was actually somewhat "routine" by that point. "They told him by that time the noninvasive [surgery option] had gotten good. And they said, 'This one may hold,' and it did hold for the rest of his life."

It was actually a bout with pneumonia that Leon caught while they were also treating his heart problems that knocked him out. Leon had his first heart attack in 1996, according to Jan. Charlene Ripley remembered subsequent heart attacks in 2008 and 2010. "He had more angioplasties after his heart trouble started," Wessel said. "He just got really cavalier about getting in the car and driving himself over there and getting another stent. I mean, he had enough balloons in his leg for a birthday party. He never had a massive cardiac arrest; he always showed up just at the onset."

Brandon Holder recalled, "We were getting ready to go out on the road one time, and we were leaving his house, and he said to me, 'My stomach doesn't feel right; it's real upset.' He went to the bathroom and came back out, sat in his chair, and said, 'I think I'm having a heart attack, boys. Take me to the hospital.'" They put in two stents, and he was back on the road in two weeks.

Matt Harris happened to be in LA in January. Jan had called him from Tennessee to explain that Leon needed brainpan surgery. "She said, 'We're going to two different doctors in Tennessee, and they want us [to cut] off the top of his head, gently remove his brain,' which was Leon's favorite phrase. 'They're gonna gently remove my brain and then patch the fucking holes in there,' right? I'm like, 'Jan, this is fucked up. We've got to go to LA and find out what's happening.' I have Lynyrd Skynyrd's plane because I'm connected through all my friends in Nashville. Within an hour, I had four different people from major bands, saying, 'We will fly him there on our private plane to take him to his brain surgery in California.' I go, 'We can't just let him get his fucking skullcap pulled off.' The whole thing about the way that brain thing should work is they scrape cartilage, and they go through his nostril, and then they patch it like you're patching a wall. They spackle it right through his nose with microsurgery instead of taking your fucking skull off and *gently removing* your brain. But we got the right doctor.

"Anyway, he gets there. He's in the hospital, just got over the brain surgery. And I happen to be in and out, and I'm so glad I'm there. He was a shell of himself. His voice was really weak. And they didn't even postpone the studio start dates with him at the Village [Village Recorders studio] with Elton and Bernie and T Bone. So he just got out of brain surgery, and he's going, 'Matt, how am I gonna do this? I've got to go in there.'"

"Elton said something when they were working together," Jan recalled. "He said he knew he had to bring his A-game. This is right after Leon had brain surgery, weeks after. He said, 'I know Leon's a competitive motherfucker.' I was like, 'Yeah, but I felt Leon's competition was always with himself.' When he was on the road with Edgar [Winter], he just became Edgar's piano player."

"And you know what? He got through it," Harris said. "He started feeling better. And it was a great experience for him. He loved the Elton experience. He was like, 'Oh, my God, this guy's an angel. God, this guy loves me, and I'm so grateful for this.'"

"When he came in finally, he had to have headphones because he couldn't hear very well anymore," Burnett recalled. "I guess he had blown his hearing out in all those live clubs. And he had to have a recliner, so he spent most of the time in the recliner with headphones on, which was strange." This was how Leon had been working for about twenty years.

Burnett said the awakening was sudden and almost miraculous. "Grace Jones came into the studio one day [brought in by Elton], and he was lying there on the recliner, and she laid down on him, like, nose to nose, fingertip to fingertip, toe to toe, just laid right down flat on him. And breathed in . . . just put some kind of life into him. It was the wildest transference of life I've ever seen; it was like *ET* or something. I want to say it aroused him, I guess. And that was the moment when he got up out of the chair and started participating again, and he started giving the background singers parts to sing, and he started really being a full force in the studio after that."

The sessions were filled with many musicians and singers. Aside from Elton and Leon, there are forty-one musicians listed in the credits. Some were familiar faces, like Marty Grebb, Rose Stone (Sly's sister), and Bill Maxwell, the vocal contractor and arranger. He and Leon had not seen each other in eighteen years. Maxwell had learned vocal arranging from his mentor, Andraé Crouch. "Andraé was the king of vocal arrangers," Maxwell explained. "That's who Quincy Jones would use with Michael Jackson. T Bone recognized that, and he started using me."

Leon also was finally convinced to play acoustic piano again. "During the sessions, I would always make him go out to the piano, sing, and play something," Maxwell said. "He got into that there, and I said he can still do it. And he started singing a gospel song. I think it might have been 'Sweeping Through the City,' and he was *smoking*, and he was playing, like, Billy Preston kind of stuff, and [his agility] was back. And I said, 'Put a click [track] to this, and it will never move.' He was right there with it. I talked to Rose Stone afterwards because Rose worked with Billy too. I said, 'Billy couldn't do this.' She said, 'I know. I've never heard anyone do what Leon just did.' Leon's talent, just as a session piano player, I've never worked with anybody that could record better. He played with absolute perfect time. He didn't budge. And I played with Billy Preston a lot. Billy was one of the greatest players ever, but Billy rushed. You had to hold Billy back. Leon never budged. He was like a machine. . . . He instinctively knew what music needed, and I'll tell you, most arrangers don't know that. Just the way he played would alter me without telling me what to do."

Leon seemed to finally, if reluctantly, fall back in love with playing an acoustic piano. Elton sent him a new piano after the sessions, the same Yamaha model he was playing in the studio. "I began to realize that I've been playing electronic pianos for so long that I had forgotten I had a whole vocabulary on real grand pianos that I'd been neglecting," Leon said.

Leon's mood shift that came with the laying-on of Grace Jones extended to working on the backing vocals with a small choir of A-list singers arranged with Maxwell. "This was the first thing; I brought the girls in," Maxwell said. "Elton wasn't there. There were no cameras at that point. I was actually putting background vocals on something on Gregg Allman's album in the other room, and then Leon saw me and said, 'Can we start on the vocals on this now?' And I said, 'Yeah, let me finish [this] song.' Leon started saying—I think the song was 'There's No Tomorrow'—'What I want is that kind of Church of God in Christ thing where somebody has this note; within the next chord they might switch harmonies so that it's loose and not defined.' I said, 'Of course, that's what we do.' We started to sing, and I looked over, and Leon was just gone. He was crying and couldn't even talk. Afterwards, I told the girls that he had been sick, and they prayed for him, and then I said, 'Okay, you've got to play us a song,' and he did 'This Masquerade' in the style of Dr. John, and they sang background, and it just lit him up. I got a call from T Bone later that night. He said, 'What'd you do to Leon? He's so happy!' Elton said, 'Use these people on everything' because it was the first time [Leon] had kind of come back to life."

It was like Old Home Week at the studio. Stevie Nicks paid a visit to tell Leon how much he has meant to her and how she and Lindsey Buckingham opened up for some of Leon's early 1970s concerts with their pre–Fleetwood Mac band, Fritz. Booker T. Jones came in to add an organ on four tracks. He asked Leon how he was doing. "I'm old," Leon answers. He was sixty-eight at the time. Sharon Stone, Jeff Bridges, LeAnn Rimes also were among the well-wishers. Don Was came in and ended up adding some bass guitar.

Leon was reunited on the sessions with Jim Keltner, but there was lingering tension between them. "I was generally happy," Keltner said of the final result. "But it would have been incredible had Leon been up and able to play live with us. That's the part I thought was too bad. But it came off all right."

Harris agreed with T Bone that Leon had a hard time hearing what was going on in the monitors. "He had a hard time remembering the songs," Harris said. "And that record, if you've heard it, it's not super hook-driven."

Keltner played drums on all the tracks, with Jay Bellerose adding additional drums and percussion on almost everything. "[Leon] said that Jay Bellerose was the best rock 'n' roll drummer he had ever worked with," T Bone said. "And that includes Jimmy Karstein and Jimmy Keltner and Jim Gordon," not to mention Ringo, Charlie Watts, Chuck Blackwell, Earl Palmer, or Hal Blaine. "So that's extremely high praise coming from Leon Russell."

Like Elton, T Bone said he was also overawed by Leon when he was a young musician. "Well, back in those days, artists were like gunslingers," Burnett said. "Mirrored sunglasses; he was unapproachable. I always held him in the absolute highest respect."

Maxwell laughed, saying, "T Bone was always so scared of him because Leon was always so mean to him in the early seventies. T Bone's the absolute sweetest guy in the world. He's been one of my best friends since 1968. He's a sweetheart. But Leon could be a little intimidating."

Leon said he didn't have a clear picture or preconceived ideas going into the project. He did arrive with the song "If It Wasn't for Bad," a funky track that opens the album. For those who had been listening to Leon's "merch records," here was a welcome return to his classic form. It's the sound of a band playing together, with an organic heft. Leon was back in a room with other people, instead of sequestered away with samples and drum programs.

"He got involved in the arrangements," T Bone said. "And he started writing. He had Bernie write for his tune ['I Should Have Sent Roses'] I think he'd just started. I think it made him feel alive again. I do think he was getting ready to die before Elton called him."

There's a moving scene in the documentary when Elton arrives at the studio in a black Adidas tracksuit to discover that Leon has written a song for him and Barbis, "In the Hands of Angels." Leon says he needs to get to a piano because he had only written it the night before at the hotel, without a piano, and wryly adds that he was "on my Ambien."

Over the evergreen gospel changes of "In the Hands of Angels," Leon sings about how "Johnny and the Governor" rescued him, making him feel kingly. Yep, he calls Elton "the Governor." The camera follows Elton as he listens on the couch, walks up to T Bone at the mixing board, and walks off into the kitchen area of the studio, overcome by emotion. "This breaks my heart," he says. "This has to go on the record. My mascara is running," he jokes. "No one had ever written a song for me before." Leon replies, "That's what you get for saving someone's life." Elton recalled that Jan told him, "You got to him just in time."

"I thought, 'What do you give a guy who's got six houses and ten of everything?'" Leon said. "The only thing I could give him would be a song. I wrote the whole song that night."

It is easy to understand why Jack Wessel, who had been by Leon's side for about thirty years, would take issue with the overarching theme of the documentary that Leon had disappeared, been forgotten about, and was asleep like Rip Van Winkle. And, indeed, Leon had a 1997 song by that name with the lines "Been asleep for a hundred years then hardly anybody know him / Recognized that the world had changed beyond his recognition." Jackie had constantly been working in the trenches with Leon over those decades. Leon was always busy on the road and recording, even if "not very impressively," Wessel acknowledged. Elton has a flair for the dramatic, with voiceovers and onscreen comments, contrasting the two men's careers. "I had already been the biggest star in the world," he says, factually. When he says Leon is not just there "to take up space; he's there to kick my ass," he is telling the truth as well. It was time for Elton to make a soulful record that he could be proud of. "You can't physically expect to be at the top of the charts when you're seventy," he says, as if consoling himself. "My album sales have been going downhill for ages."

Much of the album—which Elton characterized as "righting a wrong"—is a personal dialogue between the two men, reflecting on past glories, failures, making corrections, and moving on. Without stating as much in the film, Elton and Taupin, his songwriting partner from the beginning, wrote a song for Leon as well: "Never Too Old (to Hold Somebody)." "That was one of my favorite songs on the whole record because, you know, I'm getting up there too, but that was Leon's song," Elton explained. "Bernie and I wrote it especially for him."

Leon enjoyed writing with Elton because they both work quickly. When Elton had asked Leon to write some songs, Leon asked what kind. Elton responded, "Up-tempo, baby!" For "There's No Tomorrow," they lifted the music from "Hymn No. 5," a 1966 soul gem by the Mighty Hannibal (aka James Timothy Shaw) about the effects of the Vietnam War on soldiers. They reached out to Shaw to get his blessing and, of course, credited him on the album.

"Elton is absolutely savant when it comes to melodic songwriting," Leon marveled. "I write the first verse of a song and forget it before I get to the second one. So, I have to record while I'm writing to be able to complete the song, but Elton has such a huge amount of output and doesn't forget any of it."

The collaboration was a little different between Taupin and Leon than between Taupin and Elton. "Bernie Taupin, when he writes lyrics, he rewrites lyrics to an existing song and then gives a new lyric to Elton without telling what the existing song was," T Bone explained. "And Elton just reinvents it completely, without any idea what Bernie's been up to."

Some of Taupin's lyrics had been discarded from another project. "I was asking him for his stuff out of the trash," Leon said. "I was thinking, 'How bad could his writing be that he needed to throw [it] away?' 'I Should Have Sent Roses' was something he'd written part of some years before for a project that didn't work out, and that was the first one he gave me. I was always so jealous of Elton because I would sit around for months and wait for inspiration, and Elton had Bernie handing him lyrics all the time. What a lucky guy."

Leon finished "I Should Have Sent Roses" with Taupin. Taupin is a fan of Bob Dylan and The Band, whose Americana themes permeated the early Elton John records. Elton stated that the objective for *The Union* was to make a record that sounded like the old Leon stuff, but it was as much a return to the roots for him and Taupin as it was for Leon.

Neil Young came in to sing on "Gone to Shiloh," a minor-key Civil War song written by Bernie and Elton. Leon noted that Taupin is an expert on Civil War history. During the period they recorded *The Union*, Elton and Leon had joined a star-studded tribute to Neil as Person of the Year by the charitable MusiCares organization. Elton and Leon were joined by T Bone, Neko Case, and Sheryl Crow on a version of Young's "Helpless." T Bone suggested Neil would sound good on "Gone to Shiloh" and, re-ported Elton, "[Neil] had no hesitation about doing it. Everyone wanted Leon to succeed."

The elegiac song serves as a centerpiece on the album. Leon sings the first verse, and Elton joins Neil, and the three men intertwine their distinct voices in shiver-inducing three-part harmony for the choruses. The lyric covers similar ground as Young's "Powderfinger," and the sweeping orchestral bed hints at "Expecting to Fly" and "A Man Needs a Maid" (both of which were arranged by Leon's early champion and colleague, Jack Nitzsche). While it sounds like an homage to The Band, when each takes the lead vocal, it could be from any of their individual catalogs. "Leon was playing with people of his caliber," Elton summarized.

The most poignant moment in the film is the interaction between Leon and Brian Wilson out on the sidewalk in front of the studio. Brian has just finished arranging and adding the kind of richly stacked backing vocal parts that are his hallmark to the Elton/Bernie ballad "When Love Is Dying." Leon sings the first verse, warmly and understated, with a bit of slap-back tape echo. Elton comes in with more power and takes it to the soaring chorus against the bed of Brian's vocals. Wilson is shown nimbly layering harmonies in wide-ranging registers, from a loud clarion tenor to a low bellowing baritone, doubling them for a lush effect.

Leon is just arriving as Brian is leaving the studio. They had not seen each other in decades. To characterize their exchange as perfunctory, or even odd, would not begin to capture the depth of awkwardness involved. But it is Brian, in this case, who seems to want to make the quick getaway as if he had just ruined rather than elevated the recording. They have a brief, stiff embrace. "Go in and listen to what I did. Bye bye," Brian says as he scampers down the sunny West LA sidewalk.

"It was one of the greatest pleasures of my professional career when we were doing the album," Elton said. "Brian Wilson and Leon Russell! It's rock 'n' roll gold dust. I was lucky enough to just land on the motherlode with Leon and be there at the right place at the right time in 1970."

Things got a little tense between T Bone and Leon, and though he remained grateful for the project until the end, Leon later distanced himself from the resulting album. "He wasn't thrilled with it," Maxwell said, echoing others close to him. Leon thought there were too many chefs in that particular kitchen. Coming from the days when a producer was a person clearly running the session on one side of the glass, with the musicians and artist on the other, he seemed to be bewildered by T Bone's methods.

"He couldn't really hear what we were doing, he couldn't hear the bass very well, so I think that bothered him," Burnett said. "And, in fact, he apologized to me after the record was finished: 'I just didn't understand what you were doing, and I'm really sorry I gave you so much grief.' And I said, 'I have to tell you, Leon, I don't remember you giving me any grief at all. You were totally great the whole time.' But he had apparently felt bad about the way the record was sounding."

"The music on *The Union* is phenomenal," Elton said, "but to see someone regain their pride was the greatest experience I've had in a recording studio, and I've had some fucking wonderful experiences in the studio. And he got a new bus. I phoned him on New Year's Day, and he said, 'I got a new bus, and it's so beautiful. I can invite you on the bus now!' He said, 'You had a baby, I had a bus.'"

Chapter 38

Hall of Fame

THE UNION DEBUTED AT NUMBER three on the *Billboard* Top 200 when it was released in October 2010. "If It Wasn't for Bad" was nominated for a Grammy for Best Pop Collaboration with Vocals. *Rolling Stone* gave it a five-star review and the third slot on the 30 Best Albums of 2010. *The Guardian* gave it four out of five, and Ann Powers at the *LA Times* gave it a three out of four.

In an interview in *Rolling Stone*, Elton effused, "I'm so proud of the record. We've sold three hundred thousand copies without any airplay, and we hope to get it gold."

The album disappointed a surprising number of fans and people close to Leon. Was *The Union* perfect? No, but who realistically expects late-career records by old rock stars to be perfect? However, it was an organic, collaborative, human-sounding record, the first in many years by Leon. Such inspiration should never be taken for granted, particularly when an artist is still working in his late sixties.

Elton and Leon took a promotional victory lap of national television appearances, including *Saturday Night Live*, *Late Night with David Letterman*, *The View* (hosted by notable Leon fan Whoopi Goldberg), *CBS Sunday Morning*, and *Entertainment Tonight*.

Then they took the show on the road. The first shows were the core of T Bone Burnett's Speaking Clock Revue, with revolving artists at shows in Boston, three at the Beacon in New York, and one for Neil Young's Bridge School benefit concert in Mountain View, California. Jim Keltner, Jay Bellerose, and Marc Ribot were all on hand as well.

Leon was responsible for his old pal Keltner getting fired from those shows. "Elton fired Jim," Bill Maxwell said. "Jim is a very free drummer, and they had two drummers. . . . Jim did one of his drum fills, and Leon didn't know where one [beat] was, and they came in wrong, and it fell apart. Leon said, 'I landed on Keltner.' It should have been Jay [Bellerose] because Jay would always play the same thing on the drum, and then Leon would know where he was. But they fired Keltner and said he could play on the rest of the show, just not with Leon. That really hurt Jim, and Jim thought Leon did it on purpose. Leon was like a deer in headlights. There were two pianos and all the camera crews and everything."

As Jack Wessel observed, Leon had a dire fear of being embarrassed. Maxwell continued, "Jim said, 'We've always had times where [Leon's] done things to me.' You know, little things that would come up between them over the years that Jim would try to ignore. All those Tulsa guys were odd. All these guys would be feuding with each other. There was a whole group of people who wouldn't be talking to each other anymore."

To those close to him, Leon's singing and his usually strong left hand were noticeably weak. He complained privately about the teleprompter not scrolling quickly enough, but he would not voice his concerns or make requests to those in charge of running the show. He was unnerved. After the first show at the Beacon, Jan told one of Leon's confidants, "You've got to talk to him! He's not going to go onstage." He felt too weak and old to keep up with Elton. He could not hear things like he was used to, and he could not remember the songs. The friend assured him, "Calm down. You are Leon Russell." Leon replied, "They're gonna find out," meaning that he would be discovered as a fraud. The friend reminded him that Leon should exercise his power and tell them exactly how fast to speed up the scroll on the teleprompter, tell the monitor engineer to turn up the snare drum in his mix. "And if you don't like Jim Keltner, tell them you need a new drummer," said his friend.

After the T Bone Presents shows, Leon was back in his comfort zone with his band. And in the brand new bus, they went on tour supporting Elton and his band at arenas, starting on November 5, 2010, in Ontario, California. Leon would do five songs with his group, followed by Elton and his band doing six, then Leon would join Elton's band for a dozen, and Elton would close out with a long encore set of greatest hits.

Beau Charron was still the new guy, second guitarist to Chris Simmons, and spoke to the sudden difference in the gigs. "We had played some decent theaters, but when that Elton thing started, doing arenas . . . My first one was Ontario, California. And it was just terrifying. We're all gonna walk in this tunnel, where you could really drive a truck through, to the steps, and go to stage. Elton's just like, 'Have fun, boys. You're gonna love it. This is great.' He was excited for us. And he didn't have to be; he was just a nice guy. He'd come back to the green room every night before the show, and spend fifteen to twenty minutes talking to us, get us all laughing."

Elton recalled, "When we played our first show in a fifteen-thousand-seat arena, [Leon] said, 'Goddamn, I haven't played one of these since 1973.' And that broke my heart. And when he came onstage, people just stood up. He could die with a smile on his face because people then knew who he was."

Leon rarely gave his musicians specific feedback. "I was nervous to get on the bus every night after the show," Charron said. "Like, tonight he's gonna tell me he didn't like this or he didn't like that. And he really never did. He was always like, 'Great show, guys.' I really never took my eyes off of him. He was so quiet and just stoic most of the time. He just has a look in his eyes where you don't know if he's happy with you or not happy with you. Put some sunglasses and a hat on, and it's even more so. One time, he's like, 'Hey, I'd like it if you played this solo a little more like Freddie King.' So the next night I tried to do my best Freddie King. I walked on the bus after the show, and he handed me a hundred-dollar bill: 'Perfect.'"

Leon did give brutally blunt critiques to his kids, though. "Growing up, I really wanted to be a singer, and a musician," Coco said. "I just was terrified. And something that I didn't realize: my idea of what every musician must be like [was] what my dad was like. So I thought that every musician had perfect pitch, or just knew it off the top of their head—that they could just hear something once and then go replicate it instantly. It didn't occur to me that there are levels just like anything else. And I was looking at somebody who had just like almost an unnatural ability to understand music so well. I was measuring myself against *that*.

"My mom forced me to sing for him once when I was about eleven. He said something along the lines of, 'Oh, you have a nice tone, but you're not hitting this note, and you need to work on that. If you can't sing it, that's gonna sound wrong.' It's the first time he'd ever heard me sing. And I'm almost in tears, because I'm a very shy, introverted type of person. I didn't want to disappoint my parents. I worshipped both of them. So I stopped trying to sing for years. In fact, I'm still working on it because it's such a sore spot for me to do anything, I'm very, very insecure about it. And I don't think he did that on purpose."

Tina was also not spared Leon's critical assessment. When the tour swung through Tulsa, Tina was there and working on a recording at the Church. A local television station was interviewing Leon there. "He sat down in the control room. I play Dad my song, and the first thing he says: 'What kind of piano is that?' My dad was all about using electronic pianos, and he was like, 'You really shouldn't use those pianos because they make everything sound out of tune.' And I was just like, 'Well, thanks a lot, Dad. Tell us how you really feel about it!'"

Leon did encourage Tina's musical pursuits, though, recognizing her innate talent. "I don't know any music theory or anything like that," she said. "My brother took lessons, and a couple of my siblings have had music lessons. But my harmonies and things like that, he would just say, 'You don't know what you're doing, but not in a bad way. I mean, in a good way. You don't know the rules. You don't know how it's supposed to be, so you're just naturally writing.' It definitely made me feel good, and he trusted me musically with my own stuff, which I really appreciated."

In 2013, Willie Nelson asked Tina Rose to be on a duets album, *To All the Girls*. She sings "After the Fire Is Gone" with Willie. "I was a huge country music fan in my teens," she said. "My dad kind of got a kick out of it."

Leon had a highly refined dad-joke sense of humor. "He was dry as a bone," Matt Harris said. "There was one time we were sitting and watching the Forum footage [the *Leon Russell Festivals* DVD]. I go, 'Dude, you were the ultimate rock 'n' roll hippie.' And he goes, 'From hippie to hippo.'"

Like his family, Leon's band came to understand the different ways he would communicate. Leon gave Freddie King's Gibson to Chris Simmons. Though Simmons at first thought it was too precious to bring out on the road, Leon convinced him otherwise. "He finally asked, 'Where's that guitar? I gave it to you because Freddie would want it to be played, so do whatever you gotta do. Its value is not in its history; it's in what you do when you play it.' *That* is wisdom."

"Some nights, he'd get chatty," Charron said. "For a while there, he started taking Ambien to help him go to sleep. But if you miss your window of going to sleep on Ambien, then you kind of stay up, and you say and do things that you don't necessarily remember the next day. So late-night stories and chatting happened. We'd ask him about the Stones, you know, like, 'What did you do on this Stones song? Were you really on this?'" But he would never get into it too much, and sometimes he'd be like, 'I don't remember. I don't know.'"

"I don't know if he'd ever been diagnosed with anything officially," Holder noted. "But I mean, he had to be some sort of bipolar, manic-depressive. His mania in the later years was getting out on his scooter and hitting antique shops and restaurants. He'd get up in the morning, and the bus driver had to have that scooter waiting by the front door. He'd fly down the sidewalks, beard flapping in the wind, and just go in and buy something. 'Hey, can you boys take the gear truck down to this little antique store a couple blocks away?' 'What did you buy now?' 'Oh, a full-size wicker bicycle,' just the most random stuff."

Shopping and eating remained Leon's two addictions, or at least obsessions. His love of food was the topic one evening onstage after the Elton John tour as he welled up with emotion telling his audience about a particularly satisfying chicken Alfredo crepe he'd enjoyed earlier that day. Leon's emotions would bubble to the surface more frequently as he got into the later years, including onstage. His friends and family—Jan, Matt Harris, Steve Martin (his agent), and others—encouraged Leon to pause more between songs and tell the audience some of his great stories. Leon didn't think people wanted to hear him talk, just play. But they prevailed upon him to try it out, which he did with great returns.

"I think he got tired at some point," Jan said. "And then he got rejuvenated at another point. I said, 'You're gonna have to start talking because you're just playing your show, and it looks like you're not having fun. You're not talking to the crowd.' So he told the crowd, 'My wife says I need to start talking.' And his shows started becoming more fun again."

Wessel said, "He really liked to get those laughs. He told the same stories year in year out for a long time. But he'd get his laughs, and when he didn't, he'd be really disappointed. But mostly it worked really well. And he was surprised. That became an important thing that people were thrilled about, after going to see him for years when he didn't say 'boo.'"

The bus had long been a kind of home to Leon. Like so many senior citizens at home, he would lounge in his recliner watching the National

Geographic Channel, all-day marathons of *Pawn Stars* (and occasional porn stars), the Science Channel, Turner Classic Movies, even ESPN. He had developed a late-in-life appreciation of college football. Among his most-watched channels was MSNBC and specifically Rachel Maddow. He was such a dedicated fan of Maddow's that Brandon Holder reached out to her to invite her to a show in New York. She could not make it but wrote a gracious thank-you note expressing how much of a Leon fan she was. Jan said he only voted once that she knew of, for President Obama.

He also loved stuff on the Hallmark and Lifetime channels, movies "where love always wins, and everything turns out perfect," Jackie Wessel said with a laugh. Jan echoed Jackie. "*Friends with Benefits*, Justin Timberlake and Mila Kunis—he loved that movie. He was a romcom man through and through. He was so disappointed in me when I wouldn't watch the Hallmark channel for *hours* with him."

The Elton John tour ended, but that did not mean Elton felt his work was done. He planned on executive producing a Leon solo record as a follow-up to *The Union*. He intended to oversee the balance of Leon's career, with his team of first-class managers and agents. And he wanted Leon in the Rock & Roll Hall of Fame.

But the Hall of Fame was not something Leon gave much thought to. "Leon sure didn't worry about it," Wessel explained. "Prior to the Elton event, I'd say Leon considered his chances of even getting nominated, much less inducted, way too remote to stew over."

Elton was decisive in getting Leon inducted. "Leon was very honored and deeply moved yet again at Elton's batting for him," Wessel said.

In 2009, Anthony DeCurtis attempted to peel back the curtain on the inner workings of the secret-society-like nominating committee in an article titled, "How Do You Get into the Hall of Fame? Inside the meetings, the debates, and the secret ballots of a passionate and rigorous process." The inherent tension of the article's publication in Jann Wenner's *Rolling Stone* will not be lost on many who detect the guiding force of Wenner's hand on the levers that ultimately decide whether an artist makes the cut. "Elton John wrote a powerful letter to the committee endorsing one of his idols, Leon Russell, to little effect," DeCurtis reported.

The momentum from *The Union* and subsequent media blitz, all spearheaded by Elton, plainly made the case. "Elton doing that great album that they did together was a very nice segue into Leon being given a musical excellence award and getting into the Hall of Fame," Jon Landau acknowledged. Had his name come up in deliberations for the Hall of Fame in the past? Landau demurred, "That, I'm pretty good at *not* going into."

T Bone Burnett pointed out, "Elton campaigned very hard for him, too. He had me calling people and all of that."

Johnny Barbis said, "I was going to Robbie [Robertson] and everybody involved in the Hall of Fame, everybody. Elton worked on Jon Landau and, most importantly, Jann Wenner. It was all Elton putting it in people's faces about, 'Look what this guy's done in his career.' I mean, he campaigned for this. He was unbelievable about it."

This is not to gloss over the fact that Leon was inducted not as an artist but under the "Award for Musical Excellence" category. It had previously been the "Sidemen" category until it changed in 2010, the year Leon was nominated. You can pick many names from the list of artist inductees and shake your head in disbelief when you compare their accomplishments to those of Leon Russell. That's not fair to those others. But neither was it appropriate to limit Leon to a category with undeniably accomplished accompanists who never had significant records or headline tours of their own. "Other than saying he was the first recipient of his honor because 'they had to make up a category for me,' he was humbled and grateful enough to resist making all the great jokes he could have made about it," Wessel said.

It's better just to celebrate this redemptive denouement to the legend. It's as if all the emotion that Leon had kept at bay came over like a tsunami while he gave his acceptance speech, hitting him without warning. Then he proceeded to sing "A Song for You," and it's as if the lyric had been freshly written for this magical occasion, accompanied by tasteful licks and a particularly piquant solo from John Mayer.

Jan reported, "Paul Shaffer called him up and said, 'You need to have John Mayer play,' and Leon was like, 'I don't know who that is.' He's like, 'Trust me, you need to have him play.' He was blown away."

As Mayer wrapped it up, Leon choked up on probably the most sublime lines he ever wrote, describing a profound love that transcends the earthly bounds of time and space. It's a lyric written in his twenties about taking stock at the end of his life. And here he was singing it as an old man who looked even older than his years—the Master of Time and Space in the garb of Father Time. Not a dry eye in the house.

"All us ditch diggers were pretty choked up too," Wessel said. But like everyone else who was not there that night, the guys in the band would have to wait until the video was broadcast to see Leon's acceptance speech. "We were excited, and I thought we were going to be there," Beau Charron said. "No, we sat in the bus parked in Sam's Club in New Jersey while they went into the city and did all that stuff. He liked to play up the whole 'in the ditch on the side of the road of life' thing. Were things what they once were? No, they weren't. But he was still playing all the time. He never stopped working. But that's how he was; he could be so confident and so strong, and then other times he could make himself seem so humbled by people like Elton and Johnny coming along and doing that stuff. And he sure appreciated it. I know that he did."

"Leon could actually get very emotional, in an instant, about the whole Elton episode, even when speaking about it onstage," Wessel said. "He'd choke up, and we'd all look at each other, 'there he goes.'"

Tina Rose had observed her father getting more emotional over the years. "He would be really touched by something and cry, which was not something that I had seen before. I watched the acceptance speech, and it was so touching to see him just overwhelmed with emotion. I really could relate to that feeling cuz that's how I felt, as far as family stuff."

"I was surprised about how emotional he was about it," Jan said. "I mean, he was crying while he was playing 'A Song for You.'" Jan said that Leon had seemed satisfied with his station in life before this special night: "That's why I was so shocked about his speech at the Rock & Roll Hall of Fame, because the amount of shows that he was doing was still the same. There wasn't this huge change in our finances and the shows he did. I didn't see him as being rescued by the side of the road in the 'ditch' because he was on the road every year from the time we were together, always. There was always money."

Leon participated in an all-star jam at the ceremony with Elton, Dr. John, and Lloyd Price—whom Leon went to see as a teenager and who inspired Mad Dogs & Englishmen—singing and playing the latter's classic "Stagger Lee." Even better was Leon reprising his original piano part on the Crystals' "Da Doo Ron Ron" on the stage packed with stars, singing and playing along behind his colleague from the early days, Darlene Love, also inducted that year.

Backstage, Bruce Springsteen came to introduce himself to Leon. "The only time I ever got to say two words to him, it was in the Rock & Roll Hall of Fame," Springsteen said. "He was quite old and in the wheelchair, and his hearing wasn't that great. But I leaned over to him, and I just said, 'Hey, man, you meant a great deal to me.' I whispered in his ear. And I stood back, and he looked at me and said, 'I can't hear a damn thing you're saying,'" Springsteen said, laughing.

Leon was glad to accept the recognition, but he genuinely was happy to do without the fame aspect of it.

Elton said, "You give those people, you know, *attention*, and you give them their due, and they come alive again. I spent a lot of time with Groucho Marx in the early seventies when he was coming out and going to places, and Mae West, the same thing. They'd been forgotten about. They were hiding in their homes, and suddenly they were out and about with young people, and people were so incredibly honored, bowled over to see them both, and it made them feel young again."

Chapter 39

Life Journey

THE UNION AND INDUCTION TO the Hall of Fame was just the beginning of a few busy years of collaborations, tours, and honors for Leon. "He did get in the Rock & Roll Hall of Fame. He did get in the Songwriters Hall of Fame," Elton said. "You know, he wasn't forgotten about."

The Songwriters Hall of Fame ceremony occurred on June 16, 2011. Dwight Yoakam sang "Superstar" in tribute to Leon. He mostly stuck to the popular Carpenters arrangement. Matt Harris said Leon told him, "That guy [Richard Carpenter] made me so much money, I can't tell you, like, right at the apex of my craziness, and naked people, and drugs."

While Leon and Elton were recording *The Union*, Elvis Costello stopped by. "We were gonna write a song, and Leon and Elvis and I went in the other room, and Leon started playing the piano," Burnett recalled. "Elvis started to sing, and within about fifteen minutes, we had a song. And I said, 'Where'd that come from? What was that?' Leon said, 'Oh, I was just playing [the Beach Boys song] "Fun, Fun, Fun."'" This became "My Lovely Jezebel," which Leon performed on and got a cowriting credit for, on Costello's *National Ransom*.

Costello wrote, "The song we were cutting [with Leon] was but a trifle, a couple of groovy changes that Leon had proposed and a blue rocking rhyme that T Bone and I shot back and forth in a few minutes as pretext for watching his hands fly over the keys."

Prior to *The Union*, Leon accepted that he would ride out his life at the same below-the-radar level. But he had been given a shot in the arm and was inspired for the last leg of his life's tour. Brandon Holder explained how it changed Leon's attitude. He got some swagger back. "After the whole Elton thing, before his passing, he started doing things like wearing top hats onstage again, he wanted a real piano-looking thing, things that he hadn't done before."

The "piano-looking thing" was a portable prop to house Leon's electronic keyboards in the white shell of a baby grand piano so it at least *looked* cool and vintage. Paul Lee, Leon's sound tech, finally convinced Leon to get high-quality in-ear monitors, which allowed the stage volume to come down to levels that didn't blow out the audience or the band members. But the main benefit was that the band and Leon were able to hear everything exactly how they wanted it. Such changes helped to improve the show over the next four or five years.

Leon had started using hearing aids in the eighties. Not only had he been playing loud music his whole life, but also all the men on his father's side lost their hearing. Leon had hereditary nerve damage that resulted in hearing loss. He would take the hearing aids out onstage and crank up the monitors to deafening levels. Lee tracked down a company that made in-ears that could pump out 136 decibels. "Sometimes he would want to talk to me when he didn't have [hearing aids] in, and I'd have to yell," Jan said. "I said, 'I just don't want to yell at you.' It made me feel like I was angry."

The hearing issue made Leon seem withdrawn in social situations, especially at restaurants, where the background noise would be so loud for him that he would have to turn down or turn off his hearing aids. "So, a lot of times, he would, like, nod his head or give the wrong answer," Jan explained. "He didn't want people to know he couldn't hear. If we were out to dinner with Elton and a group of people, Elton liked to tell people where to sit. And I would be pushing Leon closer to Elton so he could hear him. I'd say, 'I'm so sorry, but Leon can't hear you if he's over there.'" Elton connected him with the Starkey Hearing Foundation, and Leon was fitted with new state-of-the-art hearing aids. He proudly emblazoned his "piano-looking thing" with a Starkey logo.

From Elton, Leon went on to open for Bob Dylan. "After Elton, we did a string of tours with Bob, then we did Little Feat, we did several of those tours with groups [like Hot Tuna and Dave Mason] that were a package deal, where we'd go out with another band so it was easier to sell," Holder said. "The Dylan one was great. We became friends with all those people."

Steve Martin had called up Dylan's agent Jeff Kramer from Leon's office. "Leon opened for Bob. We did ten or fifteen shows together. They loved each other. Bob would hang out on his bus with Leon. Jeff called me after the second or third show. He goes, 'Leon's not talking to me.' I said, 'Where were you standing when you were talking to him?' He goes, 'We were in catering. He was sitting down. I was standing on the side of him.' I said, 'Jeff, he turns his hearing aids down.'" He laughed. "'He probably couldn't hear you. Walk up to him in front and introduce yourself. I'll tell him that you're going to introduce yourself.' After that, Jeff was on the bus hearing all these great stories. He said, 'Thank you so much. It wouldn't have occurred to me.' I said, 'He shuts everybody out. If he wants to have dinner, he wants to have dinner.'"

It would not be long before Leon jerked the wheel again and drove the car back into the ditch, and it was back to cozy clubs. The honeymoon didn't even last through the tour Leon had done opening for Elton. The camaraderie dissipated as Leon bristled against the plans that Elton and his team were laying out, plans intended to help Leon sustain the success and appreciation for his legacy that he deserved.

"Johnny Barbis, Elton's manager, is a nice guy," Charron explained. "He was so good to all of us, especially me. But he really had ideas for Leon. 'We're gonna get you on these late-night TV shows. You're gonna have to stop in radio stations and do that.' And we did one or two, but Leon just didn't want to do that stuff. Johnny and Elton were really pushing him. I think, after a while, it took its toll. Leon was basically like, 'Johnny, no, I'm gonna go with somebody else.' Those guys were putting a lot of time and energy and money into Leon, and they wouldn't do that if they didn't 100 percent love him and believe in him and want him to get known to a whole new generation. That probably wasn't the best move to make, but that is classic Leon; he's going to do what he wants to do his way."

It wasn't likely so much the promo tasks they requested Leon do, though there is no disputing that he had a distaste and little energy for jumping through such hoops. It would be hard to expect someone nearing seventy to do the back-slapping, hand-shaking, and baby-kissing that major labels expect of younger and less-established artists.

More of an issue was Elton and Johnny wanting to executive produce Leon's records and artistic choices. Specifically, they wanted him to have a producer and make a rock 'n' roll "Leon record," if not with Burnett, then with someone like Don Was—these rootsy guys reconnecting legacy artists with the sound and approach of their heyday. The problem with such well-intended instincts is that they ignore another essential aspect of artists like Leon—a desire to progress, explore, find something new, and not dwell on their past glories.

Leon didn't fire Barbis on the Elton tour. And Elton would not let it go easily. Barbis continued to help Leon in the direction Leon wanted to go—a non-rock record of string-laden old standards and newer standard-like numbers.

Elton said, "We wanted to make another album, a different one than he wanted to make. The album that he wanted to make was, you know, having all the strings on it instead of doing a Leon Russell record. He went back to his old belligerent ways." He paused and, with a chuckle, continued, "His old behavior came back, and he wanted to do things his way. Johnny was great to him. Everybody within the record company—they tried to help him, but in the end, Leon wanted to do another album. It came out about two years after he made it. And it was 'Georgia on My Mind.' It was like, 'No! *No!*'" He laughed.

"Johnny wanted to make a rock record, and Leon made an NPR album, basically," explained someone who knew both men but who wanted to remain anonymous. Barbis did prevail upon Leon to hire a producer, though. Leon reconnected with his old buddy from way back, Tommy LiPuma, while he and the band were playing at the Montreux Jazz Festival.

"Elton sort of insisted that I have a producer," Leon told Dave Lawrence in a radio interview, adding, "Well, I'm not a guy that has producers."

Wessel explained, "What he wanted to say was, 'You know all those records I made that influenced you so much? I produced those.' They didn't trust him to do that. Leon came to understand that at that point in time, in the record business, a producer was a much bigger deal than it was in his day, in his time. Leon was slow to catch on to that. He ended up using Tommy LiPuma, an old friend, and started out with a great idea, and then kind of ruined the album for me by recutting a couple of his old songs. He started out with a great idea, and some of those tracks are amazing."

"I went to Capitol," Barbis said. "I asked for a one-off deal to do a new Leon record. I had it all worked out. It was going to be Don Was, to do a rock 'n' roll–type record. But Leon loved Tommy LiPuma from the Blue Thumb days."

"I've known Tommy for forty-five years," Leon said. "And he cut one of my songs that launched George Benson's career, and he cut Diana Krall, and he's just cut so many jazz artists. I was afraid there might be jazz damage there. I was really scared. When we start[ed] talking, I found out that he was a blues hound like myself. He knows all about where the bodies are buried. And it was great fun. He's the best producer I've ever worked with."

The two went back and forth on emails about song selection. One of the songs that made the cut was Billy Joel's "New York State of Mind," a suggestion from LiPuma. Leon emailed LiPuma: "I was listening to the song, I realized that Tommy, as my producer, wanted to help me become a citizen of the world instead of me being simply a hillbilly from the Southern United States, and suddenly I was extremely excited to have that kind of awareness in my life. . . . This fast lane stuff is great!!"

LiPuma came to Nashville for four or five days of preproduction sessions at Mark Lambert's studio before heading to Capitol Studios in Hollywood, where they used LiPuma's longtime engineer, Al Schmitt. LiPuma wrote in a letter to Bob Lefsetz: "We sat around playing each other songs, and at one point he asked me if I liked hillbilly music, and I pulled up on my computer one of my favorites, George Jones's 'When the Last Curtain Falls.' That pleased him immensely, and things really got relaxed after that."

Leon's road guitarist Chris Simmons was there, joining luminaries like Willie Weeks, Abe Laboriel Jr., and Robben Ford. Leon did not invite Simmons; he "crashed the session," Wessel said. Simmons explained: "I said, 'We didn't get to play on the Elton record. I think you should let us play on this.' And he said, 'Well, you know, it's executive produced by Elton, and it would be up to the producer who plays on it.'" Simmons talked his way into playing on a few songs, and Leon paid him scale, essentially breaking him even for the trip there. But that level of self-serving ambition would eventually cost Simmons his gig with Leon. He'd be canned by the end of 2012.

Leon was thrilled to be back in a fancy studio with a big budget and players with impressive pedigree. "I was talking to Tom in the preliminaries, that I was a big fan of Basie, and when I was playing my piano parts, I was basically playing the Basie parts behind my vocals," Leon said. "So next thing I knew, I had a Basie arranger and bass player [John Clayton], and the guy that was playing drums [Jeff Hamilton] played in his orchestra, too."

LiPuma had been producing sophisticated jazzy records for Diana Krall and Al Jarreau, but also funky records for Dr. John, and sophisticated, funky jazz records like Miles Davis's *Tutu*. Leon was attracted to the possibilities wrapped up in all that experience. He actually begins the album with two blues numbers, including the Robert Johnson standard "Come On in My Kitchen," featuring a lacerating slide guitar from Simmons. Leon did not love much in the way of old country blues, but he credited Eric Clapton with helping him appreciate Robert Johnson.

The record settles into proper standards with a Basie-like arrangement of "Georgia," followed by others like "That Lucky Old Sun," "Fever" (done as an upbeat blues that harkens back to the New Grass Revival days), and "I Got It Bad and That Ain't Good." They are not wholesale reinventions, but neither are they reverential museum pieces or showy, schticky production numbers. Instead, we have convincing Leon interpretations that honor his love of the songs.

In 1999, Joni Mitchell recorded a deeply moving version of her own "Both Sides Now" with the London Symphony Orchestra. The newer version cleverly leverages the title to bookend Mitchell's career. She slows down the original buoyant song, digs into the deep nicotine-stained and smoky patina of her aged voice, allowing the huskiness to serve as a counterweight of wisdom in a dialogue with her younger flawless-voiced self.

Leon pulls off a similar, if not as potent, trick here with his version of "This Masquerade Is Over," a 1938 standard that likely served as an inspiration for his own "This Masquerade." Asked if it was intended as a nod to his song, he answered, "Well, not really. I used to go to jazz jam sessions in Tulsa that started at one or two o'clock in the morning and went to two or three in the afternoon the next day. Jazz players that played Leon McAuliffe's hillbilly band were out there playing at those jam sessions. That's where I learned 'The Masquerade Is Over.' I don't think that one has anything to do with the other, it's just a consequence of having this thing learned." However, it is likely that, like Joni, Leon saw this as a fitting punctuation to his career. Indeed, he thought this might be his last album, and it was the final one released during his lifetime.

"We kind of knew it, that Leon thought it could be his final record," Al Schmitt said. "He was pretty frail. He had to come back in and lay down on the recliner to listen to the playbacks." Schmitt himself passed not long after our interview, at the age of ninety-one.

Regarding the cover of the album—a black-and-white, high-contrast extreme close-up of Leon's deeply craggy face wearing a severely serious expression, framed by his long gray hair and beard—he said, "They want everyone to look real clean and pretty, but I said there is something to be said for truth in advertising."

Tommy and Leon remained close, often grabbing lunch together when their paths crossed. Wessel got concerned one day when the two had not returned to the club where they were playing. Well past soundcheck time, Jack said, "He came in the door and I jokingly said, 'Where the hell have you been?' He goes, 'Oh Lord, I gotta go to bed right away. I'm not going to be able to play tonight. I smoked some grass.' I said, 'With who?' He said, 'With Tommy, he had one of those [vape] pens.'" Wessel laughed and then continued with the rest of what Leon said: "'What time do we play?' I said, 'Probably around eight thirty.' He said, 'I want you to get me up at six thirty. I've got to know how I'm doing.' I got him out of bed, and he was actually great that night. Of course, I told everybody in the band—these two guys in their seventies tooling around Cleveland in the afternoon, blazing."

Life Journey wasn't the sort of album that Johnny Barbis and Elton really wanted. But Charron said that while Leon was sincerely grateful to Johnny and Elton, "When it came time for him to stand his ground, especially with their management style, he was gonna stick to his guns." The final straw that made him finally decide to move on from Team Elton was the fact that they blocked out three months from the road to make the record with Tommy LiPuma. "Leon just blew his stack," Wessel said. "'Three *months*?! I can make a record in three *weeks*! Anyone who takes longer than that doesn't know what they're doing.' And it kind of built up to that point. Leon just noticed that they handled him and managed him as if he were Elton, and that just wasn't the reality. Leon wanted and *needed* to work all the time, and they tended toward, 'So, we'll be doing it this way, and you'll be where Elton is.' Leon knew who he was. And he was very grateful for all the help with that association and what it did for him. His fees had stabilized into an area that he felt was at least right—okay, if not fantastic. But then they blocked [off] three months. I guess that was just the end of a line."

Leon told Holder, "You know, once the train stops, it's really hard to get it going again." Wessel said that Leon started to get increasingly irate with management. "I remember he used to fire off letters up there in his chair on his laptop. I remember when he wrote a letter to Barbis. When he would finish off a letter, he turned around, real slow, and shared it. He'd hand me his laptop to read what he'd written."

"They took us off the road because they were trying to teach Leon a lesson, which never goes over well," Holder said with a laugh. "So they took us off the road. Well, so Leon's money dries up and he can't pay the band for sitting around the house, so we all got laid off."

Barbis sighed, saying, "Leon didn't think he needed a manager, and we amicably split up. There wasn't a problem. But we never really had a falling out. I think Leon said at one point, 'You guys made enough money off of me.'" He laughed. "He said that he could never get me on the phone."

Other friends counseled Leon similarly. When Leon said he wanted to fire Johnny because "sometimes I can't get him on the phone for a day or two," most would reply, or at least think, "That's not that long!" One friend recalled asking Leon if he had talked to Elton before firing Johnny. Nope. "Leon, you owe these calls to Elton and Johnny," said one who wished to remain anonymous. "'Don't shoot yourself in the foot here. Just when you have a wonderful record coming out. There's nobody better to do this than Johnny.' I think he called Elton after the fact and sent Johnny a note. It was, in a way, very Leon; on the verge of another success, he shot himself in the foot. That really bummed them out. It was not a financial thing. It was an emotional thing. It was like, 'Really? After all this?' They were both hurt by it. Then the album came out. If it had been promoted right, it would have been a huge record."

"He had his own way of doing things," Barbis said. "But he went along with the whole package for a couple of years and ran with it, and I think it put him back at another level of where people respected—not that he didn't have the Lifers on the road everywhere; he did. But it opened up a lot of people who didn't know who Leon Russell was."

Mark Lambert said that Leon didn't necessarily consider *Life Journey* his last record, though most artists start to think that any record could be their last once they hit a certain age, and Leon certainly felt that way. Nevertheless, he and Lambert remained busy. Leon and Willie Nelson made an album together, sending digital files back and forth, with Lambert engineering Leon's side, including most of the basic tracks. It was primarily classic country songs like "Together Again."

Leon was trying to get Willie to track to a click track. "Willie said, 'I can't play to some future time machine,'" Matt Harris said with a laugh.

"That album is still gonna come out," Willie reported. "I was just listening to it the other day."

"I actually don't listen to music very much," Leon said. Everyone in his family said the same thing. The only music he would listen to was tracks he was working on. Occasionally, he would listen to old bluegrass, which was a constant source of pleasure for him. But music was his work and silence was his hobby.

He ended up cowriting about a dozen songs with A. J. Croce, whom he had met in the nineties. "Leon and I connected on music," said Croce, an accomplished pianist and music historian. Leon told Croce to send him melodies over chords, and Leon would write him lyrics, which is a bit odd, as it was the words that usually came slower for him. "About an hour later, I got back eight verses, two possible choruses, two bridges. I ended up recording that song with Allen Toussaint." Croce proposed the idea of Leon playing on an album and having Toussaint produce. "I was playing in New Orleans, and Allen Toussaint came and sat in with me," Croce said. "And we were talking backstage. He said, 'I would love to. When I was young, I had an opportunity to work with him in the late sixties, and I really regret that I didn't.' And then, when Leon and I were sitting together in Austin, he said, 'No, I don't want to work with another producer as long as I live.'"

In 2013, Leon lost three old Tulsa friends, J. J. Cale, "Sweet" Emily Smith Miller-Mundy, and Sherman Halsey. Emily was sixty-nine and had been burning the candle at both ends from the start. "Leon was well aware of her decline in her last couple years and did keep in touch," Wessel said. "He was comforted, I think, by hearing of her asking to be taken off life support after coming out of a coma. On the day he heard of her passing he spoke of his friend onstage and from there on made a practice of dedicating and playing 'Sweet Emily' during his solo section. So that, I think, was how he managed his grief."

Halsey's death was more of a shock; he was only fifty-seven. Of the three deaths that year, Sherman's hit Leon the hardest because of the shock of it. "It was pretty brutal," Jan said. "I mean, it's one of my areas that I'm really, really guilty about and sad. I didn't want to hurt him. He was such a good guy. I never stopped loving him because he was so good to me and the best boyfriend I'd ever had up until that point." Leon performed the spiritual "His Eye Is on the Sparrow" for Sherman's memorial service, and Sherman's sister shared it online.

Leon kept a-rollin' down the road. "More and more towards the end, we would tour in Europe," Jack Wessel said. "We started going to Japan in the nineties and didn't really go anywhere else. Around 2009–2010, we started going to Europe as well. I had waited years for that because I wanted to do that kind of traveling. The last time we went to Europe was 2014."

Leon turned seventy-two in 2014, and his actual age was finally catching up with his aging body. His band members now understood well that part of their roles was taking care of and watching out for Leon. "Well, I'm in much better shape if I have my bus," Leon said that year. "If something happens to the bus, if it breaks and we have to fly, it's a nightmare because I don't like hotels very much, and I have back problems to a certain degree, and I've got my recliner on the bus."

They kept most people off the bus, but made certain exceptions. Dylan was a welcome guest, of course. Keith Richards came to a show at the Stephen Talkhouse in Amagansett, Long Island. "Someone said, 'Hey, Leon's on down the road.' And I don't often go to clubs," Richards recalled. "I hadn't seen Leon for years. . . . Leon came on and did an incredible set with a great band. I was only going to go for three numbers, but halfway through it I said, 'I'm staying for the lot; this is too good.'"

Holder said, "So we get done, and Leon heads to the bus, and we all come out the side door. Well, immediately, this guy puts me in a headlock, starts rubbing my head. He's like, 'You motherfucker.' I'm like, 'Dude, you're Keith Richards.' He goes, 'Yeah, man, let's get on the bus.'"

Charron recalled, "I'm like, 'Hey, Keith, the band's got a little fridge in the back of the bus, and we've got some beer. Do you want a beer?' He's like, 'Yeah, man, beer, weed, narcotics, you know who you're talking to!' Keith was bouncing off the walls, talking to us, taking pictures with us, drinking beer, and Leon and him sat there at the kitchen table, and it was just like they didn't know what to say to each other," Holder recalled. "It was awkward as hell. Just really minimal; just said a couple of words to each other, and he was there for maybe an hour. But really he interacted with us more than Leon. So then, after a while, Leon was like, 'I'm gonna go the bathroom. I'll be right back.' Well, like twenty minutes go by, and we're still talking with Keith, waiting for Leon to come back. He went to *bed*!"

At the Pour House in Charleston, South Carolina, Bill Murray came, danced, and bought as much as he could carry away from the merch table, brought it out to his car, and came back to buy a second load of stuff. Then he did it a third time. "The whole show, he was up front dancing, and he was buying these drinks, and he'd put the empty cup in his front shirt pocket," Holder observed. "So, by the end of the gig, he had like five cups stacked in his shirt pocket. He got on the bus, just him and Leon, and they talked, and we all stayed off the bus and let them hang out."

Leon had his systems and routines. He had an enormous amount of patience but had his limits, and all but a few adapted. Wessel said he was "a slow burn." Chris Simmons's ambition got the best of him, leading to a costly miscalculation. Not only had he invited himself onto Leon's record, but he hired a professional photographer to shoot him at a Leon show. Leon fired him. Wessel recalled, "Leon said, 'I resent that, using my gig to promote himself. Shit, I've been promoting the guy, and I just think that's sneaky and disrespectful, and I don't like that.'"

Charron recalled, "One tour manager that came along was very short-lived because he came in telling Leon, 'Everything's gonna change here,' and, 'Do things my way.' And all of us are like, 'Your days are numbered, buddy.'" Leon told the manager he did not want his teleprompters checked as baggage on planes; he could not risk losing them. "The tour manager made the mistake of arguing, and Leon stopped the whole argument by saying this to him. He said, 'I *invented* touring, so don't question me!'" Charron laughed. "'Just do what I say.'"

Chapter 40

Putting the Top Hat Back On

ALTHOUGH THE LAST TWO YEARS of Leon's life were something of a victory lap for him, he was still in a race to get out of debt. Steve and Charlene Ripley were overseeing the archives in partnership with the OKPOP Museum. Leon sold the entire warehouse full of video and audio tapes, plus assorted gear and artifacts, for $200,000. Leon retained all creative copyrights, and the organization would need permission for any commercial use, with royalties going to Leon.

The bus upkeep was a constant issue, as was Leon's general financial picture. He bought his daughters a house to share near his and Jan's home. He still wasn't out from under the setbacks he had suffered at the hands of bookkeepers who embezzled from him. Seemingly every time there was news of a new record release or reissue, Mary's attorneys would file suit.

"Leon was trying to get out of debt until the day he died," Jackie Wessel said. "When he *did* die, he wasn't out of debt, but he was closer, I think, than he ever dreamed of getting. His last accountant, Tamara Barnett, somehow showed him the light and put them on the righteous path. . . . When Leon got that money for *The Union*, it paid off a bus." Even though he retained all control over his intellectual property of the archival materials that he had granted stewardship of to the OKPOP museum—stuff that was apparently heading to the trash heap—Wessel said that Leon later had misgivings about the arrangement. "He just said, 'Oh Lord, I made another terrible deal.'" Jeff Moore—who, along with everyone at OKPOP, has been exceedingly helpful for this book—clarified, "If there was ever a request from Leon, we would have bent over backwards to do anything."

OKPOP was not yet involved when Leon finally agreed to release *A Poem Is a Naked Person*. There's a scene with Leon goofing around on "Lady Madonna" with fellow pianist David Briggs at Bradley's Barn during the *Hank Wilson's Back* sessions. They could not afford the synchronization clearance to use more than a certain "fair use" length of that Beatles song, so Leon and Harrod Blank approached Steve Ripley to see if there was anything of Leon's in those old audiotapes that they could use. Ripley said he had just the right piece, the previously unreleased demo recording of Leon playing "Hello, Little Friend" for Denny Cordell and Joe Cocker before the latter recorded his own version. Leon's wistful take sits perfectly in the film. This process happened after Ripley had possession of the tapes but before an agreement was in place with OKPOP, which would have made the process smoother.

There had only been rare bootlegs of the film. Les Blank had continued to lobby Leon for the official commercial release. He wrote him a letter in 1977 that referred to a threat from Leon's lawyers to try to halt Blank from showing the film at in-person, noncommercial appearances, which was his right. "If you don't want me showing the film, why don't you ask me yourself & grace me with the privilege of knowing why you don't want it shown? You did approve it when I finished it and gave me the go-ahead to bust my nuts in LA finishing it off in time for Cannes Film Festival and blow up to 35 mm. As an artist yourself, you must realize the frustration I feel in spending two years of the prime period my creative ability working on a project that is not released." Leon never did answer.

It was always a Leon decision; Denny Cordell wanted the film released and had written Les Blank a laudatory letter, which helped keep Blank's hope alive over the years. But Leon had retained 100 percent of the rights to the film after the Shelter split, so Denny had no standing. "It looks more like a travelogue than a Leon movie," Leon said in 2015. "But I never wanted to lose control over it. . . . I thought it might be of value in the future."

It tormented Les. Rick Huskey said Blank appeared like a ghost, un-announced, at the lake house one day in the early 2000s. "[Les] never did get to talk to Leon; Leon would not have anything to do with him," Harrod said. "So, when my father was dying, I decided on a whim that I would find Leon and write him a letter and tell him the situation and that Les had a final screening of *A Poem Is a Naked Person* at Pixar before he died. I wrote Leon to ask him if it was okay and to invite him. And he said to me, 'Thank you so much for inviting me. However, due to financial constraints, I cannot attend.' And so that said a few things to me. That said, A, he is open, and, B, he's hurting for money. And I thought that was really positive. My father was actually really happy to hear that Leon had responded to me personally. And he actually did say something to the effect of, 'Give Les my best. I'm sorry to hear about your father's cancer.'"

"[Les] felt like it was his masterpiece," said Maureen Gosling, Les Blank's assistant. "He felt like it would have been great for Leon, and it would have been great for us. I mean, *Burden of Dreams* [Les Blank's 1982 documentary about the making of Werner Herzog's film *Fitzcarraldo*] kind of saved his sanity about it. The fact that *Burden of Dreams* became so well known, got such incredible reviews, and has been regarded as a masterpiece. So it sort of made up for it, but he held that until he died."

It would take Harrod another year after Les died to actually convince Leon to approve the release of the film. On pure speculation that he could win over Leon, Harrod remastered the film per his father's instructions. "I took the Blu-Ray of the master, and sent it to Leon. And he calls me up, and he says, 'Oh my God, how do you get that to look so good?'"

Leon realized he had something that could burnish his legacy, something of high quality, and a product he could sell. But it took over a year of "courtship," in Harrod's words. A lawyer advised approaching Leon as if he were a baseball player, offering him a signing bonus. "I can't remember the actual bonus, but I think it was $25,000. And I said, 'That does not go against any royalties or anything, that's free money for you to put in your pocket and do whatever you want, with no accounting needed; it's done.' And I heard Jan in the background—and I didn't know Jan at that time—but I heard her saying, 'Do it, Leon, we need the money, do it.' And then he comes back to the phone. He goes, 'Okay, we'll do it.'"

Leon also admitted that he realized that sometimes he just ended up saying no for the sake of saying no. In an interview that Harrod did with Leon in *Rolling Stone*, Leon motioned to Harrod and said, "I met this guy, and I quite liked him more than I liked his dad."

Overall, he had warmed up to the film in his final years. When they were promoting the movie that year, Harrod and Leon were interviewed at a screening by the director Jonathan Demme. Harrod recalled, "Demme asked, 'So, Leon, how'd you like the movie when it first came out?' And

Leon says, 'I didn't.' And he said, 'How many times did you watch it?' And Leon said, 'Once was enough for me.' And Jonathan said, I'm just paraphrasing, 'Well, you know, they've kind of figured out that when you appear in a movie as yourself, you actually need to watch a movie three times before you make a judgment. The first time you watch a movie that features yourself, you're actually watching yourself and how you look, how you sound, and it's really about you. And the second time, you see yourself interacting with other characters, and you see how things are starting to fit together a little bit. But the third time you see the movie is when you start to see it as a movie as a whole, as a creation. And that's when you can make a fair judgment on the movie.' And Leon just said, 'That's very interesting. I didn't know that.' It definitely got Leon thinking, and in fact, I think that it had a big effect on him. Because he seemed to embrace the movie more and more as we went along."

It not only introduced the general public to—and reminded his fans of—Leon in his prime, but it reconnected old Leon to his younger self, from "hippo" back to "hippie." He was far enough away from that young skinny live wire that he must have seemed a stranger to himself. There would have been some deeply mixed emotions for someone not prone to nostalgia but who had begun to acknowledge the significance of his legacy as he headed for the exits. Harrod explained, "People would say, 'Well, why didn't it come out before?' and he'd say, 'This is the time. This was the time it was supposed to come out.'"

Leon went on a promo tour of film screenings, including a trip to Europe, usually with a Q&A session, and caught up with many old friends and fans along the way. He saw Maxayn Lewis at the Ace Hotel in Hollywood. "We hadn't talked in so many years because he had moved to Tennessee and had gotten remarried," Lewis recalled. "He said, 'I married a really nice lady,' and I said, 'Well, good for you!' We had so much fun talking about all the old times and crazy people that used to work for him."

The most monumental and sentimental journey to the past in 2015 was the long-awaited Mad Dogs & Englishmen reunion, which happened as a result of the efforts of the Tedeschi Trucks Band, who put together the show on September 11 for the Lockn' Festival in Virginia. "To people of a certain generation, Leon was a star, a total badass," Derek Trucks told an interviewer in 2016, shortly before Leon's death. "Then he got lost in the mix a bit. But young musicians know him. In the last five, ten years, he became a cult hero again. He was definitely behind the curtain. You don't remember the first time you heard him. But he was always there."

Trucks and his wife, guitarist-singer Susan Tedeschi, were playing with other bands. In 2005, they watched the *Mad Dogs & Englishmen* film and were smitten with the romantic view of communal early-seventies rock music and culture, the familial vibe, R&B tunes, a hippie update of Ray Charles's orchestra, "learnin' to live together." "We said, 'That looks like fun!'" Trucks told *Rolling Stone*. "Our band was loosely based on that concert footage."

Trucks's connections were myriad and deep. His uncle Butch Trucks was in the Allman Brothers Band, another family/communal band. Derek was also named after the Derek and the Dominos album, featuring his honorary uncle, Duane Allman. "I knew all of that music," Trucks told me. "Obviously, Derek and the Dominos was one of the first things that I remember, and all the Allmans stuff. I came to the Delaney and Bonnie and the Mad Dog stuff a little later, but once you start becoming aware of the history of it, it's fascinating how you can draw those direct lines, and how close it was without me knowing it at the time.

"I remember the first time I saw [Leon], I must have been eleven or twelve years old [Trucks was a child prodigy]. We played a show in Daytona Beach, Florida, down near the beach, some outdoor gig, opening for Leon, and he was one of the first musicians I ever saw who just had that presence where you were like, 'Who the *fuck* is that?' I'm guessing that had to be the early nineties, so he already had a bit of a Father Time look going. A lot of my musical taste was very much informed by the musicians I was playing with at the time, and my dad, and the things that moved them. Whenever [Leon's] name was brought up, or people talked about him, there was a certain reverence in their voices—he wasn't just another musician."

"We all grew up with that music," Tedeschi said. "And to be around somebody like Leon is just so epic for musicians to really, really connect with somebody on a musical level."

Trucks explained, "Before we played before the Lockn' thing, we did a few shows where Leon opened for our band just in theaters, at the Beacon, and I got him to sign my guitar. I guess his guy said he doesn't usually hang around and sit in, ever. But he saw the soundcheck, and I think he saw some kindred spirits up there, and he was down. He sang on 'Space Captain'—that certainly led to the Mad Dogs thing happening a few years down the road."

The story of the reunion concert can be seen in a terrific documentary by Jesse Lauter, *Learning to Live Together: The Return of Mad Dogs & Englishmen*. "It all begins with discovering Mad Dogs and Englishmen," Lauter said, "and that was the DVD reissue in 2005, I believe. I'm surprised, even a lot of muso heads and critics seem to discover or rediscover Mad Dogs. I was only eighteen years old, and it quickly resonated with me. I'm a big fan of family bands, everything from Bruce Springsteen to Sly and the Family Stone and Funkadelic. I had the thing on repeat and it's totally shaped my outlook on what's possible with large ensembles."

Lauter had always wondered why a real Mad Dogs reunion or tribute show had never taken place. "It was February or March of 2015. Pete Shapiro, the promoter and the founder of the Lockn' Festival, is an old friend of mine. The festival bill gets announced: 'Tedeschi Trucks Band presents Mad Dogs and Englishman, with Leon Russell, Rita Coolidge, Claudia Lennear, Chris Stainton,' I was just like, 'Are you fucking kidding me?' And so I call Pete immediately and said, 'I have to make a movie about this.' Pete's response was, 'Good, because I don't know what the fuck I'm doing, inviting thirty people to my festival that I never heard of. Can you explain to me what the Mad Dogs and Englishmen is?'" Lauter "piggybacked" onto the video crew that the festival hired for live-streaming the show and put together the filming of rehearsals and interviews.

Tedeschi and Trucks enlisted the Black Crowes' Chris Robinson, who said, "That album is in my DNA." As Steve Earle—who drove at age fifteen from Texas to Tulsa to catch the 1970 Mad Dogs show—points out in the documentary, "The relationship of R&B in the forties and fifties to modern rock 'n' roll hadn't been obvious to me before that, seeing it in a large-band format. I don't think anyone had done it."

Trucks and Tedeschi said that the original idea was to back Joe Cocker the year before. But he died from cancer before the show. But there was never a time when Leon and Joe both agreed to appear together at the festival. In the film, Leon reiterates something he had said privately over the years: that he hoped Joe would set the record straight about the charges leveled at Leon of using Cocker to further his own career. "I thought any moment he's gonna step up and say that's not true. However, that never happened." Jan, who accompanied him to the reunion, said, "Leon told me he loved Joe and wanted to do the best for him."

"I've been approached by people in the past who said, 'Let's do Mad Dogs & Englishmen again, and we'll get these guys and those guys,'" Leon said. "But you have to remember that all the people in the [original] band were unknown at the time. It didn't have stars. So I didn't think it could be re-created that way."

"I know Leon Russell wanted to put Mad Dogs together again; he hinted," Cocker said. "He actually left a message while I was on tour that Pam [Cocker's wife] picked up and she was going, 'Who is the Master of Space and Time?' He said, 'Let's put Mad Dogs together again!'" Joe never returned the call.

"I'm sure it stung," Trucks said, identifying with Leon as a bandleader who had to deal with that particular fallout. "The job is to put your emotions and soul on the line for all to judge. And you know, criticism is one thing, but when it hits the *reason* that you're doing it, that's a lot harder to swallow—when people question your integrity. Your head's got to be in the right place, and your heart has to be in the right place for it to really resonate. There's no way it couldn't. I think he was up against that at times."

Not only are the results of the 2015 reunion, seen in the film, heartwarming, but also the music is powerful and inspired, which perhaps should not come as a surprise given the core band backing the ever-talented veterans, most of whom had not seen each other in decades, some since 1970. "It was like a shooting star," Claudia Lennear said of the original tour. "If you saw it, great; if you missed it, it's gone." For Rita Coolidge, it was a chance to reclaim the sweet part of the bittersweet tour that she had been robbed of at the hands of the abusive Jim Gordon. "It was not meant to last, and that added urgency," she said of 1970. She said she "never dreamed" of a reunion, never mind one with such a positive outcome. "We will never recover from it," said choir member Matthew Moore. "It's never left us."

Leon appears buoyant during much of the film. At one point, he says, "It's like a high school reunion that made up for all those that I didn't go to."

When they start to play and sing, their youth roars back. Chris Stainton said, "He came in in this huge motorized wheelchair he was in, and he goes, 'Hi Chree-is.' He remembered that we wrote a song ['Dixie Lullaby'] together. He was playing okay, but I think he was having problems playing, because it hurt when he played. He had quite a few health problems over the years. But it was good. We even had Chuck Blackwell. When he came in, I didn't recognize him, so old-looking, and he was seriously ill, but he made it. Leon didn't really do much, but he was there; his presence was there."

Trucks recalled the discussion with Leon about the direction the show would take. "Knowing that it was Leon's baby the first time, I said as much to him. 'You know, this is your thing. If you want to take the reins and MD [music director] this thing, I'm here to help.' And his response was, 'Oh no, no. I did it the first time around; it's all you, baby.'" Trucks laughed. "He was very sweet about it, but he was happy to hand it to somebody else. It just gave us all the more energy to just double down and make sure that we did get it right."

"It was so cute, the relationship of Leon and Derek," Tedeschi said. "They just have a natural understanding of each other and love and respect. It's like they both have that similar thing, like a bandleader people listen to and trust because they have good instincts musically and otherwise. They all called him 'Maestro,' and they all totally respected him," Tedeschi said of the reunited Mad Dogs. "And they all acted like, 'Whatever Leon thinks, we know is right.' There was just no question there."

Pamela Polland concluded that Leon had fundamentally changed. "During the Mad Dogs tour, he was completely accessible to me, always warm. And at Lockn' he was very standoffish and really didn't get personal with me at all. So I had a few free 'hello' moments with him, and that was it. He wasn't into visiting. And, as complete opposition to that, Rita was warmer with me than she had ever been the entire two months on the road."

Rita had several reasons to be warmer, of course. She had been on guard almost the entire tour, in actual survival mode. "Rita, I call her the hero of the film," Lauter said. "She creeps up on you in the third act. A woman who experienced such deep trauma on this tour, and years and years of sitting with this, and basically being given the chance to heal from this experience thanks to the Tedeschi Trucks Band having the energy to reunite all these people, and the care and the love and the passion to make something like this happen. When she showed up, it really came together.

"Leon's energy, I thought, was just amazing," Lauter continued. "Literally the whole time, maybe up until show night, where I noticed he had a little bit of a drop before they hit the stage. But you really felt it in those practice sessions. He was being so funny, just constantly cracking jokes. And what I just love is, we had cameras following him around, and he's just shooting the same jokes to everyone. He kept saying to people, 'This is gonna be fun. Like Six Flags!'"

Rita laughed as she recounted seeing Leon again. "He wasn't especially friendly to anybody. I think he was in a lot of pain. My manager neglected to tell me when the rehearsals were. I got there the second day of rehearsals, and I guess he had a really good first day. Everybody said, 'Leon was just so great yesterday, and today he's just not the same.' He was withdrawn and closed and [had] a minimal amount of communication with everybody. But Jan was fabulous. She would just say, 'Yeah, don't pay attention to him. He's always like that.'"

It was no coincidence that Leon was more distant the day Rita arrived. He had never let go of that particular grudge. Leon was asked to accompany Rita on a song, just the two of them. Rita is shown in the film offering a staggering reading of "Bird on the Wire," which she did not solo on in 1970. Her voice dropped in her age, and the effect adds depth and soul to her take. "He was like, 'Absolutely not,'" said Coco Bridges. "He specifically sat at the keyboard, but there are cameras there, and he said he wanted to make it very clear that he wasn't playing. He was petty. And then, at the end of the song, she starts saying, 'Oh, Leon, I love you so much. You're so great.' And he's just like rolling his eyes and fuming. He was very proud of that. When he told me that story, he had a smile on. She had been so critical of him."

Rita said, "I always really loved Leon. I loved his talent. I just had a lot of compassion for him."

Lauter observed, "I think it was probably a very tough experience for him, because here he is in this room with a bunch of people that he had business relationships with, romantic relationships, people that he definitely did not ever want to see ever again. . . . In a lot of ways, I felt like he needed to do this in order to complete the circle, like 'Will the Circle Be Unbroken.' He did not want it to break."

Claudia had gone to see Leon in LA about eighteen months before the Lockn' concert. "We had maybe about an hour together just reminiscing, talking about old times, and catching up. I couldn't stop the tears coming from my eyes. It was just so lovely to be with him for that amount of time. He was like, 'Oh, so what are you doing these days?' I explained, 'Well, I teach.' He was, 'Oh, so you're an intellectual now.' He kept going on and on with that. I'm like, 'Leon, you knew back in the day I spoke French. Now, I'm teaching French.' He stopped for a moment. He didn't say anything. It was like he had to recollect. He says, 'Oh, you know, I do remember that.' Then after that, everything warmed up a little bit. He was such a sweetheart. We just couldn't live together; that was the bottom line."

Claudia said that she jumped at the chance to sing with Leon again at Lockn'. "Although I'm heartbroken that Joe is gone, I had loved the song 'Girl from the North Country' so much that when I was asked which songs would I like to sing, that was one of the first ones. . . . If I could sing one song with Leon, that would be it. And Leon welcomed me to do it. That was one of the greatest points in my musical career."

"That specifically was one of my favorite moments of that whole thing," Trucks said. "It was a dream of hers. We were playing with a full band. We had the tune worked up. But then, when she was working out the vocals with Leon, it was just him playing. And I just kind of stopped him, and I was like, 'Hey, can we just do it like this? Can this be the performance?' Leon was so just down for anything in those sessions. 'Well, sure.'" It's a moving performance, especially when Claudia and Leon hit the line "she once was a true love of mine."

Leon's playing in the film is exceptional. He thrives again, waving his arms for the band to stop during an impromptu run-through of "Jezebel." It was one of Leon's staples, and he did a version on *Anything Can Happen*. "I naturally gravitate towards gospel," Tedeschi said. "So I jumped in and started clapping and singing with him. And then he's like, 'How do you know this?' I was like, 'Well, I love gospel.' I sang in a gospel choir in college, and we got to sing with Angela Berryman, Shirley Caesar, a bunch of different mass choirs. . . . We did Shirley Caesar's 'Sweeping Through the City.'" When informed that Leon used to do that one with Patrick Henderson and Black Grass, Tedeschi replied, "I didn't even know that he did that. But of course, he has the best taste in music. He's just so on point."

The emotional heart of the whole project might just come down to Leon alone on the Festival stage giving a solo performance of the melancholy "Ballad of Mad Dogs & Englishmen."

"It sounds like it was written twenty years later, after all the chips had fallen," Trucks marveled. "It was just a last-minute idea. I think Chris Robinson came up to me. It's probably an hour before the show. Everything's rehearsed, everyone's buzzing, there's nerves, and Chris Robinson mentioned, 'You know, I saw Leon maybe a year or two ago, and he did "The Ballad of the Mad Dogs and Englishmen" solo.' I was like, 'No shit? So he's got that in his pocket.' So it was like, well, that'd be a great way to get him to end the show or, like, the song of the encore, if he's into it. So we got up the nerve to go ask him. We were kind of all the way to the stage, and he's like, 'Sure, that'll be no problem.'" Trucks laughed. "Yeah, that was quite a surprise."

The nuanced mixture of emotion, the ups and downs, is somehow all captured. Leon's voice is craggy at the higher reaches, and he uses it, leaning into the sentiment. When he wrote the song to tag it onto the credits of the original film back in 1970, it was a knowingly instant nostalgia, a wistful romantic coda for an intense tour only recently in the rearview. Singing it forty-five years later, it was a paean to their youth.

Leon's connection with Susan was extraordinary, according to Derek and Jesse. After the show, he continued to write songs for her to consider and expressed hope that they could repeat the show elsewhere. Along with *The Union*, the Lockn' reunion gave Leon a little more wind in his sails. But that energy was of a limited supply. And though he understood the end was near, Leon kept working until the end.

John Cowan remained in touch and even had Leon play piano under Cowan's version of "I Feel Like Going Home," the soulful ballad by Charlie Rich. "There are certain relationships in my life that I pursued because I didn't want to let it go," Cowan said. "And because of that—not everybody that was ever in Leon's life went on to have a friendship with him, for whatever reason. But we always were friends, and we always stayed in touch, and I always went to visit him, and he always loved me. But he was a funny guy, you know? He would have people in his life, and then he'd say, 'They were stealing from me,' and they were no longer in his life—musicians, engineers, road managers. It was a weird thing. It's why he and Denny Cordell didn't work together. Then he finally had Elton

John's manager. That was a pretty good relationship; it lifted Leon's career up out of the dregs into getting into the Rock & Roll Hall of Fame. One of the last times I saw him, I said, 'So how's things going with Johnny?' He goes, 'Oh, I fired him.' I don't know what that was about for Leon. But he would self-destruct all the time. He would self-sabotage."

For Christmas in 2015, Tina came to Nashville with her newborn. She had not been there or seen her sisters since 2005. She acknowledged, "That's just another example of things getting funky, and then me just keeping to myself, you know. We [she and Leon] literally never discussed any kind of family drama or family politics. . . . I don't really talk to anybody regularly. I haven't talked to Blue or my brother since my dad died."

Christmas would be one of the rare times Leon would sit around playing the piano for the family. "The last—I want to say, like, seven years of his life—during Christmas, he would play Christmas carols at the piano," Coco said. Tina recalled, "When we went up there for that last Christmas, or I should say that first Christmas back that I spent with him, he really wanted us to all sing classic Christmas hymns and shit, and nobody would do it. So I started singing, like in an operatic voice, being silly, and he was just like, 'Oh never mind.'"

It would be Leon's last Christmas, but he did not go gently into that good night. He might have seemed spent offstage, but he was still driven to perform, write, and record. He left it all on the big stage in that way. He was back on the road in January through the summer and managed to crank out another album, *On a Distant Shore*. "He probably played 150 days or something that year," Mark Lambert said.

One show was a benefit at the Canyon Club in Agora Hills, California, for Leon's old sideman and friend, Marty Grebb, who was sick with cancer. Ivan Neville and Bonnie Raitt were among those who performed, and Leon flew in from Nashville with his sound engineer, Paul Lee. Their plane went through a storm, causing extreme turbulence. "We finally come out of it about twenty feet above the runway, hit the runway, and then ambulances and fire trucks come to the plane," Lee recalled. People were vomiting and at least one was on the floor in the fetal position next to Leon. "He says, 'In all my fifty years of flying, that was the roughest turbulence I've ever been in.' He looked up and goes, 'Well, you hungry? They got a hell of a steak over here in the steakhouse. If we're going to get back on another plane, we might as well eat.' He bought me a seventy-dollar steak, we got back on another plane, and flew to LA."

Leon did a couple of his songs with the house band. Afterward, "Classic Leon: he rolls into the room, and within two minutes, he's got two of Bonnie's backup singers sitting in his lap and Bonnie eating out of his hand," Lee said with a chuckle. Maxayn Lewis sang with Leon that night. "The three of them would have rolled right out of there that day with him."

"We worked," Lambert said. "We cut probably twenty-five songs that he wrote." Leon had started to concentrate on writing more songs he hoped would become standards, and he specifically was hoping to get Michael Bublé to record them. Bublé had performed "A Song for You," lauding Leon as one of America's great songwriters. Leon tried to get the recordings he made with Lambert into Bublé's hands but was having no luck. He had even considered showing up at the backstage entrance to work his way to Bublé directly but wisely decided this would have been unbecoming to an artist of his stature. So, instead, Leon made his final album, which would be released posthumously.

He may or may not have designed *Life Journey* to be his final album, but the leadoff title track of *On a Distant Shore* sounds like a man saying goodbye. He even references his heart, which had seven stents in it by the time he died: "My poor heart sounds like a drum. . . . Bad news is at the door. . . ."

He laces the dark lyric with his daughters singing "dip do waddy waddy" backing vocals, like a mocking Greek chorus. It's reminiscent of Leonard Cohen, who released his own farewell album *You Want It Darker* the same year and would pass away the week before Leon. "He did have a very dark humor and wanted to put that in there," Coco said. "We definitely felt like he was knowing that it was coming to an end."

"He met an arranger named Larry Hall, who did strings and various other synth stuff in there," Lambert said. "Larry is really a talented guy, and Larry plays with a friend of mine, Ronnie Milsap. Ronnie and Leon were good friends. I was doing a record with Ronnie. It's a duet record with a whole bunch of different artists. Leon was on that too." They did Jerry Reed's "Misery Loves Company," a great 6/8 country-soul ballad.

"I loved recording with him," Milsap said. "I was working with Mark

Lambert. Leon had asked, 'Do I get to sing on this album?' and I said, 'Why Lord, yes.'"

In addition to Hall's arrangements, Leon played with talented side musicians on his final album, including Lambert himself. The drums were loops of real drums created by Gregg Morrow, which Leon would play to. Young guitar whiz Ray Goren played on "Black and Blue," recorded and mixed by the venerable Eddie Kramer in New York. Leon had met the teenage Goren when Goren opened a show in California. Leon bought an upright bass for Lambert's son, Drew, and tasked him with learning it to play on the album. "It was a handful for [Drew], but Leon was always kind of good at assigning tasks that were difficult, to make people stress a little bit," Mark said.

Leon played some of the works in progress for Taylor Hanson. "The last time I talked with him, we listened to the new record. . . . We're sitting in my car, with this legend, this genius, and he wanted to know whether *I liked it*. He just wanted to share what he was doing. It was not just, 'Taylor, what do you think?' It was, 'I'm doing something I'm excited about. I'm doing something that I'm proud of. I'm doing something I'm interested in.'"

By the time Leon went in for heart surgery in July, the album had been completed and mixed to his satisfaction. The final track on his final album was "A Song for You," which was, of course, the first song on his first album. His version is casual, almost perfunctory, one of his weaker performances of the song. It was an afterthought, one of three he recorded for Tommy LiPuma's birthday, along with "This Masquerade" and "Hummingbird." Lambert said, "He got to thinking, 'Well, I should have Larry do an arrangement on these and put them on the record,' just because he had them sitting there."

While this take on "A Song for You" might not pack the same emotional punch of Joni Mitchell on the melancholy, winter-of-her-years version of 'Both Sides Now,' it naturally stirs up a little extra emotion—if for no other reason than he chose to close out his recorded catalog with his debut track and his signature song.

Leon's final California run was in May 2016, and he astonished his band and friends with his revived energy and spirited attitude. In a shop in Big Bear, he bought an old top hat. Wessel said, "It didn't fit him very well, but he was wearing it onstage." And Leon got to see Teddy Jack again, after many years. Wessel recalled, "After a show at the Coach House, instead of the usual autograph party at the bus, he says, 'Well, I want to do a meet-and-greet, set up a table out there.' And by God, he sat there at a table, and people just went crazy. Ted came along and gave me an assist with that. Leon signed all their stuff and took pictures until the last one was gone, wearing that damn top hat," he said, laughing.

Herb Alpert had not seen his old friend in decades. "I think it was several months before he passed, he was playing at a place in Malibu here. And I was driving down Pacific Coast Highway, and I saw this big bus, and then I saw his name on the marquee. So I pulled over, knocked on the door of this bus hoping to see Leon, and he opens the door, and man, we had a great time for an hour or so. He didn't look like he was in good shape. It was hard for him to walk, and his breathing was very labored at the time, but his spirit was *right there*. And he was interested in what I was doing, and he always liked the paintings and the sculptures that I did, so I had a nice conversation with him."

Leon was not the kind of person you needed to be in touch with constantly, but you could kind of pick up where you left off. "There are a lot of musicians that are just like that," Alpert answered. "And maybe it's because I think most musicians are introverts. And I include myself in that list. I don't know of anybody that came into contact with Leon that would say a negative thing about him; he was a good guy. His talent was very widespread. I mean, he wrote some great songs."

In late May, Leon played the Simi Valley Cajun & Blues Fest along with Booker T. Jones and others. But he crashed the stage during Booker T's set, which can be seen in video online. It was completely out of character for Leon, who would only reluctantly join other performers even when invited. "For me, it's hard to watch," Wessel said. It's more than a bit rough. "He should not have done that," he said with a laugh. "But he was just full of beans! And it's really kind of funny; you wonder why people act a certain way not long before they pass. You don't think about it until they have, but on that last California run, he was really going all out on the shows, all out on the shopping. And then doing a meet-and-greet at the Coach House?! That was crazy, but you wonder what that means."

Michael Johnstone was one of Leon's friends and associates—along with Gary Busey, Harrod Blank, Maxayn Lewis, and others—who stayed in touch with Teddy over the years. Johnstone said the Simi Valley festival was the last time he saw Leon. "There's a great picture I took of Leon, taken from the back; Leon in his scooter with his top hat on going away from the camera, and Teddy walking away beside him, from the bus into the festival."

Leon had a heart attack the second week of July, and he never recovered from it. Tina Rose was en route from Indianapolis to Nashville to come and surprise her son, Payton Goodner, who had a gig. Payton had played in Leon's band a bit as a teenager. "I pull up in the driveway, and someone texted me. I think it was my stepmom. But she was like, 'I'm taking Leon to the hospital; he just had a heart attack.' And I was just like, 'Oh my God.' I still went to the show because my dad was in stable condition, and they were kind of moving him around from one hospital to the other hospital."

When he first went in, the doctors were not convinced it was a heart attack. "They thought it was a-fib [atrial fibrillation, or arrhythmia]," Wessel said. "They wanted him to stay for some tests, and it was taking too long. And he said, 'Well the hell with this; I'll come back tomorrow,' he got up and went home. It wasn't the first time he walked out of a hospital. He went back the next day, and they looked at what tests they did have, and they said, 'No, you did. You were having a heart attack when you showed up here,' and then they didn't say anything about an angio. They said, 'Time for a bypass.'"

Jan explained, "Even though when they cleared all his tests, the place where we were had to send him someplace else because [the cardiologist] said this was way above him. He knew he couldn't help him. He said anytime he'd seen a heart in that condition, that person was already dead. To him, Leon might have hours, might have days, but not more than that. It was out of his expertise. But I found out that last heart attack, they found that he'd been having mini-strokes over the years. That's what was causing a lot of the issues, and they said I probably wouldn't have noticed, but I did. And I just called him my Baby Grandpa. Because he would change, and he would not treat me very nice. And I would be like, 'I don't know who this guy is.' He was mean to me. He would drive really slow and not safe. And I would say, 'Okay, when we get where we're going, I'm driving.' And he would just say, 'Okay,' and his pace would be kind of slack. It would be for the day when he would just be mean to me and, like, accusing me of being somebody I wasn't.

"So when the doctor said it, I said, 'Oh, yeah, I know exactly those days. Because he completely changed. He was not my husband on those days.' Because on his regular days, I was everything to him. I was always the best, and he just wanted me right by his side, and I can do no wrong, and the girls can do no wrong. And on the Baby Grandpa days, we were the devils."

Tina said, "When I went to see him, there's a picture of us from that visit. He said to my stepmom, 'Take a picture of me and Tina Rose,' and I love it because that picture was at my dad's request. I love that photo of us, but he's in the hospital bed, and I'm kind of bent over, and he's holding on to my arm."

Just after he was sedated for his last surgery, Leon offered this comically profound statement to the family: "The first level is *complete satisfaction*. I am interested in seeing what working would be like with this satisfaction. Except there's no opposition. Every action has an inertial opposing section."

After the procedure, the family took turns watching over him at his bedside. Tina recalled, "On the night after the surgery, I was in there with Coco, and we were cracking up about something. My sister has this contagious laugh. And my dad was like, 'You two, hush!' And we were just like, 'Oh, shit.' My dad never reprimanded us growing up."

"When I left the hospital before he went into surgery, I was like, 'Man, I may not see the old man again,' and talked to him shortly after that," Beau Charron said. "I called him, and it was just a couple of months before he passed that my son was born. And I was so excited to tell him, and he was happy for me. My son never got to meet him. But he just kept going. I asked, 'How you feelin'?' And he's like, 'I feel okay.' I mean, considering the quadruple bypass he actually went through, he seemed great and felt great. Like, 'Well, I'm ready to get back because I got these plans. I want to work with this person, I want to do this.'"

Rather than canceling his tour dates, Leon optimistically postponed them. He was still planning to the end. "Right before he passed, we were talking about doing a one-man show at the Carlyle [Hotel in New York]," his agent Steve Martin said. "Just to showcase him playing and talking. It's just him with the piano, which I was so excited about. I said, 'And you'll make more money,' which appealed to him. We sadly never did it." Martin said there were discussions about another tour with Willie Nelson as well.

Because Leon was not one to exercise, recovery from the surgery—which would have been greatly aided by him getting up and being ambulatory—was more challenging. People started coming around to visit him. "I went a few times in hospital, and I told him if he wanted to make it, he was really gonna have to fight hard, which he didn't," said Bob Britt. "He just didn't have the fight in him. He couldn't even walk to the bathroom."

Cowan said, "I actually went out with Jan and Leon six days before he passed away. So, I was kind of shocked, but he still seemed like Leon to me."

Cowan's old partner, Sam Bush, came by as well. "At the end of his life, I was visiting him in the rehab centers. And we were visiting, and we'd have some tearful good visits, expressing love for each other. Well, I wasn't around him that much, but I knew it wasn't a good sign when he never really sat up. One day he said, 'Sammy, thank you for teaching me about bluegrass music.' And I thought, 'He's not well.' I don't think he was destined to be an old man."

But at the very end, Jan felt Leon was done fighting. "He was tired," she said. In the final days he asked her to take him on drives around the neighborhood to see the old houses and some favorite places.

Leon was in and out of care over the summer into the fall. Steve Ripley texted him on October 22, asking Leon how he was feeling, and he responded with, "Still not any better. I think they missed something."

"I don't remember exactly when he came home, but we were set to go up there for Thanksgiving that November," Tina said. "We were even considering moving up there. I really didn't want to, but I was just so concerned for my stepmom. I was just like, 'She needs help,' you know? My sisters were helping her, too. So we were set to go up there for Thanksgiving, and two weeks before that is when my dad passed, on my birthday. It was a fucked-up day.

"My stepmom had called, and she left me a voicemail, and it was really early in the morning. I listened to the voicemail, and she was just like, 'Your dad died this morning,' and it just knocked the breath out of me.

"I dream about him. My dad always comes to me in my dreams, and I feel like it's such a gift."

Tina Rose took Leon's final recliner for her living room. Someday, it should go to the Smithsonian, maybe alongside Archie Bunker's chair as a counterpoint.

Chapter 41

In a Place Where
There's No Space or Time

THE GREAT LEON RUSSELL PASSED away in his sleep on November 13, 2016.

There were two memorial services, one in Mount Juliet, Tennessee, on November 18, and one in Tulsa two days later. Both are online, thanks to Paul Lee, who observed, "Basically, Leon still had me working, full-on tour managing his funeral." He laughed. "But I wouldn't trade it for anything."

Claudia Lennear flew in from California to attend both memorials. "He was such a great guy and such a wonderful musician," Claudia said. "The world will never know one better, in my view."

Bonnie Bramlett sang "A Song for You" and "Superstar" in Tennessee, sobbing through it. Bob Britt gave a sublime performance of "Over the Rainbow." Steve Ripley spoke at length and in depth through his tears about Leon's impact on him personally and on music generally. He gave a special mention of Jackie Wessel for taking care of Leon and being by his side all those years. He read a text that Leon had sent: "The reason for connection is food, music, friendship, and tape machines. The strong stuff is just the facts of life and death; you either laugh or cry."

Britt was touring and recording with Bob Dylan when Dylan paid tribute to Leon in his 2020 song, "My Own Version of You." "Yeah, I'm not really supposed to talk about it," Britt demurred when asked.

Johnny Barbis read a letter from Elton John. Barbis prefaced it by explaining that he would never have been in the music business himself if not for Leon and joining Shelter Records in 1972. Elton's letter extolled

Leon's music as foundational to his own, "the music that turbocharged my career. . . . He was everything I wanted to be as a pianist, vocalist, and writer. His music has helped me and millions of others in the best and worst of times."

Condolences were read from Whoopi Goldberg, describing how her whole family loved Leon. "His picture sits on my piano, with the rest of my family." Tommy LiPuma exposed him as "a closet intellectual." Jackie DeShannon wrote, "Leon was one of a kind, a musical masterpiece painting. The very first time I heard him play, I knew he was a genius."

It was more of a public memorial in Tulsa, with many Leon Lifers in attendance at the Mabee Center auditorium. Leon's brother, Jerry, showed up with his wife. He and Leon had only seen each other occasionally over the years. Jan said, "I went to hug them goodbye, and they just made sure that I knew by their eyes that they were really, really mad at me. At the time, I couldn't figure out why. I didn't call him and tell him Leon had passed, but I didn't know how to call him. Leon didn't have a number for him. That was probably the sin on my part. It didn't occur to me. Nothing was occurring to me during that time. I don't remember how the funerals got planned."

Steve Ripley gave emotional remembrances, sharing some different stories than those he recounted in Nashville. He spoke about owning the Church for about twenty years and hosting Leon back there. The studio is now in Teresa Knox's loving and capable hands, with renovations and additions that have made the facility more open to fans and musicians as a living, working museum and a significant monument to Leon's legacy and that of his Tulsa colleagues. Ripley described his mentor's relentless drive, soldiering on through health challenges, and Leon's profound love of Jan and the family.

Bruce Hornsby traveled to Tulsa and offered a few of the memories that he shared for this book, plus one or two more. As she had in Tennessee, Crissy Halsey Rumford read the messages from those who could not attend, including one from Cameron Crowe and the folks at the Rock & Roll Hall of Fame, which lowered its flags and spent a day pumping Leon's music through the museum. She also read statements from his family. Honey wrote, "My father has been remembered for his impact in the music world beautifully," but she wanted to share some intimate moments she had with her father. When she was a young child on tour with him, he asked the kids to tell him which songs they wanted to hear at the shows. One time, when she was very young, she came right up to him onstage, next to his piano, watching him while he played one of her requests, "Over the Rainbow," and she remembered his beatific gaze back at her. "We are his tribe and the legacy of his heart," she concluded.

Coco was next. Leon wrote a poem for Coco after a difficult breakup. "Stay beautiful, sweet, and strong / The answer will come before too long," he wrote in verse form. "You're adored and loved, if that helps at all / And my heart bleeds and is broken too / When you think of me, know that I love you."

Coco explained that Leon's personal poetry to his family "is just so much more precious to me than any tricky little rhyme scheme or complicated riff. . . . It always loops back around to the thing that's elemental. And I wish people would think about it more like that, of the connection that it gives you."

In the early 2000s, he had written a forty-four-line poem to all of his daughters titled "A Song for My Daughters." Some of it reads:

> *Sometimes I know I've let you down. . . .*
>
> *There's so much time apart*
> *I guess I'm not like other ones*
> *And neither dears are you*
> *I don't have traits like Mother does*
> *With friends to pull me through. . . .*
>
> *I hope you'll sometimes think of me*
> *With lovelight in your eyes. . . .*

At the Tulsa memorial, Taylor Hanson gave a moving rendition of "A Song for You." He said he has never been more nervous in his life. In our visit at Grand Lake, he spoke vividly about how Leon's music continues to live on through his and subsequent generations. "It's still rippling out because of what he was about; he was about bringing people together and making stuff happen."

Hanson told me one last story: "We got the news that he'd passed, and it hit me like my dad passed, or my grandfather, really more than I even expected. He'd met my oldest son Ezra, and Ezra had become really inspired to play piano more than his dad could ever make him. He had to see it in somebody else. I walked into our house, and Ezra had no idea that Leon had passed. I kid you not, he was playing 'A Song for You.' I am still speechless when I think about it. . . . It just stopped me in my tracks. I tried to pull myself together, and I walked to the other room. He and I both had this real, genuine talk. This important figure has gone on. But what just floored me was he left something that was so alive.

"And so that's what we're doing, right? We're trying to leave something if anything. That's why I want to talk about the story of our friend Leon Russell because that's actually what he was about."

It has been a long grieving process for Jan. "Listening to Leon was . . . it was just overwhelming," she said. "But, you know, sometimes I can listen to it, like with the New Grass Revival, then it would make me laugh and be totally good, and then I burst into tears. And when I listen to his music from before me, I would be fine with that. I never know when I'm going to get a surprise. I still don't know all his music. After he died, I started looking for it everywhere. I've become his biggest fan now because he was just my mate. That's how our whole relationship was. The music was just the gold, and so beautiful.

"Towards the end, I remember him saying, 'Are you just tired of hearing me talking? Am I boring you, or do you care to hear about this?' Because he would think I wasn't interested. I would say, 'No, I'm listening,' because he would go on and on and on. We had almost a role reversal, where he was more like the woman, and I was more like the man. People were scared of him because of the way he looked, and he could have a temper, and he talked loud, but on the whole of it, he just had this sweet soul. To me, he was very tender, and I always looked out for him. I felt I had to protect him and equally felt protected by him. The way our relationship worked, and maybe the same for him, he was all things to me. He was my child, he was my mate, and he was my father. All through all of those things, the trinity in both of us played out. At first, I didn't realize how much I needed to protect him, but as the years went on, I wanted to protect him as much as I could, but he didn't come across as needing protection. The outside world would not have known. He was so sensitive. They would not have known how that affected him. I wanted to—just like I did with my girls—get up between him and other people."

Not long before he died, Leon told Jan, "Meems, I don't know why, but I breathe better when you're holding me. Isn't that weird?"

Acknowledgments

THANKS TO JAN BRIDGES AND her representatives, Bill Siddons, Dub Cornett, and Hank Teverbaugh, for trusting me for this project and their cooperation throughout. And thanks to my agent Peter McGuigan for his patience waiting for me to find just the right project.

Brant Rumble was my tireless editor who was only mildly daunted at the woolly mammoth first draft. Michaelangelo Matos showed great care in helping pare it down.

For all the Okie sweethearts! In addition to multiple late-night calls (and even old-school letters) during which he was one of the most reliable and gracious interview subjects, Jimmy Karstein gave me a driving tour around Tulsa on my first day in town while his health was failing. I felt close to him immediately, as I am sure everyone did who had the pleasure of knowing him. Losing Jimmy in 2022 hit hard.

The team at OKPOP was extremely accommodating. My visit to their super-secret archives—and unfinished museum—was a highlight of my trip to Tulsa, and I now count Jeff Moore, Mark Dempsey, Jarrod Golli-hare, and Meg Charron as friends. Mark was especially helpful with the materials and photos. Another new friend, Charlene Ripley welcomed me into her home, shared personal recordings at her studio, and even bought me lunch at Click's Steakhouse in Pawnee. Teresa Knox gave me a personal tour of the Church Studio while it was still being renovated. Rick Huskey gave me a personal tour of Leon's old Grand Lake property, which Rick has owned for decades. Rick even got me a gig singing Stones (not Leon) with Beau Charron and his band at Rick's place, Maggie's Music Box in Jenks.

Deep gratitude for the help of the following friends in connecting me to others: Morgan Neville, Teresa Knox, David Jenkins, Pat Thomas, Jesse Lauter, Teb Blackwell, Andrew Sandoval, Dennis Diken, Chris Colbourn, Tom Polce, Larry Jenkins, Tanya Donelly, Don MacKinnon, David Furnish, Larry Crane, Tom Ruprecht, Eric Van Rysdam, and Denny Tedesco, who also provided me with a transcript of a crucial candid interview with Leon.

Cameron Crowe sent me a DVD version of *The Union*, his documentary of the sessions. Rebecca Gurnee at the AFM Local 47 patiently provided me with the session contracts I requested. Andy Leach at the Rock & Roll Hall of Fame sent me valuable correspondence between Leon and Tommy LiPuma. The master Peter Guralnick and ABKO's Teri Lambi helped track down some Sam Cooke session details. Steve Hoffman, Randal Berry, Jason Odd, and Tom Sanford all provided materials or background on Leon or Leon-adjacent sessions and subjects. Laurel Stearns at Primary Wave sent publishing information and connected me with Herb Alpert's team. Alanna Nash sent her *Penthouse* interview with Leon and was highly encouraging of this project. Ned Flood gave me old articles and publications. Bob Mehr, Warren Zanes, Peter Wolf, and Duke Levine were also helpful.

I thank all the people who took the time to grant me interviews. But there was a special trust I was granted by Leon's close family and friends and for that I am most grateful.

Sources

THIS BOOK WAS WRITTEN MOSTLY over the course of 2020–2021, when Covid-19 was raging. It limited my travel, but it also kept most other people in place, so I believe I was able to get many interviews I might not have been able to arrange so easily had musicians been on the road, producers working more sessions, etcetera. Unless otherwise noted (in the text itself or below), most of the quotes are from the interviews I conducted. Approximately 137 people were interviewed. Most were phone or Zoom calls, though a few were in person. A few more were conducted via email or other digital messaging. A number of people were gracious enough to grant me multiple interviews via some combination of all these channels.

Here is the list: Elton John, Bruce Springsteen, Willie Nelson, Eric Clapton, Steve Winwood, Rita Coolidge, Randy Newman, Dave Mason, T Bone Burnett, Bruce Hornsby, Ronnie Milsap, Susan Tedeschi, Derek Trucks, Paul Shaffer, Jim Keltner, James Burton, Lenny Waronker, Jon Landau, Russ Titelman, Cheech Marin, Richard Carpenter, Glyn Johns, Steve Cropper, Terry Manning, Gary Lewis, Ian Hunter, Dwight Twilley, Van Dyke Parks, Bobby Whitlock, Dean Torrence, Taylor Hackford, Ken Burns, Don Preston, Sonny Curtis, Chris Stainton, Bobby Keys (taken from interviews for a previous book), Al Schmitt, Charlie McCoy, Sam Bush, Jim Horn, A. J. Croce, Bobby Hart, Jim Price, Roger Linn, Christine O'Dell, Johnny Barbis, Jim Halsey, Don Randi, Barney Cordell, Marc Benno, Johnny Williams, Linda Wolfe, Keith Allison, Don Nix, Steve Martin (agent, not the actor), Halen Nelah, John Gallie, Daniel Moore, Sugaree Bridges, David Teegarden, Mark Lambert, Ron Henry, Tina Rose Bridges, Wally Wilson, Charlene Ripley, David Davis, Connie

Nelson, Gordon Rudd, James Mankey, Pamela Polland, Sandy Konikoff, Bruce Robb, Stuart Margolin, Bobby Torres, Bill Bentley, Robb Royer, Syd Straw, Michael P. Graham, Alan Baker, Mary Jones, Rick Huskey, Harrod Blank, Kate Hyman, Richard Feldman, Jim Franklin, Owen Sloane, Tommy Vicari, Bob Morris, Tom Russell, Marlin Green, Harold Thompson, Maxayn Lewis, Fiona Fitzherbert, Ann Bell Nicholson, Julie Chapman, Kirk Bressler, Wayne Perkins, Mike Scott, Gary Ogan, Frank Latouf, Herb Alpert, Bob Britt, Tom Britt, Taylor Hanson, Beau Charron, Jeff Moore, Larry Shaeffer, Brandon Holder, Jack Randall, John McDonnell, Charles Thompson (aka Black Francis), Danny Campbell, Chris Simmons, Paul Lee, Jesse Lauter, Bobby Roberts, Matt Harris, Paul Brewer, Matthew Moore, Coco Bridges, Marjoe Gortner, John McEuen, Wornell Jones, Teresa Knox, and John Cowan.

Particularly helpful in bridging the timeline for me with multiple long and follow-up interviews: Jim Karstein, Jack Wessel, Maureen Gosling, Jan Bridges, Claudia Lennear, Patrick Henderson, Michael Johnstone, Don Williams, Blue Bridges-Fox, and Peter Nicholls.

Other Sources Not Otherwise Cited in the Text, by Chapter

Preface

Research on the Rock & Roll Hall of Fame nominating process includes an article by Anthony DeCurtis titled "How Do You Get into the Hall of Fame?" in the November 26, 2009, issue of *Rolling Stone*. I also include quotes from my interviews with Jon Landau and others, as cited.

Other Leon quotes come from interviews with Alanna Nash and Steve Roeser, both of whom were helpful throughout this book. Nash's "50 Years of Music" interview was for *Penthouse* magazine, January 15, 2015. Roeser's was printed in *Goldmine* magazine (Roeser, "Even Under the Guise of Hank Wilson, Leon Russell Is a Legend in His Time," *Goldmine*, September 11, 1998). Nash was kind enough to send me a PDF of her article. Roeser's piece was found on the Rock's Backpages web archive (https://www.rocksbackpages.com), which has always been helpful and which I used throughout this book.

Excerpts of Leon's speech and other parts of the Hall of Fame ceremony can be viewed on YouTube.

Chapter I: Killer Education

Nick Tosches, *Hellfire: The Jerry Lee Lewis Story* (New York: Dell, 1982).

Liza Weisstuch, "Did You Know That Tulsa Has a Wealth of Art Deco Architecture?" *Architectural Digest*, July 17, 2019.

Leon's recollections quoted in this chapter come from *Leon Russell: In His Own Words (with a Little Help from His Friends)*. This is a self-published memoir that Leon started, but never finished. It was edited and fleshed out by John Wooley, a book author and writer for the *Tulsa World* newspaper, and Steve Todoroff, who dedicated much of his life and resources to collecting Leon memorabilia, records, contracts, and related material. He also promoted Leon's Birthday Bash shows in Tulsa. I found Wooley's articles in the *Tulsa World* to be valuable resources, particularly his "Rock of Ages" series, covering the early days of rock 'n' roll in the city. Because *In His Own Words* is Leon's only written account of his life, it was valuable for this book.

Memories of and quotes from the shows with Jerry Lee Lewis come in part from my interview with Johnny Williams. Others come from Ben Fong-Torres, "Leon Russell: The Interview," *Rolling Stone*, December 10, 1970. It is an in-depth interview that is crucial for understanding Leon on the precipice of superstardom.

Craig Rosen, "Leon Russell Shares His Favorite Musical Memories," Yahoo Entertainment, April 1, 2014.

Paul Sexton, "Singing This Song for You: The Leon Russell Story," BBC Radio 2, September 29, 2010.

Teb Blackwell and Rhett Lake, *Oklahoma Guide to 45rpm Records & Bands 1955–1975* (Oklahoma Historical Society, 2014). Teb Blackwell was personally quite helpful in email correspondence as well.

Chapter 2: Okies

Denny Tedesco produced the 2008 documentary film *The Wrecking Crew!* The film was a valuable source, but Tedesco went above and beyond by providing me with a full transcript of an interview that he and the crew had with Leon on February 24, 2013. Leon is remarkably candid and it is such a rich source for Leon's memories of his session days and musical background that it is one of the most cited sources in this book. Hereafter I refer to this interview transcript as "Tedesco interview with Leon, 2013." I also cite the film *The Wrecking Crew!* by name.

US Census information was taken from ancestry.com.

Childhood memories and chronology from Bill Crawford, "Leon Russell: Superstar Child of the Electronic Age," *Lawton (OK) Sunday Constitution*, July 21, 1974.

More childhood information comes from "The Extraordinary History of Leon Russell," a presentation by Steve Todoroff that helped raise funds for a memorial for Leon in Tulsa ("The Extraordinary History of Leon Russell Presented by Steve Todoroff," YouTube video, 1:01:54, Circle Cinema, November 13, 2018, https://www.youtube.com/watch?v=FpdqInep7hs).

Steve Todoroff's liner notes from the *Gimme Shelter* greatest hits CD.

Interview with Leon by Viv Nesbitt with John Dillon for artofthesong.org.

"Joe Cocker—Mad Dogs and Englishmen—with Leon Russell," *In the Studio with Redbeard* (blog), https://www.inthestudio.net/online-only-interviews/joe-cocker-mad-dogs-englishmen/.

Leon Russell, "Still Playing A Song for You: Leon Russell on Bangladesh, Mad

Dogs and Englishmen, and His Hot New Independent Label," interview by Michael Buffalo Smith, Swampland.com, November 2001, http://swampland.com/articles /view/title:leon_russell.

Leon Russell, "Actually, I'm a Magician," interview by Nick Waterhouse, *LA Record*, July 8, 2015, https://larecord.com/archive/2015/07/08/leon-russell-interview -a-poem-is-a-naked-person-nick-waterhouse.

Alanna Nash, "50 Years of Music" interview with Leon, 2015.

Russell, *In His Own Words*.

Chapter 3: Tulsa Time

Diane Sullivan interviewing Jim Karstein and J. J. Cale, September 9, 1982, transcript, in the Steve Todoroff archives, owned by the OKPOP museum and archives.

Fong-Torres, "Leon Russell: The Interview."

Todoroff, "Extraordinary History of Leon Russell."

Willie Nelson, with David Ritz, *It's a Long Story* (Little, Brown, 2015).

John Wooley, "Rock of Ages," pts. 1–5, *Tulsa World*, 2003.

John Wooley, *From the Blue Devils to Red Dirt: The Colors of Oklahoma Music* (Hawk Publishing Group, 2006).

Alaina F. Roberts, "How Native Americans Adopted Slavery from White Settlers," Al Jazeera, December 27, 2018, https://www.aljazeera.com/opinions/2018/12/27 /how-native-americans-adopted-slavery-from-white-settlers.

Russell Cobb, *The Great Oklahoma Swindle: Race, Religion, and Lies in America's Weirdest State* (Lincoln, NE: University of Nebraska Press, 2020).

Scott Ellsworth, "Tulsa Race Massacre," *Encyclopedia of Oklahoma History and Culture*, https://www.okhistory.org/publications/enc/entry.php?entry=TU013.

Andy Wheeler, "Sounding Off on Eric Clapton and the Tulsa Sound," *Tulsa People*, March 2010.

Cleve Warren, "What Do You Know About Tulsa Time? Jimmy Karstein, Chuck Blackwell, David Teegarden, and the Unique Scene That Fueled Classic Rock," *Modern Drummer*, May 1, 2011.

Levon Helm and Stephen Davis, *This Wheel's on Fire: Levon Helm and the Story of The Band* (W. Morrow, 1993).

"Tulsa Sound Legend and Harmonica Player, Jimmy Markham, Talks Leon Russell," YouTube video, 15:12, Church Studio, November 27, 2020. Teresa Knox's interview series for the Church Studio was a valuable resource.

John Wooley, "The Axeman Cometh," *Tulsa World*, October 11, 2000.

Alice Clark, "Leon Russell's Amazing Journey," *Classic Rock*, May 20, 2014.

Fong-Torres, "Leon Russell: The Interview."

Russell, *In His Own Words*.

Blackwell and Lake, *Oklahoma Guide*.

Chapter 4: Oklahoma's Lonesome Cowboys Are Turned On in Tinseltown

Some sources have Leon arriving in LA first in 1959, some as early as 1958 (including Steve Todoroff's liner notes in *Gimme Shelter*). Leon often said he was seventeen when he went, making it 1959. But he also notes in *In His Own Words* that "except for the Jerry Lee Lewis tour, I had never been away from home." He turned eighteen in April 1960.

Some background on *Cal's Corral* came from Jason Odd, who runs "Cal's Corral—Country Music Time," a Facebook page about that scene. Included here is information from a 1973 article in the UCLA *Daily Bruin* newspaper posted there. Jerry Lee Lewis's appearance was posted on YouTube.

I contacted the American Federation of Musicians Local 47 in Los Angeles to pull contracts for sessions on which Leon is listed. Most of this session data and more was in the OKPOP archives as well.

William Sargent self-published *Superstar in a Masquerade*, which he describes as a "bio-pedia," July 27, 2021, when my manuscript was mostly finished. His research into AFM sessions seems to be the most complete that I have found, and I have used it to check and augment my own.

Quotes about the Pandora scene come from my interviews with Jim Karstein, augmented by John Wooley, "Last Man in the Band," *Oklahoma*, February 23, 2017, and Harvey Kubernik, *Turn Up the Radio! Rock, Pop, and Roll in Los Angeles 1956–1972* (Santa Monica Press, 2014).

Leon Russell, "A Song for You," interview with Andy Gill, *Uncut*, February 2017.

"Tommy Allsup, Cherokee Member and Buddy Holly's 'Crickets,' Exclusive Interview," YouTube video, 10:55, Church Studio, August 3, 2020, https://www.youtube.com/watch?v=v01_mhKyB10.

David McGee, "The Mark Lindsay Arc," Bluegrass Special, November 1998, https://web.archive.org/web/20200813075625/http://www.thebluegrassspecial.com:80/archive/2011/april2011/contentsapril2011.php.

In addition to my interview with James Burton, I referred to Ed Ward, "James Burton: The Teen Who Invented American Guitar," *Fresh Air*, NPR, May 25, 2012.

"Leon Russell Steps Up," *New Zealand Herald*, April 10, 2011.

Sharon Sheeley obituary, *The Guardian*, August 29, 2002.

"Speaking Freely: Jackie DeShannon," YouTube video, 30:31, Freedom Forum, July 11, 2016, https://www.youtube.com/watch?v=BakOtoDrqrM.

Tommy LiPuma, letter to Bob Lefsetz, *Lefsetz Letter*, November 16, 2016.

"Everly Facts," Everly Brothers session information, Everly.net.

"Jimmy Markham, Talks Leon Russell" video.

Blackwell and Lake, *Oklahoma Guide*.

Wooley, *From the Blue Devils to Red Dirt*.

Waterhouse, "Actually, I'm a Magician."

Russell, *In His Own Words*.

Roeser, "Even Under the Guise of Hank Wilson."

Tedesco interview with Leon, 2013.

The Wrecking Crew!, including outtakes.

Chapter 5: The Wall of Sound

Ken Sharp, *Sound Explosion! Inside L.A.'s Studio Factory with the Wrecking Crew* (Wrecking Crew, 2016).

The Wrecking Crew!

"Wrecking Crew Panel: Hal Blaine, Nancy Sinatra, Jeff Barry, Don Randi, Danny Tedesco," YouTube video, 42:25, NewsCraft, February 10, 2013, https://www.you tube.com/watch?v=qKGXUlBEYH8.

YouTube post by *The Wrecking Crew!* with Marty Cooper, February 15, 2018.

Hal Blaine, with David Goggin, *Hal Blaine and the Wrecking Crew* (Emeryville, CA: Mix Books, 1990).

Harvey Kubernik, "Phil Spector: Jack Nitzsche Remembers the Wall of Sound," *Goldmine*, June 17, 1988.

Philspector.com.

Mick Brown, *Tearing Down the Wall of Sound: The Rise and Fall of Phil Spector* (Vintage, 2008).

Dante Fumo, "6 Echo Chambers That Shaped the Sound of Pop Music," Reverb, February 28, 2019, https://reverb.com/news/6-echo-chambers-that-shaped -the-sound-of-popular-music.

Tom Pinnock, "The Making of the Ronettes' 'Be My Baby': 'It Was Pure Every-thing,'" *Uncut*, August 9, 2019, https://www.uncut.co.uk/features/making-ronettes -baby-pure-everything-111632/.

Russell, *In His Own Words*.

Tedesco interview with Leon, 2013.

The Wrecking Crew! Facebook page.

Phil Spector, liner notes, *Back to Mono (1958–1969)* (ABKCO, 1991).

Michael Simmons, "The Magus," *Mojo*, 2010.

Carol Kaye, email to author (her rejection of my interview request).

Marc Myers, "Who Else Made More Hit Songs?" *Wall Street Journal*, March 23, 2011.

Luis Sanchez, *The Beach Boys' Smile* (Bloomsbury, 2014), excerpted as Luis Sanchez, "Phil Spector's Famous Sound (and Cruelty) Drove the Beach Boys' Brian Wilson to Wretched Obsession," *Salon*, May 5, 2018, https://www.salon.com/2018/05/05 /phil-spectors-famous-sound-and-cruelty-drove-the-beach-boys-brian-wilson-to -wretched-obsession/.

Johnny Black, "Phil Spector's Christmas Album" (unpublished), Rock's Back-pages, December 2009.

Teri Landi (ABKO), emails to author.

Peter Guralnick, emails to author.

Mike Mettler, "Mad Dogs and Shelter People: Leon Russell Looks Back on an Amazing Life Journey," SoundBard, April 2, 2014, http://www.soundbard.com/soundbard /mad-dogs-and-shelter-people-leon-russell-looks-back-on-an-amazing-life-journey/.

Chapter 6: Playboys, Beach Boys, and Byrds

Kent Hartman, *The Wrecking Crew: The Inside Story of Rock and Roll's Best-Kept Secret* (Thomas Dunne Books, 2012).

Buzzcason.com.

Alanna Nash, "Catching Up with Leon Russell," AARP, 2014, https://www.aarp .org/entertainment/music/info-2014/leon-russell-life-journey.html.

Richard Sandomir, "Jack Good, Who Put Rock 'n' Roll on TV with 'Shindig,' Dies at 86," *New York Times*, October 6, 2017.

Stuart Grundy and John Tobler, *The Guitar Greats* (BBC Books, 1983).

David Talbot and Barbara Zheutlin, "Expecting to Fly: Jack Nitzche," *Crawdaddy*, November 1974.

Larry Crane, "Tommy 'Snuff' Garrett: A Cowboy in the Control Room," *Tape Op*, September–October 2009.

Al Kooper, *Backstage Passes & Backstabbing Bastards* (Backbeat Books, 1998).

Jim Clash, "Gary Lewis Discusses His Sixties Hit, This Diamond Ring," *Forbes*, November 8, 2020, https://www.forbes.com/sites/jimclash/2020/11/08/gary-lewis -discusses-his-no-1-sixties-hit-this-diamond-ring/?sh=73aae6f86409.

David Fricke, "Remembering Leon Russell, Rock's Behind-the-Scenes Mad Dog," *Rolling Stone*, November 22, 2016.

Johnny Rogan, *The Byrds: Timeless Flight Revisited: The Sequel* (Rogan House, 1998).

Sinatrafamily.com for session details.

Anything Can Happen: The LeonLifer Story—an amateur circa-2000 documentary by Joe Hill about a gathering of Leon fans, explained in greater detail later in the book (Joe Hill, "'*Anything Can Happen*'—the LeonLifer Story," YouTube video, 2:36:01, deepfreezevideo2, November 20, 2016, https://www.youtube.com /watch?v=FdJjkL9G5-A).

Matthew Duersten, "The Lady at the Bottom of the Groove," *LA Weekly*, April 8, 2004.

Ian S. Port, "Precision Bass: Rock 'n' Roll's Instrumental Soul," Historynet.com, May 20, 2019, https://www.historynet.com/precision-bass-the-soul-of-rock-n-roll/.

Russell, *In His Own Words*.

Kubernick, *Turn Up the Radio!*.

Tedesco interview with Leon, 2013.

The Wrecking Crew!

Hartman, *Wrecking Crew: The Inside Story.*

Roeser, "Even Under the Guise of Hank Wilson."

Rosen, "Leon Russell Shares His Favorite Musical Memories."

Sexton, "Singing This Song for You."

Chapter 7: High on Skyhill Drive

Leonrussell.com.

To Tulsa and Back: On Tour with J. J. Cale, documentary directed by Jörg Bundschuh (2005).

Ian Birch, "J. J. Acts Naturally," *Sounds*, April 17, 1976.

Waterhouse, "Actually, I'm a Magician."

"Memphis Man, Don Nix, Talks Leon Russell, Freddie King, Shelter Records & His Hit Song; Going Down," interview by Teresa Knox, YouTube video, 15:16, Church Studio, October 5, 2020, https://www.youtube.com/watch?v=kCJTSxn_kBY. Other Don Nix material comes from my interview with him.

Bobby Keys quotes from an interview I had with him, as well as his book, *Every Night's a Saturday Night: The Rock 'n' Roll Life of Legendary Sax Man Bobby Keys* (with Bill Ditenhafer, Counterpoint, 2012. Foreword by Keith Richards).

"Gary James' Interview with Gary Lewis of Gary Lewis and the Playboys," Classicbands.com, classicbands.com/GaryLewisInterview.html.

Bruce Eder, "Gary Lewis & the Playboys Biography" Allmusic.com, https://www.allmusic.com/artist/gary-lewis-the-playboys-mn0000741333/biography.

Steve Todoroff, "The Making of Longhair Music," This Land, September 11, 2013, https://thislandpress.com/2013/09/11/the-making-of-longhair-music-2/.

Duaneallman.info.

Jim Downing, "Remembering Jimmy 'Junior' Markham," *Tulsa Today*, October 8, 2018.

Lee Gabites, "A Conversation with Levon Helm," *Jawbone*, October 15, 1996, https://theband.hiof.no/articles/interview_levon_oct_96.html.

Leon Russell, interview with Mary Campbell (AP), September 1, 1971. This piece was syndicated across America.

Danny Holloway, "Lou Adler: A Music Giant," *New Musical Express*, February 5, 1972.

Sam D'Arcangelo, "Paul Simon Punishes Himself by Busting Out Classic Song That He Hates," LiveForMusic.com, May 21, 2018.

Sid Griffin, liner notes on Gene Clark, *Echoes* reissue CD, 1991.

John Einarson, *Desperados: The Roots of Country Rock* (Cooper Square Press, 2001).

Blackwell and Lake, *Oklahoma Guide.*

Gill, "A Song for You" interview with Leon.

Chapter 8: Asylum Choir

Marc Benno quotes come from my interviews and his book, *Hollywood Texas: A True Backstage Look at Love and Music Along the Rock 'n' Roll Highway: Memoirs of the Life and Times of Marc Benno* (Marno Publishing, 2013).

Randal Berry generously shared his research on the Asylum Choir and Marc Benno for a project he has been working on.

George Varga, "Leon Russell, Rock and Roll Hall of Famer, Dead at 74," *San Diego Tribune*, November 13, 2016.

Earle Mankey comments on the Gearslutz.com thread, "Beach Boys' 'Brother Studios' Setup?"

Steve Stanley, liner notes, *Daughters of Albion* CD, Now Sounds reissue, 2012.

Tedesco interview with Leon, 2013.

Nix and Knox, "Memphis Man, Don Nix, Talks Leon Russell."

Fong-Torres, "Leon Russell: The Interview."

Sargent, *Superstar in a Masquerade*.

Chapter 9: Accept No Substitute

Don Nix, *Memphis Man: Living High, Laying Low* (Sartoris Literary Group, 2015).

Bobby Whitlock, with Marc Roberty, *Bobby Whitlock: A Rock 'n' Roll Autobiography* (McFarland, 2010).

Rita Coolidge, with Michael Walker, *Delta Lady: A Memoir* (HarperCollins, 2016).

Nix, Coolidge, and Whitlock quotes and information are from their books and my own interviews with each.

David Meyer, *Twenty Thousand Roads: The Ballad of Gram Parsons and His Cosmic American Music* (Villard Books, 2008).

Chris Hillman, *Time Between: My Life as a Byrd, Burrito Brother, and Beyond* (BMG Books, 2020).

Nancy Deedrick, The Great Hollywood Hangover, http://www.hollywood hangover.com/.

Downing, "Remembering Jimmy 'Junior' Markham."

Simmons, "The Magus."

Fong-Torres, "Leon Russell: The Interview."

Nix and Knox, "Memphis Man, Don Nix, Talks Leon Russell."

Todoroff, *Gimme Shelter* liner notes.

Nash, "50 Years of Music" interview with Leon, 2015.

Chapter 10: Hello Little Friend

Every Night's a Saturday Night, documentary directed by Jeff Stacy (2018).

Chris Welch, "Delaney & Bonnie: Out of the South Comes 'The Best Band in the World,'" *Melody Maker*, October 18, 1969.

Elton John, *Me* (Macmillan, 2019).

J. P. Bean, *Joe Cocker: The Authorized Biography* (Virgin Books Limited, 2003).

Mark Plummer, "Leon Russell: King of the Delta Rockers," *Melody Maker*, August 29, 1970.

Chris O'Dell, with Katherine Ketcham, *Miss O'Dell: My Hard Days and Long Nights with The Beatles, The Stones, Bob Dylan, and Eric Clapton, and the Women They Loved* (Touchstone, 2009).

Jeff Tamarkin, "Leon Russell Talks His Career and Collaborations," Best Classic Bands, https://bestclassicbands.com/leon-russell-interview-11-13-16/.

Whitlock, *A Rock 'n' Roll Autobiography.*

Redbeard, "Joe Cocker—Mad Dogs and Englishmen—with Leon Russell."

Russell, *In His Own Words.*

Chapter 11: A Song for You

The liner notes of the CD reissue of *Leon Russell* list Sunset Sound as the studio used for "A Song for You," but remastering engineer Steve Hoffman confirmed it was A&M.

Max Bell, "The Strange Tale of Derek, Gordon, George . . . and Bobby Whitlock" (unpublished), Rock's Backpages Library, 2013, https://www.rocksbackpages.com /Library/Article/the-strange-tale-of-derek-gordon-george-and-bobby-whitlock.

Glyn Johns quoted in John Tobler and Stuart Grundy, *The Record Producers* (St. Martin's Press, 1982).

Glyn Johns, *Sound Man: A Life Recording Hits with the Rolling Stones, The Who, Led Zeppelin, the Eagles, Eric Clapton, the Faces* (Plume, 2014).

Jac Holzman and Gavan Daws, *Follow the Music: The Life and High Times of Elektra Records in the Great Years of American Pop Culture* (First Media Books, 1998).

Bill Wyman, with Richard Havers, *Rolling with the Stones* (DK, 2002).

Rob Partridge, "Leon Russell—Super Group?" *Record Mirror*, May 16, 1970.

Alan Clayson, *Ringo Starr: Straight Man or Joker?* (Paragon House Publishers, 1992).

David Fricke, "Leon Russell: The Master of Space & Time Returns," *Rolling Stone*, November 11, 2010.

Elliot Stephen Cohen, "Leon Russell: The Master of Space and Time Returns," *Keyboard*, March 2011.

Dr. John, interview by Charlie Gillett, *Let It Rock*, July 1973.

Paul Gambaccini, "The Doctor Is In—a Talk with Dr. John," *Rolling Stone*, September 27, 1973.

Jesse Lauter directed *Learning to Live Together*, a documentary about the Mad Dogs and Englishmen Reunion with the Tedeschi Trucks Band at the 2015 Lockn' Festival. He generously shared some audio interviews, including a candid one where Leon discussed Rita Coolidge.

Dave Lawrence, "Leon Russell—the Life Journey Tour in Hawai'i," interview with Leon, Hawai'i Public Radio, September 18, 2014, https://www.hawaiipublic radio.org/dave-lawrence/2014-09-18/leon-russell-the-life-journey-tour-in -hawaii.

Damian Fanelli, "George Harrison's 15 Greatest Guitar Moments After the Beatles," *Guitar World*, February 25, 2019.

Wayne Robbins, "Elton John Teams with Idol for Musical 'Union,'" *Billboard*, October 10, 2010.

Gill, "A Song for You" interview with Leon.

Roeser, "Even Under the Guise of Hank Wilson."

Fong-Torres, "Leon Russell: The Interview."

Sexton, "Singing This Song for You."

Tamarkin, "Leon Russell Talks His Career."

Plummer, "King of the Delta Rockers."

Elton John, *Me*.

Tedesco interview with Leon, 2013.

Sargent, *Superstar in a Masquerade*.

Todoroff, *Gimme Shelter* liner notes.

Chapter 12: Shelter in Place

Leon, with Harrod Blank, *A Poem Is a Naked Person* DVD extras, 2015.

The Delaney & Bonnie Fillmore West show can be heard at the online archive Wolfgang's Vault (https://www.wolfgangs.com).

Harry Shapiro, "To Forbidden Love, Made Victims of Derek and the Dominos," *Mojo*, January 2001.

Clapton quotes are from my interview with him and one he gave to Ritchie Yorke in *Circus*, October 1972.

Emily Smith was recorded in a January 29, 1989, discussion with Willie Spears, who had been a roadie for Leon, reminiscing and comparing memories.

Partridge, "Leon Russell—Super Group?"

Roeser, "Even Under the Guise of Hank Wilson."

Plummer, "King of the Delta Rockers."

Simmons, "The Magus."

Hillman, *Time Between*.

Meyer, *Twenty Thousand Roads*.

Russell, *In His Own Words*.

Chapter 13: Meet the Mad Dogs & Englishmen

Linda Wolf, *Tribute: Cocker Power* (Insight Editions, 2020). There was a live-stream Facebook event as well.

Timothy Crouse, "What's Going on Here, Joe Cocker?" *Rolling Stone*, May 25, 1972.

Barry Rehfeld, "When the Voices Took Over," *Rolling Stone*, June 6, 1985.

John Tobler, "Part Two of the Joe Cocker Story," *Blank Space*, 1979.

Herb Moss and Jacoba Atlas in A&M press kit for *Mad Dogs and Englishmen*.

Sarah Hart and Faith Phillips, "Street Cred: Leon Russell Stays True to Tulsa Sound," *Tulsa World*, August 27, 2010.

Bean, *Joe Cocker*.

Simmons, "The Magus."

Rosen, "Leon Russell Shares His Favorite Musical Memories."

Nesbitt/Dillon interview.

Russell, *In His Own Words*.

Meyer, *Twenty Thousand Roads*.

Helm and Davis, *This Wheel's on Fire*.

Fong-Torres, "Leon Russell: The Interview."

Redbeard, "Joe Cocker—Mad Dogs and Englishmen—with Leon Russell."

Chapter 14: Learning to Live Together

Learning to Live Together: The Return of Mad Dogs & Englishmen, directed by Jesse Lauter, 2021.

A&M press kit for *Mad Dogs & Englishmen*.

Chris Riemenschneider, *First Avenue: Minnesota's Mainroom* (Minnesota Historical Society Press, 2017).

Allan Holbert, "Cocker, the Grease Band [*sic*] Get the Depot Rolling," *Minneapolis Star Tribune*, April 4, 1970.

Randall J. Stephens, "Where Else Did They Copy Their Styles but from Church Groups? Rock 'n' Roll and Pentecostalism in the 1950s South," *Church History* 85, no. 1 (March 2016), 97–131. Advance online publication, February 29, 2016, https://www.cambridge.org/core/journals/church-history/article/abs/where-else-did-they-copy-their-styles-but-from-church-groups-rock-n-roll-and-pentecostalism-in-the-1950s-south/9892D9D60C00C91BF54F2DC278441A36.

"Leon Russell's 'This Masquerade' Inspiration, Carla Brown, Shares First Encounter with Leon, Part 1," interview by Teresa Knox, YouTube video, 8:14, Church Studio, September 4, 2020, https://www.youtube.com/watch?v=V0yO0Gb4myg.

Wolf, *Tribute: Cocker Power*.

Fricke, "The Master of Space & Time Returns."

Rehfeld, "When the Voices Took Over."

Chapter 15: I'm Coming Home

Bruce Springsteen, *Born to Run* (Simon & Schuster, 2016).

Mat Snow, "All Together Now: Joe Cocker," *Q* magazine, May 1992.

Fred Schruers, "Joe Cocker's Island Renaissance," *Musician*, July 1982.

Coolidge, *Delta Lady.*

Wolf, *Tribute: Cocker Power* (including an interview with Joe Cocker by Susan Viebrock, *Telluride Inside and Out*, excerpted in Wolf's book).

Redbeard, "Joe Cocker—Mad Dogs and Englishmen—with Leon Russell."

A&M press kit for *Mad Dogs & Englishmen.*

Wolfgang's Vault (https://www.wolfgangs.com).

Lauter, *Learning to Live Together.*

Plummer, "King of the Delta Rockers."

Tobler, "Part Two of the Joe Cocker Story."

Crouse, "What's Going on Here."

Waterhouse, "Actually, I'm a Magician."

Carla Brown interview, "'This Masquerade' Inspiration, Carla Brown."

Chapter 16: Shelter People

Billboard.com for chart positions.

Paul Liberator, "Kathi McDonald Solidifies Her Legacy as Rock 'n' Roll Survivor," *Marin Independent Journal* (Novato, CA), April 13, 2009.

Peter Doggett, *You Never Give Me Your Money: The Beatles After the Breakup* (HarperCollins, 2009).

Tim Stanley, "Tulsa Sound Figure 'Sweet Emily' Smith Dies at 69," *Tulsa World*, January 9, 2013.

Los Angeles Times, June 15, 1970.

Keith Phipps, interview with Randy Newman, AV Club, October 8, 2003, https://www.avclub.com/randy-newman-1798208294.

Leon's pick of his top ten favorite records in 1973 was syndicated in newspapers from an interview with Loraine Alterman.

John Tobler, "Donald Nix: Of Shoes & Sticks & Donald Nix," *ZigZag*, October 1973.

Pat Thomas, liner notes for *Motel Shot* CD, ATCO reissue, 2017.

Set lists and other artists on bills, from Songkick.com.

Elton John, "Elton John Still Uses This Tip Leon Russell Gave Him in 1970," YouTube video, 2:21, Howard Stern Show, November 19, 2020, https://www.youtube.com/watch?v=seIc5p38Gxo.

Wayne Perkins quotes are from my own interviews and Ed Reynolds, "Session Man," *Black and White*, October 29, 2009, archived on Jonimitchell.com, https://jonimitchell.com/library/view.cfm?id=2163.

Nix quotes are from my own interviews, his book (*Memphis Man: Living High, Laying Low*), and his interview with Teresa Knox ("Memphis Man, Don Nix, Talks Leon Russell," https://www.youtube.com/watch?v=kCJTSxn_kBY).

Jimmie Trammel, "Before Leon Russell Events: 10 Things to Know About Tulsa's Mayor of Rock and Roll," *Tulsa World*, April 1, 2008, https://tulsaworld.com/lifestyles/before-leon-russell-events-10-things-to-know-about-tulsas-mayor-of-rock-and-roll/article_2c7202f2-62da-54f6-9dbe-37dcfe900d99.html.

Peter Nicholls quotes are from my interviews with him along with an unpublished interview he did with Steve Todoroff in July 1987.

Jay Allen Sanford, "42 Years Ago Today: Pink Floyd's 1st San Diego Concert," *San Diego Reader*, October 18, 2012.

B. B. King, interview, *Miami News*, December 29, 1970.

"The Great Leon Russell Dallas 2014 B.B. King Tribute, et al" (November 21, 2014, concert), YouTube video, 18:50, JRGuitar, November 22, 2014, https://www.youtube.com/watch?v=3f_GjQT60vg.

Robert Gordon, *It Came from Memphis* (Faber & Faber, 1994).

Frank Mastropolo, "When Elton John Jammed with Leon Russell at Fillmore East," Ultimate Classic Rock, June 25, 2019, https://ultimateclassicrock.com/elton-john-leon-russell-fillmore-jam/.

Meyer, *Twenty Thousand Roads*.

Rosen, "Leon Russell Shares His Favorite Musical Memories."

Whitlock, *A Rock 'n' Roll Autobiography*.

Nash, "Catching Up with Leon Russell."

Fong-Torres, "Leon Russell: The Interview."

Plummer, "King of the Delta Rockers."

Elton John, *Me*.

Stanley, "Tulsa Sound Figure 'Sweet Emily' Smith."

Roeser, "Even Under the Guise of Hank Wilson."

Clark, "Leon Russell's Amazing Journey."

Chapter 17: On the Road to Bangladesh

Thomas Conner, "Willis Alan Ramsey Tells the Saga of THE Album," *Tulsa World*, May 3, 2000.

John Spong, "That '70s Show," *Texas Monthly*, April 2012.

Contractual details between Leon and Denny are from materials from Leon's archives at OKPOP, along with information in William Sargent's *Superstar in a Masquerade* (Page Publishing, 2021).

Ray Padgett, "Jim Keltner Talks Thirty Years of Drumming for Bob Dylan," Flagging Down the Double E's, July 22, 2021, https://dylanlive.substack.com/p/jim-keltner-talks-thirty-years-of.

My interviews with Peter Nicholls augmented by his interview with Todoroff.

Ben Fong-Torres, "Knockin' on Bob Dylan's Door," *Rolling Stone*, February 14, 1974.

Fong-Torres, "Leon Russell: The Interview."

George Harrison, interview by John Fugelsang, VH-1, July 24, 1997.

Harvey Kubernik, "George Harrison: All Things Must Pass at 50," *Music Connection*, November 10, 2020.

RS Editors, "The George Harrison Bangla Desh Benefit," *Rolling Stone*, September 2, 1971, https://www.rollingstone.com/music/music-news/the-george-harrison-bangla-desh-benefit-41257/.

Jonathan Cott, "I Dreamed I Saw Bob Dylan," *Rolling Stone*, September 2, 1971.

The Concert for Bangladesh, Limited Deluxe Edition (Rhino/Warner Bros., October 25, 2005), DVD extras.

Penny Valentine, "Helen Reddy: Weekend Ever Reddy," *Sounds*, February 5, 1972.

Cohen, "The Master of Space and Time Returns."

Mettler, "Leon Russell Looks Back."

Roeser, "Even Under the Guise of Hank Wilson."

Tobler, "Part Two of the Joe Cocker Story."

Simmons, "The Magus."

Chapter 18: Going Back to Tulsa

Thomas Conner, "Leon Russell Sought Shelter in Tulsa Throughout the 70s, and His Sounds Still Resonate," *Tulsa World*, December 19, 1997.

Dick Fricker, "Tulsa Recording Business Growing," *Daily Oklahoman*, May 29, 1972.

Sylvie Simmons, "J.J. Cale: The Real Slowhand," *MOJO*, September 2009.

Dan Forte, "J. J. Cale: Clapton Mentor," *Vintage Guitar*, December 2003.

Jim Edwards, "Leon: A Triumphant Return," *Tulsa People*, August 22, 2011.

Nix quotes come from my own interview with him and Tobler, "Donald Nix: Of Shoes & Sticks & Donald Nix," *ZigZag*, October 1973.

Simmons, "The Magus."

Keys, *Every Night's a Saturday Night*.

Carla Brown interview, "'This Masquerade' Inspiration, Carla Brown."

Chapter 19: Carney

Luther Brimstone, "Black Grass," *Kensington Tharunka*, November 8, 1973.

Val Wilmer, Ambrose Campbell obituary, *The Guardian*, July 7, 2006.

Harrod Blank, *A Poem Is a Naked Person* DVD extras.

Wolf, *Tribute: Cocker Power*.

Tedesco interview with Leon, 2013.

Simmons, "The Magus."

Chapter 20: Leon's Live

Engineer John LeMay told the current owner of the lake property, Rick Huskey, that Dylan recorded an entire album's worth of material there and scrapped it, making sure it was erased entirely.

Kevin Curtin, "Speaking of the Dead," *Austin Chronicle*, July 3, 2015.

Gill, "A Song for You" interview with Leon.

Roeser, "Even Under the Guise of Hank Wilson."

Nelson and Ritz, *It's a Long Story.*

Russell, *In His Own Words.*

Harrod Blank, *A Poem Is a Naked Person* DVD extras.

Chapter 21: Hank Wilson's Back

John Storms, "Panel Summons Leon Russell," *Tulsa World*, December 8, 1972.

Roadie arrest report, *Courier Journal* (Louisville, KY).

Billboard, June 23, 1973.

Michael Goldberg, "Sex, Drugs and the Devil: The Gap Band Fights for Success," *Rolling Stone*, March 1, 1984.

In addition to my interview with Ann Bell, some quotes are from the interview she did with Teresa Knox for the Church Studio video series.

Mike Ragogna, "Life Journeys: Conversations with Leon Russell, Judy Collins and John Gorka," *HuffPost*, 2014, https://www.huffpost.com/entry/life-journeys -conversatio_b_5062965.

Alanna Nash, "Sam Bush, New Grass Revival and Leon Russell," *Bluegrass Unlimited*, October 1973.

Willie Nelson told me the story about Leon being the first to sign/etch his signature in Trigger. Additional information comes from Michael Hall, "Trigger: The Life of Willie Nelson's Guitar," *Texas Monthly*, December 2012.

"Mary Rand," *Sepia Magazine Online*, http://sepiamagazineonline.net/sepia _seven/maryrand.html.

Billboard, October 20, 1973.

Spong, "That '70s Show."

Nelson and Ritz, *It's a Long Story.*

Russell, *In His Own Words.*

Sexton, "Singing This Song for You."

Waterhouse, "Actually, I'm a Magician."

Roeser, "Even Under the Guise of Hank Wilson."

Tedesco interview with Leon, 2013.

Todoroff, unpublished interview with Nicholls.

Chapter 22: Factions

"Ahmet's Aero Pact Pitch," *Billboard*, August 11, 1973.

Billboard, October 20, 1973.

Wayne Perkins quotes come from my interviews and the aforementioned Ed Reynolds piece ("Session Man," in *Black and White*).

List of players on the Jackson Browne demos comes from Mark Bego, *Jackson Browne: His Life and Music* (Citadel, 2005).

Nicholls quotes come from my own interviews as well as the unpublished interview he did with Todoroff.

Simmons, "The Magus."

Chapter 23: Stop All That Jazz

Andy Green, "Drummer Karl Himmel on His Years with Neil Young, Bob Dylan, Elvis Presley, and J. J. Cale," *Rolling Stone*, March 31, 2021.

Stephen Ford, "Shyest Stone Goes Solo," NEA syndication, July 12, 1974.

Paul Zollo, *Conversations with Tom Petty* (Omnibus Press, 2005).

Runnin' Down a Dream, documentary by Peter Bogdanovich (2007).

Andrew Bailey, "Bill Wyman Solo: It's Me, Such as I Am," *Rolling Stone*, June 6, 1974.

Marcella Detroit (aka Marcy Levy), interview by Joe Montague, *Riveting Riffs*, October 4, 2017, http://www.rivetingriffs.com/marcella_detroit.html.

Kent Jones, "*A Poem Is a Naked Person*: I Shall Be Released," Criterion, March 29, 2016, https://www.criterion.com/current/posts/3987-a-poem-is-a-naked-person -i-shall-be-released.

Eric Hynes, "Leon Russell on His Lost Doc's Long, Strange Trip," *Rolling Stone*, July 2, 2015.

Arthur Levy, "Portrait of the Artist," *Zoo World*, July 4, 1974.

Julia Lowrie Henderson, "Hit Musician Leon Russell Credits an Injury at Birth with Setting Him on His Musical Path," Studio 360, July 7, 2015, https://the world.org/stories/2015-07-07/hit-musician-leon-russell-credits-injury-birth-setting -him-his-musical-path.

Simmons, "The Magus."

Waterhouse, "Actually, I'm a Magician."

Nesbitt/Dillon interview.

Fong-Torres, "Leon Russell: The Interview."

Smith, "Still Playing a Song for You."

Chapter 24: Will O' the Wisp

Lisa Martin, "Hornet's Spook Light Has Drawn the Curious for Decades," Ozarks Alive, October 16, 2016, https://www.ozarksalive.com/stories/joplins-spook -light-has-drawn-the-curious-for-decades.

D. L. Ashliman, "Will-o'-the-Wisp, Jack-o'-Lantern, *Ignis Fatuus* (Foolish Fire): Legends About Fiery Fairies," D. L. Ashliman's Folktexts, updated February 22, 2021, https://sites.pitt.edu/~dash/willowisp.

Leon and Mary interview, by Patrick Snyder, *Rolling Stone* syndication, July 16, 1976.

Martin Hayman, "Denny Cordell: The Cordial Englishman," *Sounds*, March 30, 1974.

"Tulsa Counterculture of the 70s," Tulsa TV Memories, https://tulsatvmemories.com/harrison.html.

John Wooley, "The Lost Tapes of Mazeppa," *Tulsa World*, October 2, 1992.

Gary Busey with Ben Fong-Torres, in *Rolling Stone*, September 21, 1978.

Gary Busey, with Steffanie Sampson, *Buseyisms: Gary Busey's Basic Instructions Before Leaving Earth* (St. Martin's Press, 2018).

Dwight Twilley quotes come from my interview with him and the interview he did with Teresa Knox for the Church Studio video series ("Dwight Twilley, Legendary Power Pop Singer and Songwriter—Exclusive Interview," YouTube video, 12:02, Church Studio, August 24, 2020, https://www.youtube.com/watch?v=KRDiuTmuq_4). Another quote came from Joshua Kline, "Sound," This Land, June 23, 2010, https://thislandpress.com/2010/06/23/past-and-future-sound/. Additional background from "Dwight Twilley: The Aquarium Drunkard Interview," Aquarium Drunkard, November 20, 2014, https://aquariumdrunkard.com/2014/11/20/dwight-twilley-the-aquarium-drunkard-interview/.

Roy Jurgens, "Johnette Napolitano: Bouncing Back, Losing a Mentor, Carrying On," Buzzbands.la, November 17, 2016, https://buzzbands.la/2016/11/17/johnette-napolitano-interview/.

Tedesco interview with Leon, 2013.

Harrod Blank, *A Poem Is a Naked Person* DVD extras.

Chapter 25: Don't Fly Away

Warren Zanes, *Petty: The Biography* (Henry Holt and Company, 2015).

Linda Deutsch, "Small Record Company Owners Are Thriving" (also under various other titles), AP (syndicated nationally), May 14, 1977.

Mikal Gilmore, "Tom Petty's Real-Life Nightmares: Rocker on 'Damn the Torpedoes' Woes," *Rolling Stone*, February 21, 1980.

"Steve Ripley: Rock 'n' Roll Musician, Songwriter, Inventor," interview by John Erling, Voices of Oklahoma, June 29, 2018, https://voicesofoklahoma.com/interviews/ripley-steve/.

Chapter 26: Wedding Album

Gary Ogan quotes come from my interview with him and a piece he wrote, "Leon Russell—a Remembrance," *Oregon Music News*, January 16, 2017, https://www.oregonmusicnews.com/leon-russell-gary-ogan-remembrance.

Edwin F. McPherson, "The Talent Agencies Act: A Personal Manager's Nightmare," *Los Angeles Lawyer*, May 1994, https://mcpherson-llp.com/articles/talent-agencies-act-a-personal-managers-nightmare/.

Most of the contractual details were found in Leon's archives at OKPOP, augmented by research detailed in William Sargent's book, *Superstar in a Masquerade* (Page Publishing, 2021).

Jay Kirschenmann, "George Benson Gives Manatee County the Night," *Bradenton (FL) Herald*, June 17, 1990.

Nesbitt/Dillon interview.

Edwards, "Leon: A Triumphant Return."

Russell, *In His Own Words*.

Chapter 27: Paradise in Burbank

Roeser, "Even Under the Guise of Hank Wilson." Regarding Leon not being at the Last Waltz, Steve Roeser asked, "I have a couple of 'why weren't you' questions. Why weren't you at the Band's 'Last Waltz' [Winterland Ballroom, San Francisco, 1976]?" Leon's answer was, "I don't know. It was probably scheduling or something. They invited me to come, but I can't remember why. Probably scheduling."

"My First Real Meeting with Leon," Steve Ripley as told to Jim Edwards, *Tulsa People*, August 29, 2011.

Douglas Brinkley, "Bob Dylan's Late-Era, Old-Style American Individualism," *Rolling Stone*, May 14, 2009.

Billboard, October 21, 1978.

Ripley, interview by John Erling for Voices of Oklahoma.

Russell, *In His Own Words*.

Gary Ogan quotes come from my interview with him and a piece he wrote, "Leon Russell—a Remembrance," for *Oregon Music News*, https://www.oregonmusicnews.com/leon-russell-gary-ogan-remembrance.

Chapter 28: Paradise Lost

The information about spray-painting over the logo comes from a Facebook post made by Terry Scott, who worked for Leon.

Thomas Conner, "Leon Russell Sought Shelter in Tulsa Throughout the 70s, and His Sounds Still Resonate," *Tulsa World*, December 19, 1997.

Chapter 29: Life and Love

Smith, "Still Playing A Song for You."

Simmons, "The Magus."

Jurgens, "Johnette Napolitano."

Roeser, "Even Under the Guise of Hank Wilson."

Chapter 30: One More Love Song

J. B. Blosser, "Leon Russell Discloses His Life via Music," United Press International, December 2, 1979.

Leon Russell live review, *Sacramento Bee*, December 21, 1981.

Sexton, "Singing This Song for You."

Simmons, "The Magus."

Russell, *In His Own Words.*

Chapter 31: On the Borderline

Ellis Widner, "Leon Talks About Catfish and Life," *Tulsa Tribune*, April 20, 1987.

Ken Burns, episode 4: "'I Can't Stop Loving You' (1953–1963)," *Country Music*, 2019, https://www.pbs.org/kenburns/country-music/episode-4-i-cant-stop-loving-you-1953-1963.

"Mergeop's Interview with Jack Wessel," *Leon Russell Newsletter*, September 17, 2001.

In addition to messages I exchanged with Paul Brewer, some information is quoted from posts he shared on Facebook.

Cameron Cohick, "Leon Russell Is Dr. Feelgood," *Fort Lauderdale News*, February 24, 1982.

Bill Littleton, "Leon's Back," *Performer*, April 29, 1983.

Smith, "Still Playing A Song for You."

Tamarkin, "Leon Russell Talks His Career."

Chapter 32: Back on the Road . . . to Obscurity

Autumn Owens, "Local Discusses Musical, Acting Career and Working Through the Pain," *Weatherford (TX) Democrat*, November 7, 2019.

William Kerns, "Six Female Survivors on American Frontier Featured in One-Woman Show," *Lubbock (TX) Avalanche-Journal*, March 10, 2011.

Chapter 33: Going Down

"Leon Russell Interviewed by Bert Borth for Psycho Babble TV—2003," You-Tube video, 4:25, Bert Borth, February 2, 2011, https://www.youtube.com/watch?v=XTciYvMejLo.

Jeffrey Haas, "The Deep Freeze Story," Deep Freeze Films, http://deepfreezefilms.com/deepfreezestory.html.

Ripley, interview by John Erling for Voices of Oklahoma.

Chapter 34: Anything Can Happen

Anything Can Happen CD liner notes (Virgin, 1994).

Hornsby quotes from my interview with him and from David Fricke, "Remembering Leon Russell, Rock's Behind-the-Scenes Mad Dog," *Rolling Stone*, November 22, 2016.

Chapter 35: Just a Face in the Crowd

Robyn Lowenthal, "Willie Nelson and Leon Russell Reunite for Two Shows at the Ventura Theater," *Los Angeles Times*, February 22, 1996.

Leon Russell, *Legend in My Time: Hank Wilson, Volume 3* (ARK 21, 1998).

Background on the Lifers also came from my interview with Johnny McDonnell.

The Union CD liner notes (Decca, 2010).

"Mergeop's Interview with Jack Wessel," *Leon Russell Newsletter*.

Tedesco interview with Leon, 2013.

Tom Britt quote about the Hank Williams Jr. tour was from a post he made on Facebook.

Chapter 36: I'm Broke. My Wife and Kids Are Rich

John Wooley and Matt Gleason, "Sounds Like Ours: Where was I. J. on New Year's Eve?" *Tulsa World*, January 6, 2005.

Chris Simmons quotes come from my interview with him and from Ward Meeker, "Freddie King's Gibson ES-345 Keeps On Playin'," *Vintage Guitar*, January 2018.

Brian Lee interview on "Remembering Leon Russell with Mel Myers Podcast," for 103.3 The Eagle FM, December 2016.

"Leon Russell Crew Interviews," OKPOP.

Ripley, interview by John Erling for Voices of Oklahoma.

Tedesco interview with Leon, 2013.

Chapter 37: The Union

The Union CD liner notes (Decca, 2010).

Graham Reid, "Ever the Journeyman: Leon Russell Interviewed," Elsewhere, April 13, 2011, https://www.elsewhere.co.nz/absoluteelsewhere/3985/leon-russell-interviewed-2011-ever-the-journeyman/.

Austin Scaggs, "The *Rolling Stone* Interview: Elton John," *Rolling Stone*, February 17, 2011.

"Russell and Elton—Meeting of the Masters," Yamaha Entertainment Group, https://www.yamaha.com/allaccess/artists/pdf/issue20-russell_elton.pdf.

Cohen, "The Master of Space and Time Returns."

Nash, "50 Years of Music" interview with Leon, 2015.

Nash, "Catching Up with Leon Russell."

Simmons, "The Magus."

Mastropolo, "When Elton John Jammed."

Lawrence, "Leon Russell Speaks with Hawai'i Public Radio."

Sexton, "Singing This Song for You."

Chapter 38: Hall of Fame

Refer to the sources listed in the Preface section of these endnotes for sources in this chapter.

Chapter 39: Life Journey

The Union documentary about the recording sessions, directed by Cameron Crowe.

Elvis Costello's statement was posted on Facebook.

Mettler, "Leon Russell Looks Back."

Lawrence, "Leon Russell Speaks with Hawai'i Public Radio."

Tedesco interview with Leon, 2013.

Clark, "Leon Russell's Amazing Journey."

Nesbitt/Dillon interview.

Ragogna, "Life Journeys."

Sexton, "Singing This Song for You."

"Russell and Elton—Meeting of the Masters."

Chapter 40: Putting the Top Hat Back On

Hynes, "Leon Russell on His Lost Doc's Long, Strange Trip," *Rolling Stone*, July 2, 2015.

Tedeschi and Trucks quotes are from my interviews with them as well as from David Browne, "Inside Tedeschi Trucks Band's All-Star Joe Cocker Tribute Concert," *Rolling Stone*, July 14, 2015.

Chapter 41: In a Place Where There's No Space or Time

Carla Brown interview, "'This Masquerade' Inspiration, Carla Brown."

Selected Bibliography

Bean, J. P. *Joe Cocker: The Authorized Biography*. Virgin Books Limited, 2003.

Bego, Mark. *Jackson Browne: His Life and Music*. Citadel Press, 2005.

Benno, Marc. *Hollywood Texas: A True Backstage Look at Love and Music Along the Rock 'n' Roll Highway: Memoirs of the Life and Times of Marc Benno*. Marno Publishing, 2013.

Blackwell, Teb, and Rhett Lake. *Oklahoma Guide to 45rpm Records & Bands 1955–1975*. Oklahoma Historical Society, 2014.

Blaine, Hal, and David Goggin. *Hal Blaine and the Wrecking Crew*. Mix Books. 1990.

Brown, Mick. *Tearing Down the Wall of Sound: The Rise and Fall of Phil Spector*. Vintage, 2008.

Busey, Gary, with Steffanie Sampson. *Buseyisms: Gary Busey's Basic Instructions Before Leaving Earth*. St. Martin's Press, 2018.

Clapton, Eric. *Clapton: The Autobiography*. Broadway Books, 2007.

Clayson, Alan. *Ringo Starr: Straight Man or Joker?* Paragon House Publishers, 1992.

Cobb, Russell. *The Great Oklahoma Swindle: Race, Religion, and Lies in America's Weirdest State*. University of Nebraska Press, 2020.

Coolidge, Rita, with Michael Walker. *Delta Lady: A Memoir*. HarperCollins, 2016.

Doggett, Peter. *You Never Give Me Your Money: The Beatles After the Breakup*. HarperCollins, 2009.

Einarson, John. *Desperados: The Roots of Country Rock*. Cooper Square Press, 2001.

Fowley, Kim. *Lord of Garbage*. Kicks Books, 2013.

Gordon, Robert. *It Came from Memphis*. Faber & Faber, 1994.

Hagan, Joe. *Sticky Fingers*. Alfred A. Knopf, 2017.

Hart, Bobby. *Psychedelic Bubble Gum*. SelectBooks, 2015.

Hartman, Kent. *The Wrecking Crew: The inside Story of Rock and Roll's Best-Kept Secret*. Thomas Dunne Books, 2012.

Helm, Levon, and Stephen Davis. *This Wheel's on Fire: Levon Helm and the Story of the Band*. W. Morrow, 1993.

Hillman, Chris. *Time Between: My Life as a Byrd, Burrito Brother, and Beyond*. BMG Books, 2020.

Holzman, Jac, and Gavan Daws. *Follow the Music: The Life and High Times of Elektra Records in the Great Years of American Pop Culture*. First Media Books, 1998.

John, Elton. *Me*. Macmillan, 2019.

Johns, Glyn. *Sound Man: A Life Recording Hits with the Rolling Stones, The Who, Led Zeppelin, the Eagles, Eric Clapton, the Faces*. Plume, 2014.

Jones, Booker T. *Time Is Tight*. Little, Brown, 2019.

Keys, Bobby, and Bill Ditenhafer. *Every Night's a Saturday Night: The Rock 'n' Roll Life of Legendary Sax Man Bobby Keys*. Counterpoint, 2012.

Kooper, Al. *Backstage Passes & Backstabbing Bastards*. Backbeat Books, 2008.

Kubernik, Harvey. *Turn Up the Radio! Rock, Pop, and Roll in Los Angeles 1956–1972* Santa Monica Press, 2014.

Meyer, David N. *Twenty Thousand Roads: The Ballad of Gram Parsons and His Cosmic American Music*. Villard Books, 2008.

Nathanson, Andee. *Andee Eye*. Artifacto, 2020.

Nelson, Willie, with David Ritz. *It's a Long Story: My Life*. Little, Brown, 2015.

Nix, Don. *Memphis Man: Living High, Laying Low*. Sartoris Literary Group, 2015.

O'Dell, Chris, with Katherine Ketcham. *Miss O'Dell: My Hard Days and Long Nights with the Beatles, the Stones, Bob Dylan, and Eric Clapton, and the Women They Loved*. Touchstone, 2009.

O'Neill, Tom. *Chaos*. Little, Brown, 2019.

Riemenschneider, Chris. *First Avenue: Minnesota's Mainroom*. Minnesota Historical Society Press, 2017.

Rogan, Johnny. *The Byrds: Timeless Flight Revisited: The Sequel*. Rogan House, 1998.

Russell, Leon. *Leon Russell in His Own Words*. Edited by Steve Todoroff and John Wooley. Steve Todoroff Archives, 2019.

Sanchez, Luis. *The Beach Boys' Smile*. Bloomsbury Publishing USA, 2014.

Sargent, William. *Superstar in a Masquerade*. Page Publishing, 2021.

Sharp, Ken. *Sound Explosion! Inside L.A.'s Studio Factory with the Wrecking Crew*. Wrecking Crew, 2016.

Springsteen, Bruce. *Born to Run*. Simon & Schuster, 2016.

Tobler, John, and Stuart Grundy. *The Guitar Greats*. St. Martin's Press, 1984.

Tosches, Nick. *Hellfire: The Jerry Lee Lewis Story*. Dell, 1982.

Vanilla, Cherry. *Lick Me*. Chicago Review Press, 2010.

Whitlock, Bobby, with Marc Roberty. *Bobby Whitlock: A Rock 'n' Roll Autobiography*. McFarland, 2010.

Wolf, Linda. *Tribute: Cocker Power*. Insight Editions, 2020.

Wooley, John. *From the Blue Devils to Red Dirt: The Colors of Oklahoma Music*. Hawk Publishing Group, 2006.

Wyman, Bill, with Richard Havers. *Rolling with the Stones*. DK Publishing (Dorling Kindersley), 2002.

Yaffe, David. *Reckless Daughter*. Sarah Crichton Books, 2017.

Zanes, Warren. *Petty: The Biography*. Henry Holt and Company, 2015.

Zimmer, Dave. *Crosby, Stills & Nash*. Da Capo Press, 2008.

Zollo, Paul. *Conversations with Tom Petty*. Omnibus Press, 2005.

Index